Weaving a Program
Literate Programming in WEB

Wayne Sewell
E-Systems, Garland Division

VNR Van Nostrand Reinhold
New York

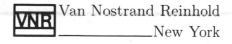

For Isic

Trademarks

METAFONT is a trademark of Addison-Wesley Publishing Company. TEX and $\mathcal{AMS}$-TEX are trademarks of the American Mathematical Society. UNIX is a trademark of AT&T Information Systems. Turbo Pascal is a trademark of Borland International. Macintosh is a trademark of Apple Computer. DECUS, VAX, and VMS are trademarks of Digital Equipment Corporation. 8086 is a trademark of Intel Corporation. VM/CMS, and MVS/TSO are trademarks of International Business Machines Corporation. MS-DOS is a trademark of Microsoft Corporation. 68000 is a trademark of Motorola, Inc.

Van Nostrand Reinhold
115 Fifth Avenue
New York, New York 10003   *9-5-91-1491556*

Van Nostrand Reinhold International Company Limited
11 New Fetter Lane
London EC4P 4EE, England

Van Nostrand Reinhold
480 La Trobe Street
Melbourne, Victoria 3000, Australia

Nelson Canada
1120 Birchmount Road
Scarborough, Ontario
Canada M1K 5G4

16 15 14 13 12 11 10 9 8 7 6 5 4 3 2 1

Library of Congress Cataloging in Publication Data

Sewell, Wayne
    Weaving a program : literate programming in WEB / Wayne Sewell.
        p.   cm.
    Bibliography: p.
    Includes index.
    ISBN 0-442-31946-0 (pbk.)
    1. WEB (Computer program language).   I. Title.
QA76.73.W24S49   1989
005.13'3—dc20   89-14740
                                              CIP

Contents

List of Figures

List of Tables

Foreword

The best way to please a person who writes software is to use that software and to admit (grudgingly) that you don't dislike it too much. Therefore, I was overjoyed to receive a letter from a person I had never met, telling me that he was not only using the WEB system I had designed, he was actually writing a book about how to use it(!) Now, a few months later, my joy is complete, because I have seen his manuscript: Not only has he captured the spirit of WEB, he has also organized its basic ideas beautifully and written a fine tutorial with grace and humor. Moreover, he has gathered together reference material from many sources, and he has been helping to make WEB available to PC users for the first time.

By a great stroke of good luck I had stumbled across the simple ideas underlying WEB about ten years ago. WEB has been my "programming language of choice" ever since for computer programs of all kinds; it has changed my life dramatically. I hope this book will stimulate a few more people to be born-again programmers, as they discover the joys of writing computer programs for human beings instead of for machines.

Donald E. Knuth
Stanford University

Preface

The WEB System of Structured Documentation was developed by Donald E. Knuth of Stanford University as part of the project to develop the TEX document compiler.

WEB is more than just a computer language or a program to process that language; it is a programming methodology, a completely new way of writing computer programs. It aids in the *design* of software rather than just the coding of it. It takes the structured programming concept of Pascal and similar languages to another level.

Above all, WEB programs are *readable*. The program listings are actually typeset and are automatically pretty-printed. The idea of literate programming is that programs can be so easy to read that they can be read for entertainment.

The WEB system provides facilities that make it easy to write portable programs, even with the multitude of Pascal dialects. WEB itself and programs written in WEB can easily be transported to new environments as long as the programs are written to take advantage of WEB's portability features.

WEB is not a stand-alone system; it is layered on top of a programming language (normally Pascal) and a documentation language (normally TEX). The WEB preprocessors, TANGLE and WEAVE, create a Pascal source file and a TEX source file from the same WEB source file. The document automatically reflects changes to the code.

WEB is in the public domain, and is easily obtainable from a number of sources (see Appendix H). It is available at very low cost for a wide variety of machines. It will work with any Pascal compiler (or C, Modula-2, or Ada compiler, for the WEB variants). In order to bring WEB to a larger audience, versions of WEB for personal computers have been developed. MS-DOS and Macintosh versions are available from Van Nostrand Reinhold.

WEB was an experiment in the design of large software systems. Knuth still considers it experimental, but that does not mean that it is not a useful tool in its present state. WEB is not a system for absolute computer novices, as it requires knowledge of Pascal (or an equivalent high-level language) and structured programming concepts in general. It is not overly user-friendly, is batch oriented, and does no handholding. However, it is a fascinating system, and provides capabilities not found in any other program development system. For people willing to endure its slight inconveniences to gain huge benefits in ease of programming, it is fully operational.

This book is intended to cover WEB in its entirety. It serves as an introduction, user's guide, and programmer's reference. In addition, it includes an advanced section containing information on the inner workings of the system and how to modify it for various purposes, including porting to different environments and converting to different computer languages.

Chapter 1 is an introduction to the WEB System for those who are unfamiliar with it. The philosophy of WEB is discussed and its basic features are described. The structure of a WEB file and the operation of the WEB processors, WEAVE and TANGLE, is presented.

Chapter 2 is a detailed description of the basic features of WEB, and includes the actual syntax of the language.

Chapter 3 discusses concepts of structured programming and how WEB supports them in a way that no other system can. The second part of the chapter describes how existing programs can be retrofitted to WEB.

Chapter 4 gives a brief overview of the language of the TeX document compiler, an integral part of the WEB system. In addition to the minimal knowledge required to use TeX, some of the more advanced features, such as multiple fonts and mathematics, are mentioned.

Chapter 5 explains the use of some of the more sophisticated features of WEB. Full utilization of WEB capabilities and WEB stylistic issues are discussed, and various tricks and traps are presented.

Chapter 6 provides information on how to actually run WEB, including command syntax for several different computers, ranging from the IBM PC and Macintosh to mainframes.

Chapter 7 discusses many of the various error conditions that can occur when using WEB, including WEB, TeX, and Pascal errors.

Chapter 8 introduces the variations of WEB for other computer languages such as C, Modula-2, and Ada.

Chapter 9 provides information on various utility programs that can be used in conjunction with WEB, including ScanTeX, WEB file merging programs, and WEB-to-C converters.

Chapter 10 surveys current research in WEB, including Marcus Brown's WEB browser and Norman Ramsey's WEB generator.

Chapter 11, the beginning of the Advanced Topics section, provides an overview of the internal operation of the WEB system. The information provided here is used in the remaining three chapters, all of which have to do with modifications to the system.

Chapter 12 provides information on how to transport the WEB system to another environment (a different computer, operating system, or compiler).

Chapter 13 discusses various ways that the user can modify the WEB system to personal preference.

Chapter 14 provides information on how to convert WEB to work with other computer languages. There is a discussion on the changes that were needed for the conversion to Modula-2. Additionally, the use of Norman Ramsey's WEB-generator (SPIDER) is described.

In the same way that television news teams have been known to influence the events they cover, this book was responsible for a modification to the WEB system itself. During the research, I became aware of an inconsistency in the way macro forward-references were handled. Upon analysis, I determined that the inconsistency could be resolved very easily, with no effect on existing programs. Professor Knuth accepted the change, resulting in TANGLE 2.9.

This book was produced in its entirety by a combination of WEB, LaTeX, and plain TeX. The sample programs were all generated from the original program source by WEB and formatted with plain TeX. The rest of the book was produced by LaTeX from the author's original machine-readable source. The bibliography, index, and glossary were produced by BibTeX, IdxTeX, and GloTeX, respectively.

Camera-ready copy was produced by the American Mathematical Society on a APS Micro-5 phototypesetter directly from the output of TeX and LaTeX, which was then reproduced by Van Nostrand Reinhold for publication.

Acknowledgments

I would like to thank Donald E. Knuth of Stanford University. If he had not developed the WEB system, this would have been a very thin book indeed.

I would also like to thank Sam Whidden of the American Mathematical Society, who was the spark that ignited this project. While I did not perceive myself as a writer, Sam thought of me as one (I still don't know which of us is correct).

I would also like to thank the following people:

- Marcus Brown (University of Alabama), Silvio Levy (Princeton), and Norman Ramsey (Princeton), who shared the fruits of their research.

- The various site coordinators of the TeX User's Group, who are responsible for distribution of the public domain implementations of TeX and WEB. Much of the information in Chapter 6 came from the site coordinators, specifically Dean Guenther, Pierre MacKay, and Craig Platt.

- Phil Wirth, for releasing the technical specifications of the Whiz-Bang 5000 computer system into the public domain.

- Brian Boyd, for his awesome proofreading skills. Brian is a filter through which no typo may pass.

The C program was written by Silvio Levy.

The SPIDER source file was supplied by Norman Ramsey.

The TANGLE and WEAVE programs were developed by Donald E. Knuth of Stanford University.

Part I

User Guide

Chapter 1

What Is WEB?

1.1 Literate Programming

The WEB System of Structured Documentation was created by Donald E. Knuth of Stanford University as part of the project to develop the TEX document compiler. Embodying the concept of *literate programming*, or programs as literature, WEB programs are at a higher level than a programming language such as Pascal or a documentation language such as TEX. In fact, WEB is a combination of the two, with a macro preprocessor thrown in.

A WEB program consists of a series of scraps of program code (referred to as *code sections*) which are combined by WEB into a compilable program and a document to describe it. Each section is a separate entity that is made up of three parts: a description part written in the TEX typesetting language (pronounced *tecch* rather than *tecks*), which describes the operation of the section; a definition part, which creates string substitution macros and formatting commands; and a program part, which contains the actual Pascal code. The code section is given a name which is typically a capsule description of what the code in the section does, such as ⟨Store the identifier in the hash table⟩. In the same way that the name of a procedure represents the code contained in the procedure, the code section name represents the code part of the section. Whenever the code section name is used in a program, the code contained in that section is expanded inline. A typical code section is shown in Figure 1.1.

A WEB file has the properties of both a program and a document. From one viewpoint, a WEB is a program with an amazingly readable listing; it is equally valid to say that the same WEB file is a document describing an algorithm and that the document can be compiled and executed. After processing, this WEB will produce a TEX source file that will become the documentation of the program and a Pascal source file that will, after compilation with an ordinary Pascal compiler, be the

16.   If this is the last queen, we have found one of the solutions. If not, call
try_queen_move recursively for the next queen.

⟨ Print the solution if last queen; try next one if not 16 ⟩ ≡
    if *queen* = *number_of_queens* **then**
      ⟨ Print one of the eight queens solutions 23 ⟩
    else *try_queen_move*(*queen* + 1);

This code is used in section 15.

Figure 1.1: Sample Code Section.

implementation of that program.

The idea behind literate programming is that a program could be considered
literature, that it could be so readable that it would actually be read for entertainment. Literate programs have a different orientation from normal programs. The
program is an expository text. The programmer tries to explain how the program
works for the benefit of another person and winds up explaining it to the computer
as well, almost incidentally.

There appears to be confusion as to the origins of the name *WEB*. Knuth himself
has supplied several different explanations for this character combination, including
the initials of his mother-in-law and the fact that it was one of the few remaining
unused mnemonics. Probably the explanation that makes the most sense is the
descriptive one: programs as webs of code joined together by connecting threads.
In any case, it is not an acronym for anything.

WEB is one of the best kept secrets around. One of the purposes of this book
is to make more people aware of WEB and what it can do for them. As part of the
project to create this book, versions of WEB for personal computers were developed,
to bring these concepts to a whole group of programmers who never had access to
them before.

The *name* of WEB is fairly well known in the TEX community, but not many
people know exactly what it is. Most people who have heard of WEB know it as
something needed to bring up TEX, but not many think of it as something that can
be used independently. Even the TEX implementors, who have to be fairly familiar
with WEB, don't normally think about it outside that context. One of the most
difficult parts of the research for this book was to get information on how to run
WEB under various computer systems (see Chapter 6). A typical dialog with one of
the site coordinators of the TEX Users Group (volunteers who provide information
about TEX on a particular computer system) would go something like this:

Author: How do you run WEB on the Whiz-Bang 5000?

Site Coordinator: Oh, it's easy. All you need to do is run **make** using makefile *whiz* and everything will be automatic.

A: How do I specify the name of the WEB file?

SC: You don't have to. The makefile will automatically use 'tex.web'.

A: How do I use something other than TEX?

SC: What do you mean?

A: Well, WEB is a general program development tool. I want to take a WEB program that I have written, something other than TEX, and run WEB on it. How do I do that?

SC: (long pause) I don't know offhand. No one ever asked that before. I'll have to look at the makefile to see how it issues the commands. Let me look it up and I'll get back to you.

1.2 Code Reorganization

WEB is unlike any other procedural programming language in that the program developer is not required to present the statements of the program in any particular order. Either top-down or bottom-up design (or both simultaneously) can be used—whatever order better describes the program logic. Knuth refers to this concept as *stream of consciousness*. Some other languages permit random ordering of procedures within a program, but WEB allows a finer granularity, position independence at the code fragment level. One ramification of this capability is that variables, types, and constants can be defined near the place where they are used, rather than being clumped together at the beginning of the program as Pascal requires. Code to initialize variables can be placed near their definitions.

One of the basic tenets of structured programming is to break apart a program into smaller, easier-to-understand pieces. The smaller the amount of code that the programmer has to view at once, the easier it is to follow. Too many levels of nested blocks on the same page obscure the program logic. The blocks can be difficult to line up, even if they are properly indented. They may even indent completely off the page.

The traditional approach is to banish inner blocks to callable procedures, thereby reducing the complexity of the outer block. The code that was in the inner block is replaced by a placeholder, the name of the procedure, that is a mnemonic representing the code that had been in the inner block.

WEB can accomplish the same objective without any performance penalty, since the code sections are expanded inline rather than called as procedures. The structure of the program exists only in the mind of the programmer, while the compiler sees the entire program as one monolithic block. Procedures are used only if they are necessary—if parameters are to be passed, to support recursion, etc.

A typical WEB program has an introduction that states what the overall program does. Since it is as much of an exposition as a program, the introduction might talk about the philosophy of the program, its history, etc. The program skeleton usually follows, although this can also be placed at the end. It doesn't really matter where it goes as long as it doesn't get in the way. The skeleton is largely irrelevant, a necessary evil to provide a framework on which to hang the real code. It doesn't change much from program to program and can be supplied via a template (see Section 5.4.1). After the skeleton and all of the other ritualistic parts such as definitions for input and output procedures, the real program follows. Central data structures are usually defined first, while descriptions of structures used in only part of the program can be deferred until that part is reached.

The data structure definitions typically describe the purpose of the records and the fields within them in detail. Following the descriptions are the actual definitions. Because of the position independence of WEB code, the types and variables for each structure can be placed into adjacent code sections (although not the same section).

After the global data structure descriptions come the major portions of the program code. The program is typically broken up into segments, where each segment corresponds to a major function of the program. For instance, one group of sections could contain the code to read and parse the input file, another major section could analyze the data and perform transformations on it, and a third could output the massaged data to a file.

1.3   Readability, or Lack Thereof

One of the principal problems with traditional computer programs is readability. Each programmer has a particular style of programming (indentation, comments, etc.), and it is difficult to read a program written by someone else. The difference in style is jarring and can interfere with understanding of the logic of the program.

The quality of the printed listing itself is also a factor in readability. Even with laser devices, the usual fixed-space typewriter-style fonts built into the printer are generally less readable than the variable-space roman fonts found in the text of this book. While some printers have variable-space fonts, use of these fonts without special software support causes even worse problems.

Programs formally published in mass media have their own additional problems with readability. Direct reproduction of computer listings, while guaranteed to match the running program if taken from the original source or compiler listing, often produces inferior results. The legibility concerns are compounded by the reproduction process. On the other hand, typesetting computer listings introduces a whole new set of problems, especially in narrow columns. Since typesetters usually are not programmers, transcription of listings often introduces errors into the syntax and/or semantics of the program. Spacing is particularly susceptible to this type of error.

WEB can solve all of these problems, as it understands both programs and type-setting.

1.4 Integral Pretty-printing

Listings generated by the WEB system are unlike any other form of program listings in existence. They resemble programs from computer science textbooks rather than listings from executable programs. WEB utilizes the TEX document compiler, which includes a typesetting command language capable of tremendous control over document appearance. Even if the author of a WEB program does not directly utilize the TEX capabilities in the source code, the combined efforts of WEB and TEX will create beautiful documents on their own. TEX automatically handles such details as microjustification, kerning, hyphenation, ligatures, and other sophisticated operations, even when the description part of the source is simple ASCII text. WEB adds functions which are specific to computer programs, such as boldface reserved words, italicized identifiers, substitution of true mathematical symbols (such as '$\neq$' for '<>' and '$\neg$' for '**not**'), and more standard pretty-printer functions such as reformatting and indentation.

The formatting of the program part of the document is under the control of WEB, but the descriptive text, including that in comments and section names, is pure TEX code. Any valid TEX command is allowed, making it possible for the program author to include complex mathematical formulas, tables, boxes, or anything else possible with plain TEX in the description of the algorithm (see Chapter 4).

Commentary may be omitted from WEB programs, as it can from ordinary languages, but the omission is so obvious that the programmer is almost compelled to write *something*. Even the author, who is not known for the quantity or quality of his commentary in traditional programming languages, does a good job of documentation when using WEB. In addition, the WEB commentary is more likely to match the code it describes. One common problem with traditional languages is that sometimes modifications are made, but the comments are not updated to reflect the change. This is still possible with WEB, but since the commentary is such an integral part of the program and is very visible, the programmer has more of a tendency to update it along with the code.

A great deal of information is added automatically to the program listing by the WEB system. All sections are numbered, and referred to by that number everywhere in the listing. All identifiers, including WEB macros, can be found in the index at the end and the line numbers on which they occur are listed. Optionally, the line on which they are defined can be flagged. Embedded within the name of each code section is the number of the section in which it appears, such as ⟨ Print the junk 3 ⟩. Each section contains a listing of all sections which reference it. "This code is used in Sections 2, 14, ... ".

1.5   Macros

Macros in WEB are similar to those found in many other languages: an equivalence is established between an identifier and a variable amount of text called a *replacement text*. When the macro is "invoked" by inserting its name into the program somewhere, the macro is "expanded" and the replacement text is inserted into the location in the program where the identifier had been. The replacement text of a macro is allowed to span multiple lines and can contain Pascal-style comments. The end of the replacement text is denoted by either the start of the next definition or the end of the definition part of the code section.

WEB contains three different macro types: numeric, simple, and parametric.

1.5.1   Numeric Macros

The replacement text of a numeric macro is actually evaluated within the WEB system during definition of the macro and is converted to a decimal number. The number, instead of the original string, becomes the replacement text. The numeric macros are similar to constants in Pascal, except that they are converted to the decimal equivalent within WEB rather than the Pascal compiler. They are primarily used in places where regular Pascal symbolic constants are not allowed, such as labels, but where the programmer would still prefer to use an identifier rather than a hard-coded number. If a symbolic label such as '*exit*:' were desired, then the following could be used:

> **define** *exit* = 10
>
> $\vdots$
>
> **label** *exit*;
>
> $\vdots$
>
> **goto** *exit*;

$\vdots$

exit:

within the program. Another use for numeric macros is to define constants with hexadecimal and octal values if the target Pascal does not support them.

The value of a numeric macro can be an expression, as long as the expression contains only addition and subtraction operators and constant values such as numbers and previously defined numeric macros. Parentheses are not allowed, the evaluation of the expression is left to right with no operator precedence, and the final value must be a signed 16-bit integer. Like other macros, numeric macros can span multiple lines and can have comments.

Forward references are not allowed for numeric macros; they must be defined before they are used.

1.5.2 Simple Macros

Simple macros are straightforward string substitution mechanisms. The replacement text, which can be several lines long, is inserted into the output file verbatim wherever the macro name appears. For example:

define *fatal_error* ≡ **begin** *print_message*; *abort*; **end**;

1.5.3 Parametric Macros

Parametric macros allow one parameter to be specified. The operation of this feature is conceptually similar to that of the preprocessor of the C language. The parameter is designated by '(#)' following the macro name. The replacement text contains one or more occurrences of '#'. When the macro is invoked, the expansion is similar to that for a simple macro, in that the replacement text is inserted where the identifier had been, except that the contents of the parentheses are substituted for '#' wherever it appears in the definition. The parentheses and their contents, along with the identifier, are replaced by the expanded text. For instance, the increment statement of Modula-2 can be simulated by using the following macro:

define *inc*(#) ≡ # ← # + 1

From that point on, '*inc(junk)*' is equivalent to '*junk* ← *junk* + 1' and output to the Pascal file as 'JUNK:=JUNK+1'.

1.5.4   Macros vs. Code Sections

The processing performed by WEB is similar for macros and for code sections—in both cases a variable amount of Pascal code is equated to a name and inserted inline anywhere that name appears in the text. However, there are several subtle differences between them:

- The macros are intended for single identifiers, expressions, or short code fragments, while the code sections are meant to be larger chunks of code consisting of algorithms or complete procedures or functions.

- Macros can have a parameter, while code sections cannot.

- Macro names must be standard identifiers consisting of only alphanumeric characters (plus the underscore), while the name of a code section can be pretty much any horizontal-mode TEX code the author desires, including blanks, punctuation, mathematical expressions, and even embedded Pascal code.

- Code sections can reference macros, but macros cannot reference code sections.

Until version 2.9 of TANGLE, there was another difference: code sections could be forward-referenced (used before they were defined), while macros could not. As of version 2.9, the restriction was removed for non-numeric macros; numeric macros are still required to be defined before use.

1.6   Portability

The macro facility of WEB, when combined with the change file mechanism described later, makes it possible to write portable programs even with the multitude of Pascal dialects. A good example of the problems related to portability is embodied in the **case** statement. The action to take when none of the cases matches the selector variable is not defined in standard Pascal. Since this is a major hole in the language, nearly all implementations try to fill it. Some compilers accept an **otherwise** or **else** clause, while other compilers use a label (such as *others:*) rather than a reserved word. Whatever action a compiler takes, it is guaranteed to be different from that of every other compiler.

This problem can be solved using WEB by creating a macro called **othercases** to represent the else/otherwise/whatever clause of a **case** statement.

In section 7 of TANGLE (see Appendix G.1.1), we find:

define *othercases* ≡ *others:*
define *endcases* ≡ **end**

>   **format** *othercases* $\equiv$ *else*
>   **format** *endcases* $\equiv$ *end*

which creates two new reserved words, **othercases** and **endcases**. The **othercases** macro is defined to be the string "*others:*", which is the mechanism used with the Pascal compiler on which WEB was developed. The first **format** command causes **othercases** to follow the same formatting conventions as the **else** clause found in **if** statements, while **endcases** is to be formatted like the regular **end** statement. Throughout the remainder of the program, **case** statements take the form:

>   **case** x **of**
>   1: $\langle$ code for $x = 1 \rangle$;
>   3: $\langle$ code for $x = 3 \rangle$;
>   **othercases** $\langle$ code for $x \neq 1$ and $x \neq 3 \rangle$
>   **endcases**

Now, in order to port the program to VAX or Microsoft Pascal, or any other Pascal that uses **otherwise** in **case** statements, we modify just one line of the source file:

>   **define** *othercases* $\equiv$ *otherwise*

rather than changing every **case** statement manually.

1.7   Conditional Compilation

WEB does not directly provide conditional compilation, but a form of it can be achieved by creative use of macros and another WEB construct known as *meta-comments*. A meta-comment is program text between the delimiters '@{' and '@}'. Regular comments are ignored by the WEB system when generating the Pascal program, but the meta-comment delimiters are passed through to the Pascal source, where they appear as the standard '{' and '}' characters. Conditional compilation is achieved by placing the optional code between two identifiers defined as WEB macros. If the conditional code is to be executed, the two macros are defined to be null, making the code visible to the compiler. If the conditional code is to be "turned off," the beginning and ending delimiters are set to meta-comments, effectively commenting out the conditional code. This technique is typically used for code to support debugging. The following code appears in TeX, METAFONT, WEAVE, TANGLE, and virtually all of the other programs from the TeX project at Stanford.

>   **define** *debug* ≡ @{
>   **define** *gubed* ≡ @}
>   **format** *debug* ≡ *begin*
>   **format** *gubed* ≡ *end*

The two macros *debug* and *gubed* (the latter is the former spelled backward) are delimiters for code used only during the debugging of the program. The **format** commands make the delimiters reserved words and format them as if they were **begin** and **end**.

At the end of section 87 in TANGLE, we find:

>   **debug if** *trouble_shooting* **then** *debug_help;* **gubed**

Under normal conditions, since the definitions of the **debug** and **gubed** macros are equal to the meta-comment delimiters, these delimiters will pass through and we will find:

>   {IF TROUBLESHOOT THEN DEBUGHELP;}[1]

in the Pascal source. Logically the debug code does not exist, even though it is physically present in the Pascal source file.

If we are debugging, we redefine the macros as:

>   **define** *debug* ≡
>   **define** *gubed* ≡

which will cause the text to appear in the Pascal source without the comment delimiters, as in:

>   IF TROUBLESHOOT THEN DEBUGHELP;

and suddenly the debug code is present. Every section of code containing a **debug-gubed** pair switches simultaneously.

1.8   Extending Pascal

The macro facilities of WEB make it possible to extend even the most primitive implementations of Pascal to a usable state. For instance, the ability to specify numeric constants as hex or octal numbers or as expressions based on other constants is often useful. While some Pascal compilers have this capability, many others do not. WEB makes these constants possible with any Pascal, since the expressions are evaluated within the WEB system and converted to decimal numbers before being passed to the Pascal file. In a similar vein, labels (used as **goto** targets) are required to be numbers in Standard Pascal. WEB allows these to be defined symbolically also.

---

[1]Identifiers are truncated to a maximum length of 12.

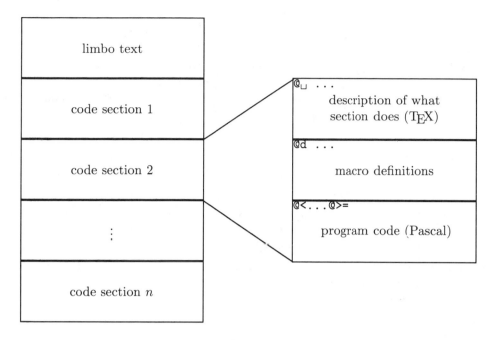

Figure 1.2: Structure of a WEB File.

1.9 Strings

WEB provides several options for handling character and string constants in the code portion of a section. String or single-character constants delimited by single quotes are passed to the output Pascal file without modification. Their use is exactly the same as for standard Pascal. When double quotes are used, however, the result is quite different. All strings delimited by double quotes are converted to *numeric* constants and can be manipulated as such in the Pascal program. Double-quoted strings of length 1 are equal to the number corresponding to the ASCII character, as if the ORD function had been performed. For example, "e" is equal to 101. For strings of length $\neq 1$, the strings are placed into a special WEB construct called the *string pool* and are written to a separate text file which can be read back in when the program is executed. In the program, the string is replaced by its index in the string pool.

1.10 WEB File Structure

A WEB source file is a plain ASCII text file consisting of a header called the *limbo section* or *limbo text*, followed by a series of code sections, each of which is an individual unit composed of WEB commands, TEX source code, and Pascal source code. Figure 1.2 illustrates this structure. In general, white space characters such as blanks, tabs, and end-of-line are not significant anywhere in a WEB program except inside string literals. Any number of consecutive white space characters is considered equivalent to one blank, except that one or more completely blank lines act as a paragraph separator in the description part of a section.

All of the Pascal code in a WEB program should be in lowercase. The reserved words *must* be lowercase or they will not be recognized as such. This is not really a big deal, because programs written entirely in uppercase are a throwback to the old teletype days. As bad as line printer listings look anyway, uppercase is not as noticeable, but in a typeset listing it really looks terrible, especially when italicized. Modula-2 and Ada use case to highlight the difference between reserved words and identifiers, but the different fonts WEB uses do so far more effectively.

The WEB commands are two-letter combinations, the first of which is always '@'. For instance, the macro definition command, which we have been displaying as it appears in the WEB listing:

define *macroname* ≡ *replacement text*

is actually entered as

```
@d macroname == replacement text
```

in the WEB source file.

This illustrates one of the unique characteristics of WEB, the fact that the listing and input source file bear only passing resemblance to each other. This causes a quandary for the author of this book: should examples appear as they would in the listing for greater readability or the way that they appear in the source file since that is what the user actually types in? Throughout the rest of this book, the examples will appear in either form, depending on what is being illustrated. The typeset form will be used unless there is a need to see the actual commands that generated that text because they don't appear in the listing (for instance, the '@p' command).

Table 1.1 and Appendix A list the commands available in the WEB language. For the commands that contain an alphabetic character ('@d', '@f', '@p', '@x', '@y', and '@z'), the letter can be either upper- or lowercase; i.e., '@d' and '@D' are equivalent. These commands will be described in detail in Chapter 2. Figure 1.3 shows what a WEB source looks like. The source code displayed corresponds to section 16 of the Eight Queens program (Appendix G.4.2). The '@␣' command ('␣' is a blank) marks the start of a new section, and the beginning of the section name ('@<') indicates the start of the Pascal code. This particular section has no definitions; if a definition

Command	Action
@@	the single character '@'
@␣	start a new section ('␣' is a blank)
@*	start a new starred (major) section
@d	macro definition
@f	format definition
@p	start Pascal part of an unnamed section
@<	start a section name
@>	end a section name or other control text
@'	octal constant
@"	hexadecimal constant
@$	string pool check sum
@{	start a "meta-comment"
@}	end a "meta-comment"
@&	concatenate two elements with no space
@~	start roman font index entry
@.	start typewriter font index entry
@:	start user-controlled-font index entry
@t	start pure TeX text
@=	start verbatim text
@\	force end-of-line here in Pascal file
@!	underline index entry (definition)
@?	cancel underline in index
@,	insert a thin space in TeX file
@/	force a line break in TeX file
@|	optional line break in TeX file
@#	force a line break with extra vertical space in TeX file
@+	cancel a pending line break in TeX file
@;	invisible semicolon in TeX file
@x	start of a change section (change files only)
@y	start of replacement text (change files only)
@z	end of a change section (change files only)
@c	C equivalent of @p (CWEB only)
@i	include a separate file (CWEB only)
@'	following character is ASCII constant (CWEB only)

Table 1.1: WEB Commands.

```
    ⋮

@ If this is the last queen, we have
found one of the solutions. If not, call
|try_queen_move| recursively for the next queen.

@<Print the solution if last queen; try
next one if not@>=

if queen = number_of_queens then
    @<Print one of the eight queens solutions@>
else
    try_queen_move(queen + 1);

    ⋮
```

Figure 1.3: WEB Input.

part had been present, the first '@d' or '@f' (**define** or **format**) would have started the definition part.

1.11   WEB **Operation**

The WEB system does not directly generate either an executable program or a printable document. WEB is not an editor of any kind; instead it consists of two preprocessors, TANGLE and WEAVE, which act as front ends for Pascal and TEX. Basic WEB processing is shown in Figure 1.4.

TANGLE is the preprocessor charged with creating the Pascal file which will eventually become the executable program. Figure 1.5 shows the Pascal source output by TANGLE (Section 16 again). It should be obvious that this file is meant to be read by compilers, not by people. In fact, the Pascal file generated by TANGLE is considered a temporary file internal to the WEB system and is normally deleted, since the WEB file is really the program source. WEB is not intended to be a one-shot program generator used to create a Pascal program once, with any further changes made directly to the Pascal file. If program modifications are to be made, they are applied to the WEB file, then a new Pascal file is generated. The Pascal file is deliberately made human-unreadable by TANGLE so no one is tempted to modify it directly.

The function of WEAVE is to take the same WEB source and create a TEX source file, which can then be passed through TEX to create the program document. Figure 1.6 shows the output of WEAVE for the section specified above. Unless the reader is

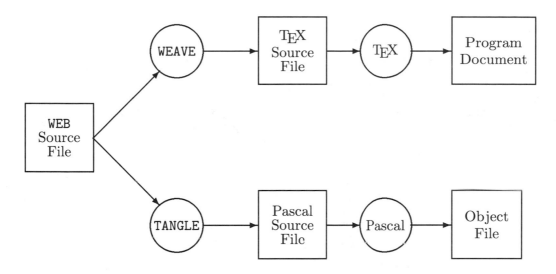

Figure 1.4: Basic WEB Data Flow.

$\vdots$

```
RIGHTDIAGHAS[COL-ROW]:=FALSE;{:12};{16:}IF COL=8 THEN{23:}
BEGIN FOR K:=1 TO 8 DO WRITE(QUEENPOS[K]:3);WRITELN;END{:23}
ELSE TRYQUEENMOVE(COL+1);{:16};{13:}NOQUEENINROW[ROW]:=TRUE;
```

$\vdots$

Figure 1.5: Pascal Code Generated by TANGLE.

intimately familiar with TEX, this code won't mean anything, except to illustrate the complexity of typesetting a computer program. Fortunately, WEAVE takes care of all that.

The TEX file generated by WEAVE is considered a temporary file like the Pascal file. It should not be directly edited for exactly the same reasons that the Pascal file should not be.

1.12 Change Files

WEB was designed to support easy portability. In addition to the facilities mentioned earlier, WEB provides another mechanism which directly supports porting programs to other computer systems: change files. A *change file* is a separate source file which contains implementation-specific code for a particular computer system or environ-

> ⋮

```
\M16. If this is the last queen, we have found one of the solutions. If not,
call
\\{try\_queen\_move} recursively for the next queen.

\Y\P$\4\X16:Print the solution if last queen; try next one if not\X\S$\6
\&{if} $\\{queen}=\\{number\_of\_queens}$ \1\&{then}\5
\X23:Print one of the eight queens solutions\X\6
\4\&{else} $\\{try\_queen\_move}(\\{queen}+1)$;\2\par
\U section~15.\fi
```

> ⋮

Figure 1.6: TₑX Code Generated by WEAVE.

ment. The main WEB file is generic in nature and is identical for all implementations, from PCs to VAXes to mainframes. The change file contains code to override the WEB file at certain key points when system dependencies are addressed, such as file handling and calls to the operating system. The main part of the WEB file, that which deals with the logic of the program and the basic algorithms, passes through unmolested by the change file. Each implementation has a different change file. Both WEAVE and TANGLE expect a WEB file and an optional change file as inputs. The implementation on which the program was developed is normally the result when no change files are applied. The processing of change files is shown in Figure 1.7 and Figure 1.8.

The change files are implemented as a series of *change sections* where each section consists of two parts: a series of lines to match the main WEB file and another series of lines to replace the lines matched. Lines containing '@x', '@y', and '@z' mark the beginning of a change section, the beginning of the replacement text, and the end of the change section, respectively. The lines between '@x' and '@y' must match the WEB file exactly and are replaced by the lines between '@y' and '@z'. The remainder of the lines containing '@x', '@y', and '@z' are ignored, as are all lines outside a change section, and can be used for comments identifying the change.

In the **othercases** example from above, the modification to make the **othercases** macro equivalent to **otherwise** is not accomplished by modifying the WEB file. The WEB file is *never* modified for implementation-dependent changes. A change file to make the **case** statement work on the VAX would contain:

```
change section for othercases (this line is a comment)

@x    ----   original line is
@d othercases == others:
@y    ---    replaced by
```

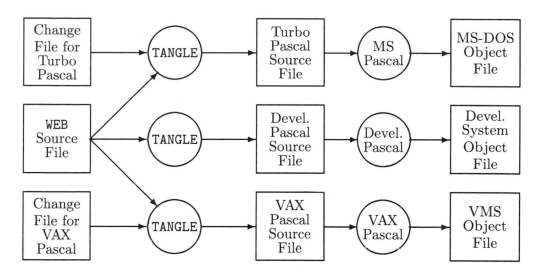

Figure 1.7: **TANGLE** Data Flow Using Change Files for Different Implementations.

```
@d othercases == otherwise
@z    ---    end of change section
```

A change file can contain as many change sections as needed. The changes are all self-contained and independent of each other. They may not overlap and must appear in the same order in the change file as the lines they replace appear in the WEB file.

1.13   Sample Listings

The complete listings of the WEB processors, **TANGLE** and **WEAVE**, plus several sample WEB programs are provided in Appendix G of this book. While reading this code, keep in mind that these listings were not touched up by the publisher or the author in any way. The output of **WEAVE** was passed through TEX directly to a digital phototypesetter to produce camera-ready copy. While a few formatting changes were made to the listings to make them compatible with the text portion of the book, all of these changes were made to the WEB source files.

Many of the parts of these listings that are not self-explanatory have already been described earlier in the text. A few minor points remain.

- In addition to those mentioned earlier, the symbol substitutions shown in Table 1.2 are performed. Most of these are obvious, but '∧' and '∨' (Boolean '**and**' and '**or**') may be unfamiliar and may cause some confusion.

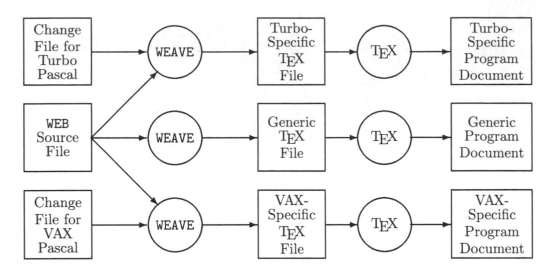

Figure 1.8: **WEAVE** Data Flow Using Change Files for Different Implementations.

- A section name followed by an equivalence sign, as in ⟨ Print the junk 3 ⟩ ≡, means that the block of text following the section name is assigned to the name and will be inserted inline anywhere it is referenced.

- A number such as '"1B' is a hexadecimal number, while ''177' is an octal number.

The reader should take this opportunity to browse through the listings in Appendix G, just to get the flavor of **WEB**. Some things that appear in the listings have not been described yet, so these should just be passed over.

It is fairly easy to navigate through a **WEB** listing. When studying a particular code section and another section is referenced, the section number embedded within the name makes it fairly easy to find that section. If the reader wishes to know where the current section is used, the message "This code is used in sections $s_1, s_2, \ldots, s_n$" at the bottom of the section will provide that information.

If the cross-referencing information is not present, then either this section has no code (contains only macro definitions and commentary) or it is a continuation section (signified by a '+≡' after the section name instead of a '≡' and by the fact that the section number within the section name is different from the number of the section itself) and the cross-references will appear in the original section. The section name will contain the number of the original section and the cross-references may be found there.

When a section name has multiple replacement texts, all of the section numbers are listed in the first occurrence of the section, in the form of "See also sections

Operation	WEB Source	WEAVE Listing
not equal	`<>`	$\neq$
less than or equal	`<=`	$\leq$
greater than or equal	`>=`	$\geq$
assignment	`:=`	$\leftarrow$
equivalence (macros)	`==`	$\equiv$
Boolean **and**	`and`	$\wedge$
Boolean **or**	`or`	$\vee$
Boolean **not**	`not`	$\neg$
inclusion in set	`in`	ϵ
Dereference of pointer	`^`	$\uparrow$

Table 1.2: WEB Operators Requiring Special Symbols.

$s_1, s_2, \ldots, s_n$". For instance, to find all of the variables of a program, one would locate ⟨ Variables of the program 10 ⟩ in the list of section names. Section 10 would contain the "See also . . ." message pointing to all of the other places in the program where ⟨ Variables of the program 10 ⟩ appears.

Code sections can easily be found by their embedded numbers, but procedures and macros don't have such a facility. The index will list all such identifiers with the numbers of the sections in which they are referenced.

While most of the examples are in regular WEB, which is based on Pascal, there are examples of WEB programs in other languages, such as Modula-2 and C.

For examples of large-scale WEB programming, the reader is referred to the listings of TeX and METAFONT, published in book form[Knu86d,Knu86b]. Some of the support programs for TeX[KF86] and METAFONT[KRS89] have also been published.

Chapter 2

Language Features

2.1 Code Sections

The *code section* is the fundamental building block of the WEB system. This construct, with its data abstraction capability, is what sets WEB apart from ordinary preprocessors and macro processors. Since the name of a code section is basically a plain-English placeholder for code defined elsewhere in the program, it allows someone to understand the essence of a program even if that person does not know Pascal.

Since a code section is complete with its own embedded description, it is a self-contained unit. The size of an individual section, whether it is at a high or low level, should always be kept as brief and concise as possible. A single code section should not span several pages of the listing. A section should fit on a single page; even better, several sections should fit on a page. If an algorithm is too complex, a logical chunk of code should be pulled out and separated into its own section with its own name and description. This keeps the individual sections precise and easy to understand and prevents "indentation creep," since the margins are reset for each section. In top-down design, the sections start out small, since most of the statements already tend to be references to other sections.

A *major section*, also known as a *starred section* because it is identified with '@*', indicates the start of a new group of related code sections. A title for the group is normally supplied with a major section. This title is set in bold font and added to the table of contents and the running heads. Additionally, a major section starts a new page in the WEAVE listing (this was overridden in the example programs in this book).

The text following the '@*' up to the first period is taken as the title of the group. This should be a fairly short phrase, since it appears in the running heads, something like '@* Main algorithm.' or '@* Generating the output.' The group title should not contain any TEX control sequences, because it is used in several different contexts: bold font within the section, forced to uppercase in the running heads, and written to a table-of-contents file. Not all control sequences will work properly in all these modes. For instance, if a TEX macro appears in the title, the expansion of the macro will be written to the contents file instead of the macro name. Normally this doesn't hurt, but occasionally it results in strange behavior when the listing is generated.

The first code section of the program should be a major section to get things started properly (i.e., so the name of the current group in the running heads will not be null on the first few pages, etc.). Also, the very last section should be a major section set aside for the index (specified by something like '`@* Index.`', which shows great imagination); otherwise the index, which will be generated in any case, will just be appended to whatever is the last section of the program and will start in the middle of a page. Using a dedicated major section for the index will force it to start on a new page and the overall appearance will be a lot better.

TEX code appears in three different contexts within a `WEB` source file. The obvious place is in the description part of a code section, but the comments within the code part of the section and the section name itself also contain TEX code. For the most part, `WEAVE` passes TEX code through to the output file unchanged, as the TEX code provided by the program author is assumed to be correct. `TANGLE`, of course, ignores the TEX code completely. Any TEX code can contain embedded Pascal code, which is delimited by vertical bar ('`|`') characters, as well.

Pascal code embedded in the TEX part of a code section is formatted similarly to the way it is handled in the Pascal part, except that special spacing, indentation, and new lines are suppressed. Identifiers are still italicized and reserved words are still set in bold. It is possible to get the same results for individual identifiers and reserved words by using the '`\\`' and '`\&`' macros, but this has the disadvantage that identifiers specified in this way are not automatically inserted in the index and underscores occurring in the identifiers are not automatically preceded with a backslash to make them compatible with TEX.

2.1.1 The Section Name

The name of the code section is significant, since it is a brief description of what the section does. Normally the first word is capitalized, while the rest are not. A code section name appears in two contexts: one or more defining occurrences and one or more references by other code sections. Wherever a section name is referenced, the Pascal text corresponding to that section is inserted into the Pascal program.

The `WEB` command '`@<`' marks the beginning of a section name and '`@>`' marks the end. The name itself can be any horizontal-mode TEX code, including blanks, punctuation, mathematics (delimited by '`$`' characters), and Pascal code (delimited by '|' characters). For instance:

> `@<Print the junk for $\sqrt{a^2+b^2}$ when |junk_ready|@>`

would result in

> ⟨Print the junk for $\sqrt{a^2 + b^2}$ when *junk_ready* 3⟩

White space characters are not significant in code section names (or anywhere else in a WEB program for that matter), as long as they are not within strings. Any number of tabs or spaces is equivalent to one space (new lines are also considered to be equivalent to a space, as long as they occur one at a time; a blank line is considered the start of a new paragraph). Therefore,

> `@<Print the junk@>` and `@<      Print      the      junk      @>`

are considered to be the same name.

After the first occurrence of a section name, subsequent appearances of the name, whether references or definitions, may be abbreviated, by using '...' to represent the rest of the name, as long as the abbreviation is not ambiguous. For instance, '`@<Print...@>`' may be used instead of '`@<Print the junk@>`' as long as only one section name begins with the word "Print." The first occurrence of the name must be spelled out, even if it is a forward reference rather than a definition. One section name cannot be a prefix of another, so '`@<Print the junk@>`' and '`@<Print the junk for the |xyz| array@>`' cannot occur in the same program.

When a section name appears at the beginning of the Pascal part of a section followed by an equal sign ('='), the Pascal text contained in that section is assigned to that name. The '=' is converted to '≡' to indicate that this is the definition of a code section rather than a reference to one.

> `@<Print the junk@>=`   would result in   ⟨Print the junk 3⟩ ≡

If other sections later in the program use the same section name when defining the code part of the section, the Pascal text from the later sections is concatenated to the text from the initial section. While each of the later sections specifies the name in the same way as the first (followed by an equal sign) all sections after the first are displayed as

> ⟨Print the junk 3⟩ +≡

The plus sign indicates that this is a continuation. The combined text of all of the sections with the same name, concatenated in the order in which they appear in the WEB file, will be inserted into the Pascal program whenever the name is referenced.

A typical use of the concatenation capability is for elements of a Pascal program which have to be inserted once in a particular place. Standard Pascal requires a rigid ordering of program components: program statement first, then constants, types, variables, procedures and functions, etc.

In a typical WEB program the first section is a template containing the structure of the main program, as in:

> **program** *doit*;
> **const** ⟨ Constants of the program 3 ⟩
> **type** ⟨ Types of the program 4 ⟩
> **var** ⟨ Variables of the program 5 ⟩
>   **begin**
>   ⟨ Do the processing 13 ⟩;
>   **end**.

Note that the entire **var** section, for instance, consists of nothing more than a **var** statement and a reference to ⟨ Variables of the program ⟩. Throughout the program, whenever variables are declared, the declarations take the form:

> **42.**   We define *counter* to count things.
> ⟨ Variables of the program 7 ⟩ +≡
> *counter*: *integer* ;

Because of the way code section definition works, all of the separate definitions of the section, each containing a small number of variables, are concatenated together, to be inserted immediately after the **var** above. The key concept is that the definitions are placed near the location where they are used, rather than being clumped together at the beginning of the program.

All Pascal code must appear in a code section. This can be either a regular named section or the *unnamed section*, a catchall code section. Code to be inserted in the unnamed section is designated by using a '@p' instead of the '@<section name@>=' that starts named sections. There has to be at least one occurrence of '@p' in a WEB program so that there is a starting point for the building of the Pascal program. The unnamed section normally contains the bare skeleton of the program, such as the one displayed above, with all of the actual code found in named sections referenced by the skeleton (see Section 2 of the Knight's Tour program in Section G.4.1). As with a regular section name, all occurrences of '@p' are concatenated together. However, unlike in named sections, there is no reference to the unnamed section anywhere in the program. There is exactly one implied reference, in that TANGLE starts with the unnamed section when building the Pascal program.

2.2   The Listing

WEB *cannot* be used without TEX or an equally powerful typesetting language. The special visual effects found in WEAVE-generated listings simply cannot be displayed on an ordinary character-cell printer.

2.2.1   Formatting Control

A lot of fine tuning of the listing can be accomplished by using WEB commands specifically provided for this purpose. For instance, '@|' can be used to encourage WEAVE to break long lines at particular points which are more aesthetically pleasing, such as between subexpressions in a complex expression. To force a line break, '@/' can be used. The '@#' command will not only force a line break but add a little extra vertical space for visual separation. This is often used to separate two short procedures contained in the same code section (longer procedures should be placed into separate code sections). The '@+' is used to tell WEAVE not to do a line break in a place where it would normally do one. This is typically used when a reserved word appears outside its normal context. For instance, if the **othercases** (see Section 1.6) for a particular Pascal compiler should be **else**, then

> **define** *othercases* ≡ **else**

would indicate that fact to WEB. However, **else** normally starts a new line, as when it occurs in its normal **if**...**then**...**else** context, causing the definition to be typeset as:

> **define** *othercases* ≡
>   **else**

The '@+' will override the line break, so use of '@+else' would prevent this from happening.

The '@+' command could be used with **else** in another way. If an **if** statement had very short one-statement **then** and **else** clauses, it could be made to print on a single line by prefixing **else** with '@+' as above, again suppressing the line break that **else** would have caused.

>   `if something then this @+else that;`

would be formatted as

> **if** *something* **then** *this* **else** *that*;

The '@,' command will generate what TEX calls a *thin space*, a separation that is narrower than a normal interword space. In a WEB program, this is often used for adjacent symbols. To illustrate use of the thin space:

    @<Cases for |open@,math|@>   becomes   ⟨ Cases for *open math* 83 ⟩

while with regular interword spacing

    @<Cases for |open math|@>   becomes   ⟨ Cases for *open math* 83 ⟩

The difference is very subtle; look closely at the space between *open* and *math* in the two lines.

The '@;' command is treated as an invisible semicolon. No character actually appears in the listing, but WEAVE pretends that one is present for formatting purposes. It is usually used for a section name which doesn't actually have a semicolon but represents code that would have had one, such as:

    @<Declaration of the |easy_cases| procedure@>@;

There are several parts of the listing that are generated automatically by WEAVE, with little or no intervention required of the programmer.

2.2.2   The Index

All identifiers used in a program, including procedures, variables, types, and macros, are automatically added to the index. All occurrences of the identifier are listed, whether in the Pascal part of a section or in a code fragment between vertical bar delimiters in the TEX part. The defining occurrence is flagged with an underline in the index. WEAVE will automatically flag identifiers which are obviously definitions, such as identifiers following **procedure**, **var**, **define**, and **format**. The programmer can mark additional identifiers as defining occurrences by placing '@!' immediately ahead of the identifier and can discourage WEAVE from flagging identifiers by using '@?' in the same way. The '@?' is typically used for references that appear to be defining references but are really not, such as the names of procedures declared with the *forward* directive. For instance,

    @!eight_bits=0..255; {unsigned one-byte quantity}
    procedure @?make_output; forward;

Arbitrary entries can be added to the index by the programmer. These can be phrases or relevant terms such as "system dependencies" or "brute force algorithm." Virtually any horizontal-mode TEX code is permitted, although it should be short enough to fit into the index easily (the index is set in double columns). The index entry consists of a starting control code ('@^', '@:', or '@.'), followed by the text to be placed in the index and a ending delimiter. The ending delimiter is the same one used for other forms of control text such as section names ('@>'). If the index is started with '@^', the entry is set in roman font. Using '@.' would create an entry in *typewriter font.* This is typically used for error messages and other text which should appear as straight ASCII. The third type of index entry is '@:', which indicates *user-controlled font.* This type of entry is typeset depending on the definition of the '\9' macro. The normal usage of this macro is to provide a way for entries like TEX to be indexed (see Section 5.2.4). Some sample index entries:

```
@^system dependencies@>
@.Long line must be truncated@>
@:TeX}{\TeX@>
```

2.2.3 The Title Page

A title page, including a table of contents, is generated by **WEAVE**. The title of the program, which is determined by the definition of the '\title' macro, appears at the top of the page in a larger font. The items listed in the table of contents correspond to the major (starred) sections of the program. Both the section and page numbers are listed for each. Although the table of contents is logically the first component of the listing, it cannot be generated as the first page because the information that appears in it, the page and section numbers of the major sections, are not yet known. Rather than generate the listing in two passes (causing TEX to be run twice), the table of contents is generated as the last page of the listing.

The title of the program is set by placing

```
\def\title{program title}
```

into the limbo section. Like the subtitles of the major sections, the title should not contain any TEX control sequences, for all the same reasons.

The title page is not present in the example programs in Appendix G, since they are included in a larger document.

2.2.4 The Running Heads

The *running heads* are the left and right headers that appear at the top of every page. In addition to appearing on the title page, the title of the program appears on the running heads, along with page number, section number, and the major section last encountered. On odd-numbered pages, the section number and title appear on the left head, while the major section and page number appear on the right. On even-numbered pages, the right and left heads are reversed.

Note that the examples in this book do not have running heads in this form. They were changed to be compatible with the text portion of the book.

2.2.5   The List of Section Names

The names of all of the sections of the program are listed as the last part of the document. It is logically the last part of the listing, although the table of contents page is physically the last. The list is alphabetized, and since the section number is always embedded within a section name, this list makes it very easy to find a particular section anywhere in the program. Each entry contains a list of all other sections in which this particular section is used.

2.3   The Pascal File

The Pascal file created by **TANGLE** is syntactically correct, although deliberately made ugly so that no one is tempted to use it as the program source. While changes of a temporary nature could be made directly to the Pascal file, any permanent changes are always made to the **WEB** file.

As **TANGLE** outputs identifiers, it transforms them into a form compatible with all Pascal compilers, including the toy ones. The identifiers are forced to uppercase, are stripped of underscore characters, and are truncated to a set length controlled by a constant called *max_id_size* (currently set to a value of 12). Throughout the remainder of this book, we will refer to *TANGLEized identifiers* as identifiers which have gone through this transformation. As the identifiers are truncated, **TANGLE** ensures that they will not become ambiguous afterward.

While most of the **WEB** commands relate to the listing produced by **WEAVE**, a few commands are used to control the output of the Pascal file.

Some implementations of Pascal allow characters such as dollar signs to appear in identifiers, usually because the standard form of identifiers in the underlying operating system contains them. Ordinarily this is not a problem as long as the programmer refrains from using these special characters within identifiers, but sometimes there is no choice, since they are used for the procedures in the run-time library, etc. For instance, the VMS operating system provides a procedure in its run-time library called *lib$signal*, which is used to terminate a program with a return code. If a return code is desired upon program exit, this procedure or one like it *must* be used, dollar sign and all. Case-sensitive identifiers, like those in Modula-2 standard libraries, fall in the same category (see Section 8.1.3), because they must not be forced to uppercase. Externally defined identifiers that are longer than **TANGLE**'s identified by '{$x}', where x is a single letter, the compiler was not able to recognize this statement as a directive and went into a frenzy of error message generation. As a side note, observe the use of the '@{' and '@}', since these braces are intended to reach the Pascal source.

2.4   In Limbo

The limbo text consists of all of the lines up to but not including the first code section. It is not really part of the program but performs necessary housekeeping, such as TeX macro and font definition and reading of TeX files such as additional macro packages. The limbo text is pure TeX code and is copied almost verbatim from the input WEB file to the output TeX file. If special fonts must be loaded for use in the description part of a code section, the '\font' command should be included in the limbo text. Since the WEAVE listing is processed in the same order as the source file (unlike the Pascal file, which is completely reordered), it is theoretically possible to define TeX macros and perform font loads in the code sections themselves as long as they are defined before use, but it is better to perform all such functions in the header. This is especially true if the macro is used in more than one section, since the sections might be reordered at some point, causing an "undefined control sequence" error.

One example of a macro defined in the limbo text of a program is the name *WEB* itself. Since it is traditionally typeset in "typewriter font," a font change is required if it occurs in ordinary roman type. The macro

    \def\web{\.{WEB}}

will allow '\web' to equate to WEB in the body of the program.

2.5   Macros

Replacement text, whether for a code section or a macro, must have balanced parentheses. WEB will not permit left parentheses to appear without an equal number of matching right parentheses within the same replacement text.

For reasons the author has not been able to determine, WEB does not allow one letter identifiers for macros. An error message is issued if one is used. This is not really a problem, since one-letter identifiers are of limited usefulness, except for anonymous loop control variables, which are not macros anyway.

While numeric macros and simple macros with numeric operands look very similar, they operate quite differently. The numeric macro evaluates an expression and comes up with a decimal value which can be used in the program anywhere a regular truncation length must be specially handled, too.

Additionally, there are other extensions to various Pascals that for one reason or another won't go through the `WEB` processors without error. In all of these cases, the '`@=`' command must be used. The purpose of this command is to define an arbitrary sequence of characters as *verbatim text*, to be left strictly alone by `WEB`. `TANGLE` will simply copy the text to the Pascal file, and `WEAVE` will format it as a literal string. As with all variable-length `WEB` commands, the '`@>`' is used to terminate the string. The procedure name above would be entered as '`@=lib$signal@>`'.

One subtlety of verbatim text is that it often must contain embedded blanks to make it work correctly. For regular Pascal code, `TANGLE` knows exactly which language elements must be separated with a blank in the Pascal file ('`WITH X DO`') and which ones can be jammed together without separators ('`J+3+(M-5)DIV(10+N)`'). The verbatim text, however, is a complete enigma, so `TANGLE` doesn't know whether to add separators or not. The lack of separators causes syntax errors in some contexts, such as when the verbatim text starts with an identifier and follows immediately after a regular identifier. In cases such as these, embedded blanks at both ends of the verbatim text will cause a manual separation, i.e., '`@=␣text␣@>`'.

For instance, a Modula-2 **import** statement contains a case-sensitive identifier ('`from @=InOut@> import @=WriteLn@>;`'). Without separators this will appear as '`FROMInOutIMPORTWriteLn`' in the output file. Adding space characters to the verbatim text in appropriate places will solve the problem, as in '`from @=␣InOut␣@> import @=␣WriteLn␣@>;`'.

The '`@\`' command is provided to force a new line in the Pascal file. Its usefulness is limited, but it does have a few applications. For instance, some debuggers allow breakpoints to be set, but only at the beginning of a source line (*source* in this case refers to the Pascal file, since the debugger knows nothing of the `WEB` file). The command is useless for pretty-printing of the Pascal file for the benefit of source level debuggers, since it would be necessary to repeat it for every source line. Not only would this be incredibly tedious, but each '`@\`' appears in the `WEAVE` listing.

The '`@&`' command is used to connect two tokens that would ordinarily be separated by a space. The algorithm that `TANGLE` uses to determine whether items should be separated or not is fairly simple, and it works for all elements found in Standard Pascal. Some of the constants found in various extensions to Pascal confuse the algorithm, and spaces are inserted where they should not be. The '`@&`' allows the programmer to specify that two tokens must be contiguous in the output file. For example, in the change file used to port `WEB` to the Macintosh, the following macro was used for breaking the program into segments:

```
@d segment(#)==@{@&$S # @}
```

Without the '`@&`', `TANGLE` inserted a space between '`{`' and '`$`' when the macro was expanded from '*segment*(*segname*)'. Since compiler directives in Turbo Pascal are numeric constant can be used. The simple macro is equated to a string. Even with the same operand, the behavior of the two macro types is different. For instance,

> **define** $xxx = 32 + 4$
> **define** $yyy \equiv 32 + 4$

In this example, xxx will be replaced anywhere it is used by the decimal number 36, while yyy is equal to the string '**32+4**'. The numeric macros are specified by '=' in the definition, while simple macros are defined with '==' (which is displayed as '$\equiv$').

Although macros are allowed no more than one parameter, it is possible to simulate multiple parameters by nesting the macros. Given the following macro definitions in a WEB program:

> **define** *third_char_matches*(**#**) $\equiv$ ($buf[ind + 2] = $ **#**)
> **define** *second_char_matches*(**#**) $\equiv$ ($buf[ind+1] = $ **#**) $\wedge$ *third_char_matches*

> **define** *char_matches*(**#**) $\equiv$ ($buf[ind] = $ **#**)
> **define** *three_chars_match*(**#**) $\equiv$ *char_matches*(**#**) $\wedge$ *second_char_matches*

and the following usage of the macros in the program part:

> **if** *three_chars_match*('b')('y')('e') **then** *do_something*;

then the Pascal output of WEB is roughly equivalent to:

```
IF((BUF[IND]='b')AND(BUF[IND+1]='y')
AND(BUF[IND+2]='e'))THEN DOSOMETHING,
```

Figure 2.1 shows how WEB performs this transformation. The first line is the starting string and the last line is the final result in the Pascal file. All of the intermediate steps are shown as pairs of lines representing the text before and after each substitution. The framing box represents the currently active area.

Figure 2.2 is another example of WEB parametric macro processing. This example comes from the part of WEAVE (see Appendix G.1.2) that stores the reserved words into the internal tables. The macro definitions for the macros are in Section 63 of WEAVE and the references to them are in 64, including the **do** reserved word. Note that the characters are converted to numeric constants rather than character ones because of the double quotes.

```
three_chars_match('b')('y')('e')
```

```
 three_chars_match('b') ('y')('e')
 char_matches('b') AND second_char_matches ('y')('e')
```

```
 char_matches('b')  AND second_char_matches('y')('e')
 (BUF[IND] = 'b')  AND second_char_matches('y')('e')
```

```
(BUF[IND] = 'b') AND  second_char_matches('y') ('e')
(BUF[IND] = 'b') AND  (BUF[IND+1] = 'y') AND third_char_matches ('e')
```

```
(BUF[IND] = 'b') AND (BUF[IND+1] = 'y') AND  third_char_matches('e')
(BUF[IND] = 'b') AND (BUF[IND+1] = 'y') AND  (BUF[IND+2] = 'e')
```

```
(BUF[IND] = 'b') AND (BUF[IND+1] = 'y') AND (BUF[IND+2] = 'e')
```

Figure 2.1: WEB Macro Parameter Processing.

2.6   The Format Command

The purpose of the **format** command is to create new reserved words and to modify or remove existing ones. *Reserved word* in this case refers to one of the word-symbols of the target language, such as **begin** and **do** in the case of Pascal. The **format** command is specified as

> **format** *new-reserved-word* ≡ *old-reserved-word*

This command tells WEAVE that it should format all occurrences of *new-reserved-word* with the same formatting rules (font, indentation, etc.) that are currently used for *old-reserved-word*. The formatting of *old-reserved-word* could have been specified in WEAVE's internal tables, or *old-reserved-word* could have itself been the object of an earlier **format** command. It is not really possible to remove a word from the internal tables, but using **format** to make it equivalent to a regular identifier such as *false* will essentially un-reserve it.

2.7   Meta-Comments and Conditional Compilation

While code for debugging is the most obvious example of conditional code, there are many other uses for this technique. Special versions of programs can easily be built. For example, there is an initialization version of TeX called IniTeX. It contains

```
id2("d")("o")
```

```
 id2 ("d")("o")
 IDFIRST := 8; sid8 ("d")("o")
```

```
IDFIRST := 8;  sid8("d") ("o")
IDFIRST := 8;  BUFFER[8] := 100; sid9 ("o")
```

```
IDFIRST := 8; BUFFER[8] := 100;  sid9("o")
IDFIRST := 8; BUFFER[8] := 100;  BUFFER[9] := 111; CURNAME := IDLOOKUP
```

```
IDFIRST := 8; BUFFER[8] := 100; BUFFER[9] := 111; CURNAME := IDLOOKUP
```

Figure 2.2: More WEB Macro Parameter Processing.

special code for reading in macro packages, hyphenation tables, and the TEX string pool in source form and then dumping them to a compressed binary form known as a *format file*. This format file is then read in by the normal production version of TEX for faster program initialization. The special dump code is not needed for the production TEX systems, so it is delimited by meta-comments "**init**" and "**tini**". When IniTEX is being built, the change file used is exactly the same as the change file for regular TEX, except that the "**init**"–"**tini**" portions are enabled.

Another use for meta-comments is in selectively generating the components of library modules in the Modula-2 version of WEB (see Section 8.1.3).

While normally meta-comments are used for conditional compilation, it would be possible to use them for code that is *never* to be compiled. For instance, part of the commentary could contain a large multiline fragment of code, i.e., "We would have done it this way, but ..." This code would probably be too big to be placed within the '|' delimiters, and wouldn't format properly anyway, since formatting by lines is turned off in that mode. The fragment would have to appear in the code part of a section, but it should not be compiled because it is really part of the description and is not meant to be executed.

It would not be possible to place the code fragment within ordinary Pascal comments, as these are TEX code rather than Pascal and the '|' delimiters would still have to be used for the code fragment.

Using meta-comments would make it invisible to the compiler. It would not be necessary to use macros for the meta-comment delimiters in this case, since the code is not conditional and is always commented out. The delimiters can be inserted directly into the code. A similar effect can be achieved by placing the code into its own code section and then not referencing it anywhere, but this will generate warning messages.

The following code section illustrates this technique:

13. The original plan was to use a **while** statement, but this was rejected because . . . .

```
@{
while something do
   whatever;
@}
```

Note that the formatting of code in meta-comments is exactly like that of any other code. As far as WEAVE is concerned, it *is* Pascal code. When the meta-comment delimiters are printed in the listing they appear with the '@' character to differentiate them from the regular comments.

Another possible use for this technique might be to document the calling mechanism for procedures declared externally. This is not needed in Pascal, because external procedures have to be declared in the program itself with the *external* directive, but Ada and Modula-2 can import procedures from other modules (packages in Ada). The imported procedures do not appear in the source of the calling program.

85. The following procedure is imported from the *godzilla* library module.

```
@{
procedure crush_tokyo(survivors_allowed: Boolean);
@}
```

2.8   Nesting of Comments

Standard Pascal does not support nested comments. This causes problems when a programmer wants to comment out a large block of code in a regular Pascal program, because these blocks often contain regular comments within them somewhere. When the ending delimiter for one of the inner comments is found, it is taken as the end of the outer comment. Not only is the outer comment terminated too soon, thereby making a portion of the commented-out code visible, but the compiler will eventually report a syntax error due to a brace mismatch.

Languages such as Modula-2, to combat this very problem, allow *nested comments*. This means that multiple levels of comments are allowed. A counter is

WEB File	Change File	Composite Text Stream
These are the lines before the change section. They will not be affected by the change section.		These are the lines before the change section. They will not be affected by the change section.
These are the lines to be matched by the change section. They will not be present in the final version of the file.	@x These are the lines to be matched by the change section. They will not be present in the final version of the file. @y These are the replacement lines. @z	These are the replacement lines.
These are the lines after the change section. They will not be affected by the change section.		These are the lines after the change section. They will not be affected by the change section.

Figure 2.3: Text Matching and Replacement When Using Change Files.

maintained, and each beginning comment delimiter increments the counter, and every ending delimiter decrements the counter. The comments can be nested to an arbitrary number of levels as long as each comment has an ending delimiter to match the beginning delimiter. Any time the nest level is greater than zero, comment(s) are in progress and no code is generated. When the counter again reaches zero, all levels of comments have ended, and the compiler resumes processing of actual code.

TANGLE provides an equivalent capability by converting all comment delimiters for the inner nest levels to '[' and ']'. This prevents the situation described above, the case where the compiler terminates the comment on the wrong ending delimiter, because the compiler does not recognize ']' as the end of a comment. The character substitution does not cause any problems with the generated code, because it only occurs within comments. The substitution takes place on all inner comments, regardless of whether they are meta-comments or the section number markers that TANGLE itself generates.

2.9 Change Files and Portability

Figure 2.3 illustrates the text matching and replacement as a change file is applied to a WEB file. The left column is the base WEB file and the middle column is the change file. The rightmost column represents the composite text that is actually processed by TANGLE and WEAVE. This text never exists as a text file, but the result of the processing is the same as if it had been the only source file.

Each change section in a change file is independent of every other change section, except that the change sections must appear in the same order as the pieces of text that they are replacing in the main WEB file. If two change sections c_1 and c_2 are out of order, c_2 will never match any lines in the WEB file because the lines it was supposed to match passed by while the search for c_1 was in progress.

Every code section that has been modified by a change file is flagged with an asterisk, making it extremely easy to identify them. The asterisk becomes bound to the section number, so it appears in all contexts where the number appears: in all occurrences of the section name, index entries, cross-references, and the list of section names. For instance, if any line of section 46 is modified, the section name will appear as ⟨ Print the junk 46* ⟩.

At the end of the listing, just before the index, the numbers of all of the modified sections are listed.

Appendix G.2.1 is an example of a program with modified sections. Only the changed sections are shown; the sections that were not modified were suppressed from the listing with ScanTEX (see Section 9.1).

Several change files can be found in Section F.2, most of which actually do something other than just be an example.

When writing a program that is intended to be portable, it is wise to keep the change file operation in mind while writing the code. For instance, when a particular system-dependent construct (such as the **otherwise** clause of a **case** statement mentioned in Chapter 1) is used, it should be defined as a macro so that the number of lines the change file must modify is reduced. Rather than changing every occurrence of the construct, only the macro definition must be modified.

The system-dependent areas of the program should be isolated to particular sections and clearly identified as sections which are likely to be modified in some way by almost any implementation. The traditional approach is to place "system dependencies" into the index for each of these sections by inserting '@^system dependencies@>' within it somewhere. This allows someone trying to introduce the program to a new system to locate the potential trouble points quickly.

2.10   Characters and Strings

If the '@' character is desired in a string, the '@@' sequence should be used. This indicates to the WEB processors that a WEB command is not being issued, but that the '@' character should be inserted into the Pascal file. This is similar to the use of adjacent single quote characters in Pascal to indicate an apostrophe rather than the end of the string. Normally, the '@@' command is found only in strings, either regular strings or preprocessed strings, since the '@' character is not used in Standard Pascal, but some compilers use '@' for special purposes. For instance, in Turbo Pascal it is used as an *address_of* function. Use of '@@' outside strings works the same way as it does in strings.

Strings of all types must end on the same line on which they begin.

When single characters are delimited by double quotes ('"') instead of the regular Pascal single quotes (''), the character is a numeric constant equal to the ordinal value of the character. This mechanism is primarily to make it possible for WEB programs to work easily with different character sets, such as ASCII and EBCDIC. All references to alphabetic characters in the program are converted to numeric values, which can then be used as indexes into a translate table containing the actual character values. Changing the contents of the translate table will allow switching of character sets. Within the program, a virtual character set (essentially ASCII) is used, and the translate table maps it to whatever character set the machine actually uses. If the character set of the machine is ASCII, each character in the translate table has the same ordinal value as its index. This concept is illustrated in the listings of both TANGLE and WEAVE.

2.10.1   The String Pool

The purpose of the string pool is to make the handling of variable-length strings a little less tedious at run-time. Within a program, it is much easier to handle constant strings, such as error messages, by index rather than by manipulating the strings themselves, especially since the current version of Standard Pascal doesn't have variable-length strings. To place an entry into the string pool, the string is placed in double quotes. Whenever TANGLE sees a string marked this way, a line is added to the *pool file*, which is a text file completely separate from the Pascal file. The first two characters of the line are decimal digits forming a number equal to the length of the string and the remainder of the line is the string itself. As the string is added to the pool, it is replaced in the program with the string pool index corresponding to the string. This is a numeric constant and can be used like one in the program, as in

```
print_error("don't do that!!");
net_message := "The network is down";
```

Note: both the variable *net_message* and the parameter of the *print_error* procedure are of type *integer*.

Of course, referring to a *preprocessed string* by index is meaningless if the string represented by the index remains in the pool file. Code must be added to the program to read the pool file and load the strings into an array of strings in memory. Then the indexes can be used to map back to the actual strings. Two adjacent double quote characters ('""') within a preprocessed string are used to signify the double quote character itself.

The last line of the pool file is a checksum, which can be used to verify that the string pool being read is the same one that was created when the program was run through **TANGLE**. The string pool checksum is represented by '**@$**', which equates to a number which should be equal to the one stored in the file. For instance,

> **if** *checksum_from_file* $\neq$ **@$ then**
>   *print_error*(`'wrong pool file'`);

The following pool file would be created if a **WEB** program contained the strings shown above:

```
15don't do that!!
19The network is down
*377506167
```

The main problem with the pool file is that it must be read every time the program is executed, so it must be kept in a location where it can always be found by the program. TEX gets around this problem by loading the strings from the pool file once when IniTEX is run and dumping them, along with all of the other preloaded tables, into a binary format file.

2.11 Extensions to Pascal

2.11.1 Constant Expressions

The evaluation of constant expressions performed by **TANGLE** is somewhat limited, but it is more than that allowed by Standard Pascal (none) and is adequate for many tasks. The expression evaluation will only handle simple add and subtract operations on adjacent constant values, but in many cases that is all that is needed. It does not handle multiplication, division, or modulo operations. The result of the expression is output to the Pascal file as a decimal number.

2.11.2 Hex and Octal Numbers

Hexadecimal and octal constants are specified by using the '**@"**' and '**@'**' commands. Like expressions, they are converted to their decimal equivalents before being placed into the Pascal file. They appear in the listing more or less as they appear in the WEB source file (but without the '@', of course). For instance, '@"1C' will be output to the Pascal file as 28 and will be typeset as "1C, while '@'177' will be output as 127 and printed as '177. Note: the hexadecimal digits A–F must be uppercase (i.e., '@"1c' will not work).

2.11.3   Simulated Control Statements

In languages such as Modula-2, the **return** and **exit** statements are used to transfer control to the end of a block. An **exit** statement can be considered equivalent to a **goto** with its destination a simulated label positioned just after the end of the closest enclosing loop structure. The **return** statement operates in a similar fashion, except that the destination is at the end of the enclosing procedure or function. While regular Pascal does not have these constructs, they can be simulated in WEB by using macros equated to regular **goto** statements, as in:

```
define proc_end = 10
define return ≡ goto proc_end
format return ≡ nil
  ⋮
procedure xyz;
label proc_end;
  begin do_something;
  if errors then return;
  do_other_stuff;
  proc_end:
  end;
```

Of course, this version of **return** is not under the direct control of the compiler like that of Modula-2, so there is more possibility of error. Also, the programmer must manually define the label in the procedure heading.

A similar method can be used to create the **loop**, **exit**, and **cycle** statements:

```
define loop_end = 20
define loop_start = 30
define exit ≡ goto loop_end
define cycle ≡ goto loop_start
define loop ≡ while true do
format exit ≡ nil
format cycle ≡ nil
format loop ≡ xclause
```

$\vdots$

label *loop_end, loop_start*;

$\vdots$

loop begin
   loop_start:
   do_something;
   if *errors* **then exit**;
   if *need_restart* **then cycle**;
   do_other_stuff;
   end;
  loop_end:

Like the **return** statement above, these homemade **exit** and **cycle** statements depend on programmer discipline rather than compiler enforcement, but they do have the advantage that the labels are visible and the target of the **goto** is obvious. One of the problems with Modula-2's **exit** statement is that the implied jump is always to the end of the innermost loop and adding an inner loop to an existing algorithm would change the meaning of any **exit** statements falling within the new loop. The **loop** statement is formatted in the same way as **xclause**, which Knuth included in the list of reserved words specifically for this purpose.

2.12   Reduction of Visual Complexity

2.12.1   Reduction with Code Sections

The whole concept of code sections, indeed of structured programming, is to reduce the amount of text that must be read in order to determine what a piece of code is doing. The code section is a form of data reduction in that the section name is a placeholder representing the code contained in that section. Anything that is logically part of the section should be moved into it, thereby reducing the complexity of the code where it is referenced.

For instance:

  if *everything_ok* **then** ⟨ Print the junk 13 ⟩
  else ⟨ Delete the junk 7 ⟩;

$\vdots$

13. ⟨ Print the junk 13 ⟩ ≡
  ⟨ Accumulate the junk 17 ⟩;
  ⟨ Ready the printer 37 ⟩;
  ⟨ Print every element of the junk array 32 ⟩

The code shown will not work, because ⟨Print the junk⟩ appears in a **then** clause and it contains more than one statement. It must be made into a compound statement using **begin** and **end**. One possible fix is:

> **if** *everything_ok* **then**
>   **begin** ⟨Print the junk 13⟩;
>   **end**
> **else** ⟨Delete the junk 7⟩;

While this will work, the **begin** and **end** clutter up the **if** statement since there is apparently only one line. However, they are necessary since the code section represented consists of multiple lines. It would be cleaner to move the **begin** and **end** to the code section itself, as in

> **if** *everything_ok* **then** ⟨Print the junk 13⟩
> **else** ⟨Delete the junk 7⟩;
>
> ⋮
>
> **13.**   ⟨Print the junk 13⟩ ≡
>   **begin**
>   ⟨Accumulate the junk 17⟩;
>   ⟨Ready the printer 37⟩;
>   ⟨Print every element of the junk array 32⟩;
>   **end**

Not only is the **if** statement simplified; the fact that the **begin** and **end** are now embedded within the section means that it can be used in any **if** statement without respecifying **begin** and **end**. Since a compound statement can be used anywhere a simple statement can, the section can be used outside an **if** statement as well. Note: the **end** must *not* have a semicolon.

2.12.2   Error Handling

Another example of the data reduction possible with WEB is in the error handling area. It is an unhappy fact that errors do occur and a production-quality program must handle them. However, the error processing has nothing to do with the basic algorithm and gets in the way of understanding it. A particular piece of code may have more lines taken up by the error handling than by the actual processing. A person looking at the code for the first time may conclude that error handling is the purpose of the code. In his original paper on literate programming [Knu84], Knuth observed that this ratio of error handling code to processing code sometimes caused programmers to cut back on the former without realizing it, because so much more error handling than processing didn't look right.

WEB can eliminate this problem very easily. All of the error handling can be reduced to a single line ⟨ Check that the input data is OK 43 ⟩, and if the reader is really interested in the error handling then section 43 can be investigated. When the error handling code is placed into its own section, and and the purpose of the section is nothing but error handling, the psychological inhibition is removed and the code is expanded to whatever degree is necessary to protect against errors completely.

2.12.3   Replacing the WITH Statement

On the topic of data reduction, one should also consider the **with** statement. The purpose of this statement is to simplify references to fields within records. Without it, each of these references must be fully qualified, or expressed completely. If the data structures are very complicated, such as nested record, array, and pointer references, and meaningful identifiers are used, the Pascal source statements can become very long and hard to follow. The following example does not use long identifiers:

$$x{\uparrow}.y.z := j{\uparrow}.k.m{\uparrow}.l\,[p].q + a.b.c{\uparrow}.d{\uparrow}.e.f$$

but one can picture the result if it did.

The **with** statement is used to specify the path to a particular record so that the fields of that record can be specified by simply using the identifier. The fragment

$$\textbf{with } a.b.c{\uparrow}d{\uparrow}.e,\ x{\uparrow}.y,\ j{\uparrow}.k.m{\uparrow}.l\,[p]\ \textbf{do}$$
$$z := q + f;$$

is equivalent to the statement above. Since the new code is actually longer than the old code, there doesn't seem to be much gained in this trivial example by using **with**, but in a real program, with many, many references to these variables, a lot of typing would be saved, since the full access paths only appear once.

One of the problems with the **with** statement is that it has a limited scope. The path to the fields of a particular record can be established only for a single statement or block, the target of the **with** statement. There is no way to establish a path to a field once for the entire program, because the **with** is an executable statement and must appear in a block of code; there is no way to extend the influence of that statement outside that block. The **with** has to be replicated for every procedure and in the main block. Also, two different records that have different fields with the same name cause confusion when two **with** statements are nested. If the bare name is used for the duplicated field it is not obvious to someone reading the program which one is intended. It is not ambiguous to the Pascal compiler, since there are definite scope rules that apply, but the default behavior may not be what the programmer intended. If the overloaded fields are of different types, then the compiler will generate errors when the wrong one is used, allowing the programmer eventually to figure it out. If both fields are of the same type, however, the compiler will quietly use the wrong one, causing a subtle logic error.

For this and other reasons, the **with** statement is not universally adored. The Ada language, which borrowed many other features from Pascal, does not have a **with** statement. Instead, Ada has **renames**: a static path that is global to the entire program and is a declaration rather than an executable statement. Another key point is that the **renames** creates a new identifier that must be unique within a scope like any other identifier. A path to a field of the same name in a different record would have a different identifier, so there is no possibility of ambiguity for the compiler or the programmer.

It is possible to duplicate the functionality of **renames** in WEB using macros. Given the following declarations:

$xrec$ = **record**
   the_field : *integer*;
  end;
x_array = **array** [1..10] **of** $xrec$;
$xrec\_ptr$ = ↑ x_array;

Assuming the existence of a variable p of type $xrec\_ptr$, accessing *the_field* for the first record in the array would require

p↑[1].*the_field*

for every access unless the **with** statement were used. However, the following macro:

define *first_field* ≡ p↑[1].*the_field*

would allow access of this field by simply specifying *first_field*. Unlike the **with** statement, it is a global declaration and can be used anywhere in the program.

The disadvantage to this technique when compared to **with** is the extra source code generated, which might be a problem in small-system environments. Also, use of **with** will allow the Pascal compiler to make certain optimizations, since by definition the path which has been opened cannot change anywhere in the scope of the statement. However, the best compilers can make these optimizations anyway.

Chapter 3

Structured Design

3.1 Designing New Programs

To obtain best results, the design of a WEB program should utilize WEB concepts from the very beginning.

Since WEB imposes no particular design order, the programmer is free to design top-down, bottom-up, or a combination of the two. The decision to design top-down or bottom-up is largely based on personal preference, although sometimes the particular program being designed is a factor. For instance, top-down would be used if the programmer does not yet have a clear idea of how most of the program will be implemented. Top-down design allows a very skeletal overview of the program to be expanded through several levels of detail to eventually become the actual program. Bottom-up design could be used in those cases where the fundamental algorithms are well understood. These algorithms are designed first, then the rest of the program is built up around them.

The order in which the sections are presented to the reader is just as important as the order in which they were written, if not more so. The ordering of the program elements in the final listing should be the order that provides the best flow for someone trying to understand the program. The two orderings do not have to be the same, because after the program is completed, any decent text editor with block move capability can be used to shuffle things around. The position independence of virtually everything that appears in a WEB program makes this very easy.

How the design process is accomplished depends a great deal on the environment in which the development takes place. Programmers working alone or in small organizations are often free to design (or not bother to design) however they wish. In a large corporation, especially a government contractor, design methodologies are usually decreed from Mount Olympus.

3.1.1   Ritualized Design

Definition of the Problem

Since the WEB program is also a document, the earlier stages consisting of descriptive text only can be written in this form. Of course, TANGLE would generate warnings because there is no code to generate, but TANGLE would not be run at this stage anyway, except to check WEB syntax. The first draft is basically a high-level description of what the program is supposed to do. As the design is expanded, the WEB program will gradually be transformed from a description of a program to an implementation of the program.

When ritualized design techniques are enforced, there are usually a series of specification documents produced, ordinarily one primary document for each phase (functional design, detail design, etc). It is possible to use WEB to generate these documents directly, although WEB's inherent readability is normally in direct opposition to the incomprehensible style such documents normally have. If WEB can't be used for the whole document, it can possibly generate portions of it for inclusion.

Functional Design

In the *functional design* phase, all of the requirements of the software are established. For large projects consisting of multiple components, the breakdown into functional units is made. The function of each component is defined, as well as its inputs and outputs, etc. This phase terminates with a ritual dog and pony show called the *preliminary design review* (PDR).

Detail Design

For a government contractor, this phase starts immediately after the PDR and continues until yet another song and dance called the *critical design review* (CDR). During the detail design, the operation of each component of the system is described at a high level.

One tool sometimes used during the detail design phase is *program design language* (PDL). PDL is a Pascal-like pseudocode language. It bears a passing resemblance to WEB in that the program statements are plain-English descriptions of what is taking place. The PDL compiler performs rudimentary pretty-printing by keying on control words such as **if** and **do** and handling indentation.

The main difference between PDL and WEB is that the PDL can't be reused in the coding phase. Once the PDL compiler creates the detail design document, its task is finished. The programmer has to start from scratch in producing the actual program code. Of course, the PDL is supposed to be used as a reference in creating the code, but there is nothing (other than manual comparison by quality assurance personnel) to ensure that the two actually match.

The hatred that many programmers, including the author, have for PDL is directly related to the wasted effort of generating the same code multiple times. Many a programmer has longed for a translator that will convert PDL into Pascal code.

Because PDL is physically separate from the code, it is not necessarily up-to-date. Theoretically, the code is derived from the PDL, and anyone wishing to understand the program should be able to read the PDL.

Many times PDL is written for a project for no other reason than that it is a requirement of the contract to do so (admittedly, that is a pretty good reason). The PDL is never read by the customer; it is simply a hefty mass that proves that something was done. It isn't read by the programmers either, because the actual code is just as easy to read as the PDL and is more likely to be up-to-date.

The PDL is supposed to be written before the actual program code and is supposed to guide the coding effort. What often happens is that the programmer decides that it is much less effort to write the code directly than to waste time doing the PDL first. The PDL is still generated, because it is required, but it is retrofitted from the actual code after the fact. Instead of the code's being derived from the PDL, the PDL is derived from the code. Unsurprisingly, PDL generated in this manner is often far too detailed for the high-level design document it is supposed to be. It doesn't really matter, because no one ever reads the PDL anyway.

In contrast to PDL, a WEB program at the detail design level can be used as a springboard in developing the final program. There is no wasted effort, as the text used in creating the detail design document can be left as is. All that is necessary is to supply the missing sections of the program.

It is not necessary to have any type of program structure during the detail design phase. It is sufficient to have nothing more than disconnected algorithms and code fragments. The main program block can be grafted on later. For the time being it can be given a section name describing the purpose of the program, such as ⟨ Do whatever it is that this program is supposed to do ⟩.

At this stage of program development, it is not necessary to write any actual program code. In fact, the choice of programming language may not have even been made. As long as the candidate language is supported by a WEB system, it is not necessary to select a language until the actual coding is started in the next phase of the project. Everything done in this phase can be accomplished solely with code section names, which are descriptive and not language-dependent. For instance, ⟨ Compute the square root of n ⟩ is the same in Pascal, Modula-2, Ada, C, or even assembly language.[1] To begin we create a single code section that represents the program as a whole, giving it a name that is a one-line summary of what the

---

[1]That brings up an interesting point. Why not have a WEB for assembly language? While the actual mnemonics for assembly languages are different, their formatting is often similar.

program does, such as ⟨ Build a data base of poets, living, dead, and other ⟩.

At this point we lay out the major parts of the program, again using plain English to state what each piece is supposed to do.

1.   ⟨ Build a data base of poets, living, dead, and other 1 ⟩ ≡
⟨ Initialize the data structures 14 ⟩
⟨ Read the poet input data 17 ⟩
⟨ Massage the data in the poet data base 24 ⟩
⟨ Output a report and store the data base in binary form 36 ⟩
⟨ Close all files and terminate 52 ⟩

Note the extremely high level of abstraction. Each of the code section names is not only a description; it is a placeholder for the actual code that will perform the function described.

The next step is to expand each of the placeholders. For each one a new code section is created with the same name, for instance ⟨ Massage the data in the poet data base ⟩. As in the previous example, the contents of the section are a list of operations to perform, at a level slightly lower than the one before, but still a very high level. For instance,

24.   ⟨ Massage the data in the poet data base 24 ⟩ ≡
⟨ Restructure the poet data base into a binary tree 25 ⟩
⟨ Remove all duplicate entries 26 ⟩
⟨ Search for the poets whose poetic license has expired and put their
        names into a "hit list" 31 ⟩
⟨ Capitalize "e. e. cummings" so that this name will sort
        properly 33 ⟩
⟨ Sort the poets by name, rank, serial number, and golf handicap 40 ⟩
⟨ Analyze the poet data for a report to be output later 44 ⟩

A similar definition is written for all of the other components of ⟨ Build a data base of poets, living, dead, and other ⟩. After all of them have been written, the next level of expansion is started; i.e., ⟨ Restructure the poet data base into a binary tree ⟩ from above is expanded.

This process continues until a sufficient level of detail has been achieved for all parts of the program. Of course, "sufficient detail" is relative and is a judgment call. It is sometimes difficult to identify the precise point at which design stops and coding starts. Many functions will be implementation details that are not relevant to the high-level functions, such as ⟨Open the input files⟩. There is no need to expand these during this phase.

As each code section is created, it must be placed somewhere in the WEB source file. While the actual position of the code section is not important at this stage, it matters a great deal in the final listing since the order of code sections is an important factor in the readability of the listing. For the time being, it is sufficient to place the sections in a hierarchical order, where the main section is first, followed by groups containing each of the second-level code sections and all of the sections they reference, etc. In later stages of the project, the second-level subheadings will probably become the major (starred) sections.

In keeping with the WEB philosophy, each section should be given a description part that states in plain English what the section does. For the higher-level functions, much of this text can be taken from the requirements document. A note describing how the code in the section meets one of the requirements is a likely candidate.

Note that none of the sample code sections seen thus far has contained a single line of Pascal code. At this level of abstraction, the language to be used for the actual coding is not relevant. A few isolated control statements may be used, but they should be kept in as generic a form as possible so that they can easily be converted to the language finally selected.

For instance, the definition of ⟨Read the poet input data⟩ could be something like:

17.   ⟨Read the poet input data 17⟩ ≡
   ⟨Open the input file containing the poet data 54⟩
   while *more_lines* **do**
      ⟨Input a data line, parse it, and store the data in the poet
         table 58⟩
   ⟨Close the poet file 126⟩

Even though the **while** statement is in Pascal form, the condition to be tested and the action to be performed are abstract. Some sort of mechanical operation by a text editor could later change all occurrences of "**while**...**do**" to the equivalent construct in Ada or C. The condition *more_lines* is also generic; since it is just an identifier, it can represent a variable, a function, or a WEB macro. In this abstract form, it just represents the condition. During the coding phase, it can be defined as any of these options with no modification to this statement, since the actual definition is elsewhere in the document.

To illustrate how language-independent this phase can be, the author has on occasion accidentally used the wrong WEB system (i.e., for the wrong language) without noticing it. While developing a program that was to be coded in Modula-2, he created a build procedure to run `TANGLE` and `WEAVE` automatically. This procedure was used throughout the detail design with no problem. Not until the coding phase, when actual Modula-2 code was inserted, was it discovered that the build procedure had been using the regular Pascal version of `WEB` all along, instead of `MWEB`, the one for Modula-2.

When the detail design of the program is run through `TANGLE` and `WEAVE`, many errors will be reported. The expected error is '`!Never defined:   <`*section_name*`>`', which means that a code section (*section_name*) was referenced but never defined. There are many code sections that will not be defined, since the lower-level code sections were deliberately not included, so the messages can be ignored. Of course, these errors will also change the error level from *success* to *warning*, which may cause problems if a command procedure or batch file performs error handling when a code other than *success* is encountered. It is possible to suppress the errors by creating the missing sections with nothing in them (except possibly **begin** and **end**), but this will clutter up the design document and there is always the possibility that someone will forget to go back and fill in the actual code during the coding phase. The error messages are a handy indicator of which sections are missing.

The '`!Never defined...`' error messages can be safely ignored, because the listing will be generated as expected. The only difference between the section names that are defined and those that are not is that the section names for the undefined sections have a section number of zero, as in ⟨ Close the poet file 0 ⟩. This is another way to locate sections which must be resolved during the coding phase easily.

If no true Pascal code is contained within the program somewhere, `TANGLE` will complain that there is no code to generate ('`!No output was specified`'). This can be ignored as well. Even if there are fragments of Pascal code within the document, the lack of an unnamed section will mean that `TANGLE` can't find them. If other error messages are shown, they probably represent real errors and should be investigated.

Some code will probably be defined as a procedure in the final program, because it requires a parameter. For instance, we may want to invert several matrices (though there probably won't be any matrix inversion in the poet data base program). It would be wasteful to have separate code sections duplicating virtually the same code, as in ⟨ Invert the *abc* matrix ⟩ and ⟨ Invert the *xyz* matrix ⟩. In this case it would be better to use a procedure-style placeholder, such as '*invert_matrix*(*abc*)', so that the code could be used with more than one matrix. While this looks like a Pascal procedure call, it is also compatible with procedure calls for many of the other languages. This format is also compatible with `WEB` parametric macros, so that avenue of expansion is open as well.

If a procedure needs to be expanded during the design phase, then it can be partially defined, with a form similar to that of code sections. The skeletal body of the procedure is placed in a code section called something such as $\langle$ Procedures and functions of the program $\rangle$.

41. $\langle$ Procedures and functions of the program $_{41}\rangle \equiv$
procedure *invert_matrix*(*mat* : *matrix*);
   begin
   $\langle$ Invert the matrix specified by *mat* $_{58}\rangle$
   end;

The definition of $\langle$ Invert the matrix specified by *mat* $\rangle$ is accomplished in the same way as for any other section, and expansion should be continued to the same level of detail as for the rest of the program. The above procedure definition is more Pascal-like than the other definitions but can be converted to other languages by the same mechanical methods discussed earlier.

The Coding Phase

During the coding phase, the skeleton program is fleshed out and all missing parts are added, resulting in a source file that will compile and link into an executable program. All of the portions of the program that are currently represented by placeholders, such as simulated procedure calls and code section names, must now be backed up with actual program code. Unlike in the detail design phase, all errors reported by the WEB processors must now be taken seriously.

Even though the project is now in the coding stage, this does not mean that everything written from now on must be actual Pascal code, instead of code section names. The process begun in the previous stage, the expansion of successive levels of detail, can be continued indefinitely. As the levels become more and more detailed, more and more Pascal code is intermixed with the abstract references to code sections.

As each placeholder is expanded, the method of replacement is determined by the type of placeholder and the size of the replacement code. For placeholders that are section names, the new code section should be created in a logical place and the real code should be inserted into this section. If the replacement code only amounts to a couple of lines and doesn't need much explanation, it can be inserted inline and the placeholder can be completely removed. If the code is referenced in many places and is more than a few lines in size, it may be feasible to change it into a procedure for reasons of code size.

For placeholders that are set up as procedure calls, the identifier used in the call must be defined. Either an actual procedure or a macro must be added to the program. If a procedure is used, and the code amounts to more than a few lines, then the procedure should be defined in a skeletal form as shown above, with the body of the procedure defined in a separate code section.

Eventually in each path of expansion a point will be reached where the action to be performed is too simple to contain references to other code sections. The terminus code section in each path will instead contain nothing but Pascal code.

About a dozen lines of code is a reasonable size for a code section. If a section is too large, some of the complexity reduction capabilities of WEB are lost and WEAVE finds the section awkward to handle during formatting. If the code sections are too small, then using them becomes too tedious, as there are too many of them and the programmer spends too much time chasing cross-references around the listing.

The Checkout Phase

Many modern program development environments permit source level debugging with integrated editors, compilers, and debuggers. The current version of WEB doesn't lend itself to this concept, since the Pascal source accessible to the debugger is virtually gibberish and bears little relation to the WEB source or the WEAVE listing the programmer sees. Multiple statements per line compound the problem, though this can be minimized by utilizing a traditional pretty-printer on the Pascal file before compiling it (one that can create a new Pascal file rather than just generate a listing).

About the only concession TANGLE makes in the debugging area is to identify the generated Pascal source code by the section number in which it appears. When TANGLE begins outputting a section, a marker in the form '{*sectionnumber*:}' is inserted into the Pascal source file. The marker is in the form of a comment so that it does not interfere with the program code. When the end of the section is reached, '{:*sectionnumber*}' is output. If a section is referenced more than once, the markers appear more than once.

It is possible to modify TANGLE to start a new Pascal line for each line of the WEB file and to provide the WEB file line number along with the section number (see Section 13.2.1)

Sample Development Project

Sample functional and detail design documents can be found in Section G.6.1 and Section G.6.2.

3.1.2 Free-form Design

A person working alone is free to design the program in any manner desired. All of the steps above, except for the reviews and formal documents, are performed, but there is much more freedom.

3.2 Programmer Teams

In today's complex world, the "one person writing one program contained in one source file" model is becoming increasingly rare. While programs of this sort are still abundant, especially utility programs, much of today's software is developed by teams of programmers (ideally) working together.

Since WEB is based on Standard Pascal and is meant to run with *any* implementation of the language, it has no provision for more modern enhancements such as separate compilation, modules, and information hiding. Therefore, the program is the smallest separable unit.

Since the vision of 70 programmers trying to edit the same source file at the same time is somewhat ludicrous, there obviously has to be some mechanism for breaking a project into assignable pieces.

The very largest projects often consist of multiple tasks, or processes, operating in multiple computers in a network, usually on mainframe or supermini computers. The work is broken down into broad functional divisions, each of which is assigned to a particular computer or group of computers. Each functional group is further divided into specific tasks, each of which operates independently and asynchronously. Communication and synchronization between processes within a particular computer and between computers are normally provided by the computer operating system and/or network software.

Smaller projects may not utilize multiple computers, but may still involve multiple processes within one computer if the application can be broken into independently operating components. Of course, programs running on systems that do not provide multitasking do not have this luxury.

On most systems, the *process*, or *task*, is the fundamental execution unit. Normally, a process indicates a serial independent instruction stream that loads a file containing executable instructions called an *executable image, load module,* or *program,* and executes the instructions therein. The process runs one program at a time; when that program completes execution, the process either goes away or finds another program to run. Meanwhile another process is executing a different program (or another instance of the same program).

A large application can be broken up into either multiple processes or one process running a large program. The nature of the application is one of the determining factors of this decision. A program such as a network gateway has a natural breakdown of independent tasks; one process could handle inbound messages, while another could route outbound traffic, and a third could provide a user interface for network control. The amount of overhead involved in multitasking is also important. If a program such as a compiler were broken into multiple processes, it would probably be less efficient than a regular single-threaded compiler because, although some processing could be performed in parallel, the overhead of communication and synchronization between the tasks would absorb the speed gained.

The point of this somewhat roundabout discussion is the following: the way that the software is to be configured determines whether Standard Pascal (and therefore regular WEB) can be used or not. In Standard Pascal, the program is the smallest discrete program unit—one WEB source file is transformed into one Pascal source file, which is compiled to become one program. If the nature of the system to be developed is such that it consists of multiple processes, each running a discrete program, and each program is of a size reasonable for one person to develop, then regular WEB is perfectly adequate for the job. If, however, the system consists of a single process running a single very large program, then it is difficult to use WEB because the entire program must be contained in a single source file, and it cannot be broken down into assignable pieces.

Even TeX is a single source file (1377 sections, 593 pages) and must be compiled in its entirety every time. Many Pascal compilers do support separate compilation in some form, but use of these features is nonportable, since all of the Pascals implement modularity differently.

One way around this problem is to use one of the WEB variations described in Chapter 8. There are versions of WEB for at least three other languages (Modula-2, Ada, and C), all of which support separate compilation.

The Modula-2 and Ada languages are especially well suited for programmer teams because their rigidly defined interfaces allow much more parallel development. The reliability is higher also, because Pascal's rigid type-checking capability is extended across module boundaries.

In Modula-2 and Ada a program can be broken up into functional units called *modules* (*packages* in Ada). These modules are more or less self-contained and independent. Each module ordinaily contains code to perform a related series of operations on a particular data type or group of data types. The definitions of both the data type and the operations to be performed on it are contained within the module. A controlled interface is provided for programs which wish to use the facilities provided by the module. Enough information is contained within the interface to allow a program to use the module, but the implementation of the module is hidden from the outside. The executable statements are always hidden, and the internal details of the data types may or may not be.

Parallel development is very easy with a modular approach. The interfaces, which are typically separate source files, are developed first, then everything else can be developed in parallel. The program that uses a module can be developed independently of the implementation of that module. If the modules are generic enough, they can be reused at a later date for another project. A library of such modules can be built up.

Pascal itself can support modular programming at the price of portability. Most production Pascal compilers provide some sort of extension for separate compilation. For instance, VAX Pascal has a module capability similar to that of Modula-2, except that it doesn't have a controlled interface; everything in the module is visible to the calling program. It is, however, separately compiled and therefore suitable for parallel development. Turbo Pascal has a "unit" construct, which does have an interface restricting access to the internals. If portability is not an issue, then some of these features can be used in a WEB program.

In the long run, Standard Pascal will eventually have modular capability as well. The Joint Pascal Standards Committee of ANSI and the IEEE is nearing completion on Extended Pascal, which includes modules as one of its many extensions to the current Pascal standard. Once Extended Pascal is accepted, WEB should be upgraded to use it as the base language.

3.3 Converting Old Programs

Not everyone is fortunate enough to write new programs all the time. Like pre-owned homes and used cars, there are always existing programs lying around that some lucky stiff is privileged to maintain.

While these programs cannot benefit from the structured design process that WEB provides, a conversion to WEB after the fact would at least make them easier to understand. The conversion might even pick up some design flaws that were always present in the program but could not be located because no one could understand the program well enough to do so.

3.3.1 Breakdown into Sections

The conversion can be done in a step by step operation, one in which the logic of the program remains identical at every stage (unless logic errors in the original program are found and corrected), but the readability increases with each iteration.

The first step of the conversion is to force the entire Pascal program into low-ercase. All of the reserved words must be lowercase to be recognized. Many text editors can force a marked block of text to lowercase in one operation. Of course, this will force comments and strings to lowercase as well. The comments will more than likely be reworked anyway to make them compatible with WEB, but the strings will probably have to be individually changed back to their original values if the case of the string matters.

The next step is to place a line containing '@␣@p' before the beginning of the program. This is really all that is necessary to convert a normal Pascal program into a crude WEB program. The '@␣' indicates the start of a code section and the '@p' begins the Pascal part of that section. The entire program becomes a single code section. Of course, a code section this size will probably not run through WEAVE successfully, since the entire section must be stored in memory at one time (see Section 11.4). Therefore, the next step is to break the program into logical pieces. The same '@␣@p' line should be placed before each function and procedure declared in the outer block and before the **begin** of the main body of the program. Additionally, one of these lines should appear before each **const**, **var**, and **type** section in the outer block (but not the ones local to procedures, etc.). Since all of the pieces are appended to the unnamed section in the order in which they appear in the source, the output of TANGLE is syntactically identical to the original program, except for the identifiers.

Since TANGLE truncates identifiers and forces them to uppercase, some of the longer identifiers may become ambiguous with each other in the overall list of identifiers (see Section 7.1.5). TANGLE will flag this as an error. If two identifiers become ambiguous, one or both of them should be renamed. Any text editor worthy of the name has a "scan for string with replace" capability. Identifiers containing dollar signs or other special characters not compatible with WEB identifiers should also be renamed. If this is not possible, they should be placed in verbatim text (see Section 2.3). After a successful run through TANGLE, the resulting program should be compiled and executed to make sure that it is syntactically and logically identical with the original. Only then should the conversion continue.

The conversion is a bottom-up data reduction process where the large blocks of the original program are broken up into discrete operations. It is the inverse of the top-down approach described earlier for designing programs. As each block is identified, it is pulled out into its own code section and given a descriptive name. The name is then inserted into the location in which the block originally appeared. Any regular Pascal comments associated with the block should be moved with it, to become the description part of the new code section, if not the section name itself. The location in the source file where the new section is placed does not matter as long as it is not inserted into the middle of an existing section. Since the '@␣@p' lines signify the start of a new section, it is safe to place the new section immediately ahead of any one of those. A better approach would be to place each new section at the very end of the program, after the final **end** statement. There is no danger of any type of collision there, and this physically separates the named sections from the unnamed sections, which will be useful for later steps.

The process can be seen in the following example. The following is a code fragment from the original program:

```
{ stuff all of the data into the array }
for n ← 1 to max do
```

```
begin
{ much code needed to initialize each cell }
x[n] ← ...
end;
```

```
{ transform the array using the Bozo Theorem. }
{    this theorem was developed by Bozo in 1822 and ... blah blah }
for n ← 1 to max do
  begin
  { much code to perform the Bozo transformation }
  end;
```

```
{ print all of the data in the array }
for n ← 1 to max do
  writeln(x[n]);
```

Since the hypothetical Bozo transformation is complex and requires a lot of instructions, we decide to make it into a code section on its own (remember, it must be moved to a point after the final **end**):

14.   The Bozo Theorem was developed by Bozo in 1822 and ... blah blah.

⟨ Transform the array according to the Bozo Theorem 14 ⟩ ≡
```
  for n ← 1 to max do
    begin
    { much code to perform the Bozo transformation }
    end;
```

and it is replaced by a reference in the original location:

```
{ stuff all of the data into the array }
for n ← 1 to max do
  begin
  { much code needed to initialize each cell }
  x[n] ← ...
  end;
```

⟨ Transform the array according to the Bozo Theorem 14 ⟩;

```
{ print all of the data in the array }
for n ← 1 to max do
  writeln(x[n]);
```

The same process is followed for the other code in the example, creating two more code sections. The code to print the array is probably too short to be given a separate code section, but we will do so anyway for illustrative purposes. After moving all three code sections out of the original block it is reduced to:

⟨ Stuff all of the data into the array 12 ⟩;
⟨ Transform the array according to the Bozo Theorem 14 ⟩;
⟨ Print all of the data in the array 15 ⟩;

This process continues throughout the program. All candidate chunks of code are pulled out into separate sections. It is an iterative process. As these blocks are replaced by placeholders, the block containing them is eventually pulled out to become a code section itself. For instance, the original block from above eventually becomes a code section:

17.   Here we stuff the x array with values, transform it using the Bozo Theorem, and print the results.
⟨ Stuff, transform, and print the x array 17 ⟩ ≡
   ⟨ Stuff all of the data into the array 12 ⟩;
   ⟨ Transform the array according to the Bozo Theorem 14 ⟩;
   ⟨ Print all of the data in the array 15 ⟩;

After continuously repeating this process, the program will eventually have no code section anywhere that is more than a dozen lines long, including the main block and each of the procedures and functions.

The next step is to determine whether any of the procedures can be converted to code sections. Any procedures which have no parameters or local variables, are not recursive, and are only called from one place can probably be converted. If the original program was designed by using structured programming principles, there is a good possibility that the only reason these procedures exist in the first place is so that the code they represent could be moved into a separate block, which is exactly what a code section does. Since the procedures to be converted should now be in code sections by themselves already, it is necessary only to replace the '@␣@p' and procedure statement with a code section name and to change the call of the procedure to a reference of a code section. The procedure should be moved to the end of the program with the other code sections, of course.

For instance, the following procedure:

```
procedure invert_main_matrix;
   begin
   { code to invert the main matrix }
   end;
```

is converted to:

> **19.** ⟨Invert the main matrix 19⟩ ≡
> **begin**
> { code to invert the main matrix }
> **end**;

and the call of the procedure:

> *invert_main_matrix*;   becomes: ⟨Invert the main matrix 19⟩;

The next step is to move the global **const**, **var**, and **type** sections out of the main block; this moves us closer to the goal of reducing the outer block to a mere skeleton. For each of these block types, a new section should be created with a name such as ⟨Variables of the program⟩ or ⟨Types in the outer block⟩ and all of the definitions in the block should be moved to the new section. The original **const**, **var**, or **type** statement should not be moved to the section but should have the section name appended to it. Assuming the current definitions are as follows:

```
@ @p
const x = 3;
   y = 2;
@ @p
type line = packed array [1..80] of char;
@ @p
var the_line : line;
```

they would be changed to

```
@ @<Constants of the program@>=
x = 3;
y = 2;
@ @<Types of the program@>=
line = packed array [1..80] of char;
@ @<Variables of the program@>=
the_line : line;
```

and would be moved to the end of the program; the original location would be changed to

```
@ @p
const @<Constants of the program@>@/
type @<Types of the program@>@/
var @<Variables of the program@>@/
```

A similar operation can be performed on all of the procedure and function definitions (the ones that were not converted to code sections). The author's personal preference is to remove all occurrences of the unnamed section from the program (except for the one containing the program skeleton). The method for doing this is the same as for **const**, etc. Each '@␣@p' ahead of a procedure or function is changed to '@␣@<Procedures and functions of the program@>=' and the procedure is moved out of the main block like all of the others. A single reference to the procedure section ('@␣@p @<Procedures and functions of the program@>') should be placed in the position in the outer block where the procedure definitions had been.

Before the procedure movement:

```
@ @p
procedure larry;
begin
{ ... }
end;

@ @p
procedure curley;
begin
{ ... }
end;
```

After the move:

46.   ⟨Procedures and functions of the program 41⟩ +≡
procedure *larry*;
   begin
   { ... }
   end;

47.   ⟨Procedures and functions of the program 41⟩ +≡
procedure *curley*;
   begin
   { ... }
   end;

The original location would contain:

```
@ @p
@<Procedures and functions of the program@>
```

The bulk of the program code should now be in named sections. The only block of executable code which should still be in the unnamed section is the main body of the program, the part which falls between the last **begin** and the last **end** (the one with a period instead of a semicolon). All of the code between the **begin** and **end** can be moved into a code section with a name that is a summation of the function the program is supposed to perform, such as ⟨Do whatever this program is supposed to do⟩.

At the conclusion of all of the frenzied moving of program code from one place to another, the result should be the following: a series of unnamed sections containing nothing but pointers to other places in the program, followed by a series of named sections containing everything else. All of the unnamed sections are contiguous and contain only one or two lines each, so they can be combined into one section, since they will be concatenated in the output file anyway. This is accomplished by removing the '@␣@p' lines from every section except for the first.

The program should now look somewhat like the Knight's Tour program in Section G.4.1: a ritual main program skeleton followed by the main part of the program in free form.

3.3.2 Refinement

We are now ready for the refinement phase. The program is fully converted to WEB and should already be more readable by an order of magnitude than in its previous life. If the conversion were to be suspended and the WEAVE-generated listing were to be distributed, many more people would be able to understand the program than before its rebirth. However, the ordering of the code sections is somewhat chaotic, as it either follows the order of the original program code or is completely random, depending on where the code sections were placed when they were moved. Also, the commentary in the description part of these sections is probably inadequate, at least by WEB standards, since it mirrors the comments from the original Pascal program, if any.

The previous phase of the conversion was somewhat mechanical, but analysis is now needed. It would be wise to run the new program through WEAVE and TEX so that a listing can be created.

In order to capture the spirit of WEB, commentary should now be added to the description part of all code sections that have none. In the case of sections in which the comments were derived from those in the original Pascal source, they should be cleaned up—i.e., transformed into regular English sentences with punctuation, first word of sentences capitalized, etc. The pidgin English usually found in program comments is often a written form of the way Tarzan talks ("sort array," "print results," "Jane make lunch," "hunters go"). While this is adequate for the crude line printer listing that people are used to, it really looks strange when typeset. Also, since WEAVE and TEX ignore white space characters and do their own line breaks and spacing, multiple line comments will run together. Making all of the comments into complete sentences with periods at the ends won't prevent the text from being reformatted, but at least the comments will make sense again (assuming they ever did). If the section name sufficiently describes what the section does, then there is probably no need for additional commentary. This part of the conversion is optional, of course, but since readability is the objective of this exercise, it is worthwhile to go the distance.

When reordering the code sections, it should be remembered that they can be placed in any order whatsoever. The only restriction is that the code sections containing procedure definitions should appear in an order that will not cause forward references when the Pascal program is built.

The global declarations of the program, the **const**, **type**, and **var** sections, have been moved out of the program skeleton and are now position-independent, but they are still monolithic blocks. If desired, these definitions can be broken up and spread throughout the program so that they are adjacent to the code in which they are used. For instance, if a particular variable is used only in a particular phase in the processing, its definition can be moved to a location immediately before or after the place where it is referenced. If that variable is the only instance of a user-defined type, then the type definition can be moved to a location adjacent to that of the variable.

When these blocks are broken up, all that is necessary is to duplicate the section name, prefixed with '@␣'. This will create a new section that is a continuation of the original section, as in

> **48.**   ⟨ Variables of the program   17 ⟩ +≡
> *x, y* : *integer*;

The only ramification of the breakup is that the order in which the declarations appear in the Pascal file may change. For each block type, the individual items appearing in continuation sections are concatenated to the block in the order of appearance in the WEB file. There is never a problem with variables, because variables are never dependent on each other, only on types. There is no danger of a variable declaration that uses a user-defined type appearing before the definition of the type, because the **type** section in its entirety appears before the **var** section.

On the other hand, if the declaration of one type is based on that of another type, such as a record containing a user-defined type, then they can be declared in the same continuation section to ensure that they appear in the proper order:

> **49.**   ⟨ Types of the program   18 ⟩ +≡
> *my_type* = 0..255;
> *my_array* = **array** [1..10] **of** *my_type*;

3.3.3 Macros and Expressions

Macros provide a data reduction capability for expressions. When complex expressions, especially Boolean expressions, are needed to implement an algorithm, they can be very difficult to follow. Too many levels of parentheses are hard to match up. If parentheses are not used, it is even harder to understand the expression, since one must be intimately familiar with the precedence rules and be able to apply them instinctively.

Programmers are often forced to break up an expression into separate statements to reduce the visual complexity. Temporary variables are sometimes used to store intermediate results. In some implementations this can cause a significant performance cost.

In the same way that code sections can reduce the complexity of a block of code, macros can be used effectively to reduce the complexity of expressions. Consider the following nightmarish Boolean expression:

$$\textbf{if } ((((ch \geq `A') \wedge (ch \leq `Z')) \vee$$
$$((ch \geq `a') \wedge (ch \leq `z'))) \vee$$
$$((ch \geq `0') \wedge (ch \leq `9')) \vee$$
$$((ch = `\$') \vee (ch = `\_'))) \wedge$$
$$(\neg ((((next \geq `A') \wedge (next \leq `Z')) \vee$$
$$((next \geq `a') \wedge (next \leq `z'))) \vee$$
$$((next > `0') \wedge (next < `9')) \vee$$
$$((next = `\$') \vee (next = `\_'))))) \textbf{ then}$$
$$\qquad do\_something;$$

While this may seem contrived, the author has seen many a statement like it.[2] It would take anywhere from several minutes to several days to determine what condition this statement is actually testing.

Part of the confusion when using WEB may be because of the special $\wedge$ and $\vee$ operators, since most programmers are not used to seeing those, but even changing them back to **and** and **or** wouldn't reduce the complexity of the expression.

$$\textbf{if } ((((ch \geq `A') \textbf{ and } (ch \leq `Z')) \textbf{ or}$$
$$((ch \geq `a') \textbf{ and } (ch \leq `z'))) \textbf{ or}$$
$$((ch \geq `0') \textbf{ and } (ch \leq `9')) \textbf{ or}$$
$$((ch = `\$') \textbf{ or } (ch = `\_'))) \textbf{ and}$$
$$(\textbf{not} ((((next \geq `A') \textbf{ and } (next \leq `Z')) \textbf{ or}$$
$$((next \geq `a') \textbf{ and } (next \leq `z'))) \textbf{ or}$$

---

[2]The author will admit to having seen such a statement but will not admit to ever having written one.

$((next \geq \text{`0'}) \textbf{ and } (next \leq \text{`9'})) \textbf{ or}$
$((next = \text{`\$'}) \textbf{ or } (next = \text{`\_'}))))\textbf{ then}$
do_something;

In an expression such as this one, it is not so much the individual subexpressions that make it so difficult to understand as the way the subexpressions relate to each other. The subexpressions themselves are not so hard to recognize, as we shall see later, but it is necessary to count parentheses to determine which subexpressions are combined in what way to form the overall expression.

On the other hand, the condition being tested in the following is obvious because the name of the identifier states specifically what is being tested.

if *network_link_is_down* **then**
⟨ Try to reconnect to the network 71 ⟩;

The definition of *network_link_is_down* could possibly be very complex. However, any complicated expression is based on subexpressions, and each of these can be given its own macro.

The breakdown process for this expression is similar to the bottom-up process used for code sections earlier. First the lowest level functions, the ones easiest to identify, are pulled out and replaced with a placeholder. This time macros are used instead of code sections, but the concept is the same.

In this expression we notice that one of the subexpressions is $(ch \geq \text{`A'}) \wedge (ch \leq \text{`Z'})$. This looks remarkably like a test for an alphabetic character, specifically an uppercase character. Suspiciously we look again, and, sure enough, we find an equivalent test for a lowercase character. Yet another subexpression is found to be testing for a digit. All of these subexpressions are converted into macros with significant names and these names replace the corresponding subexpression in the original expression. Importantly, the parentheses surrounding a subexpression go with it, so they no longer complicate the big expression. We use parametric macros because the same expressions are used with two different variables, *ch* and *next*.

define $digit(\#) \equiv ((\# \geq \text{`0'}) \wedge (\# \leq \text{`9'}))$
define $upper\_case\_alpha(\#) \equiv ((\# \geq \text{`A'}) \wedge (\# \leq \text{`Z'}))$
define $lower\_case\_alpha(\#) \equiv ((\# \geq \text{`a'}) \wedge (\# \leq \text{`z'}))$

if $((upper\_case\_alpha(ch) \vee lower\_case\_alpha(ch)) \vee digit(ch)$
$\vee ((ch = \text{`\$'}) \vee (ch = \text{`\_'}))) \wedge (\neg ((upper\_case\_alpha(next) \vee$
$lower\_case\_alpha(next)) \vee digit(next) \vee$
$((next = \text{`\$'}) \vee (next = \text{`\_'}))))\textbf{ then}$
do_something;

Since the apparent complexity of the expression has been reduced it is a little bit easier to understand. Some of the higher-level subexpressions can now be recognized. For instance, (*upper_case_alpha* ∨ *lower_case_alpha*) can be reduced to *alpha_char*. The data reduction continues as we recognize '$' and '_' as the special characters allowed in a VAX identifier.

define *alpha_char*(**#**) ≡ (*upper_case_alpha*(**#**) ∨ *lower_case_alpha*(**#**))
define *vax_spec_char*(**#**) ≡ ((**#** = '$') ∨ (**#** = '_'))

if (*alpha_char*(*ch*) ∨ *digit*(*ch*) ∨ *vax_spec_char*(*ch*)) ∧
      (¬ (*alpha_char*(*next*) ∨ *digit*(*next*)
      ∨ *vax_spec_char*(*next*))) **then**
   do_something;

After all of these subexpressions are reduced it is very easy to see that the expression is testing characters *ch* and *next* for validity as characters in a VAX identifier, so we define a macro called *vax_ident_char* that is equivalent to this expression:

define *vax_ident_char*(**#**) ≡ (*alpha_char*(**#**) ∨ *digit*(**#**)
      ∨ *vax_spec_char*(**#**))

if *vax_ident_char*(*ch*) ∧ (¬ *vax_ident_char*(*next*)) **then**
   do_something;

The puzzle has been solved. The expression is testing the current and next character in a sequence, searching for the end of a VAX identifier. If the current character is valid for a VAX identifer and the next character is not valid, then the end of an identifier has been reached. We define one final macro called *end_of_vax_identifier* that is equivalent to the entire expression:

define *end_of_vax_identifier* = (*vax_ident_char*(*ch*) ∧
      (¬ *vax_ident_char*(*next*)))

if *end_of_vax_identifier* **then**
   do_something;

Now that the expression has been completely broken down into atomic components and we can determine what it was doing, it can be reconstructed differently, if desired. The individual components can be modifed in ways that would have required a lot of editing in the original expression. For instance, some of the macros can be replaced with Boolean functions. Or, if an uppercase function (*upper*) were available, the definition of *alpha_char* could be changed to *upper_case_alpha*(*upper*(**#**)).

While we have reduced the visual complexity, the actual expression output to the Pascal file, the one the compiler sees, has not changed at all. A good compiler can optimize the huge expression, but a mediocre one would benefit from physically breaking up the expression. Now that the expression is understandable, it would be easier to restructure it.

Another ramification of the breakdown is that we now have a small library of macros (or functions, if desired) that can be used elsewhere in the program. After the reduction of the original expression (or even in conjunction with it), all of the occurrences of subexpressions like the ones shown above can be replaced with the macro equivalents throughout the entire program, thereby reducing the complexity of many expressions in parallel. The lower-level macros in particular (*alpha_char*, *digit*, etc.) can be used elsewhere, since they are parametric and will work with different character variables. As other expressions in the program are broken down in similar fashion, the macros generated by their reduction can be used in other places as well.

While this technique is most natural with Boolean expressions, it can be used for other types of expressions.

Chapter 4

Capsule Introduction to TEX

TEX is a public domain typesetting program written by Donald E. Knuth. Far more than just a simple text formatter, TEX is capable of boxes, multiple fonts in different sizes, subscripts, superscripts, mathematical symbols/formulas, and anything else a bit-mapped laser printer or photo- typesetter is capable of displaying, short of full graphics. TEX is the uppercase form of the Greek word $\tau\epsilon\chi$, the root word for technology and art, and both apply in describing it. (An expert on TEX can be referred to as a TEXnician.) The epsilon is normally printed as a subscript on hardware capable of it, and as a lowercase letter on the same line on typewriters, terminals, and line printers ('TeX').

The output of TEX is a device-independent (DVI) file which is converted to device-dependent control sequences by a device driver (not to be confused with the type of device drivers used in operating systems). There are TEX drivers available for dot-matrix printers, laser printers, and phototypesetting equipment, making it possible to use the same TEX input file (and output file, for that matter) to create rough drafts and finished documents (even typeset documents). The printed pages are guaranteed to be virtually identical on all devices supported by TEX, differing only in resolution (dots per inch). For instance, during the typesetting of this book, selected pages were test printed, first on a geriatric MX-100 dot-matrix printer, then on a laser printer, before the final typesetting run on an APS Micro-5 phototypesetter. All of this printing was from the same DVI file, generated from a single run of TEX.

The name TEX is copyrighted and may be used only if the implementor provides the full language (even on micro systems such as the IBM PC) and all functions are performed identically to all other implementations. (Knuth provides a test to define compliance with the standard.) This helps ensure compatibility among all implementations and makes it possible to transport document files between diverse systems with identical results. TEX is currently available on a wide range of systems, ranging from PCs such as the Macintosh, Amiga, and IBM PC to the big mainframes.

TEX is a *markup language.*[1] *Markup* refers to the batch approach of printing a rough draft, going through the entire document marking up changes to be made, editing in all of the changes, and printing another draft.

The relationship between TEX and WEB is very close. WEB cannot be used properly without TEX; TEX is written in WEB.

In order to utilize WEB, at least some knowledge of the TEX typesetting system is required. It is possible to get by with very little TEX knowledge and still have beautiful listings for WEB programs. For a beginning WEB programmer, it is not so much a case of knowing what to type as knowing what not to type.

4.1   TEX Input

All input to TEX is in the form of standard printable characters. Most of the input falls into three broad categories: straight text, special control characters, and control sequences.

4.1.1   Straight Text

Straight text is exactly what the name implies: ordinary ASCII character sequences made up of words, sentences, and paragraphs that are printed more or less the same way that they are entered. Most of the input to TEX falls in this category. For straight text, the TEX system performs complex typesetting functions without any action required from the programmer. Other than coming up with the text to be typeset, the only effort necessary for the programmer is to beware of entering one of the special control characters (see next section) by accident.

The text is completely free-form. TEX pays no attention to the number of blanks or tabs between words, since it handles the interword spacing anyway. Any number of them is equivalent to a single blank. One or more blank lines start a new paragraph.

4.1.2   Special Control Characters

The only pitfalls which can snare the unwary in the simple straight-text mode are the special characters which have meaning to TEX. These include the dollar sign ($), percent (%), and several others which are listed in Appendix B. All of these characters are significant to TEX. If they are used in the text, they must be preceded

---

[1] Not to be confused with a *generalized markup language* (GML), which is at a much higher level of abstraction.

by a backslash, which is the character designated as the TEX escape character, the start of a TEX control sequence. This tells TEX that you are not trying to get its attention; you just want the actual character to appear in the output.

The dollar sign is used as the beginning and ending delimiter for math mode (see Section 4.4). Two other characters associated with math mode are the underscore ('_') and the caret ('^'). Use of '_' outside math mode requires a preceding backslash. While the '^' character can be generated by entering '\char"5E', use of '$\uparrow$' will produce '↑', which is a much more pleasing character anyway.

The pound sign ('#') is used to indicate the parameter(s) of a TEX macro (see below). The percent sign marks the beginning of comments in a TEX program. Everything from the percent to the end of the line is considered a comment and is not seen by TEX.

There are a few other special control characters that are used for things that do not exist in the ASCII character set. For instance, TEX has three different kinds of dashes: hyphens, en dashes, and em dashes. The hyphen, designated by a normal ASCII '-', is used in hyphenated words such as straight-text. The en dash, entered as '--', is used in number ranges such as 50–60. The em dash, '---', separates phrases in sentences—like this.

TEX provides true 'single quotes' and "double quotes." In order to have them appear in the listing, some special character sequences must be placed in the WEB file. Unlike on typewriters and terminals, the beginning quote characters are different from the ending quote characters. The reverse quote character (' ` ') is used to generate ', while the standard quote character will generate '. Thus to put something in single quotes, 'this is quoted' will produce 'this is quoted'. Doubling the characters ''like this'' will be printed "like this".

The regular ASCII double quote character ('"') should not be used in TEX code (in a WEB program it should only be used in the Pascal code). If input, it will print as ", but it cannot be used to generate the beginning double quotes. Characters quoted "like this" will come out "like this".

4.1.3 Control Sequences

A *control sequence* is a sequence of ASCII characters beginning with an escape character, followed by either a sequence of alphabetic characters or a special character. Normally the escape character (not to be confused with the ASCII ESC control character) is the backslash ('\'). If the sequence consists of alphabetic characters it is called a *control word*, while an escape character followed by a special character is a *control symbol*. The control words are further subdivided into primitives and macros.

The most common use of control symbols is to generate the accents found in most foreign languages. For instance, the sequence '\"{o}' would be printed as 'ö'. TEX contains control symbols for all of the accents commonly found in other languages.

The concept of a TEX macro is similar to that of a `WEB` macro (and those found in many other languages as well). It is a name that is equated to a variable amount of text which replaces the macro name wherever it is referenced. The replacement text can consist of virtually any TEX code, including straight text to be typeset and other control sequences such as control symbols, primitives, and other macros. TEX macros are defined by using the '\def' primitive. A macro can have a number of parameters, which are designated by '#1', '#2', etc. For example, the following code is the definition of the '\SP' and '\H' macros from '`webmac`', the ones used to create the visible space used in strings ('␣') and hexadecimal constants:

```
\def\SP{{\tt\char`\ }} % (visible) space in a string
\def\H#1{\hbox{\rm\char"7D\tt#1}} % hexadecimal constant
```

In the '\H' macro, the '#1' represents the actual hexadecimal number to be printed and this number will be substituted when the macro is expanded.

A primitive is one of TEX's built-in functions. Each primitive performs a discrete low-level operation that is not reducible. No expansion is associated with a primitive; it equates to a procedure call within TEX itself.

4.2 Fonts

TEX has a complete family of fonts built in, including roman font (the font that appears in the text of this book), *italic*, `typewriter`, **bold**, and *slanted*. `WEB` is fully aware of these options and utilizes all of them automatically. When `WEAVE` generates the listing, the font changes are inserted as needed.

Within the TEX part of a section, the programmer is allowed to change fonts manually (the sequence '\bf' will switch to bold font). For instance, the sequence '`here we have a {\bf bold} font`' will produce 'here we have a **bold** font'. When using the bare font commands, one must remember to delimit their scope by enclosing them in braces; otherwise the remainder of the document may be in bold[2] or italic font.

The only time the `WEB` user needs to be concerned with loading fonts is the case where a special purpose font must be loaded, one that is not normally part of the TEX PLAIN macro package.

---

[2] May be emboldened? Is this what is meant by bold literature?

4.3 Boxes and Tables

Tables in TeX are created by using '\halign', which stands for "horizontal alignment." Vertical rules between the fields are optional, as are horizontal rules between the lines of the table. While a detailed description of table generation is beyond the scope of this book, several examples are provided in the Knight's Tour program in Appendix G; the WEB source code used to generate the tables is in Section F.3.1 and the result can be seen in Section G.4.1.

4.4 Math

Mathematics, in a very real sense, is the reason TeX exists in the first place. At the time it was designed, the software driving computerized typesetters produced extremely poor quality documents when trying to typeset mathematical formulas. TeX was developed specifically to overcome this problem.

Mathematical typography concepts are deeply ingrained into TeX's innards. Enclosing text in dollar signs causes the selected text to be typeset in *math mode*, a special state built into TeX.

Using an underscore in math mode causes the token following the underscore to appear as a subscript ('n_3' is set as n_3), while a caret indicates that a superscript should be used (a Valley mathematician would enter "grody to the max" as '$grody^{max}$' and it would be typeset as $grody^{max}$). TeX scoping rules apply here, so a group following a sub- or superscript command is raised or lowered as a unit ('j_{n+1}' becomes j_{n+1}). Special symbols used in mathematical formulas are generated by TeX primitive operations, such as '\infty' for ∞, '\theta' for θ, and '\sum' for $\sum$. By combining these symbols with the subscript and superscript operators, the beginnings of a mathematical formula can be formed. For instance, '$\sum_{k=0}^{n}x_{i}=\int_{-\infty}^{+\infty}f$' will produce $\sum_{k=0}^{n} x_i = \int_{-\infty}^{+\infty} f$. (The n and $k = 0$ on the summation are actually referred to as *limits*, but they are specified with the same notation as subscripts and superscripts.)

TeX has several additional modes for the formatting of mathematics. Display mode is similar to regular math mode, except that the formula is visually separated from the descriptive text. The positioning of the symbols changes slightly, as they have more vertical space and do not have to fit within a line. Use of double dollar signs identifies a formula to be displayed; otherwise the input text is exactly the same as for a formula in the "running text"; the formula in the previous paragraph would appear as

$$\sum_{k=0}^{n} x_i = \int_{-\infty}^{+\infty} f$$

when displayed. Note the repositioning of n and $k = 0$ in the summation, and the height of the summation and integral symbols compared with those in the inline formula.

If the formula is a multiline series of equations that should be aligned on the equal sign, a control sequence called '`\eqalign`' can provide this service.

The mathematical primitives found in TEX are extensive. Like table generation, they are beyond the scope of this book, but the Knight's Tour program in Appendix G contains examples of mathematical formulas. The C program in Appendix G.7 also makes heavy use of mathematics.

The $\mathcal{AMS}$-TEX macro package [Spi86] is specifically designed for documents with heavy-duty mathematics. It is possible to use the facilities of $\mathcal{AMS}$-TEX in the TEX code of a `WEB` program, within limits (see Section 5.6).

Chapter 5

Finer Points

5.1 Utilization of WEB

5.1.1 Code Sections, Macros, or Procedures?

The decision of whether to use a code section, a macro, or a procedure for a given piece of code depends primarily on three factors: the amount of code, how it is referenced, and whether it has parameters or not. All three mechanisms are roughly equivalent in that a variable amount of program code is equated to a mnemonic and use of that mnemonic in a program causes those statements to be executed.

The usage of the code is probably the primary determinant of how it should be defined. The code section is the most visible way of defining the code, and the most readable. Not only is the section name much more descriptive then even long procedure or macro identifiers, but the section number embedded in the name makes it very easy to locate the definition of the section without having to turn to the index first. The fact that forward references are allowed for everything except numeric macros simplifies matters, allowing the programmer to concentrate on the algorithm rather than positioning of code.

One thing that must be remembered about both code sections and macros is that the text is expanded inline and is therefore duplicated for every reference. If a large code section is referenced many times within the program, a huge amount of source code is created. With a procedure call, only one copy of the procedure exists in the program and is called from various locations.

If a piece of code is to be executed more than once in the same program with different input data, this is typically done by invoking it with a parameter. Since code sections have no parameter capability, this algorithm must be implemented as a procedure or macro. As above, which one is used is determined in part by the size of the code to be invoked. Macros generate more source code but execute faster

75

because there is no procedure call. If the code to be generated is short and the
amount of computer memory usage is not an issue, a macro is preferable.

5.1.2   The Procedure Shuffle

Even when using procedures, it is still possible to place the code anywhere in the
WEB program with (almost) no regard to Pascal's forward declaration policy. Procedures, like any other program text, can be placed in either a regular named section
or the catch-all unnamed section. In either case, the order in which procedures
appear in the final program is dependent on the order in which they appear in an
individual section and the place that section is inserted into the output relative to
other sections.

> **7.**   ⟨ Procedures of the program 7 ⟩ ≡
>   ⟨ Procedures for sorting 9 ⟩
>   ⟨ Procedures for analysis 8 ⟩
>
> **8.**   ⟨ Procedures for analysis 8 ⟩ ≡
> **procedure** *analyze_stuff*;
>   **begin** *sort_stuff*;
> $\vdots$
>   **end**;
>
> **9.**   ⟨ Procedures for sorting 9 ⟩ ≡
> **procedure** *sort_stuff*;
>   **begin**
> $\vdots$
>   **end**;

In the above example, the *sort_stuff* procedure is called by the *analyze_stuff*
procedure, yet *analyze_stuff* occurs earlier in the source file than *sort_stuff*. If this
were an ordinary Pascal program, this would be a forward reference and would
cause an error. However, since the section ⟨ Procedures for sorting ⟩ is referenced
by ⟨ Procedures of the program ⟩ before ⟨ Procedures for analysis ⟩, the contents of
the former (including *sort_stuff*) will be inserted into the Pascal program before the
contents of the latter, so it will not really be a forward reference after all. In the
Pascal file, *sort_stuff* will appear before it is called in *analyze_stuff*, so the Pascal
compiler will be happy.

This technique allows the programmer to group procedures by function rather
than the dictates of the Pascal compiler. Since the procedures are inserted by group,
however, sometimes a variation is needed when procedures of the two groups call

each other, or when a procedure in a group calls another procedure occurring later in the same group. Sometimes it is useful to declare a procedure in a section by itself so that it can be placed into a particular location. For instance, in section 183 of **WEAVE** we find:

⟨ Declaration of the *app_comment* procedure 195 ⟩
⟨ Declaration of the *app_octal* and *app_hex* procedures 196 ⟩
⟨ Declaration of the *easy_cases* procedure 186 ⟩
⟨ Declaration of the *sub_cases* procedure 192 ⟩
procedure *Pascal_parse*;
$\vdots$

This forces the declaration of these procedures to occur before they are used in *Pascal_parse*, even though they occur later in the source file.

5.1.3 Local Procedures

On the same general topic, that of moving procedures around in the Pascal file without really moving them, is the subject of local procedures. A *local procedure* is one that is declared within another procedure rather than in the outer block. Like other local declarations such as variable and type sections, local procedures only exist within the scope of the procedure in which they are declared and cannot be called from outside the procedure.

There are several reasons for using local procedures, including, but not limited to, the following:

- Modularity: Local procedures aid in modularity, since it is not possible for a local procedure in one scope to influence a procedure declared in another scope. This aids in the concept of information hiding.

- Access to parameters and local variables: It is not possible to access the parameters and local declarations of a procedure from outside the procedure. If the procedure calls another procedure declared in the outer block of the main program, the local variables must be passed as parameters to allow the other procedure to see them. A local procedure can access them directly.

Local procedures can themselves have local procedures. The nesting can be several levels deep, to some implementation-defined limit. The actual limit is probably adequate, since it is probably larger than the practical limit.

A procedure can access the declarations of all levels of blocks enclosing it, including the outer block, but it cannot see the declarations of blocks at the same

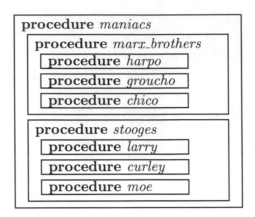

Figure 5.1: Scope of Nested Procedures.

level or at a lower level in any case, even those declared within itself, or those of outer blocks which do not enclose it.

The diagram in Figure 5.1 illustrates the scopes of nested procedures. The *groucho* procedure can access variables declared local to *marx_brothers* and *maniacs*, or the parameters of either procedure, plus the declarations in the outer block of the main program, but cannot reach the local declarations of *harpo*, *chico*, *stooges*, or any of the local procedures of *stooges*. Procedure *stooges* can see the declarations of *maniacs* and the outer block but cannot see into any other procedure. The procedure headings of *larry*, *curley*, and *moe* are visible to *stooges*, but not the internals of these procedures.

While there are many advantages to using nested procedures, readability is not one of them. When reading the listing, determining where each procedure begins and ends is not easy, even if each level of procedure is properly indented. The outer procedures are particularly hard to read, because there may be many pages of code between the procedure heading, the beginning of the procedure body, and the end of the procedure. Without marking pertinent lines with comments such as

```
end; { of moe }
```

it is almost impossible.

WEB can solve this problem in the same way that it solves all problems of visual complexity, by data reduction. All of the procedures local to a particular procedure are placed into a common code section and a reference to the code section is placed in the outer procedure, reducing all of the local procedures to a single line. In a similar way, the declarations of variables and types can also be placed into a section.

To reuse the procedure structure from above, the *maniacs* procedure is defined as follows:

14.   ⟨Procedures of the program 7⟩ +≡
procedure *maniacs*;
⟨Local variables of the *maniacs* procedure 17⟩
⟨Local procedures of the *maniacs* procedure 32⟩
  begin
  ⟨Do whatever the *maniacs* procedure is supposed to do 44⟩
  end;

The declaration of one of the procedures in the next level would be:

32.   ⟨ Local procedures of the *maniacs* procedure 32 ⟩ ≡
procedure *stooges*;
⟨Local variables of the *stooges* procedure 48⟩
⟨Local procedures of the *stooges* procedure 49⟩
  begin
  ⟨Do whatever the *stooges* procedure is supposed to do 53⟩
  end;

The other procedures would be declared in a similar manner. Each procedure is placed into the code section reserved for the local procedures of its immediately enclosing procedure and inserts it own local procedures inline by referencing the code section containing them. The relationships are easy to follow, because the code section names contain the identifier of the procedure involved. Each procedure is self-contained and position independent as is normal with WEB.

5.1.4   Getting Run Over by a Semi(colon)

Placement of semicolons can sometimes be tricky. When referencing a code section or macro, one should always keep in mind that their expansion is a simple textual substitution operation. The expansion is not line-oriented and knows nothing of statements and semicolons; it is a literal character-by-character replacement.

If the text to be expanded has multiple lines, they must be separated by semicolons in order to be valid Pascal. A natural tendency is to place one on the last line of the replacement text as well, because it looks more natural. Also, if the order of the lines is altered so that the last line is no longer last, it is not necessary to move semicolons around.

On the other hand, the place in the code where the macro or code section is referenced often has a semicolon, because it looks more natural there, too. This is especially true for macros, because they look like procedure calls and appear wrong without a semicolon. Also, the presence of a semicolon makes WEAVE format the text in a more natural way, since after a semicolon is always a good place for a line break. Code section names without semicolons tend to format strangely. If several of them are contiguous, they are run together and line breaks occur in the middle of names.

As a result of the presence of semicolons at the end of both the replacement text and the line on which it is referenced, double semicolons appear in the Pascal file. Normally this is not a problem, because the second semicolon would be considered an instance of the *empty statment*. The empty statement can appear in most contexts within a program.

If double semicolons cause problems, one way to get rid of them is to make the replacement text a compound statement with no semicolon. On the other hand, it is not really necessary to have a semicolon after a reference to a code section as long as it is formatted as if one were there. The "invisible semicolon" WEB command ('@;') serves exactly that purpose. When placed in the Pascal code, it does not appear in either the listing or the Pascal file, but the formatting algorithm behaves as if a real semicolon were present (i.e., line breaks occur at the invisible semicolon rather than in the middle of the section name). Of course, since the semicolon, invisible or otherwise, is only a separator, it is possible for more than one complete section name to appear on a line, if they are fairly short. If one name per line is desired, at the cost of more vertical space, the '@/' can be used instead of '@;'.

5.1.5   Riding Herd on Change Files

There are a few "gotchas" that crop up when change files are being used.

Matching the Right Lines

Since change files operate by text matching, rather than by a line number mechanism, it is possible for the matching operation to operate incorrectly at times. For instance, if a change section contains match text consisting of a single line and that line occurs more than once in the WEB file, the wrong line is replaced and the wrong section is modified if the first occurrence is not the one the programmer intended to match. This condition is not flagged as an error, since the WEB system has no way of knowing that the line matched is not the one that was intended.

A related problem is the case where the change consists of several lines, the first of which occurrs in several locations. As before, the match occurs at the wrong place, but at least this time the error is detected because the remaining lines in the match text will not match.

One way of getting around both problems is to start the match text a couple of lines earlier in the WEB file, beginning with a line known to be unique. Since these additional lines are not really part of the change, they must be replicated at the beginning of the replacement text as well as the match text, so that they are not inadvertently deleted.

When looking at a change file, it is very hard to correlate the various change sections with the main WEB file and with each other, since they tend to look alike. When adding a new change section, it is difficult to determine which two existing sections it should be inserted between without analysis of the WEB file, preferably with a text editor capable of string searches.

A simple technique to combat this problem is to place the section number on the '@x' line. Since anything after the '@x' is a comment, this will not cause any type of error. The section numbers make it very easy to insert new change sections in the right place. For this reason, change files should not add new code sections to the middle of the program so that the numbering of the sections in the original listing remains valid.

A new code section is created by a change file when a '@␣' or '@*' command is inserted into the text when one wasn't there before. The addition of the new section causes all of the following sections to be renumbered, making them disagree with the listing.

In order to avoid renumbering all of the code sections in the entire program, completely new sections should not be inserted into the middle of a WEB program but should be added only at the end. This ensures that the section numbers are consistent for all of the versions of a program. Programs like TANGLE and WEAVE have a specific place for new sections to be added, a code section provided for just this purpose. Except for the index, this section is the very last code section of the program, so any sections inserted after it will not affect the numbering of any previously existing sections.

How Big Should a Change Section Be?

There are two opposing philosophies regarding how change sections should be constructed in order to insert the changes with minimum hassle and yet be able to accept updates to the base WEB file. If changes are made to the base WEB file and any of the changed lines is currently in the match text of a change section, then the change section will no longer match and errors will be reported. The lines in the match text must be changed so that they again match the WEB file.

One of the two camps (which includes the author) prefers to make the change sections as small as possible, only a few lines each. If lines are to be modified in several noncontiguous locations within a code section, then the modifications are broken up into several change sections, each including only lines that have actually changed. This technique makes it easier for independent changes to interleave with each other if the changes are made to the same code sections. With smaller change sections, it is much more likely that modifications to the base WEB file will occur on lines between change sections, meaning that the change file does not have to be modified. Smaller change sections also make it easier when merging multiple change files (see Section 9.2).

The other school prefers to place an entire code section into one big change section if any line of the code section is to be changed. The code section is replaced in its entirety. Most of the lines in the replacement text are the same as those in the match text. This is almost guaranteed to conflict with other changes to the WEB file.

Making a Change in a Change File

The actual procedure of making a change to a WEB program via a change file is a fairly straightforward process, especially if a text editor which allows multiple files to be open at once is available.

The first step is to determine the change that needs to be made by looking at the listing. The number of the section in which the code appears should be noted. The reader's favorite text editor is then initiated, with the change file and the WEB file as the files to be loaded. If this is the first change, then a new change file is created. The WEB file should be loaded read-only if the editor supports this option.

An empty change section should be created, one consisting of nothing but the '@x', '@y', and '@z' lines. If this is an existing change file, the new change section should be placed between the two sections that change text before and after the target change. The section numbers on the change sections, if present, should make this easy to determine. After the new section is inserted in the proper place, the section number of the code it is to modify should be added to the '@x' line (for example, '@x [36]') to continue the tradition and make future changes easier. In addition, comments describing what change is being made are helpful. The comments may appear immediately ahead of the change section or on the end of the '@x' after the section number. They can appear anywhere except the lines between '@x' and '@y' or between '@y' and '@z'.

The lines to be matched must appear in the change section exactly as they appear in the WEB file, except for white space. While one can go to the effort of typing in these lines manually, it is far easier and more reliable to copy them from the WEB file itself. Care should be taken not to modify the WEB file. A copy operation, rather than a move, should be used. The lines should be copied twice, first to the match text part of the change section (between the '@x' and '@y'), then to the replacement text (between '@y' and '@z'). This ensures that lines are not left out of the replacement text inadvertently, thereby deleting them. If the programmer wishes to left justify the lines after they are in place, this is permissible, since WEB ignores the white space at the beginning of a line and does not use it for matching purposes. The author's preference is to leave the lines exactly as they appear in the WEB file.

The actual change can now be made by editing the replacement text. The reader should take care to modify the replacement text instead of the match text. The error is easy to make, because they are identical at first. The author has caught himself merrily editing the match text an embarrassing number of times. The error is easily detected, because the match text no longer matches the WEB file and the change fails.

Deleting Large Blocks

While the change section mechanism works fairly well for making small changes to existing text and for adding large blocks of text, it becomes very tedious when large blocks of text are to be deleted from the program with a change file. Because of the way that change sections operate, the entire block to be deleted must be included in the match text (the part between the '@x' and the '@y'). The immense size of the match text leaves the program prone to the problem mentioned in the previous section: unrelated updates to the base WEB file forcing modifications to the change file in order that the match text will still match. It is doubly irritating in this case, because the lines that are affected have been deleted by the change file and are no longer relevant.

5.1.6 Making WEAVE Do What You Want

The WEAVE processor is a very sophisticated text manipulator. Most of the time, it will do the right thing, but since it is just a computer program, sometimes it gets confused and needs assistance from a human.

The Sledge Hammer

The '@t' WEB command is provided so that the programmer can insert pure TEX code into the output file to counteract something that WEAVE has done. Since the amount of text to be inserted is variable, the end of the control text is delimited by '@>'. The TEX code is not modified by WEAVE in any way, but is inserted verbatim into the output TEX file.

Sometimes the '@/' command doesn't work, because internal massaging of the formatting codes by WEAVE cancels the line break. In cases such as these, the programmer can force the line break no matter what WEAVE thinks by using the TEX macro directly, as in '@t\6@>'. A complete list of the available brute force formatting macros can be found in Appendix C.

Another example of '@t' use is the case of procedures that are defined with the **forward** directive. When WEAVE encounters a procedure definition, it expects that the body of the procedure will follow immediately. All lines after the procedure header are indented in (right) one level, until the **end** is found. After the **end**, the indentation is set back one notch, to the level existing before the procedure. However, a procedure declared **forward** doesn't have a body, as the complete definition of the procedure occurs later in the program. Therefore, the procedure would indent in, but the lack of an **end** would mean that it would not outdent back to the previous level. Having several **forward** procedures in a row would have a stepladder effect as each one was indented another level, as in

> **procedure** x; **forward**;
>   **procedure** y; **forward**;
>   **procedure** z; **forward**;

Performing an outdent manually after each **forward** directive would solve this problem. One of the formatting macros in '`webmac`' does exactly that, so placing '`@t\2@>`' immediately after the semicolon following each **forward** would keep the indentation under control.

There are several TeX macros which can be used this way. They are listed in Appendix C. They should be used only if absolutely necessary, since it is usually better to go through normal channels.

Don't Box Me In

One side effect of verbatim text (that which appears between '`@=`' and '`@>`') that is not mentioned anywhere in the literature is the fact that in addition to typesetting the text as a string, **WEAVE** draws a box around it. For instance, the identifier from Section 2.3, '`@=lib$signal@>`', would appear in the listing as $\boxed{\texttt{lib\$signal}}$. It took the author a long time to decide whether this were a feature or not. The final decision was that it is a feature, since it highlights the fact that these strings are specially treated, but it works better when used a certain way.

If the identifier appears many times throughout the program, the resulting boxes tend to be distracting. Also, they take up slightly more vertical space, possibly causing an extra page eject on occasion. The strategy used by the author in these situations is to define a macro for each of these identifiers that appears more than once, then to use the identifier of the macro instead of the original. This means that only one box per identifier appears. The macro to generate the above identifier would be:

> **define** *signal* $\equiv \boxed{\texttt{lib\$signal}}$

Throughout the rest of the program, *signal* is used as a shorthand for *lib$signal*. Since *signal* is just an ordinary simple macro identifier, it won't be set in a box. In some situations, it is possible to get rid of the boxes entirely if desired (see Section 13.1.4).

5.2 Tricks, Traps, and Esoterica

5.2.1 Breaking Up Large TeX Files

Sometimes the TeX file for a large WEB program must be broken up into manageable pieces. For instance, TeX itself is too big to be printed successfully on many output devices, as the listing is over 500 pages. The problem is more acute on personal computers, where capacities in general are much smaller. A PC may not have the disk space to store the DVI file generated by TeX.

The WEB Manual [Knu83] describes a technique for breaking a TeX file into several pieces, running them through TeX independently, and combining the pages of the small segments into a complete document. The group of small TeX files is logically one file although it is contained in more than one physical file.

The various code sections are self-contained and can be placed in different segments as long as each section appears in its entirety and the first section in each segment is a major (starred) section. Nor is there any problem with the index and list of section names, since they are also self-contained. The table of contents, however, is created dynamically as TeX runs. Since each segment is a separate document, each will have a separate table of contents, and the page numbers of each will start at 1. The trick is to coordinate the page numbers so that one combined table of contents contains all of the segments and the page numbers are contiguous; i.e., the first page number of segment 2 is one higher than the last page of segment 1.

When breaking up the large file into pieces, all limbo text that was present in the original file should be copied to all of the segments because it may contain definitions or font loads needed by all segments. Rather than determine which definitions are needed by which segments, it is simpler to make them all the same. If the original limbo text was large, it would be much less trouble to place the limbo text in a separate file (named 'thelimbo.tex' or something similar) and add '\input thelimbo' to each segment.

The first line in each segment, however, must be '\input webmac' so that the macros that WEB itself needs will be defined. Every segment other than the last must have '\con' as the last line.

The table of contents can be combined fairly easily because it is normally output to a file anyway. It is only necessary to modify the processing of the contents text file slightly. In addition, another file is created to allow each segment to pass its ending page number to the next segment.

Two auxiliary TeX files contain the code necessary to combine the segments. The file 'getstart.tex' contains definitions to allow the segment to determine what its starting page number is; 'passlast.tex' contains code to output the starting page number of the next segment. The limbo text of all segments except the first should contain '\input getstart'; all segments except the last should have '\input `passlast`'; the middle segments should input both. Two additional statements are needed for all segments to identify the name of the current segment and that of the next segment. These should appear just ahead of the '\input' lines.

> \def\thisfilename{*this_seg*}
> \def\nextfilename{*next_seg*}

Additionally, the very last segment should contain the following to tie it all together:

> \def\readcontents{\input *firstseg*.con \input *middleseg*.con
>   \input contents}

Every contents file except the last must be listed explicitly. Here we only show three segments, but if the file were broken into 25 pieces, there would be 25 '\input' primitives.

Assume that we wish to break '`tex.tex`' into three pieces (in reality, it would probably have to be broken into about 50 pieces) that we will call '`t1.tex`', '`t2.tex`', and '`t3.tex`'. The limbo section from '`tex.tex`' is copied to a file called '`tlimbo.tex`'. The limbo section of '`t1.tex`' would contain:

> \input webmac
> \input tlimbo
> \def\thisfilename{t1}
> \def\nextfilename{t2}
> \input passlast

The execution of the TeX code within '`passlast.tex`' will cause the table of contents information to be written to '`t1.con`' instead of the normal '`contents.tex`'. An additional file ('`t2.pag`') is created and the page number of the last page of the segment plus one, i.e., the first page of the next segment, is written to it. Since this is the first segment and the starting page number is known, the '\input getstart' is not used.

The limbo text of '`t2.tex`' would contain:

> \input webmac
> \input tlimbo
> \def\thisfilename{t2}
> \def\nextfilename{t3}
> \input getstart
> \input passlast

This segment does not know its starting page number, so it must '\input getstart'. The code contained in 'getstart.tex' will read 't2.pag' and set the starting page number to that contained therein. Then the table of contents file name is set to 't2.con' and the next page number is written to 't3.pag'.

Finally, 't3.tex' would contain:

```
\input webmac
\input tlimbo
\def\thisfilename{t3}
\input getstart
\def\readcontents{\input t1.con \input t2.con
    \input contents}
```

This final segment acquires its starting page number from 't3.pag'. It does not use 'passlast.tex', because it has no following segments to pass the page number to. Since it is the segment that will actually generate the combined table of contents, if redefines '\readcontents' to input the entries from the other two segments first. Its own entries are contained in 'contents.tex', since it didn't execute 'passlast' and change the name to 't3.con'.

The contents of the 'getstart.tex' and 'passlast.tex' files can be found in Section F.1.2.

Of course, none of this would be necessary if the source file were not so big in the first place. If modular design were used, there would be several smaller WEB files instead of one big one, and the TEX files would have a corresponding configuration.

5.2.2 Having Some Reservations

Section 4 of TEX contains a trick to accomplish an unusual objective: reusing of one of Pascal's reserved words for another task. Knuth wanted to use **type** as an identifier (a parametric macro defined in section 133). However, **type** is one of Pascal's reserved words, and the compiler would not have taken kindly to its use for another purpose. Because all of the types of the program are concatenated into one code section and this code section is referenced in only one place, there is really only one occurrence of the Pascal version of **type** in the entire program. Knuth defined a new macro called *mtype*, equated to **type**, to keep the Pascal compiler happy, and used this in the proper place. However, use of *type* as the replacement text for *mtype* would cause an attempt to expand the macro *type*. So *type* is sneaked in by concatenating the letters together with TANGLE's join operation ('@&'), making *type* unrecognizable as a word. Finally *mtype* is made into a reserved word with **format** and *type* is made into an unreserved word, since it is now just an identifier.

define $mtype \equiv t@\&y@\&p@\&e$
format $mtype \equiv type$
format $type \equiv true$

$\vdots$

mtype $\langle$ Types in the outer block $7 \rangle$

5.2.3   Fun with Macros

Section 6 of TEX contains a trick that is even more exotic, one so subtle that it took the author a while to figure out how it was accomplished. In this section, some numeric macros are defined for use as Pascal labels. Two of these macros have names containing 'TEX' (*start_of_TEX* and *end_of_TEX*). The TEX logo is normally generated by the macro '\TeX', but it is against the rules of WEB to place any special characters in an identifier (i.e., '@d start_of_\TeX' would be illegal). Even if WEB were to accept such an identifier it would not remove the backslash, so the Pascal compiler would become hysterical upon encountering this identifier. An inspection of the WEB source file for TEX revealed that there was nothing unusual about the identifiers for these macros.

```
@d start_of_TEX=1
@d end_of_TEX=9998
```

With this definition, the identifiers should have appeared as *start_of_TEX* and *end_of_TEX* in the listing. The obvious (wrong) conclusion was that the TEX file had been generated by WEAVE and then doctored manually during preparation for publication. However, after running WEAVE against the TEX source file, the newly created listing also contained *start_of_TEX* and *end_of_TEX*! Where was the TEX logo coming from?

After a great deal of study, the mystery was finally solved. The following lines were discovered in the limbo section of the WEB source file for TEX:

```
\def\drop{\kern-.1667em\lower.5ex\hbox{E}\kern-.125em}
\catcode`E=13 \uppercase{\def E{e}}
\def\\#1{\hbox{\let E=\drop\it#1\/\kern.05em}}
```

The purpose of these three lines is to redefine the TEX macro responsible for italicizing identifiers of more than one character ('\\'), modifying it to drop any uppercase 'E' found in an identifier half an "ex" (a typographer's measurement equivalent to the height of the lowercase 'x' in the current font) below its normal position. Instead of specifically generating the TEX logo as expected, this code would drop *any* uppercase 'E' in *any* identifier! If the identifier *line_feed* had instead been *LINE_FEED*, it would have been displayed as *LINE_FEED* with this code in effect. This didn't cause problems elsewhere in the program because identifiers containing uppercase letters are rarely, if ever, used in WEB programs. Note that the typography in the substitute identifier is very strange. The spacing had been carefully adjusted specifically for an italic *'E'* falling between *'T'* and *'X'*; substitution of other characters fouled it up completely.

Since the '\\' macro was defined globally, even the index displayed the identifiers with the logo. The normal definition of the '\\' macro can be found in Section F.1.1. The author had so much fun with this that one of the sample programs in this book was modified in exactly the same way so that the results of this technique could be observed firsthand. The ScanTEX program had several identifiers containing 'TeX', such as *out_TeX_file* and *out_TeX_line*. The occurrences of 'TeX' in these identifiers were all changed to 'TEX' and the macro redefinitions shown above were placed into the limbo text. The results can be seen in Appendix G.5.2.

This is a prime example of the power and flexibility possible with TEX.

5.2.4 Controlling the Index

The traditional use of the user-controlled font macro is to index items that would not index properly if one of the regular index commands were used. A typical example is the TEX logo mentioned in the previous section. If TEX were indexed in the normal way with '@^\TeX@>', it would be typeset correctly in the index but would appear in the wrong position since it appears to start with '\' instead of 'T'.

The way to solve this program by using the user-controlled font mechanism is by putting TEX into the index with the following:

```
@:TeX}{\TeX@>
```

The first part of the index entry will be used to put the entry in the proper collating sequence, since the total string between the '@:' and '@>' is used for sorting purposes. and the second part will be used to typeset the entry. When WEAVE generates the index, a call to the '\9' macro is built (note that braces have been added to the entry):

```
\:\9{TeX}{\TeX}, 16.
```

What happens at this point depends on how the '\9' macro is defined. To utilize this technique, the limbo text of the program should contain the following definition:

```
\def\9#1{}
```

This definition causes the '\9' macro to be completely null. It equates to nothing—yet it has a parameter (designated by '#1'). When the macro expands to nothing, it takes the parameter with it, thereby "eating" the '{TeX}' and the code which actually executes is the equivalent of

    \:{\TeX}, 16.

The braces around '\TeX' will do nothing more than delimit a group; they will not be printed. The expansion of the '\:' will remove the comma and the period, so the following will actually appear in the index:

    TEX: 16

5.2.5   Homemade Title Page

While the WEB system will format the title page in a predefined format, it is flexible enough to allow the user to reformat it in any fashion desired. The layout of the title page is controlled by the '\topofcontents' macro. Since this is a standard TEX macro, it can be redefined in the limbo section of the program to lay out the title page in any format the programmer wishes. Typically this feature is used to add such elements as version numbers and copyright notices. There is also a '\botofcontents' macro.

Additionally, the default starting page number can be changed. Unsurprisingly, the text of the program normally starts on page 1 (the title page is numbered 0). If the program is to be included in a larger document, like the programs in this book, then the page number can be set to any value desired. In this case, the title page is given a real page number.

The following code appears in the limbo text of WEAVE:

```
\def\title{WEAVE}
\def\contentspagenumber{15} % should be odd
\def\topofcontents{\null\vfill
  \titlefalse % include headline on the contents page
  \def\rheader{\mainfont Appendix D\hfil \contentspagenumber}
  \centerline{\titlefont The {\ttitlefont WEAVE} processor}
  \vskip 15pt
  \centerline{(Version 3.1)}
  \vfill}
\pageno=\contentspagenumber \advance\pageno by 1
```

This title page was used for the WEAVE listing in the original WEB manual. The WEAVE listing that appears in this book is somewhat different, mainly because the appendix numbering is not the same and the starting page number is radically different. (The WEB file was not modified to produce the listing; a change file was used.)

5.2.6 Suppressing Unchanged Sections

Typically, a `WEB` program running on a wide range of machines (such as TEX itself) has a great number of different change files applied to it, at least one per implementation. For the most part, the main portion of the program is identical in all implementations, and certain sections, containing "system dependencies", are different for each one. Since `WEAVE` generates a complete listing every time it is run, and a program the size of `WEAVE` or `TANGLE` runs to about a hundred pages (and that is small compared to TEX or METAFONT), a lot of paper is consumed printing several large listings that are essentially the same. The author has adopted the practice of printing one full listing generated from the pure `WEB` source (the way it comes from Stanford, with no change files applied), followed by an abbreviated listing containing only changed sections for each change file applied to that program. (In fact, for the programs having published versions of the pure `WEB` source, *only* the changed sections are printed. In the case of TEX, this would be the book *TEX: The Program*; most of the other Stanford-developed programs also exist as bound documents (see Appendix H).

In order to suppress the unchanged sections, it is only necessary to add

```
\let\maybe=\iffalse
```

to the limbo text of the `WEB` file. An explanation of exactly how this works is beyond the scope of this book, but in essence a global flag is set that will tell the TEX formatting macros that only the sections modified by the change file should be output.

5.3 Stylistic Issues

5.3.1 The Elements of `WEB` Style

Section Names

While the `WEB` system will let you write programs however you want, there are several conventions that have gradually become standard practice. Whether these conventions are followed or not is optional, but programs should at least be consistent. The key word is *readability*.

The name of a section should be a short description of what the section does, in plain English. It normally is capitalized only in the first letter. A section which performs an action should have an imperative section name such as ⟨ Sort the array ⟩ rather than ⟨ Sorts the array ⟩ or ⟨ Code to sort the array ⟩, while constants, types, variables, data structures, and other definitions work better with declarative section names such as ⟨ Variables of the outer block ⟩. Procedure definitions, if placed into

named sections, fall into a middle ground, since they are considered both definitions and code. It seems to work better to treat procedures as definitions, as in
⟨Procedures to be exported⟩, especially since the name of the procedure itself is
usually imperative (*sort_array*).

Long Identifiers

Modern compilers allow much longer identifiers than in the past, allowing more
meaningful identifiers. Identifiers consisting of multiple words are typical, although
there is much controversy as to how the words are separated. One school favors
capitalization of the words, while the other prefers using underscores, as in

    IdentifierSeveralWordsLong vs. identifier_several_words_long

For readability, the underscore approach wins hands down. The only reason the
other method exists at all is that not all Pascal compilers accept the underscore
character, since it is not present in Standard Pascal (or in any version of Modula-
2). In this case the capitalization approach is the only way of separating words.
When using WEB, the underscore approach is even more preferable. Not only do the
capitalized words look even worse when italicized (*IdentifierSeveralWordsLong*), but
the WEB system removes underscores when generating the Pascal file, eliminating the
only drawback to the underscore approach.

5.3.2   Thinking in WEB

When a programmer is learning a new language, there is a tendency to avoid utilizing
the new features at first. A path of least resistance is followed, as language constructs
similar to those found in the old language are preferred. How many times have we
seen FORTRAN programs written in Pascal?

This phenomenon is much more pronounced when switching to WEB because of
the radical departure from traditional programming languages. Since WEB is based on
Pascal, many beginners write regular Pascal programs with only slight modifications
to make them compatible with WEB. Virtually no use is made of the unique WEB
features. These programs are rampant with huge code sections that span several
pages, which is in direct opposition to the WEB philosophy that sections should be
kept short and modular. The declarations are clumped together at the beginning
of the program, instead of being placed at the point of use. Instead of using the
description part of the sections to describe the program logic, the commentary is
placed in the code as ordinary Pascal comments. Utilizing the WEB system in this
manner is like buying a Maserati and then using it as a storage area for garden tools
or like hiring a nuclear physicist to wait on tables. The tool being used is adequate
for the job it has been given, but it is capable of much more.

An example of naive WEB programming can be found in Appendix G.4.4, which is logically identical to the Knight's Tour program (see Section G.4.1).

Some practices that are useful in regular Pascal turn out to be redundant or even detrimental in WEB. For instance, the practice of using comments on **end** statements to identify what they are ending, such as

```
end { procedure xxx }
end { if j < 3 }
```

is useful, even necessary, in Pascal. Sometimes it can be difficult to match **end** statements with the blocks that they terminate, especially when the blocks are very large (see Section 5.1.3). This is especially true with procedures, since procedures are potentially the largest blocks of all, sometimes larger than the main program. Procedures nested within procedures compound the problem.

This convention is not necessary in WEB, since the indentation makes it easy to determine which **begin** goes with which **end**. In fact, block identification comments can even interfere with the formatting if the comment is inserted between **end** and a semicolon, as in

```
end { procedure xxx } ;
```

If the distance between **begin** and **end** is too great to determine easily from the alignment that they are paired together, then the block is too long—some of the text within it should be pulled out and put into its own section.

Even though WEB provides complete freedom on the order of components, many programs do not take complete advantage of this. Some programs utilize named sections for pieces of code within procedures yet declare the procedures themselves within the unnamed section ('@p'). Since everything in the unnamed section is concatenated together in the order in which it appears, this means that the body of the main program must appear after all of the procedure definitions, just as in regular Pascal. If the procedures were put into named sections, such as ⟨ Procedures for searching ⟩, the positioning of the procedures could be much more flexible within the WEB file and the skeleton of the main program could be contained in one code section.

5.4 Productivity Aids

5.4.1 Template Program

When developing software in any computer language, it is useful to have a template to use as a starting point, since the overall structure is the same for all programs.

A template can be a copy of an existing program that has been reworked into a new program, or it can be a canned template created specifically for this purpose. It is less effort to use a generic template, because the code from the old program does not have to be removed each time it is used. The template contains the program structure and generic constructs that are the same in all programs, such as the increment macro and the **debug–gubed** macros. WEB lends itself to this concept nicely, since the logic of the program can be developed completely independently of the program structure. The logic can be grafted to the template as the final action.

If the program were developed without a program skeleton, only a main code section, as described in Chapter 3, the template can be merged into it very easily. It is only necessary to copy the template into the program, remove the parts that are not needed, and change the name of the generic main code section of the template's main block to match that of the actual program.

The elements contained in the template are those which are used over and over again in various programs. While not all of them are needed every time, most of them will appear in a majority of the programs. It is easier to have everything you might need in a program included in the template and delete the things that are not needed in a particular program.

A sample template is provided in Appendix G.4.3. It is intended as a guide, since space considerations precluded putting everything in it. The template should be tailored to fit the needs and/or programming style of the individual or organization who will be using it.

The local variable code section found in the sample template is a useful tool. One of the reasons why a procedure is used in a WEB program instead of a code section is so that variables can be declared local to the procedure. Programmers often use the same names more than once in a program when declaring these variables, such as n for a loop control variable. This is permissible because the scoping rules of Pascal keep local variables in one procedure completely separate from those in a different procedure or global variables in the outer block. Instead of duplicating these variables many times, they can be placed into their own code section and just referenced within each procedure.

Many of the things that are placed in the template would be more convenient if they were declared externally, when using the versions of WEB that support such things. For instance, Modula-2 and Ada provide separately compiled library modules, so the various procedures which handle text files could be placed into a separate module and imported instead of being replicated in every source program. The procedures for binary files could be placed in another module, and both modules could import a third module that declares general file handling procedures.

The include files of the C version of WEB provide a similar capability, except that they are not as efficient, because the text in the include file must be processed like the rest of the program every time the program is compiled. However, C also supports separate compilation, so it is capable of precompiled library modules as are Modula-2 and Ada.

For these languages, the template need only contain the **import** or **include** statements needed to access the external code.

5.5   Portability vs. Performance

The twin goals of portability and program efficiency are in direct conflict with each other. Each type of computer has its little quirks, and there are always cases where a certain sequence of Pascal statements will run much faster than another sequence that is logically equivalent. However, the speed gained by use of such machine-dependent features is not portable. Even though the program will run correctly on another machine, the special instructions which caused the speedup on the first machine will probably have no effect on the second. Worse, they may actually run *slower* because of the mismatch of algorithm to architecture.

Theoretically the underlying architecture of the computer system is not relevant when designing a computer program. However, the real world has a distressing tendency to poke its ugly nose into things. Production-quality programs must at least address performance issues. Hacked programs with poor design that get incorrect results at blinding speed are sometimes perceived to be of higher quality than carefully designed programs more concerned with correctness than performance. The fact that the hacked program took 20 times the effort to debug is of no concern to the users.

While the underlying computer should not be of major concern when writing abstract programs, it is always helpful to keep it in the back of the mind. While it is definitely not portable to code according to a particular architecture, there are some considerations that are common to nearly all Pascal compilers on nearly all computer systems. Use of these techniques can help performance on most computers from the same source.

Some optimizations can be performed in the change file, since it is allowed to be system-specific. For instance, every implementation of WEB I have ever seen (including the two I wrote myself) changes the procedures in TANGLE and WEAVE that read and write text files to handle a whole line at a time. The generic procedures in the main WEB files read and write one character at a time in order to be compatible with all Pascal compilers, but the speed improvement when this is changed to buffered I/O is often spectacular.

5.6   Peaceful Coexistence with LaTeX and $\mathcal{A}\mathcal{M}\mathcal{S}$-TeX

Like 'webmac', LaTeX and $\mathcal{A}\mathcal{M}\mathcal{S}$-TeX are macro packages layered on top of TeX. LaTeX provides a document structure, making it easier to produce particular document styles such as books, articles, and reports. This book was typeset by using LaTeX. $\mathcal{A}\mathcal{M}\mathcal{S}$-TeX is a system for documents containing large amounts of complex mathemetics (the AMS in $\mathcal{A}\mathcal{M}\mathcal{S}$-TeX is American Mathematical Society).

5.6.1   Including a WEB Program in a LaTeX or $\mathcal{A}\mathcal{M}\mathcal{S}$-TeX Document

While LaTeX and $\mathcal{A}\mathcal{M}\mathcal{S}$-TeX are different packages with different purposes, interfacing them with WEB programs is accomplished the same way. Throughout the remainder of this subsection, the discussion will refer to LaTeX but will be equally applicable to $\mathcal{A}\mathcal{M}\mathcal{S}$-TeX, and maybe other macro packages, as well.

There are occasions when it would be desirable to include a WEB program in a LaTeX document, such as the programs found in Appendix G. Since both LaTeX and WEB are TeX-based, this sounds simple. However, both packages expect to be the only macro package loaded into TeX and massively interfere with each other.

When a WEB program is included in a LaTeX document, the first line executed is '\input webmac'. When 'webmac.tex' executes, it defines all of the WEB macros, some of which have names already in use by LaTeX. In addition, it makes sweeping changes to fonts, spacing, and page layout. Since 'webmac' does not expect to be included in a larger document, it does not restore anything after the WEB listing is complete. When LaTeX regains control, it becomes extremely confused because all of the parameters it so carefully set appear to have changed on their own and several of its macros don't work the same as they did before. All in all, the results of the mixture are less than desirable.

Using the two packages together is possible if care is taken to prevent 'webmac' from modifying LaTeX's definitions. This is accomplished by using TeX *grouping* to limit the scope of WEB's changes. The scoping rules of TeX are similar to those of more traditional programming languages. Declarations within a particular scope are not visible outside that scope. In TeX, the characters '{' and '}' delimit a scope. After a '{' is encountered, any definitions occurring such as macros and fonts cease to exist when the matching '}' is found, and any definitions in effect at the start of the group are restored.

Another problem encountered when trying to include a WEB program in a LaTeX document is that the table of contents is placed at the end of the WEB listing. One way around this is to change the handling of the table of contents in 'webmac' to use two passes, a method which is compatible with LaTeX's own table of contents.

5.6.2 Including $\mathcal{A}_{\mathcal{M}}\mathcal{S}$-TEX in a WEB Program

The inverse operation, including a LATEX document in a WEB listing, does not work at all. Since $\mathcal{A}_{\mathcal{M}}\mathcal{S}$-TEX is structured differently than LATEX, it is sometimes possible to mix 'webmac' and $\mathcal{A}_{\mathcal{M}}\mathcal{S}$-TEX if it is done a certain way. (The C example in this book contains references to $\mathcal{A}_{\mathcal{M}}\mathcal{S}$-TEX macros.)

First, the $\mathcal{A}_{\mathcal{M}}\mathcal{S}$-TEX package must be loaded into TEX before the WEB listing. It is not possible simply to add '\input amstex' to the limbo text, because a problem similar to that described above will occur. This time it is the 'webmac' macros that will malfunction because they have been redefined. Delimiting the scope of the definitions as described above will defeat the purpose of including $\mathcal{A}_{\mathcal{M}}\mathcal{S}$-TEX in the first place, as it is the definitions that we want; we are not printing a self-contained document. It is not possible to place '\input amstex' ahead of '\input webmac', because the latter does not appear in the WEB file at all; it is added to the TEX file by WEAVE. Editing the TEX file output by WEAVE to put the '\input' of $\mathcal{A}_{\mathcal{M}}\mathcal{S}$-TEX first violates the principles of WEB.

The $\mathcal{A}_{\mathcal{M}}\mathcal{S}$-TEX package must be loaded before the WEB program TEX file. This can be done by specifying 'amstex' as the input file of TEX, then doing an interactive '\input' of the WEAVE-generated listing (be aware that the DVI file will be called 'amstex' if this approach is used). Alternatively, $\mathcal{A}_{\mathcal{M}}\mathcal{S}$-TEX can be made into a preloaded format file. The reader should bear in mind that anyone at another site wishing to print the listing of the WEB program will have to go through this same exercise. Also, some of the $\mathcal{A}_{\mathcal{M}}\mathcal{S}$-TEX macros, specifically the ones that WEB has redefined, will not be available.

5.7 The Source File

It is not required by WEB that the program text should appear in any kind of ordered fashion. Since the input is completely free-form, it can appear in any chaotic manner desired, as long as it is syntactically correct WEB, Pascal, and TEX code. WEAVE will generate the listing in exactly the same way whether the input is all jumbled together or not and TANGLE will generate the same tangled output, although if the WEB file is really disordered, it may actually be an improvement.

While the WEB processors will allow the WEB file to be constructed this way, it would be virtually impossible to maintain. Therefore, it is recommended that within the code parts of sections, the statements are placed one per line, with inner blocks indented, as in a regular Pascal program. The line breaks and indentation in the WEB source will be ignored, but at least the programmer will be able to tell what is going on when editing the file, and it will be easier to correlate the source with the listing. The indentation should not be a problem, because if there are enough nested blocks to cause indentation problems, then the code section is too big and should be broken up.

One indirect way that indenting the source can be beneficial is in the case where there is a logic error related to compound statements and blocks in a program. The indentation in the WEB file corresponds to whatever the programmer typed in, but the indentation performed by WEAVE will follow the logic of the program. The fact that the two are different can help point out the error. For instance, consider the following fragment from a WEB source file:

```
if something then
    statement1;
    statement2;
    statement3;
    end;
```

This was obviously written by a programmer who writes in both Pascal and Modula-2. This person forgot which of the two was the current language and used the Modula-2 form of the **if**, which has an **end** but no **begin**. When WEAVE sees this fragment, the formatting is as follows:

if *something* **then**
    statement1;
statement2; *statement3*;
end ;

It is easy to tell from the formatting what happened: the absence of the **begin** caused the first statement to be the clause of the **then** all by itself. The remaining statements were no longer part of the **if** statement at all. The **end**, which is dangling because the compound statement it was supposed to terminate dissolved away, is just printed where it is because WEAVE doesn't know what else to do with it.

After the missing **begin** is added:

```
if something then
    begin
    statement1;
    statement2;
    statement3;
    end;
```

The listing

> **if** *something* **then**
>   **begin** *statement1* ; *statement2* ; *statement3* ;
>   **end**;

looks much more reasonable and matches what the programmer intended.

Chapter 6

Running WEB

6.1 General Operation

This chapter describes how to run WEB on various computer systems. It does not explain how to run either TEX or the Pascal compiler. It is assumed that user guides are available for both programs. In the case of TEX, the operation should be very similar to that of WEB, because of the common origins of the programs.

All implementations of WEB perform the same basic operations. A text file containing the WEB commands is read, an optional change file is merged with it, and output text files are created. In the case of TANGLE, the files that are output are the Pascal file and the string pool file (if used). WEAVE will output a TEX source file. The WEB macro package, 'webmac', must be in a location where TEX is able to find it when a simple '\input webmac' is used. With a directory-structured file system, this is normally either the *default* directory or the one indicated by 'texinput'.

The differences between the implementations are primarily in how execution is initiated (the command line interface, etc.) and in how the various files are specified. Most implementations operate in *batch mode*. Once one of the processors is initiated, it reads its input files and writes its output files until completion. Even on the Macintosh, the actual operation of WEAVE and TANGLE is not interruptable. Selection of the files to be processed is done interactively, but once processing starts it runs to completion as in the batch environments.

6.1.1 Text Files

All files handled by the WEB processors, both for input and for output, are text files, where the meaning of text file is implementation-defined. Some systems use a combination of carriage return (CR) and line feed (LF) to mark the end of a line, while others use LF/CR or just one or the other by itself. Still other systems have no control codes at all within the line, maintaining the line length in an invisible count field preceding the line. Whatever standard format is used on a particular system shouldn't matter, as long as all programs involved (the text editor used to create the program, TeX, WEB, and the Pascal compiler) agree on the format of a text file. The only problem is in transferring text files between unlike systems, and this is a general problem affecting all programs, not just WEB. If text files are to be transferred between heterogeneous systems, a line-oriented protocol such as Kermit should be used, rather than a verbatim copy of the byte stream of the file. Kermit will always create the new file in the native text file format of the destination machine.

6.1.2   File Names

Many operating systems support the concept of file "extensions" or "types," allowing the usage of a file to be determined from its name. The format is basically the same on a number of systems: a base file name, followed by a period and the extension, as in

>   *basename.extension*

The maximum lengths of the base name and the extension vary from system to system. For instance, MS-DOS limits the base name to 8 characters and the extension to 3, while VMS will permit either to reach a length of 31. VMS also allows a *version number*, which is specified as a semicolon followed by a number appended to the end of the file name, as in

>   *basename.extension;version*

For the systems having file extensions, the particular extensions used for the various files are fairly consistent from implementation to implementation. The base WEB file is nearly always '.web' and the TeX file output by WEAVE is typically '.tex'. The Pascal file generated by TANGLE is usually '.pas', although Unix systems, cryptic to the bitter end, use '.p' as the extension. Change files are normally '.ch' or '.chg'. Since the word *pool* contains more than three letters, the pool file has the most variation as everyone abbreviates differently. The extensions '.pol' and '.poo' are used, while Clearlake VAX doesn't abbreviate at all ('.pool'), because extension length is not restricted in VMS. None of the systems (except MVS) requires all of the file names to be explicitly listed. All of them will derive the base name of the change file and the output files from that of the WEB file. In fact, many of the implementations do not provide a means to make them anything else. Many of the systems will allow using a different extension for the files and some will allow them to have a different *basename* than the main WEB file.

WEB doesn't get involved with dynamic file names, since there is no include file capability (except in CWEB; see Section 8.1.4). The WEB files are fairly portable and will normally run on all systems with no modifications. The only likely problem is with the TEX primitive '\input'. A WEB program may input a TEX file in the limbo text to load a special purpose macro package, change page dimensions, etc. Such operations are portable as long as no system dependencies are used in the file name. For instance, '\input junk' would be portable, while

```
\input [wayne.stuff]junk
\input d:\wayne\stuff\junk
\input #wayne.stuff:junk
```

would not be, since these lines use file specifications for particular computer systems. Use of the file name 'junk.xyz' would probably be okay on most systems, although a few systems (such as MVS on IBM mainframes) don't have file extensions.

A discussion of dynamic file opening really pertains more to TEX than to WEB, because the actual file operations are performed during the run of TEX. As far as WEAVE is concerned, '\input' is just part of the TEX code to be copied from the WEB file to the TEX file. However, since the file names do appear in the WEB file and their format does have a direct impact on portability, the WEB user should be made aware of the issue.

6.1.3 Null Files

For each system, there must be a way to specify lack of a change file, since it is often desirable to create a pure listing without any change files applied. Some systems with command qualifiers, modifiers, or switches have a "no change file" option, while others insist on a file name but will accept the *null device*, a pseudodevice that is always in an end-of-file state when it is an input device and will absorb any data written to it when it is an output device. If neither of these options is supplied in a particular environment, the programmer will simply have to create a dummy change file consisting of one or more blank lines, so that the WEB processors have something to open and read. It probably should have some blank lines in it, because some systems consider a zero length file the same as no file at all. It doesn't matter what text is in the file, if any, as long as it does not contain '@x', '@y', or '@z'. If the file has no change sections, it is empty as far as WEAVE and TANGLE are concerned.

Almost none of the implementations directly allows the option of suppressing the output files (the Pascal, pool, and TEX files). This seems like a peculiar feature to desire, but sometimes it is useful to run the WEB processors just to check the syntax of a program. In this case, the output files are not needed. For the implementations which have a null device, it can be used to absorb the contents of the unneeded output files.

```
This is WEAVE, Turbo Pascal Version (MS-DOS) 2.9.0
*1*11*19*29*36*55*63*65*70*93*108*121*132*139*144*183*200*218*239*258*261
*264*265
Writing the output file...*1*11*19*29*36*55*63*65*70*93*108*121*132*139*144
*183*200*218*239*258*261*264*265
Writing the index...Done.
Memory usage statistics: 737 names, 3306 cross references, 4896+4972 bytes;
parsing required 684 scraps, 1300 texts, 3766 tokens, 119 levels;
sorting required 73 levels.
(No errors were found.)
```

Figure 6.1: Terminal Log from a Run of WEAVE.

```
This is TANGLE, Turbo Pascal Version (MS-DOS) 2.9.0
*1*11*19*29*36*55*63*65*70*93*108*121*132*139*144*183*200
*218*239*258*261*264*265
Writing the output file.....500.....1000.....1500
Done.
Memory usage statistics:
694 names, 339 replacement texts;
1404+1049+1194+1212+970+861+1011+1184 bytes,
3099+4597+3478+4015+3579+3205+3668+3719 tokens.
(No errors were found.)
```

Figure 6.2: Terminal Log from a Run of TANGLE.

6.1.4   The Terminal Log

As the WEB processors execute, a synopsis of activity is written to the standard output device. If the programs are being run interactively, this device is usually the terminal. For batch jobs the output is usually to a disk file for later printing. The actual device depends on the implementation, the current operating mode, and whether I/O redirection is active or not.

Figure 6.1 is the output from a representative run of WEAVE. First is a *banner line*, which is used to identify the program and the particular version being run. When WEAVE is modified for a particular implementation, the banner line is changed as well. The numbers following the asterisks represent the major sections of the WEB program that WEAVE is processing, so that the progress of the execution can be monitored. The section numbers are listed twice, representing the multiple passes through the source file. Finally, some statistics on resource usage and the final return status are displayed.

The output from TANGLE (Figure 6.2) is pretty much the same as that of WEAVE, except that the section numbers are not listed during the second pass. Because of the massive reorganization of the program engineered by TANGLE, section numbers are meaningless during the output phase. Instead, dots indicating "I'm alive" are output, with each 500 lines of output marked.

Most of the implementations described in this chapter use some sort of command line interface. In all of the examples shown, the prompt character (such as the dollar sign for the VAX and the 'A>' or equivalent for MS-DOS) is not shown.

6.2 VAX/VMS

The two versions of WEB for VMS are similar. Both support a command line interface, although different mechanisms are used to add the commands to the system and to retrieve the command lines for use by the program.

6.2.1 Stanford

The Stanford VMS implementation uses the *foreign command* mechanism. In order for the TANGLE and WEAVE commands to be active,

```
define tex$ disk:[directory]
tangle :== $tex$:tangle
weave :== $tex$:weave
```

must appear in the 'login.com' file, where *disk*:[*directory*] is the location of the WEB software. To run the WEB processors, type

```
tangle webfile
```

```
weave webfile
```

The default extensions for the file names are '.web', '.ch', '.pas', and '.poo' for TANGLE and '.web', '.ch', and '.tex' for WEAVE. If *webfile* is omitted, the program will prompt for it.

6.2.2 Northlake Software

Northlake Software uses a Command Language Definition file ('.cld') to add the commands to run WEAVE and TANGLE to the VMS command set. The details of how to set up the system are not shown here, because this information can be found in the user guide [Nor88] supplied with the implementation.

To run TANGLE, type :

```
tangle webfile
```

Optional command qualifiers:

```
/nochange_file
/change_file=changefile
/pascal_file=pascalfile
/pool_file=poolfile
```

To run WEAVE, type

    weave *webfile*

Optional command qualifiers:

```
/nochange_file
/change_file=changefile
/tex_file=TEXfile
```

The default extensions for the file names are '.web', '.ch', '.pas', and '.pool' for TANGLE and '.web', '.ch', and '.tex' for WEAVE. Obviously, the '/nochange_file' and '/change_file=' qualifiers are mutually exclusive. There is no way to run the processors without specifying an output TEX or Pascal file ('/nopascal_file' and '/notex_file' qualifiers are not provided), but the null device can be used (as in '/tex_file=nl:') in order to check the syntax of a WEB file without generating any output.

6.3 Personal Computers

Since TEX is written in WEB and there are TEX systems running on personal computers, one would assume that WEB would have been ported first. However, most of the implementors either ran TANGLE on a development system and downloaded the Pascal file or converted TEX to another language such as C. Some of the conversions were performed manually, while others used an automated converter such as WEB-to-C or PASCHAL (see Section 9.3). In the few cases where WEB actually was ported, the implementors did not make the WEB system available to outside users, keeping it for internal use only. The systems listed here are the only ones generally available for PCs; all were developed by the author.

6.3.1 MS-DOS

The WEB processors can be run by entering:

    tangle *webfile chángefile pascalfile poolfilc*

    weave *webfile changefile TEXfile*

If there is no change file, the null device (NUL) can be used. The null device can also be used for the output files. The default extensions for the parameters are '.web', '.ch', '.pas', and '.pol' for TANGLE and '.web', '.ch', and '.tex' for WEAVE. For any parameter except *webfile*, using asterisk ('*') for a parameter or omitting it entirely means to use the same base file name as *webfile* with the default extension for that parameter; specifying an extension alone, as in '.xyz', means to use the base name plus the supplied extension. A complete file name will override both the base name and the extension. For example,

```
tangle junk * .xyz
```

would read from 'junk.web' and 'junk.ch', and would create a Pascal file named 'junk.xyz' and 'junk.pol' for the pool file.

These instructions assume that 'tangle.exe', 'weave.exe' and all of the source files are in the current directory or in the current search path.

6.3.2 Macintosh

An implementation of WEB for the Macintosh was part of the project to develop this book. Since this system is increasing in importance, the author and the publisher felt that this was essential.

Every effort was made to make WEB fit into the Macintosh environment. The operation of the WEAVE and TANGLE processors is essentially the same. In order to run either, it is only necessary to double-click on the appropriate icon. Once the processor is running, selection of the various files is accomplished via the "Files" menu. Nothing can happen until a WEB file is selected, so the "Select WEB File" option is automatically executed when the application is launched. The operation of this option is similar to "Open" on most other applications, in that a dialog box comes up allowing the user to search through the file system to select a file. Since this implementation of WEB currently does not have a built-in editor, there is no need for the "Create" option found in many Macintosh applications. After the WEB file is selected, the other file names are derived automatically from the WEB file. The currently active file names are always displayed in the main window. If the change file has a different name from the default or is in a different location from the WEB file, the "Select Change File" option will allow a search similar to that for the WEB file. The output file names can be set via the "Change xxx File" options. Any of the files other than the WEB file can be set to the null device with the "Set Null xxx" options. Once all of the file names are set as desired, either TANGLE or WEAVE can be run by selecting it from the "Build" menu.

While TANGLE or WEAVE is running, the current line numbers, code section number, and other status are displayed on the screen, along with the standard log normally output by other WEB implementations. The log will also be written to a disk file unless suppressed with the "Set Null Log" option.

The text editor used to create the WEB files should be able to create ordinary text files, since this is the type of file that the WEB processors expect. If something like MacWrite is used, the file should be saved by using the "text only" option and, in the dialog box asking where carriage returns should be put, "Paragraphs" is the proper selection. It would probably be easier to use the editor built into the Pascal compiler, like the one in Turbo Pascal. Since a Pascal compiler is required anyway, this should not be a problem.

On the Macintosh, it is possible to bind application programs to the data files that they process, so that when a data file is selected, the corresponding application is "launched" automatically. After the launched application begins execution, it can interrogate the operating system to determine the name of the file which caused it to be started and open that file automatically. For instance, when a document created by MacWrite is double-clicked from the desktop, MacWrite is started and will open the file.

TANGLE and WEAVE take advantage of this technique. The output files they create will start the associated application. Double-clicking the Pascal file created by TANGLE will launch Turbo Pascal, while the TEX file from WEAVE will bring up TEXTURES, one of the Macintosh versions of TEX. Unfortunately, since an editor is not included with the current version of Macintosh WEB, the same shortcut cannot be applied to the WEB file, because three different applications have to be used on it—an editor, TANGLE, and WEAVE. Which one should be launched?

As this book went to press, the author became aware of another implementation of WEB for the Macintosh. There was not time to include a description of it in this section, but it is listed in Appendix H.

6.3.3   Other 68000 Systems

As far as the author is aware, WEB has not been ported to other 68000 machines such as the Amiga and the Atari ST, although these machines are known to have implementations of TEX. It should not be difficult to port WEB to the 68000 architecture, since the address space has none of the restrictions of segmentation (see Chapter 12). Of course, the address space may be artificially restricted by the software. For no apparent reason, the Macintosh has a 32-kilobyte limit on the size of a segment, which is even worse than the 64K limit imposed by the 8086 family of processors!

6.4 Unix

Operation should be pretty much the same on any of the various Unix systems (after all, portability is the whole point of Unix). The WEB processors can be run by entering:

>   tangle *webfile changefile*

>   weave *webfile changefile*

If *changefile* is not specified, a file with the same name as *webfile* and an extension of '.ch' is used. If there is no change file, the null device (/bin/null) can be used. The default extensions for the parameters are '.web', '.ch', '.p', and '.pool' for TANGLE and '.web', '.ch', and '.tex' for WEAVE.

Since there are no parameters corresponding to the output files, there does not appear to be any way to change their names from something other than the base file name plus the default extension.

6.5 IBM Mainframes

For all of the other implementations of WEB, only the procedure for running them and the physical structure of text files change from system to system. The logical contents of the files, i.e., the text of the WEB program and the text that is output to the Pascal and TEX files, are identical for all systems.

There is one difference in WEB commands for the IBM mainframes, however, that must be addressed. Since these machines use EBCDIC, which has no '^' character, the WEB command to enter an index entry is '@¬' rather than '@^'.

6.5.1 MVS

Figure 6.3 shows the Job Control Language (JCL) needed to run TANGLE on MVS, while Figure 6.4 is the JCL for WEAVE. The names appearing in italics, such as *sourcefile*, should be overridden with the pertinent actual names in the 'PARM' field of the program invocation. The 'ASCIITBL' file is needed for ASCII-to-EBCDIC conversion, but it should already be present because TEX requires it as well. The null device for MVS would be specified by using 'DUMMY', as in

```
//POOL DD DUMMY,DCB=(RECFM=FB,LRECL=80,BLKSIZE=80)
```

MVS doesn't have a concept of file extensions, so of all of the implementations of TEX and WEB, it probably has the most difficulty with file names occurring in WEB programs. MVS doesn't lend itself to the concept of dynamically opened files at

```
//          JOB    ,REGION=512K
//JOBLIB DD DSN=pref.WEB.LOAD,DISP=SHR
//         EXEC PGM=TANGLE
//WEBFILE   DD DSN=sourcefile,DISP=OLD
//CHANGEFI DD DSN=changefile,DISP=OLD
//PASCALFI DD DSN=pasfile,DISP=(NEW,CATLG),
//         DCB=(RECFM=FB,LRECL=80,BLKSIZE=6080),
//         UNIT=diskunit,VOL=SER=diskvol,
//         SPACE=(TRK,(5,5))
//TTYOUT    DD SYSOUT=A
//POOL DD DSN=poolfile,DISP=(NEW,CATLG),
//         DCB=(RECFM=FB,LRECL=80,BLKSIZE=6080),
//         UNIT=diskunit,VOL=SER=diskvol,
//         SPACE=(TRK,(5,5))
//SYSPRINT DD SYSOUT=A
//ASCIITBL DD DSN=pref.TEX.ASCII.TBL,DISP=SHR
```

Figure 6.3: JCL Needed to Run TANGLE on MVS.

all, expecting every file to have a data definition (DD) in the JCL mapping the file name to an MVS dataset.

As of the July 1988 distribution, some enhancements were added to the MVS version of TeX that improve the dynamic file handling capability. For instance, if '\input junk' appears in a TeX file, MVS TeX will look for a DD name of 'JUNK' and will open the dataset associated with that name. If the DD name is not found in the JCL, a search for a catalogued dataset with the name '*prefix*.JUNK.TEX' will occur, where *prefix* is supplied by the user. If the file being input has an extension other than '.tex', i.e., '\input junkfile.dat', the DD name is constructed by taking the first 5 letters of the base name and the first 3 letters of the extension ('JUNKFDAT'), because DD names are limited to 8 characters. If not found, a search for a catalogued dataset like the one above is conducted.

For input files, the typical case, the next phase of the search is for a "library" file, a partitioned dataset whose DD name consists of the first five letters of the file extension (default or explicit), followed by 'LIB'. The base file name identifies which "member" of this partitioned dataset to use. When searching for the two names mentioned above, TeX would look for a member called 'JUNK' in the partitioned datasets pointed to by DD names 'TEXLIB' and 'DATLIB', respectively.

The library file approach appears to be the best way to handle file operations in the TeX part of a WEB program, since these operations tend to be reads rather than writes, and since no change to the JCL is needed to use library datasets. It is only necessary to store the file to be input as a member in the appropriate partitioned dataset.

```
//            JOB
//JOBLIB DD DSN=pref.WEB.LOAD,DISP=SHR
//         EXEC PGM=WEAVE
//WEBFILE   DD DSN=sourcefile,DISP=OLD
//CHANGEFI  DD DSN=changefile,DISP=OLD
//TTYOUT    DD SYSOUT=A
//SYSPRINT  DD SYSOUT=A
//TEXFILE   DD DSN=texfile,DISP=(NEW,CATLG),
//            DCB=(RECFM=FB,LRECL=80,BLKSIZE=6080),
//            UNIT=diskunit,VOL=SER=diskvol,
//            SPACE=(TRK,(5,5))
//ASCIITBL  DD DSN=pref.TEX.ASCII.TBL,DISP=SHR
```

Figure 6.4: JCL Needed to Run WEAVE on MVS.

The MVS implementation also allows completely dynamic file opens (i.e., not even a token library DD name) by use of a special syntax: pound sign ('#') followed by the complete dataset name. For a partitioned dataset, a particular member can be selected with a colon. Therefore,

```
\input #sys1.wayne.stuff.junk
\input #sys1.wayne.stuff:junk
```

would be equivalent to the dataset names

```
DSN=SYS1.WAYNE.STUFF.JUNK
DSN=SYS1.WAYNE.STUFF(JUNK)
```

and would input a sequential dataset or a member of a partitioned dataset, respectively. As with all of the other system-specific syntaxes for file names, use of this option is nonportable.

6.5.2   VM/CMS

The WEB processors can be run by entering

> **TANGLE** *webfn webft webfm chanfn chanft chanfm*

> **WEAVE** *webfn webft webfm chanfn chanft chanfm*

where the parameters are the file name, file type, and file mode of the WEB file and the change file, respectively. For instance, if the command

```
WEAVE PKTYPE
```

is entered, then `WEB` is assumed for the first file type, '`*`' is assumed for the first file mode, '`PKTYPE`' is assumed for the second file name (taking it from the first file), '`CMS-CHAN`' is assumed for the second file type, and '`*`' is assumed for the second file mode.

The '`=`' character is used in the same manner that it is normally used in CMS. For example,

```
WEAVE GFTYPE WEB K = CMS-CHAN =
```

would use '`GFTYPE`' for the second file name as well as the first, and it would use '`K`' as the file mode of both files.

6.6   Data General

The implementation of `WEB` for the Data General contains an "environment" that is basically a set of menus that walk the user through the various phases of `WEB` programming. The environment will prompt for the name of the `WEB` file, etc., and will run a text editor, `TANGLE`, `WEAVE`, TEX, and the Pascal compiler on behalf of the user.

6.7   Cray

While typesetting and program development are the last things that most people think of in regard to a Cray, implementations of `WEB` and TEX are currently running on it.

Chapter 7

Errors

In a perfect world, the concept of errors does not exist. Those who are so fortunate as to live in such a place may skip this chapter. The rest of us live in a world in which they occur all too often.

By laying out the structure of a program with glittering clarity, WEB attempts to prevent errors from happening. The purpose of this chapter is to identify the errors that slip through most often.

To program in WEB, a programmer must be proficient in three languages—WEB, TEX, and Pascal—and it is possible to make errors in all three simultaneously. Worse, the various errors that can occur are detected at different stages of the development cycle by different processors (if detected at all). WEAVE and TANGLE can only find errors in WEB commands for the most part. Pascal and TEX errors slip through to be caught by their respective compilers.

It must be kept in mind that the WEB processors basically move text around according to a set of rules. They have no real knowledge of Pascal syntax or semantics. (The author has noticed that some Pascal compilers don't either.)

While the number of different ways to do something wrong has been estimated to be $\approx 4.309184229 \times 10^{236} \pm 74$, there are certain errors that occur more often than others. This chapter will cover those most likely to pop up when using WEB.

7.1 WEB Errors

In the earlier stages of development, the program is incomplete and not in a form that would be acceptable to the Pascal compiler, so there is no real reason to generate a Pascal file. However, the WEB syntax of the embryonic program can be checked by running it through TANGLE anyway. If the implementation will allow generation of the Pascal file to be suppressed, all the better. If not, it can just be deleted without being compiled.

```
This is WEAVE, Turbo Pascal Version (MS-DOS) 2.9.0
*1*12*20*29*32*54*57*58
! Never defined: <Determine if the web file line matches>
! Never used: <Determine if the webfile line matches>
! Never defined: <Print the job |history|>
Writing the output file...*1*12*20*29*32*54
! Change file ended without @z. (change file 1.4)
 *57*58
Writing the index...Done.
Memory usage statistics: 223 names, 582 cross references, 1211+1326 bytes;
parsing required 684 scraps, 1300 texts, 3766 tokens, 104 levels;
sorting required 28 levels.
(Pardon me, but I think I spotted something wrong.)
```

Figure 7.1: Terminal Log from a Run of WEAVE with Errors.

The WEB processors attempt to catch as many errors as possible, given their limited knowledge of Pascal and TEX. Pascal syntax errors and the like are beyond them, but they can catch many of the WEB-related errors, such as malformed code section names. Most of WEB's error messages are fairly self-explanatory and state exactly what the problem is. It is always a good idea to run both TANGLE and WEAVE whenever changes have been made to a WEB program. Each of the WEB processors catches errors that the other doesn't, so errors can be caught earlier in the cycle.

A complete list of WEB error codes can be found in Appendix D.

If errors occur during the WEB processing, the output is similar to Figure 7.1. The files processed in this run contained two errors: the first is that the name of a section was not spelled exactly the same as a reference to it ("webfile" vs. "web file"), causing WEAVE to think that they were two different names.

The other error was more severe: the change file was truncated, in that its one change section had '@x' and '@y' but no '@z'. The third "never defined" message was a result of the change file problems. Note that when errors can be tied to a particular line number, the culprit is identified. (The line is not displayed on the section name mismatch errors because WEAVE has no way of knowing which one is wrong.)

The listing generated by WEAVE can aid in the debugging process in a passive sort of way. While WEB can't detect most Pascal syntax errors, the appearance of the listing can become very strange when WEAVE tries to format invalid Pascal syntax. Even when the syntax is correct, the formatting can sometimes highlight logic errors, since WEAVE formats the code that is present, not the code that was intended.

7.1.1 Errors Related to Code Sections

Section Names

There are several errors which can occur with section names, many of which are caused by improper use of abbreviation of the names ('@<Print...@>'). The error message '!Ambiguous prefix' will occur when a prefix which will match the beginning character sequence of more than one name is used, since the WEB processors cannot determine which one is being referenced. For instance, '@<Print...@>' would be ambiguous if '@<Print the junk@>' and '@<Print the stuff@>' were valid section names. The first occurrence of a section name in a WEB file must be unabbreviated. If an abbreviated name is encountered first, even if it is not ambiguous, the '!Name does not match' error will occur. This error will also occur if the unabbreviated name is not found at all.

The '!Incompatible section names' message will occur if one section name is an exact prefix of another, e.g., '@<Print the junk@>' and '@<Print the junk for all of the data@>'.

Many beginning WEB programmers forget to precede the angle brackets surrounding code sections with '@', i.e. '<...>' instead of @<...@>. This is an easy error to make, since the at signs on the delimiters don't appear in the listing. Unfortunately, the error is not always caught by WEB. However, it is most definitely caught, because the '<...>' goes into the Pascal file, causing the Pascal compiler to become hysterical. Also, the resulting listing is downright bizarre as WEAVE formats Pascal code as TEX code.

If the equals sign is left off a code section definition, (@<...@> is used instead of @<...@>=), the '!You need an = sign after the section name' message is generated.

Problems with the Unnamed Section

Forgetting the '@p' when adding code to the unnamed section is a very subtle error, but one easy to make because the '@p' does not appear in the output listing as a section name does. Normally, the input code should look like

```
@ commentary
@p
Pascal statements...
```

Omission of the '@p' would mean that the Pascal part of the code section would never start and the Pascal text would be appended to either the description part or the definition part, if present. This would probably cause an error in the former case, because WEAVE would still be in TEX mode and might choke on raw Pascal without vertical bar delimiters, but if the Pascal text appeared after a simple or parametric macro, it would simply be appended to the macro replacement text and the error would not be detected by WEB. Every time the macro was expanded, the mislaid text would be expanded with it, causing strange and wonderful results during the compilation of the Pascal program.

7.1.2 Change Files

Several errors are caused by malformed change files. Many of these occur when a change section doesn't appear in the required format ('@x', match text, '@y', replacement text, '@z'). All of the error messages are fairly self-explanatory, like '!Where is the matching @x?'. WEB will also report errors if the match text of the change section doesn't match the text in the WEB file exactly ('!Hmm... nnn of the preceding lines failed to match') or if it didn't match any lines at all ('!Change file entry did not match'). The latter message often is a result of change sections that are out of order.

7.1.3 Circular Definitions

The '!Sorry, stack capacity exceeded' error message usually happens because of some sort of circular reference, in either a macro or a code section. Either the macro or the code section references itself somewhere in the body or references another section or macro which references it directly or indirectly. The following illustrates both macro and code section circular references:

> **81.**   In this section we plan to foul things up royally.
>   **define** *Stan* $\equiv$ *buddy_of*(*Ollie*)
>   **define** *Ollie* $\equiv$ *buddy_of*(*Stan*)
> ⟨ Cause a circular reference 81 ⟩ $\equiv$
>   ⟨ Do a little of this 14 ⟩
>   ⟨ Do a little of that 52 ⟩
>   ⟨ Cause a circular reference 81 ⟩

The WEB system cannot detect this condition, especially if there are several levels of indirect referencing. The result is that TANGLE will go into a loop during the expansion of the Pascal program. The loop is not infinite, however, since TANGLE will quickly run out of resources and terminate. If a Pascal file is created (some implementations suppress the Pascal file when there are errors), the loop can be easily seen in the output because the same text sequences will appear over and over. The more direct the circular reference, the tighter the loop and the shorter the repeating text sequence. Another tipoff that a loop is occurring is the fact that the beginning marker for a section ('{*sectionnumber*:}') can be found many times, but the ending marker ('{ : *sectionnumber*}') cannot be found anywhere. On systems that suppress the Pascal file if there are errors (such as Northlake implementation for the VAX), the current line of output is displayed on the terminal with the error message. If the loop is very tight, the repetition can be seen in that line.

It is theoretically possible that the stack could be exceeded simply by having too many levels of nesting in macros or code sections, but since the stack size is set at 200 levels, it would take an absolutely humongous program, or one incredibly poorly designed, to exceed the stack. Even TeX, which has killed so many Pascal compilers with its huge size that it is often used in compiler validation suites, has no problem with the `WEB` stack.

7.1.4 Errors Related to Macros

Since none of the macros is allowed to have forward references in the original version of `WEB`, '`!This identifier has already appeared`' means that a macro was used before it was defined. To correct the error, the section containing the definition of the macro must be moved to a location in the `WEB` file ahead of the section containing the first usage of the macro. If the `WEB` system being used has been enhanced to allow forward references on non-numeric macros (version 2.9 of `TANGLE`; see Section 13.2.2), this message will only appear when a numeric macro is forward-referenced. If the message specifies a non-numeric macro, then the older version of `TANGLE` is in use. Macros of any type cannot be redefined, so '`!This identifier was defined before`' will appear if an attempt is made to do so.

7.1.5 Errors Related to Other Identifiers

Identifier length is a potential source of errors. Since `WEB` is intended to work with all versions of Pascal, including primitive ones, identifiers are forced to uppercase and truncated to a set number of characters (currently 12). This truncation causes ambiguity with long identifiers differing only at the end, such as *print_xlate_table_data* and *print_xlate_table_indexes*, which would both be output as '`PRINTXLATETA`', accompanied by '`!Identifier conflict with x`', where x is the identifier with which there was a conflict. Since some Pascal compilers consider only the first few characters significant, the true unambiguous length is much shorter than that. Therefore, `TANGLE` requires that all identifiers which appear in the Pascal program be unique within 7 characters. Fortunately, `TANGLE` keeps the complete identifiers in its tables and can easily determine that there is an ambiguity for primitive compilers. To get rid of the ambiguity the identifiers should be renamed so that they are unique in fewer characters, such as *print_data_of_xlate_table* and *print_indexes_of_xlate_table*.

The restriction of significant identifier length applies only to normal identifiers that are output to the Pascal file. The identifiers of macros are replaced by the text

```
! Missing $ inserted.
<inserted text>
                      $
<to be read again>
                      _
<argument> identifier_
                        with_underscores
\\#1->\hbox {\it #1
                  \/\kern .05em}
1.5 ...ier \\{identifier_with_underscores}
                                          using the macro instead of...

?
```

Figure 7.2: Error Dialogue from TEX.

they represent and therefore never appear in the output file, so TANGLE does not worry about their length, unambiguous or otherwise, since no Pascal compiler sees them. The only way that TANGLE will issue the "identifier conflict" message on a macro identifier is when it is forward-referenced and TANGLE doesn't realize that it is a macro because it hasn't been defined as anything yet. Spurious messages may be output if the macro identifier is ambiguous with some other identifier until TANGLE reaches the definition and discovers that it's a macro; after that they will stop. This is a slight irritation, but far better than the previous situation, where macros could not be forward-referenced at all. It is easiest just to rework the identifier spelling as shown above.

7.2   TEX Errors

Beginning WEB programmers ideally shouldn't have much difficulty with TEX errors, since they will not be using the more sophisticated features in TEX. In the straight-text mode, most of the errors should be of the "forgot a backslash" category. As the TEX usage becomes more sophisticated, the errors will become more subtle, but by that time the programmer will probably have a copy of the TEXbook [Knu86a].

Unsurprisingly, TEX errors occur primarily in the TEX part of a code section. The TEX code is written by the programmer and is copied verbatim by WEAVE to the output TEX file. Any errors present in the TEX code are copied as well. Pascal code, in all of its contexts, rarely, if ever, has TEX errors because the TEX code used to print it is under the direct control of WEAVE. No matter how garbled the Pascal syntax gets, WEAVE should still be able to produce error-free TEX code (the listing may look weird, of course, but at least TEX won't report errors or die).

The error message dialogue generated by TEX is much more complicated than that of WEB, partially because TEX provides more information and allows limited interactive correction of the error. This dialogue will look something like Figure 7.2. The nature of the error displayed is that an underscore was not preceded by a backslash; an identifer called *identifier_with_underscores* was entered as '\\{identifier_with_underscores}', where it should have been entered as either '\\{identifier_with_underscores}' or '|identifier_with_underscores|' (see Section 7.2.2). Online correction of the errors (by entering '2' and two carriage returns) can help TEX make it the rest of the way through the file, but the programmer must remember to correct the program source (the WEB file, not the TEX file), or the error will just occur again on the next run.

A partial list of TEX error codes can be found in Appendix E. A complete list of all of the error messages TEX can generate would probably exceed the capacity of this book. Some of the more common problems are described in this section.

7.2.1 Line Breaking Errors

One of the most common problems to occur in a WEB program is a bad line break. A bad line break occurs when TEX cannot find a good place to separate two lines, usually because of long words without good hyphenation breaks or long identifiers that cannot be hyphenated at all. If a program is set in narrow columns the condition is aggravated, because it is just that much harder for TEX to find a break point. It will *not* leave huge gaps as primitive word processor fill algorithms do. TEX will try to adjust the spacing between all of the words on the line to make everything come out even, but can only adjust so far before the appearance of the line starts to degrade. If the amount of justification exceeds preset limits, TEX will give up and report the error. The good news is that TEX will complain stridently when this condition occurs, making sure someone knows about it. An '!Overfull \hbox (nnnpt too wide) in paragraph at lines nn--nn' message will be reported and a "blob" (▮) will be placed in the right margin of the overfull line. The *nnn* in the error message is the number of printer's points the line extended into the margin.

To get rid of the error, the text must be reworked, by either shortening the line to make the identifier or unbreakable word fit or adding enough text to force it to the next line. The author has this problem often because of his fondness for long, descriptive identifiers.

7.2.2 Control Sequence Errors

Another typical cause of errors is accidental use of one the TEX special characters listed in Appendix B, especially the underscore character ('_'), which appears in many identifiers. Pascal code, in all of its contexts, is immune to this condition, because WEAVE makes a point of preceding all underscores within identifiers with backslashes, indicating to TEX that the underscores are to be treated as printable characters rather than as control sequences. Identifiers found in TEX code are not

so protected, even when the macro specifically for identifiers ('\\') is used, and
the backslash must be explicitly supplied by the programmer—'\\{good_stuff}'.
This does not apply to code within vertical bar characters ('|good_stuff|'), which is
actually Pascal code rather than TEX code. For this and other reasons, it is always
preferable to use '|good_stuff|' rather than '\\{good_stuff}', unless there is
some reason why the identifier should not appear in the index.

The error code reported by TEX in this case ('!Missing $ inserted') is some-
what misleading. The underscore character is used only in math mode (to denote
subscripts); when TEX finds one when not in math mode, it thinks that the programmer really meant to be in that mode and simply forgot to supply the starting
delimiter ('$').

7.2.3   Mismatched Braces

Mismatched braces are a common problem in TEX source. Every left brace ('{')
should have exactly one corresponding right brace ('}'). One typical use of braces in
the TEX part of a WEB program is one of the macros for reserved words or identifiers
('\&' or '\\'). The sequence '\&{then}}' would cause an error of this sort. TEX will
typically say exactly what is wrong, responding with things like

```
!Missing { inserted
!Missing } inserted
!I've run across a '}' that doesn't seem to match anything.
```

This is yet another reason to use the vertical bar delimiters instead of calling
the macros directly. It is possible to have mismatched vertical bars as easily as
mismatched braces, but that error is caught earlier in the cycle, by WEB.

The dollar signs used for math mode must be evenly matched like everything
else. Regular inline formulas should appear in the form '$formula$', while displayed
formulas are input as '$$formula$$'.

7.2.4   Throwing TEX for a Loop

In much the same way that circular definitions in WEB can throw TANGLE for a loop,
TEX macros can be defined in such a way as to make TEX chase its tail endlessly.
The macro definition

```
\def\expanding{forever \expanding}
```

will never finish expanding, because every expansion of the macro will trigger another expansion, none of which will ever complete. The expansions will cause TEX to
exceed its internal tables, no matter how big they are, because the replacement text

for the macro gets one word bigger with every iteration. Macros cross-referencing each other, such as

```
\def\tastesgreat{\lessfilling}
\def\lessfilling{\tastesgreat}
```

will place TeX into an infinite shouting match with itself if either macro is referenced anywhere. No extra text is expanded in this case, so the beer commercial will continue until the end of time or until TeX is halted by some external force, such as an interruption performed by the person running it.

7.3 Pascal Errors

The error messages reported by WEB and TeX are consistent from implementation to implementation, because the processing of the two programs is supposed to be identical across all systems (in the case of TeX, an implementation is *required* to be identical or it can't be called TeX).

The errors detected by Pascal, however, depend on the particular compiler involved, as do the error messages displayed. The error messages fall in a wide range of quality and usefulness. Some compilers give very descriptive error messages and may even offer a fix for the error, while others are of the "System Error #10375: something bad happened, but I don't know what" category.

7.3.1 Undeclared Identifiers

One of the most common errors trapped by the Pascal compiler when a WEB-generated program is being compiled is the case of identifiers which have not been declared. The WEB system does not detect this condition, although the index makes it easy for the programmer to check for undeclared identifiers. Similarly, usage of a WEB macro that has not been defined looks just like a procedure call and is flagged as an undefined procedure by Pascal.

As in a normal Pascal program, misspelling an identifier will also cause this error. The index is helpful in this case also, because both the correct identifier and the misspelled one will appear there, probably very close together if the misspelling is just one or two letters off and occurs later in the identifier.

7.3.2 Forward References

The topic of forward references is related to the previous one. From the viewpoint of the Pascal compiler they are the same thing. Pascal does not allow use of identifiers in a program that have not been declared before they are used. Because of the free-form nature of WEB, it is easy to cause this problem. Fortunately, it is easy to fix it with WEB as well.

7.3.3 Compound Statements

Another source of Pascal errors is use of a code section as a clause of an **if** statement where the section has more than one statement and no **begin** and **end** statements. One of the most subtle and difficult-to-find errors occurs in the following fragment:

> **if** *everything_ok* **then** ⟨ Print the junk 3 ⟩
> **else** ⟨ Delete the junk 7 ⟩;

This code is perfectly reasonable by itself. The danger is in how ⟨ Print the junk ⟩ is actually coded. Everything is fine as long as there is only one statement (simple or compound) with no semicolon. A semicolon at the end of the section would cause a Pascal syntax error because of the **else** clause. Forgetting the **begin** and **end** would have the same result if the section contained more than one statement.

Actually, we are fortunate that we are getting a syntax error in this example. If the **else** clause were not present, the error would not be detected. The first line of ⟨ Print the junk ⟩ would be executed conditionally, but the remaining lines would be executed unconditionally. The solution to this problem is to add a **begin** and **end** to the text of ⟨ Print the junk ⟩ (see Section 2.12).

7.4 Unexplained Phenomena

Sometimes a peculiar thing will occur in a WEB listing: the first page contains a few words that appear to come from nowhere and the first code section starts on the second page instead of the first. Analysis of the limbo text of the source file reveals that there are no lines consisting of regular text (only TEX commands are allowed in limbo text; plain text must be within a section). Further analysis reveals that the mysterious words occur in the end-of-line comments following one of the font loads:

```
\font\myfont specfont % this font ... blah blah ... loaded when needed
```

This appears to be OK, since the commentary is properly stowed after the TEX comment delimiter ('%' character). The problem is that the line is too long. When WEAVE copies the limbo text from the WEB file to the TEX file, it is copied *almost* verbatim. WEAVE does not like long lines and breaks them up as they are copied. Normally this does not matter because TEX accepts input in free form and spacing and line breaks don't matter. However, in this case, the break occurred in the comment. When the second part of the comment appeared on a line by itself, it no longer had a comment delimiter and therefore was no longer a comment.

```
\font\myfont specfont % this font ... blah blah ... loaded
when needed
```

When TeX processed this, the words "when needed" appeared to be normal text to be typeset. Since the start of the first code section causes a page break, these two words appeared on the first page by themselves. The solution, of course, is to have no extremely long lines in the source file.

Errors such as this are not limited to the limbo text; they can occur in any TeX code with comments at the end of a line. Such comments are more likely in the limbo text, however, because they tend to occur on definitions rather than the plain text found in the description part of code sections.

Chapter 8

Other Languages

8.1 Other Programming Languages

Even though WEB appears to be hopelessly locked into Pascal, this is not the case. The system can be adapted to other programming languages. TANGLE and WEAVE do not really understand Pascal. TANGLE merely identifies scraps of text tied to names, reorders the scraps on the basis of how they are referenced, and outputs them to another file. Certain operations are performed on identifiers, such as forcing them to uppercase and removing underlines, but identifiers are basically the same in every language. Nonalphabetic tokens are passed through verbatim.

WEAVE has more understanding of the language, since it recognizes reserved words, but these words are merely entries in a table, as are the formatting rules. The tables can be modified to handle a new language, with different reserved words and different rules for formatting, without affecting the program logic.

While WEB was designed for ALGOL-like languages, the author can see no reason why it couldn't be adapted to interpretive languages or artificial intelligence languages such as Prolog. It really could be adapted to any language in which the source file is stored as a normal ASCII source file. Of course, the programmer might have difficulty resisting modifications to the program source file while in the interactive environment.

8.1.1 Why Adapt WEB to Other Languages?

Standard Pascal is an incomplete language from a real-world production software point of view. This is not surprising, since the language was originally designed by Niklaus Wirth as a tool for teaching structured programming and was never intended for development of production code. The only reason for the widespread use of Pascal is that the various implementors extended the language tremendously

125

when they developed their compilers. VAX Pascal is a good example of a full-featured production compiler. Its many extensions to Pascal allow sophisticated systems to be developed with it. Virtually *every* implementation of Pascal has to extend it in some way, since a compiler that implements Standard Pascal and only Standard Pascal (if one exists) is virtually useless for real programming projects. While the extensions make Pascal a viable language, portability suffers because each of the implementors extended the language a different way, resulting in a Babel of dialects that is surpassed only by the BASIC language. Porting a program from one Pascal to another can be a major effort, even on the same machine. Typical of the problems encountered is the **case** statement. The action to be performed if none of the cases match is not defined in Standard Pascal. Since this is a major hole in the language, most implementations try to fill it. Some provide an **else** or **otherwise** clause, others use labels (such as *others:* or *otherwise:*). Whatever mechanism a compiler uses, it is different from what every other compiler uses.

The WEB system tries to counteract the portability problem by using macros for constructs that should have been addressed in the language and then redefining the macros in the implementation-specific change files to generate the correct code, allowing the generic WEB file to remain constant for all implementations. While this makes it possible to write portable Pascal programs, it would still be much less work if the language extensions themselves were more standardized.

While WEB does a tremendous job of overcoming the deficiencies of Pascal, there are limits to what can be accomplished. For instance, Standard Pascal does not support separate compilation. A Pascal program is a monolithic block which must be compiled as a unit. *Include files*, which allow a program to be broken up into more than one source file, do not change this fact because the program is still logically one large block and must be compiled as such.

Variables not local to a procedure are global to the entire program and are therefore available for accidental modification. Unrelated parts of the program can interact in unexpected ways, especially if the same variable names are used in more than one place. For example, forgetting to declare a variable which should be defined local to a procedure will be detected immediately by the compiler *unless* a variable of a compatible type with the same name is declared globally. The result is that the wrong variable, one unrelated to the procedure, will be modified. Errors of this nature can be very difficult to find. The WEB system can help detect this type of error (if the programmer happens to notice the inconsistencies in the cross-reference listing) but will not prevent it from happening.

8.1.2   The WEB Variants

Note that the versions of WEB for other languages are not translators of any kind. All of them expect the source code to contain valid instructions for their target language.

Many people misunderstand the purpose of these systems, expecting them to take a regular WEB program containing Pascal code and generate C, Modula-2, or Ada source code from it by converting the Pascal. While there are some programs that provide a capability similar to that (see Section 9.3), the programs described in this chapter are not of that category. The source files for CWEB should contain valid C code, etc. If the programmer wishes to convert an existing WEB program to Modula-2, the conversion must be performed manually by editing the source code.

There is an ambiguity that occurs when discussing conversion of WEB to another language, because conversion in this context has two different, though related, meanings. Conversion of the WEB *language* refers to modification of the TANGLE and WEAVE processors to handle WEB programs written in a language other than Pascal while the processors themselves remain Pascal. Conversion of the WEB *processors* refers to complete rewriting of WEAVE and TANGLE themselves in the new WEB language. In most cases, the WEB language conversion must be performed first, because without a working WEB system for the new language, the converted WEAVE and TANGLE cannot be processed.

Operation of the WEB variations which support languages other than Pascal is pretty much the same as for the original. The basic functions of WEB, such as expansion of macros and code sections, are applicable to any programming language. Referencing a code section is language-independent, since ⟨ Print the junk ⟩ means the same thing in C that it does in Modula-2. The actual statements found in the code part of the sections are different, of course, but all of the WEB mechanisms (except for macros in C) operate in basically the same way. Therefore, most of the User Guide portion of this book is valid for the WEB variants. The differences are described in the following sections.

8.1.3 Modula-2

One of the problems with WEB is actually a limitation of Pascal rather than of WEB. Specifically, the problem of huge monolithic programs can be easily solved with Modula-2. The author has developed a Modula-2 version of WEB [Sew87a] by transforming WEAVE and TANGLE into MWEAVE and MANGLE. Not only does Modula-2 provide for separate compilation, but several other deficiencies of Pascal are corrected. On the other hand, Modula-2 introduces a few problems of its own, such as case sensitivity and lack of underlines in identifiers. MWEB fixes these problems the same way that Modula-2 and regular WEB fix Pascal, resulting in a system with the advantages of both WEB and Modula-2 and few of the disadvantages of either.

The language Modula-2 was designed by Wirth to be the successor to Pascal. Unlike the original Pascal, it was designed to be used for developing real software. Most of the problems with Pascal are corrected by Modula-2, including the **case** problem mentioned above. The syntax is more straightforward, with less likelihood of ambiguity. The most important contribution of Modula-2 is that embodied in the name—the module concept. Modula-2 makes it possible to break up a large programming project into smaller independent pieces, called *modules*, each logically isolated from the others via the software engineering principle of *information hiding*.

The Modula-2 language is much more standardized than Pascal. Since the language is much more powerful, there is less need to extend it. Input and output, the bane of portability, are completely removed from the language definition itself and are instead banished to library procedures that are more-or-less standardized.

While Modula-2 fixes most of the problems of Pascal and nearly all of the differences between Modula-2 and Pascal are improvements, a couple of the features of the language are steps backward. Case sensitivity is one of the nonenhancements. In a Modula-2 program, *junk*, *Junk*, and *JUNK* would be considered three different variables. The reason for this change from Pascal, if any, is not obvious. The author has never heard a *reasonable* explanation for it. Equally annoying, all of the Modula-2 reserved words are required to be in uppercase. This one almost makes sense, since having the reserved words stand out in this way would make a regular ASCII listing more readable. However, this slight benefit is not worth the extra effort involved in writing a program. Using a powerful editor with macro and/or template capability which can fill in the reserved words on behalf of the programmer would make this less painful, but not necessarily enjoyable.

MWEB is a version of the WEB system which has been customized for the language Modula-2. Many of the deficiencies of Pascal that are repaired by the WEB system are unnecessary in MWEB, since Modula-2 fixes most of them in the language definition itself. Some examples are the **else** clause on a **case** statement, the standard procedure to increment a variable (INC), and the **loop**, **exit**, and **return** instructions. To counteract the new problems introduced by the language, MWEB was designed to fix Modula-2 in the same way that Modula-2 and standard WEB fix Pascal. The effort expended by MWEB in this effort is small compared to the lengths necessary to bring Standard Pascal to a usable state. The result of the merger of Modula-2 and MWEB is a programming system that has the advantages of both and few of the disadvantages.

Identifier Length

The maximum size of an identifier is larger in MWEB. The TANGLE limit was insufficient, since some of the standard Modula-2 library modules had identifiers far longer and the truncated identifiers would not match. Unlike Pascal, Modula-2 does not specify a maximum identifier length; all characters in an identifier are considered significant. However, since it is difficult to use ∞ as a constant in a computer program, arbitrary numbers were selected—31 characters maximum length, 20 for unambiguous length.

Compound Statements

The problems caused by lack of a **begin-end** pair on code sections which may be used as compound statements (see Section 7.3.3) are not applicable to Modula-2 since this language doesn't have compound statements. Rather, all **if** statements and other control statements are always compound. In Pascal, the clause associated with a **then**, **else**, or **do** can either be a single statement or a series of statements between **begin** and **end**, as in:

        if *condition* **then**
            begin *statement*; *statement*;
            end
        else *statement*;

        while *condition* **do**
            begin *statement*; *statement*;
            end;

        while *condition* **do**
            statement;

The equivalent statements in Modula-2 never have a **begin** and always have an **end**, even if there is only one statement. For instance,

        if *condition* **then**
            statement;
        else
            statement; *statement*;
        end;

        while *condition* **do**
            statement; *statement*;
        end;

Therefore, the tedium of worrying about **begin** and **end** on sections which may be used in control statements is unnecessary.

Comments

While Pascal can have comments delimited by either '(* *)' or '{ }', Modula 2 uses only the former, since the braces are used elsewhere in the language definition (as set delimiters). The meta-comment delimiters are still '@{' and '@}', although they are converted to '(*' and '*)' when output. It was not worth the effort to change the delimiters to '@(*' and '@*)', since it would require three-letter commands, not to mention the ambiguity of '@*)' with the already existing '@*'.

Case Sensitivity

Like `TANGLE`, the `MANGLE` processor forces everything to uppercase. All occurrences of an identifier, definition and references alike, are forced to uppercase on an equal basis. If definition modules, implementation modules, and client modules are all `MANGLED`, all instances of an identifier will still match, as they would all be forced to uppercase and truncated together. This automatic forcing to uppercase removes (actually, satisfies) the requirement of Modula-2 that reserved words be in uppercase in the source. As described above, the uppercase words are for readability, but the bold font used by `MWEB` is much more readable. Leaving `MANGLE`'s uppercase mechanism intact disables the ability of Modula-2 to have multiple identifiers in a program differing only in case (*junk*, *Junk*, and *JUNK*), but this is a poor practice anyway. (The author will stop just short of saying that anyone who does it deserves whatever happens to him.) The only real problem with the uppercase identifiers occurs with imported modules which were not generated with the `MWEB` system (such as the library modules supplied with the compiler). For identifiers such as these, which *must* contain lower- or mixed case, the `WEB` command to "pass through" Pascal code without modification ('@=*verbatim text*@>') must be used.

For example:

```
from @=␣InOut␣@> import @=␣WriteString␣@>;
```

Some predefined identifiers are all uppercase to begin with, such as the primary library module SYSTEM or the increment instruction INC. These can be left alone.

Vertical Bar Character

The vertical bar character ('|') is specially handled, since it is used by both Modula-2 and `WEB` for different purposes. `WEB` uses it to delimit Pascal code embedded within TEX code, while Modula-2 uses it to mark the end of the statement sequence following a case label (except for the last one), as in

```
case junk of
1: r := 10;
   m := 60  |
2: k := 7    |
3: m := 6
end;
```

A true conflict between the two usages is unlikely, because Pascal code within TEX code usually consists of short expressions or simple variable names rather than compound statements such as **case**. MWEAVE can identify the usage of the vertical bar by context and will use the Modula-2 version in the code part of a section and the WEB version within TEX code (including code section names and comments in the code part of a section). If for some reason a **case** statement is needed within TEX code, two adjacent bar characters ('||') are used to represent the Modula-2 case separator and are compressed by MWEAVE into an internal character which is displayed as the regular vertical bar character.

Underline Character

The usage of the underline character in identifiers, absent from the Modula-2 language definition as it is from Standard Pascal, is provided by MWEB. MANGLE removes the underlines before passing the program to the compiler, as TANGLE does.

Other Special Characters

In Modula-2, some new special characters are provided for optionally replacing tokens which require a two-character combination or a reserved word in Pascal ('#' for '<>', '~' for **not**, and '&' for **and**). The '&' and '~' operators are no problem, but '#' is already used by the WEB system for macro parameters. For example, the two definitions

```
@d test(#)==m[#] <> x[j+#]
@d test(#)==m[#] #  x[j+#]
```

are logically equivalent from a Modula-2 standpoint, but the output generated by the regular TANGLE and WEAVE for the second would not be what the programmer expected. The parsers of the two programs would not be able to differentiate between the middle '#' which means $\neq$, and those in the array index expressions, which are intended to be replaced by the macro parameter. To resolve this ambiguity, MANGLE and MWEAVE will accept the Modula-2 version of '#' anywhere in a WEB program *except* within a macro definition, where '#' will continue to represent the parameter.

Of course, the old Pascal symbols still work. These new symbols are largely irrelevant when the WEB system is being used, because MWEAVE will convert them to $\neq$, $\neg$, and $\wedge$ anyway. The MWEB operators are shown in Table 8.1.

Quotes

The Modula-2 language allows strings to be delimited by either single or double quotes ('' or '"'). While this is a definite improvement, it does conflict with WEB,

Operation	Source File	WEAVE Listing
not equal	`<>`	$\neq$
not equal	`#`	$\neq$
less than or equal	`<=`	$\leq$
greater than or equal	`>=`	$\geq$
assignment	`:=`	$\leftarrow$
equivalence (macros)	`==`	$\equiv$
Boolean **and**	`and`	$\wedge$
Boolean **and**	`&`	$\wedge$
Boolean **or**	`or`	$\vee$
Boolean **not**	`not`	$\neg$
Boolean **not**	`~`	$\neg$
inclusion in set	`in`	ϵ
dereference of pointer	`^`	$\uparrow$

Table 8.1: `MWEB` Operators Requiring Special Symbols.

in which single quotes delimit regular strings, while double quotes identify strings destined for the string pool. Rather than disable the string pool, I reluctantly decided that the user would just have to continue using single quotes as in Pascal.

On the other hand, MWEB is the only WEB variation that retains the string pool. CWEB and the WEB systems generated by SPIDER (see Section 10.2.2) do not bother with it. After several years, the author is not aware of any programs other than TEX or METAFONT that have ever utilized the string pool. Maybe the next version of MWEB should drop it as well.

Sample Programs

As can be seen from the listings of the sample MWEB programs in Section G.5, MWEB is not *that* different; on first glance, it could be mistaken for standard WEB. Closer inspection would reveal the differences in reserved words, in comments, and in compound statements. Note the use of the **elsif** statement. The boxes around words such as 'WriteString' are an unforeseen side effect of use of the "pass through" WEB command described above to prevent selected words from being forced to uppercase. While startling, it does point out which identifiers require special treatment. I highly recommend using the approach taken in ScanTEX: define simple macros equivalent to each of these external identifiers and use the macro everywhere else in the program, including the **import** statement. This isolates the boxes to the section containing the definitions rather than sprinkling them throughout the program (see Section 5.1.6).

```
         .
         .
         .
@ @<Scan the line@>=
temp_index := 1; (* preset comparison index to second character position *)
if (current_line_len > 3) and (buffer[0] = '\')  then
    if ( char_matches('M') or char_matches('N')  )
                                    and numeric_digit_at(2) then
        @<Search for '\.{\\*.}'; set |output_enabled| if found@>;
    elsif three_chars_match('i')('n')('x') then
        output_enabled := false;
        input_has_ended := true;
    end;
end;


         .
         .
         .
```

Figure 8.1: MWEB Input.

Figure 8.1 is a fragment of Modula-2 code from ScanTEX.

Modules

In Modula-2 a source file can either be a complete program module or a library module, which consists of two parts: a definition module and an implementation module. The definition module contains the interfaces that are visible to the outside world. The implementation module contains the actual code. The Modula-2 language specification requires that the two parts of the library module reside in separate source files, for reasons such as version checking. However, care must be taken to ensure that the definitions in these files agree. While the Modula-2 compiler catches the errors that occur when they are not the same, it would be convenient if the two sets of definitions were driven from the same source.

The combination of Modula-2 and WEB allows for a technique of building library modules that is much less haphazard than the standard method. The Table Handler module of Appendix G.5.1 is such a module. It is constructed in such a way that both the definition module and the implementation module can be driven from the same set of declarations.

The entire text of both the definition module and the implementation module is contained within the WEB source file. Using WEB's meta-comment facility, either the definition module or the implementation module is completely commented out when the other is being generated. The default case is for the implementation module to be generated and the definition module to be commented out, since the latter is generated much less often.

For example,

    define *defmod* ≡ @{

define *enddef* ≡ @}
define *impmod* ≡
define *endimp* ≡

will create two sets of meta-comment delimiters, one set for the implementation module and another set for the definition module.

defmod
⟨ The definition module 11 ⟩
enddef
impmod
⟨ The implementation module 9 ⟩
endimp

Note that since the entire text of the implementation module is contained in ⟨ The implementation module ⟩, placing the single reference to that code section between **impmod** and **endimp** will cause the entire implementation module to be commented out as a whole.

In order to generate the definition module rather than the implementation module, a generic change file is used to reverse the definition of the meta-comment macros and comment out the implementation module instead of the definition module. For example,

```
@x
@d  defmod==@{
@d  enddef==@}
@d  impmod==
@d  endimp==
@y
@d  defmod==
@d  enddef==
@d  impmod==@{
@d  endimp==@}
@z
```

would comment out the implementation module and uncomment the definition module.

If the identifiers of the meta-comment macros are always the same for all modules (e.g., **impmod** and **endimp**), then a generic "create definition module" change file containing the above lines can be used.

Since two different Modula-2 source files are driven from the same MWEB source, it is helpful if the implementation of MANGLE will allow the output file name to be overridden, especially the file extension. Typically the definition module for 'junk.web' will be 'junk.def' and the implementation module will be 'junk.mod'. In the Turbo Pascal version of MANGLE for MS-DOS, they would be generated by

```
mangle junk * .mod
mangle junk defmod .def
```

assuming that the implementation change file to be applied is 'junk.ch'. There is really nothing implementation-dependent about the definition module (except possibly whether there is an export list or not), so the implementation change file is not needed when building the definition module and can be replaced by 'defmod.ch'.

When building library modules by using this technique, one should be careful not to build a definition module unless the source code to be placed in the definition module has actually changed. The creation of a new '.def' file will cause **make**-style programs to compile the definition module, because they typically go by the time stamp of the file rather than the contents when deciding whether to process the file or not. Because most Modula-2 compilers do version checking, a recompilation of the definition module will require a recompilation of all modules that import it—explicit imports by other definition and implementation modules and the implicit import performed by its own implementation module. All of these must be recompiled. If this causes any other definition modules to be recompiled, then all of their dependent modules must be recompiled, etc. A likely result is a rebuilding of the entire system.

Another factor that the programmer should be aware of is that the definition and implementation modules take up twice the disk space when compared with the standard method, because both Modula-2 source files contain the complete source text of both modules. The only difference between the two is a total of eight characters— the '(* *)' surrounding the implementation module in the '.def' file, and the same characters surrounding the definition module in the '.mod' file.

Each procedure to be exported from a module appears twice: the procedure heading appears in the definition module and the full procedure in the implementation module. The two occurrences of the procedure heading must match exactly. Using the technique described here, they are not only identical, but the same physical code. The procedure heading is placed into a code section by itself, which is then referenced by both the definition module and the implementation module, causing the heading to be expanded inline in both places.

One unique feature of building modules this way is that, as everywhere else in WEB, all uses of a particular thing can be kept physically close together. For instance, in the module example the procedure heading of an exported procedure is followed immediately by the definition module occurrence of that procedure heading, which is itself followed immediately by the full procedure to appear in the implementation module. Any declarations such as types that are used only by this procedure could be declared here also, to be placed into either ⟨Types to be exported⟩ or ⟨Types local to the module⟩, depending on whether they need to be exported or not.

41. ⟨Procedure heading of the *zyz* procedure 41⟩ ≡
procedure *xyz*(*num*: *integer*);

44. ⟨Procedure heading declarations of the definition module 17⟩ +≡
⟨Procedure heading of the *zyz* procedure 41⟩

45. ⟨Full procedure declarations of the implement. module 18⟩ +≡
⟨Procedure heading of the *zyz* procedure 41⟩
  begin
  { ... }
  end *xyz*;

Opaque types are handled somewhat like exported procedures, in that there are two defining occurrences of the identifier, one in the definition module and the other in the implementation module. The exported type consists of an identifier only, since the details of the type are hidden from the outside world. The full declaration occurs in the implementation module. In MWEB, the two definitions can be adjacent for documentation purposes. In the sample module, *symbol_table* is an opaque type declared in this manner (see Sections 14 and 15 of Appendix G.5.1).

14. ⟨Types local to the module 9⟩ +≡
tableptr = **pointer to** *table_record*;
symbol_table = *tableptr*;

15. ⟨Types to be exported 10⟩ +≡
symbol_table;

The complete structure of a definition module is as follows:

11. ⟨The definition module 11⟩ ≡
definition module *alpha*;
⟨Import list of the definition module 12⟩
export qualified ⟨Identifiers to be exported 15⟩;
const ⟨Constants to be exported 6⟩
type ⟨Types to be exported 9⟩
var ⟨Variables to be exported 8⟩
⟨Procedure heading declarations of the definition module 42⟩
end *alpha*.

The structure of an implementation module is as follows:

9. ⟨ The implementation module 9 ⟩ ≡
implementation module *alpha*;
⟨ Import list of the implementation module 12 ⟩
const ⟨ Constants local to the module 6 ⟩
type ⟨ Types local to the module 9 ⟩
var ⟨ Variables local to the module 8 ⟩
⟨ Full procedure declarations of the implement. module 43 ⟩
begin
⟨ Initialize the module 83 ⟩;
end *alpha*.

Both the implementation module and the definition module can have import lists, but they should be different. The list for the implementation module imports all procedures called from the module, all of the types needed for the parameters of these procedures, etc. The identifiers it imports are from system modules and from other user-written modules. The import list of the definition module should be much smaller, importing only the things actually used in the definition of procedure headings, etc. No procedure names should appear in the import list of a definition module because it has no executable code and cannot call any procedures. Normally, the definition module doesn't have an import list at all, but if a procedure has parameters of a type defined in another module, then the type must be imported. Unnecessary imports (importing of identifiers not actually used in the definition module) cause unnecessary dependencies and may even lead to circular imports (two modules importing each other, directly or indirectly), which are impossible to compile and link without errors.

In the older version of Modula-2 described in the second edition of Wirth's book, all of the identifiers to be visible outside a module must be explicitly exported by appearing in an export list. If an identifier is not in the list, it cannot be imported by another module, even though the definition is present within the definition module.

The maintenance of this list is somewhat tiresome. The author has lost track of the number of times that he has added a new procedure to a module and has forgotten to add the new name to the export list. No errors are reported when the definition module is compiled, but plenty of errors are reported when another module tries to import the new procedure.

The export list for definition modules was dropped when Modula-2 was revised (third edition of Wirth's book), although it is still used for local modules. All identifiers appearing within the definition module are now implicitly exported. Many of the compilers will still accept an export list, so that older programs can be compiled without modification. Depending on the compiler, the export list either overrides the implicit exports or is ignored.

If a program is to be compatible with all Modula-2 compilers, the export list must be provided. It can either be placed in the main **WEB** file or appear in the change file of each implementation that needs an export list.

The export list, if provided at all, can be incrementally built in the same way that the procedure definitions themselves are built. An export list is formatted as follows:

> **export qualified** ⟨ Identifiers to be exported 15 ⟩;

In the part of the program where each identifier is defined, the identifier can be added to the export list as well. For instance, immediately after ⟨ Procedure heading of the *zyz* procedure 41 ⟩ above would be

> **42.**   ⟨ Identifiers to be exported   15 ⟩ +≡
>
> *xyz,*

Note that the identifier is followed by a comma. This is necessary because the names in the list must be separated by commas. However, the very last exported identifier in the program must not have a comma because it would cause a syntax error when the list is built.

8.1.4   C

There are at least three different versions of **WEB** for the C language[Thi86a,GS86, Lev87], two of which were developed in Europe and one at Princeton. The three **CWEB** systems share some similarities, such as the feature that all three use the macros supplied by the C preprocessor rather than the **WEB** version. Since the C macros allow more than one parameter, it is not necessary to perform the gyrations needed for multiple parameters in **WEB**. To keep the three versions separate, we will refer to Thimbleby's version as Cweb, and the other two as German **CWEB** and Levy **CWEB** (Silvio Levy of Princeton).

Cweb will not be covered in great detail, since it is radically different from all of the other **WEB** systems, has a lot of incompatible commands, and is crippled by being based on Troff instead of TEX (see Section 8.2).

About the only feature in Cweb that would be nice to have in other versions of **WEB** is the ability to "cite" a code section from elsewhere in the program. The cross-referencing capabilities of regular **WEB** are limited to the Pascal part of a program. When one code section is referenced by another, a "This code is used in Section *n*" message is generated in the section being referenced. However, a code section cannot be mentioned by either name or number from the description part of a section, because section names are not allowed in either the description part or the definition part (the reason, of course, is that the appearance of a section name would start the code part of the section prematurely; the WEB processors would not know until the end of the name whether it is a definition or a reference, i.e., followed by a '=' or not). Cweb provides a series of commands to allow the description part to reference another code section. The '@#<' command, when used in the TeX part of a section, indicates that the following code section name should be replaced with its section number, for use in messages such as "Topic x is discussed in section 132." The section name is terminated with '@>', like all other control text. The '@$<' command is used in the same way, but it is replaced with the section name itself, and the '@#<$' command equates to both. When any of these commands is used, a "Cited by Section *n*" message appears in the cross reference part of the code section being referenced.

The Levy version of CWEB is probably the best known, primarily because it is included in the TeX distribution for Unix.

Several of the features found in regular WEB were not carried over to CWEB. These include the string pool, meta-comments, and constants in octal or hex.

Hexadecimal and octal constants are handled differently for CWEB than they are for regular WEB. The '@'' and '@"' commands, which convert these numbers to decimal, are not defined in CWEB (the '@"' isn't, anyway; the '@'' is reused for another purpose, as shown below), since the standard C language supports other number bases directly. Instead, the standard C notation is used (e.g., '040' for 40_8).

The **format** command works the same way that it does for regular WEB, allowing words to be reserved or unreserved. This is not necessary very often, since CWEAVE recognizes **typedef** and automatically makes identifiers defined this way into reserved words.

Unlike regular WEB, CWEB places each statement in the output file on a separate line, although it doesn't go any further toward pretty-printing the source file. Additionally, C **#line** statements are added to identify the corresponding line in the WEB source file. The '@\' command (force end of line in program file) is not supported, since it is unnecessary. While on the subject of the C output file, it should be noted that CTANGLE does not force identifiers to uppercase, truncate them, or remove underscores as the original TANGLE does.

CWEB does not provide the same macro capability that regular WEB does. Instead, the macros of the underlying C language are used. The '@d' command is converted to the equivalent **#define**. Instead of the three WEB macro types, the standard C macros, which can accept multiple parameters, are used. The syntax of the macros is

> @d *identifier*   *replacement text*

if there are no parameters (note that this syntax is the same as that for simple macros in regular WEB, except that there is no '==') and

Operation	Source File	WEAVE Listing
not equal	!=	$\neq$
less than or equal	<=	$\leq$
greater than or equal	>=	$\geq$
equal	==	$\equiv$
Boolean **and**	&&	$\wedge$
Boolean **or**	||	$\vee$
Boolean **not**	!	$\neg$
right arrow	->	$\Rightarrow$

Table 8.2: CWEB Operators Requiring Special Symbols.

$$\text{@d } identifier(param_1, \ldots, param_n) \qquad replacement\ text$$

if parameters are needed. The usage is the same as for regular C, except that it is not necessary to protect new lines with backslashes in the replacement text, as CTANGLE will handle that automatically. There is no equivalent to the WEB numeric macro.

All of the **#define** commands are automatically moved to the beginning of the C program. If for some reason the **#define** should appear in the part of the program in which it is defined, it can be moved from the definition part of the section to the code part and converted to regular C syntax. Then it becomes regular C code.

CWEB does not implement the string pool construct, so normal strings are delimited by either '"' or '''. Single characters are specified either by ''*letter*'' or by '@'*letter*'. Use of ''a'' represents the letter 'a' in the machine's native character set. If '@'a' is used, however, the character represents the letter 'a' in the ASCII character set no matter what character set the machine normally uses. This is roughly equivalent to regular WEB's double-quoted characters ('"a"'), except that the CWEB version is a character constant, while those in WEB are numeric constants.

CWEB provides an "include file" capability. When a '@i' command is encountered, input from the currently active WEB file is suspended. The file indicated by the file name following the '@i' command is opened and input comes from that file. When the end of the included file is reached, the input resumes with the file active at the time that file was opened. Included files can themselves include files. The file names can optionally be delimited by double quotes.

The CWEB operators are shown in Table 8.2. As can be expected, the differences between these operators and those of regular WEB are primarily the differences between C and Pascal operators. A sample CWEB listing (the Homotopy program) can be found in Appendix G.7. Part of a code section from the CWEB source file (Section 7) used to generate this listing can be seen in Figure 8.2.

⋮

is, by definition, 2π times the turning number.

```
@d pi 3.1415916535897
@d poltoc(a,r,theta) (a).x=r*cos(theta), (a).y=r*sin(theta);

@<Function definitions@>=
calc_turning_no(prime)
tang_map prime; /* derivative map of curve under consideration */
{
  int i;
  for (i=1;i<n_pts;i++)
    prime[i].arg-=2*pi*rint((prime[i].arg-prime[i-1].arg)/(2*pi));
  return -(int) rint((prime[0].arg-prime[n_pts-1].arg)/(2*pi));
}
```

⋮

Figure 8.2: CWEB Input.

8.1.5 Ada

The Ada language is increasing in importance. Many programming organizations are turning to this language, in some cases because of the features it provides, in other cases because use of the language was dictated by the customer (for instance, the Department of Defense). Whatever the reason, more programs are being written in Ada. Ada is already used as a PDL in some locations, and an Ada WEB fits in with this concept nicely.

The Ada WEB system is one of the first products of the SPIDER WEB-generator described in Section 10.2.2. Since Ada WEB came from SPIDER, which was itself derived from Levy CWEB, the same features that were dropped from CWEB are not available in Ada WEB. Features such as the hex and octal constants will not be missed, since the Ada language provides a way to specify them.

Operation	Source File	WEAVE Listing
not equal	/=	≠
less than or equal	<=	≤
greater than or equal	>=	≥
arrow	=>	⟹
open label	<<	≪
close label	>>	≫
separator				

Table 8.3: Ada WEB Operators Requiring Special Symbols.

The meta-comment capability is not directly provided by SPIDER-generated systems, although it is possible to handle meta-comments with creative use of the language specification input to SPIDER. There is a version of Ada WEB with a meta-comment facility, although it is separate from the regular Ada WEB.

Like Modula-2, Ada provides a capability for separating the interface into a module (or *package*, to use the Ada term) from its implementation. The method described in the Modula-2 section above for driving the interface and the implementation from the same source can be used in Ada, although it must be implemented differently. Since meta-comments are not available in the regular Ada WEB, the technique of commenting out either the definition module (called the *package specification* in Ada) or the implementation module (the *package body*) is not possible. However, since Ada doesn't require that the two be in separate source files as Modula-2 does, it isn't needed anyway. The main concept, that of using the same definitions twice, can be used, but it must be modified slightly, since the definitions are not specified in quite the same way. In the package specification, the procedure header is followed by a semicolon (**procedure** x;), while its redefinition in the package body replaces the semicolon with a reserved word (**procedure** x **is**). This means that the semicolon must not be placed on the procedure heading itself, but must be moved to the reference of the header in the package specification.

41.   ⟨ Procedure heading of the *zyz* procedure   41 ⟩ ≡
procedure *xyz*(*num*: **in** *abc_type*)

42.   ⟨ Procedure heading declarations of the package spec   42 ⟩ ≡
⟨ Procedure heading of the *zyz* procedure 41 ⟩ ;

43.   ⟨ Full procedure declarations of the package body   43 ⟩ ≡
⟨ Procedure heading of the *zyz* procedure 41 ⟩ **is**
   begin
   { ... }
   end *xyz*;

The Ada equivalent of Modula-2's opaque types are the private and limited private types. As in Modula-2, the declaration must physically appear in a certain place in the program.

14.   ⟨ Full declarations of the private types   9 ⟩ +≡
   type *symbol_table* **is access** *table_record*;

15.   ⟨ Private types   10 ⟩ +≡
   type *symbol_table* **is limited private**;

The structure of a package specification is as follows:

package *beta* **is**
⟨ Visible declarations of the package 6 ⟩
⟨ Private types 9 ⟩
⟨ Procedure heading declarations of the package spec 42 ⟩
private
⟨ Full declarations of the private types 9 ⟩
end *beta*;

The structure of a package body is as follows:

package body *beta* **is**
⟨ Declarations local to the package 6 ⟩
⟨ Full procedure declarations of the package body 43 ⟩
end *beta*;

8.1.6   Extended Pascal

It may seem peculiar to list Pascal as an alternative to Pascal, but in many respects, Extended Pascal is a new language.

Much of the commentary on Modula-2 and Ada applies equally well to Extended Pascal, since many of the features of these languages, most importantly modules with controlled interfaces, can be found in Extended Pascal. In fact, Extended Pascal's module implementation is more sophisticated than Modula-2's or Ada's in some ways. At some point, WEB will need to be modified to work with Extended Pascal, but there is no point in starting this project until the new language stabilizes and is accepted as a standard.

8.2   Other Documentation Languages

With the exception of Thimbleby's system[Thi86a,Thi86c,Thi86b], which is based on the Unix Nroff/Troff language, all of the WEB derivatives change only the programming language, while the documentation system remains TEX. WEAVE doesn't really generate TEX primitives. Nearly all of the formatting commands placed into the document source are actually in the form of TEX macros (for instance, '\&{else}' produces **else**), which could theoretically be converted to a different typesetting language by another preprocessor, although it is doubtful that the language could duplicate the sheer power of TEX, especially where mathematics is concerned. Conversion to another document language could be accomplished at one of three different levels: a level completely external to WEB; definitions of the formatting macros; or actual modification of WEAVE to generate different codes.

While it is possible to use a language other than TEX, it is uncertain whether use of a different documentation system is worth the effort involved. Thimbleby[Thi86c] discussed the difficulties of the conversion to Troff and estimated that fully 95 percent of the implementation effort of Cweb was in this area. Troff is not flexible enough to handle all of the typesetting features WEB needs.

As described in Section 11.5, much of the complexity of typesetting the WEB listing is handled within TEX by powerful macros contained within the 'webmac' package. For many of the functions, WEAVE only has to supply the information and the macros actually do the typesetting. Without the power of TEX, a lot more work would have to be done within WEAVE and it would be many times more complex than it is already.

Chapter 9

WEB Utilities

9.1 ScanTEX

The MWEB sample program ScanTEX actually performs a useful function. It scans a
TEX file generated by WEAVE (or MWEAVE, of course) and copies only the sections which
have been modified by a change file to a new TEX file, resulting in an abbreviated
program listing containing only the changes. The unchanged sections are not copied,
nor are the cross-references, the section names, or the title page, which includes the
table of contents.

The reasons why this is useful are discussed in Section 5.2.6.

Experienced WEB users may wonder why the author went to the trouble of writing
a program to duplicate a function already provided by the WEB system itself, since
the suppression of unchanged sections can be accomplished by placing

```
\let\maybe=\iffalse
```

into the limbo section of the WEB file. The reasons were the following:

1. ScanTEX does not print the index. Since the index contains entries for the full
   listing rather than just the abbreviated one, a program the size of TEX can
   have an index that is much longer than the rest of the listing.

2. Since ScanTEX is an external program that can either be run or not run,
   neither the WEB file nor the change file must be modified to turn suppression
   on or off.

3. If the TEX file is to be saved for a period of time, the reduced version generated by ScanTEX takes up much less disk space. The unmodified sections
   are physically removed from the TEX file by ScanTEX, rather than just being
   disabled.

4. The author was unaware that the built-in mechanism existed when he wrote
   ScanTEX (the real reason). Since it is buried deep in Appendix G of the WEB
   manual, it is easy to miss.

During the development of this book, an enhancement (designated version 1.1)
was added to the program. The normal handling of major sections by 'webmac'
is not valid in the abbreviated listing generated by ScanTEX. In a regular listing,
the major sections force a new page and add the group title to the running heads.
However, this works best when every major section is present. In the abbreviated
listing, only the changed sections appear, whether they are major sections or normal
ones. This causes haphazard operation of the page ejects and changes to the running
heads, since some major sections will be present and others will not.

The modification to ScanTEX will eliminate this condition. Immediately after the
'\input webmac', several lines of code are generated to override some of the macros
that 'webmac' defines. The result of these redefinitions is that major sections, instead
of starting new pages as they normally do, are treated exactly like regular sections,
except that the group title still appears in bold font. Also, the running heads are
modified to display "Modified Sections Only" instead of the current major section.

9.2   Multiple Change File Utilities

The subject of multiple change files for the same WEB program has appeared several
times in TUGboat [AH86,GR86,Sew87b,Bre88]. The fact that TANGLE and WEAVE
allow only one change file per WEB file sometimes causes problems.

9.2.1   Why Merge Change Files?

Sometimes it is desirable to create a special purpose variation of a program, such
as a version of TEX with an extended character set to handle Japanese characters.
Such a program may be only slightly different from the original, so a change file is
a reasonable way to build it, for all the same reasons that change files simplify the
implementation-dependent changes. Changes to the base WEB file would automatically be picked up when the program is run through TANGLE again.

Some of the enhancements to the WEB processors discussed in Section 13.2 are
examples of slight modifications that lend themselves to change files. Also, the
Modula-2 WEB system described in Section 8.1.3 (MWEB) was implemented as a pair
of change files applied to TANGLE and WEAVE, containing the modifications to allow
WEB to work with the language Modula- 2. The bulk of the processing for MWEB is
identical to that of regular WEB, so the change files are fairly small.

However, virtually every implementation of a WEB program written for portability requires a change file to tailor the program to the target system. The two sets

of changes are independent and (ideally) mutually exclusive, since the enhancement changes are related to the program logic and the implementation changes deal primarily with the interface to the operating environment, but both must be applied to the same WEB source file. TANGLE and WEAVE, the WEB processors, expect only one change file containing all of the changes to be incorporated.

When the merging is done manually, it is a tedious, error-prone exercise. The individual changes from the two files must be interleaved, since they must appear in the combined change file in the same order in which the code they are to modify appears in the base WEB file. The operation is less tiresome if the convention of marking changes with the number of the section that they modify is followed, but it never reaches the point of being fun. Even then, the section numbers don't help if both change files modify the same section. Analysis is required to place the changes within the section in the proper order.

This operation must be repeated for every implementation change file, each of which is different and may modify different sections of the program. Worse, if the enhancement change file is updated at some later date, it is necessary to go back and make the same update to every one of the composite change files. Conversely, if one of the implementation change files is updated, the composite change file for that implementation must be modified.

Some of the enhancement change files can be used in conjunction with each other, if the enhancements they provide do not conflict with each other. When multiple enhancements are taken into account, the number of separate change files to maintain, already unmanageable, becomes impossible.

Another reason for multiple change files is supplied by Appelt and Horn[AH86]. The example is a site running TeX on several different computers with different operating systems $(s_1, \ldots, s_n)$, each of which can print on several output devices $(o_1, \ldots, o_m)$. The TeX *device driver* (a program used to convert the TeX device-independent document into printer-specific control codes) for each output device is created by modifying the device driver template DVItype, with a change file containing the code to handle that particular device. However, DVItype, like other programs, needs a change file for each operating system on which it is to run. Therefore, the number of unique change files is the number of operating systems times the number of printer types.

As a side note, keeping listings for a myriad different versions of the program is an exercise for the truly masochistic, even if the listings are made shorter by suppression of unchanged sections (see Section 9.1 and Section 5.2.6).

9.2.2 Automated Merge Programs

The programs described below are designed to automate this process by combining two or more change files into a single file acceptable to TANGLE and WEAVE. Each of the files to be merged is maintained as a separate file, and the merge program will accept multiple change files and create a new change file containing the combined changes. This combined file is then used as input to `TANGLE` and `WEAVE`. After running the `WEB` processors, this file may be deleted for the same reason that the Pascal and TEX files output by `WEB` may be deleted after use: it is an intermediate file that can easily be regenerated and should not be considered a true source file. Using this approach, it is only necessary to keep a master copy of each input change file. Everything else is derived.

Most of the programs described below can build a new `WEB` file as an option, one with all of the changes merged in. This feature is normally used for permanent changes to the base `WEB` file, like the upgrade from version 2.8 of `TANGLE` to 2.9 in Section F.2.1 (see Section 13.2.2). Changes to Stanford-supplied programs are often published in TUGboat in change file form. These change files are not intended to be used as input to `TANGLE` and `WEAVE` but are printed as if they were change files to guide the installer in making the changes directly to the `WEB` files with a text editor. These merge programs can be used to process them in the same way as any other change file to create a new `WEB` file.

9.2.3   Parallel vs. Sequential Merging

The are two basic philosophies used for merging change files—parallel and sequential. The primary difference between the two is in how the multiple change files relate to each other. The operation should be pretty much the same when the changes are to different parts of the program, but the two methodologies operate very differently when change conflicts occur (when more than one of the change files tries to modify the same lines of code).

Conflicts often occur when merging change files. While significant conflicts are (ideally) not very likely, since the changes being merged are normally for different purposes and modify different portions of the code, conflicts of a trivial nature occur often. For instance, many `WEB` programs follow the example of Stanford and output a "banner line" to the terminal to identify the program and its version level, as in

```
@d banner=='This is WEAVE, Version X.X'
```

Nearly all change files modify this line to reflect the change they are making to the program, such as

```
@d banner=='This is WEAVE with hyperspace option, ...'
@d banner=='This is MWEAVE, Modula-2 WEAVE, ...'
```

for modifications to the logic of the program itself or

```
@d banner=='This is WEAVE, VAX/VMS Version ...'
@d banner=='This is WEAVE, Turbo Pascal Version ...'
```

for the various implementation change files. However, when multiple change files are being merged, the banner line of none of them is correct, since the version of the program actually executing is a combination of the two, and should be something like

```
@d banner=='This is MWEAVE, VAX/VMS Version ...'
```

The '\title' command in the limbo portion of a WEB program falls in the same category as the banner line, since it is also a target common to many change files.

The solution to this problem is to create a *third* change file containing nothing but conflict resolutions. For lack of a better term, we will refer to this file as a *referee file*. Its change sections would consist only of the composite banner line and title. It should be placed in the list of change files in a position where its changes will override all of the others. Since the conflicts it addresses are expected, the warning messages can be ignored. (It goes without saying that any *unexpected* conflicts which surface must be analyzed to ensure that they don't change the logic of the program to an uncompilable or unexecutable state.)

For smoothest operation the change sections for banner line, title, etc., should be moved out of the implementation and enhancement change files entirely, letting the referee files set the unique banner line for each combination. The uncharitable might point out that a myriad change files is what using a merge program was supposed to prevent. The difference is that the referee files are only a few lines long, just one or two change sections, and don't change unless a new version of something comes out. In fact, they are the *only* change files that have to be modified in this case if the version-dependent changes are moved out of the main change files.

The merge programs are split equally between the two modes of operation; WEBMERGE and KNIT/TWIST operate in the parallel mode, while TIE and PATCH are sequential processors.

Sequential Merging

In the sequential approach, "the addition of change file f_{i+1} behaves as if the change files f_1 to f_i had been merged into the WEB program before." In other words, the changes from the first change file are applied to the base WEB file, then the changes from the second change file are applied to the composite result, the changes from the third are applied to that, and so on.

The problem with this approach is that it requires the change files to be aware of the existence of each other. In other words, if change files f_1 and f_2 modify the same parts of a program, file f_2 must be written to modify the lines from f_1 rather than the WEB file itself. This precludes using f_2 without f_1. If the changes made by the two change files are truly independent, then it should be possible to handle them independently as well. It might be desirable to apply f_2 with a different f_1 or by itself. To use the example of MWEB, change files 'weave.vax' and 'mweave.ch' exist, both based on 'weave.web'. Applying 'mweave.ch' to 'weave.web' produces the generic version of MWEAVE (Modula-2 WEAVE). Applying 'weave.vax' to 'weave.web' results in the VAX-specific version of regular WEAVE. Merging 'weave.vax' and 'mweave.ch' results in 'mweave.vax', which can then be used to create the VAX version of MWEAVE. Either of these change files can be used alone or with the other with no modifications. Also, 'mweave.ch' can be merged with a completely different implementation change file to produce MWEAVE for another environment, without changing either file.

Change conflict resolution in a sequential merge program is similar to that for parallel programs, in that a third special change file is built for this purpose. The ordering of the change files is reversed, however. The referee file should be the last in the list so that it can override the changes made by the others. If the primary change files are written so that there is no conflict between them, i.e., the referee file is the only one that modifies the banner line or the '\title' in the first place, then there are no change conflicts at all and the change files can be specified in any order. If change files are written this way, then it doesn't matter whether a parallel or sequential merge program is used, because the result is exactly the same.

Parallel Merging

In contrast to sequential merge, the other approach applies all of the change files to the original WEB file in parallel. If a conflict occurs, one of the change files is selected to apply that change, and the others are flushed (in this case, "flushing" a change file means discarding the current change section for that file and moving ahead to the next one). A warning message is sent to the screen identifying which two files had a conflict, which file was flushed, and the source line on which the conflict occurred.

Which file is used and which ones are flushed depend on how the conflict occurs. Two rules apply: a change file with a matching operation already in progress has precedence over any others which match later lines; if no change is currently in progress and more than one file matches on the same line of the WEB file, the higher-priority change file is used. *Priority* refers to position within the list of change files (f_1 would have a higher priority than f_2). Therefore, change files intended for conflict resolution should appear first in the list.

If the sequential approach of change file merging is truly needed, the case in which one change file needs to be fully applied before the second one is applied to the result of the first, this can be accomplished serially by using WEBMERGE to create an intermediate WEB file and then applying the second change file to it. Of course, this does require additional steps, but that's what batch files and command procedures are for.

The author has had only one occasion, after more than two years of using WEBMERGE, when a situation that would have been easier to handle with a sequential merge program arose. When 'mangle.ch', the change file to convert TANGLE to Modula-2, was being merged with the various implementation change files for TANGLE, it would have been handy to override the specification of '.pas' as the default file type, replacing it with '.mod', in the VAX and MS-DOS implementations. However, since the lines to be modified were in the implementation change file rather than the base WEB file, they were out of the reach of WEBMERGE. A referee file could have been used, but it would have had to duplicate much of the implementation change file. The lines containing '.pas' were in the largest section, the last one, where all of the new code was added. A sequential program, since it modifies the result of all of the other change files, could have easily changed '.pas' to '.mod' in the one place it occurred.

9.2.4 Stand-alone vs. Integrated

The merge programs are divided into two groups in another way.[1] TIE and WEBMERGE are stand-alone programs that are completely external to the WEB system, while the other two are actually modified versions of the WEB processors themselves. (Actually, PATCH can operate in both modes. From the vantage point of being the last one developed, it was able to incorporate many of the best features of its predecessors.)

The stand-alone programs apply multiple change files to a WEB file and generate either a new WEB or a composite change file containing the combined changes. One interesting property of the stand-alone merge programs is that they can be used with text files other than WEB source files. Change files can be written for regular languages or even data files. Whatever text appears between '@x' and '@y' in a change section will be matched with the input source file and this text will be replaced by whatever lines appear between '@y' and '@z', whether they consist of WEB source code, regular Ada source code, or telephone numbers.

TWIST and KNIT are themselves implemented as change files. Applying 'knit.chg' to 'tangle.web' creates 'knit.pas', while 'twist.chg' is used to generate TWIST from WEAVE. One additional feature that TWIST provides from its vantage point as part of WEAVE is that the changed code sections are not only marked with an asterisk, but with the number of the change file which caused the modification. Of course, since the change flag is on a section-by-section basis, it is uncertain what happens

---

[1]One is reminded of the old joke: There are two types of people in this world—those who divide everyone into two groups and those who don't.

when two different change files modify the same section.

PATCH was a stand-alone program, which was later used to create TPATCH and WPATCH from TANGLE and WEAVE.

9.2.5   PATCH

The PATCH processor provides an additional capability for change files: include files. As in regular programming languages, include files can be very useful when the same source code appears in more than one program. For instance, many parts of WEAVE and TANGLE are identical, such as the merging of lines from the WEB file and the change file. Other good examples are the description of the internal format of the DVI file which appears in TEX and DVItype, the description of TFM (TEX Font Metric) files duplicated in TEX and METAFONT, the description of GF (Generic Font) files in METAFONT, GFtype, GFtoPK, and so on. In all of these cases a large section of text is copied verbatim into the WEB source file for more than one program. Any changes to the common text must be painstakingly applied to every file.

It would be much more convenient if these common blocks of text could be placed into separate files, to be included by TANGLE and WEAVE during processing. There would be only one copy of the text to be included, with a corresponding reduction of disk space required, and any changes to the include file would automatically be picked up by all programs using it.

The PATCH processor inputs a base WEB file and applies various *patches* to it. A patch is another WEB file with a series of associated change files, which are applied one after the other. Each patch has a *patch file* specifying the file names of the WEB file and all of the change files.

A patch is initiated by a '@i' followed by the file name of the patch file. The specified WEB file and all of its change files are inserted at the point at which the '@i' occurred. A patch may itself contain secondary patches, again indicated by '@i'.

PATCH has three modes of operation. *Merge mode* applies all patches and creates a WEB file and one change file suitable for input to the regular TANGLE and WEAVE. *Insert mode* creates a new pure WEB file with all changes and patches applied, similar to the WEB file generated by WEBMERGE. In *update mode* all changes are applied to the primary patch, while secondary patches are applied directly to the WEB file, for incorporation of frozen changes to a baseline.

9.3   C Postprocessors

Some sites do not have Pascal compilers but would like to use WEB anyway. This section describes a pair of utilities, WEB-to-C and PASCHAL, that take normal WEB as input and generate C source code instead of Pascal. This is a completely different concept from the CWEB systems described in Section 8.1.4, which require manual conversion of the WEB source to C. Both WEB-to-C and PASCHAL are somewhat limited, since they are specifically designed to handle TEX rather than programs in general. Features of Pascal not used by TEX are not necessarily supported.

Rather than converting WEB source files directly into C, these programs are instead Pascal-to-C converters. The WEB file is run through TANGLE in the usual manner, then the Pascal file created by TANGLE is run through the converter to create a C source file.

When dealing with TEX and related programs, it makes sense to use these programs, because any enhancements to the base system are picked up automatically, while the changes must be made manually for the versions of TEX that were converted to other languages by hand.

For general programming, i.e., user-written programs as opposed to TEX, it makes more sense to write the program directly in CWEB, if C is the desired language, rather than going through the extra steps involved with these translator programs.

WEB-to-C is provided with the standard UNIX distribution of TEX, while PASCHAL is distributed with TurboTEX, one of the implementations for the IBM PC.

Chapter 10

On the Horizon

10.1 What Is Needed

In the short term, there are a number of incremental changes which could be made to the baseline WEB processors. These modifications would be comparatively easy to make, would greatly improve the utility of the system in a production environment, and would be compatible with existing WEB programs. This wish list includes, but is not limited to, the following:

- Forward references for numeric macros: Because of the way that numeric macros are implemented in WEB, this would be a much more complicated change than the one for non-numeric macros but would still be worthwhile. Incorporation of this change would permit *complete* position independence of all elements of a WEB program.

- Include file capability: This feature is partially provided by CWEB, but it would be nice if it were available in the base WEB system.

- Block delete for change files: The problems associated with deleting large blocks of text via the change file mechanism are discussed in Section 5.1.5. It would be useful to add some new commands to WEB specifically to handle this case. For instance, an alternate form for change sections could be a delete-lines change section consisting a command (such as '@r' for remove?) that would identify a delete range as the two lines immediately following that command: the first of the two lines would match the first line of the WEB file that was to be deleted, and the second line would match the last line to be deleted. This would be equivalent to a huge change section with a match text consisting of all of the lines to be deleted and no replacement text. For instance,

```
@r
first line to be deleted
last line to be deleted
```

10.2   Current Research

10.2.1   Interactive WEB

The complicated syntax of strongly typed languages like Pascal puts off many people because the typing in of the various elements can be tedious. The syntax of WEB can be even more tedious, since WEB syntax is a combination of the syntaxes of Pascal and TeX, with a few more commands added.

The WEB Tool was developed by Marcus Brown while working on a doctorate at Texas A & M. The tool is an interactive WEB browser, a program which loads in a WEB source file and retains the structure. The operator is allowed to view the program in several different ways, including a tree structure and individual sections.

The relationships among the sections are maintained. Using the mouse, the user can browse through the program by following the logical links. The entire program can be displayed in a graphical tree form and individual code sections can be called up in another window for display. The sections can also be called up from an alphabetical list of section names or from the index. In the case of a section name, moving the cursor into that name and clicking the mouse calls up the code section associated with the name. Moving the cursor into one of the section numbers in a particular index entry also calls up the code section.

When a code section is displayed, most of the WEB commands are removed to prevent cluttering up the display. The WEB tool provides an ASCII approximation of the way the section would look in the listing. Much of the information normally provided in the listing by WEAVE is displayed, such as an equivalent of the "This code is used in Sections ..." messages. Since every section starts with a '@␣' or '@*', these commands can be left implicit. The '@<' and '@>' are removed from section names and replaced with '<<' and '>>'. The '@d' and '@f' commands are replaced with 'Define:' and 'Format:'.

The three components of a section are placed in separate subwindows with independent scroll bars. From any code section, movement to the next section or the previous section is accomplished by clicking on a button with the mouse. Moving the cursor into the name of a code section referenced within the current section calls up the new section.

The WEB tool runs under Unix on the Sun workstation, although it should be possible to port it to other windowing systems, such as X-Windows or the Macintosh. The current version is a browser only and has no edit capability.

The WEB browser is a prototype system. It is an interesting program, but its lack of editing capability means that it can't be used as a stand-alone tool. It could be used to study a program and determine where changes should be made, but those changes would have to be incorporated with a traditional text editor.

A WEB editor based on this prototype would be a great program development environment. The author can envision a function key or mouse button which would create a placeholder in the cursor position. After prompting for the code section name (which would not need the '@<' and '@>' delimiters), this function would automatically create a new code section with the specified name and would put a placeholder for the code section in the original position. If the programmer wanted to expand the new code section, the regular function to open a code section could be used.

Code section numbers would not be relevant while in the editor and would not be displayed. The program could be stored in tree form and a regular WEB file suitable for processing by TANGLE and WEAVE could be output on command. All of the WEB commands could be added to the file as it is built; e.g., the '@<' and '@>' would be added to section names as they went by and '@␣' would precede each section ('@*' for major sections).

10.2.2 Generic WEB

Work is being done by Norman Ramsey of Princeton, based on earlier work by Silvio Levy of the same institution, on a language-independent version of WEB: more specifically, a version of the WEB processors that can be quickly adapted to new languages.

This is accomplished by separating the data structures containing WEB's knowledge of a particular language from the procedures that manipulate these structures. As stated in Chapter 8, WEB really knows nothing of computer languages; it manipulates text according to a set of rules (see Chapter 11). The rules are currently hard-coded into the program itself, but if they were separated and a method for building new rule sets independently were developed, then the same WEB processors could be used with more than one language.

A program to generate a language-specific version of the WEB system from a language specification has been developed. Since it generates a WEB system, the program was christened SPIDER.[1]

The SPIDER processor does not generate the entire WEB system. Rather it creates an *instance* of the portions of WEAVE and TANGLE that are language-specific. Each language is a different instance and has a different pair of language modules. This code is then combined with the generic part of the WEB processors.

---

[1]The SPIDER Manual is stored as 'spiderman.tex', with apologies to Stan Lee and Marvel Comics.

The role of **SPIDER** exactly corresponds to that of automatic parser generators. These programs take a language definition and generate source code to parse that language. This code is then included in a larger program such as a compiler.

The input to **SPIDER** is a text file containing commands which define the language to be processed. This is not a language definition in a syntactic or semantic sense, as would be needed to generate a compiler, but is a simpler definition that contains just the information needed by **TANGLE** and **WEAVE**.

The development of **SPIDER** dramatically changes the procedure used to convert **WEB** to other computer languages. Much of the more difficult parts of the conversion are semiautomated.

While use of **SPIDER** does not relieve the implementor of the need to understand the internal operation of **WEB**, it does eliminate some of the tedium of the actual coding. Instead of putting in code to handle the language-specific parts, the implementor may create a text file containing a language specification that will allow **SPIDER** to generate this code.

The bulk of the **WEB** system is already language-independent. This part of the code is maintained as a pair of independent source files (referred to as the master **WEAVE** and the master **TANGLE**) and does not change from language to language. The language-dependent part is generated by **SPIDER** from the language specification, and the two parts are combined to become a running **WEB** system.

Using the Ada language as an example, the procedure is as follows:

1. A language specification is created and given a name like 'ada.spider' or equivalent.

2. From this source file **SPIDER** builds 'adat.web' and 'adaw.web', the source files, in **CWEB**, containing the language-dependent code. These two files are in the form of include files, and the master **WEAVE** and **TANGLE** files contain the '@i' commands necessary to include them.

3. **CTANGLE** is run on the master **TANGLE** and **WEAVE**, which then include 'adat.web' and 'adaw.web'; 'adatangle.c' and 'adaweave.c' are created.

4. Compiling and linking these two C files produce the executable programs 'adatangle' and 'adaweave', which are then used to process Ada **WEB** programs.

The language definition contains information such as '+' is a token, **case** is a reserved word, **procedure** starts on a new line. Detailed explanation of the language definition is not appropriate for this chapter and is deferred to Section 14.3 in "Advanced Topics".

SPIDER has already been used to generate WEB systems for Ada, C, and AWK, and there is no reason why someone can't sit down and create a language specification for any language whatsoever.

The main drawback to SPIDER is that it is implemented in AWK and is therefore available only on UNIX systems. There is no middle ground where UNIX is concerned—people either love it or hate it; there is no in-between.

Since the master TANGLE and WEAVE are based on Levy CWEB, the operation of SPIDER-generated WEB is similar to that version of WEB. While that this means that SPIDER has some features that are provided by CWEB, such as separate lines corresponding to source lines and include files, it also means that some of the features of the original WEB are not available because they were not carried over when CWEB was developed. These features were dropped because they were not needed in C. However, the purpose of SPIDER is to generate WEB for new languages, and some of these languages could possibly have made use of some of the features available in the original WEB system.

As a future extension of the SPIDER concept, the WEB processors could be given the capability of loading the language data at run-time, allowing them to change languages on the fly. This would allow multiple computer languages to be combined in the same WEB program. Of course, some method for producing multiple output files would have to be added to TANGLE, because few compilers are happy when fed languages other than their own.

Part II

Advanced Topics

Chapter 11

Internal Operation of WEB

While most people are happy to use the WEB software as distributed, there are several reasons why someone would want to modify it. These reasons include:

1. porting the system to a new environment, such as a new computer, or a different compiler or operating system on the same machine

2. making modifications to WEB for personal preference

3. making WEB work with new languages

These three topics are covered in the following chapters. Except for item 2, in which changes can be made at several different levels, these modifications require changes to the WEB processors, TANGLE and WEAVE, using change files.

Before modifying the WEB system, it may be advantageous to learn how it works in the first place. This chapter provides an overview of the internals of the WEB processors. It does not describe them in massive detail, since the complete source listings of TANGLE and WEAVE are provided in Appendix G, Sections G.1.1 and G.1.2, and they do a pretty good job of describing themselves (which, of course, is what WEB is all about).

11.1 Overview

The processing of WEAVE and TANGLE, while similar in parts, is quite different because of the different functions of the two programs. TANGLE generates the Pascal file and is uninterested in anything related to the formatting of the listing. It completely ignores the comments (except meta-comments) and all other TEX code within the WEB file and is concerned only with the actual program code. The orientation of WEAVE, of course, is just the opposite. Like TANGLE, it concentrates most of its effort on the Pascal code but is concerned with which fonts the various elements should have, the spacing between them, etc.

11.2   Code Common to TANGLE and WEAVE

The similarities between TANGLE and WEAVE are in the way tables in memory are allocated (although not the contents of the tables) and in the input and output processing, especially input of the WEB and change files.

11.2.1   Data Structures

Both of the WEB processors utilize large arrays containing all of the elements they are manipulating.

All textual items, such as identifiers, code section names, and reserved words, are stored in the *byte_mem* array. WEAVE additionally stores items manually indexed by the programmer (via '@:', '@^', or '@.'). Since most of the processing treats all of these textual elements in a similar fashion, we will refer to them collectively as *names*. These names are stored sequentially in the order in which they are encountered. There is no separation between the name entries; they are jammed together as one huge stream of bytes. Beginning position, length, and other information about the names are maintained in separate arrays containing offsets into *byte_mem*. Because of the number of module names and identifiers possible in a large program, the bounds of this array can exceed the capacity of many Pascal compilers. Many compilers are limited to 16-bit indexes by the architecture of their target machine. Therefore *byte_mem* is split up into segments to reduce the size of the index needed to reference an array element. It is defined as a two-dimensional array, where the first index represents the segment and the second is the byte offset within that segment.

The *byte_start* array locates the various text elements in *byte_mem*. For each section name or identifier, *byte_start* contains the starting offset within *byte_mem*. The length of the name can be obtained by subtracting the offset of the next entry from the offset of the current entry. The segment of *byte_mem* in which to store the name is determined by performing a modulo operation on the current name index. This causes the names to be distributed evenly among the segments.

Several other arrays contain information associated with a particular name. All of these arrays share a common index, the unique number assigned to each name. The *link* array contains the forward links to allow an associated group of names to be chained together. The *ilk* array provides a category for the name (both WEAVE and TANGLE use this array, but the usages are different).

While section names and identifiers are stored in memory in a similar way, accessing them is completely different. As each element is encountered, a search is performed to determine whether this element has already occurred. Because identifiers are typically shorter than section names and are always referenced as a complete unit (they cannot be abbreviated as section names can), they lend themselves to a hashing algorithm. A hash value is computed for each identifier and this value is used as an index into a hash table. The value in the selected entry is the head of a chain of name indexes. The chain (which is contained in the *link* array mentioned above) only contains forward links, rather than both directions, and the search follows the chain until either the name or a null index is found.

The section names are stored as a binary tree. They cannot be hashed as the identifiers can because they are often referenced by only a prefix of the name, as in '@<Print...@>', and hash codes include all of the characters in the name. A binary tree needs two links per node, rather than just a forward link. The *link* array above is used for the left links of the tree, and the *ilk* array, which is not needed for section names, stores the right links.

11.2.2 Input File Processing

The procedures which actually read lines from the WEB file and merge lines from the change file with them are identical in the two processors. Once the current line is available, only then does the logic diverge.

The *changing* flag is used to determine whether the next line is to be read from the main WEB file or the change file. Only one change file can be opened during a run of one of the WEB processors (for information on handling of multiple change files, see Section 9.2).

During program initialization, the change file is opened and all of the lines up to and including the '@x' marking the first change section are read. The first actual line of the change section, the one after '@x', is also read and stored for matching purposes. Whenever a change section is pending, each line of the main WEB file is compared with the first line of the change section until a match occurs. After the first match, all following lines up to the '@y' must match exactly. Lines are read from the two files and compared without any further processing, since the lines being read are the ones to be replaced and will not appear in the merged text.

When the '@y' is found, any lines that didn't match are reported as warnings and the *changing* flag is set, indicating that input lines should now be read from the change file. After each line of the replacement text is read in, processing of the line is the same as when the input was coming from the main WEB file.

When the line containing '@z' is encountered, the current change section has been completely processed. Lines are read from the change file until the next '@x' is read or until the end of the change file is reached. The *changing* flag is turned

off, causing input to come from the WEB file again. As before, the first line of the
change section is stored, to be matched with each line of the main WEB file.

If no more change sections are present in the file, the length of the buffer normally
containing the match line is set to zero so that it can never match anything; change
file processing is complete. The remaining input will come only from the WEB file.

During the termination of the program, the length of the match line is checked.
Since the end-of-file processing for the change file sets this variable to zero, the
presence of a nonzero value indicates that the currently active change section never
matched any line in the WEB file: an error.

11.3   Internals of TANGLE

11.3.1   Data Structures

In addition to *byte_mem*, TANGLE contains a similar array called *tok_mem*, which
contains all of the tokens of the source program. All of the tokens are compressed
into as few bytes as possible. Identifiers and strings are represented by their index,
section names are represented by the section number, two-character tokens such as
':=' are compressed into a 1-byte internal code, and single-character tokens such as
'+' are represented by the numeric equivalent of the ASCII character.

In the same way that *byte_mem* is a monolithic block containing all of the identifiers, section names, strings, etc., of the program all jammed together, *tok_mem*
contains all of the replacement texts of the program in one large stream. There is
no movement of data within *tok_mem* after the input file has been read in; all of the
tokens remain in their original positions.

The *tok_start* array provides the same service for *tok_mem* that *byte_start* does
for *byte_mem*: it separates the bulk into its individual components, the replacement
texts.

All Pascal code in a WEB program (the "real" code, not that occurring in comments) is part of some replacement text, either that of a macro or that of a code
section (possibly the unnamed section corresponding to the main program).

The *equiv* array, which is indexed by name, is used to associate a code section
or macro to its replacement text. The entry for a given name contains the index of
that particular replacement text. For a numeric macro, the entry in *equiv* contains
the actual numeric value associated with the macro.

A code section can actually have more than one replacement text. The same
code section can be defined many times in the program, and each new replacement
text is considered a continuation of the first, although each text is logically separate
and has a different text index number.

The *text_link* array, which is indexed by replacement text index rather than by name index, is used to chain multiple replacement texts together. If the entry for a given replacement text has an index in it, then another replacement text is to be chained to this one. The value contained in the *equiv* entry for the name is the index of the first replacement text.

TANGLE actually contains two hash tables, one for the full identifiers and another for the version of the identifier sent to the output file, which is truncated, forced to uppercase, and without underscores. The actual identifier doesn't appear twice in *byte_mem*; the same entry is pointed to from two different directions.

In TANGLE, all identifiers have an associated value called an *ilk*, which can be either *normal* or one of the three macro types. The identifier is stored on its first occurrence, and the *ilk* is also stored. Identifiers of *ilk* other than normal have no entry in the chopped identifier hash table (*chop_hash*), because macro identifiers do not appear in the Pascal program and do not have to be chopped.

On subsequent lookups of the identifier, the *ilk* of the new occurrence is compared with the original *ilk*. The normal case is for all occurrences to be of normal *ilk* (this is a regular nonmacro identifier) or for the first occurrence to be of one of the three macro types and all subsequent occurrences to be of normal *ilk*, i.e., uses of the macro. If the previous *ilk* was normal and the new *ilk* is a macro *ilk*, then this is a forward reference of a macro. In the case of simple and parametric macros, this is allowed (version 2.9 or later) so the *ilk* is simply changed. Forward references are not allowed on numeric macros so an error message is generated if one is attempted. In either case, the identifer now has a macro *ilk*, so it is removed from the hash table for chopped identifiers. If the previous *ilk* was a macro type and the new *ilk* is also a macro type, then an illegal macro redefinition has occurred. This is not allowed for any macro type, whether it is being redefined with the same type or a different type.

11.3.2 Operation

TANGLE reads the source files during the first pass and converts all of the input to tokens stored in *tok_mem*. The tokenization of the replacement texts is very similar for code sections and for simple and parametric macros. In fact, the same procedure (*scan_repl*) is used for all three (numeric macros have their own scan procedure). As macros are scanned, the '=', '==', or '(#)==' following the identifier is not stored; it is only used to determine the type of the macro. When scanning a parametric macro, any occurrences of '#' in the definition are stored as a *param* token. These will be replaced by the parameter when the macro is later expanded.

When a non-numeric macro is referenced in a replacement text, the token corresponding to the macro is simply stored. No further processing is done, as expansion occurs during output of the replacement text. The parameter of a macro is tokenized along with the macro identifier, including the parentheses around it.

Numeric macros are not tokenized in the same way that other macros and code sections are. Instead, the expression is evaluated during the scan, and the resulting 16-bit signed number is stored in *equiv*. The expressions occurring in numeric macro definitions are limited, so the only input tokens that should be encountered during evaluation are integer constants, plus or minus operators, or previously defined numeric macro identifiers.

The processing of constant expressions within numeric macros is similar to that performed for expressions found in the text of the program. In both cases, the processing is limited to addition and subtraction of adjacent constant values. Neither type of expression allows parentheses, multiplication, division, or modulo operations. The main difference between the two is the point at which the evaluation occurs. The expression evaluation in numeric macros takes place during scanning of the macro definition in the first pass, while evaluation of general constant expressions occurs during the output phase.

Whenever a '{' is encountered during scanning, whether in a code section or in a macro, an ordinary comment has been found, so TANGLE scans at high speed for the matching '}'. All text between them is ignored, as TANGLE does not process regular comments. This does not apply to meta-comments; '@{' and '@}' are compressed into internal tokens that will actually be output as '{' and '}'.

During the second pass, the Pascal code is generated by spilling the contents of *tok_mem* to the output file by expansion of all replacement texts. The output starts with the replacement text of the "unnamed section." As each token is encountered, it is output to the Pascal file. Ordinary tokens such as identifiers, numeric macros, special characters, and numbers are simply output. When the token indicating a code section or a non-numeric macro is encountered, this indicates that a new replacement text is to be started. The pointer to the current replacement text in *tok_mem* is pushed onto a stack and scanning of the new replacement text is started. Processing of tokens in the new replacement text continues as before and references to other macros or code sections cause another level to be pushed onto the stack and yet another replacement text to be started. Each time the end of a replacement text is encountered, TANGLE checks for continuation replacement texts (this can only occur for code section replacement texts; macros cannot be continued later in the program). If a continuation is found, the token pointer is reset to the beginning of the continuation text and the expansion continues with no change in the nesting level. If there is no continuation, then the stack is popped and token processing continues at the token after the token which caused the just-completed expansion.

When the token corresponding to an identifier that has been defined as a parametric macro is encountered during expansion, special processing is required for the parameter. The parameter is handled somewhat like a dynamically defined simple macro, where '#' (actually the *param* token resulting from '#') is the macro and the parameter, minus its enclosing parentheses, is the replacement text. In fact, the parameter is copied into *tok_mem* like the other replacement texts, in the first position following all of the permanent replacement texts. It is even given its own index.

Once the parameter has been copied into *tok_mem*, the expansion of the replacement text of the parametric macro begins. Each time that the *param* token is encountered (corresponding to '#' in the macro definition), the text of the parameter is expanded. The processing is exactly the same as for a simple macro in that the output of tokens in the parametric macro is halted, the current token pointer is pushed onto the stack, and expansion begins with the new replacement text (the parameter). When the end of the replacement text is reached the stack is popped as with any replacement text, and output continues with the token after *param*. When the end of the parametric macro's replacement text is reached, the replacement text of the parameter is removed from *tok_mem* before the stack is popped.

Since the replacement text for one macro can contain a call to another, it is possible for more than one parameter replacement text to be active, although only the one for the innermost macro can actually expand at any given time.

TANGLE maintains a count of the current nest level of comment delimiters, because Pascal does not allow nested comments so it would be undesirable to start a new comment while one is already in progress. As each beginning delimiter is output, the level is incremented; each ending delimiter decrements the counter. If the nest level is not zero—i.e., this is an inner comment—the '[' and ']' characters are output instead of '{' and '}'. This applies to all comment delimiters which are actually output to the Pascal file, including user-supplied meta-comments and internally generated comments containing section numbers found at the beginning and end of a code section expansion.

11.4 Internals of WEAVE

11.4.1 Data Structures

Identifiers in WEAVE also have an *ilk* value, but the usage is completely different. The *ilk* of a WEAVE identifier is either the font in which it is to be typeset (normal, roman, user-controlled, or typewriter) or the group of reserved words to which it belongs (for-like, proc-like, etc.).

The cross-referencing information is stored in *xmem*, which is an array of records containing two fields, *num* and *link*, both of which are 16-bit integers. The *num* field is the number of the code section in which this element is either defined or referenced. If this is a definition, the value stored in *num* is the section number plus the constant *def_flag*. The value for a reference is just the section number. The *link* field is used to chain all of the entries for a particular name together.

The *xref* array, which is indexed by a name such as *ilk* or *tok_start*, contains an index into the *xmem* array, pointing to the first cross-reference entry for that name.

Like **TANGLE**, **WEAVE** has a *tok_mem* array. However, it is much smaller because **WEAVE** doesn't have to store the text of the entire program, just the Pascal text currently being processed. Since **WEAVE** doesn't have to worry about inter-section relationships, each code section is a self-contained unit that can be formatted independently of all other sections. Therefore, after processing is completed on a particular section, its tokens can be thrown away and the same space can be reused for the next Pascal text.

The Pascal text being processed by **WEAVE** is broken into "scraps" of text. Each scrap has exactly one *category*, which identifies the type of scrap, and a variable number of tokens called a *translation*. The *cat* array is used to store the category codes of the scraps, while the *trans* array is used to store the index of the first token of the translation of a scrap within the *tok_mem* array.

11.4.2   Operation

Like the **TANGLE** processor, **WEAVE** makes several passes over the **WEB** program. However, **WEAVE** actually reads the source file twice. The first pass is used to store all of the cross-references, and the second actually does the transformation into TEX form.

For the most part, **WEAVE** performs no processing on TEX code in a **WEB** program, other than simply to copy this text directly to the output file. TEX code is scanned, however, for embedded Pascal code ('|...|'). While in the TEX part of a code section, scanning occurs at fairly high speed and continues until either the end of the TEX part is found (signified by the '@d' or '@f' commands starting the definition part, the '@p' or '@<' commands starting the Pascal part, or the '@*' or '@␣' commands starting the next section) or a vertical bar ('|') character is encountered. When a '|' character is found, the Pascal code up to the next '|' is processed, then the high-speed scan starts again. In a similar fashion, comments in Pascal code and code section names are also TEX code and the fast scan is performed for them also, including the detection of the '|'.

The scanning of the Pascal code is similar to that of the TEX code in that scanning continues until the end of the current piece of Pascal code. Unsurprisingly, the terminators of the Pascal scan are pretty much the inverse of those that terminate the TEX scan, except that both stop at the end of a section. Scanning of Pascal code stops when a '{' character (start of a comment) or a '|' character (end of Pascal code within TEX code) is found. **WEAVE** continuously switches between TEX and Pascal code until the end of the section is reached.

11.4.3 The Cross-referencing Pass

The purpose of the cross-referencing pass is to handle forward references of code sections and non-numeric macros (forward references of numeric macros are disallowed) and assign numbers to all of the code sections. During this pass, only programmer-specified index entries (using '@.', etc.), identifiers in Pascal code, and section names are relevant, and everything else is ignored. Nothing is written to the output file. At the end of the pass, a consistency check is made to ensure that there are no undefined or unused code sections. TeX code is completely ignored during the cross-referencing pass.

11.4.4 The Code Generation Pass

The input files are read a second time for the code generation pass. During this pass, the conversion from Pascal to TeX code is accomplished. The processing is performed one section at a time. The code for a section in read in, converted, and output to the TeX file. After the processing for that section is complete, the next section is processed.

The description part of the section is scanned at high speed in much the same way as during the first pass, except that the TeX code is copied to the output TeX file as it goes by.

11.4.5 Input Tokenization

As the Pascal part of the section is read in, it is tokenized. As in **TANGLE**, two-letter symbols are compressed and section names and identifiers are converted to their identifying numbers. Each token is then converted to one or more "scraps" corresponding to what will actually be output. Each scrap has a *category* and a *translation*. The category of a scrap, which corresponds to a syntactic class, determines how it will be handled during later processing. The translation of a scrap is a variable number of output tokens, stored in *tok_mem*, corresponding to the actual TeX code to be output by **WEAVE**.

In addition to the actual language element, these translations include tokens that are formatting control codes associated with the element. For instance, many of the control statements start on a new line, so the first token is *force*, which will eventually cause '\6' to be issued and a new line to be started. The formatting control codes are *indent*, *outdent*, *opt*, *backup*, *break_space*, *force*, *big_force*, *math_rel*, *math_bin*, *math_op*, *cancel*, and *big_cancel*. These are all 1-byte binary numbers in the range above 127.

These tokens appear in Table 11.1. For each discrete operation, the table shows the **WEB** command, the name of the input token it is converted to on input, the name

Cmd	In token	Out token	Output as	Action
		indent	'\1'	indent one more em
		outdent	'\2'	indent one less em
'@|'	math_break	opt	'\3'	opt. line break
		backup	'\4'	backspace of one em
		break_space	'\5'	opt. line break or en space
'@/'	line_break	force	'\6'	line break
'@#'	big_line_break	big_force	'\7'	line break w/extra space
'@,'	thin_space		'\,'	TEX thin space
		math_rel	'\mathrel{'	math relational operator
		math_bin	'\mathbin{'	math binary operator
		math_op	'\mathop{'	math operator
		cancel		cancels *force*, *big_force*
'@+'	no_line_break	big_cancel		cancels spaces too

Table 11.1: **WEAVE** Formatting Codes.

of the output token that appears in the translation, and the sequence of ASCII characters output when that token is written to the TEX file. The codes which have no **WEB** command or input token are generated internally by **WEAVE** as part of the translation of another input token. The *cancel* and *big_cancel* codes have no output sequence because they are not actually output themselves; they inhibit other tokens from being output by their presence in an adjacent location. The *thin_space* input token has no corresponding output token because the output sequence itself ('\,') is put directly into the translation. The meanings of all of the formatting codes are discussed in **WEAVE** Section 141.

For reserved words and other identifiers, the *category* is typically derived from the *ilk*, and the tokens that are placed in *tok_mem* are always the same for a particular *ilk*. A list of the categories and translations for all of the input tokens can be found in Section 142 of **WEAVE**.

In many cases, the relationship between the input sequence, the token, the scrap, and the translation (the output tokens) is fairly straightforward. For instance, the ':=' sequence is converted to a internal token called *left_arrow*. This token becomes a single scrap with a category of *math* and a translation consisting of the output tokens '\' and 'K' ('\K' is a TEX control sequence that will generate '←'). Some tokens generate more than one scrap, depending on the complexity of the token.

11.4.6 Transformation of the Tokens

If a one-on-one mapping from the input token to the output tokens were sufficient to format computer programs, then WEAVE would be a much smaller, simpler program. However, the formatting of various language elements is dependent in part on the program context in which they appear. For instance, the **var** reserved word starts a new line when it begins a list of variables, but it does not do so when it precedes a variable parameter in a procedure declaration. The following shows **var** used both ways:

procedure x(**var** n : *integer*);
var m : *integer*;

In order to format **var** properly, WEAVE must be able to differentiate between the two usages.

After the list of scraps has been built from the input tokens, WEAVE then scans the list and looks for certain patterns of category codes. This is the most complex part of WEAVE (indeed, in all of WEB). A list of *productions* guides WEAVE in this endeavor. Each production consists of a left-hand part, which is a list of category codes to search for, and a right-hand side specifying a new list of category codes to replace the first. If one of the productions contains on its left-hand side a category sequence that matches the current sequence of scraps, the production "fires" and the old sequence of category codes is replaced with the sequence on the right-hand side of the production. A list of the productions can be found in Section 143 of WEAVE.

Since the number of scrap category codes on the right side of a production is always less than or equal to the number on the left side, the firing of the productions is a data reduction process as lower-level scraps are combined into higher-level ones. The complexity reduction doesn't change the translations of the old scraps; all of the output tokens they contain are left intact. However, new output tokens may be inserted between them, since a production may optionally specify additional output tokens to insert between the translations of the old scraps. Hence, the number of output tokens increases while the number of scraps decreases.

Since the old translations are not modified in any way, it is not possible to delete any of the tokens they contain. However, they can be logically deleted by precise placement of new tokens. For instance, inserting a *cancel* token immediately ahead of a *force* token will effectively delete the *force* token, even though it is still physically present in the translation.

WEAVE will always try to match the longer productions first. If one production is a subset of another, i.e., the first n scraps of production x are the same as all of production y, then x will be used instead of y, though both match the input scraps.

Also, the transformation of the input scraps as productions fire means that some productions may now match the input scraps where they didn't before. The scrap pointer is backed up after the firing of most productions, because the new scraps resulting from the transformation may be combinable with scraps that have already been passed by. The code for the productions instructs WEAVE how many scraps to back up the pointer after a given production fires.

For instance, assume a series of input scraps $s_1, \ldots, s_n$. WEAVE first compares all of the productions in the list with $s_1, \ldots, s_n$. If no match is found, then the productions are compared with $s_2, \ldots, s_n$. Still no match, so the pointer is incremented again and $s_3, \ldots, s_n$ is compared. This time a match is found, as the scraps s_3, s_4, s_5 are the same as one of the productions. As the production fires, s_4 and s_5 are combined into a new scrap s_4, one with a different category. Since the code for the production knows that this change could cause other productions to fire, it instructs WEAVE to back up the scrap pointer one position. After backing up, the pointer is again pointing at s_1, and the matching process starts again. Because the category of s_4 has changed from what it was the first time through, scraps s_2, s_3, s_4 cause another production to fire, and the scrap configuration is changed again.

The combination of scraps continues until either all of the code has been reduced to a single scrap, normally of category *stmt*, with a translation containing all of the output tokens or no more reducible sequences can be found. Irreducible sequences occur when the firing of productions is disrupted because a code section contains incomplete code such as a **begin** with no **end** or because a code section name appeared in a place where something else was expected.

The ability to insert new tokens between existing scraps as they are absorbed into larger ones is the primary reason that the scrap data reduction is performed in the first place. Otherwise the translation of the single conglomerate scrap would be exactly equivalent to the combined translations of all the original scraps.

To see how this adjustment is useful, let us consider TEX math mode. Much of the text in the Pascal part of a code section must be in math mode. For instance, the '$\neq$', '$\leq$', and '$\leftarrow$' operators are available *only* in math mode. On the other hand, a lot of the other tokens found in Pascal code are not typeset in math mode. Therefore, the TEX source code generated by WEAVE contains a lot of dollar sign characters representing shifts in and out of math mode.

The tokens in a piece of program code can appear in any order whatever, whether valid Pascal or not. The program may contain errors of Pascal syntax, but it must be typeset anyway so that the programmer can see what the problem is. Since every token is self-contained and can appear anywhere in the program, it ordinarily would have to have dollar signs before and after the actual token string everywhere it appears, in order to make absolutely sure that TEX was in math mode at the time the token was encountered. However, since math tokens are often adjacent in the output, there would be a huge number of unnecessary dollar signs, since sequences such as '$ $token_1$ $ $ $token_2$ $ $ $token_3$ $' would appear. This sequence should really appear with one set of delimiters for each complete mathematical expression, as in '$ $token_1$ $token_2$ $token_3$ $'.

One of the purposes of the scrap data reduction is to combine tokens that are typographically equivalent into a larger scrap that can be handled as a unit. For instance, to handle the case above, the production

$$math\ math \rightarrow math \qquad\qquad (\text{Prod } 20^1)$$

means "anytime two scraps of category *math* are adjacent, they should be combined into one scrap, also of category *math*." If another *math* scrap appears after the newly formed one, it too should be absorbed by using the same production rule. This process continues until all of the *math* scraps in a particular sequence have been combined, and the result is a single large *math* scrap, surrounded by scraps that have a category other than *math*. Note that no dollar signs have been added during the combination of *math* scraps (the individual math scraps don't have dollar signs embedded in their translations, either). Only one pair is needed for the big scrap, and how they are added depends on how the single *math* scrap is absorbed into a higher-level one. For instance, if the scrap were followed by a scrap of category *terminator*, which corresponds to a semicolon or equivalent, then a complete statement has been found. The production

$$math\ terminator \rightarrow stmt \qquad [\![S = \$\,M\,\$\,T]\!] \qquad (\text{Prod } 23)$$

would fire and both scraps would be transformed into a single scrap of category *stmt*. As part of the conversion, the dollar signs would be added before and after the disappearing *math* scrap, since it can't be combined with any more *math* scraps. In fact, after the firing of this production, it isn't even a *math* scrap any more. The associated rule to combine the translations appears between $[\![$ and $]\!]$ and states that the translation of *stmt* S should be dollar sign, the original translation of the *math* scrap M, another dollar sign, and the translation of *terminator* T.

Another example of how the productions work relates to the way the **var** reserved word mentioned earlier is formatted. The **var** word has its own *ilk* called *var_like*, since it operates differently from any other word. When **var** is tokenized, its translation includes the tokens *force* and *backup* ahead of the token representing the word **var** itself. It is given two scraps, with category codes of *var_head* and *intro*. All three of the output tokens are contained in the translation of the *var_head* scrap; the *intro* doesn't have a translation. The *force* and *backup* tokens are always

---

[1]See the list of productions and their associated translation rules in Section 143 of **WEAVE**.

included in the translation, even for a procedure parameter variable, because at time of tokenization it is not known how **var** will be used.

If this particular **var** is a procedure parameter it will follow immediately after a left parenthesis, which has a category of *open*. Thus the sequence of category codes for these two elements is *open*, *var_head*, and *intro*, which just happens to match Production 37:

$$open \; var\_head \; intro \rightarrow open \; math \; [\![M = math\_op \; cancel \, V \; \}]\!] \; (\text{Prod 37})$$

As the production fires, it converts *var_head* and *intro* to *math* (*open* is left alone) and inserts *math_op* and *cancel* ahead of the translation of *var_head*. The *cancel* code, true to its name, cancels the *force* and *backup* control codes in the translation of *var_head*. Note that this new translation makes *var_head* into a math operator, which is appropriate as it is now part of a math scrap. The preceding *math_op* code will be output as '`\mathop{`', and a right brace (the one after V above) is added when the production fires. Therefore, when **var** is output later, it will appear as '`\mathop{\&{var}}`'.

Occurrences of **var** that are not procedure parameters would never be preceded by a parenthesis; therefore the sequence of events just described could never occur because the action is based on the scrap sequence *open*, *var_head*, and *intro*, and a different sequence would result without the parenthesis. If Production 37 did not fire, the *cancel* would not be inserted, the *force* would take effect, and **var** would appear on a new line.

There are some undocumented `WEB` commands used only for debugging of `WEAVE`. They are not mentioned anywhere in the `WEB` manual (not in the text anyway; they are discussed in the comments of the `WEAVE` listing) or in the user guide portion of this book, because they are not readily available to the user. They cannot be used unless `WEAVE` debugging is turned on, or unless `WEAVE` is modified to turn them on regardless of debug mode, and either of these changes require `WEAVE` to be modified and rebuilt. If this option is enabled, `WEAVE` will output tracing information to the terminal if '`@1`' (partial trace) or '`@2`' (full trace) is found in the `WEB` source file. The '`@0`' command will turn tracing off again.

The data reduction process can be observed in action in Figure 11.1, which is a listing generated by `WEAVE` when '`@2`' is placed in the `WEB` file. The code being processed corresponds to Section 16 of the Eight Queens program, ⟨ Print the solution if last queen; try next one if not 16 ⟩. The '`*`' character represents the current position of the scrap pointer, while the 'n:' is the number of the production that just fired.

Figure 11.2 is a more readable explanation of what is happening, a cleaned-up version of the same data. Each line represents the firing of a production. In the left column is the current list of scrap category codes "before firing"; the right column

```
Tracing after 1.170:|try_queen_move|
48:*stmt
Tracing after 1.180:@
25:*simp math semi cond...
45:*math semi cond...
42:*math terminator cond alpha simp...
23:*stmt cond alpha simp...
4: stmt cond*alpha math math simp...
20: stmt cond*alpha math simp omega...
21: stmt cond*alpha math omega module...
2:*stmt cond clause module...
24: stmt*cond clause stmt elsie simp...
13:*stmt clause simp...
35: stmt clause simp*open math math simp...
20: stmt clause simp*open math simp close...
21: stmt clause simp*open math close semi
29: stmt clause*simp math semi
45: stmt*clause math semi
42:*stmt clause math terminator
23:*stmt clause stmt
11:*stmt stmt
49:*stmt
```

Figure 11.1: **WEAVE** Output When *tracing* = 2.

shows the list "after firing." The center field identifies the production that fired. The framing boxes highlight the scraps matching the left side of the production and the scraps that they are transformed into after the firing.

11.4.7 Output of the Tokens

After the data reduction is complete, the output of the accumulated tokens begins. Compared to the analysis phase, this part is almost trivial. At this point there will either be a single scrap containing the combined translations of all of the original scraps or a series of irreducible scraps with separate translations. In either case there is a string of tokens to be output one at a time. The output tokens consist of single characters, control codes such as *indent* and *outdent*, and codes for section names and identifiers. As identifers are output, any underscore characters appearing within them are preceded by backslashes to pacify TEX. Most of the language elements that were single tokens during input do not appear as single tokens in the output; they were converted to sequences of ordinary character tokens and are no different from any other character tokens when output. For instance, the *left_arrow* mentioned earlier is output as two separate character tokens, '\' and 'K'.

The beginning of the code section is indicated by outputting a '\M' macro (or '\N' macro for a major section). As identifiers (including reserved words) are output, they are encapsulated as the parameter of a '\&', '\\', or '\|' macro. Strings are output by using the '\.' macro. Section names are output as '\X*nn*:The name of

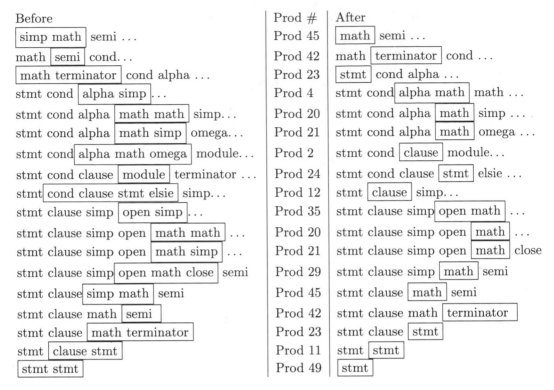

Figure 11.2: **WEAVE** Data Reduction.

the section\X', where *nn* is the number of the section. Control codes are converted to the equivalent macro; i.e., a *force* code is output as '\6'. Comments are output in the form '\C{...}'.

After all of the tokens have been output, the cross-references are generated, if this is the first defining occurrence of a particular section name. Two types of messages are generated: a message that points to continuations of the same code section, if any ("See also sections $s_1, s_2, \ldots, s_n$."), and a list of the sections that reference this one ("This code is used in sections $s_1, s_2, \ldots, s_n$.").

After these messages are generated, the processing for the code section is complete. The cycle begins again as the tokens for the next section are read in.

11.4.8   Output of the Index

After all of the sections of the program have been processed, the automatically generated parts of the listing are output. If any code sections of the program were modified by a change file, then a list of these sections is output, preceded by '\ch'.

The index follows immediately after the changed section list. A '\inx' macro marks the beginning of the index. All of the entries are sorted, then output based on their *ilk*. For each entry, '\:' is output first, then either '\\', '\|', '\.', '\&', or '\9', depending on the *ilk* of the entry, followed by the entry itself in braces, for instance, '\:\|{j}'. A list of section numbers follows the item. The entries are output one a time. WEAVE doesn't worry about setting them up in double columns, as this is handled by 'webmac'. The section numbers of the defining occurrences are surrounded by '\[*nn*]', which causes them to be underlined.

After all of the index entries have been output, the list of code section names is output, preceded by '\fin'. Since the names are stored as a binary tree, they are already in alphabetical order, so they are simply output in the same form in which they appear in the program part, with the '\X' macro. Finally, a '\con' command is added as the very last line of the file, to instruct 'webmac' to print the table of contents and terminate.

11.5 WEB Macros

The 'webmac' macro package contains all of the definitions for the TEX macros that WEAVE generates. The existence of this package allows WEAVE to be greatly simplified, since a lot of processing can be performed by a sequence consisting of only a few characters. For instance, the '\&', '\\', and '\.' macros generate reserved words (bold), identifiers (italics), and typewriter font strings. More complicated macros generate structures such as the index ('\inx') and table of contents ('\con').

Besides defining all of the TEX macros that a WEAVE-generated source file could invoke, 'webmac' also performs initialization of several other key elements. All of the needed fonts are loaded and important formatting parameters such as page width and height and running headers are initialized.

Use of 'webmac' is more or less transparent to the programmer because its actions go on behind the scenes. WEAVE automatically inserts '\input webmac' as the first line of the TEX file, followed by the contents of the limbo section of the input WEB file.

The table of contents is handled entirely within 'webmac'. As each major section is encountered, a line is added to a text file called 'contents.tex'. Each line contains the name given to the major section (the text between '@*' and '.' in the original WEB file) and the section and page numbers of the major section. At the end of the TEX file the '\con' macro is encountered. The contents file is closed and read back in to generate the table of contents.

Chapter 12

Porting to Other Environments

The information in this user guide portion of this book is of limited usefulness if the reader has no access to a machine on which the WEB system will run. This chapter has been added to aid in transporting WEB to new environments.

12.1 Issues in Porting

12.1.1 Porting in General

The WEB software was written in such a way that porting it to different machines is easy when compared to porting other programs of equivalent size and complexity. It makes no use of features not found in Standard Pascal, making it completely compatible with nearly all Pascal compilers. In fact, it doesn't take advantage of many features common to all versions of Pascal, such as pointers, so that it can be converted to languages not having these features.

The system-dependent portions of the programs are isolated to specific sections and are flagged as *system dependencies* in the index. Unsurprisingly, the system dependencies are primarily the low-level input/output routines and other interfaces to the underlying operating system.

The porting process doesn't involve the target machine as much as it does the target compiler. For instance, there are at least two different ports to the IBM PC: one for Microsoft Pascal and the other for Turbo Pascal. On the other hand, since Turbo Pascal also runs on the Macintosh, the port to Turbo on the Mac is very similar to that on the PC, except for calls to the operating system.

A sample implementation change file, one which modifies TANGLE to work on the hypothetical Whiz-Bang 5000 computer, can be found in Section F.2.1, and the modified listing resulting from these changes can be found in Appendix G.2.1.

12.1.2   Opening Files

The specification of the names of the various files used by the WEB processors and the opening of those files are among the most system-dependent operations in Pascal. Many systems are similar in the way that the file name is logically connected to the Pascal file, such as something like

$$assign(webfile, \text{‘junk.web’}); \; reset(webfile);$$

but they are nearly always different in subtle ways, and still other systems are totally off the wall in the way that they perform this function.

There is even more variation in how the names of the files are acquired from the operator. The unmodified processors use the Standard Pascal approach of simply declaring the file names in the program header, then performing a *reset* or *rewrite* on them, leaving the connection of the files to external file names to the operating environment. If this works in the target environment, it is adequate for a preliminary implementation used to bootstrap the WEB system on the target machine. If there are more sophisticated ways to handle file names available on the system, they can be investigated during the refinement phase of the port.

If the program header method doesn't work right in the target environment, the flint knife approach of prompting for a file name via the *writeln* procedure and reading the result with the *readln* procedure can be used for the bootstrap version, although ideally something more elegant can be developed later.

Many environments provide some sort of access to the command line, such as the command line interpreter (CLI) procedures in the VMS Run-time Library and Turbo Pascal's *ParamCnt* and *ParamStr* variables.

12.1.3   Case Sensitivity

Some environments are case-sensitive in the handling of identifiers and have system procedure names containing lower- or mixed case. Since TANGLE forces everything to uppercase, these procedures can't be called because the uppercase version of the identifier is not recognized.

This problem can be resolved in one of two ways: by using the WEB "verbatim text" command ('@=') or by disabling TANGLE's uppercase function. TANGLE.does not modify verbatim text in any way but simply passes it through to the Pascal file. Lower- and mixed case strings in verbatim text are not forced to uppercase as other strings are. The difficulty with this approach is that it must be utilized for *all* system calls in *all* programs and can become very tedious. Both of the WEB processors themselves during the porting process and all user programs after the system is operational must be modified in this way. Also, the verbatim strings are framed by boxes , which can be distracting.

The uppercase mechanism can be disabled in TANGLE, to eliminate the problem. The Data General implementation incorporated this modification. Most of the C implementations do also, since C is case-sensitive. However, caution must be taken when making changes to the WEB processors. A subtle bug was introduced into TANGLE on some of the systems implementing this particular modification [Rei87]. TANGLE was not recognizing the lowercase forms of **div** and **mod**, causing incorrect results from constant expressions under certain conditions.

12.1.4 Small Systems

Memory Allocation

Porting WEB to larger systems such as a mainframe or a VAX is comparatively easy. The difficulty arises when trying to shoehorn it into limited architectures such as the 8086 series of processors. The WEB data structures are implemented as large arrays, some of which are by themselves larger than the 64-kilobyte limit on the data segment of the 8086. This limit is not a restriction of the compiler, but of the underlying architecture of the processor. The Macintosh is even worse, with an arbitrary 32K limit imposed by the operating system. The 68000 processor itself does not impose such a restriction. While difficult, this problem is not insurmountable. The restriction is on the data segment, not the overall memory space of the machine. If the arrays are changed from static variables to pointers to those variables, then they can be dynamically allocated on the heap, thereby bypassing the data segment restriction (provided the particular compiler supports a "long heap" falling outside the data segment). The *byte_mem* and *tok_mem* arrays pose a special problem, because there is still a 64-kilobyte limit on an individual data element, even one allocated on the long heap. The arrays are normally defined as an array of byte arrays, and the total size is well above the limit. However, if they are changed to an array of pointers to byte arrays, then there is no longer a problem. The array of pointers takes up hardly any static memory, and each of the byte arrays is a separate data element.

In TANGLE, the number of bytes available for storage of tokens in each segment of *tok_mem* is controlled by the constant *max_toks*, while the number of segments is equal to *zz*. Thus the total size of the *tok_mem* array is *max_toks* × *zz* (in TANGLE 2.9, the value of *max_toks is 50000, while zz = 2*, unless modified by the change file). If *tok_mem* is converted to an array of pointers, then there will be *zz* number of pointers, each pointing to an array of size *max_toks*, which are allocated independently. As long as *max_toks* does not exceed the size of a segment, the actual memory available in the machine is the only limiting factor. If *max_toks* is too big to fit in a segment of memory (as on the Macintosh), then the value of *max_toks* must be decreased. At the same time, *zz* should be increased. When this occurs, the size of a individual segment decreases while the number of segments increases. If the two are coordinated properly, i.e., *zz* is doubled while *max_toks* is halved, the total amount of token memory remains constant. The value of *zz* should always be a power of 2, because it is used in **div** and **mod** operations, and many compilers can do such calculations more efficiently with bit shifts.

In order to implement this change, all references to the particular array must be converted from $x[index]$ to $x{\uparrow}[index]$. The macro capability can assist in what would be an extremely tedious task, to find and modify every reference to these arrays. To perform this change, we provide a new identifier for the pointer to the array, then make the original identifier into a macro which expands into a reference to the pointer. For instance, if the array *x* is currently defined as **array** [0..5000] **of** *integer*, and references are of the form $x[n]$, we would redefine *x* as follows:

> **define** $x \equiv ad\_x{\uparrow}$

where *ad_x* is a pointer to *x_type* and *x_type* is **array** [0..5000] **of** *integer*. All of the places in the program where $x[n]$ appears will expand to $ad\_x{\uparrow}[n]$. It will be necessary to remember to perform a *new* or equivalent memory allocation procedure on the pointer. This only has to be performed once, during program initialization.

Unfortunately, it is not possible to use the macros for all of the arrays. The two-dimensional arrays, *byte_mem* and *tok_mem*, resist this technique. In order to handle the segmentation problem above, they must be changed from a two-dimensional array to an array of pointers, so the code to dereference an element of *tok_mem* must be changed from $tok\_mem[n,m]$ to $tok\_mem[n]{\uparrow}[m]$. Since the macro technique described above can only affect the identifier, it cannot be used to change the ',' between *n* and *m* to ']^[', which is the modification needed. The implementor has no choice other than to go through the entire program and add a change section for every access (or every group of accesses) of *tok_mem*. Since these changes are in a part of the program not usually affected by implementation change files, there is more chance of conflict with changes to the baseline **WEB** file, or with any other change files being merged with the implementation change file (see Section 9.2).

Integer Size

Another problem which arises when trying to port to one of the smaller machines is integer size. **TANGLE** and **WEAVE** make use of 32-bit integers and 16-bit unsigned values (range of 0–65535). While some of the Pascal compilers on small systems support one or the other of these two ordinal types, most don't support both, thus guaranteeing a great deal of work not needed on larger systems. Even when the longer integers are supported, they are often not compatible with the regular integers, requiring a lot of conversions and typecasting. Like the conversion of *tok_mem* to an array of pointers, this causes a lot of changes in a part of the program not normally touched by implementation change files.

12.1.5 Closing Files

Neither of the WEB processors performs a "close" operation on any of the files that it uses. While many operating systems, especially on the larger machines, perform this function automatically upon termination of the program, many others do not. Since file operations on input files are basically read-only windows into an existing disk file, terminating the program without closing them usually causes no severe damage. The pointer to the file is lost, but the actual disk file is not affected. Possibly some of the file system's internal data structures are not deallocated, but this may not cause a problem until later.

Output files are another matter. On some systems, terminating a program without closing output files causes the file to be incomplete. Any buffered data which has not been written to the physical file is simply dropped. Directory information for the file is probably incorrect and the length field, if any, is almost guaranteed to be wrong. Worse, the length may be zero, yet the blocks allocated to the file when it was created are still tied up. To be on the safe side, all files, both input and output, should be closed.

Reading the input files twice, as WEAVE does, causes problems on at least one system if the files are not closed between the two calls to *reset*.

12.1.6 Refinements

There are sometimes two phases to a port of a WEB program. The first phase is the effort to make the program run at all. Until the fundamental changes such as **othercases** are handled, the program is not going to compile, much less run. The **othercases** modification is needed on nearly all computer systems, since the Stanford development system is probably the only one which uses *others:* rather than **otherwise** or **else**.

After the program is running and is producing the correct results, other modifications can be made, such as performance improvements and enhancement of the interface to the operating system. As always in a program development environment, the older version of a program should not be discarded until its replacement has been thoroughly tested and shown to be fully operational.

One change made to nearly all implementations of WEB is to add text file buffering. The generic versions of WEAVE and TANGLE read text files one character at a time, primarily because each character is converted to its numeric equivalent before it is stored. However, most Pascal compilers can read an entire line with one procedure call (*readln*), and this call is usually faster than reading individual characters, in some cases overwhelmingly so. Therefore, most implementations of WEB modify the *input_ln* procedure to read a line into a local string variable, then loop through the string to convert the individual characters to their numeric values. A similar modification is usually made to the *flush_buffer* procedure, the one that outputs a line.

Since the change file is allowed to take advantage of features provided by the implementation, it is useful to place procedures and other definitions that can be used by more than one program into a separate program unit such as a module or equivalent construct, for implementations that support modularity. For instance, procedures to access the command line, assign file names, etc., could be made generic enough that TANGLE, WEAVE, TEX, and even user-written programs could use them. Therefore, rather than duplicate this code for every program, it is only necessary to place the procedures into a separately compiled module and interface to it from each program, using **extern**, **import**, **inherit**, or whatever mechanism the implementation uses. The sample implementation change file uses this technique; the *setup_text_file* procedure is declared as an external procedure.

12.2   The Porting Procedure

The easiest way to port the WEB system to a new environment, such as a different computer, operating system, or Pascal compiler, is to bootstrap it from a running WEB system. The procedure is similar to that of porting a compiler.

If the system already running WEB (which we will hereafter refer to as the *boot system*) is freely available during the port and transfer of text files between the two machines is not difficult, then the porting operation is comparatively hassle-free, as long as the target system has a halfway decent Pascal compiler. Porting TANGLE is the first step, since it is the bootstrap for everything else. The sequence of steps is as follows:

1. Create a new change file for TANGLE containing the modifications necessary to run TANGLE on the target system ('`tangle.tar`'). The change file for the boot system ('`tangle.boo`') can be used as a guide, and the sections most likely to need changes are identified by "system dependencies" in the index. Do *not* change '`tangle.web`', ever! All modifications are made via the change file.

2. On the boot system, run TANGLE on itself, using '`tangle.web`' and the newly created change file ('`tangle.tar`') as inputs. This will produce a TANGLE Pascal source file ('`tangle.pas`') tailored to the target system. (Warning: if the boot system's own Pascal file is still present on the system, care must be taken not to overwrite it with the new one, since the two files have the same

name. Of course, Pascal files are really temporary files in the WEB system, so the old Pascal file for the boot system may not be around anyway.)

3. Copy the new Pascal file ('`tangle.pas`'), '`tangle.web`', and the new change file ('`tangle.tar`') to the target system. These are all text files, so any line-oriented text file transfer mechanism can be used, as long as the files are created in the target system's native format. Kermit is a likely candidate. The WEB file only has to be copied once, since it is not going to be changing during this procedure. Whenever this step is repeated, only the change file and the Pascal file need to be copied again.

4. Compile the Pascal program on the target system. If no compile errors occur, link the program and prepare it for execution. If errors were found during any phase, determine the problem, go back to the boot system, correct '`tangle.tar`', and go back to Step 2.

5. Run the new TANGLE executable on its own source file and change file (the output Pascal file should be given a different name to prevent destruction of the source created by the boot system). Assuming the fledgling TANGLE didn't die or have any other execution errors, compare the Pascal file it created with the one transferred over from the boot system.

6. If the two source files are identical (every single byte should match), then the port of TANGLE is probably complete. If errors occurred at any step, or if the files are not identical, then the entire procedure must be repeated. After determining what the problem is, go back to the boot system and correct the target system's change file. Again, do *not* change the WEB file. The steps from 2 on should be repeated until the output of the target TANGLE is identical to that of the boot TANGLE. A "differences" program, one which compares text files line by line and reports on the differences between them, would be helpful here.

   For further verification, every available WEB file should be run through both TANGLE processors, with every valid combination of WEB file and change file. While TANGLE's own WEB file is a good test, building TEX and METAFONT is the ultimate test. If *all* Pascal files created by the target TANGLE match exactly those created by the boot TANGLE, then the target TANGLE is fully operational.

7. The next step is to port WEAVE. The procedure is basically the same except that the boot system is no longer needed to run TANGLE, since the target version can now be used. All of the steps can be performed directly on the target machine, including creation of the implementation change file for the target system. The boot system is needed only during the verification phase, to create TEX files

to compare with the output of the target WEAVE. The TEX files created on the boot system for comparison during the testing only have to be generated and copied once, since they won't be constantly changing during development as the Pascal file was for TANGLE. The boot system WEAVE can be run with its own change file as input (since that won't be changing during the port, unlike the target change file) and the output copied over to the target system for comparison with the output of target WEAVE. As with TANGLE, all possible WEB file/change file combinations, including TEX and METAFONT, should be processed by WEAVE on both systems. Once the TEX output of target WEAVE is identical to that of the boot WEAVE for all programs, then the WEB system has been fully ported and is available for user programs.

If file transfer between the two systems is not available on a continuous basis, it is necessary to transfer as many pertinent files as possible while the path is established, including all of the files needed for verification. It is still advisable to create a first cut of the change file for the target system on the boot system and to build a Pascal file from it. However, since the file transfer is a one-shot, the change file and resulting Pascal file for the target system are only approximations.

Once on the target system, all further modifications to TANGLE have to be performed directly on the Pascal file since the boot TANGLE is not available to generate a new one. Before modifying the Pascal file, however, both it and the first-cut change file should be saved for the purpose of later verification. Making changes directly to the Pascal source is much more difficult because of its extreme unreadability. This file should be renamed something like 'ptangle' (for Proto-TANGLE) so that is won't be confused with the final version. The only purpose of Proto-TANGLE is to bootstrap the regular TANGLE by building a system-specific Pascal file. Proto-TANGLE doesn't have to be fully operational, as long as the parts it needs to build TANGLE work properly. For instance, TANGLE makes no use of the string pool, so it doesn't matter whether the Proto-TANGLE code that handles the string pool works or not.

All changes necessary to make Proto-TANGLE work should be carefully noted, because the same changes will be needed for the real TANGLE. Each modification should be added to the change file for the target system as it is made to the Pascal file for Proto-TANGLE.

The verification of Proto-TANGLE is similar to that of real TANGLE described above. The only Pascal file currently present on the target system that was actually built on the boot system (and therefore the only one useful for verification purposes) is the first-cut Pascal file, the one saved before hand modifications were made. With 'tangle.web' and the first-cut change file as inputs, the Pascal file created by Proto-TANGLE should be identical to the first-cut Pascal file brought over from the boot system. Once these two are identical, the Proto-TANGLE can probably be trusted enough to generate the real TANGLE. The most current change file, the one that ideally reflects all of the manual changes to Proto-TANGLE, should be used to create real TANGLE. Since this should be a full-powered version of TANGLE, the verification process should include all available WEB and changes files as above.

The new TANGLE can now be used to build WEAVE and any other WEB files that were brought over from the boot system. Proto-TANGLE can be set aside but should not be deleted until TANGLE has had a burn-in period.

If there is no running TANGLE (i.e., there is no boot system), but the WEB source files are available, then the bootstrapping is still possible as long as the generic 'tangle.pas' (the one with no system-dependent change files applied) is included. The procedure is similar to that specified above in that the Pascal source is directly modified to create the Proto-TANGLE used to build the real TANGLE.

As before, the original Pascal file should be saved for matching purposes.

However, WEB cannot be used without TeX. If the target system does not have TeX, then that will have to be ported also. The procedure for porting TeX is logically similar to that for porting the WEAVE processor, in that a new change file is written and a system-specific Pascal file is created. Many of the changes appearing in the change file for TeX are similar to those made for the WEB processors. The size and complexity of TeX, however, are both an order of magnitude greater. Pascal compilers live in fear of TeX, viewing it as something akin to "The Terminator." TeX will find bugs in a Pascal compiler that have lain dormant for years.

Once TeX is built, make a copy of the implementation change file ('tex.tar') and call it 'initex.tar'. This change file will be used to build IniTeX, the initialization version of TeX, while the original will build the production version. The two will be exactly the same, except that 'initex.tar' contains an extra change section that redefines the **init** and **tini** macros to be null strings, thus enabling all of the initialization code. The Pascal file and resulting executable should be called 'initex'. The production version should be named 'virtex' (virgin TeX). IniTeX is used to build the format file ('.fmt'), compressed binary versions of macro packages such as 'PLAIN' and LaTeX. It is not used for printing documents; VirTeX is the program used for that, after loading the format files created by IniTeX.

TANGLE and WEAVE are hard enough to port to limited architectures such as the 8086. Porting TeX to these systems makes building the Pyramids seem like making birdhouses. It can be done, because these systems have versions of TeX running on them, at least two of which were built with WEB, but the programming effort was probably such that the implementation change files are more than likely bigger than the WEB file. In these cases, it is easier simply to buy one of the commercial versions of TeX than to port it yourself.

Chapter 13

Tailoring to Personal Preference

The operation of the WEB system is extremely flexible. This chapter illustrates ways that it can be modified.

It should be pointed out that any changes to the way WEB operates are possibly nonportable and may not run properly on another system.

Modifications to the WEB system can be performed at three levels:

1. Dynamic formatting changes in a WEB source file (or in a separate TeX file input by a WEB source file). Changes such as these are portable as long as they use no system-dependent features such as weird fonts. If a separate TeX file is input, it must be distributed along with the WEB file.

2. Semipermanent formatting changes in the macro package ('webmac.tex').

3. Permanent changes in the WEB processors themselves.

Most of the nonpermanent changes are used to alter the way the document is formatted, since there is really no way to control generation of the output Pascal file from the WEB source file except for usage of the '@=' and '@\' commands on an individual basis, a very limited form of control. There is, of course, no external file corresponding to 'webmac.tex'.

The changes shown here are only representative, to give the reader an idea of what modifications are possible with the WEB system.

13.1 Modification of Formatting

All of the TeX code in this section can be used at level 1 or 2 above. Be aware that any changes to 'webmac' will have an effect on all of the WEB users at a site.

13.1.1 Regular Operators

The WEB system converts some of the Pascal operators to generic pseudocode forms, such as '$\neq$' for '<>'. While this makes the program look more polished and aids in readability (especially for people who do not know Pascal but are familiar with the mathematical symbols), in some applications it can cause a problem. The most common problem is the case in which a program is intended specifically to illustrate use of Pascal rather than general programming concepts. The special operators only confuse the issue, since they are not Pascal and the user cannot type them in to run the program. One can picture a beginning programmer who is having a nervous breakdown trying to find the '$\neq$' key on a standard ASCII keyboard.

The WEAVE processor does not really generate either the Pascal operators or the generic ones when creating the TeX file. Instead, the text actually output consists of TeX control sequences. The following commands, which equate TeX standard math operators to various control sequence names, appear in 'webmac':

```
\let\G=\ge % greater than or equal sign
\let\I=\ne % unequal sign
\let\K=\gets % left arrow
\let\L=\le % less than or equal sign
\let\R=\lnot % logical not
\let\V=\lor % logical or
\let\W=\land % logical and
```

Since the TeX code output by WEAVE uses these control sequences whenever referring to the operators, the control sequences that generate the generic operators can be redefined to generate the standard Pascal operators instead.

In order to return to the regular operators, place '\input regpas' in the limbo section of the WEB file, where 'regpas.tex' consists of the following:

```
\def\G{>=} % greater than or equal sign
\def\I{<>} % unequal sign
\def\K{:=} % left arrow
\def\L{<=} % less than or equal sign
\def\R{\mathop{\&{not}}} % logical not
\def\V{\mathbin{\&{or}}} % logical or
\def\W{\mathbin{\&{and}}} % logical and
```

The resulting text is not as pretty, but it is pure Pascal.

13.1.2 Changing of Page Size

The default page settings for WEB are adjusted for a regular $8\ 1/2 \times 11$ page. However, if the program is to be printed in a different format (such as the $7\ 1/2 \times 9\ 1/4$ page size of this book), the dimensions can be adjusted to whatever size is required.

This is accomplished by changing '\pageheight', '\pagewidth', etc., as needed, then performing a call to the '\setpage' macro to lock them in. For instance,

```
\newdimen\pagewidth \pagewidth=5.5in
\newdimen\pageheight \pageheight=7.625in
\newdimen\fullpageheight \fullpageheight=7.925in
\newdimen\pageshift \pageshift=.5in
\setpage
```

was placed into the limbo text of all the WEB programs in this book.

Be aware that, while all of the text will adjust to the new margins automatically, the number of pages will change and some lines may now fall on bad line breaks (see Section 7.2). Manual adjustment of the text may be required to make it fit comfortably in the new margins.

There is a built-in magnification macro in 'webmac'. It can increase the size of all fonts used by WEB. Listings are easier to read at the larger size, although the magnification should probably be used only with shorter listings because of the paper consumption. To magnify the print size, use:

```
\magnify{\magstep1}
\setpage
```

in the limbo text.

13.1.3 Double Columns

The WEB system by its very nature encourages verbose commentary, since the elaborate description of the algorithms is one of the main objectives of the system. The data structures and algorithms tend to be more spread out than is typical in ordinary computer programs. Also, because code sections are not split across pages, larger sections can cause a lot of white space in the listing as sections are forced to a new page.

Since a properly written WEB program doesn't have many levels of indentation in a given code section, the sections tend to expand vertically rather than horizontally and most of the time don't use the full width of the page. MWEB exhibits this behavior even more, because it performs many more new-line operations during formatting.

The net result is that WEB programs can take up a lot of pages of output, much of which is wasted by white space. This normally isn't a problem, but sometimes printing costs necessitate more efficient use of pages. Given that WEB programs tend to be more vertical than horizontal, using double columns is one means of better utilization of papyrus real estate.

The double-column macros can be found in Section F.1.2. In order to utilize them, '\input webdoub' should be included in the limbo section.

13.1.4   Getting Rid of Boxes

If a program has a large amount of verbatim text, the framing boxes added to verbatim strings by WEAVE can be distracting. If there are a lot of identifiers containing dollar signs or other special characters and these identifiers occur throughout the program, it can seem that the program contains nothing but boxes. While using the technique described in Section 5.1.6 will reduce the number of boxes, it requires a macro definition for each identifier. Environments such as VAX/VMS, where all identifiers provided by the operating system contain dollar signs, would require a significant amount of effort to define all of them.

Verbatim text *must* be used for the VMS identifiers, because WEB does not accept dollar signs in identifiers, but there is really no reason to highlight them. They should be displayed in the same way as any other identifier, if possible.

When WEAVE outputs a verbatim string, it doesn't output the complex series of '\hbox', '\vbox', '\hrule', and '\vrule' primitives needed to draw the box. Instead, as with other complicated typesetting functions, it simply encapsulates the string as the parameter of a macro ('\='), leaving the dirty work to 'webmac'. Therefore, changing the definition of the '\=' macro modifies the handling of verbatim strings throughout the program.

Because of the large number of identifiers containing dollar signs in the VMS environment, the Northlake VAX implementation change files modify the verbatim text macro to treat the VMS identifiers as ordinary identifiers, by inserting the following macro definition into the limbo text of all WEB programs:

```
\def\=#1{\hbox{{\it
    \def\${{\sl\char'\$}}#1\/\kern.05em}}}
```

With this definition, the identifier '@=sts$k_warning@>', which would appear in the listing as $\boxed{\tt sts\$k\_warning}$ with the standard definition of '\=', is instead set as '*sts$k_warning*', making it appear similar to normal identifiers.

As a side note, identifiers declared this way don't appear in the index, as verbatim text is not placed into the index by WEAVE, and must be indexed manually. Since the character sequence to print the identifier starts with '\=', the user-controlled indexing command ('@:') must be used, as described in Section 5.2.4. The index entry would be specified as '@:sts\$k_warning}{\={sts\$k_warning}@>'.

This technique will only work if all of the verbatim text is of the same type, such as the VAX identifiers, since it globally changes the way verbatim text is formatted. If there are other types of verbatim text within the same program, they may be formatted strangely. It would be possible to redefine the '\=' macro several times throughout the program, but this is probably more trouble than it is worth.

13.2   Permanent Changes

It is possible to change the operation of TANGLE and WEAVE permanently if a Pascal compiler and the system-specific change files are available (see Chapter 12). Like all changes to TANGLE and WEAVE not coming from Stanford, the changes should not be made to the WEB files but should be placed in a change file. While it is possible to change the implementation-dependent change file, it is preferable to place the new changes in a separate change file and use a change file merge program to combine the two sets of changes into a temporary file for use with TANGLE (see Section 9.2). In the same way that modified versions of TEX are no longer called TEX, a modified TANGLE or WEAVE should also be given a different name and kept separate from the original.

13.2.1   Semireadable Pascal Output

The Pascal file generated by TANGLE is absolutely useless for trying to understand the program. This is deliberate, so that no one is tempted to modify the Pascal file. The WEB file is the program source, and the Pascal file is considered a temporary file to be deleted after compilation. However, the number of programs that run correctly the first time can be counted on the fingers of one foot, so a debugging phase is almost always required. Many modern computer systems have powerful source-level debuggers that are made almost useless by the fact that the Pascal file is virtual gibberish. Stepping through the program is made more difficult because TANGLE puts multiple statements on a line and spans single statements across lines.

While pretty-printing the Pascal program is not necessary, it would be useful at least to change the line breaking so that there is only one statement per line for debugging purposes, as in C WEB.

In order to provide this modification, we take advantage of a facility already present in TANGLE, the WEB command to force a new line in the Pascal file ('@\'). The processing performed when this command is found in the WEB file is almost what is desired. After a couple of slight modifications to the way it operates, it will provide the desired behavior. The *force_line* token is normally placed into *tok_mem* in response to a '@\', but if the procedure used to tokenize a replacement text (*repl_text*) is modified to detect that the current input line has changed, we can add a simulated *force_line* token for every line of the input file (the ones with Pascal code, anyway—we don't need to handle the lines containing TEX code). A new line is detected by the fact that the line number changes (on the off chance that the WEB file and the change file are at the same line number, the *changing* flag is tested also). Since this change is by itself a useful feature, we will provide a change file for it separately, so that it can be implemented separately (see Section F.2.1).

However, there is more that we can do. If we would like the Pascal program to point back to the WEB source file by displaying the line numbers (in the form of comments, as section numbers are currently displayed), that is possible also. In addition to the code described above, which does the line breaking, we add some code to store the line number as just another token in *tok_mem*. More accurately, we store the line number as part of the *force_line* token, redefining *force_line* as a 3-byte token. The first byte is the original code for *force_line* and the other 2 bytes form a 16-bit number corresponding to the source line.

Since we have two ranges of line numbers, those of the base WEB file and those of the change file, we need a scheme to keep them separate. Therefore, we use the range of the number to differentiate between them. If the number is less than 32768 (the high bit is clear), then the line is from the WEB file. If the number is greater than 32768 (the high bit is set), then the line is from the change file. (Ideally the program won't have more than 32767 lines in either the WEB file or the change file.) If the line number is 0, the *force_line* does not correspond to a source line at all; this is used for the original manual *force_line* issued in response to a '@\'.

During the output of the *force_line* token, the output routine will now extract the 2 bytes immediately following this token and combine them to get the line number. After testing and then removing the high bit, the line number is output to the Pascal file as a comment (if the line number is not 0). A 'W' or 'C' is output before the line number to identify which file the line came from.

The change file to implement this enhancement can be found in Section F.2.1. Be aware that since the line numbers are tokens contained in the replacement text of the code section, they will be output in the same way as any other token when the replacement text is expanded. Therefore, if a code section is referenced more than once in a program, the line number information will appear for each occurrence. The line numbers don't appear on macro expansions, because macros tend to be used more times in a program and because macros are referenced from the middle of a statement more often. If the reader would prefer that line numbers appear on macro expansions as well as code sections, then the following modification should be made to both of the change files: remove 'and (t = module_name)' from the 'if' statment in Section 165.

Unlike some of the other modifications in this section, this change has no compatibility problems with unmodified WEB systems. The Pascal file is logically identical to the output of the normal TANGLE. It does take up slightly more disk space, but this shouldn't be a problem because the Pascal file is normally deleted after use anyway.

13.2.2 Forward References for Macros

The modification described in this section started out as an user-installed enhancement to TANGLE like the others in this section, but seemed to be such a definite improvement that it was incorporated into TANGLE as a permanent change. After discussion with Professor Knuth during the development of this book, it was agreed that the change would be incorporated into the baseline TANGLE at Stanford.

The change is in this book because once the TANGLE on the Stanford distribution is updated, it will take time for the new version (2.9) to be filtered through the implementors and site coordinators to reach the user sites. If anyone wishes to install the mod to a current TANGLE, the instructions at the beginning of this section may be followed.

The fact that TANGLE evaluates numeric macros during the first pass is a good reason why they are not allowed to have forward references. This reason does not apply to other macro types, however. The former restriction on forward references was an artificial one for macros other than numeric macros.

This restriction was originally applied so that the behavior of the macros would be the same for all macro types. While it is true that forbidding forward references on numeric macros while allowing them on other macro types causes an inconsistency, there was already a much worse inconsistency in that the operation of the macros in this respect was quite different from that of the code sections, which were otherwise very similar.

Both macros and code sections allow a variable amount of text to be equated to a name, and this text is expanded into the output file each time the name is referenced. Intuitively, the decision as to whether to use a code section or a macro for a given piece of text should depend on the amount of text to be equated, whether it consists of complete statements or merely of a phrase or fragment, and whether a parameter is needed or not. Otherwise the two mechanisms should be interchangeable.

However, there are no restrictions of any kind on the placement of code sections, but macros could not be forward-referenced. This went against the whole philosophy of WEB, the concept of ordering things in a way that contributes to the exposition, rather than bending to the dictates of the system. Everything else in WEB allows the programmer to disregard Pascal's "declare-em-up-front" syndrome and concentrate on the algorithm. The author cannot count the number of times he had forgotten that macros behave differently from code sections and had merrily moved things around to improve the flow of the exposition, only to see the dreaded '!This identifier has already appeared' when a macro was carried along in the move.

A programmer could simply have ignored the error message, of course, since TANGLE would have done exactly what was intended anyway, but this is not a good practice since it will have a tendency to mask real errors.

Upon analysis of the identifier processing code in TANGLE, the actual modification turned out to be fairly trivial. The nature of the change was simply to suppress the error message generated when a forward reference of a non-numeric macro is detected (the *ilk* of an identifier changes from normal to simple or parametric). During expansion, the code generated will be what the programmer expects. Forward references to a numeric macro and redefinition of a macro to the same or a different type will still cause an error.

This change will have no effect on existing WEB programs, since it merely removes a restriction that was in effect when those programs were written. The expansion of old programs would be exactly the same.

Programs developed by using the new TANGLE may not be compatible with the older versions of TANGLE (pre-2.9). The word *may* is used because the programs are incompatible only if they contain forward references of non-numeric macros, and the programmer doesn't necessarily know whether these are present are not. The whole point of the change is that the programmer shouldn't have to keep up with such things. Of course, the worst that can happen is that an error message may appear.

The change file 'forward.ch' in Section F.2.1 can be used to upgrade TANGLE from version 2.8 to 2.9. The banner line that is output when TANGLE runs will contain the current version number.

13.2.3   Longer Identifiers

Lengthening identifiers is a fairly simple change. Since TANGLE is meant to support all Pascal compilers, including the toy ones, the significant length of identifiers is kept very short. There are actually two lengths associated with identifiers: an actual length and a truncated unambiguous length. This corresponds to some Pascal compilers that will allow identifiers of virtually unlimited length, yet only so many of those characters are significant. Two different identifiers which started with the same set of characters would be considered the same identifier.

The following change file will modify TANGLE to increase the size of identifiers:

```
@x [8]
@!max_id_length=12; {long identifiers are chopped to this length, which must
  not exceed |line_length|}
@!unambig_length=7; {identifiers must be unique if chopped to this length}
  {note that 7 is more strict than \PASCAL's 8, but this can be varied}
@y
@!max_id_length=40; {long identifiers are chopped to this length, which must
  not exceed |line_length|}
@!unambig_length=20; {identifiers must be unique if chopped to this length}
@z
```

Note that programs that are written to take advantage of the longer *unambig_length* may have errors if they are run through a WEB system that does not have this modification. If portability is a concern, this change should not be made.

Chapter 14

Conversion to Other Languages

This chapter describes the process of converting the WEB system to process programs in other languages. The techniques used to produce some of the variations in Chapter 8 are presented.

14.1 General Language Conversion Issues

The following issues are likely to come up when converting WEB to a new language.

- Identifier length: The size of an identifier may have to be increased. There are two lengths for identifiers, *max_id_length* and *unambig_length*. For reasons of portability, both should be compatible with the smallest values for all known compilers for that language.

- Reserved words: The new language will have reserved words different from those of Pascal. Addition of these words can be accomplished with the built-in mechanisms of WEB, such as the formatting command

    format *module* $\equiv$ *program*

  which creates a new reserved word **module** and causes it to be formatted as if it were **program**. The problem of this approach is that it has to be duplicated in every source file, putting the burden of implementing MWEB on the user rather than the implementor.

  Additionally, this technique only allows reserved words to be formatted in a manner similar to an already existing reserved word. It does not allow words to be given a formatting behavior different from anything currently defined.

  The length of reserved words may also have to be increased if the new language has longer reserved words than Pascal. The new reserved words will have to

199

be assigned an *ilk*. The new tokens must be given a *cat*, either an existing one or a newly created one.

- Formatting codes: If the new reserved words are different, it is a certainty that they are formatted differently. The list of productions will probably have to be modified, as will the translations of the tokens and *ilk* codes.

- Comments: Since every language handles comments differently, all code related to comments will probably have to be changed.

- Special characters: If a special character is used by both WEB and the target language, this must be resolved.

14.2   Modula-2

The transformation from WEB to MWEB was comparatively easy—Pascal and Modula-2 are much alike, at least syntactically. In fact, Modula-2 is actually less complicated than Pascal and has a cleaner syntax with fewer ambiguities.

MANGLE and MWEAVE were created by modifying their regular WEB counterparts with a standard change file. The author wanted to minimize the modifications to the code, limiting them to those absolutely necessary to process Modula-2.

Very few modifications were required to transform TANGLE into MANGLE. Many more changes had to be made to WEAVE to support Modula-2, since WEAVE has to know enough about the language to format it properly.

The following issues surfaced during the implementation of MWEB:

14.2.1   Identifier Length

The size of an identifier had to be increased. The values selected for *max_id_length* and *unambig_length*, 31 and 20, should be reasonable for Modula-2.

Increasing the size of the reserved words was a little more effort. The macros used to insert reserved words (*sid1–sid9*, section 63 of WEAVE) had to be expanded because they wouldn't handle words longer than nine characters, thus making **implementation** rather difficult to insert. Macros *sid10–sid14* were added and *id_loc* was changed from 10 to 15. Possibly the method of storing reserved words should have been altered, but the author did not want to make radical changes, at least not in this version of MWEB.

14.2.2   Formatting Tables

The Modula-2 reserved words were added to the internal tables. Several new reserved words were added (**return**, **exit**, **by**, **import**, etc.) and others not needed for Modula-2 were dropped (**goto**, **label**, **downto**, **file**, and others).

A couple of new *ilk* codes were added, one was dropped, and many of the reserved words were shuffled from one *ilk* to another. Most of the *ilk* codes were given new translations.

Because of the simpler syntax of the Modula-2 control statements, and because the author simplified the formatting even more to impose his personal preferences (for instance, always forcing a new line after **begin**, **do**, **repeat**, **then**, etc.), the formatting information stored in the internal tables was much smaller. No new productions were added; in fact, many of the existing productions are not needed for Modula-2 and can never fire because the category sequences that trigger them cannot be generated. The code to process these "dead code" productions would have been deleted, except for the extra effort involved in deleting code with change files (see Section 5.1.5).

14.2.3 Comments

All code related to comments had to be changed. While Pascal can have comments delimited by either '(* *)' or '{ }', Modula-2 uses only the former, since the braces are used elsewhere in the language definition (as set delimiters). Fortunately, this is a common and well-documented modification to TANGLE, since some of the more primitive Pascal systems have the same restriction. On the other hand, Modula-2 allows nested comments, so the comment-handling code in MANGLE could be simplified (the comment delimiters for the inner nest levels no longer have to be converted to '[ ]' for the program to compile).

New token codes corresponding to '(*' and '*)' were added, and since '{' and '}' are just regular tokens in MWEB, they had to be added to the list. All of these new tokens were given translations, category codes, etc.

14.2.4 Vertical Bar Character

The vertical bar character ('|') had to be specially handled, since it is used by both Modula-2 and WEB for different purposes. Code was added to identify the usage of the character by context. A new token was created for the double vertical bar, the regular single vertical bar was added to the list of tokens (normally it is filtered out by the scan), and both were given a translation of '\VB' (see the section on 'mwebmac' below).

14.2.5 Other Special Characters

Modifying MANGLE and MWEAVE to handle '#' and '~' was no problem, but '#' is already used by the WEB system for macro parameters. To resolve this ambiguity,

MANGLE and MWEAVE were modified to accept the Modula-2 version of '#' anywhere in a WEB program *except* within a macro definition. This is the only really ugly part of the conversion; a couple of state variables were added to identify the context of '#'.

14.2.6   The Macro Package

A new file, 'mwebmac.tex', inputs the original 'webmac.tex', then redefines one macro and adds one new one. The comment macro ('\C{...}') was redefined to generate '(* *)' instead of '{ }', and '\VB' was added to generate the vertical bar character. WEAVE normally generates '\input webmac' as the first line of the output TEX file; this was changed to input 'mwebmac' instead.

14.3   Use of SPIDER

An overview of SPIDER operation can be found in Section 10.2.2. The following is a description of the language specification.

Unsurprisingly, the information contained in the language specification that is input by SPIDER directly parallels that found in the internal tables of the WEB processors.

In all of the following command definitions, *id* is a standard identifier.

A translation (*trans*) is a (possibly empty) sequence of *translation pieces* delimited by angle brackets. The pieces of the list are separated by dashes ('-') and can be any one of the following, in any order:

- A string, delimited by double quotes. This string may contain embedded quotes ('"') escaped by '\', but it *must not* contain embedded white space or an embedded dash. Unfortunately, the escape character for SPIDER is the same as that for TEX control sequences, so all occurrences of '\' in the string must appear as '\\'.

- The "self" marker ('*'), which refers to the sequence of characters making up the token being translated. The self marker is permitted only in certain contexts, and its precise meaning depends on the context.

- A digit.

- A keyword.

  The keywords known to SPIDER are *space*, which stands for one space ('␣'), and *dash* ('-').

The other keywords (*break_space, force, big_force, opt, backup, cancel, indent, outdent, math_rel, math_bin*, and *math_op*) are passed on to WEAVE. The meaning of these keywords is exactly the same as that described in Section 141 of WEAVE (see Appendix G.1.2).

The *only* keywords that will work properly in math mode are *indent* and *outdent*, so when defining the translations of tokens *mathness no* must be used if the translations contain other keywords. Any recognized keywords may be used in the translations of a production; there the mathness is automatically handled.

Here are some example translations:

```
<"\\"-space>
<indent-force>
<"{\\let\\\\=\\bf"-space>
<"}"-indent-"{}"-space>
```

A restricted translation (*restrans*) is a translation that is only allowed to contain quoted strings and the keywords *space* and *dash*. It contains only printable ASCII characters.

The first phase of the specification is to define of the individual language elements, such as tokens and reserved words. The format of the **token** statement is

> **token** *tok* **category** *id* [**translation** *trans*] [**name** *id*]
> [**tangleto** *restrans*] [**mathness** *mathopt*]

The *tok* is the actual token, such as '+' or '['. The meaning of **category** is the same as that described in Section 11.4. The **translation** is the character sequence to be output by WEAVE for this token. If not specified, the translation is the same as the token. The **tangleto** sequence is the sequence of characters to be output by TANGLE for this token, if it is different from the token itself. The *mathopt* can be yes, no, or maybe, meaning that this token must always be used in math mode, can never be used in math mode, or can be used in either math mode or horizontal mode, respectively. The **name** is used primarily during debugging of SPIDER or the new WEB. It assigns an identifier to the token that can be found in the generated code.

The special keywords *identifier, number, newline*, and *pseudo_semi* can be used for *tok*, allowing the translation and other properties of these built-in tokens to be set in the same way as those of any other token.

It doesn't matter whether one token is a prefix of another, because the WEB processors generated by SPIDER will use the longer of the two when scanning. For instance, the sequence '<=' will be taken as a single token rather than as a '<' followed by a '='.

Ordinarily the character sequence output for a given token is the token itself. TANGLE has a fairly simple algorithm to determine when to separate tokens with blanks. If identifiers (including reserved words) or numeric constants are adjacent, they can be ambiguous. For instance, "**if** *true* **then**" becomes the new identifier "*iftruethen*" without the separating blanks, and "**for** *j* := *n* **to** 100 **do** *oper*;" is transformed into the assignment statement "*forj* := *nto100dooper*;". All other token combinations are output in a continuous stream, without separators. This works 99% of the time, but occasionally problems occur. For instance, in C the string '=-' can be ambiguous when using older compilers. The purpose of the **tangleto** is to provide an override for the character sequence to be output for a token. Use of '**tangleto** <"="-space>' would prevent the ambiguity because the '=' token would always be output as '=␣'.

The following are sample token statements:

```
token + category unorbinop
token = category equals translation <"\\K">
token <= name lt_eq translation <"\\L"> category binop
```

The reserved words are not defined via the **token** command, since they are a subset of the token *identifier*. The reserved words are handled with a combination of the **reserved** and **ilk** commands. The **ilk** command is used to define a new *ilk*, or syntactic class. Its format is

> **ilk** *id* **category** *id*

The category of an **ilk** command is equivalent to that of a **token** command. To create a new reserved word and associate it with a particular *ilk*, the **reserved** command is used:

> **reserved** *id* **ilk** *id*

Typically several reserved words have the same *ilk*. The following sample **ilk** and **reserved** commands

```
ilk for_like category for
reserved for ilk for_like
reserved while ilk for_like
```

would create new reserved words **for** and **while**, give them both an *ilk* of *for_like*, and give *for_like* a category of *for*.

In the same way that the productions are the most difficult part of WEAVE to describe, the commands to generate them are the most difficult to define. The information contained in the command is roughly equivalent to the production itself, in that there is a left side consisting of category codes to match and a right side containing another list of codes with which to replace them. The format is

$$c_1 \; c_2 \; \ldots \; c_n \; \text{-->} \; c_1 \; c_2 \; \ldots \; c_n$$

Any translation to be applied when the production is fired should be placed between the proper two category codes on the left side. Some simple production definitions would be

```
math simp --> math
stmt <break_space> stmt --> stmt
```

The first production implements WEAVE's rule 20 (see Section 143 of Appendix G.1.2), while the second corresponds to rule 49—two consecutive statements can be combined by putting an optional line break between them.

There are a couple of special operators that can be used on the left-hand side of a production. The '?' is used as a "wild card" category code; it will match any single scrap with any category code. The '!' is a **not** operator modifying the category code which immediately follows it. A match occurs if the category of the input scrap is *not* the same as the specified category.

When there is only one scrap category on the right side of a production, all of the scraps on the left side are to be combined into that one scrap (*math simp* → *math*). The firing of a production is also straightforward if the number of scraps is the same on both sides, since there is no ambiguity as to which left-side scraps become which right-side scraps (*alpha simp* → *alpha math*). However, if the number of scraps on the right side is less than the number on the left, yet greater than one, there is an ambiguity. Some of the left-hand scraps must be combined into one right-hand scrap, but which ones into what scrap? For instance, in the Ada production '*when math terminator* → *math terminator*', the first two scraps (*when* and *math*) are converted to category *math*; on the other hand, the production '*open math semi* → *open math*' combines the second and third scraps into a single scrap (*math* and *semi* become *math*). Which scraps to combine is somewhat intuitive to a human, but SPIDER must be told explicitly what the relationships are. This is accomplished by placing square brackets around the scraps that should be reduced to one scrap. The example productions from above would be entered as

```
[ when math ] terminator --> math terminator
open [ math semi ] --> open math
```

The wild card scrap designator can allow one production to handle language constructs that would require several similar productions without it. For instance, the reserved word **end** is used in many different contexts in Ada, such as **end loop**, **end if**, and **end** *procname*. Ordinarily there would have to be separate productions for each of these variations, because the reserved words such as **loop** and **if** have different category codes. If the wild card operator is used, however, all of these can be replaced by the following lines, which appear in the SPIDER file for Ada (see Section F.4)

```
close semi --> ending
close <"\\"-space> ?  semi --> ending
```

where *close* is the category corresponding to the **end** reserved word. The first production handles **end** by itself (followed immediately by a semicolon), while the second handles all of the **end** *something* cases. The new translations, which appear between the angle brackets, do nothing more than insert '\␣' between the scraps. Note that all forms of **end** wind up with a category of *ending*.

For languages that support line numbers, line number information can be inserted into the output of TANGLE for debugging purposes, providing pointers to lines in the WEB file. The **line** command determines the character sequences before and after the line number. The format is

line begin *restrans* **end** *restrans*

In C, the *restrans* for **begin** is '#line', and the ending *restrans* is empty. In other languages, this can be made into a comment containing the line number, similar to the comments containing the section number currently output by the regular TANGLE processor. Note: this command is not really optional, because TANGLE will output the line number in any case. If the line number is not embedded in a comment or '#line' statement, it will appear in the text of the program, causing a syntax error.

```
line begin <"#line"> end <"">
line begin <"{"-"line"> end <"}">
line begin <dash-dash-"line"> end <"">
```

will generate line information for C, Pascal, and Ada, respectively, where it will be output as '#line *nnn*', '{line *nnn*}', and '--line *nnn*'.

Each language needs special purpose TEX macros, if for no other reason than to define the special operators that it uses. SPIDER permits these macros to be appended to the language-independent macro kernel ('webkernel.tex'), creating an instance of 'webmac' for the target language. All source lines between 'macros begin' and 'macros end' will be added to the macro package.

```
macros begin
\def\xyz{} % this line will be added to webmac
macros end
```

There can be several groups of macros appearing in a SPIDER file; they don't have to be all clumped together. Each group must be delimited by 'macros begin' and 'macros end' as shown above. All of the groups are concatenated together before being added to the kernel macro package.

Since the beginning and ending delimiters for comments are different for every language, SPIDER provides a mechanism for defining them:

comment begin *restrans* **end** *endopt*

The *endopt* can either be a *restrans* or the keyword *newline*. For languages such as Ada, in which the end of the current line is the comment terminator, *newline* would be used; otherwise the actual character sequence should appear. As far as the actual typesetting of the comments is concerned, the '\commentbegin' and '\commentend' macros should be defined in the language-dependent macro code (i.e., between the 'macros begin' and 'macros end' mentioned above) to generate the correct delimiters for the language. For instance, Ada comments would be defined as follows:

```
comment begin <dash-dash> end newline
macros begin
\def\commentbegin{{\tt --}}
macros end
```

At some point, it would be useful to let SPIDER know what language is being generated. The command to accomplish this is

language *name* [**extension** *name*] [**version** *name*]

where *name* is the language to be generated, such as C or Ada. If specified, **extension** is the file extension to be used for files generated by TANGLE and **version** will appear in the banner line. The **extension** will default to be the same as the name of the language. For example:

```
language Ada extension ada
language Pascal extension pas
```

The **at_sign** command makes it possible to use a character other than '@' for WEB commands. The format is

at_sign *char*

For instance, to change the command character to '!', use

```
at_sign !
```

The **module** command is used to set the category code for code section names (also known as *modules*). A different category can be given to the definition of the code section and uses of the code section. The format is

module [**definition** *catid*] [**use** *catid*]

The default behavior can be defined with

```
module definition stmt use stmt
```

Default values can be set for **translation** and **mathness**, for the case where a preponderance of the tokens have the same setting for these parameters. Once the defaults are set, the individual **token** and **ilk** commands don't have to specify **translation** or **mathness** if they are the same as the default. The format of the **default** statement is

default [**translation** *trans*] [**mathness** *mathopt*]

The comment character for the SPIDER language is the pound sign ('**#**'). Anything following this character on a line is ignored.

Appendix A

Command Summary

A.1   Regular WEB Commands

'@@' — **the single character '@'** —

This code is the only means by which the character '@' can be included in a WEB program.

'@␣' — **start a new section** —

This code marks the beginning of a section other than a major section ('␣' is a blank).

'@*' — **start a new starred (major) section** —

This code marks the beginning of a major section, one that starts a new topic.

'@d' — **macro definition** —

Definition of a numeric, string, or parametric macro.

'@f' — **format definition** —

This identifier is to be formatted as if it were the target reserved word.

'@p' — **start Pascal part of an unnamed section** —

The Pascal part of this code section is to be appended to the "unnamed section," the one corresponding to the main program.

'@<' — **start a section name** —

This is the beginning of a section name.

209

'@>' — end a section name or other control text —

This code is used as an ending delimiter for variable-length strings such as section names, index entries, pure TEX strings, and verbatim strings.

'@'' — octal constant —

The octal digits which follow this code are to be converted to decimal equivalents before being passed to the Pascal compiler.

'@"' — hexadecimal constant —

The hexadecimal digits which follow this code are to be converted to decimal equivalents before being passed to the Pascal compiler.

'@$' — string pool check sum —

This code is converted to the numeric value stored with the string pool when it was created. Comparing the value of this constant with the one in the pool file allows a program to determine whether the correct pool file is being used.

'@{' — start a "meta-comment" —

This is the beginning of a meta-comment. Unlike regular comments, this delimiter is passed through to the Pascal source, where it appears as '{'.

'@}' — end a "meta-comment" —

This is the end of a meta-comment. Unlike regular comments, this delimiter is passed through to the Pascal source, where it appears as '}'.

'@&' — concatenate two elements with no space —

The two syntactic elements on either side of the '@&' are to be placed into the Pascal file without an intervening space.

'@^' — start Roman font index entry —

Place an entry into the index in regular roman font.

'@.' — start typewriter font index entry —

Place an entry into the index in `typewriter` font.

'@:' — start user-controlled-font index entry —

Place an entry into the index in the user-controlled font. The action taken depends on the definition of the '\9' macro.

'@t' — start pure TEX text —

This command allows the insertion of arbitrary TEX code into the listing in case WEAVE doesn't do quite what is desired. It is a manual override. The end of the sequence is '@>'.

'@=' — start verbatim text —

This command allows the insertion of arbitrary text into the Pascal program. Manual override.

'@\' — force end-of-line here in Pascal file —

Start a new line in the Pascal output file.

'@!' — underline index entry (definition) —

Underline this entry in the index, indicating that this is the defining occurrence.

'@?' — cancel underline in index —

Cancel underline for index entries automatically underlined, such as identifiers following **var**.

'@,' — insert a thin space in TEX file —

A TEX thin space is to be inserted into the listing at the current location.

'@/' — force a line break —

Do a line break here regardless of the formatting.

'@|' — optional line break —

Tell WEAVE that this is a good place for a line break.

'@#' — force a line break with extra vertical space —

Start a new line and add a little bit more vertical space.

'@+' — cancel a pending line break —

Discourage WEAVE from putting a line break here.

'@;' — invisible semicolon —

There is no semicolon at this position in the program, but format as if there were.

A.2   Commands Found Only in Change Files

'@x' — start of a change section —

This command marks the beginning of a change section. The lines following the '@x', referred to as the *match text*, must appear within the WEB file
somewhere.

'@y' — start of replacement text —

The lines following this command are the replacement text and will be inserted
into the input stream in place of the lines that were matched.

'@z' — end of a change section —

This command marks the end of the replacement text and of the change section.

A.3   Additional Commands for CWEB

A.3.1   German CWEB

'@h' — start of function heading —

This command marks the start of a function heading in a declaration.

A.3.2   Levy CWEB

'@i' — include a file —

This command includes a file into WEB's input.

'@c' — start C part of an unnamed section —

Same function that '@p' performs for regular WEB.

'@'' — ASCII constant —

The character which follows this code is an ASCII character constant, no
matter what the character set of the machine is.

Appendix B

Special Characters Used by TEX

\ — TEX escape character

& — used as field separator in tables

— used for parameters of macros

$ — beginning and ending delimiter for math mode

% — TEX comment marker—everything from this character to end of line is a comment

^ — in math mode, the following character or group is a superscript

_ — in math mode, the following character or group is a subscript

` ` — two single reverse quotes are equivalent to "

' ' — two single apostrophes are equivalent to "

` — a single reverse quote is equivalent to '

' — a single apostrophe is equivalent to '

- — a single dash is equivalent to -

-- — a double dash is equivalent to –

--- — a triple dash is equivalent to —

{ — start a group

} — end a group

~ — unbreakable space

Appendix C

Formatting Macros

The actual definitions of the macros listed here can be found in the listing of 'webmac.tex' in Section F.1.1. Most of the macros in 'webmac' are not really useful when invoked directly by the programmer, since most of them require special context and work better under the direct control of WEAVE. The ones listed below have some utility.

\\{*identifier*} — italic type for identifiers

\|{*letter*} — math italic for one-letter identifiers

\&{*resword*} — boldface type for reserved words

\.{*string*} — typewriter type for strings

\1 — indent one more notch

\2 — indent one less notch

\3 — optional break within a statement

\4 — backspace one notch

\5 — optional break—equivalent to '@|', except cannot be cancelled by WEAVE

\6 — forced break—equivalent to '@/', except cannot be cancelled by WEAVE

\7 — forced break and a little extra space—equivalent to '@#', except cannot be cancelled by WEAVE

Appendix D

WEB Error Codes

D.1   Errors Detected by Both `TANGLE` and `WEAVE`

`!Ambiguous prefix` —

> A section name was abbreviated with '...', but the abbreviation matched more than one section name.

`!Change file ended after @x` —

> The change file was truncated. A change section was started with '@x', but the end of the file was reached before any match lines were found.

`!Change file ended before @y` —

> The change file was truncated. A change section was started with '@x' and contained lines to match with the main WEB file, but the end of the file was reached before '@y' was found.

`!Change file ended without @z` —

> The change file was truncated. A change section was started with '@x' and contained lines to match with the main WEB file, '@y', and replacement lines, but the end of the file was reached before '@z' was found.

`!Change file entry did not match` —

> The first line after '@x' didn't match any line in the main WEB file. Either the match text actually does not match or the change sections are out of order.

`!Hmm... nnn of the preceding lines failed to match` —

> The first line after '@x' matched a line in the WEB file, but one or more of the lines (*nnn* is the number of lines) before '@y' didn't match.

217

`!Incompatible section names` —

A section name was defined that was a prefix or an extension of an already existing section name.

`!Input ended in mid-comment` —

The `WEB` file was truncated; the end of the file was reached in the middle of a comment.

`!Input ended in section name` —

The `WEB` file was truncated; the end of the file was reached in the middle of a section name, possibly because the name didn't have a proper ending delimiter ('`@>`').

`!Input line too long` —

The input line was longer than the maximum length allowed.

`!Name does not match` —

A section name was abbreviated with '...', but the complete name was never found.

`!Section name didn't end` —

A section name was started and the end was never found, possibly because the name didn't have a proper ending delimiter ('`@>`').

`!Section name too long` —

A section name was longer than the maximum length allowed.

`!Sorry, x capacity exceeded` —

One of the limits of `TANGLE` or `WEAVE`, such as token memory or number of identifiers, was exceeded. Either the program is really too big for the `WEB` system to handle or there is something wrong with it, such as an error making it seem too big or poor structure (too much code in a single section instead of being broken up into multiple sections). The x identifies the particular capacity which has been exceeded.

`!String constant didn't end` —

A string was started and the end was never found, possibly because the string didn't have a proper ending delimiter ('`'`).

`!This can't happen(xxx)` —

> Logic error in the code of TANGLE or WEAVE, most likely introduced when WEB was being ported to a new system rather than present in the original version. There is probably nothing the user can do to resolve it; show the error message to the system person maintaining WEB. It will probably have to be reported to the implementor or vendor.

`!Verbatim string didn't end` —

> A verbatim text string was started and the end was never found, possibly because the string didn't have a proper ending delimiter ('"').

`!WEB file ended during a change` —

> The change file was truncated. A change section was started with '@x' and contained lines to match with the main WEB file, but the WEB file ended before all of the lines before '@y' were matched.

`!Where is the matching @x?` —

> A '@y' or '@z' was found in a change file when '@x' was expected.

`!Where is the matching @y?` —

> A '@x' or '@z' was found in a change file when '@y' was expected.

`!Where is the matching @z?` —

> A '@x' or '@y' was found in a change file when '@z' was expected.

D.2 Errors Specific to TANGLE

`!@d is ignored in Pascal text`

> A WEB macro definition occurred in Pascal code, where it is not allowed. Macros can only occur in the definition part of a section.

`!@f is ignored in Pascal text` —

> A **format** command definition occurred in Pascal code, where it is not allowed. It can only occur in the definition part of a section.

`!@p is ignored in Pascal text` —

> The WEB command that indicates the start of Pascal code for an unnamed section ('@p') occurred when already in Pascal code.

`!Can't output ASCII code nnn —`

An invalid ASCII code appeared in the source file. WEB files should consist only of printable ASCII characters. The number *nnn* is the decimal equivalent of the actual code found.

`!Constant too big —`

A decimal, octal, or hexadecimal constant is too large for a 32-bit integer value $(2^{31} - 1)$.

`!Definition flushed since it starts badly —`

A macro definition didn't start with '=', '==', or '(#)' after the identifier.

`!Definition flushed, must start with identifier of length > 1 —`

A macro definition or format command started with something other than an identifier, or the identifier was only one character in length (not permitted).

`!Double @ sign missing —`

If the '@' character appears in a string to be placed into the string pool, it should appear as '@@' so that it is not mistaken for a WEB command.

`!Extra ) —`

Parentheses nesting error; more right parentheses found than left ones.

`!Extra @} —`

An ending delimiter for meta-comments ('@}') was found when no meta-comment was in progress.

`!Fraction too long —`

A fraction extended past the end of an input line.

`!Identifier conflict with x —`

The current identifier is ambiguous with previously defined identifier *x*.

`!Improper @ within control text —`

The '@' character is not allowed in a section name or other control text. It should be replaced by '@@'.

`!Improper numeric definition will be flushed —`

Something other than a digit, identifier, or math operator was found while scanning a numeric expression.

`!Long line must be truncated` —

A line in the source file was longer than the maximum line length.

`!Missing ) ` —

During a macro definition, the replacement text had one less right parenthesis then left.

`!Missing nn )'s ` —

During a macro definition, the replacement text had *nn* less right parentheses then left.

`!No output was specified` —

There was no Pascal code in the entire source file, or there was no occurrence of the unnamed section ('`@p`') and therefore no starting point for building the Pascal program.

`!No parameter was given for x` —

The macro *x* was defined as parametric, but when the macro was used, a parameter was not supplied.

`!Not present:  <section_name>` —

A section was referenced but never defined. The actual section name replaces '*<section_name>*'.

`!Omit semicolon in numeric definition` —

A semicolon is not valid in the definition of numeric macros, since they are expressions rather than statements.

`!Pascal text flushed, = sign is missing` —

The section name beginning the code part of a section isn't followed by '='.

`!Preprocessed string is too long` —

A preprocessed string (one which goes in the string pool) has *length* > 99.

`!Program ended at brace level nnn` —

End-of-file was found with meta-comments in progress. The nesting level is designated by *nnn*.

`!Section ended in mid-comment` —

'`@␣`' or '`@*`' or the end of the file was found while a comment was in progress.

`!String didn't end` —

> A string was started and the end of the line was reached without finding the ending delimiter of the string.

`!String too long` —

> A string was longer than the maximum length allowed.

`!This identifier has already appeared` —

> A numeric macro has been referenced before it is defined. Forward references are not allowed for numeric macros.

`!This identifier was defined before` —

> A macro is being defined with the same identifier as one already defined. Macros cannot be redefined.

`!Two numbers occurred without a sign between them` —

> Invalid syntax occurred in an expression.

`!Use == for macros` —

> A double equal sign ('==') must be used for simple and parametric macros.

`!Value too big: nnnn` —

> The current value of the accumulator for a numeric expression is too large for a 16-bit integer value ($2^{15} - 1$). *nnnn* is the actual value that wouldn't fit.

`!Verbatim string too long` —

> A verbatim string was longer than the maximum length allowed.

`!You should double @ signs in strings` —

> If the '@' character appears in a string, it should appear as '@@' so that it is not mistaken for a WEB command.

`!You should double @ signs in verbatim strings` —

> If the '@' character appears in a verbatim string, it should appear as '@@' so that it is not mistaken for a WEB command.

D.3 Errors Specific to WEAVE

`!Control codes are forbidden in control text —`

> If the '`@`' character appears in control text, it should appear as '`@@`' so that it is not mistaken for a WEB command.

`!Control text didn't end —`

> Control text was started and the end was never found, possibly because the name didn't have a proper ending delimiter ('`@>`').

`!Double @ required outside of sections —`

> If the '`@`' character appears in limbo text, it should appear as '`@@`' so that it is not mistaken for a WEB command.

`!Double @ should be used in strings —`

> If the '`@`' character appears in a string, it should appear as '`@@`' so that it is not mistaken for a WEB command.

`!Extra @> —`

> An ending delimiter for control text ('`@>`') was found when control text was not in progress.

`!Illegal use of @ in comment —`

> The '`@`' character is not allowed in comments. It should be replaced by '`@@`'.

`!Improper format definition —`

> An identifier didn't follow '`@f`'.

`!Improper macro definition —`

> An identifier didn't follow '`@d`'.

`!Line had to be broken —`

> WEAVE could not find a good breaking point for an output line (because of long strings, etc.) and finally picked an arbitrary place. The line should be restructured.

`!Missing "|" after Pascal text —`

> Pascal code in TEX code must be delimited by '`|`'.

`!Never defined:` <*section_name*> `—`

> A section was referenced but never defined.

`!Never used:` *<section_name>* —

A section was defined but never referenced.

`!TeX string should be in Pascal text only` —

'@t' was found when already in TEX portion of section.

`!Unknown control code` —

An invalid control code was detected: '@' followed by a character not listed in Appendix A.

`!You can't do that in Pascal text` —

One of the WEB commands valid only in Pascal code was used in TEX code.

`!You can't do that in TeX text` —

One of the WEB commands valid only in TEX code was used in Pascal code.

`!You need an = sign after the section name` —

The proper syntax for the definition of a section is '@<name@>='. The equal sign was omitted.

Appendix E

TₑX Error Codes

The error messages listed here are the ones most often seen when running TₑX on a file generated by WEAVE.

!Emergency stop —

> TₑX is halting with a fatal error, as a result of either an error in the source file or internal inconsistencies.

!Extra }, or forgotten $ —

> Some type of brace mismatch.

!I can't find file xxx —

> A file specified by a '\input' command couldn't be found.

!* (job aborted, file error in nonstop mode) —**

> Some sort of error occurred while attempting to open a file, such as trying to '\input' a nonexistent file. Since TₑX is in currently in nonstop (batch) mode, it is unable to prompt for the correct name.

!Missing { inserted —

> A left brace was expected, but was not found. TₑX pretended that one was present and continued.

!Missing $ inserted —

> A sequence valid only in math mode has been issued when TₑX was not currently in math mode, possibly because an underscore was found without a preceding backslash.

`!Missing } inserted` —

A right brace was expected, but was not found. TEX pretended that one was present and continued.

`!Overfull \hbox (nnnpt too wide) in paragraph at lines nn--nn` —

TEX could not find a good place to break a line, probably because of unbreakable items such as `WEB` identifiers. The *nnn*pt indicates how much too wide the box was.

`!Text line contains an invalid character` —

A non-ASCII character was found in the TEX source file.

`!TeX capacity exceeded, sorry` —

One of TEX's resources has apparently been exhausted (the actual message will say which one). Possible candidates are number of strings, pool size, main memory size, hash size, font memory, exception dictionary, input stack size, semantic nest size, parameter stack size, buffer size, save size, text input levels, grouping levels, and pattern memory.

`!This can't happen` —

There is a bug in this version of TEX, probably in the implementation-specific code rather than in the main logic. Contact the implementor, as there is probably nothing that the user can do.

`!Undefined control sequence` —

This control sequence (macro, control symbol, etc.) has never been defined. Make sure the spelling is correct.

`!Underfull \hbox (badness nnn) in paragraph at lines nn--nn` —

This line has too much empty space in it.

`!Underfull \vbox (badness nnn) has occurred while \output is active` —

This page has too much white space in it.

`!Use of xxx doesn't match its definition` —

A control sequence has been defined as one type of control and has been used as if it were a different type. For instance, a macro has been used in a context requiring a control symbol.

`!xxx not loadable:  Bad metric (TFM) file` —

There is something wrong with the TeX font metric file for the requested font. It is either corrupted, incompatible with the current version of TeX, or not a metric file.

`!xxx not loadable:  Metric (TFM) file not found` —

The TeX font metric file for the requested font could not be found at the specified magnification.

`!Font xxx not loaded:  Not enough room left` —

Too many different fonts were loaded into TeX at once. This problem doesn't often happen with `WEB`, since `WEAVE` handles fonts automatically, but having a large number of user-loaded fonts in the limbo section could cause it.

Appendix F

Various Text Files

F.1 Source Code for WEB Macros

F.1.1 Language Macro Packages

Regular WEB

The following file, `webmac.tex`, is the source file for the WEB macros. Note: there are two font families currently in used with the TeX system: the Computer Modern (CM) fonts and the earlier Almost Modern (AM) fonts. Which one you use depends on which one is installed on your system. IF the AM fonts are in use, the file listed below will have to be modified (in all of the '`\font`' commands, change 'cm' to 'am'). If both font families are available, the CM fonts are recommended, not just for WEB but for all uses of TeX, because the AM fonts are considered obsolete and should be retired.

Contents of text file '`webmac.tex`':

```
% standard macros for WEB listings (in addition to PLAIN.TEX)
\xdef\fmtversion{\fmtversion+WEBMAC1.4}
\parskip 0pt % no stretch between paragraphs
\parindent 1em % for paragraphs and for the first line of Pascal text

\font\eightrm=cmr8
\let\sc=\eightrm \let\mainfont=\tenrm
\font\titlefont=cmr7 scaled\magstep4 % title on the contents page
\font\ttitlefont=cmtt10 scaled\magstep2 % typewriter type in title
\font\tentex=cmtex10 % TeX extended character set (used in strings)

\def\\#1{\hbox{\it#1\/\kern.05em}} % italic type for identifiers
\def\|#1{\hbox{$#1$}} % one-letter identifiers look a bit better this way
\def\&#1{\hbox{\bf#1\/}} % boldface type for reserved words
\def\.#1{\hbox{\tentex % typewriter type for strings
```

```
  \let\\=\BS % backslash in a string
  \let\'=\RQ % right quote in a string
  \let\`=\LQ % left quote in a string
  \let\{=\LB % left brace in a string
  \let\}=\RB % right brace in a string
  \let\~=\TL % tilde in a string
  \let\ =\SP % space in a string
  \let\_=\UL % underline in a string
  \let\&=\AM % ampersand in a string
  #1}}
\def\#{\hbox{\tt\char'\#}} % parameter sign
\def\${\hbox{\tt\char'\$}} % dollar sign
\def\%{\hbox{\tt\char'\%}} % percent sign
\def\^{\ifmmode\mathchar"222 \else\char'^ \fi} % pointer or hat
% circumflex accents can be obtained from \^^D instead of \^
\def\AT!{@} % at sign for control text

\chardef\AM='\& % ampersand character in a string
\chardef\BS='\\ % backslash in a string
\chardef\LB='\{ % left brace in a string
\def\LQ{{\tt\char'22}} % left quote in a string
\chardef\RB='\} % right brace in a string
\def\RQ{{\tt\char'23}} % right quote in a string
\def\SP{{\tt\char'\ }} % (visible) space in a string
\chardef\TL='\~ % tilde in a string
\chardef\UL='\_ % underline character in a string

\newbox\bak \setbox\bak=\hbox to -1em{} % backspace one em
\newbox\bakk\setbox\bakk=\hbox to -2em{} % backspace two ems

\newcount\ind % current indentation in ems
\def\1{\global\advance\ind by1\hangindent\ind em} % indent one more notch
\def\2{\global\advance\ind by-1} % indent one less notch
\def\3#1{\hfil\penalty#10\hfilneg} % optional break within a statement
\def\4{\copy\bak} % backspace one notch
\def\5{\hfil\penalty-1\hfilneg\kern2.5em\copy\bakk\ignorespaces}% optional break
\def\6{\ifmmode\else\par % forced break
  \hangindent\ind em\noindent\kern\ind em\copy\bakk\ignorespaces\fi}
\def\7{\Y\6} % forced break and a little extra space

\let\yskip=\smallskip
\def\to{\mathrel{.\,.}} % double dot, used only in math mode
\def\note#1#2.{\Y\noindent{\hangindent2em\baselineskip10pt\eightrm#1 #2.\par}}
\def\lapstar{\rlap{*}}
\def\startsection{\Q\noindent{\let\*=\lapstar\bf\modstar.\quad}}
\def\defin#1{\global\advance\ind by 2 \1\&{#1 }} % begin `define' or `format'
\def\A{\note{See also}} % cross-reference for multiply defined section names
\def\B{\mathopen\.{@\{}}} % begin controlled comment
\def\C#1{\ifmmode\gdef\XX{\null$\null}\else\gdef\XX{}\fi % Pascal comments
  \XX\hfil\penalty-1\hfilneg\quad$\{\,$#1$\,\}$\XX}
\def\D{\defin{define}} % macro definition
\def\E{\cdot10^} % exponent in floating point constant
\def\F{\defin{format}} % format definition
\let\G=\ge % greater than or equal sign
\def\H#1{\hbox{\rm\char"7D\tt#1}} % hexadecimal constant
\let\I=\ne % unequal sign
\def\J{\.{@\&}} % TANGLE's join operation
\let\K=\gets % left arrow
\let\L=\le % less than or equal sign
\outer\def\M#1.{\MN#1.\ifon\vfil\penalty-100\vfilneg % beginning of section
  \vskip12ptminus3pt\startsection\ignorespaces}
```

```
\outer\def\N#1.#2.{\MN#1.\vfil\eject % beginning of starred section
  \def\rhead{\uppercase{\ignorespaces#2}} % define running headline
  \message{*\modno} % progress report
  \edef\next{\write\cont{\Z{#2}{\modno}{\the\pageno}}}\ next% to contents file
  \ifon\startsection{\bf\ignorespaces#2.\quad}\ignorespaces}
\def\MN#1.{\par % common code for \M, \N
  {\xdef\modstar{#1}\let\*=\empty\xdef\modno{#1}}
  \ifx\modno\modstar \onmaybe \else\ontrue \fi \mark{\modno}}
\def\O#1{\hbox{\rm\char'23\kern-.2em\it#1\/\kern.05em}} % octal constant
\dof\P{\rightskip=0pt plus 100pt minus 10pt % go into Pascal mode
  \sfcode';=3000
  \pretolerance .10000
  \hyphenpenalty 10000 \exhyphenpenalty 10000
  \global\ind=2 \1\ \unskip}
\def\Q{\rightskip=0pt % get out of Pascal mode
  \sfcode';=1500 \pretolerance 200 \hyphenpenalty 50 \exhyphenpenalty 50 }
\let\R=\lnot % logical not
\let\S=\equiv % equivalence sign
\def\T{\mathclose{\.{@\}}}} % terminate controlled comment
\def\U{\note{This code is used in}} % cross-reference for uses of sections
\let\V=\lor % logical or
\let\W=\land % logical and
\def\X#1:#2\X{\ifmmode\gdef\XX{\null$\null}\else\gdef\XX{}\ fi% section name
  \XX$\langle\,$#2{\eightrm\kern.5em#1}$\,\rangle$\XX}
\def\Y{\par\yskip}
\let\Z=\let % now you can \send the control sequence \Z
\def\){\hbox{\.{@\$}}} % sign for string pool check sum
\def\]{\hbox{\.{@\\}}} % sign for forced line break
\def\=#1{\kern2pt\hbox{\vrule\vtop{\vbox{\hrule
      \hbox{\strut\kern2pt\.{#1}\kern2pt}}
    \hrule}\vrule}\kern2pt} % verbatim string
\let\~=\ignorespaces
\let\*=*

\def\onmaybe{\let\ifon=\maybe} \let\maybe=\iftrue
\newif\ifon \newif\iftitle \newif\ifpagesaved
\def\lheader{\mainfont\the\pageno\eightrm\qquad\rhead\hfill\title\qquad
  \tensy x\mainfont\topmark} % top line on left-hand pages
\def\rheader{\tensy x\mainfont\topmark\eightrm\qquad\title\hfill\rhead
  \qquad\mainfont\the\pageno} % top line on right-hand pages
\def\page{\box255 }
\def\normaloutput#1#2#3{\ifodd\pageno\hoffset=\pageshift\fi
  \shipout\vbox{
    \vbox to\fullpageheight{
      \iftitle\global\titlefalse
      \else\hbox to\pagewidth{\vbox to10pt{}\ifodd\pageno #3\else#2\fi}\fi
      \vfill#1}} % parameter #1 is the page itself
  \global\advance\pageno by1}

\def\rhead{\.{WEB} OUTPUT} % this running head is reset by starred sections
\def\title{} % an optional title can be set by the user
\def\topofcontents{\centerline{\titlefont\title}
  \vfill} % this material will start the table of contents page
\def\botofcontents{\vfill} % this material will end the table of contents page
\def\contentspagenumber{0} % default page number for table of contents
\newdimen\pagewidth \pagewidth=6.5in % the width of each page
\newdimen\pageheight \pageheight=8.7in % the height of each page
\newdimen\fullpageheight \fullpageheight=9in % page height including headlines
\newdimen\pageshift \pageshift=0in % shift righthand pages wrt lefthand ones
\def\magnify#1{\mag=#1\pagewidth=6.5truein\pageheight=8.7truein
  \fullpageheight=9truein\setpage}
```

```
\def\setpage{\hsize\pagewidth\vsize\pageheight} % use after changing page size
\def\contentsfile{CONTENTS} % file that gets table of contents info
\def\readcontents{\input CONTENTS}

\newwrite\cont
\output{\setbox0=\page % the first page is garbage
  \openout\cont=\contentsfile
  \global\output{\normaloutput\page\lheader\rheader}}
\setpage
\vbox to \vsize{} % the first \topmark won't be null

\def\ch{\note{The following sections were changed by the change file:}
  \let\*=\relax}
\newbox\sbox % saved box preceding the index
\newbox\lbox % lefthand column in the index
\def\inx{\par\vskip6pt plus 1fil % we are beginning the index
  \write\cont{} % ensure that the contents file isn't empty
  \closeout\cont % the contents information has been fully gathered
  \output{\ifpagesaved\normaloutput{\box\sbox}\lheader\rheader\fi
    \global\setbox\sbox=\page \global\pagesavedtrue}
  \pagesavedfalse \eject % eject the page-so-far and predecessors
  \setbox\sbox\vbox{\unvbox\sbox} % take it out of its box
  \vsize=\pageheight \advance\vsize by -\ht\sbox % the remaining height
  \hsize=.5\pagewidth \advance\hsize by -10pt
    % column width for the index (20pt between cols)
  \parfillskip 0pt plus .6\hsize % try to avoid almost empty lines
  \def\lr{L} % this tells whether the left or right column is next
  \output{\if L\lr\global\setbox\lbox=\page \gdef\lr{R}
    \else\normaloutput{\vbox to\pageheight{\box\sbox\vss
        \hbox to\pagewidth{\box\lbox\hfil\page}}}\lheader\rheader
    \global\vsize\pageheight\gdef\lr{L}\global\pagesavedfalse\fi}
  \message{Index:}
  \parskip 0pt plus .5pt
  \outer\def\:##1, {\par\hangindent2em\noindent##1:\kern1em} % index entry
  \let\ttentry=\. \def\.##1{\ttentry{##1\kern.2em}} % give \tt a little room
  \def\[##1]{$\underline{##1}$} % underlined index item
  \rm \rightskip0pt plus 2.5em \tolerance 10000 \let\*=\lapstar
  \hyphenpenalty 10000 \parindent0pt}
\def\fin{\par\vfill\eject % this is done when we are ending the index
  \ifpagesaved\null\vfill\eject\fi % output a null index column
  \if L\lr\else\null\vfill\eject\fi % finish the current page
  \parfillskip 0pt plus 1fil
  \def\rhead{NAMES OF THE SECTIONS}
  \message{Section names:}
  \output{\normaloutput\page\lheader\rheader}
  \setpage
  \def\note##1##2.{\hfil\penalty-1\hfilneg\quad{\eightrm##1 ##2.}}
  \linepenalty=10 % try to conserve lines
  \def\U{\note{Used in}} % cross-reference for uses of sections
  \def\:{\par\hangindent 2em}\let\*=*\let\.=\ttentry}
\def\con{\par\vfill\eject % finish the section names
  \rightskip 0pt \hyphenpenalty 50 \tolerance 200
  \setpage
  \output{\normaloutput\page\lheader\rheader}
  \titletrue % prepare to output the table of contents
  \pageno=\contentspagenumber \def\rhead{TABLE OF CONTENTS}
  \message{Table of contents:}
  \topofcontents
  \line{\hfil Section\hbox to3em{\hss Page}}
  \def\Z##1##2##3{\line{\ignorespaces##1
    \leaders\hbox to .5em{.\hfil}\hfil\ ##2\hbox to3em{\hss##3}}}
```

```
\readcontents\relax % read the contents info
\botofcontents \end} % print the contents page(s) and terminate
```

End of text file 'webmac.tex'

Modula-2 WEB

The following file, `mwebmac.tex`, contains the additional macros needed for MWEB. The regular `webmac.tex` is used as a base.

Contents of text file 'mwebmac.tex':

```
\input webmac

\def\C#1{\ifmmode\gdef\XX{\null$\null}\else\gdef\XX{}\fi % Pascal comments
  \XX\hfil\penalty-1\hfilneg\quad$(*\,$#1$\,*)$\XX}

\def\VB{\ifmmode\gdef\XX{\null$\null}\else\gdef\XX{}\fi % Pascal comments
  \XX\hfil\penalty-1\hfilneg\quad$|$\XX}
```

End of text file 'mwebmac.tex'

C WEB

The following file, `cwebmac.tex`, contains the additional macros needed for C WEB.

Contents of text file 'cwebmac.tex':

```
% standard macros for WEB listings (in addition to PLAIN.TEX)
% $Revision: 1.8 $
\let\amp=\&
\parskip 0pt % no stretch between paragraphs
\parindent 1em % for paragraphs and for the first line of C text

\font\eightrm=cmr8 % this will eventually become cmr8
\let\sc=\eightrm \let\mainfont=\tenrm
\font\titlefont=cmr7 scaled\magstep4 % title on the contents page
\font\ttitlefont=cmtt10 scaled\magstep2 % typewriter type in title
```

```
\font\tentex=cmtex10 % TeX extended character set (used in strings)

\def\~{\char`\~}
\def\\#1{\leavevmode\hbox{\it#1\/\kern.05em}} % italic type for identifiers
\def\|#1{\leavevmode\hbox{$#1$}} % one-letter identifiers look better this way
\def\&#1{\leavevmode\hbox{\bf#1\/}} % boldface type for reserved words
\def\.#1{\leavevmode\hbox{\tentex % typewriter type for strings
  \let\\=\BS % backslash in a string
  \let\'=\RQ % right quote in a string
  \let\`=\LQ % left quote in a string
  \let\{=\LB % left brace in a string
  \let\}=\RB % right brace in a string
  \let\~=\TL % tilde in a string
  \let\ =\SP % space in a string
  \let\_=\UL % underline in a string
  \let\&=\AM % ampersand in a string
  #1}}
\def\nxt#1{\ifx#1\egroup#1\else#1\discretionary{\\}{}{}\expand after\nxt\fi}
\def\)#1{\leavevmode\bgroup\tentex % breakable typewriter type
  \let\\=\BS % backslash in a string
  \let\'=\RQ % right quote in a string
  \let\`=\LQ % left quote in a string
  \let\{=\LB % left brace in a string
  \let\}=\RB % right brace in a string
  \let\~=\TL % tilde in a string
  \let\ =\SP % space in a string
  \let\_=\UL % underline in a string
  \let\&=\AM % ampersand in a string
  \nxt#1\egroup}
\def\^{\ifmmode\mathchar"222 \else\char`^ \fi} % pointer or hat
% circumflex accents can be obtained from \^^D instead of \^
\def\AT{@} % at sign for control text

\chardef\AM=`\& % ampersand character in a string
\chardef\BS=`\\ % backslash in a string
\chardef\LB=`\{ % left brace in a string
\def\LQ{{\tt\char'22}} % left quote in a string
\chardef\RB=`\} % right brace in a string
\def\RQ{{\tt\char'23}} % right quote in a string
\def\SP{{\tt\char`\ }} % (visible) space in a string
\chardef\TL=`\~ % tilde in a string
\chardef\UL=`\_ % underline character in a string

\newbox\bak \setbox\bak=\hbox to -1em{} % backspace one em
\newbox\bakk\setbox\bakk=\hbox to -2em{} % backspace two ems

\newcount\ind % current indentation in ems
\def\1{\global\advance\ind by1\hangindent\ind em} % indent one more notch
\def\2{\global\advance\ind by-1} % indent one less notch
\def\3#1{\hfil\penalty#10\hfilneg} % optional break within a statement
\def\4{\copy\bak} % backspace one notch
\def\5{\hfil\penalty-1\hfilneg\kern2.5em\copy\bakk\ignorespaces}% optional break
\def\6{\ifmmode\else\par % forced break
  \hangindent\ind em\noindent\kern\ind em\copy\bakk\ignorespaces\fi}
\def\7{\Y\6} % forced break and a little extra space
\def\8{\hskip-\ind em\hskip 2em} % no indentation

\let\yskip=\smallskip
\def\?{\mathrel?}
\def\note#1#2.{\Y\noindent{\hangindent2em\baselineskip10pt\eightrm#1 #2.\par}}
\def\lapstar{\rlap{*}}
```

```
\def\startsection{\Q\noindent{\let\*=\lapstar\bf\modstar.\quad}}
\def\defin#1{\global\advance\ind by 2 \1\&{#1 }} % begin 'define' or 'format'
\def\A{\note{See also}} % cross-reference for multiply defined section names
\def\B{\mathopen{\.{@/\ast}}} % begin controlled comment
\def\C#1{\ifmmode\gdef\XX{\null$\null}\else\gdef\XX{}\fi % C comments
  \XX\hfil\penalty-1\hfilneg\quad$/\ast\,$#1$\,\ast/$\XX}
\def\D{\defin{\#define} } % macro definition
\def\F{\defin{format}} % format definition
\let\G=\ge % greater than or equal sign
\let\I=\ne % unequal sign
\def\J{\.{@\&}} % TANGLE's join operation
\let\K== % can be changed to left arrow, if desired
\let\L=\le % less than or equal sign
\outer\def\M#1.{\MN#1.\ifon\vfil\penalty-100\vfilneg % beginning of section
  \vskip12ptminus3pt\startsection\ignorespaces}
\outer\def\N#1.#2.{\MN#1.\vfil\eject % beginning of starred section
  \def\rhead{\uppercase{\ignorespaces#2}} % define running headline
  \message{*\modno} % progress report
  \edef\next{\write\cont{\Z{#2}{\modno}{\the\pageno}}}\ next% to contents file
  \ifon\startsection{\bf\ignorespaces#2.\quad}\ignorespaces}
\def\MN#1.{\par % common code for \M, \N
  {\xdef\modstar{#1}\let\*=\empty\xdef\modno{#1}}
  \ifx\modno\modstar \onmaybe \else\ontrue \fi \mark{\modno}}
\def\O#1{% octal, hex or decimal constant
  {\def\?{\kern.2em}%
  \def\${\ell}% long constant
  \def\_{\cdot 10^{\aftergroup}}% power of ten
  \def\~{\hbox{\rm\char'23\kern-.2em\it\aftergroup\?\aftergroup} }%octal
  \def\"{\hbox{\rm\char"7D\tt\aftergroup}}#1}}% double quotes for hex constant
\def\P{\rightskip=0pt plus 100pt minus 10pt % go into C mode
  \sfcode`;=3000
  \pretolerance 10000
  \hyphenpenalty 9999 % so strings can be broken (a discretionary \ is inserted)
  \exhyphenpenalty 10000
  \global\ind=2 \1\ \unskip}
\def\Q{\rightskip=0pt % get out of C mode
  \sfcode`;=1500 \pretolerance 200 \hyphenpenalty 50 \exhyphenpenalty 50 }
\let\R=\lnot % logical not
\let\S=\equiv % equivalence sign
\def\T{\mathclose{\.{@\ast/}}} % terminate controlled comment
\def\U{\note{This code is used in}} % cross-reference for uses of sections
\let\V=\lor % logical or
\let\W=\land % logical and
\def\X#1:#2\X{\ifmmode\gdef\XX{\null$\null}\else\gdef\XX{}\fi% section name
  \XX$\langle\,$#2{\eightrm\kern.5em#1}$\,\rangle$\XX}
\def\Y{\par\yskip}
\let\Z=\let % now you can \send the control sequence \Z
\def\]{\hbox{\.{@\\}}} % sign for forced line break
\def\=#1{\kern2pt\hbox{\vrule\vtop{\vbox{\hrule
        \hbox{\strut\kern2pt\.{#1}\kern2pt}}
      \hrule}\vrule}\kern2pt} % verbatim string
\let\*=*

\def\onmaybe{\let\ifon=\maybe} \let\maybe=\iftrue
\newif\ifon \newif\iftitle \newif\ifpagesaved
\def\lheader{\mainfont\the\pageno\eightrm\qquad\rhead\hfill\title\qquad
  \tensy x\mainfont\topmark} % top line on left-hand pages
\def\rheader{\tensy x\mainfont\topmark\eightrm\qquad\title\hfill\rhead
  \qquad\mainfont\the\pageno} % top line on right-hand pages
\def\page{\box255 }
\def\normaloutput#1#2#3{\shipout\vbox{
```

```
\ifodd\pageno\hoffset=\pageshift\fi
\vbox to\fullpageheight{
\iftitle\global\titlefalse
\else\hbox to\pagewidth{\vbox to10pt{}\ifodd\pageno #3\else#2\fi}\fi
\vfill#1}} % parameter #1 is the page itself
\global\advance\pageno by1}

\def\rhead{\.{WEB} OUTPUT} % this running head is reset by starred sections
\def\title{} % an optional title can be set by the user
\def\topofcontents{\centerline{\titlefont\title}
 \vfill} % this material will start the table of contents page
\def\botofcontents{\vfill} % this material will end the table of contents page
\def\contentspagenumber{0} % default page number for table of contents
\newdimen\pagewidth \pagewidth=6.5in % the width of each page
\newdimen\pageheight \pageheight=8.7in % the height of each page
\newdimen\fullpageheight \fullpageheight=9in % page height including headlines
\newdimen\pageshift \pageshift=0in % shift righthand pages wrt lefthand ones
\def\magnify#1{\mag=#1\pagewidth=6.5truein\pageheight=8.7truein
 \fullpageheight=9truein\setpage}
\def\setpage{\hsize\pagewidth\vsize\pageheight} % use after changing page size
\def\contentsfile{\jobname.toc} % file that gets table of contents info
\def\readcontents{\input \jobname.toc}

\newwrite\cont
\output{\setbox0=\page % the first page is garbage
 \openout\cont=\contentsfile
 \global\output{\normaloutput\page\lheader\rheader}}
\setpage
\vbox to \vsize{} % the first \topmark won't be null

\def\ch{\note{The following sections were changed by the change file:}
 \let\*=\relax}
\newbox\sbox % saved box preceding the index
\newbox\lbox % lefthand column in the index
\def\inx{\par\vskip6pt plus 1fil % we are beginning the index
 \write\cont{} % ensure that the contents file isn't empty
 \closeout\cont % the contents information has been fully gathered
 \output{\ifpagesaved\normaloutput{\box\sbox}\lheader\rheader\fi
   \global\setbox\sbox=\page \global\pagesavedtrue}
 \pagesavedfalse \eject % eject the page-so-far and predecessors
 \setbox\sbox\vbox{\unvbox\sbox} % take it out of its box
 \vsize=\pageheight \advance\vsize by -\ht\sbox % the remaining height
 \hsize=.5\pagewidth \advance\hsize by -10pt
   % column width for the index (20pt between cols)
 \parfillskip 0pt plus .6\hsize % try to avoid almost empty lines
 \def\lr{L} % this tells whether the left or right column is next
 \output{\if L\lr\global\setbox\lbox=\page \gdef\lr{R}
   \else\normaloutput{\vbox to\pageheight{\box\sbox\vss
       \hbox to\pagewidth{\box\lbox\hfil\page}}}\lheader\rheader
   \global\vsize\pageheight\gdef\lr{L}\global\pagesavedfalse\fi}
 \message{Index:}
 \parskip 0pt plus .5pt
 \outer\def\:##1, {\par\hangindent2em\noindent##1:\kern1em} % index entry
 \def\[##1]{$\underline{##1}$} % underlined index item
 \rm \rightskip0pt plus 2.5em \tolerance 10000 \let\*=\lapstar
 \hyphenpenalty 10000 \parindent0pt}
\def\fin{\par\vfill\eject % this is done when we are ending the index
 \ifpagesaved\null\vfill\eject\fi % output a null index column
 \if L\lr\else\null\vfill\eject\fi % finish the current page
 \parfillskip 0pt plus 1fil
 \def\rhead{NAMES OF THE SECTIONS}
```

```
    \message{Section names:}
    \output{\normaloutput\page\lheader\rheader}
    \setpage
    \def\note##1##2.{\quad{\eightrm##1 ##2.}}
    \def\U{\note{Used in}} % cross-reference for uses of sections
    \def\:{\par\hangindent 2em}\let\*=*}
\def\con{\par\vfill\eject % finish the section names
    \rightskip 0pt \hyphenpenalty 50 \tolerance 200
    \setpage
    \output{\normaloutput\page\lheader\rheader}
    \titletrue % prepare to output the table of contents
    \pageno=\contentspagenumber \def\rhead{TABLE OF CONTENTS}
    \message{Table of contents:}
    \topofcontents
    \line{\hfil Section\hbox to3em{\hss Page}}
    \def\Z##1##2##3{\line{\ignorespaces##1
      \leaders\hbox to .5em{.\hfil}\hfil\ ##2\hbox to3em{\hss##3}}}
    \readcontents\relax % read the contents info
    \botofcontents \end} % print the contents page(s) and terminate
\tracingstats1 % temporary (during development)
\def\FE{\mathrel{/=}}
\def\PP{\mathord{++}}
\def\PE{\mathrel{+=}}
\def\MM{\mathord{--}}
\def\ME{\mathrel{-=}}
\def\MG{\mathrel{\to}}
\def\GG{\mathrel{>\!>}}
\def\LL{\mathrel{<\!<}}
\def\TE{\mathrel{\ast=}}
\def\CE{\mathrel{\%=}}
\def\HE{\mathrel{\uparrow=}}
\def\AE{\mathrel{\&=}}
\def\OE{\mathrel{|=}}
\let\openbraces=\{
\let\closebraces=\}
\def\{{\ifmmode\openbraces\else$\openbraces$\fi}
\def\}{\ifmmode\closebraces\else$\closebraces$\fi}
```

End of text file 'cwebmac.tex'

Macro Kernel for WEB Systems Generated by SPIDER

The following file contains the generic macros used for all versions of WEB generated by SPIDER. The additional language-specific macros found in the SPIDER input file for a language ('.spi') are appended to it to become an instance of 'webmac' for that language.

Contents of text file 'webkernel.tex':

```
%\let\plainmark=\mark
%\def\mark#1{\message{(Marking ''#1'')}\plainmark{#1}}

% standard macros for WEB listings (in addition to PLAIN.TEX)
% rename some old favorites
\let\amp=\&
\let\SS=\S
\let\PP=\P
\let\em=\it % compatibility with latex

\newif\iftwoside\twosidefalse
\parskip 0pt % .1pt plus 0.1pt mins 0.1pt % no stretch between paragraphs
\parindent 1em % for paragraphs and for the first line of Pascal text

\font\eightrm=cmr8
\font\sc=cmcsc10
\let\mainfont=\tenrm
\font\titlefont=cmr7 scaled\magstep4 % title on the contents page
\font\ttitlefont=cmtt10 scaled\magstep2 % typewriter type in title
\font\tentex=cmtex10 % TeX extended character set (used in strings)
\let\idfont\it
\let\reservedfont\bf

\def\today{\ifcase\month\or
  January\or February\or March\or April\or May\or June\or
  July\or August\or September\or October\or November\or December\fi
  \space\number\day, \number\year}

\def\\#1{\leavevmode\hbox{\idfont#1\/\kern.05em}} % italic type for identifiers
\def\|#1{\leavevmode\hbox{$#1$}} % one-letter identifiers look better this way
\def\&#1{\leavevmode\hbox{\reservedfont#1\/}} % boldface type for reserved words
\def\.#1{\leavevmode\hbox{\tentex % typewriter type for strings
  \let\\=\BS % backslash in a string
  \let\'=\RQ % right quote in a string
  \let\`=\LQ % left quote in a string
  \let\{=\LB % left brace in a string
  \let\}=\RB % right brace in a string
  \let\~=\TL % tilde in a string
  \let\ =\SP % space in a string
  \let\_=\UL % underline in a string
  \let\&=\AM % ampersand in a string
  #1}}
\def\#{\hbox{\tt\char'\#}} % parameter sign
\def\${\hbox{\tt\char'\$}} % dollar sign
\def\%{\hbox{\tt\char'\%}} % percent sign
\def\^{\ifmmode\mathchar"222 \else\char'^ \fi} % pointer or hat
% circumflex accents can be obtained from \^^D instead of \^
\def\AT!{@} % at sign for control text
\def\@{@} % at sign in strings
% EVERY WEAVE MUST DEFINE \? WHERE ? IS THE AT SIGN!!!!

% Macros to surround text in |...|
\def\CD{\relax\ifmmode\let\DC\egroup\hbox\bgroup\else\let\DC\relax\fi}

\chardef\AM='\& % ampersand character in a string
\chardef\BS='\\ % backslash in a string
\chardef\LB='\{ % left brace in a string
\def\LQ{{\tt\char'22}} % left quote in a string
```

```
\chardef\RB=`\} % right brace in a string
\def\RQ{{\tt\char'23}} % right quote in a string
\def\SP{{\tt\char`\ }} % (visible) space in a string
\chardef\TL=`\~ % tilde in a string
\chardef\UL=`\_ % underline character in a string

\newbox\bak \setbox\bak=\hbox to -1em{} % backspace one em
\newbox\bakk\setbox\bakk=\hbox to -2em{} % backspace two ems

\newcount\ind % current indentation in ems
\def\0{\ifmmode\ifinner$\par % forced break
  \hangindent\ind em\noindent\kern\ind em\ignorespaces$\fi
  \else\par % forced break
  \hangindent\ind em\noindent\kern\ind em\ignorespaces\fi}
\def\1{\global\advance\ind by1\hangindent\ind em} % indent one more notch
\def\2{\global\advance\ind by-1} % indent one less notch
\def\3#1{\hfil\penalty#10\hfilneg} % optional break within a statement
\def\4{\copy\bak} % backspace one notch
\def\5{\hfil\penalty-1\hfilneg\kern2.5em\copy\bakk\ignorespaces}% optional break
%\def\6{\ifmmode\else\par % forced break with no indentation
%  \hangindent\ind em\noindent\kern\ind em\copy\bakk\ignorespaces\fi}
\def\6{\ifmmode\else\par % forced break with no indentation
  \hangindent\ind em\startline\ignorespaces\fi}
\def\7{\Y\6} % forced break and a little extra space
\def\8{\unskip} % no indentation--works only in code, not in |...|
\def\startline{\noindent
  \count255=\ind\advance\count255by-2
  \hskip\count255 em}

\let\yskip=\smallskip
\def\note#1#2.{\Y\noindent{\hangindent2em\baselineskip10pt\eightrm#1 #2.\par}}
\def\lapstar{\rlap{*}}
\def\startsection{\Q\noindent{\let\*=\lapstar\bf\modstar.\quad}}
\def\defin#1{\global\advance\ind by 2 \1\&{#1 }} % begin `define' or `format'
\def\A{\note{See also}} % cross-reference for multiply defined section names
\def\B{\mathopen{\.{@\commentbegin}}} % begin controlled comment
\def\C#1{\ifmmode\gdef\XX{\null$\null}\else\gdef\XX{}\fi % C comments
  \XX\hfil\penalty-1\hfilneg\quad
        $\commentbegin\,${#1}$\,\commentend$\XX}
\def\D{\defin{define}} % macro definition
\def\F{\defin{format}} % format definition
\def\J{\.{@\&}} % TANGLE's join operation
\outer\def\M#1 {\MN#1.\ifon\vfil\penalty-100\vfilneg % beginning of section
  \vskip12ptminus3pt\startsection\ignorespaces}
\outer\def\N#1.#2.{\MN#1.\headcheck#2\headcheck
  \edef\rhead{\uppercase{\ignorespaces\themodtitle}} % define running headline
  \message{*\modno} % progress report
  \edef\next{\write\cont{\thetocskip
        \Z{\theopen\relax
                \themodtitle}{\modno}{\the\pageno}}}\next % to contents file
  \ifon\startsection{\bf\ignorespaces\themodtitle.\quad}\ignorespaces}
\def\MN#1.{\par % common code for \M, \N
  {\xdef\modstar{#1}\let\*=\empty\xdef\modno{#1}}
  \ifx\modno\modstar \onmaybe \else \ontrue \fi \mark{\modno}}
\def\O#1{% octal, hex or decimal constant
  {\def\?{\kern.2em}%
  \def\$[{\ell]}% long constant
  \def\_{\cdot 10^{\aftergroup}}% power of ten
  \def\~{\hbox{\rm\char'23\kern-.2em\it\aftergroup\?\aftergroup} }%octal
  \def\^{\hbox{\rm\char"7D\tt\aftergroup}}% double quotes for hex constant
  #1}}
```

```
\def\P{\rightskip=0pt plus 100pt minus 10pt % go into Pascal mode
  \sfcode`;=3000
  \pretolerance 10000
  \hyphenpenalty 10000 \exhyphenpenalty 10000
  \global\ind=2 \1\ \unskip}
\def\Q{\rightskip=0pt % get out of Pascal mode
  \sfcode`;=1500 \pretolerance 200 \hyphenpenalty 50 \exhyphenpenalty 50 }
\def\T{\mathclose{\.{@\commentend}}} % terminate controlled comment
\def\U{\note{This code is used in}} % cross-reference for uses of sections
\def\X#1:#2\X{\ifmmode\gdef\XX{\null$\null}\else\gdef\XX{}\ fi% section name
  \XX$\langle\,$#2{\eightrm\kern.5em#1}$\,\rangle$\XX}
\def\XF#1:#2\XF{\ifmmode\gdef\XX{\null$\null}\else\gdef\XX{}\fi % section name
  \XX{\tt(#2{\eightrm\kern.5em#1})}\XX}
\def\Y{\par\yskip}
\def\){\hbox{\.{@\$}}} % sign for string pool check sum
\def\]{\hbox{\.{@\\}}} % sign for forced line break
\def\=#1{\kern2pt\hbox{\vrule\vtop{\vbox{\hrule
        \hbox{\strut\kern2pt\.{#1}\kern2pt}}
      \hrule}\vrule}\kern2pt} % verbatim string
\let\~=\ignorespaces
\let\*=*


\def\DO{\hbox{\sl\char'044}} % slant dollar sign
\let\G=\ge % greater than or equal sign
\def\H{{\rm\char'136}} % hat
\let\I=\ne % unequal sign
\let\K=\gets % left arrow
\let\L=\le % less than or equal sign
\let\R=\lnot % logical not
\let\S=\equiv % equivalence sign
\let\TI\sim % tilde
\let\V=\lor % logical or
\let\W=\land % logical and
\let\Z=\let % now you can \send the control sequence \Z


\def\onmaybe{\let\ifon=\maybe} \let\maybe=\iftrue
\newif\ifon \newif\iftitle \newif\ifpagesaved
\def\lheader{\mainfont\the\pageno\eightrm\qquad\rhead\hfill\title\qquad
  \tensy x\mainfont\topmark} % top line on left-hand pages
\def\rheader{\tensy x\mainfont\topmark\eightrm\qquad\title\hfill\rhead
  \qquad\mainfont\the\pageno} % top line on right-hand pages
\def\lfooter{\hfil} % bottom line on left-hand-pages
\def\rfooter{\hfil} % bottom line on left-hand-pages
\def\page{\box255 }
\def\normaloutput#1#2#3#4#5{%
%\message{(At start top, first, and bottom marks: \topmark, \firstmark, \botmark
)}%
\shipout\vbox{
  \iftwoside\else\ifodd\pageno\hoffset=\pageshift\fi\fi
  \vbox to\fullpageheight{
     \iftitle
     \else\hbox to\pagewidth{\vbox to10pt{}%
        \ifodd\pageno#3\else
               \iftwoside#2\else#3\fi
        \fi}%
     \fi
     \vfill#1% parameter #1 is the page itself
     \iftitle\global\titlefalse
     \else\baselineskip=24pt\hbox to\pagewidth{\strut % see TeXbook p256
```

```
            \ifodd\pageno#5\else
                    \iftwoside#4\else#5\fi
            \fi}%
        \fi
    }%
}%
\global\advance\pageno by1
%\message{(At end top, first, and bottom marks: \topmark, \firstmark, \botmark)}
%
}


\def\rhead{\.{WEB} OUTPUT} % this running head is reset by starred sections
\def\title{} % an optional title can be set by the user
\def\topofcontents{\centerline{\titlefont\title}
  \vfill} % this material will start the table of contents page
\def\botofcontents{\vfill} % this material will end the table of contents page
\def\contentspagenumber{0} % default page number for table of contents
\newdimen\pagewidth \pagewidth=6.5in % the width of each page
\newdimen\pageheight \pageheight=8.4in % the height of each page
\newdimen\fullpageheight \fullpageheight=9in % page height including
                                        % headlines and footlines
\newdimen\pageshift \pageshift=0in % shift righthand pages wrt lefthand ones
\catcode'\@=11 % make at letter
\def\m@g{\mag=\count@\pagewidth=6.5truein\pageheight=8.4truein
  \fullpageheight=9truein\setpage}
\catcode'\@=12 % make at other
\def\setpage{\hsize\pagewidth\vsize\pageheight} % use after changing page size

\edef\contentsfile{\jobname.toc } % file that gets table of contents info
\def\readcontents{\expandafter\input \contentsfile}

\newwrite\cont
\output{\setbox0=\page % the first page is garbage
  \openout\cont=\contentsfile
  \global\output{\normaloutput\page\lheader\rheader\lfooter\rfooter}}
\setpage
\vbox to \vsize{} % the first \topmark won't be null
\eject
\write\cont{\string\catcode'\string\@=11}% a hack to make contents
                                    % take stuff in \.{---}

\def\ch{\note{The following sections were changed by the change file:}
  \let\*=\relax}
\newbox\sbox % saved box preceding the index
\newbox\lbox % lefthand column in the index
\def\inx{\par\vskip6pt plus 1fil % we are beginning the index
  \write\cont{} % ensure that the contents file isn't empty
  \closeout\cont % the contents information has been fully gathered
  \output{\ifpagesaved\normaloutput{\box\sbox}\lheader\rheader
                \lfooter\rfooter\fi
    \global\setbox\sbox=\page \global\pagesavedtrue}
  \pagesavedfalse \eject % eject the page-so-far and predecessors
  \setbox\sbox\vbox{\unvbox\sbox} % take it out of its box
  \vsize=\pageheight \advance\vsize by -\ht\sbox % the remaining height
  \hsize=.5\pagewidth \advance\hsize by -10pt
    % column width for the index (20pt between cols)
  \parfillskip 0pt plus .6\hsize % try to avoid almost empty lines
  \def\lr{L} % this tells whether the left or right column is next
  \output{\if L\lr\global\setbox\lbox=\page \gdef\lr{R}
    \else\normaloutput{\vbox to\pageheight{\box\sbox\vss
```

```
        \hbox to\pagewidth{\box\lbox\hfil\page}}}\lheader\rheader
        \lfooter\rfooter
    \global\vsize\pageheight\gdef\lr{L}\global\pagesavedfalse\fi}
  \message{Index:}
  \parskip 0pt plus .5pt
  \outer\def\:##1, {\par\hangindent2em\noindent##1:\kern1em} % index entry
  \def\[##1]{$\underline{##1}$} % underlined index item
  \rm \rightskip0pt plus 2.5em \tolerance 10000 \let\*=\lapstar
  \hyphenpenalty 10000 \parindent0pt}
\def\fin{\par\vfill\eject % this is done when we are ending the index
  \ifpagesaved\null\vfill\eject\fi % output a null index column
  \if L\lr\else\null\vfill\eject\fi % finish the current page
  \parfillskip 0pt plus 1fil
  \def\rhead{NAMES OF THE SECTIONS}
  \message{Section names:}
  \output{\normaloutput\page\lheader\rheader\lfooter\rfooter}
  \setpage
  \def\note##1##2.{\quad{\eightrm##1 ##2.}}
  \def\U{\note{Used in}} % cross-reference for uses of sections
  \def\:{\par\hangindent 2em}\let\*=*}
\def\con{\par\vfill\eject % finish the section names
  \rightskip 0pt \hyphenpenalty 50 \tolerance 200
  \setpage
  \output{\normaloutput\page\lheader\rheader\lfooter\rfooter}
  \titletrue % prepare to output the table of contents
  \pageno=\contentspagenumber \def\rhead{TABLE OF CONTENTS}
  \message{Table of contents:}
  \topofcontents
  \line{\hfil Section\hbox to3em{\hss Page}}
  \def\Z##1##2##3{\line{{\ignorespaces##1}
    \leaders\hbox to .5em{.\hfil}\hfil\ ##2\hbox to3em{\hss##3}}}
  \readcontents\relax % read the contents info
  \botofcontents \end} % print the contents page(s) and terminate
%\tracingstats1 % temporary (during development)


\def\vert{|}

%%% this stuff is to allow inital =,1,2,3,4 in starred modules
%%%     = means ''part'', don't skip page
%%%     normal starred module is 0
%%%         1,2,3,4 are submodules, and are indented
%%%
%%%     @*=     bold name in table of contents
%%%             causes page eject
%%%             suppresses page eject following
%%%
%%%     @*1,2   first level of indentation
%%%     @*3,4   second level of indentation
%%%
%%%     @*1,3   cause page eject
%%%     @*2,4   don't cause page eject
%%%


\newif\ifcancel\cancelfalse
\catcode`\@=11
\def\ifnextchar#1#2#3{\let\@tempe=#1\def\@tempa{#2}\def\@tempb{#3}\@ ifnch}
\def\@ifnch{\ifx \@tempc \@tempe\let\@tempd\@tempa\else\let\@tempd\@tempb\fi
     \@tempd}
\def\makethechar#1{\let\@tempc=#1}
```

```
\catcode'\@=12

\def\headcheck#1#2\headcheck{%
        \makethechar{#1}%
        \def\theskipper{\vfil\penalty-100\vfilneg\vskip12ptminus3pt}%
                            % skip before new module
        \def\theopen{}% opening skip in toc entry
        \def\thetocskip{}% vertical skip before toc entry
        \def\themodtitle{{#2}}
        \ifnextchar=[%
                \def\theskipper{\vfil\eject}%
                \canceltrue
                \def\theopen{\bf}%
                \def\thetocskip{\vskip3ptplus1in\penalty-100
                        \vskip0ptplus-1in}%
        }{\ifnextchar1{%
                \cancelfalse
                \def\theskipper{\vfil\eject}%
                \def\theopen{\hskip2em}%
        }{\ifnextchar2{%
                \cancelfalse
                \def\theopen{\hskip2em}%
        }{\ifnextchar3{%
                \cancelfalse
                \def\theskipper{\vfil\eject}%
                \def\theopen{\hskip4em}%
        }{\ifnextchar4{%
                \cancelfalse
                \def\theopen{\hskip4em}%
        }{% else
                \ifcancel\else
                        \def\theskipper{\vfil\eject}%
                \fi
                \cancelfalse
                \def\themodtitle{#1{#2}}%
        }}}}}%
        \theskipper
}


%%%%%%% for verbatim quoting of code
% The following are copied from manmanc.tex and are taken from p421 of
% the TeXbook  ... modified to \verbatim...\endverbatim
% macros for verbatim scanning
\chardef\other=12
\def\ttverbatim{\begingroup
  \catcode'\|=\other
  \catcode'\\=\other
  \catcode'\{=\other
  \catcode'\}=\other
  \catcode'\$=\other
  \catcode'\&=\other
  \catcode'\#=\other
  \catcode'\%=\other
  \catcode'\~=\other
  \catcode'\_=\other
  \catcode'\^=\other
  \obeyspaces \obeylines \tt}
{\obeyspaces\global\let =\ } % from texbook, p 381
```

```
%\outer\def\verbatim{$$\let\par=\endgraf \ttverbatim \parskip=0pt
%  \catcode'\|=0 \rightskip-5pc \ttfinish}
%{\catcode'\|=0 |catcode'|\=\other % | is temporary escape character
%   |obeylines % end of line is active
%   |gdef|ttfinish#1^^M#2\endverbatim{#1|vbox{#2}|endgroup$$}}

\outer\def\verbatimcode{\par\ttverbatim\leftskip=2em\parskip=0pt
  \ttfinishcode}
{\catcode'\|=0 |catcode'|\=\other % | is temporary escape character
  |obeylines % end of line is active
  |gdef|ttfinishcode#1^^M#2\endverbatimcode{#1|vbox{#2}|endgroup}}


% end of manmac stuff
```

End of text file '`webkernel.tex`'

F.1.2   Special Purpose Macro Packages

Double-column Formatting

The following file, `webdoub.tex`, is the source file for the double-column formatting macros.

Contents of text file '`webdoub.tex`':

```
\hsize 84mm

\output{\setbox0=\box255}\eject % get rid of spurious WEBMAC page


\newdimen\pagewidth \newdimen\pageheight \newdimen\ruleht
\hsize=177mm  \vsize=240mm
\parindent=1em % this is needed for WEB output
\pagewidth=\hsize \pageheight=\vsize \ruleht=1pt
\abovedisplayskip=11pt plus 3pt minus 8pt
\abovedisplayshortskip=0pt plus 3pt
\belowdisplayskip=11pt plus 3pt minus 8pt
\belowdisplayshortskip=6pt plus 3pt minus 3pt

\newif\iftitle
\def\titlepage{\global\titletrue} % for pages without headlines

\def\leftheadline{\hbox to \pagewidth{\mainfont\the\pageno\hfill\title}}
\def\rightheadline{\hbox to \pagewidth{\title\hfill\mainfont\the\pageno}}
\hoffset=-.25in \voffset=-.6in
```

```
\newinsert\lefttop \newinsert\righttop
\count\lefttop=1000 \count\righttop=1000
\dimen\lefttop=\maxdimen \dimen\righttop=\maxdimen
\skip\lefttop=25pt plus 3pt minus 3pt
\skip\righttop=\skip\lefttop

\def\onepageout#1{\shipout\vbox{ % here we define one page of output
    \offinterlineskip % butt the boxes together
    \vbox to 9mm{ % this part goes on top of the regular pages
      \iftitle % the next is used for title pages
        \global\titlefalse % reset the titlepage switch
        \hbox to\pagewidth{\leaders\doubrule\hfill}
      \else\ifodd\pageno \rightheadline\else\leftheadline\fi\fi
      \vfill} % this completes the \vbox to 9mm
    \vbox to \pageheight{
      #1 % now insert the main information
      \boxmaxdepth=\maxdepth
      } % this completes the \vbox to \pageheight
    \baselineskip=7mm \lineskiplimit=0pt
    }
  \advancepageno}

\output{\onepageout{\unvbox255}}

\newbox\partialpage

\def\begindoublecolumns{
\output={\global\setbox\partialpage=\vbox{\unvbox255}}\eject
  \output={\doublecolumnout} \hsize=84mm \vsize=510mm}

\def\doublecolumnout{\dimen0=\pageheight
  \advance\dimen0 by-\ht\partialpage \splittopskip=\topskip
  \ifdim\ht\lefttop>0pt \setbox255=\vbox{\unvbox\lefttop
    \setbox0=\lastbox\unvbox0\vskip\skip\lefttop\unvbox255}\fi
  \setbox0=\vsplit255 to\dimen0
  \ifdim\ht\righttop>0pt \setbox255=\vbox{\unvbox\righttop
    \setbox0=\lastbox\unvbox0\vskip\skip\righttop\unvbox255}\fi
  \setbox2=\vsplit255 to\dimen0
  \onepageout\pagesofar
  \unvbox255 \penalty\outputpenalty}
\def\pagesofar{\unvbox\partialpage
  \wd0=\hsize \wd2=\hsize \hbox to\pagewidth{\box0\hfil\box2}}
\def\balancecolumns{\setbox0=\vbox{\unvbox255} \dimen0=\ht0
  \advance\dimen0 by\topskip \advance\dimen0 by-\baselineskip
  \divide\dimen0 by2 \splittopskip=\topskip
  {\vbadness=10000 \loop \global\setbox3=\copy0
    \global\setbox1=\vsplit3 to\dimen0
    \ifdim\ht3>\dimen0 \global\advance\dimen0 by1pt \repeat}
  \setbox0=\vbox to\dimen0{\unvbox1}
  \setbox2=\vbox to\dimen0{\unvbox3}
  \pagesofar}

\def\doubrule{\hrule height\ruleht}
\baselineskip=11pt
\parskip=0pt plus 1pt
\def\dotitle{\goodbreak\vskip9mm plus4mm minus 2mm
  \vbox{\doubrule width \hsize \kern5pt}
  \kern-3pt
  \nointerlineskip
  \leftline{\strut\bf \title}
```

```
\doubrule
\kern12pt\nobreak\noindent\ignorespaces}

\begindoublecolumns

\hyphenchar\tentt=-1 % no hyphenation in the typewriter font

\def\Z#1#2#3{\dotitle\def\dotitle{\null}\line{\ignorespaces#1\ \dotfill\ {\tensy x}#2}}
\def\M#1.{\MN#1.\iftrue\medbreak\startsection\ignorespaces}
\def\firstmod{1}
\def\N#1.#2.{\MN#1.\iftrue\nobreak
  \ifx\modno\firstmod\medskip\else\bigskip\fi
  \message{*\modno} % progress report
  \doubrule\medbreak\startsection
  {\bf\ignorespaces#2.\quad}\ignorespaces}
\def\inx{\par\medbreak
  \def\:##1, {\par\hangindent2em\noindent##1:\kern1em}
  \def\[##1]{$\underline{##1}$}
  \rm \rightskip0pt plus2.5em \tolerance10000 \let\*=\lapstar
  \hyphenpenalty10000 \parindent0pt}
\def\fin{\par\bigskip\doubrule\medbreak
  \parfillskip0pt plus1fil
  \def\note##1##2.{\hfil\penalty-1\hfilneg\quad{\eightrm##1 ##2.}}
  \def\U{\note{Used in}}
  \def\:{\par\hangindent 2em}\let\*=*}
\let\con=\bye
\parskip=0pt
\input contents.tex
```

End of text file 'webdoub.tex'

Regular Pascal Operators

The following file, `regpas.tex`, is the source file for the macros used to restore the regular Pascal operators to a listing.

Contents of text file 'regpas.tex':

```
\def\G{>=} % greater than or equal sign
\def\I{<>} % unequal sign
\def\K{:=} % left arrow
\def\L{<=} % less than or equal sign
\def\R{\mathop{\&{not}}} % logical not
\def\V{\mathbin{\&{or}}} % logical or
\def\W{\mathbin{\&{and}}} % logical and
```

End of text file 'regpas.tex'

TeX File Concatenation

The following files, getstart.tex and passlast.tex, are the source files for the macros used to make it possible to concatenate separate TeX files together.

Contents of text file 'getstart.tex':

```
\newcount\pagecount
\newwrite\cont
\newread\pcount \newcount\pagecount
\def\countfile{\thisfilename.pag}
\openin\pcount=\countfile
\read\pcount to\pagecount
\closein\pcount
\pageno=\pagecount \advance\pageno by 1
```

End of text file 'getstart.tex'

Contents of text file 'passlast.tex':

```
\def\pagecountfile{\nextfilename.pag}
\def\contentsfile{\thisfilename.con}
\countdef\temppageno=0
\newwrite\pfile
\def\con{\par
  \temppageno=\pageno
  \advance\temppageno by 1
  \openout\pfile=\pagecountfile
  \write\pfile{\the\temppageno}
  \closeout\pfile % the pagecount information has been fully gathered
  \vfill\eject % finish the section names
  \end} % terminate
```

End of text file 'passlast.tex'

F.2   Change Files

F.2.1   Changes to TANGLE

Implementation Change File

Contents of text file 'tangle.wiz':

```
@x [limbo]
\def\title{TANGLE}
@y
\def\title{TANGLE for the Whiz-Bang 5000}
@z


@x [1]
This program converts a \.{WEB} file to a \PASCAL\ file. It was written
by D. E. Knuth in September, 1981; a somewhat similar {\mc SAIL} program had
been developed in March, 1979. Since this program describes itself, a
bootstrapping process involving hand-translation had to be used to get started.
@y
This program converts a \.{WEB} file to a \PASCAL\ file. It is a modified form
of a program written by D. E. Knuth in September, 1981.
@z


@x [1]
@d banner=='This is TANGLE, Version 3'
@y
We add a second decimal point and number to the main version number,
so we can differentiate between changes to the standard \.{TANGLE}\
and changes local to the version for the hypothetical Whiz-Bang 5000
super-mini-micro-hyper-maxi-omni-computer.
@d banner=='This is TANGLE, Whiz-Bang 5000 Version 3.0.0'
@z


@x [2] part 1
calls the '|jump_out|' procedure, which goes to the label |end_of_TANGLE|.

@d end_of_TANGLE = 9999 {go here to wrap it up}

@p @t\4@>@<Compiler directives@>@/
program TANGLE(@!web_file,@!change_file,@!Pascal_file,@!pool);
label end_of_TANGLE; {go here to finish}
@y
calls the '|jump_out|' procedure, which aborts the program.

@p @t\4@>@<Compiler directives@>@/
program TANGLE;
@z


@x [2] part 2
@<Error handling procedures@>@/
@y
@<Whiz-Bang 5000 procedures@>@/
@<Error handling procedures@>@/
@z
```

```
@x [3]
@d stat==@{ {change this to '$\\{stat}\equiv\null$'
  when gathering usage statistics}
@d tats==@t@>@} {change this to '$\\{tats}\equiv\null$'
  when gathering usage statistics}
@y
@d stat== {change this to '$\\{stat}\equiv\null$'
  when gathering usage statistics}
@d tats== {change this to '$\\{tats}\equiv\null$'
  when gathering usage statistics}
@z

@x [7]
@d othercases == others: {default for cases not listed explicitly}
@y
@d othercases == otherwise {default for cases not listed explicitly}
@z

@x [12]
@d last_text_char=127 {ordinal number of the largest element of |text_char|}

@<Types...@>=
@!text_file=packed file of text_char;
@y
@d last_text_char=127 {ordinal number of the largest element of |text_char|}

@d text_file==text
@z

@x [21] part 1
on the \PASCAL\ system that was used in \.{TANGLE}'s initial development:
@y
when using Whiz-Bang Pascal:
@z

@x [21] part 2
rewrite(term_out,'TTY:'); {send |term_out| output to the terminal}
@y
assign(term_out,'console_dev');
rewrite(term_out); {send |term_out| output to the terminal}
@z

@x [22]
actually left the computer's internal buffers and been sent.
@^system dependencies@>

@d update_terminal == break(term_out) {empty the terminal output buffer}
@y
actually left the computer's internal buffers and been sent. The Whiz-Bang
always updates the terminal, so we will make the procedure null.
@^system dependencies@>

@d update_terminal ==
@z

@x [26]
@ The following code opens |Pascal_file| and |pool|.
Since these files were listed in the program header, we assume that the
\PASCAL\ runtime system has checked that suitable external file names have
```

```
been given.
@^system dependencies@>

@<Set init...@>=
rewrite(Pascal_file); rewrite(pool);
@y
@ The following code opens |Pascal_file| and |pool|.
@^system dependencies@>

@<Set init...@>=
@<Set up all of the files, both input and output@>;
rewrite(Pascal_file); rewrite(pool);
@z

@x [28]
var final_limit:0..buf_size; {|limit| without trailing blanks}
begin limit:=0; final_limit:=0;
if eof(f) then input_ln:=false
else  begin while not eoln(f) do
    begin buffer[limit]:=xord[f^]; get(f);
    incr(limit);
    if buffer[limit-1]<>" " then final_limit:=limit;
    if limit=buf_size then
      begin while not eoln(f) do get(f);
      decr(limit); {keep |buffer[buf_size]| empty}
      if final_limit>limit then final_limit:=limit;
      print_nl('! Input line too long'); loc:=0; error;
@.Input line too long@>
      end;
    end;
  read_ln(f); limit:=final_limit; input_ln:=true;
  end;
end;
@y
label done;
var @!temp_buf:string[buf_size]; {intermediate input buffer}
  k:0..buf_size; {index into |buffer|}
begin limit:=0;
if eof(f) then input_ln:=false
else
  begin read_ln(f,temp_buf); limit:=length(temp_buf);
  if limit>=buf_size then
    begin print_nl('! Input line too long'); loc:=0; error;
@.Input line too long@>
    limit:=buf_size-1;
    end;
  for k:=1 to limit do buffer[k-1]:=xord[temp_buf[k]];
  while limit>1 do if buffer[limit-1]=" " then decr(limit) @+else goto done;
done:
  input_ln:=true;
  end;
end;
@z


@x [30] part 1
that terminates the program.
@y
that terminates the program. This is the case with the Whiz-Bang.
@z
```

```
@x [30] part 2
begin goto end_of_TANGLE;
end;
@y
begin
stat @<Print statistics about memory usage@>;@+tats@;@/
@<Close the files since the Whiz-Bang 5000 requires it@>;
@<Print the job |history|@>;
halt(history);
end;
@z
```

```
@x [97] part 1
@d check_break==if out_ptr>line_length then flush_buffer
@y
```

The Whiz-Bang 5000 allows us to use a '|string|' to write an entire line
at once, rather than character by character. The maximum size of the string is
fixed, but the current size is dynamic and can be set by
accessing |temp_buf.length|, a simulated field within the string data type.

```
@d check_break==if out_ptr>line_length then flush_buffer
@z
```

```
@x [97] part 2
@!b:0..out_buf_size; {value of |break_ptr| upon entry}
@y
@!b:0..out_buf_size; {value of |break_ptr| upon entry}
@!temp_buf:string[out_buf_size]; {intermediate input buffer}
@z
```

```
@x [97] part 3
for k:=1 to break_ptr do write(Pascal_file,xchr[out_buf[k-1]]);
write_ln(Pascal_file); incr(line);
@y
for k:=1 to break_ptr do temp_buf[k]:=xchr[out_buf[k-1]];
temp_buf.length := break_ptr;
write_ln(Pascal_file,temp_buf); incr(line);
@z
```

```
@x [180]
reset(term_in,'TTY:','/I'); {open |term_in| as the terminal, don't do a |get|}
@y
assign(term_in,'console_dev');
reset(term_in); {open |term_in| as the terminal}
@z
```

```
@x [182]  part 1
end_of_TANGLE:
@y
@z
```

```
@x [182]  part 2
@t\4\4@>{here files should be closed if the operating system requires it}
@<Print the job |history|@>;
end.
@y
@<Close the files since the Whiz-Bang 5000 requires it@>;
```

```
@<Print the job |history|@>;
halt(history);
end.
@z

@x [188]
This module should be replaced, if necessary, by changes to the program
that are necessary to make \.{TANGLE} work at a particular installation.
It is usually best to design your change file so that all changes to
previous modules preserve the module numbering; then everybody's version
will be consistent with the printed program. More extensive changes,
which introduce new modules, can be inserted here; then only the index
itself will get a new module number.
@y
Here will be the changes to the program
that are necessary to make \.{TANGLE} work with the Whiz-Bang 5000.
@^system dependencies@>
@<Types...@>=
@!str255=string[255]; {long string type}

@ The Whiz-Bang 5000 doesn't automatically close files, so we have to close them
manually to keep the output files from being truncated.
@<Close the files since the Whiz-Bang 5000 requires it@>=
close(web_file);
close(change_file);
close(Pascal_file);
close(pool);

@ This procedure appends a default file extension to a file name.
We determine the file name based on the default extension, the base
file name, and whatever was input on the command line. The |main| flag
indiciates that this is the base file name that the others are derived
from.
@^system dependencies@>
@<Whiz-Bang 5000 procedures@>=
procedure setup_text_file(var @!the_file : text_file; @!def_ext :str255;
        @!descr_str : str255; @!main : boolean); extern;
@ @<Set up all of the files, both input and output@>=
setup_text_file(web_file,'web','web',true);
setup_text_file(change_file,'ch','change',false);
setup_text_file(Pascal_file,'pas','Pascal',false);
setup_text_file(pool,'pol','string pool',false);
@z
```

End of text file 'tangle.wiz'

New Lines in Pascal Output

Contents of text file 'pasforce.ch':

```
@x [165]
@!b:ASCII_code; {a character from the buffer}
@!bal:eight_bits; {left parentheses minus right parentheses}
begin bal:=0;
loop@+  begin continue: a:=get_next;
@y
@!b:ASCII_code; {a character from the buffer}
@!bal:eight_bits; {left parentheses minus right parentheses}
@!saved_line: integer;
@!saved_ch_flag: boolean;
begin bal:=0;
saved_line := -1;
loop@+  begin continue: a:=get_next;
if ((saved_line <> line) or (saved_ch_flag <> changing) ) and (t = module_name) then
    begin
    saved_ch_flag := changing;
    saved_line := line; app_repl(force_line);
    end;
@z
```

End of text file 'pasforce.ch'

New Lines plus Line Numbers

Contents of text file 'paslines.ch':

```
@x [1]
This program converts a \.{WEB} file to a \PASCAL\ file. It was written
by D. E. Knuth in September, 1981; a somewhat similar {\mc SAIL} program had
been developed in March, 1979. Since this program describes itself, a
bootstrapping process involving hand-translation had to be used to get started.
@y
This program converts a \.{WEB} file to a \PASCAL\ file. It is a modified form
of a program written by D. E. Knuth in September, 1981.
@z

@x [1]
@d banner=='This is TANGLE, Version 3'
@y
@d banner=='This is TANGLE, Line Numbers Version 3'
@z

@x [122]
  flush_buffer;
  end;
out_state:=misc;
@y
  flush_buffer;
```

```
   end;
if (tok_mem[zo,cur_byte] <> 0) or (tok_mem[zo,cur_byte+1] <> 0) then begin
   n := tok_mem[zo,cur_byte] ;
   if brace_level=0 then send_out(misc,"{")
   else send_out(misc,"[");
   if n>=@"80 then
      begin
      send_out(misc,"C"); n := (n - @"80) ;
      end
   else send_out(misc,"W");
   n := n * @"100 + tok_mem[zo,cur_byte+1] ;
   send_val(n);
   if brace_level=0 then send_out(misc,"}")
   end;
cur_byte := cur_byte + 2;
out_state:=misc;
@z

@x [165]
@!b:ASCII_code; {a character from the buffer}
@!bal:eight_bits; {left parentheses minus right parentheses}
begin bal:=0;
loop@+  begin continue: a:=get_next;
   case a of
@y
@!b:ASCII_code; {a character from the buffer}
@!bal:eight_bits; {left parentheses minus right parentheses}
@!saved_line: integer;
@!saved_ch_flag: boolean;
begin bal:=0;
saved_line := -1;
loop@+  begin continue: a:=get_next;
if ((saved_line <> line) or (saved_ch_flag <> changing) ) and (t = module_name) then
    begin
    saved_ch_flag := changing;
    saved_line := line; app_repl(force_line);
    if changing then app_repl((line div @"100)+@"80)
    else app_repl(line div @"100);
    app_repl(line mod @"100);
    end;
   case a of
   force_line:
      begin
      app_repl(force_line);
      app_repl(0);
      a := 0;
      end;
@z
```

End of text file 'paslines.ch'

Upgrade of TANGLE from 2.8 to 2.9

Contents of text file 'forward.ch':

```
@x [limbo]
% Version 2.8 fixed a bug in change_buffer movement (August, 1985).
@y
% Version 2.8 fixed a bug in change_buffer movement (August, 1985).
% Version 2.9 allows nonnumeric macros before their definition (December, 1988).
@z

@x [limbo]
  \centerline{(Version 2.8)}
@y
  \centerline{(Version 2.9)}
@z

@x [1]
@d banner=='This is TANGLE, Version 2.8'
@y
@d banner=='This is TANGLE, Version 2.9'
@z

@x [57]
if p<>name_ptr then @<Give double-definition error and change |p| to type |t|@>
@y
if p<>name_ptr then @<Give double-definition error, if necessary, and
      change |p| to type |t|@>
@z

@x [59] part 1
@ If a macro has appeared before it was defined, \.{TANGLE} will
@y
@ If a nonnumeric macro has appeared before it was defined, \.{TANGLE} will
@z

@x [59] part 2
so \.{TANGLE} finds it simplest to make a blanket rule that macros should
@y
so \.{TANGLE} finds it simplest to make a blanket rule that numeric macros should
@z

@x [59] part 3
  begin err_print('! This identifier has already appeared');
@y
  begin
    if t = numeric then
      err_print('! This identifier has already appeared');
@z
```

End of text file 'forward.ch'

F.3 Files Related to Knight's Tour

F.3.1 WEB Source File

Contents of text file 'knights.web':

```
% limbo material
\def\WEB{{\tt WEB}}
\def\title{The Knight's Tour}
\def\9#1{} % this is used for sort keys in the index via @@:sort key}{entry@@>

% Note: the following commands set up the page dimensions for the
%    WEB book.  To use a regular 8 1/2 by 11 page they can be removed,
%    but be aware that some bad line breaks will occur.  The program
%    text is adjusted to the funny dimensions below and will need a little
%    fiddling to be printed on a regular page.

\newdimen\pagewidth \pagewidth=5.5in % the width of each page
\newdimen\pageheight \pageheight=7.625in % the height of each page
\newdimen\fullpageheight \fullpageheight=7.925in
\newdimen\pageshift \pageshift=.5in % shift righthand pages wrt lefthand ones
\setpage


%\def\append{G}

\def\smalline{height2pt&\omit&&&&&&&&\cr}
\def\hrline{\multispan{11}\hrulefill\cr}

@* Introduction.
The following program is based on the ``Knight's Tour'' algorithm
@^Knight's Tour@>
found on pages 137--142 of Niklaus Wirth's {\sl Algorithms + Data
@^Wirth, Niklaus@>
Structures = Programs}
(pages 148--152 in the 1986 edition, renamed {\sl Algorithms and Data
Structures}),
translated into the \WEB\ language. @.WEB@>


@ This program has no input, because we want to keep it rather simple.
The result of the program will be the solution to the
problem, which will be written to the |output| file.

In true top-down tradition, we lay out the entire program as
a skeleton which will be filled in later.

@p
program knights_tour(@!output);
const @<Constants of the program@>@;
type @<Types of the program@>@;
```

```
var @<Variables of the program@>@;@/
@<Recursive procedure definitions@>
begin @/
@<Initialize the data structures@>;
@<Perform the Knight's Tour and print the results@>;
end.
```

@ Here are some macros for common programming idioms.

```
@d incr(#) == #:=#+1 {increase a variable by unity}
@d decr(#) == #:=#-1 {decrease a variable by unity}
```

@ We shall proceed to build the program in pieces, following the text of
Wirth's book and describing the structures and algorithms in more or less the same
order in which he describes them. Part of the time we will be designing
top-down; at other times, bottom-up; but always in the order that contributes
more to the understanding of the program. One difference between this
description and Wirth's is that we will use meaningful variable names (rather
than names such as |u,v,a,b,c|). We can get away with this
because we don't have to worry about the entire program's being listed in one
place in narrow columns. It is broken up into small pieces and
spread over several pages.

@* The Tour.
@!@^Knight's Tour@>
For those not familiar with the Knight's Tour, it is a classic computer science
problem involving a knight, moving according to the rules of chess, which
attempts to move to every square of a chessboard once and
only once.
To implement it, we use what is known as a ``backtracking'' algorithm,
@!@^backtracking algorithm@>
which is a trial-and-error search for a solution, sometimes referred to as a
``brute force'' approach. We start at a beginning position and try every path
leading from that position (there are 8 possible knight moves from a given
position) and then every path from each of those positions, etc. We follow
every path until either a complete solution is found or the first failure occurs
(the square is not on the board or has already been visited). If we
get a failure, we ``backtrack'' to the previous good move and start again from
there.
```

@ The board is a $max \times max$ square and the
number of squares is $|max|^2$.
Since this program has no input, we declare the value |max=5| as a compile-time
constant.

```
@<Constants of the program@>=
@!max = 5;
@!number_of_squares = 25;
```

@ The obvious way to define the board is
as a array of two dimensions where the indexes range from 1 to |max|.

```
@<Types of the program@>=
@!index = 1..max ;
```

@ Boolean values for the squares would be sufficient if we only wanted to know
which squares had been visited, but we also wish to know the {\it order} of
the visits, so we define |board| as a two-dimensional array of
ordinal values ranging from 0 to |number_of_squares|.
If the value at |board[row,col]=0|
then the square at that position has not been visited and
is a candidate for a visit. Otherwise |board[row,col]=i|, which indicates
that the square was visited on the |i|th move. The total number of moves
(including the first one) |=number_of_squares|.

```
@d empty=0
@<Variables of the program@>=
```
```

```
@!board : array [index,index] of empty .. number_of_squares;
@ Here we initialize all positions on the board to |empty|.
This code is placed in a
program scrap separate from all of the other initialization code
for reasons explained later.
@<Initialize the Knight's Tour board@>=
for i := 1 to max do
  for j := 1 to max do
    board[i,j] := empty ;
@ Two local variables, |targ_row| and |targ_col|, are the
coordinates of |target_square|, the one to which we wish to move next.
Before we attempt the move, we must first ensure that
|target_square| is on the board (|1<=targ_row<=max| and
|1<=targ_col<=max|). Then we must determine whether it is available
for knight placement (|target_square=empty|).
We provide some macros for manipulation
of |target_square|.

Side note: in Wirth's  book,
the |target_position_valid| test is later changed to be a check
for inclusion in the set |[1..max]| rather than discrete comparisons to 1 and
|max|. While this is more efficient, it does not necessarily aid understanding
of the algorithm, so we will not bother.
@d valid_row_or_column(#)== @|
( (1 <= #) and (# <= max) )
@d target_position_valid== @|
(valid_row_or_column(targ_row) and @|
valid_row_or_column(targ_col) )
@d target_square==board[targ_row,targ_col]
@d target_empty== @| (target_square = empty)
@d set_square_to(#)== @| target_square := #
@<Local variables of the Knight's Tour procedure@>=
@!targ_row,@!targ_col : integer ; {row and column of target square}
@ There are 8 possible knight moves from any given position.
Since we normally are going to attempt all 8, we will
define |candidate_move| to hold the move index.
@d number_of_legal_knight_moves=8
@<Local variables of the Knight's Tour procedure@>=
@!candidate_move : 0..number_of_legal_knight_moves ;

@ We are ready to define the procedure which actually does the search.
It must be declared as a procedure rather than as simple inline code, since it
is recursive. As the procedure is entered for a particular move number and
current position, the moves possible from that position are attempted.
The Boolean result |successful| is set if one of the 8 paths results
in a solution.
The procedure passes the value of |successful| back to
the calling procedure, which will pass it to its own caller, etc., all the
way back up to the original call.
@<Recursive procedure definitions@>=
procedure try_knight_move(@!move_number:integer ;
                @!row,@!col:index ;
                var successful:Boolean) ;

var @<Local variables of the Knight's Tour procedure@>

begin
@<Try the moves possible from the current position until solution is found
or all have been tried@>;
end ;
@ Each of the 8 possible moves is attempted.
```

If the move can be made, it is recorded and a
move from the new position is attempted.
If |successful| is ever |true|,
it can only mean that a complete solution has
been found and the search is terminated.
If |successful| is false, the remaining
candidate moves are tried.

```
@d no_more_candidates== @|
(candidate_move = number_of_legal_knight_moves)

@<Try the moves...@>=
candidate_move := 0 ;
repeat
  incr(candidate_move) ;
  successful := false ;
  @<Set the coordinates of the next move as defined
        by the rules of chess@>;
  @<Record the move if acceptable and try to make
       further moves; set |successful| if
       solution is found@>;
until successful or no_more_candidates ;
```

@ The condition \\{move_is_acceptable} is equivalent to the combination
of the conditions |(target_position_valid and target_empty)|.
Because of the realities of computer memory addressing, if
we find that the condition |target_position_valid|
is not |true|, then we cannot perform the second test because
the array indexes |targ_row| or |targ_col| are not valid and
the contents of |target_square| cannot be accessed.
We have to test these two conditions with separate nested |if| statements
(''|if target_position_valid then if target_empty then|'').
In the future, when the ANSI Extended Pascal Standard is adopted, its
short-circuiting \&{and_then} operator will make this unnecessary, but we have
to handle it manually in the meantime.

Once we have determined that the move is acceptable we record it. If
|board_not_full| is true, we try the next knight move.
If |board_not_full| is false (i.e., the board {\it is} full),
it means we have found a solution to the
problem, so we set |successful| to true, which will terminate the tour.

```
@d board_not_full==@|
move_number < number_of_squares
@d record_move== @| set_square_to(move_number)
@<Record the move if...@>=
if target_position_valid then
  if target_empty then
   begin
   record_move ;
   if board_not_full then @|
       @<Try further knight moves and erase this move if not successful@>
   else
       successful := true;

   end;
```

@ Here we try the next move by having the procedure call itself recursively,
with the |move_number| incremented by one and
|targ_row,targ_col| as the position of the move.
If a failure occurs on that move or any move that follows it
(|successful=false|), we erase the move we just made (this is the
''backtracking'' part) and continue looking.

```
@^backtracking algorithm@>
```

Important note: the |begin| and
|end| statements are {\it critical} for this particular section, since it
is used as a |then| clause in the previous section
and the program text is simply inserted verbatim.
Without the |begin| and |end| the call to the |try_knight_move| procedure
alone becomes
the |then| clause, which will cause a syntax error when the dangling
|else| clause is processed.
```
@d next_move==move_number + 1
@d erase_move==set_square_to(empty)
@<Try further...@>=
begin
try_knight_move(next_move,targ_row,targ_col,successful) ;
if not successful then
     erase_move;
end
@ We now consider the moves
```
a knight is allowed to make. From any given
position there are 8 possible moves, not all of which are necessarily on
the board. A knight makes a two-part L-shaped move, where the first part
is either one or two squares in a nondiagonal direction, and the second
part is one or two squares in a direction perpendicular to the first.
The number of squares
is never the same for the two parts; if the knight is moved one square during
the first part, then it is moved two squares during the second, and vice versa.

```
$$\vbox{
\offinterlineskip
\halign{ \vrule # & \strut\  # \  & \vrule # & \  # \  &
     \vrule # & \  # & \vrule # & \  # & \vrule # & \  # & \vrule # \cr
\hrline\smalline
&&&  $\odot$ && $\Longleftrightarrow$   && $\odot$ &&& \cr
\smalline\hrline\smalline
& $\odot$  &&&& $\Uparrow$   &&&& $\odot$ & \cr
\smalline\hrline\smalline
& $\Updownarrow$  && $\Leftarrow$  && $\spadesuit$ &&
      $\Rightarrow$    && $\Updownarrow$   & \cr
\smalline\hrline\smalline
& $\odot$ &&&& $\Downarrow$   &&&& $\odot$ & \cr
\smalline\hrline\smalline
&&& $\odot$ &&  $\Longleftrightarrow$ && $\odot$ &&& \cr
\smalline\hrline
}}$$
```

The '$\spadesuit$' represents a knight. Doesn't it sort
of look like one? (You have to use some imagination. Okay, a {\it lot}
of imagination.) The '$\odot$' characters represent the legal
destinations from the current position.

@ Rather than go through a complicated algorithm, we simply
initialize a pair of tables, |row_deltas| and |col_deltas|, containing
values to be added to the current position to get the target position.
For each of the 8 moves which are possible from the current position,
|row_deltas[candidate_move]| is added to the current row to get |targ_row| and
|col_deltas[candidate_move]| provides the same service for |targ_col|.
```
@<Set the coordinates of the next move as defined by the rules of chess@>=
targ_row := row + row_deltas[candidate_move] ;
targ_col := col + col_deltas[candidate_move] ;
```

@ If we are going to use these arrays, it might be helpful to define them
to prevent the Pascal compiler from complaining bitterly.
@<Variables of the program@>=
@!row_deltas,@!col_deltas : @|
array @| [1..number_of_legal_knight_moves] @| of @| -2..2 ;
@ Even though the compiler is now happy, if we don't initialize the arrays with
the proper delta values, we will take the knight on a route more like the
Drunkard's Walk than the Knight's Tour.
@^Drunkard's Walk@>
@^Knight's Tour@>
@<Initialize the data structures@>=
```
    row_deltas[1] := 2 ;    col_deltas[1] := 1 ;@|
    row_deltas[2] := 1 ;    col_deltas[2] := 2 ;@|
    row_deltas[3] := - 1 ;  col_deltas[3] := 2 ;@|
    row_deltas[4] := - 2 ;  col_deltas[4] := 1 ;@|
    row_deltas[5] := - 2 ;  col_deltas[5] := - 1 ;@|
    row_deltas[6] := - 1 ;  col_deltas[6] := - 2 ;@|
    row_deltas[7] := 1 ;    col_deltas[7] := - 2 ;@|
    row_deltas[8] := 2 ;    col_deltas[8] := - 1 ;
```
@ Now it's time to start the tour. For starting position $x_{0}y_{0}$
@^Knight's Tour@>
we select (1,1). Since this is the first move, we set |board[1,1]=1|. We
then call the |try_knight_move| procedure
with the proper parameters for move 2 to set events in
motion. After all of the moves have been completed, we print out the board.
The result should be the same as the first part of Table 3.1 on page 141
(page 151, 1986 edition) of
Wirth's book, which is reproduced here.

```
$$\vbox{
\offinterlineskip
\halign{ \vrule # & \strut\ # \ & \vrule # & \ # \ &
    \vrule # & \ # & \vrule # & \ # & \vrule # & \ # & \vrule # \cr
\hrline\smalline
& 1  && 6  && 15 && 10 && 21 & \cr
\smalline\hrline\smalline
& 14 && 9  && 20 && 5  && 16 & \cr
\smalline\hrline\smalline
& 19 && 2  && 7  && 22 && 11 & \cr
\smalline\hrline\smalline
& 8  && 13 && 24 && 17 && 4  & \cr
\smalline\hrline\smalline
& 25 && 18 && 3  && 12 && 23 & \cr
\smalline\hrline
}}$$
```

@ We define a macro to initialize the first move and start the tour.
Note: the call to |try_knight_move| in the definition
of |do_the_tour_starting_at| appears to have
the wrong number of parameters. This procedure requires four parameters and
we seem to be passing only three. However, since a macro parameter is really
just a simple string substitution, we will really be replacing the \#
character with two parameters at once: the row and column of the starting
position. Since the comma is included in the substitution, the expanded text
will have the proper four parameters.
@d do_the_tour_starting_at(#)==board[#] := 1 ;try_knight_move(2,#,successful) ;
@<Perform the Knight's Tour and print the results@>=
@<Initialize the Knight's Tour board@>,
do_the_tour_starting_at(1,1) ;
@<Print the results of the Knight's Tour@>;

@ Since Table 3.1 in the book shows a second solution obtained with
a different first move (3,3),

```
$$\vbox{
\offinterlineskip
\halign{ \vrule # & \strut\  # \   & \vrule # & \  # \   &
      \vrule # & \   # & \vrule # & \   # & \vrule # & \   # & \vrule # \cr
\hrline\smalline
& 23  && 10 && 15 &&  4 && 25 & \cr
\smalline\hrline\smalline
& 16  &&  5 && 24 &&  9 && 14   & \cr
\smalline\hrline\smalline
& 11  && 22 &&  1 && 18 &&  3   & \cr
\smalline\hrline\smalline
& 6   && 17 && 20 && 13 &&  8 & \cr
\smalline\hrline\smalline
& 21  && 12 &&  7 &&  2 && 19 & \cr
\smalline\hrline
}}$$
```

\noindent we decide to run the tour
again to duplicate that result as well. We decline the third test in
Table 3.1, because it requires a different value of |max|, which we cannot
change at run-time as the program is currently designed.
Before rerunning the test, we must remember to
reinitialize the board. This is the reason that the board initialization
code was separated from all of the other initializations; it is executed more
than once.
We use the same name when defining
the code for this section as for the previous section,
which will cause the second test to follow
immediately after the first in the Pascal program.
@^Knight's Tour@>
@<Perform the Knight's Tour and print the results@>=
@<Initialize the Knight's Tour board@>;
do_the_tour_starting_at(3,3) ;
@<Print the results of the Knight's Tour@>;
@ The 1986 edition shows yet another solution, with (2,4) as the
starting move.

```
$$\vbox{
\offinterlineskip
\halign{ \vrule # & \strut\  # \   & \vrule # & \  # \   &
      \vrule # & \   # & \vrule # & \   # & \vrule # & \   # & \vrule # \cr
\hrline\smalline
& 23  && 4  && 9  && 14 && 25 & \cr
\smalline\hrline\smalline
& 10  && 15 && 24 &&  1 && 8    & \cr
\smalline\hrline\smalline
& 5   && 22 &&  3 && 18 && 13   & \cr
\smalline\hrline\smalline
& 16  && 11 && 20 && 7  &&  2 & \cr
\smalline\hrline\smalline
& 21  && 6  && 17 && 12 && 19 & \cr
\smalline\hrline
}}$$
```

@<Perform the Knight's Tour and print the results@>=
@<Initialize the Knight's Tour board@>;
do_the_tour_starting_at(2,4) ;

```
@<Print the results of the Knight's Tour@>;
@* The output phase.
The job of printing is not as interesting as the problem itself, but it must be
done sooner or later, so we may as well get it over with.


@ In order to keep this program reasonably free of notations that
are uniquely Pascalesque, a few macro definitions for low-level output
instructions are introduced here. All of the output-oriented commands
in the remainder of the program will be stated in terms of three
simple primitives called |new_line|, |print_string|, and
|print_integer|.
@^system dependencies@>

@d width=3 {width of an integer field}
@d print_string(#)==write(#) {put a given string into the |output| file}
@d print_integer(#)==write(#:width) {print an integer of |width| character
    positions }
@d new_line==write_ln {advance to a new line in the |output| file}


@ @<Print the results of the Knight's Tour@>=
if successful then
    for i := 1 to max do
        begin @/
          for j := 1 to max do
            print_integer(board[i,j]) ;
          new_line;
        end
else
    print_string('no solution') ;
@.no solution@>
new_line;
new_line;
@ We define a few more odd variables.
@<Variables of the program@>=
@!i,@!j : index ; {temporary index variables}
@!successful : Boolean ; {The Knight's Tour was successful }
@* A little math.
Just as the movies have gratuitous sex and violence, this program has
gratuitous mathematics. The following sections in this group have
nothing to do with the program and are here only to illustrate the
power of \TeX\ in typesetting mathematics. (This is an example, after all!)
Since the problem of the Knight's Tour is more logical than
mathematical, there was no need to tap the power of \TeX\ math.
Warning: the following formulas were lifted from several documents and are
out of context, so they may or may not make sense.
(They sure look nice, though.)

@ If this program had been mathematical in nature, we could have displayed
the formula in its true form:

$$\eqalign{\sin[(2n+1)\theta]&=\Im(e^{(2n+1)i\theta})\cr
  &=\Im\{[\cos(\theta) + i \sin(\theta)]^{2n+1}\}\cr
  &=\sum_{k=0}^n(-1)^k{{2n+1}\choose{2k+1}}\sin^{2k+1} (\theta)\cos^{2(n-k)}
(\theta)\cr
  &=\Bigl[\sum_{k=0}^n (-1)^k{{2n+1}\choose{2k+1}}\cot^{2(n-k)}(\theta)
\Bigr]\Bigl[\sin^{2n+1}(\theta)\Bigr]\cr}$$

\noindent rather than some line-printer approximation of it.
@ Since $\sin({{k\pi}\over{2n+1}})\neq 0$ for $k=1,\dots,n$, the roots of
```

```
$p(x)=\sum_{k=0}^n{{2n+1}\choose{2k+1}} (-1)^kx^{n-k}$ are exactly $\cot^2(
\theta_k)$.

@ Matrices are fun (and good for you, too).
$$A=\pmatrix{a_{11}&a_{12}&\ldots&a_{1n}\cr
             a_{21}&a_{22}&\ldots&a_{2n}\cr
             \vdots&\vdots&\ddots&\vdots\cr
             a_{m1}&a_{m2}&\ldots&a_{mn}\cr}$$

@ I have heard that the risk-adjusted
 present discount value of firm $j$ in period $t, MV_{j,t}$ is given by
\def\one{\sum_{r=0}^\infty{\displaystyle{E(\hbox{\it cash payout})_{t+\tau}}
\over{\displaystyle{(1+R_f)^{r}}}}}
\def\two{{\beta_{j}}{\sum_{r=0}^\infty{{\displaystyle {K_{j,t+\tau}}\three}\over{\four}}}}
\def\three{\Big({{\displaystyle{1-\delta^{2r}}}\over{\displaysty le{1-\delta^{2}}
}}\Big)^{1/2}}
\def\four{\displaystyle{(1+R_{f})^{r}}}
$$MV_{j,t}={\one} - {\theta}{\two} $$
where $R_f$ is the (assumed constant) risk-free discount rate and $\theta$ is
the price of risk $\gamma$ multiplied by $\sigma(\varepsilon_{mt})$.

@ Dividing both sides of equation 4 by the expected value of future cash flows
allows $Z$ for each firm to be calculated as a function of $R_f$ and $\theta$:
$$\eqalign {Z_{j,t}(R_{f},\theta) &\equiv  {{MV_{j,t}}\over {\one}}\cr
&= 1 - \theta{ {\two} \over{\one}}\cr} $$
I think that's wonderful.

@ Finally we have
$$e^x=\int_{-\infty}^x\sum_{n=0}^\infty {\lambda^n\over n!}d\lambda$$



@* Index.
Every identifier used in this program is shown here together with a list
of the section numbers where that identifier appears. The section number
is underlined if the identifier was defined in that section. However,
one-letter identifiers are indexed only at their point of definition,
since such identifiers tend to appear almost everywhere.

This index also refers to other topics that appear in the documentation
(e.g., 'backtracking algorithm').
```

End of text file 'knights.web'

F.3.2   Pascal File Generated by TANGLE

Contents of text file 'knights.pas':

```
{2:}PROGRAM KNIGHTSTOUR(OUTPUT);CONST{6:}MAX=5;NUMBEROFSQUA=25;{:6}
TYPE{7:}INDEX=1..MAX;{:7}VAR{8:}
```

```
BOARD:ARRAY[INDEX,INDEX]OF 0..NUMBEROFSQUA;{:8}{18:}
ROWDELTAS,COLDELTAS:ARRAY[1..8]OF-2..2;{:18}{27:}I,J:INDEX;
SUCCESSFUL:BOOLEAN;{:27}{12:}PROCEDURE TRYKNIGHTMOV(MOVENUMBER:INTEGER;
ROW,COL:INDEX;VAR SUCCESSFUL:BOOLEAN);VAR{10:}TARGROW,TARGCOL:INTEGER;
{:10}{11:}CANDIDATEMOV:0..8;{:11}BEGIN{13:}CANDIDATEMOV:=0;
REPEAT CANDIDATEMOV:=CANDIDATEMOV+1;SUCCESSFUL:=FALSE;{17:}
TARGROW:=ROW+ROWDELTAS[CANDIDATEMOV];
TARGCOL:=COL+COLDELTAS[CANDIDATEMOV];{:17};{14:}
IF(((1<=TARGROW)AND(TARGROW<=MAX))AND((1<=TARGCOL)AND(TARGCOL<=MA X)))
THEN IF(BOARD[TARGROW,TARGCOL]=0)THEN BEGIN BOARD[TARGROW,TARGCOL]:=
MOVENUMBER;IF MOVENUMBER<NUMBEROFSQUA THEN{15:}
BEGIN TRYKNIGHTMOV(MOVENUMBER+1,TARGROW,TARGCOL,SUCCESSFUL);
IF NOT SUCCESSFUL THEN BOARD[TARGROW,TARGCOL]:=0;END{:15}
ELSE SUCCESSFUL:=TRUE;END,[:14];UNTIL SUCCESSFUL OR(CANDIDATEMOV=8);
{:13};END;{:12}BEGIN{19:}ROWDELTAS[1]:=2;COLDELTAS[1]:=1;
ROWDELTAS[2]:=1;COLDELTAS[2]:=2;ROWDELTAS[3]:=-1;COLDELTAS[3]:=2;
ROWDELTAS[4]:=-2;COLDELTAS[4]:=1;ROWDELTAS[5]:=-2;COLDELTAS[5]:=-1;
ROWDELTAS[6]:=-1;COLDELTAS[6]:=-2;ROWDELTAS[7]:=1;COLDELTAS[7]:=-2;
ROWDELTAS[8]:=2;COLDELTAS[8]:=-1;{:19};{21:}{9:}
FOR I:=1 TO MAX DO FOR J:=1 TO MAX DO BOARD[I,J]:=0;{:9};BOARD[1,1]:=1;
TRYKNIGHTMOV(2,1,1,SUCCESSFUL);;{26:]
IF SUCCESSFUL THEN FOR I:=1 TO MAX DO BEGIN FOR J:=1 TO MAX DO WRITE(
BOARD[I,J]:3);WRITELN;END ELSE WRITE('no solution');WRITELN;WRITELN;
{:26};{:21}{22:}{9:}FOR I:=1 TO MAX DO FOR J:=1 TO MAX DO BOARD[I,J]:=0;
{:9};BOARD[3,3]:=1;TRYKNIGHTMOV(2,3,3,SUCCESSFUL);;{26:}
IF SUCCESSFUL THEN FOR I:=1 TO MAX DO BEGIN FOR J:=1 TO MAX DO WRITE(
BOARD[I,J]:3);WRITELN;END ELSE WRITE('no solution');WRITELN;WRITELN;
{:26};{:22}{23:}{9:}FOR I:=1 TO MAX DO FOR J:=1 TO MAX DO BOARD[I,J]:=0;
{:9};BOARD[2,4]:=1;TRYKNIGHTMOV(2,2,4,SUCCESSFUL);;{26:}
IF SUCCESSFUL THEN FOR I:=1 TO MAX DO BEGIN FOR J:=1 TO MAX DO WRITE(
BOARD[I,J]:3);WRITELN;END ELSE WRITE('no solution');WRITELN;WRITELN;
{:26};{:23};END.{:2}
```

End of text file 'knights.pas'

F.4   SPIDER Source File for Ada

Contents of text file 'ada.spi':

```
language Ada extension ada

at_sign @

module definition stmt use math

comment begin <dash-dash> end newline
macros begin
\def\commentbegin{{\tt -- }}
macros end
```

```
line begin <dash-dash-"line"> end <"">

default translation <*> mathness yes

token identifier category math mathness maybe
token number category math mathness yes
token newline category ignore_scrap translation <> mathness maybe
token pseudo_semi translation <> category semi mathness maybe

macros begin
\let\R\relax
macros end

# Delimiters
token & category binop translation <"\\amp">
token ( category open
token ) category close
token * category binop
token + category unorbinop
token , category binop translation <",\\,"-opt-3>
token - category unorbinop
token . category binop
token / category binop
token : category binop
token ; category semi translation <";"-space-opt-2>
token < category binop
token = category binop
token > category binop
token | category binop translation <"\\mid">

# Compound delimiters

token => category arrow translation <"\\AR">
token .. category binop translation <"\\.{..}">
token ** category binop
token := category binop translation <"\\mathbin{:=}">
token /= translation <"\\I"> category binop
token >= translation <"\\G"> category binop
token <= translation <"\\L"> category binop
token << translation <"\\ll"> category openlabel
token >> translation <"\\gg"> category closelabel
token <> translation <"\\LG"> category math

# Hacks no ', and this becomes a binary op
token ' category binop mathness no

token # category math translation <"\\#">



default mathness maybe translation <*>

reserved abort ilk math_like
reserved abs ilk unop_like
reserved accept ilk proc_like
reserved access ilk math_like
reserved all ilk math_like
reserved and ilk and_like
reserved array ilk math_like
```

```
reserved at ilk at_like
reserved begin ilk begin_like
reserved body ilk math_like
reserved case ilk case_like
reserved constant ilk math_like
reserved declare ilk decl_like
reserved delay ilk math_like
reserved delta ilk math_like
reserved digits ilk math_like
reserved do ilk is_like
reserved else ilk else_like
reserved elsif ilk elsif_like
reserved end ilk end_like
reserved entry ilk proc_like
reserved exception ilk ex_like
reserved exit ilk math_like
reserved for ilk math_like
reserved function ilk proc_like
reserved generic ilk gen_like
reserved goto ilk math_like
reserved if ilk if_like
reserved in ilk unorbinop_like
reserved is ilk is_like
reserved limited ilk math_like
reserved loop ilk loop_like
reserved mod ilk binop_like
reserved new ilk separate_like
reserved not ilk unop_like
reserved null ilk math_like
reserved of ilk math_like
reserved or ilk or_like
reserved others ilk math_like
reserved out ilk math_like
reserved package ilk proc_like
reserved pragma ilk math_like
reserved private ilk private_like
reserved procedure ilk proc_like
reserved raise ilk math_like
reserved range ilk math_like
reserved record ilk record_like
reserved rem ilk binop_like
reserved renames ilk math_like
reserved return ilk math_like
reserved reverse ilk math_like
reserved select ilk begin_like
reserved separate ilk separate_like
reserved subtype ilk math_like
reserved task ilk proc_like
reserved terminate ilk math_like
reserved then ilk then_like
reserved type ilk math_like
reserved use ilk math_like
reserved when ilk when_like
reserved while ilk math_like
reserved with ilk with_like
reserved xor ilk binop_like

ilk and_like translation <*> category and
ilk at_like translation <*> category at
ilk begin_like translation <*-indent> category beginning
ilk binop_like translation <"\\"-space-*-"\\"-space> category binop
```

```
ilk case_like translation <*> category case
ilk decl_like translation <*-indent> category declaration
ilk else_like translation <*> category else
ilk elsif_like translation <*> category elsif
ilk end_like translation <*> category close
ilk ex_like translation <*> category exception
ilk gen_like translation <*-indent> category generic
ilk if_like translation <*> category if
ilk is_like translation <*> category is
ilk loop_like translation <*> category loop
ilk math_like translation <*> category math
ilk or_like translation <*> category or
ilk private_like translation <*> category private
ilk proc_like translation <*> category proc
ilk record_like translation <*> category record
ilk separate_like translation <*> category separate
ilk then_like translation <*> category then
ilk unop_like translation <*-"\\"-space> category unop
ilk unorbinop_like translation <"\\"-space-*-"\\"-space> category resunorbinop
ilk when_like translation <*> category when
ilk with_like translation <*> category with


# \MC means ''math close'' and sets \MS to ''math set''
macros begin
\def\MC{\ifmmode\global\let\MS$\else\global\let\MS\relax\fi\relax\MS}
\def\LG{\mathord{<}\mathord{>}}
\let\IG=\ignorespaces
macros end



beginning <outdent-force> continuation <outdent-force> ending --> stmt
beginning <outdent-force> ending --> stmt
# beginning <force> (stmt|ignore_scrap) --> beginning
beginning <force> stmt --> beginning

case <"\\"-space> math <"\\"-space> is <indent-force> --> beginning

close semi --> ending
close <"\\"-space> ? semi --> ending
close <"\\"-space> ? <"\\"-space> ? semi --> ending

continuation <force> stmt --> continuation
continuation <outdent-force> continuation --> continuation


declaration <outdent-force> beginning <outdent-force> continuation <outdent-forc
e> ending --> stmt
declaration <outdent-force> beginning <outdent-force> ending --> stmt
declaration <outdent-force> ending --> stmt
declaration <force> stmt --> declaration

else <indent-force> --> continuation
elsif <"\\"-space> math <"\\"-space> then <indent-force> --> continuation

exception <indent-force> --> continuation

generic <outdent-force> declaration --> declaration
generic <force> stmt --> generic
```

```
if <"\\"-space> math <"\\"-space> then --> ifthen
ifthen <indent-force> stmt --> beginning
ifthen <indent-force> <"\\"-space> math <"\\"-space> <outdent-force> else --> if
then
ifthen <indent-force> <"\\"-space> math <"\\"-space> <outdent-force> close <"\\"
-space> if --> math
ifthen <indent-force> <"\\"-space> math <"\\"-space> <outdent-force> elsif --> i
f


is --> math

loop <indent-force> --> beginning

math [ <"\\"-space> and <"\\"-space> then <"\\"-space> ] --> math binop
math [ <"\\"-space> and <"\\"-space> ] --> math binop

math (binop|unorbinop) math --> math
math <"\\"-space> resunorbinop <"\\"-space>  math --> math
(unorbinop|unop) math --> math
resunorbinop <"\\"-space>  math --> math
# This doesn't apply in Ada:  math unop --> math

math arrow --> math
math binop <"\\"-space> exception --> math
math <"\\"-space> is --> math
math <"\\"-space> loop --> loop
math <"\\"-space> math --> math
math [ <"\\"-space> or <"\\"-space> else <"\\"-space> ] --> math binop
math [ <"\\"-space> or <"\\"-space> ] --> math binop
math <"\\"-space> private --> math
math <"\\"-space> separate --> math
math <indent-force> stmt <outdent-force> --> stmt
math terminator --> stmt

open close --> math
open math close --> math
open [ math semi ] --> open math

<force-backup> openlabel math closelabel <force> --> math

or <indent-force> --> continuation

private <indent-force> --> beginning

proc <"\\"-space> math <"\\"-space> is <"\\"-space> separate --> math
proc <"\\"-space> math <"\\"-space> is <indent-force> --> declaration
proc <"\\"-space> math terminator --> stmt

record <"\\"-space> at <"\\"-space> math terminator <indent-force> --> beginning
record <indent-force> --> beginning

semi --> terminator

stmt <force> stmt --> stmt

when <"\\"-space> math arrow <indent-force> --> whengroup
[ when <"\\"-space> math ] terminator   > math terminator
whengroup stmt <outdent-force> ending --> ending
whengroup stmt <outdent-force> whengroup --> whengroup
```

```
with <"\\"-space> math --> math
with <"\\"-space> proc <"\\"-space> math --> math

? ignore_scrap --> #1

macros begin
\let\AR=\Longrightarrow
macros end
```

Appendix G

Listings

G.1 WEB Processors

This section contains the listings for the WEB processors themselves, TANGLE and WEAVE. Their author, Donald E. Knuth, placed them in the public domain for the benefit of all. While he was perfectly willing to allow their inclusion here, he preferred that they be accompanied by the following caveat:

> These programs were my very first attempt at literate programming, and my style was constantly evolving during the two months that I was writing them; nowadays I would be able to do much better. Still, those programs may provide motivation for the readers who discover that they can do the job much more elegantly than I did.

G.1.1   Source Listing for TANGLE

1.   Introduction.   This program converts a WEB file to a Pascal file. It was written by
D. E. Knuth in September, 1981; a somewhat similar SAIL program had been developed in
March, 1979. Since this program describes itself, a bootstrapping process involving hand-
translation had to be used to get started.

   For large WEB files one should have a large memory, since TANGLE keeps all the Pascal text
in memory (in an abbreviated form). The program uses a few features of the local Pascal
compiler that may need to be changed in other installations:

   1) Case statements have a default.
   2) Input-output routines may need to be adapted for use with a particular character set
       and/or for printing messages on the user's terminal.

These features are also present in the Pascal version of TₑX, where they are used in a similar
(but more complex) way. System-dependent portions of TANGLE can be identified by looking
at the entries for 'system dependencies' in the index below.

   The "banner line" defined here should be changed whenever TANGLE is modified.

   define *banner* ≡ ´This␣is␣TANGLE,␣Version␣3´

2.   The program begins with a fairly normal header, made up of pieces that will mostly be
filled in later. The WEB input comes from files *web_file* and *change_file*, the Pascal output
goes to file *Pascal_file*, and the string pool output goes to file *pool*.

   If it is necessary to abort the job because of a fatal error, the program calls the '*jump_out*'
procedure, which goes to the label *end_of_TANGLE*.

   define *end_of_TANGLE* = 9999   { go here to wrap it up }

⟨ Compiler directives 4 ⟩
program *TANGLE*(*web_file*, *change_file*, *Pascal_file*, *pool*);
   label *end_of_TANGLE*;   { go here to finish }
   const ⟨ Constants in the outer block 8 ⟩
   type ⟨ Types in the outer block 11 ⟩
   var ⟨ Globals in the outer block 9 ⟩
     ⟨ Error handling procedures 30 ⟩
   procedure *initialize*;
     var ⟨ Local variables for initialization 16 ⟩
     begin ⟨ Set initial values 10 ⟩
     end;

3.   Some of this code is optional for use when debugging only; such material is enclosed
between the delimiters **debug** and **gubed**. Other parts, delimited by **stat** and **tats**, are
optionally included if statistics about TANGLE's memory usage are desired.

define *debug* ≡ @{   { change this to '*debug* ≡ ' when debugging }
define *gubed* ≡ @}   { change this to '*gubed* ≡ ' when debugging }
format *debug* ≡ *begin*
format *gubed* ≡ *end*

define *stat* ≡ @{   { change this to '*stat* ≡ ' when gathering usage statistics }
define *tats* ≡ @}   { change this to '*tats* ≡ ' when gathering usage statistics }
format *stat* ≡ *begin*
format *tats* ≡ *end*

4. The Pascal compiler used to develop this system has "compiler directives" that can appear in comments whose first character is a dollar sign. In production versions of TANGLE these directives tell the compiler that it is safe to avoid range checks and to leave out the extra code it inserts for the Pascal debugger's benefit, although interrupts will occur if there is arithmetic overflow.

⟨ Compiler directives 4 ⟩ ≡
   @{@&$C−, A+, D−@}   { no range check, catch arithmetic overflow, no debug overhead }
   debug @{@&$C+, D+@} *gubed*   { but turn everything on when debugging }

This code is used in section 2.

5. Labels are given symbolic names by the following definitions. We insert the label '*exit*:' just before the '**end**' of a procedure in which we have used the '**return**' statement defined below; the label '*restart*' is occasionally used at the very beginning of a procedure; and the label '*reswitch*' is occasionally used just prior to a **case** statement in which some cases change the conditions and we wish to branch to the newly applicable case. Loops that are set up with the **loop** construction defined below are commonly exited by going to '*done*' or to '*found*' or to '*not_found*', and they are sometimes repeated by going to '*continue*'.

define *exit* = 10   { go here to leave a procedure }
define *restart* = 20   { go here to start a procedure again }
define *reswitch* = 21   { go here to start a case statement again }
define *continue* = 22   { go here to resume a loop }
define *done* = 30   { go here to exit a loop }
define *found* = 31   { go here when you've found it }
define *not_found* = 32   { go here when you've found something else }

6. Here are some macros for common programming idioms.

define *incr*(#) ≡ # ← # + 1   { increase a variable by unity }
define *decr*(#) ≡ # ← # − 1   { decrease a variable by unity }
define *loop* ≡ **while** *true* **do**   { repeat over and over until a **goto** happens }
define *do_nothing* ≡   { empty statement }
define *return* ≡ **goto** *exit*   { terminate a procedure call }
format *return* ≡ *nil*
format *loop* ≡ *xclause*

7. We assume that **case** statements may include a default case that applies if no matching label is found. Thus, we shall use constructions like

$$
\begin{aligned}
&\textbf{case } x \textbf{ of}\\
&1: \ \langle\,\text{code for } x = 1\,\rangle;\\
&3: \ \langle\,\text{code for } x = 3\,\rangle;\\
&\textbf{othercases } \langle\,\text{code for } x \neq 1 \text{ and } x \neq 3\,\rangle\\
&\textbf{endcases}
\end{aligned}
$$

since most Pascal compilers have plugged this hole in the language by incorporating some sort of default mechanism. For example, the compiler used to develop WEB and TEX allows '*others:*' as a default label, and other Pascals allow syntaxes like '**else**' or '**otherwise**' or '*otherwise:*', etc. The definitions of **othercases** and **endcases** should be changed to agree with local conventions. (Of course, if no default mechanism is available, the **case** statements of this program must be extended by listing all remaining cases. The author would have taken the trouble to modify TANGLE so that such extensions were done automatically, if he had not wanted to encourage Pascal compiler writers to make this important change in Pascal, where it belongs.)

define *othercases* $\equiv$ *others*:   { default for cases not listed explicitly }
define *endcases* $\equiv$ **end**   { follows the default case in an extended **case** statement }
format *othercases* $\equiv$ *else*
format *endcases* $\equiv$ *end*

8.   The following parameters are set big enough to handle TEX, so they should be sufficient for most applications of TANGLE.

$\langle$ Constants in the outer block 8 $\rangle \equiv$
  buf_size = 100;   { maximum length of input line }
  max_bytes = 45000;   { $1/ww$ times the number of bytes in identifiers, strings, and module
      names; must be less than 65536 }
  max_toks = 50000;
      { $1/zz$ times the number of bytes in compressed Pascal code; must be less than 65536 }
  max_names = 4000;   { number of identifiers, strings, module names; must be less than 10240 }
  max_texts = 2000;   { number of replacement texts, must be less than 10240 }
  hash_size = 353;   { should be prime }
  longest_name = 400;   { module names shouldn't be longer than this }
  line_length = 72;   { lines of Pascal output have at most this many characters }
  out_buf_size = 144;   { length of output buffer, should be twice *line_length* }
  stack_size = 50;   { number of simultaneous levels of macro expansion }
  max_id_length = 12;
      { long identifiers are chopped to this length, which must not exceed *line_length* }
  unambig_length = 7;   { identifiers must be unique if chopped to this length }
      { note that 7 is more strict than Pascal's 8, but this can be varied }
This code is used in section 2.

9.   A global variable called *history* will contain one of four values at the end of every run: *spotless* means that no unusual messages were printed; *harmless_message* means that a message of possible interest was printed but no serious errors were detected; *error_message* means that at least one error was found; *fatal_message* means that the program terminated abnormally. The value of *history* does not influence the behavior of the program; it is simply computed for the convenience of systems that might want to use such information.

> **define** *spotless* = 0   { *history* value for normal jobs }
> **define** *harmless_message* = 1   { *history* value when non-serious info was printed }
> **define** *error_message* = 2   { *history* value when an error was noted }
> **define** *fatal_message* = 3   { *history* value when we had to stop prematurely }

> **define** *mark_harmless* ≡ **if** *history* = *spotless* **then** *history* ← *harmless_message*
> **define** *mark_error* ≡ *history* ← *error_message*
> **define** *mark_fatal* ≡ *history* ← *fatal_message*

⟨ Globals in the outer block 9 ⟩ ≡
history: *spotless* .. *fatal_message*;   { how bad was this run? }

See also sections 13, 20, 23, 25, 27, 29, 38, 40, 44, 50, 65, 70, 79, 80, 82, 86, 94, 95, 100, 124, 126, 143, 156, 164, 171, 179, and 185.

This code is used in section 2.

10.   ⟨ Set initial values 10 ⟩ ≡
history ← *spotless*;

See also sections 14, 17, 18, 21, 26, 42, 46, 48, 52, 71, 144, 152, and 180.

This code is used in section 2.

11.   The character set.   One of the main goals in the design of WEB has been to make it readily portable between a wide variety of computers. Yet WEB by its very nature must use a greater variety of characters than most computer programs deal with, and character encoding is one of the areas in which existing machines differ most widely from each other.

To resolve this problem, all input to WEAVE and TANGLE is converted to an internal seven-bit code that is essentially standard ASCII, the "American Standard Code for Information Interchange." The conversion is done immediately when each character is read in. Conversely, characters are converted from ASCII to the user's external representation just before they are output.

Such an internal code is relevant to users of WEB only because it is the code used for preprocessed constants like "A". If you are writing a program in WEB that makes use of such one-character constants, you should convert your input to ASCII form, like WEAVE and TANGLE do. Otherwise WEB's internal coding scheme does not affect you.

Here is a table of the standard visible ASCII codes:

	0	1	2	3	4	5	6	7
´040	␣	!	"	#	$	%	&	´
´050	(	)	*	+	,	-	.	/
´060	0	1	2	3	4	5	6	7
´070	8	9	:	;	<	=	>	?
´100	@	A	B	C	D	E	F	G
´110	H	I	J	K	L	M	N	O
´120	P	Q	R	S	T	U	V	W
´130	X	Y	Z	[	\	]	^	_
´140	`	a	b	c	d	e	f	g
´150	h	i	j	k	l	m	n	o
´160	p	q	r	s	t	u	v	w
´170	x	y	z	{	|	}	~	

(Actually, of course, code ´040 is an invisible blank space.) Code ´136 was once an upward arrow (↑), and code ´137 was once a left arrow (←), in olden times when the first draft of ASCII code was prepared; but WEB works with today's standard ASCII in which those codes represent circumflex and underline as shown.

⟨ Types in the outer block 11 ⟩ ≡
    $ASCII\_code = 0 .. 127;$ { seven-bit numbers, a subrange of the integers }

See also sections 12, 37, 39, 43, and 78.

This code is used in section 2.

12.   The original Pascal compiler was designed in the late 60s, when six-bit character sets were common, so it did not make provision for lowercase letters. Nowadays, of course, we need to deal with both capital and small letters in a convenient way, so WEB assumes that it is being used with a Pascal whose character set contains at least the characters of standard ASCII as listed above. Some Pascal compilers use the original name *char* for the data type associated with the characters in text files, while other Pascals consider *char* to be a 64-element subrange of a larger data type that has some other name.

In order to accommodate this difference, we shall use the name *text_char* to stand for the data type of the characters in the input and output files. We shall also assume that *text_char* consists of the elements *chr*(*first_text_char*) through *chr*(*last_text_char*), inclusive. The following definitions should be adjusted if necessary.

    define *text_char* ≡ *char*   { the data type of characters in text files }
    define *first_text_char* = 0   { ordinal number of the smallest element of *text_char* }
    define *last_text_char* = 127   { ordinal number of the largest element of *text_char* }

⟨ Types in the outer block 11 ⟩ +≡
    text_file = **packed file of** *text_char*;

13. The `WEAVE` and `TANGLE` processors convert between ASCII code and the user's external character set by means of arrays *xord* and *xchr* that are analogous to Pascal's *ord* and *chr* functions.

⟨ Globals in the outer block 9 ⟩ +≡
xord: **array** [*text_char*] **of** *ASCII_code*;   { specifies conversion of input characters }
xchr: **array** [*ASCII_code*] **of** *text_char*;   { specifies conversion of output characters }

14. If we assume that every system using `WEB` is able to read and write the visible characters of standard ASCII (although not necessarily using the ASCII codes to represent them), the following assignment statements initialize most of the *xchr* array properly, without needing any system-dependent changes. For example, the statement `xchr[@´101]:=´A´` that appears in the present `WEB` file might be encoded in, say, EBCDIC code on the external medium on which it resides, but `TANGLE` will convert from this external code to ASCII and back again. Therefore the assignment statement `XCHR[65]:=´A´` will appear in the corresponding Pascal file, and Pascal will compile this statement so that *xchr*[65] receives the character A in the external (*char*) code. Note that it would be quite incorrect to say `xchr[@´101]:="A"`, because "A" is a constant of type *integer*, not *char*, and because we have "A" = 65 regardless of the external character set.

⟨ Set initial values 10 ⟩ +≡
   xchr[´40] ← ´␣´; *xchr*[´41] ← ´!´; *xchr*[´42] ← ´"´; *xchr*[´43] ← ´#´; *xchr*[´44] ← ´$´;
   xchr[´45] ← ´%´; *xchr*[´46] ← ´&´; *xchr*[´47] ← ´´´;
   xchr[´50] ← ´(´; *xchr*[´51] ← ´)´; *xchr*[´52] ← ´*´; *xchr*[´53] ← ´+´; *xchr*[´54] ← ´,´;
   xchr[´55] ← ´-´; *xchr*[´56] ← ´.´; *xchr*[´57] ← ´/´;
   xchr[´60] ← ´0´; *xchr*[´61] ← ´1´; *xchr*[´62] ← ´2´; *xchr*[´63] ← ´3´; *xchr*[´64] ← ´4´;
   xchr[´65] ← ´5´; *xchr*[´66] ← ´6´; *xchr*[´67] ← ´7´;
   xchr[´70] ← ´8´; *xchr*[´71] ← ´9´; *xchr*[´72] ← ´:´; *xchr*[´73] ← ´;´; *xchr*[´74] ← ´<´;
   xchr[´75] ← ´=´; *xchr*[´76] ← ´>´; *xchr*[´77] ← ´?´;
   xchr[´100] ← ´@´; *xchr*[´101] ← ´A´; *xchr*[´102] ← ´B´; *xchr*[´103] ← ´C´; *xchr*[´104] ← ´D´;
   xchr[´105] ← ´E´; *xchr*[´106] ← ´F´; *xchr*[´107] ← ´G´;
   xchr[´110] ← ´H´; *xchr*[´111] ← ´I´; *xchr*[´112] ← ´J´; *xchr*[´113] ← ´K´; *xchr*[´114] ← ´L´;
   xchr[´115] ← ´M´; *xchr*[´116] ← ´N´; *xchr*[´117] ← ´O´;
   xchr[´120] ← ´P´; *xchr*[´121] ← ´Q´; *xchr*[´122] ← ´R´; *xchr*[´123] ← ´S´; *xchr*[´124] ← ´T´;
   xchr[´125] ← ´U´; *xchr*[´126] ← ´V´; *xchr*[´127] ← ´W´;
   xchr[´130] ← ´X´; *xchr*[´131] ← ´Y´; *xchr*[´132] ← ´Z´; *xchr*[´133] ← ´[´; *xchr*[´134] ← ´\´;
   xchr[´135] ← ´]´; *xchr*[´136] ← ´^´; *xchr*[´137] ← ´_´;
   xchr[´140] ← ´`´; *xchr*[´141] ← ´a´; *xchr*[´142] ← ´b´; *xchr*[´143] ← ´c´; *xchr*[´144] ← ´d´;
   xchr[´145] ← ´e´; *xchr*[´146] ← ´f´; *xchr*[´147] ← ´g´;
   xchr[´150] ← ´h´; *xchr*[´151] ← ´i´; *xchr*[´152] ← ´j´; *xchr*[´153] ← ´k´; *xchr*[´154] ← ´l´;
   xchr[´155] ← ´m´; *xchr*[´156] ← ´n´; *xchr*[´157] ← ´o´;
   xchr[´160] ← ´p´; *xchr*[´161] ← ´q´; *xchr*[´162] ← ´r´; *xchr*[´163] ← ´s´; *xchr*[´164] ← ´t´;
   xchr[´165] ← ´u´; *xchr*[´166] ← ´v´; *xchr*[´167] ← ´w´;
   xchr[´170] ← ´x´; *xchr*[´171] ← ´y´; *xchr*[´172] ← ´z´; *xchr*[´173] ← ´{´; *xchr*[´174] ← ´|´;
   xchr[´175] ← ´}´; *xchr*[´176] ← ´~´;
   xchr[0] ← ´␣´; *xchr*[´177] ← ´␣´;   { these ASCII codes are not used }

15. Some of the ASCII codes below ´40 have been given symbolic names in `WEAVE` and `TANGLE` because they are used with a special meaning.

  define *and_sign* = ´4   { equivalent to 'and' }

define *not_sign* = ´5   { equivalent to 'not' }
define *set_element_sign* = ´6   { equivalent to 'in' }
define *tab_mark* = ´11   { ASCII code used as tab-skip }
define *line_feed* = ´12   { ASCII code thrown away at end of line }
define *form_feed* = ´14   { ASCII code used at end of page }
define *carriage_return* = ´15   { ASCII code used at end of line }
define *left_arrow* = ´30   { equivalent to ':=' }
define *not_equal* = ´32   { equivalent to '<>' }
define *less_or_equal* = ´34   { equivalent to '<=' }
define *greater_or_equal* = ´35   { equivalent to '>=' }
define *equivalence_sign* = ´36   { equivalent to '==' }
define *or_sign* = ´37   { equivalent to 'or' }

16.   When we initialize the *xord* array and the remaining parts of *xchr*, it will be convenient to make use of an index variable, i.

⟨ Local variables for initialization 16 ⟩ ≡
i: 0 .. *last_text_char*;

See also sections 41, 45, and 51.

This code is used in section 2.

17.   Here now is the system-dependent part of the character set. If WEB is being implemented on a garden-variety Pascal for which only standard ASCII codes will appear in the input and output files, you don't need to make any changes here. But at MIT, for example, the code in this module should be changed to

$$\textbf{for } i \leftarrow 1 \textbf{ to } ´37 \textbf{ do } xchr[i] \leftarrow chr(i);$$

WEB's character set is essentially identical to MIT's, even with respect to characters less than ´40.

Changes to the present module will make WEB more friendly on computers that have an extended character set, so that one can type things like ≠ instead of <>. If you have an extended set of characters that are easily incorporated into text files, you can assign codes arbitrarily here, giving an *xchr* equivalent to whatever characters the users of WEB are allowed to have in their input files, provided that unsuitable characters do not correspond to special codes like *carriage_return* that are listed above.

(The present file TANGLE.WEB does not contain any of the non-ASCII characters, because it is intended to be used with all implementations of WEB. It was originally created on a Stanford system that has a convenient extended character set, then "sanitized" by applying another program that transliterated all of the non-standard characters into standard equivalents.)

⟨ Set initial values 10 ⟩ +≡
   for *i* ← 1 **to** ´37 **do** *xchr*[*i*] ← ´␣´;

18.   The following system-independent code makes the *xord* array contain a suitable inverse to the information in *xchr*.

⟨ Set initial values 10 ⟩ +≡
   for *i* ← *first_text_char* **to** *last_text_char* **do** *xord*[*chr*(*i*)] ← ´40;
   for *i* ← 1 **to** ´176 **do** *xord*[*xchr*[*i*]] ← *i*;

19. Input and output. The input conventions of this program are intended to be very much like those of TₑX (except, of course, that they are much simpler, because much less needs to be done). Furthermore they are identical to those of WEAVE. Therefore people who need to make modifications to all three systems should be able to do so without too many headaches.

We use the standard Pascal input/output procedures in several places that TₑX cannot, since TANGLE does not have to deal with files that are named dynamically by the user, and since there is no input from the terminal.

20. Terminal output is done by writing on file *term_out*, which is assumed to consist of characters of type *text_char*.

define *print*(#) ≡ *write*(*term_out*, #)   {'*print*' means write on the terminal}
define *print_ln*(#) ≡ *write_ln*(*term_out*, #)   {'*print*' and then start new line}
define *new_line* ≡ *write_ln*(*term_out*)   {start new line}
define *print_nl*(#) ≡   {print information starting on a new line}
        begin *new_line*; *print*(#);
        end
⟨Globals in the outer block 9⟩ +≡
term_out: *text_file*;   {the terminal as an output file}

21. Different systems have different ways of specifying that the output on a certain file will appear on the user's terminal. Here is one way to do this on the Pascal system that was used in TANGLE's initial development:

⟨Set initial values 10⟩ +≡
  rewrite(*term_out*, ˋTTY:ˊ);   {send *term_out* output to the terminal}

22. The *update_terminal* procedure is called when we want to make sure that everything we have output to the terminal so far has actually left the computer's internal buffers and been sent.

define *update_terminal* ≡ *break*(*term_out*)   {empty the terminal output buffer}

23. The main input comes from *web_file*; this input may be overridden by changes in *change_file*. (If *change_file* is empty, there are no changes.)

⟨Globals in the outer block 9⟩ +≡
web_file: *text_file*;   {primary input}
change_file: *text_file*;   {updates}

24. The following code opens the input files. Since these files were listed in the program header, we assume that the Pascal runtime system has already checked that suitable file names have been given; therefore no additional error checking needs to be done.

procedure *open_input*;   {prepare to read *web_file* and *change_file*}
  begin *reset*(*web_file*); *reset*(*change_file*);
  end;

25. The main output goes to *Pascal_file*, and string pool constants are written to the *pool* file.

⟨Globals in the outer block 9⟩ +≡
Pascal_file: *text_file*;
pool: *text_file*;

26.   The following code opens *Pascal_file* and *pool*. Since these files were listed in the program header, we assume that the Pascal runtime system has checked that suitable external file names have been given.

⟨Set initial values 10⟩ +≡
   rewrite(*Pascal_file*); *rewrite*(*pool*);

27.   Input goes into an array called *buffer*.

⟨Globals in the outer block 9⟩ +≡
buffer: **array** [0 .. *buf_size*] **of** *ASCII_code*;

28.   The *input_ln* procedure brings the next line of input from the specified file into the *buffer* array and returns the value *true*, unless the file has already been entirely read, in which case it returns *false*. The conventions of TeX are followed; i.e., *ASCII_code* numbers representing the next line of the file are input into *buffer*[0], *buffer*[1], ..., *buffer*[*limit* − 1]; trailing blanks are ignored; and the global variable *limit* is set to the length of the line. The value of *limit* must be strictly less than *buf_size*.

   We assume that none of the *ASCII_code* values of *buffer*[*j*] for $0 \le j < limit$ is equal to 0, ´177, *line_feed*, *form_feed*, or *carriage_return*.

function *input_ln*(**var** *f* : *text_file*): *boolean*;   { inputs a line or returns *false* }
   var *final_limit*: 0 .. *buf_size*;   { *limit* without trailing blanks }
   begin *limit* ← 0; *final_limit* ← 0;
   if *eof*(*f*) **then** *input_ln* ← *false*
   else begin while ¬*eoln*(*f*) **do**
         begin *buffer*[*limit*] ← *xord*[*f*↑]; *get*(*f*); *incr*(*limit*);
         if *buffer*[*limit* − 1] ≠ "␣" **then** *final_limit* ← *limit*;
         if *limit* = *buf_size* **then**
            begin while ¬*eoln*(*f*) **do** *get*(*f*);
            decr(*limit*);   { keep *buffer*[*buf_size*] empty }
            if *final_limit* > *limit* **then** *final_limit* ← *limit*;
            print_nl(´!␣Input␣line␣too␣long´); *loc* ← 0; *error*;
            end;
         end;
      read_ln(*f*); *limit* ← *final_limit*; *input_ln* ← *true*;
      end;
   end;

29. Reporting errors to the user.   The TANGLE processor operates in two phases: first it inputs the source file and stores a compressed representation of the program, then it produces the Pascal output from the compressed representation.

   The global variable *phase_one* tells whether we are in Phase I or not.

⟨Globals in the outer block 9⟩ +≡
phase_one: *boolean*;   { *true* in Phase I, *false* in Phase II }

30. If an error is detected while we are debugging, we usually want to look at the contents of memory. A special procedure will be declared later for this purpose.

⟨ Error handling procedures 30 ⟩ ≡
    debug **procedure** *debug_help*; *forward*; **gubed**

See also sections 31 and 34.

This code is used in section 2.

31. During the first phase, syntax errors are reported to the user by saying

$$`err\_print(\ `!\textrm{Error message}`)\textrm',$$

followed by '*jump_out*' if no recovery from the error is provided. This will print the error message followed by an indication of where the error was spotted in the source file. Note that no period follows the error message, since the error routine will automatically supply a period.

Errors that are noticed during the second phase are reported to the user in the same fashion, but the error message will be followed by an indication of where the error was spotted in the output file.

The actual error indications are provided by a procedure called *error*.

    define *err_print*(**#**) ≡
            begin *new_line*; *print*(**#**); *error*;
            end

⟨ Error handling procedures 30 ⟩ +≡
procedure *error*;   { prints '.' and location of error message }
    var *j*: 0 .. *out_buf_size*;   { index into *out_buf* }
    k, l: 0 .. *buf_size*;   { indices into *buffer* }
    begin if *phase_one* **then** ⟨ Print error location based on input buffer 32 ⟩
    else ⟨ Print error location based on output buffer 33 ⟩;
    update_terminal; *mark_error*;
    debug *debug_help*; **gubed**
    end;

32. The error locations during Phase I can be indicated by using the global variables *loc*, *line*, and *changing*, which tell respectively the first unlooked-at position in *buffer*, the current line number, and whether or not the current line is from *change_file* or *web_file*. This routine should be modified on systems whose standard text editor has special line-numbering conventions.

⟨ Print error location based on input buffer 32 ⟩ ≡
    begin if *changing* **then** *print*(´. (change file ´) **else** *print*(´. (´);
    print_ln(´l. ´, *line* : 1, ´)´);
    if *loc* ≥ *limit* **then** *l* ← *limit*
    else *l* ← *loc*;
    for *k* ← 1 **to** *l* **do**
      if *buffer*[*k* − 1] = *tab_mark* **then** *print*(´ ´)
      else *print*(*xchr*[*buffer*[*k* − 1]]);   { print the characters already read }
    new_line;
    for *k* ← 1 **to** *l* **do** *print*(´ ´);   { space out the next line }

for $k \leftarrow l + 1$ **to** *limit* **do** *print*(*xchr*[*buffer*[$k - 1$]]);   { print the part not yet read }
print(´␣´);   { this space separates the message from future asterisks }
end

This code is used in section 31.

33.   The position of errors detected during the second phase can be indicated by outputting the partially-filled output buffer, which contains *out_ptr* entries.

⟨ Print error location based on output buffer 33 ⟩ ≡
  begin *print_ln*(´.␣(1.´, *line* : 1, ´)´);
  for $j \leftarrow 1$ **to** *out_ptr* **do** *print*(*xchr*[*out_buf*[$j - 1$]]);   { print current partial line }
  print(´...␣´);   { indicate that this information is partial }
  end

This code is used in section 31.

34.   The *jump_out* procedure just cuts across all active procedure levels and jumps out of the program. This is the only non-local **goto** statement in TANGLE. It is used when no recovery from a particular error has been provided.

Some Pascal compilers do not implement non-local **goto** statements. In such cases the code that appears at label *end_of_TANGLE* should be copied into the *jump_out* procedure, followed by a call to a system procedure that terminates the program.

  define *fatal_error*(#) ≡
              begin *new_line*; *print*(#); *error*; *mark_fatal*; *jump_out*;
              end

⟨ Error handling procedures 30 ⟩ +≡
procedure *jump_out*;
  begin goto *end_of_TANGLE*;
  end;

35.   Sometimes the program's behavior is far different from what it should be, and TANGLE prints an error message that is really for the TANGLE maintenance person, not the user. In such cases the program says *confusion*(´indication␣of␣where␣we␣are´).

  define *confusion*(#) ≡ *fatal_error*(´!␣This␣can´´t␣happen␣(´, #, ´)´)

36.   An overflow stop occurs if TANGLE's tables aren't large enough.

  define *overflow*(#) ≡ *fatal_error*(´!␣Sorry,␣´, #, ´␣capacity␣exceeded´)

37.   Data structures.   Most of the user's Pascal code is packed into seven- or eight-bit integers in two large arrays called *byte_mem* and *tok_mem*. The *byte_mem* array holds the names of identifiers, strings, and modules; the *tok_mem* array holds the replacement texts for macros and modules. Allocation is sequential, since things are deleted only during Phase II, and only in a last-in-first-out manner.

Auxiliary arrays *byte_start* and *tok_start* are directories to *byte_mem* and *tok_mem*, and the *link*, *ilk*, *equiv*, and *text_link* arrays give further information about names. These auxiliary arrays consist of sixteen-bit items.

⟨ Types in the outer block 11 ⟩ +≡
  eight_bits = 0 .. 255;   { unsigned one-byte quantity }
  sixteen_bits = 0 .. 65535;   { unsigned two-byte quantity }

38. TANGLE has been designed to avoid the need for indices that are more than sixteen bits wide, so that it can be used on most computers. But there are programs that need more than 65536 tokens, and some programs even need more than 65536 bytes; TeX is one of these. To get around this problem, a slight complication has been added to the data structures: *byte_mem* and *tok_mem* are two-dimensional arrays, whose first index is either 0 or 1. (For generality, the first index is actually allowed to run between 0 and $ww - 1$ in *byte_mem*, or between 0 and $zz - 1$ in *tok_mem*, where ww and zz are set to 2 and 3; the program will work for any positive values of ww and zz, and it can be simplified in obvious ways if $ww = 1$ or $zz = 1$.)

> **define** $ww = 2$ { we multiply the byte capacity by approximately this amount }
> **define** $zz = 3$ { we multiply the token capacity by approximately this amount }

⟨ Globals in the outer block 9 ⟩ +≡
byte_mem: **packed array** $[0 .. ww - 1, 0 .. max\_bytes]$ **of** *ASCII_code*;   { characters of names }
tok_mem: **packed array** $[0 .. zz - 1, 0 .. max\_toks]$ **of** *eight_bits*;   { tokens }
byte_start: **array** $[0 .. max\_names]$ **of** *sixteen_bits*;   { directory into *byte_mem* }
tok_start: **array** $[0 .. max\_texts]$ **of** *sixteen_bits*;   { directory into *tok_mem* }
link: **array** $[0 .. max\_names]$ **of** *sixteen_bits*;   { hash table or tree links }
ilk: **array** $[0 .. max\_names]$ **of** *sixteen_bits*;   { type codes or tree links }
equiv: **array** $[0 .. max\_names]$ **of** *sixteen_bits*;   { info corresponding to names }
text_link: **array** $[0 .. max\_texts]$ **of** *sixteen_bits*;   { relates replacement texts }

39. The names of identifiers are found by computing a hash address h and then looking at strings of bytes signified by $hash[h]$, $link[hash[h]]$, $link[link[hash[h]]]$, ..., until either finding the desired name or encountering a zero.

A '*name_pointer*' variable, which signifies a name, is an index into *byte_start*. The actual sequence of characters in the name pointed to by p appears in positions $byte\_start[p]$ to $byte\_start[p + ww] - 1$, inclusive, in the segment of *byte_mem* whose first index is $p \bmod ww$. Thus, when $ww = 2$ the even-numbered name bytes appear in $byte\_mem[0, *]$ and the odd-numbered ones appear in $byte\_mem[1, *]$. The pointer 0 is used for undefined module names; we don't want to use it for the names of identifiers, since 0 stands for a null pointer in a linked list.

Strings are treated like identifiers; the first character (a double-quote) distinguishes a string from an alphabetic name, but for TANGLE's purposes strings behave like numeric macros. (A 'string' here refers to the strings delimited by double-quotes that TANGLE processes. Pascal string constants delimited by single-quote marks are not given such special treatment; they simply appear as sequences of characters in the Pascal texts.) The total number of strings in the string pool is called *string_ptr*, and the total number of names in *byte_mem* is called *name_ptr*. The total number of bytes occupied in $byte\_mem[w, *]$ is called $byte\_ptr[w]$.

We usually have $byte\_start[name\_ptr + w] = byte\_ptr[(name\_ptr + w) \bmod ww]$ for $0 \leq w < ww$, since these are the starting positions for the next ww names to be stored in *byte_mem*.

> **define** $length(\#) \equiv byte\_start[\# + ww] - byte\_start[\#]$ { the length of a name }

⟨ Types in the outer block 11 ⟩ +≡
    name_pointer = $0 .. max\_names$;   { identifies a name }

40.   ⟨ Globals in the outer block 9 ⟩ +≡

name_ptr: *name_pointer*;   { first unused position in *byte_start* }
string_ptr: *name_pointer*;   { next number to be given to a string of length $\neq 1$ }
byte_ptr: **array** $[0 \dots ww - 1]$ **of** $0 \dots max\_bytes$;   { first unused position in *byte_mem* }
pool_check_sum: *integer*;   { sort of a hash for the whole string pool }

41.   ⟨ Local variables for initialization 16 ⟩ +≡
wi: $0 \dots ww - 1$;   { to initialize the *byte_mem* indices }

42.   ⟨ Set initial values 10 ⟩ +≡
  for $wi \leftarrow 0$ **to** $ww - 1$ **do**
    begin $byte\_start[wi] \leftarrow 0$; $byte\_ptr[wi] \leftarrow 0$;
    end;
  $byte\_start[ww] \leftarrow 0$;   { this makes name 0 of length zero }
  $name\_ptr \leftarrow 1$; $string\_ptr \leftarrow 128$; $pool\_check\_sum \leftarrow 271828$;

43.   Replacement texts are stored in *tok_mem*, using similar conventions. A '*text_pointer*' variable is an index into *tok_start*, and the replacement text that corresponds to p runs from positions $tok\_start[p]$ to $tok\_start[p + zz] - 1$, inclusive, in the segment of *tok_mem* whose first index is $p \bmod zz$. Thus, when $zz = 2$ the even-numbered replacement texts appear in $tok\_mem[0, *]$ and the odd-numbered ones appear in $tok\_mem[1, *]$. Furthermore, $text\_link[p]$ is used to connect pieces of text that have the same name, as we shall see later. The pointer 0 is used for undefined replacement texts.

  The first position of $tok\_mem[z, *]$ that is unoccupied by replacement text is called $tok\_ptr[z]$, and the first unused location of *tok_start* is called *text_ptr*. We usually have the identity $tok\_start[text\_ptr + z] = tok\_ptr[(text\_ptr + z) \bmod zz]$, for $0 \le z < zz$, since these are the starting positions for the next *ww* replacement texts to be stored in *tok_mem*.

⟨ Types in the outer block 11 ⟩ +≡
  text_pointer = $0 \dots max\_texts$;   { identifies a replacement text }

44.   It is convenient to maintain a variable z that is equal to $text\_ptr \bmod zz$, so that we always insert tokens into segment z of *tok_mem*.

⟨ Globals in the outer block 9 ⟩ +≡
  text_ptr: *text_pointer*;   { first unused position in *tok_start* }
  tok_ptr: **array** $[0 \dots zz - 1]$ **of** $0 \dots max\_toks$;
        { first unused position in a given segment of *tok_mem* }
  z: $0 \dots zz - 1$;   { current segment of *tok_mem* }
  stat *max_tok_ptr*: **array** $[0 \dots zz - 1]$ **of** $0 \dots max\_toks$;   { largest values assumed by *tok_ptr* }
  tats

45.   ⟨ Local variables for initialization 16 ⟩ +≡
zi: $0 \dots zz - 1$;   { to initialize the *tok_mem* indices }

46.   ⟨ Set initial values 10 ⟩ +≡
  for $zi \leftarrow 0$ **to** $zz - 1$ **do**
    begin $tok\_start[zi] \leftarrow 0$; $tok\_ptr[zi] \leftarrow 0$;
    end;
  $tok\_start[zz] \leftarrow 0$;   { this makes replacement text 0 of length zero }
  $text\_ptr \leftarrow 1$; $z \leftarrow 1 \bmod zz$;

47. Four types of identifiers are distinguished by their *ilk*:

normal identifiers will appear in the Pascal program as ordinary identifiers since they have not been defined to be macros; the corresponding value in the *equiv* array for such identifiers is a link in a secondary hash table that is used to check whether any two of them agree in their first *unambig_length* characters after underline symbols are removed and lowercase letters are changed to uppercase.

numeric identifiers have been defined to be numeric macros; their *equiv* value contains the corresponding numeric value plus 2^{15}. Strings are treated as numeric macros.

simple identifiers have been defined to be simple macros; their *equiv* value points to the corresponding replacement text.

parametric identifiers have been defined to be parametric macros, like simple identifiers, their *equiv* value points to the replacement text.

define *normal* = 0   { ordinary identifiers have *normal* ilk }
define *numeric* = 1   { numeric macros and strings have *numeric* ilk }
define *simple* = 2   { simple macros have *simple* ilk }
define *parametric* = 3   { parametric macros have *parametric* ilk }

48. The names of modules are stored in *byte_mem* together with the identifier names, but a hash table is not used for them because **TANGLE** needs to be able to recognize a module name when given a prefix of that name. A conventional binary seach tree is used to retrieve module names, with fields called *llink* and *rlink* in place of *link* and *ilk*. The root of this tree is *rlink*[0]. If p is a pointer to a module name, *equiv*[p] points to its replacement text, just as in simple and parametric macros, unless this replacement text has not yet been defined (in which case *equiv*[p] = 0).

define *llink* ≡ *link*   { left link in binary search tree for module names }
define *rlink* ≡ *ilk*   { right link in binary search tree for module names }
⟨ Set initial values 10 ⟩ +≡
   rlink[0] ← 0;   { the binary search tree starts out with nothing in it }
   equiv[0] ← 0;   { the undefined module has no replacement text }

49. Here is a little procedure that prints the text of a given name.

procedure *print_id*(p : *name_pointer*);   { print identifier or module name }
   var k: 0 .. *max_bytes*;   { index into *byte_mem* }
      w: 0 .. *ww* − 1;   { segment of *byte_mem* }
   begin if $p \geq$ *name_ptr* **then** *print*(´IMPOSSIBLE´)
   else begin $w \leftarrow p$ **mod** *ww*;
      for $k \leftarrow$ *byte_start*[p] **to** *byte_start*[$p + ww$] − 1 **do** *print*(*xchr*[*byte_mem*[w, k]]);
      end;
   end;

50. Searching for identifiers. The hash table described above is updated by the *id_lookup* procedure, which finds a given identifier and returns a pointer to its index in *byte_start*. If the identifier was not already present, it is inserted with a given *ilk* code; and an error message is printed if the identifier is being doubly defined.

Because of the way **TANGLE**'s scanning mechanism works, it is most convenient to let *id_lookup* search for an identifier that is present in the *buffer* array. Two other global variables specify its position in the buffer: the first character is $buffer[id\_first]$, and the last is $buffer[id\_loc - 1]$. Furthermore, if the identifier is really a string, the global variable $double\_chars$ tells how many of the characters in the buffer appear twice (namely @@ and ""), since this additional information makes it easy to calculate the true length of the string. The final double-quote of the string is not included in its "identifier," but the first one is, so the string length is $id\_loc - id\_first - double\_chars - 1$.

We have mentioned that *normal* identifiers belong to two hash tables, one for their true names as they appear in the WEB file and the other when they have been reduced to their first $unambig\_length$ characters. The hash tables are kept by the method of simple chaining, where the heads of the individual lists appear in the *hash* and *chop_hash* arrays. If h is a hash code, the primary hash table list starts at $hash[h]$ and proceeds through *link* pointers; the secondary hash table list starts at $chop\_hash[h]$ and proceeds through *equiv* pointers. Of course, the same identifier will probably have two different values of h.

The *id_lookup* procedure uses an auxiliary array called *chopped_id* to contain up to $unambig\_length$ characters of the current identifier, if it is necessary to compute the secondary hash code. (This array could be declared local to *id_lookup*, but in general we are making all array declarations global in this program, because some compilers and some machine architectures make dynamic array allocation inefficient.)

⟨ Globals in the outer block 9 ⟩ +≡
id_first: $0 .. buf\_size$;   { where the current identifier begins in the buffer }
id_loc: $0 .. buf\_size$;   { just after the current identifier in the buffer }
double_chars: $0 .. buf\_size$;   { correction to length in case of strings }

hash, *chop_hash*: **array** $[0 .. hash\_size]$ **of** *sixteen_bits*;   { heads of hash lists }
chopped_id: **array** $[0 .. unambig\_length]$ **of** *ASCII_code*;   { chopped identifier }

51.   Initially all the hash lists are empty.

⟨ Local variables for initialization 16 ⟩ +≡
h: $0 .. hash\_size$;   { index into hash-head arrays }

52.   ⟨ Set initial values 10 ⟩ +≡
  for $h \leftarrow 0$ **to** $hash\_size - 1$ **do**
    begin $hash[h] \leftarrow 0$; $chop\_hash[h] \leftarrow 0$;
    end;

53.   Here now is the main procedure for finding identifiers (and strings). The parameter t is set to *normal* except when the identifier is a macro name that is just being defined; in the latter case, t will be *numeric*, *simple*, or *parametric*.

function $id\_lookup(t : eight\_bits)$: *name_pointer*;   { finds current identifier }
  label *found*, *not_found*;
  var *c*: *eight_bits*;   { byte being chopped }
    i: $0 .. buf\_size$;   { index into *buffer* }
    h: $0 .. hash\_size$;   { hash code }
    k: $0 .. max\_bytes$;   { index into *byte_mem* }
    w: $0 .. ww - 1$;   { segment of *byte_mem* }
    l: $0 .. buf\_size$;   { length of the given identifier }
    p, *q*: *name_pointer*;   { where the identifier is being sought }
    s: $0 .. unambig\_length$;   { index into *chopped_id* }

begin $l \leftarrow id\_loc - id\_first$; { compute the length }
⟨ Compute the hash code h 54 ⟩;
⟨ Compute the name location p 55 ⟩;
if $(p = name\_ptr) \lor (t \neq normal)$ then ⟨ Update the tables and check for possible errors 57 ⟩;
$id\_lookup \leftarrow p$;
end;

54. A simple hash code is used: If the sequence of ASCII codes is $c_1 c_2 \dots c_m$, its hash value will be

$$(2^{n-1} c_1 + 2^{n-2} c_2 + \cdots + c_n) \bmod hash\_size.$$

⟨ Compute the hash code h 54 ⟩ ≡
  $h \leftarrow buffer[id\_first]$; $i \leftarrow id\_first + 1$;
  while $i < id\_loc$ do
    begin $h \leftarrow (h + h + buffer[i]) \bmod hash\_size$; $incr(i)$;
    end

This code is used in section 53.

55. If the identifier is new, it will be placed in position $p = name\_ptr$, otherwise p will point to its existing location.

⟨ Compute the name location p 55 ⟩ ≡
  $p \leftarrow hash[h]$;
  while $p \neq 0$ do
    begin if $length(p) = l$ then
        ⟨ Compare name p with current identifier, **goto** *found* if equal 56 ⟩;
      $p \leftarrow link[p]$;
      end;
    $p \leftarrow name\_ptr$; { the current identifier is new }
    $link[p] \leftarrow hash[h]$; $hash[h] \leftarrow p$; { insert p at beginning of hash list }
  found:

This code is used in section 53.

56. ⟨ Compare name p with current identifier, **goto** *found* if equal 56 ⟩ ≡
  begin $i \leftarrow id\_first$; $k \leftarrow byte\_start[p]$; $w \leftarrow p \bmod ww$;
  while $(i < id\_loc) \land (buffer[i] = byte\_mem[w, k])$ do
    begin $incr(i)$; $incr(k)$;
    end;
  if $i = id\_loc$ then goto *found*; { all characters agree }
  end

This code is used in section 55.

57. ⟨ Update the tables and check for possible errors 57 ⟩ ≡
  begin if $((p \neq name\_ptr) \land (t \neq normal) \land (ilk[p] = normal)) \lor ((p = name\_ptr) \land (t = normal) \land (buffer[id\_first] \neq """"))$ then ⟨ Compute the secondary hash code h and put the first characters into the auxiliary array *chopped_id* 58 ⟩;
  if $p \neq name\_ptr$ then ⟨ Give double-definition error, if necessary, and change p to type t 59 ⟩
  else ⟨ Enter a new identifier into the table at position p 61 ⟩;
  end

This code is used in section 53.

58.   The following routine, which is called into play when it is necessary to look at the secondary hash table, computes the same hash function as before (but on the chopped data), and places a zero after the chopped identifier in *chopped_id* to serve as a convenient sentinel.

⟨ Compute the secondary hash code *h* and put the first characters into the auxiliary array
        chopped_id 58 ⟩ ≡
  begin *i* ← *id_first*; *s* ← 0; *h* ← 0;
  while (*i* < *id_loc*) ∧ (*s* < *unambig_length*) **do**
    begin if *buffer*[*i*] ≠ "_" **then**
      begin if *buffer*[*i*] ≥ "a" **then** *chopped_id*[*s*] ← *buffer*[*i*] − ´40
      else *chopped_id*[*s*] ← *buffer*[*i*];
      h ← (*h* + *h* + *chopped_id*[*s*]) **mod** *hash_size*; *incr*(*s*);
      end;
    incr(*i*);
    end;
  chopped_id[*s*] ← 0;
  end

This code is used in section 57.

59.   If a nonnumeric macro has appeared before it was defined, `TANGLE` will still work all right; after all, such behavior is typical of the replacement texts for modules, which act very much like macros. However, an undefined numeric macro may not be used on the right-hand side of another numeric macro definition, so `TANGLE` finds it simplest to make a blanket rule that numeric macros should be defined before they are used. The following routine gives an error message and also fixes up any damage that may have been caused.

⟨ Give double-definition error, if necessary, and change *p* to type *t* 59 ⟩ ≡
  { now *p* ≠ *name_ptr* and *t* ≠ *normal* }
  begin if *ilk*[*p*] = *normal* **then**
    begin if *t* = *numeric* **then** *err_print*(´!␣This␣identifier␣has␣already␣appeared´);
    ⟨ Remove *p* from secondary hash table 60 ⟩;
    end
  else *err_print*(´!␣This␣identifier␣was␣defined␣before´);
  ilk[*p*] ← *t*;
  end

This code is used in section 57.

60.   When we have to remove a secondary hash entry, because a *normal* identifier is changing to another *ilk*, the hash code *h* and chopped identifier have already been computed.

⟨ Remove *p* from secondary hash table 60 ⟩ ≡
  q ← *chop_hash*[*h*];
  if *q* = *p* **then** *chop_hash*[*h*] ← *equiv*[*p*]
  else begin while *equiv*[*q*] ≠ *p* **do** *q* ← *equiv*[*q*];
    equiv[*q*] ← *equiv*[*p*];
    end

This code is used in section 59.

61.   The following routine could make good use of a generalized *pack* procedure that puts items into just part of a packed array instead of the whole thing.

⟨ Enter a new identifier into the table at position p 61 ⟩ ≡
  begin if $(t = normal) \wedge (buffer[id\_first] \neq """")$ **then**
    ⟨ Check for ambiguity and update secondary hash 62 ⟩;
  $w \leftarrow name\_ptr \bmod ww$; $k \leftarrow byte\_ptr[w]$;
  if $k + l > max\_bytes$ **then** $overflow($ ´byte␣memory´ $)$;
  if $name\_ptr > max\_names - ww$ **then** $overflow($ ´name´ $)$;
  $i \leftarrow id\_first$; { get ready to move the identifier into $byte\_mem$ }
  while $i < id\_loc$ **do**
    begin $byte\_mem[w, k] \leftarrow buffer[i]$; $incr(k)$; $incr(i)$;
    end;
  $byte\_ptr[w] \leftarrow k$; $byte\_start[name\_ptr + ww] \leftarrow k$; $incr(name\_ptr)$;
  if $buffer[id\_first] \neq """"$ **then** $ilk[p] \leftarrow t$
  else ⟨ Define and output a new string of the pool 64 ⟩;
  end

This code is used in section 57.

62. ⟨ Check for ambiguity and update secondary hash 62 ⟩ ≡
  begin $q \leftarrow chop\_hash[h]$;
  while $q \neq 0$ **do**
    begin ⟨ Check if q conflicts with p 63 ⟩;
    $q \leftarrow equiv[q]$;
    end;
  $equiv[p] \leftarrow chop\_hash[h]$; $chop\_hash[h] \leftarrow p$; { put p at front of secondary list }
  end

This code is used in section 61.

63. ⟨ Check if q conflicts with p 63 ⟩ ≡
  begin $k \leftarrow byte\_start[q]$; $s \leftarrow 0$; $w \leftarrow q \bmod ww$;
  while $(k < byte\_start[q + ww]) \wedge (s < unambig\_length)$ **do**
    begin $c \leftarrow byte\_mem[w, k]$;
    if $c \neq$ "_" **then**
      begin if $c \geq$ "a" **then** $c \leftarrow c -$ ´40; { convert to uppercase }
      if $chopped\_id[s] \neq c$ **then goto** not_found;
      $incr(s)$;
      end;
    $incr(k)$;
    end;
  if $(k = byte\_start[q + ww]) \wedge (chopped\_id[s] \neq 0)$ **then goto** not_found;
  $print\_nl($ ´!␣Identifier␣conflict␣with␣´ $)$;
  for $k \leftarrow byte\_start[q]$ **to** $byte\_start[q + ww] - 1$ **do** $print(xchr[byte\_mem[w, k]])$;
  $error$; $q \leftarrow 0$; { only one conflict will be printed, since $equiv[0] = 0$ }
$not\_found:$ **end**

This code is used in section 62.

64. We compute the string pool check sum by working modulo a prime number that
large but not so large that overflow might occur.
  define $check\_sum\_prime \equiv$ ´3777777667 { $2^{29} - 73$ }
⟨ Define and output a new string of the pool 64 ⟩ ≡
  begin $ilk[p] \leftarrow numeric$; { strings are like numeric macros }

if $l - double\_chars = 2$ then   { this string is for a single character }
  $equiv[p] \leftarrow buffer[id\_first + 1] + \,'100000$
else begin $equiv[p] \leftarrow string\_ptr + \,'100000$; $\ l \leftarrow l - double\_chars - 1$;
  if $l > 99$ then $\ err\_print(\,'!\textvisiblespace Preprocessed\textvisiblespace string\textvisiblespace is\textvisiblespace too\textvisiblespace long\,')$;
  $incr(string\_ptr)$; $\ write(pool, xchr["0" + l\,\mathbf{div}\,10], xchr["0" + l\,\mathbf{mod}\,10])$;   { output the length }
  $pool\_check\_sum \leftarrow pool\_check\_sum + pool\_check\_sum + l$;
  while $pool\_check\_sum > check\_sum\_prime$ do
    $pool\_check\_sum \leftarrow pool\_check\_sum - check\_sum\_prime$;
  $i \leftarrow id\_first + 1$;
  while $i < id\_loc$ do
    begin $write(pool, xchr[buffer[i]])$;   { output characters of string }
    $pool\_check\_sum \leftarrow pool\_check\_sum + pool\_check\_sum + buffer[i]$;
    while $pool\_check\_sum > check\_sum\_prime$ do
      $pool\_check\_sum \leftarrow pool\_check\_sum - check\_sum\_prime$;
    if $(buffer[i] = """")\ \lor\ (buffer[i] = "@")$ then $\ i \leftarrow i + 2$
      { omit second appearance of doubled character }
    else $incr(i)$;
    end;
  $write\_ln(pool)$;
  end;
end

This code is used in section 61.

65.   Searching for module names.   The *mod_lookup* procedure finds the module
name $mod\_text[1 .. l]$ in the search tree, after inserting it if necessary, and returns a pointer
to where it was found.

⟨ Globals in the outer block 9 ⟩ $+\equiv$
mod_text: **array** $[0 .. longest\_name]$ **of** *ASCII_code*;   { name being sought for }

66.   According to the rules of WEB, no module name should be a proper prefix of another,
so a "clean" comparison should occur between any two names. The result of *mod_lookup* is
0 if this prefix condition is violated. An error message is printed when such violations are
detected during phase two of WEAVE.

  define *less* = 0   { the first name is lexicographically less than the second }
  define *equal* = 1   { the first name is equal to the second }
  define *greater* = 2   { the first name is lexicographically greater than the second }
  define *prefix* = 3   { the first name is a proper prefix of the second }
  define *extension* = 4   { the first name is a proper extension of the second }
function $mod\_lookup(l : sixteen\_bits)$: *name_pointer*;   { finds module name }
  label *found*;
  var *c*: *less* .. *extension*;   { comparison between two names }
    j: $0 .. longest\_name$;   { index into *mod_text* }
    k: $0 .. max\_bytes$;   { index into *byte_mem* }
    w: $0 .. ww - 1$;   { segment of *byte_mem* }
    p: *name_pointer*;   { current node of the search tree }
    q: *name_pointer*;   { father of node *p* }
  begin $c \leftarrow greater$; $\ q \leftarrow 0$; $\ p \leftarrow rlink[0]$;   { $rlink[0]$ is the root of the tree }
  while $p \neq 0$ **do**

begin ⟨ Set c to the result of comparing the given name to name p 68 ⟩;
  $q \leftarrow p$;
  if $c = less$ **then** $p \leftarrow llink[q]$
  else if $c = greater$ **then** $p \leftarrow rlink[q]$
    else goto *found*;
  end;
⟨ Enter a new module name into the tree 67 ⟩;
found: **if** $c \neq equal$ **then**
  begin $err\_print(\text{`!}_\sqcup\text{Incompatible}_\sqcup\text{section}_\sqcup\text{names'})$; $p \leftarrow 0$;
  end;
$mod\_lookup \leftarrow p$;
end;

67. ⟨ Enter a new module name into the tree 67 ⟩ ≡
  $w \leftarrow name\_ptr$ **mod** ww; $k \leftarrow byte\_ptr[w]$;
  if $k + l > max\_bytes$ **then** $overflow(\text{`byte}_\sqcup\text{memory'})$;
  if $name\_ptr > max\_names - ww$ **then** $overflow(\text{`name'})$;
  $p \leftarrow name\_ptr$;
  if $c = less$ **then** $llink[q] \leftarrow p$
  else $rlink[q] \leftarrow p$;
  $llink[p] \leftarrow 0$; $rlink[p] \leftarrow 0$; $c \leftarrow equal$; $equiv[p] \leftarrow 0$;
  for $j \leftarrow 1$ **to** l **do** $byte\_mem[w, k + j - 1] \leftarrow mod\_text[j]$;
  $byte\_ptr[w] \leftarrow k + l$; $byte\_start[name\_ptr + ww] \leftarrow k + l$; $incr(name\_ptr)$;
This code is used in section 66.

68. ⟨ Set c to the result of comparing the given name to name p 68 ⟩ ≡
  begin $k \leftarrow byte\_start[p]$; $w \leftarrow p$ **mod** ww; $c \leftarrow equal$; $j \leftarrow 1$;
  while $(k < byte\_start[p + ww]) \wedge (j \leq l) \wedge (mod\_text[j] = byte\_mem[w, k])$ **do**
    begin $incr(k)$; $incr(j)$;
    end;
  if $k = byte\_start[p + ww]$ **then**
    if $j > l$ **then** $c \leftarrow equal$
    else $c \leftarrow extension$
  else if $j > l$ **then** $c \leftarrow prefix$
    else if $mod\_text[j] < byte\_mem[w, k]$ **then** $c \leftarrow less$
      else $c \leftarrow greater$;
  end
This code is used in sections 66 and 69.

69. The *prefix_lookup* procedure is supposed to find exactly one module name that has $mod\_text[1 .. l]$ as a prefix. Actually the algorithm silently accepts also the situation that some module name is a prefix of $mod\_text[1 .. l]$, because the user who painstakingly typed in more than necessary probably doesn't want to be told about the wasted effort.

function $prefix\_lookup(l : sixteen\_bits): name\_pointer$; { finds name extension }
  var c: $less .. extension$; { comparison between two names }
    $count$: $0 .. max\_names$; { the number of hits }
    j: $0 .. longest\_name$; { index into mod_text }
    k: $0 .. max\_bytes$; { index into $byte\_mem$ }
    w: $0 .. ww - 1$; { segment of $byte\_mem$ }

```
    p: name_pointer;   { current node of the search tree }
    q: name_pointer;   { another place to resume the search after one branch is done }
    r: name_pointer;   { extension found }
begin q ← 0; p ← rlink[0]; count ← 0; r ← 0;   { begin search at root of tree }
while p ≠ 0 do
    begin ⟨ Set c to the result of comparing the given name to name p 68 ⟩;
    if c = less then  p ← llink[p]
    else if c = greater then  p ← rlink[p]
        else begin r ← p; incr(count); q ← rlink[p]; p ← llink[p];
            end;
    if p = 0 then
        begin p ← q; q ← 0;
        end;
    end;
if count ≠ 1 then
    if count = 0 then  err_print(´!␣Name␣does␣not␣match´)
    else err_print(´!␣Ambiguous␣prefix´);
prefix_lookup ← r;   { the result will be 0 if there was no match }
end;
```

70. Tokens.   Replacement texts, which represent Pascal code in a compressed format, appear in *tok_mem* as mentioned above. The codes in these texts are called 'tokens'; some tokens occupy two consecutive eight-bit byte positions, and the others take just one byte.

If $p > 0$ points to a replacement text, *tok_start*$[p]$ is the *tok_mem* position of the first eight-bit code of that text. If *text_link*$[p] = 0$, this is the replacement text for a macro, otherwise it is the replacement text for a module. In the latter case *text_link*$[p]$ is either equal to *module_flag*, which means that there is no further text for this module, or *text_link*$[p]$ points to a continuation of this replacement text; such links are created when several modules have Pascal texts with the same name, and they also tie together all the Pascal texts of unnamed modules. The replacement text pointer for the first unnamed module appears in *text_link*$[0]$, and the most recent such pointer is *last_unnamed*.

define *module_flag* $\equiv$ *max_texts*   { final *text_link* in module replacement texts }

⟨ Globals in the outer block 9 ⟩ +≡
last_unnamed: *text_pointer*;   { most recent replacement text of unnamed module }

71.   ⟨ Set initial values 10 ⟩ +≡
    last_unnamed ← 0; *text_link*[0] ← 0;

72.   If the first byte of a token is less than ´200, the token occupies a single byte. Otherwise we make a sixteen-bit token by combining two consecutive bytes a and b. If ´200 $\leq a <$ ´250, then $(a -$ ´200$) \times 2^8 + b$ points to an identifier; if ´250 $\leq a <$ ´320, then $(a -$ ´250$) \times 2^8 + b$ points to a module name; otherwise, i.e., if ´320 $\leq a <$ ´400, then $(a -$ ´320$) \times 2^8 + b$ is the number of the module in which the current replacement text appears.

Codes less than ´200 are 7-bit ASCII codes that represent themselves. In particular, a single-character identifier like 'x' will be a one-byte token, while all longer identifiers will occupy two bytes.

Some of the 7-bit ASCII codes will not be present, however, so we can use them for special purposes. The following symbolic names are used:

param denotes insertion of a parameter. This occurs only in the replacement texts of parametric macros, outside of single-quoted strings in those texts.

begin_comment denotes @{, which will become either { or [.

end_comment denotes @}, which will become either } or].

octal denotes the @´ that precedes an octal constant.

hex denotes the @" that precedes a hexadecimal constant.

check_sum denotes the @$ that denotes the string pool check sum.

join denotes the concatenation of adjacent items with no space or line breaks allowed between them (the @& operation of WEB).

double_dot denotes '..' in Pascal.

verbatim denotes the @= that begins a verbatim Pascal string. It is also used for the end of the string.

force_line denotes the @\ that forces a new line in the Pascal output.

define *param* $= 0$ { ASCII null code will not appear }
define *verbatim* $= $ '2 { extended ASCII alpha should not appear }
define *force_line* $= $ '3 { extended ASCII beta should not appear }
define *begin_comment* $= $ '11 { ASCII tab mark will not appear }
define *end_comment* $= $ '12 { ASCII line feed will not appear }
define *octal* $= $ '14 { ASCII form feed will not appear }
define *hex* $= $ '15 { ASCII carriage return will not appear }
define *double_dot* $= $ '40 { ASCII space will not appear except in strings }
define *check_sum* $= $ '175 { will not be confused with right brace }
define *join* $= $ '177 { ASCII delete will not appear }

73. The following procedure is used to enter a two-byte value into *tok_mem* when a replacement text is being generated.

procedure *store_two_bytes*(*x* : *sixteen_bits*); { stores high byte, then low byte }
  begin if *tok_ptr*[*z*] $+ 2 >$ *max_toks* **then** *overflow*(´token´);
  tok_mem[*z*, *tok_ptr*[*z*]] $\leftarrow x$ **div** '400; { this could be done by a shift command }
  tok_mem[*z*, *tok_ptr*[*z*] $+ 1$] $\leftarrow x$ **mod** '400; { this could be done by a logical and }
  tok_ptr[*z*] $\leftarrow$ *tok_ptr*[*z*] $+ 2$;
  end;

74. When TANGLE is being operated in debug mode, it has a procedure to display a replacement text in symbolic form. This procedure has not been spruced up to generate a real great format, but at least the results are not as bad as a memory dump.

debug procedure *print_repl*(*p* : *text_pointer*);
var *k*: $0 .. $ *max_toks*; { index into *tok_mem* }
  a: *sixteen_bits*; { current byte(s) }
  zp: $0 .. zz - 1$; { segment of *tok_mem* being accessed }
begin if $p \geq$ *text_ptr* **then** *print*(´BAD´)
else begin $k \leftarrow$ *tok_start*[*p*]; *zp* $\leftarrow p$ **mod** *zz*;
  while $k < $ *tok_start*[*p* $+ zz$] **do**
    begin *a* $\leftarrow$ *tok_mem*[*zp*, *k*];
    if $a \geq$ '200 **then** ⟨ Display two-byte token starting with *a* 75 ⟩
    else ⟨ Display one-byte token *a* 76 ⟩;
    incr(*k*);
    end;

```
      end;
   end;
 gubed
```

75. ⟨ Display two-byte token starting with a 75 ⟩ ≡
```
  begin incr(k);
  if a < '250 then   { identifier or string }
     begin a ← (a − '200) ∗ '400 + tok_mem[zp, k]; print_id(a);
     if byte_mem[a mod ww, byte_start[a]] = """" then print('"')
     else print('␣');
     end
  else if a < '320 then   { module name }
        begin print('@<'); print_id((a − '250) ∗ '400 + tok_mem[zp, k]); print('@>');
        end
     else begin a ← (a − '320) ∗ '400 + tok_mem[zp, k];   { module number }
        print('@', xchr["{"], a : 1, '@', xchr["}"]);
              { can't use right brace between debug and gubed }
        end;
  end
```
This code is used in section 74.

76. ⟨ Display one-byte token a 76 ⟩ ≡
```
  case a of
  begin_comment: print('@', xchr["{"]);
  end_comment: print('@', xchr["}"]);   { can't use right brace between debug and gubed }
  octal: print('@´´');
  hex: print('@"');
  check_sum: print('@$');
  param: print('#');
  "@": print('@@');
  verbatim: print('@=');
  force_line: print('@\');
  othercases print(xchr[a])
  endcases
```
This code is used in section 74.

77. Stacks for output.   Let's make sure that our data structures contain enough information to produce the entire Pascal program as desired, by working next on the algorithms that actually do produce that program.

78.   The output process uses a stack to keep track of what is going on at different "levels" as the macros are being expanded. Entries on this stack have five parts:

end_field is the *tok_mem* location where the replacement text of a particular level will end;

byte_field is the *tok_mem* location from which the next token on a particular level will be read;

name_field points to the name corresponding to a particular level;

repl_field points to the replacement text currently being read at a particular level.

mod_field is the module number, or zero if this is a macro.

The current values of these five quantities are referred to quite frequently, so they are stored in a separate place instead of in the *stack* array. We call the current values *cur_end*, *cur_byte*, *cur_name*, *cur_repl*, and *cur_mod*.

The global variable *stack_ptr* tells how many levels of output are currently in progress. The end of all output occurs when the stack is empty, i.e., when $stack\_ptr = 0$.

⟨ Types in the outer block 11 ⟩ +≡
output_state = **record** *end_field*: *sixteen_bits*;   { ending location of replacement text }
    byte_field: *sixteen_bits*;   { present location within replacement text }
    name_field: *name_pointer*;   { *byte_start* index for text being output }
    repl_field: *text_pointer*;   { *tok_start* index for text being output }
    mod_field: 0 .. '27777;   { module number or zero if not a module }
    end;

79.   **define** *cur_end* ≡ *cur_state.end_field*   { current ending location in *tok_mem* }
  define *cur_byte* ≡ *cur_state.byte_field*   { location of next output byte in *tok_mem* }
  define *cur_name* = *cur_state.name_field*   { pointer to current name being expanded }
  define *cur_repl* ≡ *cur_state.repl_field*   { pointer to current replacement text }
  define *cur_mod* ≡ *cur_state.mod_field*   { current module number being expanded }

⟨ Globals in the outer block 9 ⟩ +≡
cur_state: *output_state*;   { *cur_end*, *cur_byte*, *cur_name*, *cur_repl* }
stack: **array** [1 .. *stack_size*] **of** *output_state*;   { info for non-current levels }
stack_ptr: 0 .. *stack_size*;   { first unused location in the output state stack }

80.   It is convenient to keep a global variable *zo* equal to *cur_repl* **mod** *zz*.

⟨ Globals in the outer block 9 ⟩ +≡
zo: 0 .. *zz* − 1;   { the segment of *tok_mem* from which output is coming }

81.   Parameters must also be stacked. They are placed in *tok_mem* just above the other replacement texts, and dummy parameter 'names' are placed in *byte_start* just after the other names. The variables *text_ptr* and *tok_ptr* [*z*] essentially serve as parameter stack pointers during the output phase, so there is no need for a separate data structure to handle this problem.

82.   There is an implicit stack corresponding to meta-comments that are output via @[and @}. But this stack need not be represented in detail, because we only need to know whether it is empty or not. A global variable *brace_level* tells how many items would be on this stack if it were present.

⟨ Globals in the outer block 9 ⟩ +≡
brace_level: *eight_bits*;   { current depth of @{ ... @} nesting }

83.   To get the output process started, we will perform the following initialization steps. We may assume that *text_link* [0] is nonzero, since it points to the Pascal text in the first unnamed module that generates code; if there are no such modules, there is nothing to output, and an error message will have been generated before we do any of the initialization.

⟨ Initialize the output stacks 83 ⟩ ≡

$stack\_ptr \leftarrow 1;\; brace\_level \leftarrow 0;\; cur\_name \leftarrow 0;\; cur\_repl \leftarrow text\_link[0];\; zo \leftarrow cur\_repl \bmod zz;$
$cur\_byte \leftarrow tok\_start[cur\_repl];\; cur\_end \leftarrow tok\_start[cur\_repl + zz];\; cur\_mod \leftarrow 0;$

This code is used in section 112.

84.   When the replacement text for name p is to be inserted into the output, the following subroutine is called to save the old level of output and get the new one going.

procedure $push\_level(p : name\_pointer);$ { suspends the current level }
    begin if $stack\_ptr = stack\_size$ **then** $overflow(\text{`stack'})$
    else begin $stack[stack\_ptr] \leftarrow cur\_state;$ { save cur_end, cur_byte, etc. }
        $incr(stack\_ptr);\; cur\_name \leftarrow p;\; cur\_repl \leftarrow equiv[p];\; zo \leftarrow cur\_repl \bmod zz;$
        $cur\_byte \leftarrow tok\_start[cur\_repl];\; cur\_end \leftarrow tok\_start[cur\_repl + zz];\; cur\_mod \leftarrow 0;$
        end;
    end;

85.   When we come to the end of a replacement text, the pop_level subroutine does the right thing: It either moves to the continuation of this replacement text or returns the state to the most recently stacked level. Part of this subroutine, which updates the parameter stack, will be given later when we study the parameter stack in more detail.

procedure $pop\_level;$ { do this when cur_byte reaches cur_end }
    label $exit;$
    begin if $text\_link[cur\_repl] = 0$ **then**   { end of macro expansion }
        begin if $ilk[cur\_name] = parametric$ **then**
            ⟨ Remove a parameter from the parameter stack 91 ⟩;
        end
    else if $text\_link[cur\_repl] < module\_flag$ **then**   { link to a continuation }
            begin $cur\_repl \leftarrow text\_link[cur\_repl];$ { we will stay on the same level }
            $zo \leftarrow cur\_repl \bmod zz;\; cur\_byte \leftarrow tok\_start[cur\_repl];\; cur\_end \leftarrow tok\_start[cur\_repl + zz];$
            return;
            end;
    $decr(stack\_ptr);$ { we will go down to the previous level }
    if $stack\_ptr > 0$ **then**
        begin $cur\_state \leftarrow stack[stack\_ptr];\; zo \leftarrow cur\_repl \bmod zz;$
        end;
$exit:$ **end**;

86.   The heart of the output procedure is the get_output routine, which produces the next token of output that is not a reference to a macro. This procedure handles all the stacking and unstacking that is necessary. It returns the value $number$ if the next output has a numeric value (the value of a numeric macro or string), in which case cur_val has been set to the number in question. The procedure also returns the value $module\_number$ if the next output begins or ends the replacement text of some module, in which case cur_val is that module's number (if beginning) or the negative of that value (if ending). And it returns the value $identifier$ if the next output is an identifier of length two or more, in which case cur_val points to that identifier name.

define $number = \text{'}200$ { code returned by get_output when next output is numeric }
define $module\_number = \text{'}201$ { code returned by get_output for module numbers }
define $identifier = \text{'}202$ { code returned by get_output for identifiers }

⟨ Globals in the outer block 9 ⟩ +≡
cur_val: *integer*;   { additional information corresponding to output token }

87.   If *get_output* finds that no more output remains, it returns the value zero.

function *get_output*: *sixteen_bits*;   { returns next token after macro expansion }
  label *restart*, *done*, *found*;
  var *a*: *sixteen_bits*;   { value of current byte }
    b: *eight_bits*;   { byte being copied }
    bal: *sixteen_bits*;   { excess of (versus) while copying a parameter }
    k: 0 .. *max_bytes*;   { index into *byte_mem* }
    w: 0 .. *ww* − 1;   { segment of *byte_mem* }
  begin *restart*: **if** *stack_ptr* = 0 **then**
    begin *a* ← 0; **goto** *found*;
    end;
  if *cur_byte* = *cur_end* **then**
    begin *cur_val* ← −*cur_mod*; *pop_level*;
    if *cur_val* = 0 **then goto** *restart*;
    a ← *module_number*; **goto** *found*;
    end;
  a ← *tok_mem*[*zo*, *cur_byte*]; *incr*(*cur_byte*);
  if *a* < '200 **then**   { one-byte token }
    if *a* = *param* **then** ⟨Start scanning current macro parameter, **goto** *restart* 92⟩
    else goto *found*;
  a ← (*a* − '200) ∗ '400 + *tok_mem*[*zo*, *cur_byte*]; *incr*(*cur_byte*);
  if *a* < '24000 **then**   { '24000 = ('250 − '200) ∗ '400 }
    ⟨Expand macro *a* and **goto** *found*, or **goto** *restart* if no output found 89⟩;
  if *a* < '50000 **then**   { '50000 = ('320 − '200) ∗ '400 }
    ⟨Expand module *a* − '24000, **goto** *restart* 88⟩;
  cur_val ← *a* − '50000; *a* ← *module_number*; *cur_mod* ← *cur_val*;
found: **debug if** *trouble_shooting* **then** *debug_help*; **gubed**
  get_output ← *a*;
  end;

88.   The user may have forgotten to give any Pascal text for a module name, or the Pascal text may have been associated with a different name by mistake.

⟨ Expand module *a* − '24000, **goto** *restart* 88 ⟩ ≡
  begin *a* ← *a* − '24000;
  if *equiv*[*a*] ≠ 0 **then** *push_level*(*a*)
  else if *a* ≠ 0 **then**
      begin *print_nl*('!␣Not␣present:␣<'); *print_id*(*a*); *print*('>'); *error*;
      end;
  goto *restart*;
  end
This code is used in section 87.

89.   ⟨Expand macro *a* and **goto** *found*, or **goto** *restart* if no output found 89⟩ ≡
  begin case *ilk*[*a*] **of**
  normal: **begin** *cur_val* ← *a*; *a* ← *identifier*;
    end;

numeric: **begin** *cur_val* ← *equiv*[a] − ´*100000*; *a* ← *number*;
　　end;
simple: **begin** *push_level*(a); **goto** *restart*;
　　end;
parametric: **begin** ⟨ Put a parameter on the parameter stack, or **goto** *restart* if error occurs 90 ⟩;
　　push_level(a); **goto** *restart*;
　　end;
othercases *confusion*(´output´)
endcases;
goto *found*;
end

This code is used in section 87.

90.　　We come now to the interesting part, the job of putting a parameter on the parameter stack. First we pop the stack if necessary until getting to a level that hasn't ended. Then the next character must be a '('; and since parentheses are balanced on each level, the entire parameter must be present, so we can copy it without difficulty.

⟨ Put a parameter on the parameter stack, or **goto** *restart* if error occurs 90 ⟩ ≡
　　while (*cur_byte* = *cur_end*) ∧ (*stack_ptr* > 0) **do** *pop_level*;
　　if (*stack_ptr* = 0) ∨ (*tok_mem*[*zo*, *cur_byte*] ≠ "(") **then**
　　　　begin *print_nl*(´!␣No␣parameter␣given␣for␣´); *print_id*(a); *error*; **goto** *restart*;
　　　　end;
　　⟨ Copy the parameter into *tok_mem* 93 ⟩;
　　equiv[*name_ptr*] ← *text_ptr*; *ilk*[*name_ptr*] ← *simple*; *w* ← *name_ptr* **mod** *ww*;
　　k ← *byte_ptr*[w];
　　debug if *k* = *max_bytes* **then** *overflow*(´byte␣memory´);
　　byte_mem[w, k] ← "#"; *incr*(k); *byte_ptr*[w] ← *k*;
　　gubed　　{ this code has set the parameter identifier for debugging printouts }
　　if *name_ptr* > *max_names* − *ww* **then** *overflow*(´name´);
　　byte_start[*name_ptr* + *ww*] ← *k*; *incr*(*name_ptr*);
　　if *text_ptr* > *max_texts* − *zz* **then** *overflow*(´text´);
　　text_link[*text_ptr*] ← 0; *tok_start*[*text_ptr* + *zz*] ← *tok_ptr*[z]; *incr*(*text_ptr*);
　　z ← *text_ptr* **mod** *zz*

This code is used in section 89.

91.　　The *pop_level* routine undoes the effect of parameter-pushing when a parameter macro is finished:

⟨ Remove a parameter from the parameter stack 91 ⟩ ≡
　　begin *decr*(*name_ptr*); *decr*(*text_ptr*); *z* ← *text_ptr* **mod** *zz*;
　　stat if *tok_ptr*[z] > *max_tok_ptr*[z] **then** *max_tok_ptr*[z] ← *tok_ptr*[z];
　　tats　　{ the maximum value of *tok_ptr* occurs just before parameter popping }
　　tok_ptr[z] ← *tok_start*[*text_ptr*];
　　debug *decr*(*byte_ptr*[*name_ptr* **mod** *ww*]); **gubed**
　　end

This code is used in section 85.

92.　　When a parameter occurs in a replacement text, we treat it as a simple macro in position (*name_ptr* − 1):

⟨ Start scanning current macro parameter, **goto** *restart* 92 ⟩ ≡
  begin *push_level*(*name_ptr* − 1); **goto** *restart*;
  end

This code is used in section 87.

93. Similarly, a *param* token encountered as we copy a parameter is converted into a simple macro call for *name_ptr* −1. Some care is needed to handle cases like *macro*(#; *print*(`'#'`)); the # token will have been changed to *param* outside of strings, but we still must distinguish 'real' parentheses from those in strings.

define *app_repl*(#) ≡
      begin if *tok_ptr*[*z*] = *max_toks* **then** *overflow*(`'token'`);
      tok_mem[*z*, *tok_ptr*[*z*]] ← #; *incr*(*tok_ptr*[*z*]);
      end

⟨ Copy the parameter into *tok_mem* 93 ⟩ ≡
  bal ← 1; *incr*(*cur_byte*);   { skip the opening '(' }
  loop begin *b* ← *tok_mem*[*zo*, *cur_byte*]; *incr*(*cur_byte*);
    if *b* = *param* **then** *store_two_bytes*(*name_ptr* + ′77777)
    else begin if *b* ≥ ′200 **then**
        begin *app_repl*(*b*); *b* ← *tok_mem*[*zo*, *cur_byte*]; *incr*(*cur_byte*);
        end
      else case *b* **of**
        "(": *incr*(*bal*);
        ")": **begin** *decr*(*bal*);
          if *bal* = 0 **then goto** *done*;
          end;
        "'": **repeat** *app_repl*(*b*); *b* ← *tok_mem*[*zo*, *cur_byte*]; *incr*(*cur_byte*);
          until *b* = "'";   { copy string, don't change *bal* }
        othercases *do_nothing*
        endcases;
      app_repl(*b*);
      end;
    end;
done:

This code is used in section 90.

94. Producing the output.   The *get_output* routine above handles most of the complexity of output generation, but there are two further considerations that have a nontrivial effect on **TANGLE**'s algorithms.

First, we want to make sure that the output is broken into lines not exceeding *line_length* characters per line, where these breaks occur at valid places (e.g., not in the middle of a string or a constant or an identifier, not between '<' and '>', not at a '**@&**' position where quantities are being joined together). Therefore we assemble the output into a buffer before deciding where the line breaks will appear. However, we make very little attempt to make "logical" line breaks that would enhance the readability of the output; people are supposed to read the input of **TANGLE** or the TEXed output of **WEAVE**, but not the tangled-up output. The only concession to readability is that a break after a semicolon will be made if possible, since commonly used "pretty printing" routines give better results in such cases.

Second, we want to decimalize non-decimal constants, and to combine integer quantities that are added or subtracted, because Pascal doesn't allow constant expressions in subrange types or in case labels. This means we want to have a procedure that treats a construction like `(E-15+17)` as equivalent to '`(E+2)`', while also leaving '`(1E-15+17)`' and '`(E-15+17*y)`' untouched. Consider also '`-15+17.5`' versus '`-15+17..5`'. We shall not combine integers preceding or following `*`, `/`, `div`, `mod`, or `@&`. Note that if y has been defined to equal -2, we must expand '`x*y`' into '`x*(-2)`'; but '`x-y`' can expand into '`x+2`' and we can even change '`x - y mod z`' to '`x + 2 mod z`' because Pascal has a nonstandard **mod** operation!

The following solution to these problems has been adopted: An array *out_buf* contains characters that have been generated but not yet output, and there are three pointers into this array. One of these, *out_ptr*, is the number of characters currently in the buffer, and we will have $1 \leq out\_ptr \leq line\_length$ most of the time. The second is *break_ptr*, which is the largest value $\leq out\_ptr$ such that we are definitely entitled to end a line by outputting the characters $out\_buf[1 .. (break\_ptr - 1)]$; we will always have $break\_ptr \leq line\_length$. Finally, *semi_ptr* is either zero or the largest known value of a legal break after a semicolon or comment on the current line; we will always have $semi\_ptr \leq break\_ptr$.

⟨Globals in the outer block 9⟩ +≡
out_buf: **array** [0 .. *out_buf_size*] **of** *ASCII_code*;   {assembled characters}
out_ptr: 0 .. *out_buf_size*;   {first available place in *out_buf* }
break_ptr: 0 .. *out_buf_size*;   {last breaking place in *out_buf* }
semi_ptr: 0 .. *out_buf_size*;   {last semicolon breaking place in *out_buf* }

95.   Besides having those three pointers, the output process is in one of several states:

num_or_id means that the last item in the buffer is a number or identifier, hence a blank space or line break must be inserted if the next item is also a number or identifier.

unbreakable means that the last item in the buffer was followed by the `@&` operation that inhibits spaces between it and the next item.

sign means that the last item in the buffer is to be followed by `+` or `-`, depending on whether *out_app* is positive or negative.

sign_val means that the decimal equivalent of $|out\_val|$ should be appended to the buffer. If $out\_val < 0$, or if $out\_val = 0$ and $last\_sign < 0$, the number should be preceded by a minus sign. Otherwise it should be preceded by the character *out_sign* unless $out\_sign = 0$; the *out_sign* variable is either 0 or "␣" or "+".

sign_val_sign is like *sign_val*, but also append `+` or `-` afterwards, depending on whether *out_app* is positive or negative.

sign_val_val is like *sign_val*, but also append the decimal equivalent of *out_app* including its sign, using *last_sign* in case $out\_app = 0$.

misc means none of the above.

For example, the output buffer and output state run through the following sequence as we generate characters from '(x-15+19-2)':

output	out_buf	out_state	out_sign	out_val	out_app	last_sign
(	(	*misc*				
x	(x	*num_or_id*				
−	(x	*sign*			−1	−1
15	(x	*sign_val*	"+"	−15		−15
+	(x	*sign_val_sign*	"+"	−15	+1	+1
19	(x	*sign_val_val*	"+"	−15	+19	+1
−	(x	*sign_val_sign*	"+"	+4	−1	−1
2	(x	*sign_val_val*	"+"	+4	−2	−2
)	(x+2)	*misc*				

At each stage we have put as much into the buffer as possible without knowing what is coming next. Examples like 'x-0.1' indicate why *last_sign* is needed to associate the proper sign with an output of zero.

In states *num_or_id*, *unbreakable*, and *misc* the last item in the buffer lies between *break_ptr* and *out_ptr* − 1, inclusive; in the other states we have *break_ptr* = *out_ptr*.

The numeric values assigned to *num_or_id*, etc., have been chosen to shorten some of the program logic; for example, the program makes use of the fact that *sign* + 2 = *sign_val_sign*.

define *misc* = 0   { state associated with special characters }
define *num_or_id* = 1   { state associated with numbers and identifiers }
define *sign* = 2   { state associated with pending + or - }
define *sign_val* = *num_or_id* + 2   { state associated with pending sign and value }
define *sign_val_sign* = *sign* + 2   { *sign_val* followed by another pending sign }
define *sign_val_val* = *sign_val* + 2   { *sign_val* followed by another pending value }
define *unbreakable* = *sign_val_val* + 1   { state associated with @& }

⟨ Globals in the outer block 9 ⟩ +≡
out_state: *eight_bits*;   { current status of partial output }
out_val, *out_app*: *integer*;   { pending values }
out_sign: *ASCII_code*;   { sign to use if appending *out_val* ≥ 0 }
last_sign: −1 .. +1;   { sign to use if appending a zero }

06.   During the output process, *line* will equal the number of the next line to be output.
⟨ Initialize the output buffer 96 ⟩ ≡
    out_state ← *misc*;   *out_ptr* ← 0;   *break_ptr* ← 0;   *semi_ptr* ← 0;   *out_buf*[0] ← 0;   *line* ← 1;
This code is used in section 112.

97.   Here is a routine that is invoked when *out_ptr* > *line_length* or when it is time to flush out the final line. The *flush_buffer* procedure often writes out the line up to the current *break_ptr* position, then moves the remaining information to the front of *out_buf*. However, it prefers to write only up to *semi_ptr*, if the residual line won't be too long.

define *check_break* ≡
        if *out_ptr* > *line_length* **then** *flush_buffer*

procedure *flush_buffer*;   { writes one line to output file }
  var *k*: 0 .. *out_buf_size*;   { index into *out_buf* }

> b: $0 \mathrel{..} out\_buf\_size$;   { value of $break\_ptr$ upon entry }

begin $b \leftarrow break\_ptr$;
if $(semi\_ptr \neq 0) \wedge (out\_ptr - semi\_ptr \leq line\_length)$ **then** $break\_ptr \leftarrow semi\_ptr$;
for $k \leftarrow 1$ **to** $break\_ptr$ **do** $write(Pascal\_file, xchr[out\_buf[k-1]])$;
$write\_ln(Pascal\_file)$; $incr(line)$;
if $line \bmod 100 = 0$ **then**
  begin $print('\,.\,')$;
  if $line \bmod 500 = 0$ **then** $print(line : 1)$;
  $update\_terminal$;   { progress report }
  end;
if $break\_ptr < out\_ptr$ **then**
  begin if $out_buf[break_ptr] = $ "␣" **then**
    begin $incr(break\_ptr)$;   { drop space at break }
    if $break\_ptr > b$ **then** $b \leftarrow break\_ptr$;
    end;
  for $k \leftarrow break\_ptr$ **to** $out\_ptr - 1$ **do** $out\_buf[k - break\_ptr] \leftarrow out\_buf[k]$;
  end;
$out\_ptr \leftarrow out\_ptr - break\_ptr$; $break\_ptr \leftarrow b - break\_ptr$; $semi\_ptr \leftarrow 0$;
if $out\_ptr > line\_length$ **then**
  begin $err\_print('!\,Long\,line\,must\,be\,truncated')$; $out\_ptr \leftarrow line\_length$;
  end;
end;

98. ⟨ Empty the last line from the buffer 98 ⟩ ≡
$break\_ptr \leftarrow out\_ptr$; $semi\_ptr \leftarrow 0$; $flush\_buffer$;
if $brace\_level \neq 0$ **then** $err\_print('!\,Program\,ended\,at\,brace\,level\,', brace\_level : 1)$;

This code is used in section 112.

99.   Another simple and useful routine appends the decimal equivalent of a nonnegative integer to the output buffer.

define $app(\#) \equiv$
        begin $out\_buf[out\_ptr] \leftarrow \#$; $incr(out\_ptr)$;   { append a single character }
        end
procedure $app\_val(v : integer)$;   { puts v into buffer, assumes $v \geq 0$ }
  var k: $0 \mathrel{..} out\_buf\_size$;   { index into out_buf }
  begin $k \leftarrow out\_buf\_size$;   { first we put the digits at the very end of out_buf }
  repeat $out\_buf[k] \leftarrow v \bmod 10$; $v \leftarrow v \mathbin{\textbf{div}} 10$; $decr(k)$;
  until $v = 0$;
  repeat $incr(k)$; $app(out_buf[k] + $ "0"$)$;
  until $k = out\_buf\_size$;   { then we append them, most significant first }
  end;

100.   The output states are kept up to date by the output routines, which are called $send\_out$, $send\_val$, and $send\_sign$. The $send\_out$ procedure has two parameters: t tells the type of information being sent and v contains the information proper. Some information may also be passed in the array $out\_contrib$.

If $t = misc$ then v is a character to be output.
If $t = str$ then v is the length of a string or something like '<>' in $out\_contrib$.

If $t = ident$ then v is the length of an identifier in *out_contrib*.

If $t = frac$ then v is the length of a fraction and/or exponent in *out_contrib*.

define $str = 1$ { *send_out* code for a string }
define $ident = 2$ { *send_out* code for an identifier }
define $frac = 3$ { *send_out* code for a fraction }

⟨ Globals in the outer block 9 ⟩ +≡
out_contrib: **array** [1 .. *line_length*] **of** *ASCII_code*; { a contribution to *out_buf* }

101. A slightly subtle point in the following code is that the user may ask for a *join* operation (i.e., **@&**) following whatever is being sent out. We will see later that *join* is implemented in part by calling *send_out*(*frac*, 0).

procedure *send_out*(*t* : *eight_bits*; *v* : *sixteen_bits*); { outputs *v* of type *t* }
   label *restart*;
   var *k*: 0 .. *line_length*; { index into *out_contrib* }
   begin ⟨ Get the buffer ready for appending the new information 102 ⟩;
   if $t \neq misc$ **then**
      for $k \leftarrow 1$ **to** v **do** *app*(*out_contrib*[*k*])
   else *app*(*v*);
   check_break;
   if $(t = misc) \wedge ((v = ";") \vee (v = "\}"))$ **then**
      begin *semi_ptr* ← *out_ptr*; *break_ptr* ← *out_ptr*;
      end;
   if $t \geq ident$ **then** *out_state* ← *num_or_id* { $t = ident$ or *frac* }
   else *out_state* ← *misc* { $t = str$ or *misc* }
   end;

102. Here is where the buffer states for signs and values collapse into simpler states, because we are about to append something that doesn't combine with the previous integer constants.

We use an ASCII-code trick: Since "," − 1 = "+" and "," + 1 = "-", we have "," − *c* = sign of *c*, when $|c| = 1$.

⟨ Get the buffer ready for appending the new information 102 ⟩ ≡
restart: **case** *out_state* **of**
  num_or_id: **if** $t \neq frac$ **then**
     begin *break_ptr* ← *out_ptr*;
     if $t = ident$ **then** *app*("␣");
     end;
  sign: **begin** *app*("," − *out_app*); *check_break*; *break_ptr* ← *out_ptr*;
    end;
  sign_val, *sign_val_sign*: **begin** ⟨ Append *out_val* to buffer 103 ⟩;
    out_state ← *out_state* − 2; **goto** *restart*;
    end;
  sign_val_val: ⟨ Reduce *sign_val_val* to *sign_val* and **goto** *restart* 104 ⟩;
  misc: **if** $t \neq frac$ **then** *break_ptr* ← *out_ptr*;
    othercases *do_nothing* { this is for *unbreakable* state }
  endcases

This code is used in section 101.

103. ⟨ Append *out_val* to buffer 103 ⟩ ≡
  if (*out_val* < 0) ∨ ((*out_val* = 0) ∧ (*last_sign* < 0)) **then** *app*("-")
  else if *out_sign* > 0 **then** *app*(*out_sign*);
  app_val(*abs*(*out_val*)); *check_break*;

This code is used in sections 102 and 104.

104. ⟨ Reduce *sign_val_val* to *sign_val* and **goto** *restart* 104 ⟩ ≡
  begin if (*t* = *frac*) ∨ ((⟨ Contribution is * or / or DIV or MOD 105 ⟩) **then**
    begin ⟨ Append *out_val* to buffer 103 ⟩;
    out_sign ← "+"; *out_val* ← *out_app*;
    end
  else *out_val* ← *out_val* + *out_app*;
  out_state ← *sign_val*; **goto** *restart*;
  end

This code is used in section 102.

105. ⟨ Contribution is * or / or DIV or MOD 105 ⟩ ≡
  ((*t* = *ident*) ∧ (*v* = 3) ∧
      (((*out_contrib*[1] = "D") ∧ (*out_contrib*[2] = "I") ∧ (*out_contrib*[3] = "V")) ∨
      ((*out_contrib*[1] = "M") ∧ (*out_contrib*[2] = "O") ∧ (*out_contrib*[3] = "D")))) ∨
      ((*t* = *misc*) ∧ ((*v* = "*") ∨ (*v* = "/"))))

This code is used in section 104.

106.   The following routine is called with $v = \pm 1$ when a plus or minus sign is appended to
the output. It extends Pascal to allow repeated signs (e.g., '--' is equivalent to '+'), rather
than to give an error message. The signs following 'E' in real constants are treated as part
of a fraction, so they are not seen by this routine.

procedure *send_sign*(*v* : *integer*);
  begin case *out_state* **of**
  sign, *sign_val_sign*: *out_app* ← *out_app* * *v*;
  sign_val: **begin** *out_app* ← *v*; *out_state* ← *sign_val_sign*;
    end;
  sign_val_val: **begin** *out_val* ← *out_val* + *out_app*; *out_app* ← *v*; *out_state* ← *sign_val_sign*;
    end;
  othercases begin *break_ptr* ← *out_ptr*; *out_app* ← *v*; *out_state* ← *sign*;
    end
  endcases;
  last_sign ← *out_app*;
  end;

107.   When a (signed) integer value is to be output, we call *send_val*.

  define *bad_case* = 666   { this is a label used below }

procedure *send_val*(*v* : *integer*);   { output the (signed) value *v* }
  label *bad_case*,   { go here if we can't keep *v* in the output state }
      exit;
  begin case *out_state* **of**
  num_or_id: **begin** ⟨ If previous output was DIV or MOD, **goto** *bad_case* 110 ⟩;
      out_sign ← "␣"; *out_state* ← *sign_val*; *out_val* ← *v*; *break_ptr* ← *out_ptr*; *last_sign* ← +1;

```
      end;
  misc: begin ⟨If previous output was * or /, goto bad_case 109⟩;
      out_sign ← 0; out_state ← sign_val; out_val ← v; break_ptr ← out_ptr; last_sign ← +1;
      end;
  ⟨Handle cases of send_val when out_state contains a sign 108⟩
  othercases goto bad_case
  endcases;
  return;
bad_case: ⟨Append the decimal value of v, with parentheses if negative 111⟩;
exit: end;
```

108. ⟨Handle cases of *send_val* when *out_state* contains a sign 108⟩ ≡

```
sign: begin out_sign ← "+"; out_state ← sign_val; out_val ← out_app * v;
    end;
sign_val: begin out_state ← sign_val_val; out_app ← v;
    err_print(´!␣Two␣numbers␣occurred␣without␣a␣sign␣between␣them´);
    end;
sign_val_sign: begin out_state ← sign_val_val; out_app ← out_app * v;
    end;
sign_val_val: begin out_val ← out_val + out_app; out_app ← v;
    err_print(´!␣Two␣numbers␣occurred␣without␣a␣sign␣between␣them´);
    end;
```

This code is used in section 107.

109. ⟨If previous output was * or /, goto *bad_case* 109⟩ ≡

```
  if (out_ptr = break_ptr + 1) ∧ ((out_buf[break_ptr] = "*") ∨ (out_buf[break_ptr] = "/")) then
      goto bad_case
```

This code is used in section 107.

110. ⟨If previous output was DIV or MOD, goto *bad_case* 110⟩ ≡

```
  if (out_ptr = break_ptr + 3) ∨ ((out_ptr = break_ptr + 4) ∧ (out_buf[break_ptr] = "␣")) then
      if ((out_buf[out_ptr − 3] = "D") ∧ (out_buf[out_ptr − 2] = "I") ∧ (out_buf[out_ptr − 1] = "V"))∨
          ((out_buf[out_ptr − 3] = "M") ∧ (out_buf[out_ptr − 2] = "O") ∧ (out_buf[out_ptr − 1] = "D"))
              then
      goto bad_case
```

This code is used in section 107.

111. ⟨Append the decimal value of v, with parentheses if negative 111⟩ ≡

```
  if v ≥ 0 then
      begin if out_state = num_or_id then
          begin break_ptr ← out_ptr; app("␣");
          end;
      app_val(v); check_break; out_state ← num_or_id;
      end
  else begin app("("); app("−"); app_val(−v); app(")"); check_break; out_state ← misc;
      end
```

This code is used in section 107.

112.   The big output switch.   To complete the output process, we need a routine that takes the results of *get_output* and feeds them to *send_out*, *send_val*, or *send_sign*. This procedure '*send_the_output*' will be invoked just once, as follows:

⟨ Phase II: Output the contents of the compressed tables 112 ⟩ ≡
  if *text_link*[0] = 0 **then**
    begin *print_nl*(´!␣No␣output␣was␣specified.´); *mark_harmless*;
    end
  else begin *print_nl*(´Writing␣the␣output␣file´); *update_terminal*;
    ⟨ Initialize the output stacks 83 ⟩;
    ⟨ Initialize the output buffer 96 ⟩;
    send_the_output;
    ⟨ Empty the last line from the buffer 98 ⟩;
    print_nl(´Done.´);
    end

This code is used in section 182.

113.   A many-way switch is used to send the output:

  define *get_fraction* = 2   { this label is used below }
procedure *send_the_output*;
  label *get_fraction*,   { go here to finish scanning a real constant }
    reswitch, *continue*;
  var *cur_char*: *eight_bits*;   { the latest character received }
    k: 0 .. *line_length*;   { index into *out_contrib* }
    j: 0 .. *max_bytes*;   { index into *byte_mem* }
    w: 0 .. *ww* − 1;   { segment of *byte_mem* }
    n: *integer*;   { number being scanned }
  begin while *stack_ptr* > 0 **do**
    begin *cur_char* ← *get_output*;
  reswitch: **case** *cur_char* **of**
    0: *do_nothing*;   { this case might arise if output ends unexpectedly }
    ⟨ Cases related to identifiers 116 ⟩
    ⟨ Cases related to constants, possibly leading to *get_fraction* or *reswitch* 119 ⟩
    "+","-": *send_sign*("," − *cur_char*);
    ⟨ Cases like <> and := 114 ⟩
    "´": ⟨ Send a string, **goto** *reswitch* 117 ⟩;
    ⟨ Other printable characters 115 ⟩: *send_out*(*misc*, *cur_char*);
    ⟨ Cases involving @{ and @} 121 ⟩
    join: **begin** *send_out*(*frac*, 0); *out_state* ← *unbreakable*;
      end;
    verbatim: ⟨ Send verbatim string 118 ⟩;
    force_line: ⟨ Force a line break 122 ⟩;
    othercases *err_print*(´!␣Can´´t␣output␣ASCII␣code␣´, *cur_char* : 1)
    endcases;
    goto *continue*;
  get_fraction: ⟨ Special code to finish real constants 120 ⟩;
  continue: **end**;
  end;

114.   ⟨ Cases like <> and := 114 ⟩ ≡

and_sign: **begin** *out_contrib*[1] ← "A"; *out_contrib*[2] ← "N"; *out_contrib*[3] ← "D";
  send_out(*ident*, 3);
  end;
not_sign: **begin** *out_contrib*[1] ← "N"; *out_contrib*[2] ← "O"; *out_contrib*[3] ← "T";
  send_out(*ident*, 3);
  end;
set_element_sign: **begin** *out_contrib*[1] ← "I"; *out_contrib*[2] ← "N"; *send_out*(*ident*, 2);
  end;
or_sign: **begin** *out_contrib*[1] ← "O"; *out_contrib*[2] ← "R"; *send_out*(*ident*, 2);
  end;
left_arrow: **begin** *out_contrib*[1] ← ":"; *out_contrib*[2] ← "="; *send_out*(*str*, 2);
  end;
not_equal: **begin** *out_contrib*[1] ← "<"; *out_contrib*[2] ← ">"; *send_out*(*str*, 2);
  end;
less_or_equal: **begin** *out_contrib*[1] ← "<"; *out_contrib*[2] ← "="; *send_out*(*str*, 2);
  end;
greater_or_equal: **begin** *out_contrib*[1] ← ">"; *out_contrib*[2] ← "="; *send_out*(*str*, 2);
  end;
equivalence_sign: **begin** *out_contrib*[1] ← "="; *out_contrib*[2] ← "="; *send_out*(*str*, 2);
  end;
double_dot: **begin** *out_contrib*[1] ← "."; *out_contrib*[2] ← "."; *send_out*(*str*, 2);
  end;

This code is used in section 113.

115. Please don't ask how all of the following characters can actually get through **TANGLE** outside of strings. It seems that """" and "{" cannot actually occur at this point of the program, but they have been included just in case **TANGLE** changes.

If **TANGLE** is producing code for a Pascal compiler that uses '(.' and '.)' instead of square brackets (e.g., on machines with EBCDIC code), one should remove "[" and "]" from this list and put them into the preceding module in the appropriate way. Similarly, some compilers want '^' to be converted to '@'.

⟨ Other printable characters 115 ⟩ ≡
  "!", """", "#", "$", "%", "&", "(", ")", "*", ",", "/", ":", ";", "<", "=", ">", "?", "@", "[", "\", "]",
  "^", "_", "`", "{", "|"

This code is used in section 113.

116. Single-character identifiers represent themselves, while longer ones can be found in the *byte_mem* array. All must be converted to uppercase, with underlines removed. Extremely long identifiers must be chopped.

(Some Pascal compilers work with lowercase letters instead of uppercase. If this module of **TANGLE** is changed, it's also necessary to change from uppercase to lowercase in the modules that are listed in the index under "uppercase".)

define *up_to*(#) ≡ # − 24, # − 23, # − 22, # − 21, # − 20, # − 19, # − 18, # − 17, # − 16, # − 15, # − 14,
  # − 13, # − 12, # − 11, # − 10, # − 9, # − 8, # − 7, # − 6, # − 5, # − 4, # − 3, # − 2, # − 1, #

⟨ Cases related to identifiers 116 ⟩ ≡
"A", *up_to*("Z"): **begin** *out_contrib*[1] ← *cur_char*; *send_out*(*ident*, 1);
  end;
"a", *up_to*("z"): **begin** *out_contrib*[1] ← *cur_char* − '40; *send_out*(*ident*, 1);

```
  end;
identifier: begin k ← 0; j ← byte_start[cur_val]; w ← cur_val mod ww;
  while (k < max_id_length) ∧ (j < byte_start[cur_val + ww]) do
    begin incr(k); out_contrib[k] ← byte_mem[w, j]; incr(j);
    if out_contrib[k] ≥ "a" then out_contrib[k] ← out_contrib[k] − '40
    else if out_contrib[k] = "_" then decr(k);
    end;
  send_out(ident, k);
  end;
```

This code is used in section 113.

117.   After sending a string, we need to look ahead at the next character, in order to see if there were two consecutive single-quote marks. Afterwards we go to *reswitch* to process the next character.

⟨Send a string, **goto** *reswitch* 117⟩ ≡
```
  begin k ← 1; out_contrib[1] ← "´";
  repeat if k < line_length then incr(k);
    out_contrib[k] ← get_output;
  until (out_contrib[k] = "´") ∨ (stack_ptr = 0);
  if k = line_length then err_print('!␣String␣too␣long');
  send_out(str, k); cur_char ← get_output;
  if cur_char = "´" then out_state ← unbreakable;
  goto reswitch;
  end
```

This code is used in section 113.

118.   Sending a verbatim string is similar, but we don't have to look ahead.

⟨Send verbatim string 118⟩ ≡
```
  begin k ← 0;
  repeat if k < line_length then incr(k);
    out_contrib[k] ← get_output;
  until (out_contrib[k] = verbatim) ∨ (stack_ptr = 0);
  if k = line_length then err_print('!␣Verbatim␣string␣too␣long');
  send_out(str, k − 1);
  end
```

This code is used in section 113.

119.   In order to encourage portable software, `TANGLE` complains if the constants get dangerously close to the largest value representable on a 32-bit computer ($2^{31} − 1$).

define *digits* ≡ "0", "1", "2", "3", "4", "5", "6", "7", "8", "9"

⟨Cases related to constants, possibly leading to *get_fraction* or *reswitch* 119⟩ ≡
```
digits: begin n ← 0;
  repeat cur_char ← cur_char − "0";
    if n ≥ '14631463146 then err_print('!␣Constant␣too␣big')
    else n ← 10 ∗ n + cur_char;
    cur_char ← get_output;
  until (cur_char > "9") ∨ (cur_char < "0");
  send_val(n); k ← 0;
```

```
  if cur_char = "e" then  cur_char ← "E";
  if cur_char = "E" then goto get_fraction
  else goto reswitch;
  end;
check_sum: send_val(pool_check_sum);
octal: begin n ← 0;  cur_char ← "0";
  repeat cur_char ← cur_char − "0";
    if n ≥ '2000000000 then  err_print('!␣Constant␣too␣big')
    else n ← 8 ∗ n + cur_char;
    cur_char ← get_output;
  until  (cur_char > "7") ∨ (cur_char < "0");
  send_val(n);  goto reswitch;
  end;
hex: begin n ← 0;  cur_char ← "0";
  repeat if cur_char ≥ "A" then  cur_char ← cur_char + 10 − "A"
    else cur_char ← cur_char − "0";
    if n ≥ "8000000 then  err_print('!␣Constant␣too␣big')
    else n ← 16 ∗ n + cur_char;
    cur_char ← get_output;
  until  (cur_char > "F") ∨ (cur_char < "0") ∨ ((cur_char > "9") ∧ (cur_char < "A"));
  send_val(n);  goto reswitch;
  end;
number: send_val(cur_val);
".": begin k ← 1;  out_contrib[1] ← ".";  cur_char ← get_output;
  if cur_char = "." then
    begin out_contrib[2] ← ".";  send_out(str, 2);
    end
  else if  (cur_char ≥ "0") ∧ (cur_char ≤ "9") then  goto get_fraction
    else begin send_out(misc, ".");  goto reswitch;
      end;
  end;
```
This code is used in section 113.

120. The following code appears at label '*get_fraction*', when we want to scan to the end of a real constant. The first k characters of a fraction have already been placed in *out_contrib*, and *cur_char* is the next character.

⟨ Special code to finish real constants 120 ⟩ ≡
```
  repeat if k < line_length then  incr(k);
    out_contrib[k] ← cur_char;  cur_char ← get_output;
    if  (out_contrib[k] = "E") ∧ ((cur_char = "+") ∨ (cur_char = "-")) then
      begin if k < line_length then  incr(k);
      out_contrib[k] ← cur_char;  cur_char ← get_output;
      end
    else if cur_char = "e" then  cur_char ← "E";
  until  (cur_char ≠ "E") ∧ ((cur_char < "0") ∨ (cur_char > "9"));
  if k = line_length then  err_print('!␣Fraction␣too␣long');
  send_out(frac, k);  goto reswitch
```
This code is used in section 113.

121. Some Pascal compilers do not recognize comments in braces, so the comments must be delimited by '(*' and '*)'. In such cases the statement '*send_out*(*misc*, "{")' that appears here should be replaced by '**begin** *out_contrib*[1] ← "("; *out_contrib*[2] ← "*"; *send_out*(*str*, 2); **end**', and a similar change should be made to '*send_out*(*misc*, "}")'.

⟨Cases involving @{ and @} 121⟩ ≡
begin_comment: **begin if** *brace_level* = 0 **then** *send_out*(*misc*, "{")
  else *send_out*(*misc*, "[");
  incr(*brace_level*);
  end;
end_comment: **if** *brace_level* > 0 **then**
    begin *decr*(*brace_level*);
    if *brace_level* = 0 **then** *send_out*(*misc*, "}")
    else *send_out*(*misc*, "]");
    end
  else *err_print*(´!␣Extra␣@}´);
module_number: **begin if** *brace_level* = 0 **then** *send_out*(*misc*, "{")
  else *send_out*(*misc*, "[");
  if *cur_val* < 0 **then**
    begin *send_out*(*misc*, ":"); *send_val*(−*cur_val*);
    end
  else begin *send_val*(*cur_val*); *send_out*(*misc*, ":");
    end;
  if *brace_level* = 0 **then** *send_out*(*misc*, "}")
  else *send_out*(*misc*, "]");
  end;

This code is used in section 113.

122. ⟨Force a line break 122⟩ ≡
  begin *send_out*(*str*, 0); { normalize the buffer }
  while *out_ptr* > 0 **do**
    begin if *out_ptr* ≤ *line_length* **then** *break_ptr* ← *out_ptr*;
    flush_buffer;
    end;
  out_state ← *misc*;
  end

This code is used in section 113.

123.   Introduction to the input phase.   We have now seen that TANGLE will be able to output the full Pascal program, if we can only get that program into the byte memory in the proper format. The input process is something like the output process in reverse, since we compress the text as we read it in and we expand it as we write it out.

    There are three main input routines. The most interesting is the one that gets the next token of a Pascal text; the other two are used to scan rapidly past TEX text in the WEB source code. One of the latter routines will jump to the next token that starts with '@', and the other skips to the end of a Pascal comment.

124.   But first we need to consider the low-level routine *get_line* that takes care of merging *change_file* into *web_file*. The *get_line* procedure also updates the line numbers for error messages.

⟨ Globals in the outer block 9 ⟩ +≡
line: *integer*;   { the number of the current line in the current file }
other_line: *integer*;
        { the number of the current line in the input file that is not currently being read }
temp_line: *integer*;   { used when interchanging *line* with *other_line* }
limit: 0 .. *buf_size*;   { the last character position occupied in the buffer }
loc: 0 .. *buf_size*;   { the next character position to be read from the buffer }
input_has_ended: *boolean*;   { if *true*, there is no more input }
changing: *boolean*;   { if *true*, the current line is from *change_file* }

125. As we change *changing* from *true* to *false* and back again, we must remember to
swap the values of *line* and *other_line* so that the *err_print* routine will be sure to report
the correct line number.

  define *change_changing* ≡ *changing* ← ¬*changing*; *temp_line* ← *other_line*; *other_line* ← *line*;
        line ← *temp_line*   { *line* ↔ *other_line* }

126. When *changing* is *false*, the next line of *change_file* is kept in *change_buffer*[0 ..
change_limit], for purposes of comparison with the next line of *web_file*. After the change
file has been completely input, we set *change_limit* ← 0, so that no further matches will be
made.

⟨ Globals in the outer block 9 ⟩ +≡
change_buffer: **array** [0 .. *buf_size*] **of** *ASCII_code*;
change_limit: 0 .. *buf_size*;   { the last position occupied in *change_buffer* }

127. Here's a simple function that checks if the two buffers are different.
function *lines_dont_match*: *boolean*;
  label *exit*;
  var *k*: 0 .. *buf_size*;   { index into the buffers }
  begin *lines_dont_match* ← *true*;
  if *change_limit* ≠ *limit* **then return**;
  if *limit* > 0 **then**
    for *k* ← 0 **to** *limit* − 1 **do**
      if *change_buffer*[*k*] ≠ *buffer*[*k*] **then return**;
  lines_dont_match ← *false*;
exit: **end**;

128. Procedure *prime_the_change_buffer* sets *change_buffer* in preparation for the next
matching operation. Since blank lines in the change file are not used for matching, we have
(*change_limit* = 0) ∧ ¬*changing* if and only if the change file is exhausted. This procedure
is called only when *changing* is true; hence error messages will be reported correctly.

procedure *prime_the_change_buffer*;
  label *continue*, *done*, *exit*;
  var *k*: 0 .. *buf_size*;   { index into the buffers }
  begin *change_limit* ← 0;   { this value will be used if the change file ends }
  ⟨ Skip over comment lines in the change file; **return** if end of file 129 ⟩;
  ⟨ Skip to the next nonblank line; **return** if end of file 130 ⟩;
  ⟨ Move *buffer* and *limit* to *change_buffer* and *change_limit* 131 ⟩;
exit: **end**;

129.   While looking for a line that begins with **@x** in the change file, we allow lines that begin with **@**, as long as they don't begin with **@y** or **@z** (which would probably indicate that the change file is fouled up).

⟨ Skip over comment lines in the change file; **return** if end of file 129 ⟩ ≡
    loop begin *incr*(*line*);
        if ¬*input_ln*(*change_file*) **then return**;
        if *limit* < 2 **then goto** *continue*;
        if *buffer*[0] ≠ "@" **then goto** *continue*;
        if (*buffer*[1] ≥ "X") ∧ (*buffer*[1] ≤ "Z") **then** *buffer*[1] ← *buffer*[1] + "z" − "Z";
            { lowercasify }
        if *buffer*[1] = "x" **then goto** *done*;
        if (*buffer*[1] = "y") ∨ (*buffer*[1] = "z") **then**
           begin *loc* ← 2; *err_print*(´!␣Where␣is␣the␣matching␣@x?´);
           end;
    continue: **end**;
  done:

This code is used in section 128.

130.   Here we are looking at lines following the **@x**.

⟨ Skip to the next nonblank line; **return** if end of file 130 ⟩ ≡
    repeat *incr*(*line*);
        if ¬*input_ln*(*change_file*) **then**
           begin *err_print*(´!␣Change␣file␣ended␣after␣@x´); **return**;
           end;
    until *limit* > 0;

This code is used in section 128.

131.   ⟨ Move *buffer* and *limit* to *change_buffer* and *change_limit* 131 ⟩ ≡
    begin *change_limit* ← *limit*;
    if *limit* > 0 **then**
        for *k* ← 0 **to** *limit* − 1 **do** *change_buffer*[*k*] ← *buffer*[*k*];
    end

This code is used in sections 128 and 132.

132.   The following procedure is used to see if the next change entry should go into effect; it is called only when *changing* is false. The idea is to test whether or not the current contents of *buffer* matches the current contents of *change_buffer*. If not, there's nothing more to do; but if so, a change is called for: All of the text down to the **@y** is supposed to match. An error message is issued if any discrepancy is found. Then the procedure prepares to read the next line from *change_file*.

procedure *check_change*;   { switches to *change_file* if the buffers match }
    label *exit*;
    var *n*: *integer*;   { the number of discrepancies found }
      k: 0 .. *buf_size*;   { index into the buffers }
    begin if *lines_dont_match* **then return**;
    n ← 0;
    loop begin *change_changing*;   { now it's *true* }
      incr(*line*);

```
        if ¬input_ln(change_file) then
           begin err_print(´! Change file ended before @y´); change_limit ← 0;
           change_changing;  { false again }
           return;
           end;
        ⟨ If the current line starts with @y, report any discrepancies and return 133 ⟩;
        ⟨ Move buffer and limit to change_buffer and change_limit 131 ⟩;
        change_changing;  { now it's false }
        incr(line);
        if ¬input_ln(web_file) then
           begin err_print(´! WEB file ended during a change´); input_has_ended ← true;
           return;
           end;
        if lines_dont_match then incr(n);
        end;
exit: end;
```

133. ⟨ If the current line starts with @y, report any discrepancies and return 133 ⟩ ≡

```
  if limit > 1 then
     if buffer[0] = "@" then
        begin if (buffer[1] ≥ "X") ∧ (buffer[1] ≤ "Z") then buffer[1] ← buffer[1] + "z" − "Z";
               { lowercasify }
        if (buffer[1] = "x") ∨ (buffer[1] = "z") then
           begin loc ← 2; err_print(´! Where is the matching @y?´);
           end
        else if buffer[1] = "y" then
              begin if n > 0 then
                 begin loc ← 2;
                 err_print(´! Hmm... ´, n : 1, ´ of the preceding lines failed to match´);
                 end;
              return;
              end
        end
```

This code is used in section 132.

134. ⟨ Initialize the input system 134 ⟩ ≡

```
  open_input; line ← 0; other_line ← 0;
  changing ← true; prime_the_change_buffer; change_changing;
  limit ← 0; loc ← 1; buffer[0] ← " "; input_has_ended ← false;
```

This code is used in section 182.

135. The *get_line* procedure is called when $loc > limit$; it puts the next line of merged input into the buffer and updates the other variables appropriately. A space is placed at the right end of the line.

```
procedure get_line;  { inputs the next line }
  label restart;
  begin restart: if changing then ⟨ Read from change_file and maybe turn off changing 137 ⟩;
  if ¬changing then
     begin ⟨ Read from web_file and maybe turn on changing 136 ⟩;
```

>   **if** *changing* **then goto** *restart*;
>   **end**;
>   *loc* $\leftarrow$ 0; *buffer*[*limit*] $\leftarrow$ "␣";
>   **end**;

136. $\langle$ Read from *web_file* and maybe turn on *changing* 136 $\rangle \equiv$
  begin *incr*(*line*);
  if $\neg$*input_ln*(*web_file*) **then** *input_has_ended* $\leftarrow$ *true*
  else if *limit* = *change_limit* **then**
     if *buffer*[0] = *change_buffer*[0] **then**
       if *change_limit* > 0 **then** *check_change*;
  end

This code is used in section 135.

137. $\langle$ Read from *change_file* and maybe turn off *changing* 137 $\rangle \equiv$
  begin *incr*(*line*);
  if $\neg$*input_ln*(*change_file*) **then**
    begin *err_print*(`!␣Change␣file␣ended␣without␣@z`); *buffer*[0] $\leftarrow$ "@"; *buffer*[1] $\leftarrow$ "z";
    limit $\leftarrow$ 2;
    end;
  if *limit* > 1 **then** { check if the change has ended }
    if *buffer*[0] = "@" **then**
     begin if (*buffer*[1] $\geq$ "X") $\wedge$ (*buffer*[1] $\leq$ "Z") **then** *buffer*[1] $\leftarrow$ *buffer*[1] + "z" − "Z";
        { lowercasify }
     if (*buffer*[1] = "x") $\vee$ (*buffer*[1] = "y") **then**
      begin *loc* $\leftarrow$ 2; *err_print*(`!␣Where␣is␣the␣matching␣@z?`);
      end
     else if *buffer*[1] = "z" **then**
       begin *prime_the_change_buffer*; *change_changing*;
       end;
     end;
  end

This code is used in section 135.

138. At the end of the program, we will tell the user if the change file had a line that didn't match any relevant line in *web_file*.

$\langle$ Check that all changes have been read 138 $\rangle \equiv$
  if *change_limit* $\neq$ 0 **then** { *changing* is false }
    begin for *loc* $\leftarrow$ 0 **to** *change_limit* **do** *buffer*[*loc*] $\leftarrow$ *change_buffer*[*loc*];
    limit $\leftarrow$ *change_limit*; *changing* $\leftarrow$ *true*; *line* $\leftarrow$ *other_line*; *loc* $\leftarrow$ *change_limit*;
    err_print(`!␣Change␣file␣entry␣did␣not␣match`);
    end

This code is used in section 183.

139. Important milestones are reached during the input phase when certain control codes are sensed.

Control codes in WEB begin with '@', and the next character identifies the code. Some of these are of interest only to WEAVE, so TANGLE ignores them; the others are converted by TANGLE into internal code numbers by the *control_code* function below. The ordering of these internal code numbers has been chosen to simplify the program logic; larger numbers are given to the control codes that denote more significant milestones.

> **define** *ignore* = 0   { control code of no interest to TANGLE }
> **define** *control_text* = '203   { control code for '@t', '@^', etc. }
> **define** *format* = '204   { control code for '@f' }
> **define** *definition* = '205   { control code for '@d' }
> **define** *begin_Pascal* = '206   { control code for '@p' }
> **define** *module_name* = '207   { control code for '@<' }
> **define** *new_module* = '210   { control code for '@␣' and '@*' }

function *control_code*(*c* : *ASCII_code*): *eight_bits*;   { convert *c* after @ }
   begin case *c* **of**
   "@": *control_code* ← "@";   { 'quoted' at sign }
   "`": *control_code* ← *octal*;   { precedes octal constant }
   """": *control_code* ← *hex*;   { precedes hexadecimal constant }
   "$": *control_code* ← *check_sum*;   { string pool check sum }
   "␣", *tab_mark*: *control_code* ← *new_module*;   { beginning of a new module }
   "*": **begin** *print*(´*´, *module_count* + 1 : 1); *update_terminal*;   { print a progress report }
     control_code ← *new_module*;   { beginning of a new module }
     end;
   "D", "d": *control_code* ← *definition*;   { macro definition }
   "F", "f": *control_code* ← *format*;   { format definition }
   "{": *control_code* ← *begin_comment*;   { begin-comment delimiter }
   "}": *control_code* ← *end_comment*;   { end-comment delimiter }
   "P", "p": *control_code* ← *begin_Pascal*;   { Pascal text in unnamed module }
   "T", "t", "^", ".", ":": *control_code* ← *control_text*;   { control text to be ignored }
   "&": *control_code* ← *join*;   { concatenate two tokens }
   "<": *control_code* ← *module_name*;   { beginning of a module name }
   "=": *control_code* ← *verbatim*;   { beginning of Pascal verbatim mode }
   "\": *control_code* ← *force_line*;   { force a new line in Pascal output }
   othercases *control_code* ← *ignore*   { ignore all other cases }
   endcases;
   end;

140. The *skip_ahead* procedure reads through the input at fairly high speed until finding the next non-ignorable control code, which it returns.

function *skip_ahead*: *eight_bits*;   { skip to next control code }
   label *done*;
   var *c*: *eight_bits*;   { control code found }
   begin loop
     begin if *loc* > *limit* **then**
       begin *get_line*;
       if *input_has_ended* **then**
         begin *c* ← *new_module*; **goto** *done*;
         end;
       end;
     buffer[*limit* + 1] ← "@";
     while *buffer*[*loc*] ≠ "@" **do** *incr*(*loc*);
     if *loc* ≤ *limit* **then**

```
    begin loc ← loc + 2;  c ← control_code(buffer[loc − 1]);
    if (c ≠ ignore) ∨ (buffer[loc − 1] = ">") then goto done;
    end;
  end;
done: skip_ahead ← c;
  end;
```

141. The *skip_comment* procedure reads through the input at somewhat high speed until finding the first unmatched right brace or until coming to the end of the file. It ignores characters following '\' characters, since all braces that aren't nested are supposed to be hidden in that way. For example, consider the process of skipping the first comment below, where the string containing the right brace has been typed as `\.\}` in the WEB file.

```
procedure skip_comment;   { skips to next unmatched '}' }
  label exit;
  var bal: eight_bits;   { excess of left braces }
    c: ASCII_code;   { current character }
  begin bal ← 0;
  loop begin if loc > limit then
      begin get_line;
      if input_has_ended then
        begin err_print('! Input ended in mid-comment'); return;
        end;
      end;
    c ← buffer[loc];  incr(loc);
    ⟨ Do special things when c = "@", "\", "{", "}"; return at end 142 ⟩;
    end;
exit: end;
```

142. ⟨ Do special things when c = "@", "\", "{", "}"; return at end 142 ⟩ ≡
```
  if c = "@" then
    begin c ← buffer[loc];
    if (c ≠ " ") ∧ (c ≠ tab_mark) ∧ (c ≠ "*") ∧ (c ≠ "z") ∧ (c ≠ "Z") then incr(loc)
    else begin err_print('! Section ended in mid-comment'); decr(loc); return;
      end
    end
  else if (c = "\") ∧ (buffer[loc] ≠ "@") then incr(loc)
    else if c = "{" then incr(bal)
      else if c = "}" then
          begin if bal = 0 then return;
          decr(bal);
          end
```
This code is used in section 141.

143. Inputting the next token.   As stated above, TANGLE's most interesting input procedure is the *get_next* routine that inputs the next token. However, the procedure isn't especially difficult.

In most cases the tokens output by *get_next* have the form used in replacement texts, except that two-byte tokens are not produced. An identifier that isn't one letter long is represented by the output '*identifier*', and in such a case the global variables *id_first* and *id_loc* will have been set to the appropriate values needed by the *id_lookup* procedure. A string that begins with a double-quote is also considered an *identifier*, and in such a case the global variable *double_chars* will also have been set appropriately. Control codes produce the corresponding output of the *control_code* function above; and if that code is *module_name*, the value of *cur_module* will point to the *byte_start* entry for that module name.

Another global variable, *scanning_hex*, is *true* during the time that the letters A through F should be treated as if they were digits.

⟨ Globals in the outer block 9 ⟩ +≡
cur_module: *name_pointer*;   { name of module just scanned }
scanning_hex: *boolean*;   { are we scanning a hexadecimal constant? }

144.   ⟨ Set initial values 10 ⟩ +=
scanning_hex ← *false*;

145.   At the top level, *get_next* is a multi-way switch based on the next character in the input buffer. A *new_module* code is inserted at the very end of the input file.

```
function get_next: eight_bits;    { produces the next input token }
  label restart, done, found;
  var c: eight_bits;    { the current character }
    d: eight_bits;    { the next character }
    j, k: 0 .. longest_name;    { indices into mod_text }
  begin restart: if loc > limit then
    begin get_line;
    if input_has_ended then
      begin c ← new_module; goto found;
      end;
    end;
  c ← buffer[loc]; incr(loc);
  if scanning_hex then
    ⟨ Go to found if c is a hexadecimal digit, otherwise set scanning_hex ← false 146 ⟩;
  case c of
  "A", up_to("Z"), "a", up_to("z"): ⟨ Get an identifier 148 ⟩;
  """": ⟨ Get a preprocessed string 149 ⟩;
  "@": ⟨ Get control code and possible module name 150 ⟩;
  ⟨ Compress two-symbol combinations like ':=' 147 ⟩
  "␣", tab_mark: goto restart;    { ignore spaces and tabs }
  "{": begin skip_comment; goto restart;
    end;
  othercases do_nothing
  endcases;
found: debug if trouble_shooting then debug_help; gubed
  get_next ← c;
  end;
```

146.   ⟨ Go to *found* if *c* is a hexadecimal digit, otherwise set *scanning_hex* ← *false* 146 ⟩ ≡
if $((c \geq$ "0"$) \wedge (c <$ "9"$)) \vee ((c \geq$ "A"$) \wedge (c \leq$ "F"$))$ then goto *found*
else *scanning_hex* ← *false*

This code is used in section 145.

147. Note that the following code substitutes @{ and @} for the respective combinations
'(*' and '*)'. Explicit braces should be used for TEX comments in Pascal text.

> **define** *compress*(#) ≡
> > **begin if** *loc* ≤ *limit* **then**
> > > **begin** *c* ← #; *incr*(*loc*);
> > > **end**;
> > **end**

⟨ Compress two-symbol combinations like ':=' 147 ⟩ ≡
".": **if** *buffer*[*loc*] = "." **then** *compress*(*double_dot*)
  else if *buffer*[*loc*] = ")" **then** *compress*("]");
":": **if** *buffer*[*loc*] = "=" **then** *compress*(*left_arrow*);
"=": **if** *buffer*[*loc*] = "=" **then** *compress*(*equivalence_sign*);
">": **if** *buffer*[*loc*] = "=" **then** *compress*(*greater_or_equal*);
"<": **if** *buffer*[*loc*] = "=" **then** *compress*(*less_or_equal*)
  else if *buffer*[*loc*] = ">" **then** *compress*(*not_equal*);
"(": **if** *buffer*[*loc*] = "*" **then** *compress*(*begin_comment*)
  else if *buffer*[*loc*] = "." **then** *compress*("[");
"*": **if** *buffer*[*loc*] = ")" **then** *compress*(*end_comment*);

This code is used in section 145.

148. We have to look at the preceding character to make sure this isn't part of a real
constant, before trying to find an identifier starting with 'e' or 'E'.

⟨ Get an identifier 148 ⟩ ≡
  begin if ((*c* = "e") ∨ (*c* = "E")) ∧ (*loc* > 1) **then**
    if (*buffer*[*loc* − 2] ≤ "9") ∧ (*buffer*[*loc* − 2] ≥ "0") **then** *c* ← 0;
  if *c* ≠ 0 **then**
    begin *decr*(*loc*); *id_first* ← *loc*;
    repeat *incr*(*loc*); *d* ← *buffer*[*loc*];
    until ((*d* < "0") ∨ ((*d* > "9") ∧ (*d* < "A")) ∨ ((*d* > "Z") ∧ (*d* < "a")) ∨ (*d* > "z")) ∧ (*d* ≠ "_");
    if *loc* > *id_first* + 1 **then**
      begin *c* ← *identifier*; *id_loc* ← *loc*;
      end;
    end
  else *c* ← "E"; { exponent of a real constant }
  end

This code is used in section 145.

149. A string that starts and ends with double-quote marks is converted into an identifier
that behaves like a numeric macro by means of the following piece of the program.

⟨ Get a preprocessed string 149 ⟩ ≡
  begin *double_chars* ← 0; *id_first* ← *loc* − 1;
  repeat *d* ← *buffer*[*loc*]; *incr*(*loc*);
    if (*d* = """") ∨ (*d* = "@") **then**
      if *buffer*[*loc*] = *d* **then**
        begin *incr*(*loc*); *d* ← 0; *incr*(*double_chars*);
        end
      else begin if *d* = "@" **then** *err_print*(´!␣Double␣@␣sign␣missing´)
        end

```
      else if loc > limit then
          begin err_print(´!␣String␣constant␣didn´´t␣end´); d ← """";
          end;
    until d = """";
    id_loc ← loc − 1;  c ← identifier;
    end
```

This code is used in section 145.

150. After an @ sign has been scanned, the next character tells us whether there is more work to do.

⟨ Get control code and possible module name 150 ⟩ ≡
```
    begin c ← control_code(buffer[loc]);  incr(loc);
    if c = ignore then goto restart
    else if c = hex then  scanning_hex ← true
        else if c = module_name then ⟨ Scan the module name and make cur_module point to it 151 ⟩
            else if c = control_text then
                begin repeat c ← skip_ahead;
                until c ≠ "@";
                if buffer[loc − 1] ≠ ">" then  err_print(´!␣Improper␣@␣within␣control␣text´);
                goto restart;
                end;
    end
```

This code is used in section 145.

151. ⟨ Scan the module name and make *cur_module* point to it 151 ⟩ ≡
```
    begin ⟨ Put module name into mod_text[1 .. k] 153 ⟩;
    if k > 3 then
        begin if (mod_text[k] = ".") ∧ (mod_text[k − 1] = ".") ∧ (mod_text[k − 2] = ".") then
            cur_module ← prefix_lookup(k − 3)
        else cur_module ← mod_lookup(k);
        end
    else cur_module ← mod_lookup(k);
    end
```

This code is used in section 150.

152. Module names are placed into the *mod_text* array with consecutive spaces, tabs, and carriage-returns replaced by single spaces. There will be no spaces at the beginning or the end. (We set *mod_text*[0] ← "␣" to facilitate this, since the *mod_lookup* routine uses *mod_text*[1] as the first character of the name.)

⟨ Set initial values 10 ⟩ +≡
```
    mod_text[0] ← "␣";
```

153. ⟨ Put module name into *mod_text*[1 .. k] 153 ⟩ ≡
```
    k ← 0;
    loop begin if loc > limit then
            begin get_line;
            if input_has_ended then
                begin err_print(´!␣Input␣ended␣in␣section␣name´); goto done;
```

```
        end;
      end;
  d ← buffer[loc]; ⟨If end of name, goto done 154⟩;
  incr(loc);
  if k < longest_name − 1 then incr(k);
  if (d = "␣") ∨ (d = tab_mark) then
      begin d ← "␣";
      if mod_text[k − 1] = "␣" then decr(k);
      end;
  mod_text[k] ← d;
  end;
done: ⟨Check for overlong name 155⟩;
  if (mod_text[k] = "␣") ∧ (k > 0) then decr(k);
```
This code is used in section 151.

154.   ⟨If end of name, goto done 154⟩ ≡
```
  if d = "@" then
      begin d ← buffer[loc + 1];
      if d = ">" then
          begin loc ← loc + 2; goto done;
          end;
      if (d = "␣") ∨ (d = tab_mark) ∨ (d = "*") then
          begin err_print(´!␣Section␣name␣didn´´t␣end´); goto done;
          end;
      incr(k); mod_text[k] ← "@"; incr(loc);  { now d = buffer[loc] again }
      end
```
This code is used in section 153.

155.   ⟨Check for overlong name 155⟩ ≡
```
  if k ≥ longest_name − 2 then
      begin print_nl(´!␣Section␣name␣too␣long:␣´);
      for j ← 1 to 25 do print(xchr[mod_text[j]]);
      print(´...´); mark_harmless;
      end
```
This code is used in section 153.

156.   Scanning a numeric definition.   When **TANGLE** looks at the Pascal text follow-ing the '=' of a numeric macro definition, it calls on the procedure $scan\_numeric(p)$, where p points to the name that is to be defined. This procedure evaluates the right-hand side, which must consist entirely of integer constants and defined numeric macros connected with + and − signs (no parentheses). It also sets the global variable $next\_control$ to the control code that terminated this definition.

A definition ends with the control codes $definition$, $format$, $module\_name$, $begin\_Pascal$, and new_module, all of which can be recognized by the fact that they are the largest values get_next can return.

define $end\_of\_definition(\#) ≡ (\# ≥ format)$ { is # a control code ending a definition? }

⟨Globals in the outer block 9⟩ +≡
$next\_control$: $eight\_bits$;   { control code waiting to be acted upon }

157. The evaluation of a numeric expression makes use of two variables called the *next_sign* and the *accumulator*. At the beginning, *next_sign* is +1 and *accumulator* is zero. When a + or – is scanned, *next_sign* is multiplied by the value of that sign. When a numeric value is scanned, it is multiplied by *next_sign* and added to the *accumulator*; then *next_sign* is reset to +1.

> **define** *add_in*(#) ≡
> > **begin** *accumulator* ← *accumulator* + *next_sign* ∗ (#); *next_sign* ← +1;
> > **end**

procedure *scan_numeric*(*p* : *name_pointer*);   { defines numeric macros }
  label *reswitch*, *done*;
  var *accumulator*: *integer*;   { accumulates sums }
    next_sign: −1 .. +1;   { sign to attach to next value }
    q: *name_pointer*;   { points to identifiers being evaluated }
    val: *integer*;   { constants being evaluated }
  begin ⟨ Set *accumulator* to the value of the right-hand side 158 ⟩;
  if *abs*(*accumulator*) ≥ ´100000 **then**
    begin *err_print*(´!␣Value␣too␣big:␣´, *accumulator* : 1); *accumulator* ← 0;
    end;
  equiv[*p*] ← *accumulator* + ´100000;   { name *p* now is defined to equal *accumulator* }
  end;

158. ⟨ Set *accumulator* to the value of the right-hand side 158 ⟩ ≡
  accumulator ← 0; *next_sign* ← +1;
  loop begin *next_control* ← *get_next*;
  reswitch: **case** *next_control* **of**
    digits: **begin** ⟨ Set *val* to value of decimal constant, and set *next_control* to the following
        token 160 ⟩;
      add_in(*val*); **goto** *reswitch*;
      end;
    octal: **begin** ⟨ Set *val* to value of octal constant, and set *next_control* to the following
        token 161 ⟩;
      add_in(*val*); **goto** *reswitch*;
      end;
    hex: **begin** ⟨ Set *val* to value of hexadecimal constant, and set *next_control* to the following
        token 162 ⟩;
      add_in(*val*); **goto** *reswitch*;
      end;
    identifier: **begin** *q* ← *id_lookup*(*normal*);
      if *ilk*[*q*] ≠ *numeric* **then**
        begin *next_control* ← "∗"; **goto** *reswitch*;   { leads to error }
        end;
      add_in(*equiv*[*q*] − ´100000);
      end;
    "+": *do_nothing*;
    "−": *next_sign* ← −*next_sign*;
    format, *definition*, *module_name*, *begin_Pascal*, *new_module*: **goto** *done*;
    ";": *err_print*(´!␣Omit␣semicolon␣in␣numeric␣definition´);
    othercases ⟨ Signal error, flush rest of the definition 159 ⟩
    endcases;

>   **end**;
> *done*:

This code is used in section 157.

159. ⟨ Signal error, flush rest of the definition 159 ⟩ ≡
>   **begin** *err_print*(´!␣Improper␣numeric␣definition␣will␣be␣flushed´);
>   **repeat** *next_control* ← *skip_ahead*
>   **until** *end_of_definition*(*next_control*);
>   **if** *next_control* = *module_name* **then**
>   **begin**   { we want to scan the module name too }
>   *loc* ← *loc* − 2; *next_control* ← *get_next*;
>   **end**;
>   *accumulator* ← 0; **goto** *done*;
>   **end**

This code is used in section 158.

160. ⟨ Set *val* to value of decimal constant, and set *next_control* to the following token 160 ⟩ ≡
>   *val* ← 0;
>   **repeat** *val* ← 10 ∗ *val* + *next_control* − "0"; *next_control* ← *get_next*;
>   **until** (*next_control* > "9") ∨ (*next_control* < "0")

This code is used in section 158.

161. ⟨ Set *val* to value of octal constant, and set *next_control* to the following token 161 ⟩ ≡
>   *val* ← 0; *next_control* ← "0";
>   **repeat** *val* ← 8 ∗ *val* + *next_control* − "0"; *next_control* ← *get_next*;
>   **until** (*next_control* > "7") ∨ (*next_control* < "0")

This code is used in section 158.

162. ⟨ Set *val* to value of hexadecimal constant, and set *next_control* to the following
>   token 162 ⟩ ≡
>   *val* ← 0; *next_control* ← "0";
>   **repeat if** *next_control* ≥ "A" **then** *next_control* ← *next_control* + "0" + 10 − "A";
>   *val* ← 16 ∗ *val* + *next_control* − "0"; *next_control* ← *get_next*;
>   **until** (*next_control* > "F") ∨ (*next_control* < "0") ∨ ((*next_control* > "9") ∧ (*next_control* < "A"))

This code is used in section 158.

163. Scanning a macro definition.   The rules for generating the replacement texts corresponding to simple macros, parametric macros, and Pascal texts of a module are almost identical, so a single procedure is used for all three cases. The differences are that

  a) The sign # denotes a parameter only when it appears outside of strings in a parametric macro; otherwise it stands for the ASCII character #. (This is not used in standard Pascal, but some Pascals allow, for example, '/#' after a certain kind of file name.)

  b) Module names are not allowed in simple macros or parametric macros; in fact, the appearance of a module name terminates such macros and denotes the name of the current module.

  c) The symbols @d and @f and @p are not allowed after module names, while they terminate macro definitions.

164. Therefore there is a procedure *scan_repl* whose parameter *t* specifies either *simple* or *parametric* or *module_name*. After *scan_repl* has acted, *cur_repl_text* will point to the replacement text just generated, and *next_control* will contain the control code that terminated the activity.

⟨ Globals in the outer block 9 ⟩ +≡
cur_repl_text: *text_pointer*;   { replacement text formed by *scan_repl* }

165.
procedure *scan_repl*(*t* : *eight_bits*);   { creates a replacement text }
  label *continue*, *done*, *found*;
  var *a*: *sixteen_bits*;   { the current token }
    b: *ASCII_code*;   { a character from the buffer }
    bal: *eight_bits*;   { left parentheses minus right parentheses }
  begin *bal* ← 0;
  loop begin *continue*: *a* ← *get_next*;
    case *a* **of**
    "(": *incr*(*bal*);
    ")": **if** *bal* = 0 **then** *err_print*(´!␣Extra␣)´)
      else *decr*(*bal*);
    "´": ⟨ Copy a string from the buffer to *tok_mem* 168 ⟩;
    "#": **if** *t* = *parametric* **then** *a* ← *param*;
    ⟨ In cases that *a* is a non-ASCII token (*identifier*, *module_name*, etc.), either process it and
        change *a* to a byte that should be stored, or **goto** *continue* if *a* should be ignored, or
        goto *done* if *a* signals the end of this replacement text 167 ⟩
    othercases *do_nothing*
    endcases;
    app_repl(*a*);   { store *a* in *tok_mem* }
    end;
  done: *next_control* ← *a*; ⟨ Make sure the parentheses balance 166 ⟩;
    if *text_ptr* > *max_texts* − *zz* **then** *overflow*(´text´);
    cur_repl_text ← *text_ptr*; *tok_start*[*text_ptr* + *zz*] ← *tok_ptr*[*z*]; *incr*(*text_ptr*);
    if *z* = *zz* − 1 **then** *z* ← 0 **else** *incr*(*z*);
  end;

166.   ⟨ Make sure the parentheses balance 166 ⟩ ≡
  if *bal* > 0 **then**
    begin if *bal* = 1 **then** *err_print*(´!␣Missing␣)´)
    else *err_print*(´!␣Missing␣´, *bal* : 1, ´␣´)´´s´);
    while *bal* > 0 **do**
      begin *app_repl*(")"); *decr*(*bal*);
      end;
    end

This code is used in section 165.

167.   ⟨ In cases that *a* is a non-ASCII token (*identifier*, *module_name*, etc.), either process it
      and change *a* to a byte that should be stored, or **goto** *continue* if *a* should be ignored, or
      goto *done* if *a* signals the end of this replacement text 167 ⟩ ≡
identifier: **begin** *a* ← *id_lookup*(*normal*); *app_repl*((*a* **div** ´400) + ´200); *a* ← *a* **mod** ´400;
  end;

module_name: **if** $t \neq$ *module_name* **then goto** *done*
  else begin *app_repl*((*cur_module* **div** ´*400*) + ´*250*); $a \leftarrow$ *cur_module* **mod** ´*400*;
    end;
verbatim: ⟨ Copy verbatim string from the buffer to *tok_mem* 169 ⟩;
definition, *format*, *begin_Pascal*: **if** $t \neq$ *module_name* **then goto** *done*
  else begin *err_print*(´!␣@´, *xchr*[*buffer*[*loc* − 1]], ´␣is␣ignored␣in␣Pascal␣text´);
    goto *continue*;
    end;
new_module: **goto** *done*;

This code is used in section 165.

168. ⟨ Copy a string from the buffer to *tok_mem* 168 ⟩ ≡
  begin $b \leftarrow$ "´";
  loop begin *app_repl*(b);
    if $b =$ "@" **then**
      if *buffer*[*loc*] = "@" **then** *incr*(*loc*)   { store only one @ }
      else *err_print*(´!␣You␣should␣double␣@␣signs␣in␣strings´);
    if *loc* = *limit* **then**
      begin *err_print*(´!␣String␣didn´´t␣end´); *buffer*[*loc*] $\leftarrow$ "´"; *buffer*[*loc* + 1] $\leftarrow$ 0;
      end;
    $b \leftarrow$ *buffer*[*loc*]; *incr*(*loc*);
    if $b =$ "´" **then**
      begin if *buffer*[*loc*] $\neq$ "´" **then goto** *found*
      else begin *incr*(*loc*); *app_repl*("´");
        end;
      end;
    end;
found: **end**   { now *a* holds the final "´" that will be stored }

This code is used in section 165.

169. ⟨ Copy verbatim string from the buffer to *tok_mem* 169 ⟩ ≡
  begin *app_repl*(*verbatim*); *buffer*[*limit* + 1] $\leftarrow$ "@";
  while *buffer*[*loc*] $\neq$ "@" **do**
    begin *app_repl*(*buffer*[*loc*]); *incr*(*loc*);
    if *loc* < *limit* **then**
      if (*buffer*[*loc*] = "@") ∧ (*buffer*[*loc* + 1] = "@") **then**
        begin *app_repl*("@"); *loc* $\leftarrow$ *loc* + 2;
        end;
    end;
  if *loc* ≥ *limit* **then** *err_print*(´!␣Verbatim␣string␣didn´´t␣end´)
  else if *buffer*[*loc* + 1] $\neq$ ">" **then**
    err_print(´!␣You␣should␣double␣@␣signs␣in␣verbatim␣strings´);
  loc $\leftarrow$ *loc* + 2;
  end   { another *verbatim* byte will be stored, since *a* = *verbatim* }

This code is used in section 167.

170.   The following procedure is used to define a simple or parametric macro, just after
the '==' of its definition has been scanned.

procedure *define_macro*(*t* : *eight_bits*);

var *p*: *name_pointer*; { the identifier being defined }
begin *p* ← *id_lookup*(*t*); *scan_repl*(*t*);
equiv[*p*] ← *cur_repl_text*; *text_link*[*cur_repl_text*] ← 0;
end;

171. Scanning a module. The *scan_module* procedure starts when '`@␣`' or '`@*`' has been sensed in the input, and it proceeds until the end of that module. It uses *module_count* to keep track of the current module number; with luck, WEAVE and TANGLE will both assign the same numbers to modules.

⟨ Globals in the outer block 9 ⟩ +≡
module_count: 0 .. ′27777;   { the current module number }

172. The top level of *scan_module* is trivial.

procedure *scan_module*;
  label *continue*, *done*, *exit*;
  var *p*: *name_pointer*;   { module name for the current module }
  begin *incr*(*module_count*); ⟨ Scan the definition part of the current module 173 ⟩;
  ⟨ Scan the Pascal part of the current module 175 ⟩;
exit: **end**;

173. ⟨ Scan the definition part of the current module 173 ⟩ ≡
  next_control ← 0;
  loop begin *continue*: **while** *next_control* ≤ *format* **do**
      begin *next_control* ← *skip_ahead*;
      if *next_control* = *module_name* **then**
        begin   { we want to scan the module name too }
        loc ← *loc* − 2; *next_control* ← *get_next*;
        end;
      end;
    if *next_control* ≠ *definition* **then goto** *done*;
    next_control ← *get_next*;   { get identifier name }
    if *next_control* ≠ *identifier* **then**
      begin *err_print*(´!␣Definition␣flushed,␣must␣start␣with␣´,
          ´identifier␣of␣length␣>␣1´); **goto** *continue*;
      end;
    next_control ← *get_next*;   { get token after the identifier }
    if *next_control* = "=" **then**
      begin *scan_numeric*(*id_lookup*(*numeric*)); **goto** *continue*;
      end
    else if *next_control* = *equivalence_sign* **then**
        begin *define_macro*(*simple*); **goto** *continue*;
        end
      else ⟨ If the next text is '(#) ≡', call *define_macro* and **goto** *continue* 174 ⟩;
    err_print(´!␣Definition␣flushed␣since␣it␣starts␣badly´);
    end;
done:
This code is used in section 172.

174. ⟨ If the next text is '(#) ≡', call *define_macro* and **goto** *continue* 174 ⟩ ≡

```
if next_control = "(" then
  begin next_control ← get_next;
  if next_control = "#" then
    begin next_control ← get_next;
    if next_control = ")" then
      begin next_control ← get_next;
      if next_control = "=" then
        begin err_print(´!␣Use␣==␣for␣macros´); next_control ← equivalence_sign;
        end;
      if next_control = equivalence_sign then
        begin define_macro(parametric); goto continue;
        end;
      end;
    end;
  end;
```

This code is used in section 173.

175.   ⟨ Scan the Pascal part of the current module 175 ⟩ ≡
```
case next_control of
begin_Pascal: p ← 0;
module_name: begin p ← cur_module;
  ⟨ Check that = or ≡ follows this module name, otherwise return 176 ⟩;
  end;
othercases return
endcases;
⟨ Insert the module number into tok_mem 177 ⟩;
scan_repl(module_name);   { now cur_repl_text points to the replacement text }
⟨ Update the data structure so that the replacement text is accessible 178 ⟩;
```
This code is used in section 172.

176.   ⟨ Check that = or ≡ follows this module name, otherwise return 176 ⟩ ≡
```
repeat next_control ← get_next;
until next_control ≠ "+";   { allow optional '+=' }
if (next_control ≠ "=") ∧ (next_control ≠ equivalence_sign) then
  begin err_print(´!␣Pascal␣text␣flushed,␣=␣sign␣is␣missing´);
  repeat next_control ← skip_ahead;
  until next_control = new_module;
  return;
  end
```
This code is used in section 175.

177.   ⟨ Insert the module number into tok_mem 177 ⟩ ≡
```
store_two_bytes(´150000 + module_count);   { ´150000 = ´320 ∗ ´400 }
```
This code is used in section 175.

178.   ⟨ Update the data structure so that the replacement text is accessible 178 ⟩ ≡
```
if p = 0 then   { unnamed module }
  begin text_link[last_unnamed] ← cur_repl_text; last_unnamed ← cur_repl_text;
  end
```

> else if $equiv[p] = 0$ then $equiv[p] \leftarrow cur\_repl\_text$ { first module of this name }
>> else begin $p \leftarrow equiv[p]$;
>>> while $text\_link[p] < module\_flag$ do $p \leftarrow text\_link[p]$;   { find end of list }
>>> $text\_link[p] \leftarrow cur\_repl\_text$;
>> end;
> $text\_link[cur\_repl\_text] \leftarrow module\_flag$;   { mark this replacement text as a nonmacro }

This code is used in section 175.

179. Debugging. The Pascal debugger with which TANGLE was developed allows breakpoints to be set, and variables can be read and changed, but procedures cannot be executed. Therefore a '*debug_help*' procedure has been inserted in the main loops of each phase of the program; when *ddt* and *dd* are set to appropriate values, symbolic printouts of various tables will appear.

The idea is to set a breakpoint inside the *debug_help* routine, at the place of '*breakpoint*:' below. Then when *debug_help* is to be activated, set *trouble_shooting* equal to *true*. The *debug_help* routine will prompt you for values of *ddt* and *dd*, discontinuing this when $ddt \leq 0$; thus you type $2n + 1$ integers, ending with zero or a negative number. Then control either passes to the breakpoint, allowing you to look at and/or change variables (if you typed zero), or to exit the routine (if you typed a negative value).

Another global variable, *debug_cycle*, can be used to skip silently past calls on *debug_help*. If you set $debug\_cycle > 1$, the program stops only every *debug_cycle* times *debug_help* is called; however, any error stop will set *debug_cycle* to zero.

⟨ Globals in the outer block 9 ⟩ +≡
   debug *trouble_shooting*: *boolean*;   { is *debug_help* wanted? }
ddt: *integer*;   { operation code for the *debug_help* routine }
dd: *integer*;   { operand in procedures performed by *debug_help* }
debug_cycle: *integer*;   { threshold for *debug_help* stopping }
debug_skipped: *integer*;   { we have skipped this many *debug_help* calls }
term_in: *text_file*;   { the user's terminal as an input file }
   gubed

180. The debugging routine needs to read from the user's terminal.

⟨ Set initial values 10 ⟩ +≡
   dobug *trouble_shooting* ← *true*; *debug_cycle* ← 1; *debug_skipped* ← 0;
trouble_shooting ← *false*; *debug_cycle* ← 99999;   { use these when it almost works }
reset(*term_in*, ´TTY:´, ´/I´);   { open *term_in* as the terminal, don't do a *get* }
   gubed

181.   **define** *breakpoint* = 888   { place where a breakpoint is desirable }

debug procedure *debug_help*;   { routine to display various things }
label *breakpoint*, *exit*;
var *k*: *integer*;   { index into various arrays }
begin *incr*(*debug_skipped*);
if $debug\_skipped < debug\_cycle$ **then return**;
debug_skipped ← 0;
loop begin *write*(*term_out*, ´#´); *update_terminal*;   { prompt }
   read(*term_in*, *ddt*);   { read a list of integers }
   if $ddt < 0$ **then return**

```
        else if ddt = 0 then
            begin goto breakpoint; @\   { go to every label at least once }
        breakpoint: ddt ← 0; @\
            end
        else begin read(term_in, dd);
            case ddt of
            1: print_id(dd);
            2: print_repl(dd);
            3: for k ← 1 to dd do  print(xchr[buffer[k]]);
            4: for k ← 1 to dd do  print(xchr[mod_text[k]]);
            5: for k ← 1 to out_ptr do  print(xchr[out_buf[k]]);
            6: for k ← 1 to dd do  print(xchr[out_contrib[k]]);
            othercases print(´?´)
            endcases;
            end;
        end;
exit: end;
    gubed
```

182. The main program.   We have defined plenty of procedures, and it is time to put the last pieces of the puzzle in place. Here is where TANGLE starts, and where it ends.

```
    begin initialize; ⟨Initialize the input system 134⟩;
    print_ln(banner);   { print a "banner line" }
    ⟨Phase I: Read all the user's text and compress it into tok_mem 183⟩;
    stat for zo ← 0 to zz − 1 do  max_tok_ptr[zo] ← tok_ptr[zo];
    tats
    ⟨Phase II: Output the contents of the compressed tables 112⟩;
end_of_TANGLE: if string_ptr > 128 then  ⟨Finish off the string pool file 184⟩;
    stat ⟨Print statistics about memory usage 186⟩; tats
{ here files should be closed if the operating system requires it }
    ⟨Print the job history 187⟩;
    end.
```

183.   ⟨Phase I: Read all the user's text and compress it into tok_mem 183⟩ ≡
```
    phase_one ← true; module_count ← 0;
    repeat next_control ← skip_ahead;
    until next_control = new_module;
    while ¬input_has_ended do  scan_module;
    ⟨Check that all changes have been read 138⟩;
    phase_one ← false;
```
This code is used in section 182.

184.   ⟨Finish off the string pool file 184⟩ ≡
```
    begin print_nl(string_ptr − 128 : 1, ´␣strings␣written␣to␣string␣pool␣file.´);
    write(pool, ´*´);
    for string_ptr ← 1 to 9 do
        begin out_buf[string_ptr] ← pool_check_sum mod 10;
        pool_check_sum ← pool_check_sum div 10;
        end;
```

> **for** *string_ptr* ← 9 **downto** 1 **do** *write*(*pool*, *xchr*["0" + *out_buf*[*string_ptr*]]);
> *write_ln*(*pool*);
> **end**

This code is used in section 182.

185. ⟨Globals in the outer block 9⟩ +≡
stat *wo*: 0 .. *ww* − 1; {segment of memory for which statistics are being printed}
tats

186. ⟨Print statistics about memory usage 186⟩ ≡
print_nl(´Memory␣usage␣statistics:´);
print_nl(*name_ptr* : 1, ´␣names,␣´, *text_ptr* . 1, ´␣replacement␣texts;´);
print_nl(*byte_ptr*[0] : 1);
for *wo* ← 1 **to** *ww* − 1 **do** *print*(´+´, *byte_ptr*[*wo*] : 1);
print(´␣bytes,␣´, *max_tok_ptr*[0] : 1);
for *zo* ← 1 **to** *zz* − 1 **do** *print*(´+´, *max_tok_ptr*[*zo*] : 1);
print(´␣tokens.´);

This code is used in section 182.

187. Some implementations may wish to pass the *history* value to the operating system so that it can be used to govern whether or not other programs are started. Here we simply report the history to the user.

⟨Print the job *history* 187⟩ ≡
case *history* **of**
spotless: *print_nl*(´(No␣errors␣were␣found.)´);
harmless message: *print_nl*(´(Did␣you␣see␣the␣warning␣message␣above?)´);
error_message: *print_nl*(´(Pardon␣me,␣but␣I␣think␣I␣spotted␣something␣wrong.)´);
fatal_message: *print_nl*(´(That␣was␣a␣fatal␣error,␣my␣friend.)´);
end {there are no other cases}

This code is used in section 182.

188. System-dependent changes. This module should be replaced, if necessary, by changes to the program that are necessary to make TANGLE work at a particular installation. It is usually best to design your change file so that all changes to previous modules preserve the module numbering; then everybody's version will be consistent with the printed program. More extensive changes, which introduce new modules, can be inserted here; then only the index itself will get a new module number.

189. Index. Here is a cross-reference table for the TANGLE processor. All modules in which an identifier is used are listed with that identifier, except that reserved words are indexed only when they appear in format definitions, and the appearances of identifiers in module names are not indexed. Underlined entries correspond to where the identifier was declared. Error messages and a few other things like "ASCII code" are indexed here too.

⟨ Append *out_val* to buffer 103 ⟩ Used in sections 102 and 104.

⟨ Append the decimal value of v, with parentheses if negative 111 ⟩ Used in section 107.

⟨ Cases involving @{ and @} 121 ⟩ Used in section 113.

⟨ Cases like <> and := 114 ⟩ Used in section 113.

⟨ Cases related to constants, possibly leading to *get_fraction* or *reswitch* 119 ⟩
     Used in section 113.

⟨ Cases related to identifiers 116 ⟩ Used in section 113.

⟨ Check for ambiguity and update secondary hash 62 ⟩ Used in section 61.

⟨ Check for overlong name 155 ⟩ Used in section 153.

⟨ Check if q conflicts with p 63 ⟩ Used in section 62.

⟨ Check that all changes have been read 138 ⟩ Used in section 183.

⟨ Check that = or ≡ follows this module name, otherwise **return** 176 ⟩ Used in section 175.

⟨ Compare name p with current identifier, **goto** *found* if equal 56 ⟩ Used in section 55.

⟨ Compiler directives 4 ⟩ Used in section 2.

⟨ Compress two-symbol combinations like ':=' 147 ⟩ Used in section 145.

⟨ Compute the hash code h 54 ⟩ Used in section 53.

⟨ Compute the name location p 55 ⟩ Used in section 53.

⟨ Compute the secondary hash code h and put the first characters into the auxiliary array
     chopped_id 58 ⟩ Used in section 57.

⟨ Constants in the outer block 8 ⟩ Used in section 2.

⟨ Contribution is * or / or DIV or MOD 105 ⟩ Used in section 104.

⟨ Copy a string from the buffer to *tok_mem* 168 ⟩ Used in section 165.

⟨ Copy the parameter into *tok_mem* 93 ⟩ Used in section 90.

⟨ Copy verbatim string from the buffer to *tok_mem* 169 ⟩ Used in section 167.

⟨ Define and output a new string of the pool 64 ⟩ Used in section 61.

⟨ Display one-byte token a 76 ⟩ Used in section 74.

⟨ Display two-byte token starting with a 75 ⟩ Used in section 74.

⟨ Do special things when $c =$ "@","\","{","}"; **return** at end 142 ⟩ Used in section 141.

⟨ Empty the last line from the buffer 98 ⟩ Used in section 112.

⟨ Enter a new identifier into the table at position p 61 ⟩ Used in section 57.

⟨ Enter a new module name into the tree 67 ⟩ Used in section 66.

⟨ Error handling procedures 30, 31, 34 ⟩ Used in section 2.

⟨ Expand macro a and **goto** *found*, or **goto** *restart* if no output found 89 ⟩
     Used in section 87.

⟨ Expand module $a -$ '24000, **goto** *restart* 88 ⟩ Used in section 87.

⟨ Finish off the string pool file 184 ⟩ Used in section 182.

⟨ Force a line break 122 ⟩ Used in section 113.

⟨ Get a preprocessed string 149 ⟩ Used in section 145.

⟨ Get an identifier 148 ⟩ Used in section 145.

⟨ Get control code and possible module name 150 ⟩ Used in section 145.

⟨ Get the buffer ready for appending the new information 102 ⟩ Used in section 101.

⟨ Give double-definition error, if necessary, and change p to type t 59 ⟩ Used in section 57.

⟨ Globals in the outer block 9, 13, 20, 23, 25, 27, 29, 38, 40, 44, 50, 65, 70, 79, 80, 82, 86, 94, 95, 100,
     124, 126, 143, 156, 164, 171, 179, 185 ⟩ Used in section 2.

⟨ Go to *found* if c is a hexadecimal digit, otherwise set *scanning_hex* ← *false* 146 ⟩
     Used in section 145.

⟨Signal error, flush rest of the definition 159⟩ Used in section 158.
⟨Skip over comment lines in the change file; **return** if end of file 129⟩ Used in section 128.
⟨Skip to the next nonblank line; **return** if end of file 130⟩ Used in section 128.
⟨Special code to finish real constants 120⟩ Used in section 113.
⟨Start scanning current macro parameter, **goto** *restart* 92⟩ Used in section 87.
⟨Types in the outer block 11, 12, 37, 39, 43, 78⟩ Used in section 2.
⟨Update the data structure so that the replacement text is accessible 178⟩
    Used in section 175.
⟨Update the tables and check for possible errors 57⟩ Used in section 53.

G.1.2   Source Listing for WEAVE

1.   Introduction.   This program converts a WEB file to a TEX file. It was written by
D. E. Knuth in October, 1981; a somewhat similar SAIL program had been developed in
March, 1979, although the earlier program used a top-down parsing method that is quite
different from the present scheme.

   The code uses a few features of the local Pascal compiler that may need to be changed in
other installations:

   1) Case statements have a default.
   2) Input-output routines may need to be adapted for use with a particular character set
       and/or for printing messages on the user's terminal.

These features are also present in the Pascal version of TEX, where they are used in a similar
(but more complex) way. System-dependent portions of WEAVE can be identified by looking
at the entries for 'system dependencies' in the index below.

   The "banner line" defined here should be changed whenever WEAVE is modified.

   define *banner* ≡ ´This␣is␣WEAVE,␣Version␣3.1´

2.   The program begins with a fairly normal header, made up of pieces that will mostly be
filled in later. The WEB input comes from files *web_file* and *change_file*, and the TEX output
goes to file *tex_file*.

   If it is necessary to abort the job because of a fatal error, the program calls the '*jump_out*'
procedure, which goes to the label *end_of_WEAVE*.

   define *end_of_WEAVE* = 9999   { go here to wrap it up }

⟨Compiler directives 4⟩
program *WEAVE*(*web_file*, *change_file*, *tex_file*);
  label *end_of_WEAVE*;   { go here to finish }
  const ⟨Constants in the outer block 8⟩
  type ⟨Types in the outer block 11⟩
  var ⟨Globals in the outer block 9⟩
    ⟨Error handling procedures 30⟩
  procedure *initialize*;
    var ⟨Local variables for initialization 16⟩
    begin ⟨Set initial values 10⟩
    end;

3.   Some of this code is optional for use when debugging only; such material is enclosed
between the delimiters **debug** and **gubed**. Other parts, delimited by **stat** and **tats**, are
optionally included if statistics about WEAVE's memory usage are desired.

   define *debug* ≡ @{   { change this to '*debug* ≡ ' when debugging }

define *gubed* ≡ **@}**   { change this to '*gubed* ≡ ' when debugging }
format *debug* ≡ *begin*
format *gubed* ≡ *end*

define *stat* ≡ **@{**   { change this to '*stat* ≡ ' when gathering usage statistics }
define *tats* ≡ **@}**   { change this to '*tats* ≡ ' when gathering usage statistics }
format *stat* ≡ *begin*
format *tats* ≡ *end*

4.   The Pascal compiler used to develop this system has "compiler directives" that can appear in comments whose first character is a dollar sign. In production versions of WEAVE these directives tell the compiler that it is safe to avoid range checks and to leave out the extra code it inserts for the Pascal debugger's benefit, although interrupts will occur if there is arithmetic overflow.

⟨ Compiler directives 4 ⟩ ≡
  @{@&\$$C-, A+, D-$**@}**   { no range check, catch arithmetic overflow, no debug overhead }
  debug @{@&\$$C+, D+$**@} gubed**   { but turn everything on when debugging }

This code is used in section 2.

5.   Labels are given symbolic names by the following definitions. We insert the label '*exit*:' just before the '**end**' of a procedure in which we have used the '**return**' statement defined below; the label '*restart*' is occasionally used at the very beginning of a procedure; and the label '*reswitch*' is occasionally used just prior to a **case** statement in which some cases change the conditions and we wish to branch to the newly applicable case. Loops that are set up with the **loop** construction defined below are commonly exited by going to '*done*' or to '*found*' or to '*not_found*', and they are sometimes repeated by going to '*continue*'.

define *exit* = 10   { go here to leave a procedure }
define *restart* = 20   { go here to start a procedure again }
define *reswitch* = 21   { go here to start a case statement again }
define *continue* = 22   { go here to resume a loop }
define *done* = 30   { go here to exit a loop }
define *found* = 31   { go here when you've found it }
define *not_found* = 32   { go here when you've found something else }

6.   Here are some macros for common programming idioms.

define *incr*(**#**) ≡ **#** ← **#** + 1   { increase a variable by unity }
define *decr*(**#**) ≡ **#** ← **#** − 1   { decrease a variable by unity }
define *loop* ≡ **while** *true* **do**   { repeat over and over until a **goto** happens }
define *do_nothing* ≡   { empty statement }
define *return* ≡ **goto** *exit*   { terminate a procedure call }
format *return* ≡ *nil*
format *loop* ≡ *xclause*

7.   We assume that **case** statements may include a default case that applies if no matching label is found. Thus, we shall use constructions like

> **case** x **of**
> 1: ⟨code for $x = 1$⟩;
> 3: ⟨code for $x = 3$⟩;
> **othercases** ⟨code for $x \neq 1$ and $x \neq 3$⟩
> **endcases**

since most Pascal compilers have plugged this hole in the language by incorporating some
sort of default mechanism. For example, the compiler used to develop WEB and TeX allows
'*others*:' as a default label, and other Pascals allow syntaxes like '**else**' or '**otherwise**' or
'*otherwise*:', etc. The definitions of **othercases** and **endcases** should be changed to agree
with local conventions. (Of course, if no default mechanism is available, the **case** statements
of this program must be extended by listing all remaining cases.)

> **define** *othercases* ≡ *others*:   { default for cases not listed explicitly }
> **define** *endcases* ≡ **end**   { follows the default case in an extended **case** statement }
> **format** *othercases* ≡ *else*
> **format** *endcases* ≡ *end*

8.   The following parameters are set big enough to handle TeX, so they should be sufficient
for most applications of WEAVE.

⟨Constants in the outer block 8⟩ ≡
> $max\_bytes = 45000$;   { $1/ww$ times the number of bytes in identifiers, index entries, and module
>   names; must be less than 65536 }
> $max\_names = 5000$;
>   { number of identifiers, index entries, and module names; must be less than 10240 }
> $max\_modules = 2000$;   { greater than the total number of modules }
> $hash\_size = 353$;   { should be prime }
> $buf\_size = 100$;   { maximum length of input line }
> $longest\_name = 400$;   { module names shouldn't be longer than this }
> $long\_buf\_size = 500$;   { $buf\_size + longest\_name$ }
> $line\_length = 80$;
>   { lines of TeX output have at most this many characters, should be less than 256 }
> $max\_refs = 30000$;   { number of cross references; must be less than 65536 }
> $max\_toks = 30000$;   { number of symbols in Pascal texts being parsed; must be less than 65536 }
> $max\_texts = 2000$;   { number of phrases in Pascal texts being parsed; must be less than 10240 }
> $max\_scraps = 1000$;   { number of tokens in Pascal texts being parsed }
> $stack\_size = 200$;   { number of simultaneous output levels }

This code is used in section 2.

9.   A global variable called *history* will contain one of four values at the end of every run:
spotless means that no unusual messages were printed; *harmless_message* means that a
message of possible interest was printed but no serious errors were detected; *error_message*
means that at least one error was found; *fatal_message* means that the program terminated
abnormally. The value of *history* does not influence the behavior of the program; it is simply
computed for the convenience of systems that might want to use such information.

> **define** *spotless* = 0   { *history* value for normal jobs }

define *harmless_message* = 1   { *history* value when non-serious info was printed }
define *error_message* = 2   { *history* value when an error was noted }
define *fatal_message* = 3   { *history* value when we had to stop prematurely }

define *mark_harmless* ≡ **if** *history* = *spotless* **then** *history* ← *harmless_message*
define *mark_error* ≡ *history* ← *error_message*
define *mark_fatal* ≡ *history* ← *fatal_message*

⟨ Globals in the outer block 9 ⟩ ≡
history: *spotless* .. *fatal_message*;   { how bad was this run? }

See also sections 13, 20, 23, 25, 27, 29, 37, 39, 45, 48, 53, 55, 63, 65, 71, 73, 93, 108, 114, 118, 121, 129, 144, 177, 202, 219, 229, 234, 240, 242, 244, 246, and 258.

This code is used in section 2.

10.   ⟨ Set initial values 10 ⟩ ≡
history ← *spotless*;

See also sections 14, 17, 18, 21, 26, 41, 43, 49, 54, 57, 94, 102, 124, 126, 145, 203, 245, 248, and 259.

This code is used in section 2.

11.   **The character set.**   One of the main goals in the design of WEB has been to make it readily portable between a wide variety of computers. Yet WEB by its very nature must use a greater variety of characters than most computer programs deal with, and character encoding is one of the areas in which existing machines differ most widely from each other.

To resolve this problem, all input to WEAVE and TANGLE is converted to an internal seven-bit code that is essentially standard ASCII, the "American Standard Code for Information Interchange." The conversion is done immediately when each character is read in. Conversely, characters are converted from ASCII to the user's external representation just before they are output.

Such an internal code is relevant to users of WEB only because it is the code used for preprocessed constants like "A". If you are writing a program in WEB that makes use of such one-character constants, you should convert your input to ASCII form, like WEAVE and TANGLE do. Otherwise WEB's internal coding scheme does not affect you.

Here is a table of the standard visible ASCII codes:

	0	*1*	*2*	*3*	*4*	*5*	*6*	*7*
'040	␣	!	"	#	$	%	&	'
'050	(	)	*	+	,	–	.	/
'060	0	1	2	3	4	5	6	7
'070	8	9	:	;	<	=	>	?
'100	@	A	B	C	D	E	F	G
'110	H	I	J	K	L	M	N	O
'120	P	Q	R	S	T	U	V	W
'130	X	Y	Z	[	\	]	^	_
'140	`	a	b	c	d	e	f	g
'150	h	i	j	k	l	m	n	o
'160	p	q	r	s	t	u	v	w
'170	x	y	z	{			}	~	

(Actually, of course, code *'040* is an invisible blank space.) Code *'136* was once an upward arrow (↑), and code *'137* was once a left arrow (←), in olden times when the first draft of ASCII code was prepared; but WEB works with today's standard ASCII in which those codes represent circumflex and underline as shown.

⟨ Types in the outer block 11 ⟩ ≡
    ASCII_code = 0 .. 127;   { seven-bit numbers, a subrange of the integers }

See also sections 12, 36, 38, 47, 52, and 201.

This code is used in section 2.

12.   The original Pascal compiler was designed in the late 60s, when six-bit character sets were common, so it did not make provision for lowercase letters. Nowadays, of course, we need to deal with both capital and small letters in a convenient way, so WEB assumes that it is being used with a Pascal whose character set contains at least the characters of standard ASCII as listed above. Some Pascal compilers use the original name *char* for the data type associated with the characters in text files, while other Pascals consider *char* to be a 64-element subrange of a larger data type that has some other name.

In order to accommodate this difference, we shall use the name *text_char* to stand for the data type of the characters in the input and output files. We shall also assume that *text_char* consists of the elements *chr*(*first_text_char*) through *chr*(*last_text_char*), inclusive. The following definitions should be adjusted if necessary.

    define *text_char* ≡ *char*   { the data type of characters in text files }
    define *first_text_char* = 0   { ordinal number of the smallest element of *text_char* }
    define *last_text_char* = 127   { ordinal number of the largest element of *text_char* }

⟨ Types in the outer block 11 ⟩ +≡
    text_file = **packed file of** *text_char*;

13. The WEAVE and TANGLE processors convert between ASCII code and the user's external character set by means of arrays *xord* and *xchr* that are analogous to Pascal's *ord* and *chr* functions.

⟨ Globals in the outer block 9 ⟩ +≡
xord: **array** [*text_char*] **of** *ASCII_code*;   { specifies conversion of input characters }
xchr: **array** [*ASCII_code*] **of** *text_char*;   { specifies conversion of output characters }

14. If we assume that every system using WEB is able to read and write the visible characters of standard ASCII (although not necessarily using the ASCII codes to represent them), the following assignment statements initialize most of the *xchr* array properly, without needing any system-dependent changes. For example, the statement xchr[@´101]:=´A´ that appears in the present WEB file might be encoded in, say, EBCDIC code on the external medium on which it resides, but TANGLE will convert from this external code to ASCII and back again. Therefore the assignment statement XCHR[65]:=´A´ will appear in the corresponding Pascal file, and Pascal will compile this statement so that *xchr*[65] receives the character A in the external (*char*) code. Note that it would be quite incorrect to say xchr[@´101]:="A", because "A" is a constant of type *integer*, not *char*, and because we have "A" = 65 regardless of the external character set.

⟨ Set initial values 10 ⟩ +≡
  xchr[´40] ← ´␣´; *xchr*[´41] ← ´!´; *xchr*[´42] ← ´"´; *xchr*[´43] ← ´#´; *xchr*[´44] ← ´$´;
  xchr[´45] ← ´%´; *xchr*[´46] ← ´&´; *xchr*[´47] ← ´´´;
  xchr[´50] ← ´(´; *xchr*[´51] ← ´)´; *xchr*[´52] ← ´*´; *xchr*[´53] ← ´+´; *xchr*[´54] ← ´,´;
  xchr[´55] ← ´-´; *xchr*[´56] ← ´.´; *xchr*[´57] ← ´/´;
  xchr[´60] ← ´0´; *xchr*[´61] ← ´1´; *xchr*[´62] ← ´2´; *xchr*[´63] ← ´3´; *xchr*[´64] ← ´4´;
  xchr[´65] ← ´5´; *xchr*[´66] ← ´6´; *xchr*[´67] ← ´7´;
  xchr[´70] ← ´8´; *xchr*[´71] ← ´9´; *xchr*[´72] ← ´:´; *xchr*[´73] ← ´;´; *xchr*[´74] ← ´<´;
  xchr[´75] ← ´=´; *xchr*[´76] ← ´>´; *xchr*[´77] ← ´?´;
  xchr[´100] ← ´@´; *xchr*[´101] ← ´A´; *xchr*[´102] ← ´B´; *xchr*[´103] ← ´C´; *xchr*[´104] ← ´D´;
  xchr[´105] ← ´E´; *xchr*[´106] ← ´F´; *xchr*[´107] ← ´G´;
  xchr[´110] ← ´H´; *xchr*[´111] ← ´I´; *xchr*[´112] ← ´J´; *xchr*[´113] ← ´K´; *xchr*[´114] ← ´L´;
  xchr[´115] ← ´M´; *xchr*[´116] ← ´N´; *xchr*[´117] ← ´O´;
  xchr[´120] ← ´P´; *xchr*[´121] ← ´Q´; *xchr*[´122] ← ´R´; *xchr*[´123] ← ´S´; *xchr*[´124] ← ´T´;
  xchr[´125] ← ´U´; *xchr*[´126] ← ´V´; *xchr*[´127] ← ´W´;
  xchr[´130] ← ´X´; *xchr*[´131] ← ´Y´; *xchr*[´132] ← ´Z´; *xchr*[´133] ← ´[´; *xchr*[´134] ← ´\´;
  xchr[´135] ← ´]´; *xchr*[´136] ← ´^´; *xchr*[´137] ← ´_´;
  xchr[´140] ← ´`´; *xchr*[´141] ← ´a´; *xchr*[´142] ← ´b´; *xchr*[´143] ← ´c´; *xchr*[´144] ← ´d´;
  xchr[´145] ← ´e´; *xchr*[´146] ← ´f´; *xchr*[´147] ← ´g´;
  xchr[´150] ← ´h´; *xchr*[´151] ← ´i´; *xchr*[´152] ← ´j´; *xchr*[´153] ← ´k´; *xchr*[´154] ← ´l´;
  xchr[´155] ← ´m´; *xchr*[´156] ← ´n´; *xchr*[´157] ← ´o´;
  xchr[´160] ← ´p´; *xchr*[´161] ← ´q´; *xchr*[´162] ← ´r´; *xchr*[´163] ← ´s´; *xchr*[´164] ← ´t´;
  xchr[´165] ← ´u´; *xchr*[´166] ← ´v´; *xchr*[´167] ← ´w´;
  xchr[´170] ← ´x´; *xchr*[´171] ← ´y´; *xchr*[´172] ← ´z´; *xchr*[´173] ← ´{´; *xchr*[´174] ← ´|´;
  xchr[´175] ← ´}´; *xchr*[´176] ← ´~´;
  xchr[0] ← ´␣´; *xchr*[´177] ← ´␣´;   { these ASCII codes are not used }

15. Some of the ASCII codes below ´40 have been given symbolic names in WEAVE and TANGLE because they are used with a special meaning.

  define *and_sign* = ´4   { equivalent to 'and' }

define *not_sign* = ´5   { equivalent to 'not' }
define *set_element_sign* = ´6   { equivalent to 'in' }
define *tab_mark* = ´11   { ASCII code used as tab-skip }
define *line_feed* = ´12   { ASCII code thrown away at end of line }
define *form_feed* = ´14   { ASCII code used at end of page }
define *carriage_return* = ´15   { ASCII code used at end of line }
define *left_arrow* = ´30   { equivalent to ':=' }
define *not_equal* = ´32   { equivalent to '<>' }
define *less_or_equal* = ´34   { equivalent to '<=' }
define *greater_or_equal* = ´35   { equivalent to '>=' }
define *equivalence_sign* = ´36   { equivalent to '==' }
define *or_sign* = ´37   { equivalent to 'or' }

16.   When we initialize the *xord* array and the remaining parts of *xchr*, it will be convenient to make use of an index variable, *i*.

⟨ Local variables for initialization 16 ⟩ ≡
i: 0 .. *last_text_char*;

See also sections 40, 56, and 247.

This code is used in section 2.

17.   Here now is the system-dependent part of the character set. If WEB is being implemented on a garden-variety Pascal for which only standard ASCII codes will appear in the input and output files, you don't need to make any changes here. But at MIT, for example, the code in this module should be changed to

$$\textbf{for } i \leftarrow 1 \textbf{ to } ´37 \textbf{ do } xchr[i] \leftarrow chr(i);$$

WEB's character set is essentially identical to MIT's, even with respect to characters less than ´40.

Changes to the present module will make WEB more friendly on computers that have an extended character set, so that one can type things like ≠ instead of <>. If you have an extended set of characters that are easily incorporated into text files, you can assign codes arbitrarily here, giving an *xchr* equivalent to whatever characters the users of WEB are allowed to have in their input files, provided that unsuitable characters do not correspond to special codes like *carriage_return* that are listed above.

(The present file WEAVE.WEB does not contain any of the non-ASCII characters, because it is intended to be used with all implementations of WEB. It was originally created on a Stanford system that has a convenient extended character set, then "sanitized" by applying another program that transliterated all of the non-standard characters into standard equivalents.)

⟨ Set initial values 10 ⟩ +≡
for *i* ← 1 **to** ´37 **do** *xchr*[*i*] ← ´␣´;

18.   The following system-independent code makes the *xord* array contain a suitable inverse to the information in *xchr*.

⟨ Set initial values 10 ⟩ +≡
for *i* ← *first_text_char* **to** *last_text_char* **do** *xord*[*chr*(*i*)] ← ´40;
for *i* ← 1 **to** ´176 **do** *xord*[*xchr*[*i*]] ← *i*;

19. Input and output. The input conventions of this program are intended to be very much like those of TEX (except, of course, that they are much simpler, because much less needs to be done). Furthermore they are identical to those of **TANGLE**. Therefore people who need to make modifications to all three systems should be able to do so without too many headaches.

We use the standard Pascal input/output procedures in several places that TEX cannot, since **WEAVE** does not have to deal with files that are named dynamically by the user, and since there is no input from the terminal.

20. Terminal output is done by writing on file *term_out*, which is assumed to consist of characters of type *text_char*:

> **define** *print*(#) ≡ *write*(*term_out*, #)   { '*print*' means write on the terminal }
> **define** *print_ln*(#) ≡ *write_ln*(*term_out*, #)   { '*print*' and then start new line }
> **define** *new_line* ≡ *write_ln*(*term_out*)   { start new line }
> **define** *print_nl*(#) ≡   { print information starting on a new line }
>   **begin** *new_line*; *print*(#);
>   **end**

⟨ Globals in the outer block 9 ⟩ +≡
term_out: *text_file*;   { the terminal as an output file }

21. Different systems have different ways of specifying that the output on a certain file will appear on the user's terminal. Here is one way to do this on the Pascal system that was used in **TANGLE**'s initial development:

⟨ Set initial values 10 ⟩ +≡
  rewrite(*term_out*, 'TTY:');   { send *term_out* output to the terminal }

22. The *update_terminal* procedure is called when we want to make sure that everything we have output to the terminal so far has actually left the computer's internal buffers and been sent.

> **define** *update_terminal* ≡ *break*(*term_out*)   { empty the terminal output buffer }

23. The main input comes from *web_file*; this input may be overridden by changes in *change_file*. (If *change_file* is empty, there are no changes.)

⟨ Globals in the outer block 9 ⟩ +≡
web_file: *text_file*;   { primary input }
change_file: *text_file*;   { updates }

24. The following code opens the input files. Since these files were listed in the program header, we assume that the Pascal runtime system has already checked that suitable file names have been given; therefore no additional error checking needs to be done. We will see below that **WEAVE** reads through the entire input twice.

procedure *open_input*;   { prepare to read *web_file* and *change_file* }
  begin *reset*(*web_file*); *reset*(*change_file*);
  end;

25. The main output goes to *tex_file*.

⟨ Globals in the outer block 9 ⟩ +≡
tex_file: *text_file*;

26.   The following code opens *tex_file*. Since this file was listed in the program header, we assume that the Pascal runtime system has checked that a suitable external file name has been given.

⟨ Set initial values 10 ⟩ +≡
    rewrite(*tex_file*);

27.   Input goes into an array called *buffer*.

⟨ Globals in the outer block 9 ⟩ +≡
buffer: **array** [0 .. *long_buf_size*] **of** *ASCII_code*;

28.   The *input_ln* procedure brings the next line of input from the specified file into the *buffer* array and returns the value *true*, unless the file has already been entirely read, in which case it returns *false*. The conventions of TEX are followed; i.e., *ASCII_code* numbers representing the next line of the file are input into *buffer*[0], *buffer*[1], ..., *buffer*[*limit* − 1]; trailing blanks are ignored; and the global variable *limit* is set to the length of the line. The value of *limit* must be strictly less than *buf_size*.

We assume that none of the *ASCII_code* values of *buffer*[*j*] for $0 \leq j < limit$ is equal to 0, ´177, *line_feed*, *form_feed*, or *carriage_return*. Since *buf_size* is strictly less than *long_buf_size*, some of WEAVE's routines use the fact that it is safe to refer to *buffer*[*limit* + 2] without overstepping the bounds of the array.

function *input_ln*(**var** *f* : *text_file*): *boolean*;   { inputs a line or returns *false* }
    var *final_limit*: 0 .. *buf_size*;   { *limit* without trailing blanks }
    begin *limit* ← 0; *final_limit* ← 0;
    if *eof*(*f*) **then** *input_ln* ← *false*
    else begin while ¬*eoln*(*f*) **do**
            begin *buffer*[*limit*] ← *xord*[*f*↑]; *get*(*f*); *incr*(*limit*);
            if *buffer*[*limit* − 1] ≠ "␣" **then** *final_limit* ← *limit*;
            if *limit* = *buf_size* **then**
                begin while ¬*eoln*(*f*) **do** *get*(*f*);
                decr(*limit*);   { keep *buffer*[*buf_size*] empty }
                if *final_limit* > *limit* **then** *final_limit* ← *limit*;
                print_nl(´!␣Input␣line␣too␣long´); *loc* ← 0; *error*;
                end;
            end;
        read_ln(*f*); *limit* ← *final_limit*; *input_ln* ← *true*;
        end;
    end;

29. Reporting errors to the user.   The WEAVE processor operates in three phases: first it inputs the source file and stores cross-reference data, then it inputs the source once again and produces the TEX output file, and finally it sorts and outputs the index.

The global variables *phase_one* and *phase_three* tell which Phase we are in.

⟨ Globals in the outer block 9 ⟩ +≡
phase_one: *boolean*;   { *true* in Phase I, *false* in Phases II and III }
phase_three: *boolean*;   { *true* in Phase III, *false* in Phases I and II }

30.   If an error is detected while we are debugging, we usually want to look at the contents of memory. A special procedure will be declared later for this purpose.

⟨ Error handling procedures 30 ⟩ ≡
   debug **procedure** *debug_help*; *forward*; **gubed**

See also sections 31 and 33.

This code is used in section 2.

---

31. The command '*err_print*(´!␣**Error**␣**message**´)' will report a syntax error to the user, by printing the error message at the beginning of a new line and then giving an indication of where the error was spotted in the source file. Note that no period follows the error message, since the error routine will automatically supply a period.

The actual error indications are provided by a procedure called *error*. However, error messages are not actually reported during phase one, since errors detected on the first pass will be detected again during the second.

   define *err_print*(**#**) ≡
         begin if ¬*phase_one* **then**
            begin *new_line*; *print*(**#**); *error*;
            end;
         end

⟨ Error handling procedures 30 ⟩ +≡
procedure *error*; { prints '.' and location of error message }
   var *k, l*: 0 .. *long_buf_size*; { indices into *buffer* }
   begin ⟨ Print error location based on input buffer 32 ⟩;
   update_terminal; *mark_error*;
   debug *debug_skipped* ← *debug_cycle*; *debug_help*; **gubed**
   end;

---

32. The error locations can be indicated by using the global variables *loc*, *line*, and *changing*, which tell respectively the first unlooked-at position in *buffer*, the current line number, and whether or not the current line is from *change_file* or *web_file*. This routine should be modified on systems whose standard text editor has special line-numbering conventions.

⟨ Print error location based on input buffer 32 ⟩ ≡
   begin if *changing* **then** *print*(´.␣(change␣file␣´) **else** *print*(´.␣(´);
   print_ln(´l.´, *line* : 1, ´)´);
   if *loc* > *limit* **then** *l* ← *limit*
   else *l* ← *loc*;
   for *k* ← 1 **to** *l* **do**
      if *buffer*[*k* − 1] = *tab_mark* **then** *print*(´␣´)
      else *print*(*xchr*[*buffer*[*k* − 1]]); { print the characters already read }
   new_line;
   for *k* ← 1 **to** *l* **do** *print*(´␣´); { space out the next line }
   for *k* ← *l* + 1 **to** *limit* **do** *print*(*xchr*[*buffer*[*k* − 1]]); { print the part not yet read }
   if *buffer*[*limit*] = "|" **then** *print*(*xchr*["|"]); { end of Pascal text in module names }
   print(´␣´); { this space separates the message from future asterisks }
   end

This code is used in section 31.

---

33. The *jump_out* procedure just cuts across all active procedure levels and jumps out of the program. This is the only non-local **goto** statement in WEAVE. It is used when no recovery from a particular error has been provided.

Some Pascal compilers do not implement non-local **goto** statements. In such cases the code that appears at label *end_of_WEAVE* should be copied into the *jump_out* procedure, followed by a call to a system procedure that terminates the program.

> **define** *fatal_error*(#) ≡
>   **begin** *new_line*; *print*(#); *error*; *mark_fatal*; *jump_out*;
>   **end**

⟨ Error handling procedures 30 ⟩ +≡
procedure *jump_out*;
   begin goto *end_of_WEAVE*;
   end;

34.   Sometimes the program's behavior is far different from what it should be, and WEAVE prints an error message that is really for the WEAVE maintenance person, not the user. In such cases the program says *confusion*(ˊindication␣of␣where␣we␣areˊ).

> **define** *confusion*(#) ≡ *fatal_error*(ˊ!␣This␣canˊˊt␣happen␣(ˊ,#,ˊ)ˊ)

35.   An overflow stop occurs if WEAVE's tables aren't large enough.

> **define** *overflow*(#) ≡ *fatal_error*(ˊ!␣Sorry,␣ˊ,#,ˊ␣capacity␣exceededˊ)

36.   Data structures.   During the first phase of its processing, WEAVE puts identifier names, index entries, and module names into the large *byte_mem* array, which is packed with seven-bit integers. Allocation is sequential, since names are never deleted.

An auxiliary array *byte_start* is used as a directory for *byte_mem*, and the *link*, *ilk*, and *xref* arrays give further information about names. These auxiliary arrays consist of sixteen-bit items.

⟨ Types in the outer block 11 ⟩ +≡
   eight_bits = 0 .. 255;   { unsigned one-byte quantity }
   sixteen_bits = 0 .. 65535;   { unsigned two-byte quantity }

37.   WEAVE has been designed to avoid the need for indices that are more than sixteen bits wide, so that it can be used on most computers. But there are programs that need more than 65536 bytes; TₑX is one of these. To get around this problem, a slight complication has been added to the data structures: *byte_mem* is a two-dimensional array, whose first index is either 0 or 1. (For generality, the first index is actually allowed to run between 0 and *ww* − 1, where *ww* is defined to be 2; the program will work for any positive value of *ww*, and it can be simplified in obvious ways if *ww* = 1.)

> **define** *ww* = 2   { we multiply the byte capacity by approximately this amount }

⟨ Globals in the outer block 9 ⟩ +≡
byte_mem: **packed array** [0 .. *ww* − 1, 0 .. *max_bytes*] **of** *ASCII_code*;   { characters of names }
byte_start: **array** [0 .. *max_names*] **of** *sixteen_bits*;   { directory into *byte_mem* }
link: **array** [0 .. *max_names*] **of** *sixteen_bits*;   { hash table or tree links }
ilk: **array** [0 .. *max_names*] **of** *sixteen_bits*;   { type codes or tree links }
xref: **array** [0 .. *max_names*] **of** *sixteen_bits*;   { heads of cross-reference lists }

38. The names of identifiers are found by computing a hash address h and then looking at strings of bytes signified by $hash[h]$, $link[hash[h]]$, $link[link[hash[h]]]$, ..., until either finding the desired name or encountering a zero.

A '*name_pointer*' variable, which signifies a name, is an index into *byte_start*. The actual sequence of characters in the name pointed to by p appears in positions $byte\_start[p]$ to $byte\_start[p+ww]-1$, inclusive, in the segment of *byte_mem* whose first index is $p \bmod ww$. Thus, when $ww = 2$ the even-numbered name bytes appear in $byte\_mem[0, *]$ and the odd-numbered ones appear in $byte\_mem[1, *]$. The pointer 0 is used for undefined module names; we don't want to use it for the names of identifiers, since 0 stands for a null pointer in a linked list.

We usually have $byte\_start[name\_ptr + w] = byte\_ptr[(name\_ptr + w) \bmod ww]$ for $0 \le w < ww$, since these are the starting positions for the next ww names to be stored in *byte_mem*.

> **define** $length(\#) \equiv byte\_start[\# + ww] - byte\_start[\#]$ { the length of a name }

⟨ Types in the outer block 11 ⟩ +≡
  $name\_pointer = 0 .. max\_names$;   { identifies a name }

39. ⟨ Globals in the outer block 9 ⟩ +≡
$name\_ptr$: $name\_pointer$;   { first unused position in *byte_start* }
$byte\_ptr$: **array** $[0 .. ww - 1]$ **of** $0 .. max\_bytes$;   { first unused position in *byte_mem* }

40. ⟨ Local variables for initialization 16 ⟩ +≡
wi: $0 .. ww - 1$;   { to initialize the *byte_mem* indices }

41. ⟨ Set initial values 10 ⟩ +≡
  for $wi \leftarrow 0$ **to** $ww - 1$ **do**
    begin $byte\_start[wi] \leftarrow 0$; $byte\_ptr[wi] \leftarrow 0$;
    end;
  $byte\_start[ww] \leftarrow 0$;   { this makes name 0 of length zero }
  $name\_ptr \leftarrow 1$;

42. Several types of identifiers are distinguished by their *ilk*:

normal identifiers are part of the Pascal program and will appear in italic type.

roman identifiers are index entries that appear after `@^` in the WEB file.

wildcard identifiers are index entries that appear after `@:` in the WEB file.

typewriter identifiers are index entries that appear after `@.` in the WEB file.

array_like, *begin_like*, ..., *var_like* identifiers are Pascal reserved words whose *ilk* explains how they are to be treated when Pascal code is being formatted.

Finally, if c is an ASCII code, an *ilk* equal to *char_like* $+ c$ denotes a reserved word that will be converted to character c.

> **define** $normal = 0$ { ordinary identifiers have *normal* ilk }
> **define** $roman = 1$ { normal index entries have *roman* ilk }
> **define** $wildcard = 2$ { user-formatted index entries have *wildcard* ilk }
> **define** $typewriter = 3$ { 'typewriter type' entries have *typewriter* ilk }
> **define** $reserved(\#) \equiv (ilk[\#] > typewriter)$ { tells if a name is a reserved word }
> **define** $array\_like = 4$ { **array, file, set** }

define *begin_like* = 5   { begin }
define *case_like* = 6   { case }
define *const_like* = 7   { const, label, type }
define *div_like* = 8   { div, mod }
define *do_like* = 9   { do, of, then }
define *else_like* = 10   { else }
define *end_like* = 11   { end }
define *for_like* = 12   { for, while, with }
define *goto_like* = 13   { goto, packed }
define *if_like* = 14   { if }
define *in_like* = 15   { in }
define *nil_like* = 16   { nil }
define *proc_like* = 17   { function, procedure, program }
define *record_like* = 18   { record }
define *repeat_like* = 19   { repeat }
define *to_like* = 20   { downto, to }
define *until_like* = 21   { until }
define *var_like* = 22   { var }
define *loop_like* = 23   { loop, xclause }
define *char_like* = 24   { and, or, not, in }

43.   The names of modules are stored in *byte_mem* together with the identifier names, but a hash table is not used for them because WEAVE needs to be able to recognize a module name when given a prefix of that name. A conventional binary seach tree is used to retrieve module names, with fields called *llink* and *rlink* in place of *link* and *ilk*. The root of this tree is *rlink*[0].

define *llink* ≡ *link*   { left link in binary search tree for module names }
define *rlink* ≡ *ilk*   { right link in binary search tree for module names }
define *root* ≡ *rlink*[0]   { the root of the binary search tree for module names }

⟨ Set initial values 10 ⟩ +≡
   root ← 0;   { the binary search tree starts out with nothing in it }

44.   Here is a little procedure that prints the text of a given name on the user's terminal.

procedure *print_id*(*p* : *name_pointer*);   { print identifier or module name }
   var *k*: 0 .. *max_bytes*;   { index into *byte_mem* }
      w: 0 .. *ww* − 1;   { row of *byte_mem* }
   begin if *p* ≥ *name_ptr* **then** *print*(´IMPOSSIBLE´)
   else begin *w* ← *p* **mod** *ww*;
      for *k* ← *byte_start*[*p*] **to** *byte_start*[*p* + *ww*] − 1 **do** *print*(*xchr*[*byte_mem*[*w*, *k*]]);
      end;
   end;

45.   We keep track of the current module number in *module_count*, which is the total number of modules that have started. Modules which have been altered by a change file entry have their *changed_module* flag turned on during the first phase.

⟨ Globals in the outer block 9 ⟩ +≡
module_count: 0 .. *max_modules*;   { the current module number }
changed_module: **packed array** [0 .. *max_modules*] **of** *boolean*;   { is it changed? }
change_exists: *boolean*;   { has any module changed? }

46. The other large memory area in WEAVE keeps the cross-reference data. All uses of the name p are recorded in a linked list beginning at $xref[p]$, which points into the $xmem$ array. Entries in $xmem$ consist of two sixteen-bit items per word, called the num and $xlink$ fields. If x is an index into $xmem$, reached from name p, the value of $num(x)$ is either a module number where p is used, or it is def_flag plus a module number where p is defined; and $xlink(x)$ points to the next such cross reference for p, if any. This list of cross references is in decreasing order by module number. The current number of cross references is $xref\_ptr$.

The global variable $xref\_switch$ is set either to def_flag or to zero, depending on whether the next cross reference to an identifier is to be underlined or not in the index. This switch is set to def_flag when @! or @d or @f is scanned, and it is cleared to zero when the next identifier or index entry cross reference has been made. Similarly, the global variable mod_xref_switch is either def_flag or zero, depending on whether a module name is being defined or used.

> **define** $num(\#) \equiv xmem[\#].num\_field$
> **define** $xlink(\#) \equiv xmem[\#].xlink\_field$
> **define** $def\_flag = 10240$ { must be strictly larger than $max\_modules$ }

47. ⟨ Types in the outer block 11 ⟩ +≡
$xref\_number = 0 .. max\_refs;$

48. ⟨ Globals in the outer block 9 ⟩ +≡
$xmem$: **array** $[xref\_number]$ **of packed record**
  num_field: $sixteen\_bits$;   { module number plus zero or def_flag }
  $xlink\_field$: $sixteen\_bits$;   { pointer to the previous cross reference }
  end;
$xref\_ptr$: $xref\_number$;   { the largest occupied position in $xmem$ }
$xref\_switch, mod\_xref\_switch$: $0 .. def\_flag$;   { either zero or def_flag }

49. ⟨ Set initial values 10 ⟩ +≡
$xref\_ptr \leftarrow 0$; $xref\_switch \leftarrow 0$; $mod\_xref\_switch \leftarrow 0$; $num(0) \leftarrow 0$; $xref[0] \leftarrow 0$;
  { cross references to undefined modules }

50. A new cross reference for an identifier is formed by calling new_xref, which discards duplicate entries and ignores non-underlined references to one-letter identifiers or Pascal's reserved words.

> **define** $append\_xref(\#) \equiv$
>   **if** $xref\_ptr = max\_refs$ **then** $overflow(\text{´cross}_\sqcup\text{reference´})$
>   **else begin** $incr(xref\_ptr)$; $num(xref\_ptr) \leftarrow \#$;
>   **end**

procedure $new\_xref(p : name\_pointer)$;
  label $exit$;
  var q: $xref\_number$;   { pointer to previous cross reference }
    m, n: $sixteen\_bits$;   { new and previous cross-reference value }
  begin if $(reserved(p) \vee (byte\_start[p] + 1 = byte\_start[p + ww])) \wedge (xref\_switch = 0)$ **then**
    return;
  $m \leftarrow module\_count + xref\_switch$; $xref\_switch \leftarrow 0$; $q \leftarrow xref[p]$;
  if $q > 0$ **then**
    begin $n \leftarrow num(q)$;

```
    if (n = m) ∨ (n = m + def_flag) then return
    else if m = n + def_flag then
        begin num(q) ← m; return;
        end;
    end;
  append_xref(m); xlink(xref_ptr) ← q; xref[p] ← xref_ptr;
exit: end;
```

51. The cross reference lists for module names are slightly different. Suppose that a module name is defined in modules $m_1, \ldots, m_k$ and used in modules $n_1, \ldots, n_l$. Then its list will contain $m_1 + def\_flag$, $m_k + def\_flag$, $\ldots$, $m_2 + def\_flag$, n_l, $\ldots$, n_1, in this order. After Phase II, however, the order will be $m_1 + def\_flag$, $\ldots$, $m_k + def\_flag$, n_1, $\ldots$, n_l.

```
procedure new_mod_xref(p : name_pointer);
  var q, r: xref_number;   { pointers to previous cross references }
  begin q ← xref[p]; r ← 0;
  if q > 0 then
    begin if mod_xref_switch = 0 then
      while num(q) ≥ def_flag do
        begin r ← q; q ← xlink(q);
        end
    else if num(q) ≥ def_flag then
        begin r ← q; q ← xlink(q);
        end;
    end;
  append_xref(module_count + mod_xref_switch); xlink(xref_ptr) ← q; mod_xref_switch ← 0;
  if r = 0 then xref[p] ← xref_ptr
  else xlink(r) ← xref_ptr;
  end;
```

52. A third large area of memory is used for sixteen-bit 'tokens', which appear in short lists similar to the strings of characters in *byte_mem*. Token lists are used to contain the result of Pascal code translated into TeX form; further details about them will be explained later. A *text_pointer* variable is an index into *tok_start*.

⟨ Types in the outer block 11 ⟩ +≡
    text_pointer = 0 .. *max_texts*;   { identifies a token list }

53. The first position of *tok_mem* that is unoccupied by replacement text is called *tok_ptr*, and the first unused location of *tok_start* is called *text_ptr*. Thus, we usually have the condition *tok_start*[*text_ptr*] = *tok_ptr*.

⟨ Globals in the outer block 9 ⟩ +≡
    tok_mem: **packed array** [0 .. *max_toks*] **of** *sixteen_bits*;   { tokens }
    tok_start: **array** [*text_pointer*] **of** *sixteen_bits*;   { directory into *tok_mem* }
    text_ptr: *text_pointer*;   { first unused position in *tok_start* }
    tok_ptr: 0 .. *max_toks*;   { first unused position in *tok_mem* }
    stat *max_tok_ptr*, *max_txt_ptr*: 0 .. *max_toks*;   { largest values occurring }
    tats

54. ⟨ Set initial values 10 ⟩ +≡

$tok\_ptr \leftarrow 1$; $text\_ptr \leftarrow 1$; $tok\_start[0] \leftarrow 1$; $tok\_start[1] \leftarrow 1$;
stat $max\_tok\_ptr \leftarrow 1$; $max\_txt\_ptr \leftarrow 1$; **tats**

55. Searching for identifiers.

The hash table described above is updated by the *id_lookup* procedure, which finds a given identifier and returns a pointer to its index in *byte_start*. The identifier is supposed to match character by character and it is also supposed to have a given *ilk* code; the same name may be present more than once if it is supposed to appear in the index with different typesetting conventions. If the identifier was not already present, it is inserted into the table.

Because of the way WEAVE's scanning mechanism works, it is most convenient to let *id_lookup* search for an identifier that is present in the *buffer* array. Two other global variables specify its position in the buffer: the first character is *buffer*[*id_first*], and the last is *buffer*[*id_loc* − 1].

⟨ Globals in the outer block 9 ⟩ +≡
id_first: 0 .. *long_buf_size*;   { where the current identifier begins in the buffer }
id_loc: 0 .. *long_buf_size*;   { just after the current identifier in the buffer }

hash: **array** [0 .. *hash_size*] **of** *sixteen_bits*;   { heads of hash lists }

56. Initially all the hash lists are empty.

⟨ Local variables for initialization 16 ⟩ +≡
h: 0 .. *hash_size*;   { index into hash-head array }

57. ⟨ Set initial values 10 ⟩ +≡
   for $h \leftarrow 0$ **to** $hash\_size - 1$ **do** $hash[h] \leftarrow 0$;

58.

Here now is the main procedure for finding identifiers (and index entries). The parameter *t* is set to the desired *ilk* code. The identifier must either have *ilk* = *t*, or we must have *t* = *normal* and the identifier must be a reserved word.

function *id_lookup*(*t* : *eight_bits*): *name_pointer*;   { finds current identifier }
   label *found*;
   var *i*: 0 .. *long_buf_size*;   { index into *buffer* }
      h: 0 .. *hash_size*;   { hash code }
      k: 0 .. *max_bytes*;   { index into *byte_mem* }
      w: 0 .. *ww* − 1;   { row of *byte_mem* }
      l: 0 .. *long_buf_size*;   { length of the given identifier }
      p: *name_pointer*;   { where the identifier is being sought }
   begin $l \leftarrow id\_loc - id\_first$;   { compute the length }
   ⟨ Compute the hash code *h* 59 ⟩;
   ⟨ Compute the name location *p* 60 ⟩;
   if $p = name\_ptr$ **then** ⟨ Enter a new name into the table at position *p* 62 ⟩;
   $id\_lookup \leftarrow p$;
   end;

59.

A simple hash code is used: If the sequence of ASCII codes is $c_1 c_2 \ldots c_m$, its hash value will be

$$(2^{n-1}c_1 + 2^{n-2}c_2 + \cdots + c_n) \bmod hash\_size.$$

⟨ Compute the hash code *h* 59 ⟩ ≡

$h \leftarrow buffer[id\_first]; \ i \leftarrow id\_first + 1;$
while $i < id\_loc$ **do**
 begin $h \leftarrow (h + h + buffer[i]) \bmod hash\_size; \ incr(i);$
 end

This code is used in section 58.

60. If the identifier is new, it will be placed in position $p = name\_ptr$, otherwise p will point to its existing location.

$\langle$ Compute the name location p 60 $\rangle \equiv$
 $p \leftarrow hash[h];$
 while $p \neq 0$ **do**
  begin if $(length(p) = l) \wedge ((ilk[p] = t) \vee ((t = normal) \wedge reserved(p)))$ **then**
   $\langle$ Compare name p with current identifier, **goto** *found* if equal 61 $\rangle$;
  $p \leftarrow link[p];$
  end;
 $p \leftarrow name\_ptr;$ $\{$ the current identifier is new $\}$
 $link[p] \leftarrow hash[h]; \ hash[h] \leftarrow p;$ $\{$ insert p at beginning of hash list $\}$
found:

This code is used in section 58.

61. $\langle$ Compare name p with current identifier, **goto** *found* if equal 61 $\rangle \equiv$
 begin $i \leftarrow id\_first; \ k \leftarrow byte\_start[p]; \ w \leftarrow p \bmod ww;$
 while $(i < id\_loc) \wedge (buffer[i] = byte\_mem[w, k])$ **do**
  begin $incr(i); \ incr(k);$
  end;
 if $i = id\_loc$ **then goto** *found*; $\{$ all characters agree $\}$
 end

This code is used in section 60.

62. When we begin the following segment of the program, $p = name\_ptr$.

$\langle$ Enter a new name into the table at position p 62 $\rangle \equiv$
 begin $w \leftarrow name\_ptr \bmod ww;$
 if $byte\_ptr[w] + l > max\_bytes$ **then** $overflow(\text{`byte}_{\sqcup}\text{memory'});$
 if $name\_ptr + ww > max\_names$ **then** $overflow(\text{`name'});$
 $i \leftarrow id\_first; \ k \leftarrow byte\_ptr[w];$ $\{$ get ready to move the identifier into $byte\_mem$ $\}$
 while $i < id\_loc$ **do**
  begin $byte\_mem[w, k] \leftarrow buffer[i]; \ incr(k); \ incr(i);$
  end;
 $byte\_ptr[w] \leftarrow k; \ byte\_start[name\_ptr + ww] \leftarrow k; \ incr(name\_ptr); \ ilk[p] \leftarrow t; \ xref[p] \leftarrow 0;$
 end

This code is used in section 58.

63. Initializing the table of reserved words. We have to get Pascal's reserved words into the hash table, and the simplest way to do this is to insert them every time **WEAVE** is run. A few macros permit us to do the initialization with a compact program.

 define $sid9(\#) \equiv buffer[9] \leftarrow \#; \ cur\_name \leftarrow id\_lookup$
 define $sid8(\#) \equiv buffer[8] \leftarrow \#; \ sid9$
 define $sid7(\#) \equiv buffer[7] \leftarrow \#; \ sid8$

define $sid6\,(\#) \equiv buffer\,[6] \leftarrow \#;\ \ sid7$
define $sid5\,(\#) \equiv buffer\,[5] \leftarrow \#;\ \ sid6$
define $sid4\,(\#) \equiv buffer\,[4] \leftarrow \#;\ \ sid5$
define $sid3\,(\#) \equiv buffer\,[3] \leftarrow \#;\ \ sid4$
define $sid2\,(\#) \equiv buffer\,[2] \leftarrow \#;\ \ sid3$
define $sid1\,(\#) \equiv buffer\,[1] \leftarrow \#;\ \ sid2$
define $id2 \equiv id\_first \leftarrow 8;\ \ sid8$
define $id3 \equiv id\_first \leftarrow 7;\ \ sid7$
define $id4 \equiv id\_first \leftarrow 6;\ \ sid6$
define $id5 \equiv id\_first \leftarrow 5;\ \ sid5$
define $id6 \equiv id\_first \leftarrow 4;\ \ sid4$
define $id7 \equiv id\_first \leftarrow 3;\ \ sid3$
define $id8 \equiv id\_first \leftarrow 2;\ \ sid2$
define $id9 \equiv id\_first \leftarrow 1;\ \ sid1$

⟨ Globals in the outer block 9 ⟩ +≡
cur_name: $name\_pointer$; { points to the identifier just inserted }

64. The intended use of the macros above might not be immediately obvious, but the riddle is answered by the following:

⟨ Store all the reserved words 64 ⟩ ≡
  $id\_loc \leftarrow 10;$
  $id3\,("a")("n")("d")(char\_like + and\_sign);$
  $id5\,("a")("r")("r")("a")("y")(array\_like);$
  $id5\,("b")("e")("g")("i")("n")(begin\_like);$
  $id4\,("c")("a")("s")("e")(case\_like);$
  $id5\,("c")("o")("n")("s")("t")(const\_like);$
  $id3\,("d")("i")("v")(div\_like);$
  $id2\,("d")("o")(do\_like);$
  $id6\,("d")("o")("w")("n")("t")("o")(to\_like);$
  $id4\,("e")("l")("s")("e")(else\_like);$
  $id3\,("e")("n")("d")(end\_like);$
  $id4\,("f")("i")("l")("e")(array\_like);$
  $id3\,("f")("o")("r")(for\_like);$
  $id8\,("f")("u")("n")("c")("t")("i")("o")("n")(proc\_like);$
  $id4\,("g")("o")("t")("o")(goto\_like);$
  $id2\,("i")("f")(if\_like);$
  $id2\,("i")("n")(char\_like + set\_element\_sign);$
  $id5\,("l")("a")("b")("e")("l")(const\_like);$
  $id3\,("m")("o")("d")(div\_like);$
  $id3\,("n")("i")("l")(nil\_like);$
  $id3\,("n")("o")("t")(char\_like + not\_sign);$
  $id2\,("o")("f")(do\_like);$
  $id2\,("o")("r")(char\_like + or\_sign);$
  $id6\,("p")("a")("c")("k")("e")("d")(goto\_like);$
  $id9\,("p")("r")("o")("c")("e")("d")("u")("r")("e")(proc\_like);$
  $id7\,("p")("r")("o")("g")("r")("a")("m")(proc\_like);$
  $id6\,("r")("e")("c")("o")("r")("d")(record\_like);$
  $id6\,("r")("e")("p")("e")("a")("t")(repeat\_like);$
  $id3\,("s")("e")("t")(array\_like);$

$id4\,("\texttt{t}")("\texttt{h}")("\texttt{e}")("\texttt{n}")(do\_like)$;
$id2\,("\texttt{t}")("\texttt{o}")(to\_like)$;
$id4\,("\texttt{t}")("\texttt{y}")("\texttt{p}")("\texttt{e}")(const\_like)$;
$id5\,("\texttt{u}")("\texttt{n}")("\texttt{t}")("\texttt{i}")("\texttt{l}")(until\_like)$;
$id3\,("\texttt{v}")("\texttt{a}")("\texttt{r}")(var\_like)$;
$id5\,("\texttt{w}")("\texttt{h}")("\texttt{i}")("\texttt{l}")("\texttt{e}")(for\_like)$;
$id4\,("\texttt{w}")("\texttt{i}")("\texttt{t}")("\texttt{h}")(for\_like)$;
$id7("\texttt{x}")("\texttt{c}")("\texttt{l}")("\texttt{a}")("\texttt{u}")("\texttt{s}")("\texttt{e}")(loop\_like)$;

This code is used in section 261.

65. Searching for module names.   The *mod_lookup* procedure finds the module name $mod\_text[1 \mathbin{..} l]$ in the search tree, after inserting it if necessary, and returns a pointer to where it was found.

⟨ Globals in the outer block 9 ⟩ +≡
mod_text: **array** $[0 \mathbin{..} longest\_name]$ **of** *ASCII_code*;   { name being sought for }

66.   According to the rules of WEB, no module name should be a proper prefix of another, so a "clean" comparison should occur between any two names. The result of *mod_lookup* is 0 if this prefix condition is violated. An error message is printed when such violations are detected during phase two of WEAVE.

define *less* = 0   { the first name is lexicographically less than the second }
define *equal* = 1   { the first name is equal to the second }
define *greater* = 2   { the first name is lexicographically greater than the second }
define *prefix* = 3   { the first name is a proper prefix of the second }
define *extension* = 4   { the first name is a proper extension of the second }

function $mod\_lookup(l : sixteen\_bits): name\_pointer$;   { finds module name }
　label *found*;
　var c: *less* .. *extension*;   { comparison between two names }
　　j: $0 \mathbin{..} longest\_name$;   { index into *mod_text* }
　　k: $0 \mathbin{..} max\_bytes$;   { index into *byte_mem* }
　　w: $0 \mathbin{..} ww - 1$;   { row of *byte_mem* }
　　p: *name_pointer*;   { current node of the search tree }
　　q: *name_pointer*;   { father of node p }
　begin $c \leftarrow greater$; $q \leftarrow 0$; $p \leftarrow root$;
　while $p \neq 0$ **do**
　　begin ⟨ Set variable c to the result of comparing the given name to name p 68 ⟩;
　　$q \leftarrow p$;
　　if $c = less$ **then** $p \leftarrow llink[q]$
　　else if $c = greater$ **then** $p \leftarrow rlink[q]$
　　　else goto *found*;
　　end;
　⟨ Enter a new module name into the tree 67 ⟩;
found: **if** $c \neq equal$ **then**
　　begin $err\_print(\texttt{`!\textvisiblespace Incompatible\textvisiblespace section\textvisiblespace names'})$; $p \leftarrow 0$;
　　end;
　$mod\_lookup \leftarrow p$;
　end;

67.   ⟨ Enter a new module name into the tree 67 ⟩ ≡
  $w \leftarrow name\_ptr \bmod ww$; $k \leftarrow byte\_ptr[w]$;
  if $k + l > max\_bytes$ **then** $overflow(\texttt{'byte}_\sqcup\texttt{memory'})$;
  if $name\_ptr > max\_names - ww$ **then** $overflow(\texttt{'name'})$;
  $p \leftarrow name\_ptr$;
  if $c = less$ **then** $llink[q] \leftarrow p$
  else $rlink[q] \leftarrow p$;
  $llink[p] \leftarrow 0$; $rlink[p] \leftarrow 0$; $xref[p] \leftarrow 0$; $c \leftarrow equal$;
  for $j \leftarrow 1$ **to** l **do** $byte\_mem[w, k + j - 1] \leftarrow mod\_text[j]$;
  $byte\_ptr[w] \leftarrow k + l$; $byte\_start[name\_ptr + ww] \leftarrow k + l$; $incr(name\_ptr)$;
This code is used in section 66.

68.   ⟨ Set variable c to the result of comparing the given name to name p 68 ⟩ ≡
  begin $k \leftarrow byte\_start[p]$; $w \leftarrow p \bmod ww$; $c \leftarrow equal$; $j \leftarrow 1$;
  while $(k < byte\_start[p + ww]) \wedge (j \leq l) \wedge (mod\_text[j] = byte\_mem[w, k])$ **do**
    begin $incr(k)$; $incr(j)$;
    end;
  if $k = byte\_start[p + ww]$ **then**
    if $j > l$ **then** $c \leftarrow equal$
    else $c \leftarrow extension$
  else if $j > l$ **then** $c \leftarrow prefix$
    else if $mod\_text[j] < byte\_mem[w, k]$ **then** $c \leftarrow less$
      else $c \leftarrow greater$;
  end
This code is used in sections 66 and 69.

69.   The *prefix_lookup* procedure is supposed to find exactly one module name that has
$mod\_text[1 .. l]$ as a prefix. Actually the algorithm silently accepts also the situation that
some module name is a prefix of $mod\_text[1 .. l]$, because the user who painstakingly typed
in more than necessary probably doesn't want to be told about the wasted effort.

Recall that error messages are not printed during phase one. It is possible that the
prefix_lookup procedure will fail on the first pass, because there is no match, yet the second
pass might detect no error if a matching module name has occurred after the offending
prefix. In such a case the cross-reference information will be incorrect and **WEAVE** will report
no error. However, such a mistake will be detected by the **TANGLE** processor.

function *prefix_lookup*(l : *sixteen_bits*): *name_pointer*;   { finds name extension }
  var c: $less .. extension$;   { comparison between two names }
    $count$: $0 .. max\_names$;   { the number of hits }
    j: $0 .. longest\_name$;   { index into *mod_text* }
    k: $0 .. max\_bytes$;   { index into *byte_mem* }
    w: $0 .. ww - 1$;   { row of *byte_mem* }
    p: *name_pointer*;   { current node of the search tree }
    q: *name_pointer*;   { another place to resume the search after one branch is done }
    r: *name_pointer*;   { extension found }
  begin $q \leftarrow 0$; $p \leftarrow root$; $count \leftarrow 0$; $r \leftarrow 0$;   { begin search at root of tree }
  while $p \neq 0$ **do**
    begin ⟨ Set variable c to the result of comparing the given name to name p 68 ⟩;
    if $c = less$ **then** $p \leftarrow llink[p]$
    else if $c = greater$ **then** $p \leftarrow rlink[p]$

```
      else begin r ← p; incr(count);  q ← rlink[p];  p ← llink[p];
        end;
    if p = 0 then
      begin p ← q;  q ← 0;
      end;
    end;
  if count ≠ 1 then
    if count = 0 then  err_print(´!␣Name␣does␣not␣match´)
    else err_print(´!␣Ambiguous␣prefix´);
  prefix_lookup ← r;   { the result will be 0 if there was no match }
  end;
```

70. Lexical scanning.   Let us now consider the subroutines that read the `WEB` source
file and break it into meaningful units. There are four such procedures: One simply skips to
the next '`@␣`' or '`@*`' that begins a module; another passes over the TeX text at the beginning
of a module; the third passes over the TeX text in a Pascal comment; and the last, which is
the most interesting, gets the next token of a Pascal text.

71.   But first we need to consider the low-level routine *get_line* that takes care of merging
change_file into *web_file*. The *get_line* procedure also updates the line numbers for error
messages.

⟨ Globals in the outer block 9 ⟩ +≡
line: *integer*;   { the number of the current line in the current file }
other_line: *integer*;
          { the number of the current line in the input file that is not currently being read }
temp_line: *integer*;   { used when interchanging *line* with *other_line* }
limit: 0 .. *long_buf_size*;   { the last character position occupied in the buffer }
loc: 0 .. *long_buf_size*;   { the next character position to be read from the buffer }
input_has_ended: *boolean*;   { if *true*, there is no more input }
changing: *boolean*;   { if *true*, the current line is from *change_file* }

72.   As we change *changing* from *true* to *false* and back again, we must remember to
swap the values of *line* and *other_line* so that the *err_print* routine will be sure to report
the correct line number.

  define *change_changing* ≡ *changing* ← ¬*changing*; *temp_line* ← *other_line*; *other_line* ← *line*;
            line ← *temp_line*   { *line* ↔ *other_line* }

73.   When *changing* is *false*, the next line of *change_file* is kept in *change_buffer*[0 ..
change_limit], for purposes of comparison with the next line of *web_file*. After the change
file has been completely input, we set *change_limit* ← 0, so that no further matches will be
made.

⟨ Globals in the outer block 9 ⟩ +≡
change_buffer: **array** [0 .. *buf_size*] **of** *ASCII_code*;
change_limit: 0 .. *buf_size*;   { the last position occupied in *change_buffer* }

74.   Here's a simple function that checks if the two buffers are different.

function *lines_dont_match*: *boolean*;

```
      label exit;
      var k: 0 .. buf_size;   {index into the buffers}
      begin lines_dont_match ← true;
      if change_limit ≠ limit then return;
      if limit > 0 then
        for k ← 0 to limit − 1 do
          if change_buffer[k] ≠ buffer[k] then return;
      lines_dont_match ← false;
exit: end;
```

75. Procedure *prime_the_change_buffer* sets *change_buffer* in preparation for the next matching operation. Since blank lines in the change file are not used for matching, we have (*change_limit* = 0) ∧ ¬*changing* if and only if the change file is exhausted. This procedure is called only when *changing* is true; hence error messages will be reported correctly.

```
procedure prime_the_change_buffer;
  label continue, done, exit;
  var k: 0 .. buf_size;   {index into the buffers}
  begin change_limit ← 0;   {this value will be used if the change file ends}
  ⟨Skip over comment lines in the change file; return if end of file 76⟩;
  ⟨Skip to the next nonblank line; return if end of file 77⟩;
  ⟨Move buffer and limit to change_buffer and change_limit 78⟩;
exit: end;
```

76. While looking for a line that begins with @x in the change file, we allow lines that begin with @, as long as they don't begin with @y or @z (which would probably indicate that the change file is fouled up).

⟨Skip over comment lines in the change file; **return** if end of file 76⟩ ≡
```
  loop begin incr(line);
    if ¬input_ln(change_file) then return;
    if limit < 2 then goto continue;
    if buffer[0] ≠ "@" then goto continue;
    if (buffer[1] ≥ "X") ∧ (buffer[1] ≤ "Z") then buffer[1] ← buffer[1] + "z" − "Z";
          {lowercasify}
    if buffer[1] = "x" then goto done;
    if (buffer[1] = "y") ∨ (buffer[1] = "z") then
      begin loc ← 2; err_print(´!␣Where␣is␣the␣matching␣@x?´);
      end;
  continue: end;
done:
```
This code is used in section 75.

77. Here we are looking at lines following the @x.

⟨Skip to the next nonblank line; **return** if end of file 77⟩ ≡
```
  repeat incr(line);
    if ¬input_ln(change_file) then
      begin err_print(´!␣Change␣file␣ended␣after␣@x´); return;
      end;
  until limit > 0;
```
This code is used in section 75.

78. ⟨ Move *buffer* and *limit* to *change_buffer* and *change_limit* 78 ⟩ ≡
  begin *change_limit* ← *limit*;
  if *limit* > 0 **then**
    for *k* ← 0 **to** *limit* − 1 **do** *change_buffer*[*k*] ← *buffer*[*k*];
  end

This code is used in sections 75 and 79.

79. The following procedure is used to see if the next change entry should go into effect; it is called only when *changing* is false. The idea is to test whether or not the current contents of *buffer* matches the current contents of *change_buffer*. If not, there's nothing more to do; but if so, a change is called for: All of the text down to the @y is supposed to match. An error message is issued if any discrepancy is found. Then the procedure prepares to read the next line from *change_file*.

procedure *check_change*; { switches to *change_file* if the buffers match }
  label *exit*;
  var *n*: *integer*; { the number of discrepancies found }
    k: 0 .. *buf_size*; { index into the buffers }
  begin if *lines_dont_match* **then return**;
  n ← 0;
  loop begin *change_changing*; { now it's *true* }
    incr(*line*);
    if ¬*input_ln*(*change_file*) **then**
      begin *err_print*(´!␣Change␣file␣ended␣before␣@y´); *change_limit* ← 0;
      change_changing; { *false* again }
      return;
      end;
    ⟨ If the current line starts with @y, report any discrepancies and **return** 80 ⟩;
    ⟨ Move *buffer* and *limit* to *change_buffer* and *change_limit* 78 ⟩;
    change_changing; { now it's *false* }
    incr(*line*);
    if ¬*input_ln*(*web_file*) **then**
      begin *err_print*(´!␣WEB␣file␣ended␣during␣a␣change´); *input_has_ended* ← *true*;
      return;
      end;
    if *lines_dont_match* **then** *incr*(*n*);
    end;
exit: **end**;

80. ⟨ If the current line starts with @y, report any discrepancies and **return** 80 ⟩ ≡
  if *limit* > 1 **then**
    if *buffer*[0] = "@" **then**
      begin if (*buffer*[1] ≥ "X") ∧ (*buffer*[1] ≤ "Z") **then** *buffer*[1] ← *buffer*[1] + "z" − "Z";
        { lowercasify }
      if (*buffer*[1] = "x") ∨ (*buffer*[1] = "z") **then**
        begin *loc* ← 2; *err_print*(´!␣Where␣is␣the␣matching␣@y?´);
        end
      else if *buffer*[1] = "y" **then**
        begin if *n* > 0 **then**

```
            begin loc ← 2;
            err_print(´!␣Hmm...␣´, n : 1, ´␣of␣the␣preceding␣lines␣failed␣to␣match´);
            end;
        return;
        end;
    end
```

This code is used in section 79.

81. The *reset_input* procedure, which gets WEAVE ready to read the user's WEB input, is used at the beginning of phases one and two.

```
procedure reset_input;
    begin open_input; line ← 0; other_line ← 0;
    changing ← true; prime_the_change_buffer; change_changing;
    limit ← 0; loc ← 1; buffer[0] ← "␣"; input_has_ended ← false;
    end;
```

82. The *get_line* procedure is called when *loc* > *limit*; it puts the next line of merged input into the buffer and updates the other variables appropriately. A space is placed at the right end of the line.

```
procedure get_line;    { inputs the next line }
    label restart;
    begin restart: if changing then changed_module[module_count] ← true
    else ⟨ Read from web_file and maybe turn on changing 83 ⟩;
    if changing then
        begin ⟨ Read from change_file and maybe turn off changing 84 ⟩;
        if ¬changing then
            begin changed_module[module_count] ← true; goto restart;
            end;
        end;
    loc ← 0; buffer[limit] ← "␣";
    end;
```

83. ⟨ Read from *web_file* and maybe turn on *changing* 83 ⟩ ≡
```
    begin incr(line);
    if ¬input_ln(web_file) then input_has_ended ← true
    else if limit = change_limit then
        if buffer[0] = change_buffer[0] then
            if change_limit > 0 then check_change;
    end
```
This code is used in section 82.

84. ⟨ Read from *change_file* and maybe turn off *changing* 84 ⟩ ≡
```
    begin incr(line);
    if ¬input_ln(change_file) then
        begin err_print(´!␣Change␣file␣ended␣without␣@z´); buffer[0] ← "@"; buffer[1] ← "z";
        limit ← 2;
        end;
    if limit > 1 then    { check if the change has ended }
```

```
    if buffer[0] = "@" then
      begin if (buffer[1] ≥ "X") ∧ (buffer[1] ≤ "Z") then buffer[1] ← buffer[1] + "z" − "Z";
                  { lowercasify }
        if (buffer[1] = "x") ∨ (buffer[1] = "y") then
          begin loc ← 2; err_print(´! Where is the matching @z?´);
          end
        else if buffer[1] = "z" then
              begin prime_the_change_buffer; change_changing;
              end;
      end;
    end
```

This code is used in section 82.

85. At the end of the program, we will tell the user if the change file had a line that didn't match any relevant line in *web_file*.

⟨ Check that all changes have been read 85 ⟩ ≡

```
    if change_limit ≠ 0 then   { changing is false }
      begin for loc ← 0 to change_limit do buffer[loc] ← change_buffer[loc];
      limit ← change_limit; changing ← true; line ← other_line; loc ← change_limit;
      err_print(´! Change file entry did not match´);
      end
```

This code is used in section 261.

86. Control codes in WEB, which begin with '@', are converted into a numeric code designed to simplify WEAVE's logic; for example, larger numbers are given to the control codes that denote more significant milestones, and the code of *new_module* should be the largest of all. Some of these numeric control codes take the place of ASCII control codes that will not otherwise appear in the output of the scanning routines.

```
    define ignore = 0    { control code of no interest to WEAVE }
    define verbatim = ´2    { extended ASCII alpha will not appear }
    define force_line = ´3    { extended ASCII beta will not appear }
    define begin_comment = ´11    { ASCII tab mark will not appear }
    define end_comment = ´12    { ASCII line feed will not appear }
    define octal = ´14    { ASCII form feed will not appear }
    define hex = ´15    { ASCII carriage return will not appear }
    define double_dot = ´40    { ASCII space will not appear except in strings }
    define no_underline = ´175    { this code will be intercepted without confusion }
    define underline = ´176    { this code will be intercepted without confusion }
    define param = ´177    { ASCII delete will not appear }
    define xref_roman = ´203    { control code for '@^' }
    define xref_wildcard = ´204    { control code for '@:' }
    define xref_typewriter = ´205    { control code for '@.' }
    define TeX_string = ´206    { control code for '@t' }
    define check_sum = ´207    { control code for '@$' }
    define join = ´210    { control code for '@&' }
    define thin_space = ´211    { control code for '@,' }
    define math_break = ´212    { control code for '@|' }
    define line_break = ´213    { control code for '@/' }
```

define *big_line_break* = '214   { control code for '@#' }
define *no_line_break* = '215   { control code for '@+' }
define *pseudo_semi* = '216   { control code for '@;' }
define *format* = '217   { control code for '@f' }
define *definition* = '220   { control code for '@d' }
define *begin_Pascal* = '221   { control code for '@p' }
define *module_name* = '222   { control code for '@<' }
define *new_module* = '223   { control code for '@␣' and '@*' }

87. Control codes are converted from ASCII to WEAVE's internal representation by the *control_code* routine.

function *control_code*(*c* : *ASCII_code*): *eight_bits*;   { convert *c* after @ }
  begin case *c* **of**
  "@": *control_code* ← "@";   { 'quoted' at sign }
  "'": *control_code* ← *octal*;   { precedes octal constant }
  """": *control_code* ← *hex*;   { precedes hexadecimal constant }
  "$": *control_code* ← *check_sum*;   { precedes check sum constant }
  "␣", *tab_mark*, "*": *control_code* ← *new_module*;   { beginning of a new module }
  "=": *control_code* ← *verbatim*;
  "\": *control_code* ← *force_line*;
  "D", "d": *control_code* ← *definition*;   { macro definition }
  "F", "f": *control_code* ← *format*;   { format definition }
  "{": *control_code* ← *begin_comment*;   { begin-comment delimiter }
  "}": *control_code* ← *end_comment*;   { end-comment delimiter }
  "P", "p": *control_code* ← *begin_Pascal*;   { Pascal text in unnamed module }
  "&": *control_code* ← *join*;   { concatenate two tokens }
  "<": *control_code* ← *module_name*;   { beginning of a module name }
  ">": **begin** *err_print*('!␣Extra␣@>'); *control_code* ← *ignore*;
    end;   { end of module name should not be discovered in this way }
  "T", "t": *control_code* ← *TeX_string*;   { TEX box within Pascal }
  "!": *control_code* ← *underline*;   { set definition flag }
  "?": *control_code* ← *no_underline*;   { reset definition flag }
  "^": *control_code* ← *xref_roman*;   { index entry to be typeset normally }
  ":": *control_code* ← *xref_wildcard*;   { index entry to be in user format }
  ".": *control_code* ← *xref_typewriter*;   { index entry to be in typewriter type }
  ",": *control_code* ← *thin_space*;   { puts extra space in Pascal format }
  "|": *control_code* ← *math_break*;   { allows a break in a formula }
  "/": *control_code* ← *line_break*;   { forces end-of-line in Pascal format }
  "#": *control_code* ← *big_line_break*;   { forces end-of-line and some space besides }
  "+": *control_code* ← *no_line_break*;   { cancels end-of-line down to single space }
  ";": *control_code* ← *pseudo_semi*;   { acts like a semicolon, but is invisible }
  ⟨ Special control codes allowed only when debugging 88 ⟩
  othercases begin *err_print*('!␣Unknown␣control␣code'); *control_code* ← *ignore*;
    end
  endcases;
  end;

88. If WEAVE is compiled with debugging commands, one can write @2, @1, and @0 to turn tracing fully on, partly on, and off, respectively.

⟨ Special control codes allowed only when debugging 88 ⟩ ≡
    debug
"0", "1", "2": **begin** *tracing* ← *c* − "0"; *control_code* ← *ignore*;
    end;
    gubed

This code is used in section 87.

89. The *skip_limbo* routine is used on the first pass to skip through portions of the input that are not in any modules, i.e., that precede the first module. After this procedure has been called, the value of *input_has_ended* will tell whether or not a new module has actually been found.

procedure *skip_limbo*;   { skip to next module }
  label *exit*;
  var *c*: *ASCII_code*;   { character following @ }
  begin loop
    if *loc* > *limit* **then**
      begin *get_line*;
      if *input_has_ended* **then return**;
      end
    else begin *buffer*[*limit* + 1] ← "@";
      while *buffer*[*loc*] ≠ "@" **do** *incr*(*loc*);
      if *loc* ≤ *limit* **then**
        begin *loc* ← *loc* + 2; *c* ← *buffer*[*loc* − 1];
        if (*c* = "␣") ∨ (*c* = *tab_mark*) ∨ (*c* = "*") **then return**;
        end;
      end;
exit: **end**;

90. The *skip_TeX* routine is used on the first pass to skip through the TeX code at the beginning of a module. It returns the next control code or '|' found in the input. A *new_module* is assumed to exist at the very end of the file.

function *skip_TeX*: *eight_bits*;   { skip past pure TeX code }
  label *done*;
  var *c*: *eight_bits*;   { control code found }
  begin loop
    begin if *loc* > *limit* **then**
      begin *get_line*;
      if *input_has_ended* **then**
        begin *c* ← *new_module*; **goto** *done*;
        end;
      end;
    buffer[*limit* + 1] ← "@";
    repeat *c* ← *buffer*[*loc*]; *incr*(*loc*);
      if *c* = "|" **then goto** *done*;
    until *c* = "@";
    if *loc* ≤ *limit* **then**
      begin *c* ← *control_code*(*buffer*[*loc*]); *incr*(*loc*); **goto** *done*;
      end;
    end;

done: *skip_TeX* ← *c*;
   end;

91. The *skip_comment* routine is used on the first pass to skip through TEX code in Pascal comments. The *bal* parameter tells how many left braces are assumed to have been scanned when this routine is called, and the procedure returns a corresponding value of *bal* at the point that scanning has stopped. Scanning stops either at a '|' that introduces Pascal text, in which case the returned value is positive, or it stops at the end of the comment, in which case the returned value is zero. The scanning also stops in anomalous situations when the comment doesn't end or when it contains an illegal use of @. One should call *skip_comment*(1) when beginning to scan a comment.

function *skip_comment*(*bal* : *eight_bits*): *eight_bits*;   { skips TEX code in comments }
   label *done*,
   var *c*: *ASCII_code*;   { the current character }
   begin loop
     begin if *loc* > *limit* **then**
      begin *get_line*;
      if *input_has_ended* **then**
       begin *bal* ← 0; **goto** *done*;
       end;   { an error message will occur in phase two }
      end;
    c ← *buffer*[*loc*]; *incr*(*loc*);
    if *c* = "|" **then goto** *done*;
    ⟨ Do special things when *c* = "@", "\", "{", "}"; **goto** *done* at end 92 ⟩;
    end;
done: *skip_comment* ← *bal*;
   end;

92. ⟨ Do special things when *c* = "@", "\", "{", "}"; **goto** *done* at end 92 ⟩ ≡
  if *c* = "@" **then**
   begin *c* ← *buffer*[*loc*];
   if (*c* ≠ "␣") ∧ (*c* ≠ *tab_mark*) ∧ (*c* ≠ "*") **then** *incr*(*loc*)
   else begin *decr*(*loc*); *bal* ← 0; **goto** *done*;
    end   { an error message will occur in phase two }
   end
  else if (*c* = "\") ∧ (*buffer*[*loc*] ≠ "@") **then** *incr*(*loc*)
   else if *c* = "{" **then** *incr*(*bal*)
    else if *c* = "}" **then**
     begin *decr*(*bal*);
     if *bal* = 0 **then goto** *done*;
     end

This code is used in section 91.

93. Inputting the next token. As stated above, WEAVE's most interesting lexical scanning routine is the *get_next* function that inputs the next token of Pascal input. However, *get_next* is not especially complicated.

The result of *get_next* is either an ASCII code for some special character, or it is a special code representing a pair of characters (e.g., ':=' or '..'), or it is the numeric value computed by the *control_code* procedure, or it is one of the following special codes:

exponent: The 'E' in a real constant.

identifier: In this case the global variables *id_first* and *id_loc* will have been set to the appropriate values needed by the *id_lookup* routine.

string: In this case the global variables *id_first* and *id_loc* will have been set to the beginning and ending-plus-one locations in the buffer. The string ends with the first reappearance of its initial delimiter; thus, for example,

$$\text{\textasciiacute This isn\textasciiacute\textasciiacute t a single string\textasciiacute}$$

will be treated as two consecutive strings, the first being ´This isn´.

Furthermore, some of the control codes cause *get_next* to take additional actions:

xref_roman, *xref_wildcard*, *xref_typewriter*, *TeX_string*: The values of *id_first* and *id_loc* will be set so that the string in question appears in *buffer*[*id_first* .. (*id_loc* − 1)].

module_name: In this case the global variable *cur_module* will point to the *byte_start* entry for the module name that has just been scanned.

If *get_next* sees '@!' or '@?', it sets *xref_switch* to *def_flag* or zero and goes on to the next token.

A global variable called *scanning_hex* is set *true* during the time that the letters A through F should be treated as if they were digits.

define *exponent* = ´200   { E or e following a digit }
define *string* = ´201   { Pascal string or WEB precomputed string }
define *identifier* = ´202   { Pascal identifier or reserved word }

⟨ Globals in the outer block 9 ⟩ +≡
cur_module: *name_pointer*;   { name of module just scanned }
scanning_hex: *boolean*;   { are we scanning a hexadecimal constant? }

94.   ⟨ Set initial values 10 ⟩ +≡
  scanning_hex ← *false*;

95.   As one might expect, *get_next* consists mostly of a big switch that branches to the various special cases that can arise.

define *up_to*(#) ≡ # − 24, # − 23, # − 22, # − 21, # − 20, # − 19, # − 18, # − 17, # − 16, # − 15, # − 14, # − 13, # − 12, # − 11, # − 10, # − 9, # − 8, # − 7, # − 6, # − 5, # − 4, # − 3, # − 2, # − 1, #

function *get_next*: *eight_bits*;   { produces the next input token }
  label *restart*, *done*, *found*;
  var *c*: *eight_bits*;   { the current character }
    d: *eight_bits*;   { the next character }
    j, *k*: 0 .. *longest_name*;   { indices into *mod_text* }
  begin *restart*: **if** *loc* > *limit* **then**
    begin *get_line*;
    if *input_has_ended* **then**
      begin *c* ← *new_module*; **goto** *found*;
      end;
    end;
  c ← *buffer*[*loc*]; *incr*(*loc*);

   if *scanning_hex* **then**
     ⟨Go to *found* if *c* is a hexadecimal digit, otherwise set *scanning_hex* ← *false* 96⟩;
   case *c* **of**
   "A", *up_to*("Z"), "a", *up_to*("z"): ⟨Get an identifier 98⟩;
   "`", """": ⟨Get a string 99⟩;
   "@": ⟨Get control code and possible module name 100⟩;
   ⟨Compress two-symbol combinations like ':=' 97⟩
   "␣", *tab_mark*: **goto** *restart*;   {ignore spaces and tabs}
   othercases *do_nothing*
   endcases;
found: **debug if** *trouble_shooting* **then** *debug_help*; **gubed**
   get_next ← *c*;
   end;

96.   ⟨Go to *found* if *c* is a hexadecimal digit, otherwise set *scanning_hex* ← *false* 96⟩ ≡
   if $((c \geq$ "0"$) \wedge (c \leq$ "9"$)) \vee ((c \geq$ "A"$) \wedge (c \leq$ "F"$))$ **then goto** *found*
   else *scanning_hex* ← *false*

This code is used in section 95.

97.   Note that the following code substitutes @{ and @} for the respective combinations '(*' and '*)'. Explicit braces should be used for TeX comments in Pascal text.
   define *compress*(**#**) ≡
          begin if *loc* ≤ *limit* **then**
            begin *c* ← **#**; *incr*(*loc*);
            end;
          end
⟨Compress two-symbol combinations like ':=' 97⟩ ≡
   ".": **if** *buffer*[*loc*] = "." **then** *compress*(*double_dot*)
     else if *buffer*[*loc*] = ")" **then** *compress*("]");
   ":": **if** *buffer*[*loc*] = "=" **then** *compress*(*left_arrow*);
   "=": **if** *buffer*[*loc*] = "=" **then** *compress*(*equivalence_sign*);
   ">": **if** *buffer*[*loc*] = "=" **then** *compress*(*greater_or_equal*);
   "<": **if** *buffer*[*loc*] = "=" **then** *compress*(*less_or_equal*)
     else if *buffer*[*loc*] = ">" **then** *compress*(*not_equal*);
   "(": **if** *buffer*[*loc*] = "*" **then** *compress*(*begin_comment*)
     else if *buffer*[*loc*] = "." **then** *compress*("[");
   "*": **if** *buffer*[*loc*] = ")" **then** *compress*(*end_comment*);

This code is used in section 95.

98.   ⟨Get an identifier 98⟩ ≡
   begin if $((c =$ "E"$) \vee (c =$ "e"$)) \wedge (loc > 1)$ **then**
     if $(buffer[loc - 2] \leq$ "9"$) \wedge (buffer[loc - 2] \geq$ "0"$)$ **then** *c* ← *exponent*;
   if *c* ≠ *exponent* **then**
     begin *decr*(*loc*); *id_first* ← *loc*;
     repeat *incr*(*loc*); *d* ← *buffer*[*loc*];
     until $((d <$ "0"$) \vee ((d >$ "9"$) \wedge (d <$ "A"$)) \vee ((d >$ "Z"$) \wedge (d <$ "a"$)) \vee (d >$ "z"$)) \wedge (d \neq$ "_"$)$;
     c ← *identifier*; *id_loc* ← *loc*;
     end;
   end

This code is used in section 95.

99.   A string that starts and ends with single or double quote marks is scanned by the following piece of the program.

⟨ Get a string 99 ⟩ ≡
  begin *id_first* ← *loc* − 1;
  repeat *d* ← *buffer* [*loc*]; *incr* (*loc*);
    if *loc* > *limit* **then**
      begin *err_print* (´!␣String␣constant␣didn´´t␣end´); *loc* ← *limit*; *d* ← *c*;
      end;
  until *d* = *c*;
  id_loc ← *loc*; *c* ← *string*;
  end

This code is used in section 95.

100.   After an **©** sign has been scanned, the next character tells us whether there is more work to do.

⟨ Get control code and possible module name 100 ⟩ ≡
  begin *c* ← *control_code* (*buffer* [*loc*]); *incr* (*loc*);
  if *c* = *underline* **then**
    begin *xref_switch* ← *def_flag*; **goto** *restart*;
    end
  else if *c* = *no_underline* **then**
      begin *xref_switch* ← 0; **goto** *restart*;
      end
    else if (*c* ≤ *TeX_string*) ∧ (*c* ≥ *xref_roman*) **then** ⟨ Scan to the next **©>** 106 ⟩
      else if *c* = *hex* **then** *scanning_hex* ← *true*
        else if *c* = *module_name* **then**
          ⟨ Scan the module name and make *cur_module* point to it 101 ⟩
          else if *c* = *verbatim* **then** ⟨ Scan a verbatim string 107 ⟩;
  end

This code is used in section 95.

101.   The occurrence of a module name sets *xref_switch* to zero, because the module name might (for example) follow **var**.

⟨ Scan the module name and make *cur_module* point to it 101 ⟩ ≡
  begin ⟨ Put module name into *mod_text* [1 .. *k*] 103 ⟩;
  if *k* > 3 **then**
    begin if (*mod_text* [*k*] = ".") ∧ (*mod_text* [*k* − 1] = ".") ∧ (*mod_text* [*k* − 2] = ".") **then**
      cur_module ← *prefix_lookup* (*k* − 3)
    else *cur_module* ← *mod_lookup* (*k*);
    end
  else *cur_module* ← *mod_lookup* (*k*);
  xref_switch ← 0;
  end

This code is used in section 100.

102.   Module names are placed into the *mod_text* array with consecutive spaces, tabs, and carriage-returns replaced by single spaces. There will be no spaces at the beginning or the end. (We set $mod\_text[0] \leftarrow$ "␣" to facilitate this, since the mod_lookup routine uses $mod\_text[1]$ as the first character of the name.)

⟨Set initial values 10⟩ +≡
$mod\_text[0] \leftarrow$ "␣";

103. ⟨Put module name into $mod\_text[1 .. k]$ 103⟩ ≡
$k \leftarrow 0$;
loop begin if $loc > limit$ **then**
    begin gct_linc;
    if $input\_has\_ended$ **then**
      begin $err\_print($´!␣Input␣ended␣in␣section␣name´$)$; $loc \leftarrow 1$; **goto** $done$;
      end;
    end;
$d \leftarrow buffer[loc]$; ⟨If end of name, **goto** $done$ 104⟩;
$incr(loc)$;
if $k < longest\_name - 1$ **then** $incr(k)$;
if $(d =$ "␣"$) \vee (d = tab\_mark)$ **then**
    begin $d \leftarrow$ "␣";
    if $mod\_text[k-1] =$ "␣" **then** $decr(k)$;
    end;
$mod\_text[k] \leftarrow d$;
end;
$done$: ⟨Check for overlong name 105⟩;
if $(mod\_text[k] =$ "␣"$) \wedge (k > 0)$ **then** $decr(k)$

This code is used in section 101.

104. ⟨If end of name, **goto** $done$ 104⟩ ≡
if $d =$ "@" **then**
  begin $d \leftarrow buffer[loc + 1]$;
  if $d =$ ">" **then**
    begin $loc \leftarrow loc + 2$; **goto** $done$;
    end;
  if $(d =$ "␣"$) \vee (d = tab\_mark) \vee (d =$ "*"$)$ **then**
    begin $err\_print($´!␣Section␣name␣didn´´t␣end´$)$; **goto** $done$;
    end;
  $incr(k)$; $mod\_text[k] \leftarrow$ "@"; $incr(loc)$; { now $d = buffer[loc]$ again }
  end

This code is used in section 103.

105. ⟨Check for overlong name 105⟩ ≡
if $k \geq longest\_name - 2$ **then**
  begin $print\_nl($´!␣Section␣name␣too␣long:␣´$)$;
  for $j \leftarrow 1$ **to** 25 **do** $print(xchr[mod\_text[j]])$;
  $print($´...´$)$; $mark\_harmless$;
  end

This code is used in section 103.

106. ⟨Scan to the next @> 106⟩ ≡
begin $id\_first \leftarrow loc$; $buffer[limit + 1] \leftarrow$ "@";

```
while buffer[loc] ≠ "@" do incr(loc);
id_loc ← loc;
if loc > limit then
   begin err_print(´!␣Control␣text␣didn´´t␣end´); loc ← limit;
   end
else begin loc ← loc + 2;
   if buffer[loc − 1] ≠ ">" then
      err_print(´!␣Control␣codes␣are␣forbidden␣in␣control␣text´);
   end;
end
```

This code is used in section 100.

107. A verbatim Pascal string will be treated like ordinary strings, but with no surrounding delimiters. At the present point in the program we have $buffer[loc − 1] = verbatim$; we must set id_first to the beginning of the string itself, and id_loc to its ending-plus-one location in the buffer. We also set loc to the position just after the ending delimiter.

⟨ Scan a verbatim string 107 ⟩ ≡
```
   begin id_first ← loc; incr(loc); buffer[limit + 1] ← "@"; buffer[limit + 2] ← ">";
   while (buffer[loc] ≠ "@") ∨ (buffer[loc + 1] ≠ ">") do incr(loc);
   if loc ≥ limit then err_print(´!␣Verbatim␣string␣didn´´t␣end´);
   id_loc ← loc; loc ← loc + 2;
   end
```

This code is used in section 100.

108. Phase one processing. We now have accumulated enough subroutines to make it possible to carry out WEAVE's first pass over the source file. If everything works right, both phase one and phase two of WEAVE will assign the same numbers to modules, and these numbers will agree with what TANGLE does.

The global variable $next\_control$ often contains the most recent output of get_next; in interesting cases, this will be the control code that ended a module or part of a module.

⟨ Globals in the outer block 9 ⟩ +≡
$next\_control$: $eight\_bits$;   { control code waiting to be acting upon }

109. The overall processing strategy in phase one has the following straightforward outline.

⟨ Phase I: Read all the user's text and store the cross references 109 ⟩ ≡
```
   phase_one ← true; phase_three ← false; reset_input; module_count ← 0; skip_limbo;
   change_exists ← false;
   while ¬input_has_ended do ⟨ Store cross reference data for the current module 110 ⟩;
   changed_module[module_count] ← change_exists;   { the index changes if anything does }
   phase_one ← false;   { prepare for second phase }
   ⟨ Print error messages about unused or undefined module names 120 ⟩;
```

This code is used in section 261.

110. ⟨ Store cross reference data for the current module 110 ⟩ ≡
```
   begin incr(module_count);
   if module_count = max_modules then overflow(´section␣number´);
   changed_module[module_count] ← false;   { it will become true if any line changes }
```

```
  if buffer[loc − 1] = "*" then
     begin print(´*´, module_count : 1); update_terminal;   { print a progress report }
     end;
⟨ Store cross references in the TEX part of a module 113 ⟩;
⟨ Store cross references in the definition part of a module 115 ⟩;
⟨ Store cross references in the Pascal part of a module 117 ⟩;
  if changed_module[module_count] then change_exists ← true;
  end
```

This code is used in section 109.

111. The *Pascal_xref* subroutine stores references to identifiers in Pascal text material beginning with the current value of *next_control* and continuing until *next_control* is '{' or '|', or until the next "milestone" is passed (i.e., *next_control* $\geq$ *format*). If *next_control* $\geq$ *format* when *Pascal_xref* is called, nothing will happen; but if *next_control* = "|" upon entry, the procedure assumes that this is the '|' preceding Pascal text that is to be processed.

The program uses the fact that our internal code numbers satisfy the following relations:

$xref\_roman = identifier + roman;$

$xref\_wildcard = identifier + wildcard;$

$xref\_typewriter = identifier + typewriter;$

$normal = 0.$

An implied '@!' is inserted after **function**, **procedure**, **program**, and **var**.

```
procedure Pascal_xref;   { makes cross references for Pascal identifiers }
  label exit;
  var p: name_pointer;   { a referenced name }
  begin while next_control < format do
     begin if (next_control ≥ identifier) ∧ (next_control ≤ xref_typewriter) then
        begin p ← id_lookup(next_control − identifier); new_xref(p);
        if (ilk[p] = proc_like) ∨ (ilk[p] = var_like) then xref_switch ← def_flag;   { implied '@!' }
        end;
     next_control ← get_next;
     if (next_control = "|") ∨ (next_control = "{") then return;
     end;
exit: end;
```

112. The *outer_xref* subroutine is like *Pascal_xref* but it begins with *next_control* $\neq$ "|" and ends with *next_control* $\geq$ *format*. Thus, it handles Pascal text with embedded comments.

```
procedure outer_xref;   { extension of Pascal_xref }
  var bal: eight_bits;   { brace level in comment }
  begin while next_control < format do
     if next_control ≠ "{" then Pascal_xref
     else begin bal ← skip_comment(1); next_control ← "|";
        while bal > 0 do
           begin Pascal_xref;
           if next_control = "|" then bal ← skip_comment(bal)
           else bal ← 0;   { an error will be reported in phase two }
           end;
```

```
          end;
      end;
```

113.   In the TeX part of a module, cross reference entries are made only for the identifiers
in Pascal texts enclosed in | ... |, or for control texts enclosed in @^ ... @> or @. ... @> or
@: ... @>.

⟨ Store cross references in the TeX part of a module 113 ⟩ ≡
   repeat *next_control* ← *skip_TeX*;
     case *next_control* **of**
     underline: *xref_switch* ← *def_flag*;
     no_underline: *xref_switch* ← 0;
     "|": *Pascal_xref*;
     xref_roman, *xref_wildcard*, *xref_typewriter*, *module_name*: **begin** *loc* ← *loc* − 2;
        next_control ← *get_next*;   { scan to @> }
        if *next_control* ≠ *module_name* **then** *new_xref*(*id_lookup*(*next_control* − *identifier*));
        end;
     othercases *do_nothing*
     endcases;
   until *next_control* ≥ *format*

This code is used in section 110.

114.   During the definition and Pascal parts of a module, cross references are made for all
identifiers except reserved words; however, the identifiers in a format definition are referenced
even if they are reserved. The TeX code in comments is, of course, ignored, except for Pascal
portions enclosed in | ... |; the text of a module name is skipped entirely, even if it contains
| ... | constructions.

   The variables *lhs* and *rhs* point to the respective identifiers involved in a format definition.

⟨ Globals in the outer block 9 ⟩ +≡
lhs, *rhs*: *name_pointer*;   { indices into *byte_start* for format identifiers }

115.   When we get to the following code we have *next_control* ≥ *format*.

⟨ Store cross references in the definition part of a module 115 ⟩ ≡
   while *next_control* ≤ *definition* **do**   { *format* or *definition* }
     begin *xref_switch* ← *def_flag*;   { implied @! }
     if *next_control* = *definition* **then** *next_control* ← *get_next*
     else ⟨ Process a format definition 116 ⟩;
     outer_xref;
     end

This code is used in section 110.

116.   Error messages for improper format definitions will be issued in phase two. Our job
in phase one is to define the *ilk* of a properly formatted identifier, and to fool the *new_xref*
routine into thinking that the identifier on the right-hand side of the format definition is
not a reserved word.

⟨ Process a format definition 116 ⟩ ≡
   begin *next_control* ← *get_next*;
   if *next_control* = *identifier* **then**
```
```

> begin *lhs* ← *id_lookup*(*normal*); *ilk*[*lhs*] ← *normal*; *new_xref*(*lhs*); *next_control* ← *get_next*;
> if *next_control* = *equivalence_sign* then
>   begin *next_control* ← *get_next*;
>   if *next_control* = *identifier* then
>   begin *rhs* ← *id_lookup*(*normal*); *ilk*[*lhs*] ← *ilk*[*rhs*]; *ilk*[*rhs*] ← *normal*; *new_xref*(*rhs*);
>   *ilk*[*rhs*] ← *ilk*[*lhs*]; *next_control* ← *get_next*;
>   end;
>   end;
> end;
> end

This code is used in section 115.

---

117. Finally, when the TEX and definition parts have been treated, we have *next_control* ≥ *begin_Pascal*.

⟨ Store cross references in the Pascal part of a module 117 ⟩ ≡
> if *next_control* ≤ *module_name* then   { *begin_Pascal* or *module_name* }
>   begin if *next_control* = *begin_Pascal* then *mod_xref_switch* ← 0
>   else *mod_xref_switch* ← *def_flag*;
>   repeat if *next_control* = *module_name* then *new_mod_xref*(*cur_module*);
>   *next_control* ← *get_next*; *outer_xref*;
>   until *next_control* > *module_name*;
>   end

This code is used in section 110.

---

118. After phase one has looked at everything, we want to check that each module name was both defined and used. The variable *cur_xref* will point to cross references for the current module name of interest.

⟨ Globals in the outer block 9 ⟩ +≡
cur_xref: *xref_number*;   { temporary cross reference pointer }

---

119. The following recursive procedure walks through the tree of module names and prints out anomalies.

procedure *mod_check*(*p* : *name_pointer*);   { print anomalies in subtree *p* }
> begin if *p* > 0 then
>   begin *mod_check*(*llink*[*p*]);
>   *cur_xref* ← *xref*[*p*];
>   if *num*(*cur_xref*) < *def_flag* then
>   begin *print_nl*(´!␣Never␣defined:␣<´); *print_id*(*p*); *print*(´>´); *mark_harmless*;
>   end;
>   while *num*(*cur_xref*) ≥ *def_flag* do *cur_xref* ← *xlink*(*cur_xref*);
>   if *cur_xref* = 0 then
>   begin *print_nl*(´!␣Never␣used:␣<´); *print_id*(*p*); *print*(´>´); *mark_harmless*;
>   end;
>   *mod_check*(*rlink*[*p*]);
>   end;
> end;

---

120. ⟨ Print error messages about unused or undefined module names 120 ⟩ ≡ *mod_check*(*root*)
This code is used in section 109.

121.   Low-level output routines.   The TeX output is supposed to appear in lines at most *line_length* characters long, so we place it into an output buffer. During the output process, *out_line* will hold the current line number of the line about to be output.

⟨ Globals in the outer block 9 ⟩ +≡
out_buf: **array** [0 .. *line_length*] **of** *ASCII_code*;   { assembled characters }
out_ptr: 0 .. *line_length*;   { number of characters in *out_buf* }
out_line: *integer*;   { coordinates of next line to be output }

122.   The *flush_buffer* routine empties the buffer up to a given breakpoint, and moves any remaining characters to the beginning of the next line. If the *per_cent* parameter is *true*, a "%" is appended to the line that is being output; in this case the breakpoint b should be strictly less than *line_length*. If the *per_cent* parameter is *false*, trailing blanks are suppressed. The characters emptied from the buffer form a new line of output.

procedure *flush_buffer*(b : *eight_bits*; *per_cent* : *boolean*);
                { outputs *out_buf*[1 .. b], where $b \leq$ *out_ptr* }
   label *done*;
   var j, k: 0 .. *line_length*;
   begin $j \leftarrow b$;
   if ¬*per_cent* **then**   { remove trailing blanks }
      loop begin if $j = 0$ **then goto** *done*;
         if *out_buf*[j] ≠ "␣" **then goto** *done*;
         decr(j);
         end;
done: **for** $k \leftarrow 1$ **to** j **do** *write*(*tex_file*, *xchr*[*out_buf*[k]]);
   if *per_cent* **then** *write*(*tex_file*, *xchr*["%"]);
   write_ln(*tex_file*); *incr*(*out_line*);
   if $b <$ *out_ptr* **then**
      for $k \leftarrow b + 1$ **to** *out_ptr* **do** *out_buf*[$k - b$] $\leftarrow$ *out_buf*[k];
   out_ptr $\leftarrow$ *out_ptr* $- b$;
   end;

123.   When we are copying TeX source material, we retain line breaks that occur in the input, except that an empty line is not output when the TeX source line was nonempty. For example, a line of the TeX file that contains only an index cross-reference entry will not be copied. The *finish_line* routine is called just before *get_line* inputs a new line, and just after a line break token has been emitted during the output of translated Pascal text.

procedure *finish_line*;   { do this at the end of a line }
   label *exit*;
   var k: 0 .. *buf_size*;   { index into *buffer* }
   begin if *out_ptr* > 0 **then** *flush_buffer*(*out_ptr*, *false*)
   else begin for $k \leftarrow 0$ **to** *limit* **do**
      if (*buffer*[k] ≠ "␣") ∧ (*buffer*[k] ≠ *tab_mark*) **then return**;
      flush_buffer(0, *false*);
      end;
exit: **end**;

124.   In particular, the *finish_line* procedure is called near the very beginning of phase two. We initialize the output variables in a slightly tricky way so that the first line of the output file will be '\input webmac'.

⟨ Set initial values 10 ⟩ +≡
  $out\_ptr \leftarrow 1$; $out\_line \leftarrow 1$; $out\_buf[1] \leftarrow$ "c"; $write(tex\_file, \text{`}\backslash\text{input}_{\sqcup}\text{webma'})$;

125. When we wish to append the character c to the output buffer, we write '$out(c)$'; this will cause the buffer to be emptied if it was already full. Similarly, '$out2(c_1)(c_2)$' appends a pair of characters. A line break will occur at a space or after a single-nonletter TEX control sequence.

  define $oot(\#) \equiv$
      if $out\_ptr = line\_length$ **then** $break\_out$;
      $incr(out\_ptr)$; $out\_buf[out\_ptr] \leftarrow \#$;
  define $oot1(\#) \equiv oot(\#)$ **end**
  define $oot2(\#) \equiv oot(\#)$ $oot1$
  define $oot3(\#) \equiv oot(\#)$ $oot2$
  define $oot4(\#) \equiv oot(\#)$ $oot3$
  define $oot5(\#) \equiv oot(\#)$ $oot4$
  define $out \equiv$ **begin** $oot1$
  define $out2 \equiv$ **begin** $oot2$
  define $out3 \equiv$ **begin** $oot3$
  define $out4 \equiv$ **begin** $oot4$
  define $out5 \equiv$ **begin** $oot5$

126. The $break\_out$ routine is called just before the output buffer is about to overflow. To make this routine a little faster, we initialize position 0 of the output buffer to '$\backslash$'; this character isn't really output.

⟨ Set initial values 10 ⟩ +≡
  $out\_buf[0] \leftarrow$ "$\backslash$";

127. A long line is broken at a blank space or just before a backslash that isn't preceded by another backslash. In the latter case, a "%" is output at the break.

procedure $break\_out$; { finds a way to break the output line }
  label $exit$;
  var k: $0 .. line\_length$; { index into out_buf }
    c, d: $ASCII\_code$; { characters from the buffer }
  begin $k \leftarrow out\_ptr$;
  loop begin if $k = 0$ **then** ⟨ Print warning message, break the line, **return** 128 ⟩;
    $d \leftarrow out\_buf[k]$;
    if $d =$ "$\sqcup$" **then**
      begin $flush\_buffer(k, false)$; **return**;
      end;
    if $(d =$ "$\backslash$"$) \wedge (out\_buf[k-1] \neq$ "$\backslash$"$)$ **then**   { in this case $k > 1$ }
      begin $flush\_buffer(k-1, true)$; **return**;
      end;
    $decr(k)$;
    end;
$exit$: **end**;

128. We get to this module only in unusual cases that the entire output line consists of a string of backslashes followed by a string of nonblank non-backslashes. In such cases it is almost always safe to break the line by putting a "%" just before the last character.

⟨ Print warning message, break the line, **return** 128 ⟩ ≡
 begin *print_nl*(´ !␣Line␣had␣to␣be␣broken␣(output␣l.´, *out_line* : 1); *print_ln*(´):´);
 for *k* ← 1 **to** *out_ptr* − 1 **do** *print*(*xchr*[*out_buf*[*k*]]);
 new_line; *mark_harmless*; *flush_buffer*(*out_ptr* − 1, *true*); **return**;
 end

This code is used in section 127.

129. Here is a procedure that outputs a module number in decimal notation.

⟨ Globals in the outer block 9 ⟩ +≡
dig: **array** [0 .. 4] **of** 0 .. 9; { digits to output }

130. The number to be converted by *out_mod* is known to be less than *def_flag*, so it cannot have more than five decimal digits. If the module is changed, we output '*' just after the number.

procedure *out_mod*(*m* : *integer*); { output a module number }
 var *k*: 0 .. 5; { index into *dig* }
  a: *integer*; { accumulator }
 begin *k* ← 0; *a* ← *m*;
 repeat *dig*[*k*] ← *a* **mod** 10; *a* ← *a* **div** 10; *incr*(*k*);
 until *a* = 0;
 repeat *decr*(*k*); *out*(*dig*[*k*] + "0");
 until *k* = 0;
 if *changed_module*[*m*] **then** *out2*("\")("*");
 end;

131. The *out_name* subroutine is used to output an identifier or index entry, enclosing it in braces.

procedure *out_name*(*p* : *name_pointer*); { outputs a name }
 var *k*: 0 .. *max_bytes*; { index into *byte_mem* }
  w: 0 .. *ww* − 1; { row of *byte_mem* }
 begin *out*("{"); *w* ← *p* **mod** *ww*;
 for *k* ← *byte_start*[*p*] **to** *byte_start*[*p* + *ww*] − 1 **do**
  begin if *byte_mem*[*w*, *k*] = "_" **then** *out*("\");
  out(*byte_mem*[*w*, *k*]);
  end;
 out("}");
 end;

132. Routines that copy TₑX material. During phase two, we use the subroutines *copy_limbo*, *copy_TeX*, and *copy_comment* in place of the analogous *skip_limbo*, *skip_TeX*, and *skip_comment* that were used in phase one.

The *copy_limbo* routine, for example, takes TₑX material that is not part of any module and transcribes it almost verbatim to the output file. No '@' signs should occur in such material except in '@@' pairs; such pairs are replaced by singletons.

procedure *copy_limbo*; { copy TₑX code until the next module begins }
 label *exit*;
 var *c*: *ASCII_code*; { character following @ sign }

```
      begin loop
        if loc > limit then
          begin finish_line; get_line;
          if input_has_ended then return;
          end
        else begin buffer[limit + 1] ← "@"; ⟨Copy up to control code, return if finished 133⟩;
          end;
exit: end;
```

133. ⟨Copy up to control code, **return** if finished 133⟩ ≡

```
  while buffer[loc] ≠ "@" do
    begin out(buffer[loc]); incr(loc);
    end;
  if loc ≤ limit then
    begin loc ← loc + 2; c ← buffer[loc − 1];
    if (c = "⊔") ∨ (c = tab_mark) ∨ (c = "*") then return;
    if (c ≠ "z") ∧ (c ≠ "Z") then
      begin out("@");
      if c ≠ "@" then err_print(´!⊔Double⊔@⊔required⊔outside⊔of⊔sections´);
      end;
    end
```

This code is used in section 132.

134. The *copy_TeX* routine processes the TeX code at the beginning of a module; for example, the words you are now reading were copied in this way. It returns the next control code or '|' found in the input.

```
function copy_TeX: eight_bits;   {copy pure TeX material}
  label done;
  var c: eight_bits;   {control code found}
  begin loop
    begin if loc > limit then
      begin finish_line; get_line;
      if input_has_ended then
        begin c ← new_module; goto done;
        end;
      end,
    buffer[limit + 1] ← "@"; ⟨Copy up to '|' or control code, goto done if finished 135⟩;
    end;
done: copy_TeX ← c;
  end;
```

135. We don't copy spaces or tab marks into the beginning of a line. This makes the test for empty lines in *finish_line* work.

⟨Copy up to '|' or control code, **goto** *done* if finished 135⟩ ≡

```
  repeat c ← buffer[loc]; incr(loc);
    if c = "|" then goto done;
    if c ≠ "@" then
      begin out(c);
      if (out_ptr = 1) ∧ ((c = "⊔") ∨ (c = tab_mark)) then decr(out_ptr);
```

```
        end;
    until  c = "@";
    if loc ≤ limit then
        begin c ← control_code(buffer[loc]); incr(loc); goto done;
        end
```

This code is used in section 134.

136.   The *copy_comment* uses and returns a brace-balance value, following the conventions of *skip_comment* above. Instead of copying the TeX material into the output buffer, this procedure copies it into the token memory. The abbreviation *app_tok*(*t*) is used to append token *t* to the current token list, and it also makes sure that it is possible to append at least one further token without overflow.

```
    define app_tok(#) ≡
            begin if tok_ptr + 2 > max_toks then overflow(´token´);
            tok_mem[tok_ptr] ← #; incr(tok_ptr);
            end
function copy_comment(bal : eight_bits): eight_bits;   { copies TeX code in comments }
    label done;
    var c: ASCII_code;   { current character being copied }
    begin loop
        begin if loc > limit then
            begin get_line;
            if input_has_ended then
                begin err_print(´!␣Input␣ended␣in␣mid-comment´); loc ← 1;
                ⟨ Clear bal and goto done 138 ⟩;
                end;
            end;
        c ← buffer[loc]; incr(loc);
        if c = "|" then goto done;
        app_tok(c); ⟨ Copy special things when c = "@", "\", "{", "}"; goto done at end 137 ⟩;
        end;
done: copy_comment ← bal;
    end;
```

137.   ⟨ Copy special things when c = "@", "\", "{", "}"; goto done at end 137 ⟩ ≡
```
    if c = "@" then
        begin incr(loc);
        if buffer[loc − 1] ≠ "@" then
            begin err_print(´!␣Illegal␣use␣of␣@␣in␣comment´); loc ← loc − 2; decr(tok_ptr);
            ⟨ Clear bal and goto done 138 ⟩;
            end;
        end
    else if (c = "\") ∧ (buffer[loc] ≠ "@") then
            begin app_tok(buffer[loc]); incr(loc);
            end
    else if c = "{" then incr(bal)
        else if c = "}" then
                begin decr(bal);
                if bal = 0 then goto done;
```

end

This code is used in section 136.

138. When the comment has terminated abruptly due to an error, we output enough right braces to keep TₑX happy.

⟨ Clear *bal* and **goto** *done* 138 ⟩ ≡
  app_tok("␣"); { this is done in case the previous character was '\' }
  repeat *app_tok*("}"); *decr*(*bal*);
  until *bal* = 0;
  goto *done*;

This code is used in sections 136 and 137.

139. Parsing. The most intricate part of WEAVE is its mechanism for converting Pascal-like code into TₑX code, and we might as well plunge into this aspect of the program now. A "bottom up" approach is used to parse the Pascal-like material, since WEAVE must deal with fragmentary constructions whose overall "part of speech" is not known.

At the lowest level, the input is represented as a sequence of entities that we shall call *scraps*, where each scrap of information consists of two parts, its *category* and its *translation*. The category is essentially a syntactic class, and the translation is a token list that represents TₑX code. Rules of syntax and semantics tell us how to combine adjacent scraps into larger ones, and if we are lucky an entire Pascal text that starts out as hundreds of small scraps will join together into one gigantic scrap whose translation is the desired TₑX code. If we are unlucky, we will be left with several scraps that don't combine; their translations will simply be output, one by one.

The combination rules are given as context-sensitive productions that are applied from left to right. Suppose that we are currently working on the sequence of scraps $s_1 s_2 \ldots s_n$. We try first to find the longest production that applies to an initial substring $s_1 s_2 \ldots$; but if no such productions exist, we find to find the longest production applicable to the next substring $s_2 s_3 \ldots$; and if that fails, we try to match $s_3 s_4 \ldots$, etc.

A production applies if the category codes have a given pattern. For example, one of the productions is

$$open \; math \; semi \; \rightarrow \; open \; math$$

and it means that three consecutive scraps whose respective categories are *open*, *math*, and *semi* are converted to two scraps whose categories are *open* and *math*. This production also has an associated rule that tells how to combine the translation parts:

$$O_2 = O_1$$
$$M_2 = M_1 \, S \, \backslash, \, opt \, 5$$

This means that the *open* scrap has not changed, while the new *math* scrap has a translation M_2 composed of the translation M_1 of the original *math* scrap followed by the translation S of the *semi* scrap followed by '\,' followed by '*opt*' followed by '5'. (In the TₑX file, this will specify an additional thin space after the semicolon, followed by an optional line break with penalty 50.) Translation rules use subscripts to distinguish between translations of scraps whose categories have the same initial letter; these subscripts are assigned from left to right.

WEAVE also has the production rule

$$semi \;\rightarrow\; terminator$$

(meaning that a semicolon can terminate a Pascal statement). Since productions are applied from left to right, this rule will be activated only if the *semi* is not preceded by scraps that match other productions; in particular, a *semi* that is preceded by '*open math*' will have disappeared because of the production above, and such semicolons do not act as statement terminators. This incidentally is how WEAVE is able to treat semicolons in two distinctly different ways, the first of which is intended for semicolons in the parameter list of a procedure declaration.

The translation rule corresponding to *semi* $\rightarrow$ *terminator* is

$$T = S$$

but we shall not mention translation rules in the common case that the translation of the new scrap on the right-hand side is simply the concatenation of the disappearing scraps on the left-hand side.

140. Here is a list of the category codes that scraps can have.

> **define** *simp* = 1
>> { the translation can be used both in horizontal mode and in math mode of TEX }
>
> **define** *math* = 2   { the translation should be used only in TEX math mode }
> **define** *intro* = 3   { a statement is expected to follow this, after a space and an optional break }
> **define** *open* = 4   { denotes an incomplete parenthesized quantity to be used in math mode }
> **define** *beginning* = 5
>> { denotes an incomplete compound statement to be used in horizontal mode }
>
> **define** *close* = 6   { ends a parenthesis or compound statement }
> **define** *alpha* = 7   { denotes the beginning of a clause }
> **define** *omega* = 8   { denotes the ending of a clause and possible comment following }
> **define** *semi* = 9   { denotes a semicolon and possible comment following it }
> **define** *terminator* = 10   { something that ends a statement or declaration }
> **define** *stmt* = 11   { denotes a statement or declaration including its terminator }
> **define** *cond* = 12   { precedes an **if** clause that might have a matching **else** }
> **define** *clause* = 13   { precedes a statement after which indentation ends }
> **define** *colon* = 14   { denotes a colon }
> **define** *exp* = 15   { stands for the E in a floating point constant }
> **define** *proc* = 16   { denotes a procedure or program or function heading }
> **define** *case_head* = 17   { denotes a case statement or record heading }
> **define** *record_head* = 18   { denotes a record heading without indentation }
> **define** *var_head* = 19   { denotes a variable declaration heading }
> **define** *elsie* = 20   { **else** }
> **define** *casey* = 21   { **case** }
> **define** *mod_scrap* = 22   { denotes a module name }
>
> **debug procedure** *print_cat*(*c* : *eight_bits*);   { symbolic printout of a category }
> **begin case** *c* **of**
> *simp*: *print*(´simp´);
> *math*: *print*(´math´);

```
intro: print('intro');
open: print('open');
beginning: print('beginning');
close: print('close');
alpha: print('alpha');
omega: print('omega');
semi: print('semi');
terminator: print('terminator');
stmt: print('stmt');
cond: print('cond');
clause: print('clause');
colon: print('colon');
exp: print('exp');
proc: print('proc');
case_head: print('casehead');
record_head: print('recordhead');
var_head: print('varhead');
elsie: print('elsie');
casey: print('casey');
mod_scrap: print('module');
othercases print('UNKNOWN')
endcases;
end;
gubed
```

141. The token lists for translated TEX output contain some special control symbols as well as ordinary characters. These control symbols are interpreted by WEAVE before they are written to the output file.

break_space denotes an optional line break or an en space;

force denotes a line break;

big_force denotes a line break with additional vertical space;

opt denotes an optional line break (with the continuation line indented two ems with respect to the normal starting position)—this code is followed by an integer n, and the break will occur with penalty $10n$;

backup denotes a backspace of one em;

cancel obliterates any *break_space* or *force* or *big_force* tokens that immediately precede or follow it and also cancels any *backup* tokens that follow it;

indent causes future lines to be indented one more em;

outdent causes future lines to be indented one less em.

All of these tokens are removed from the TEX output that comes from Pascal text between | . . . | signs; *break_space* and *force* and *big_force* become single spaces in this mode. The translation of other Pascal texts results in TEX control sequences \1, \2, \3, \4, \5, \6, \7 corresponding respectively to *indent*, *outdent*, *opt*, *backup*, *break_space*, *force*, and *big_force*. However, a sequence of consecutive '␣', *break_space*, *force*, and/or *big_force* tokens is first replaced by a single token (the maximum of the given ones).

The tokens *math_rel*, *math_bin*, *math_op* will be translated into \mathrel{, \mathbin{, and \mathop{, respectively. Other control sequences in the TEX output will be '\\{...}' surrounding identifiers, '\&{...}' surrounding reserved words, '\.{...}' surrounding strings, '\C{...}*force*' surrounding comments, and '\X*n*:...\X' surrounding module names, where *n* is the module number.

> **define** *math_bin* = '203
> **define** *math_rel* = '204
> **define** *math_op* = '205
> **define** *big_cancel* = '206   { like *cancel*, also overrides spaces }
> **define** *cancel* = '207   { overrides *backup*, *break_space*, *force*, *big_force* }
> **define** *indent* = *cancel* + 1   { one more tab (\1) }
> **define** *outdent* = *cancel* + 2   { one less tab (\2) }
> **define** *opt* = *cancel* + 3   { optional break in mid-statement (\3) }
> **define** *backup* = *cancel* + 4   { stick out one unit to the left (\4) }
> **define** *break_space* = *cancel* + 5   { optional break between statements (\5) }
> **define** *force* = *cancel* + 6   { forced break between statements (\6) }
> **define** *big_force* = *cancel* + 7   { forced break with additional space (\7) }
> **define** *end_translation* = *big_force* + 1   { special sentinel token at end of list }

142.   The raw input is converted into scraps according to the following table, which gives category codes followed by the translations. Sometimes a single item of input produces more than one scrap. (The symbol '******' stands for '\&{identifier}', i.e., the identifier itself treated as a reserved word. In a few cases the category is given as '*comment*'; this is not an actual category code, it means that the translation will be treated as a comment, as explained below.)

<>	*math*: \I
<=	*math*: \L
>=	*math*: \G
:=	*math*: \K
==	*math*: \S
(*	*math*: \B
*)	*math*: \T
(.	*open*: [
.)	*close*:]
" string "	*simp*: \.{" modified string "}
´ string ´	*simp*: \.{\´ modified string \´}
@= string @>	*simp*: \={ modified string }
#	*math*: \#
$	*math*: \$
_	*math*: _
%	*math*: \%
^	*math*: \^
(	*open*: (
)	*close*:)
[	*open*: [
]	*close*:]
*	*math*: \ast

,	*math*: , *opt* 9
..	*math*: \to
.	*simp*: .
:	*colon*: :
;	*semi*: ;
identifier	*simp*: \\{ identifier }
E in constant	*exp*: \E{
digit *d*	*simp*: *d*
other character *c*	*math*: *c*
and	*math*: \W
array	*alpha*: **
begin	*beginning*: *force* ** *cancel*　　*intro*:
case	*casey*:　　*alpha*: *force* **
const	*intro*: *force backup* **
div	*math*: *math_bin* ** }
do	*omega*: **
downto	*math*: *math_rel* ** }
else	*terminator*:　　*elsie*: *force backup* **
end	*terminator*:　　*close*: *force* **
file	*alpha*: **
for	*alpha*: *force* **
function	*proc*: *force backup* ** *cancel*　　*intro*: *indent* \␣
goto	*intro*: **
if	*cond*:　　*alpha*: *force* **
in	*math*: \in
label	*intro*: *force backup* **
mod	*math*: *math_bin* ** }
nil	*simp*: **
not	*math*: \R
of	*omega*: **
or	*math*: \V
packed	*intro*: **
procedure	*proc*: *force backup* ** *cancel*　　*intro*: *indent* \␣
program	*proc*: *force backup* ** *cancel*　　*intro*: *indent* \␣
record	*record_head*. **　　*intro*:
repeat	*beginning*: *force indent* ** *cancel*　　*intro*:
set	*alpha*: **
then	*omega*: **
to	*math*: *math_rel* ** }
type	*intro*: *force backup* **
until	*terminator*:　　*close*: *force backup* **　　*clause*:
var	*var_head*: *force backup* ** *cancel*　　*intro*:
while	*alpha*: *force* **
with	*alpha*: *force* **
xclause	*alpha*: *force* \~　　*omega*: **
@' const	*simp*: \O{const}

`@"` const	*simp*: `\H{const}`
`@$`	*simp*: `\)`
`@\`	*simp*: `\]`
`@,`	*math*: `\,`
`@t` stuff `@>`	*simp*: `\hbox{` stuff `}`
`@<` module `@>`	*mod_scrap*: `\Xn`: module `\X`
`@#`	*comment*: *big_force*
`@/`	*comment*: *force*
`@|`	*simp*: *opt* 0
`@+`	*comment*: *big_cancel* `\`␣ *big_cancel*
`@;`	*semi*:
`@&`	*math*: `\J`
`@{`	*math*: `\B`
`@}`	*math*: `\T`

When a string is output, certain characters are preceded by '`\`' signs so that they will print properly.

A comment in the input will be combined with the preceding *omega* or *semi* scrap, or with the following *terminator* scrap, if possible; otherwise it will be inserted as a separate *terminator* scrap. An additional "comment" is effectively appended at the end of the Pascal text, just before translation begins; this consists of a *cancel* token in the case of Pascal text in | ... |, otherwise it consists of a *force* token.

From this table it is evident that WEAVE will parse a lot of non-Pascal programs. For example, the reserved words '`for`' and '`array`' are treated in an identical way by WEAVE from a syntactic standpoint, and semantically they are equivalent except that a forced line break occurs just before '**for**'; Pascal programmers may well be surprised at this similarity. The idea is to keep WEAVE's rules as simple as possible, consistent with doing a reasonable job on syntactically correct Pascal programs. The production rules below have been formulated in the same spirit of "almost anything goes."

143.   Here is a table of all the productions. The reader can best get a feel for how they work by trying them out by hand on small examples; no amount of explanation will be as effective as watching the rules in action. Parsing can also be watched by debugging with '`@2`'.

Production categories [[translations]]	Remarks
1 alpha math colon → *alpha math*	e.g., **case** v : *boolean* **of**
2 alpha math omega → *clause* [[$C = A$ ␣ \$ M \$ ␣ *indent* O]]	e.g., **while** $x > 0$ **do**
3 alpha omega → *clause* [[$C = A$ ␣ *indent* O]]	e.g., **file of**
4 alpha simp → *alpha math*	convert to math mode
5 beginning close (*terminator* or *stmt*) → *stmt*	compound statement ends
6 beginning stmt → *beginning* [[$B_2 = B_1$ *break_space* S]]	compound statement grows
7 case_head casey clause → *case_head* [[$C_4 = C_1$ *outdent* $C_2 C_3$]]	variant records
8 case_head close terminator → *stmt* [[$S = C_1$ *cancel outdent* $C_2 T$]]	end of case statement
9 case_head stmt → *case_head* [[$C_2 = C_1$ *force* S]]	case statement grows

10 casey clause → *case_head* — beginning of case statement

11 clause stmt → *stmt*

$$[\![S_2 = C \ break\_space \ S_1 \ cancel \ outdent \ force]\!]$$ — end of controlled statement

12 cond clause stmt elsie → *clause*

$$[\![C_3 = C_1 \ C_2 \ break\_space \ S \ E \sqcup cancel]\!]$$ — complete conditional

13 cond clause stmt → *stmt*

$$[\![S_2 = C_1 \ C_2 \ break\_space \ S_1 \ cancel \ outdent \ force]\!]$$ — incomplete conditional

14 elsie → *intro* — unmatched else

15 exp math simp* → *math* $\quad [\![M_2 = E \ M_1 \ S\, \}]\!]$ — signed exponent

16 exp simp* → *math* $\quad [\![M = E \ S\, \}]\!]$ — unsigned exponent

17 intro stmt → *stmt* $\quad [\![S_2 = I \sqcup opt \ 7 \ cancel \ S_1]\!]$ — labeled statement, etc.

18 math close → *stmt close* $\quad [\![S = \$ \ M \ \$]\!]$ — end of field list

19 math colon → *intro* $\quad [\![I = force \ backup \ \$ \ M \ \$ \ C]\!]$ — compound label

20 math math → *math* — simple concatenation

21 math simp → *math* — simple concatenation

22 math stmt → *stmt*

$$[\![S_2 = \$ \ M \ \$ \ indent \ break\_space \ S_1 \ cancel \ outdent \ force]\!]$$ — macro or type definition

23 math terminator → *stmt* $\quad [\![S = \$ \ M \ \$ \ T]\!]$ — statement involving math

24 mod_scrap (terminator or semi) → *stmt*

$$[\![S = M \ T \ force]\!]$$ — module like a statement

25 mod_scrap → *simp* — module unlike a statement

26 open case_head close → *math*

$$[\![M = O \ \$ \ cancel \ C_1 \ cancel \ outdent \ \$ \ C_2]\!]$$ — case in field list

27 open close → *math* $\quad [\![M = O \setminus , \ C]\!]$ — empty set []

28 open math case_head close → *math*

$$[\![M_2 = O \ M_1 \ \$ \ cancel \ C_1 \ cancel \ outdent \ \$ \ C_2]\!]$$ — case in field list

29 open math close → *math* — parenthesized group

30 open math colon → *open math* — colon in parentheses

31 open math proc intro → *open math*

$$[\![M_2 = M_1 \ math\_op \ cancel \ P\, \}]\!]$$ — **procedure** in parentheses

32 open math semi → *open math* $\quad [\![M_2 = M_1 \ S \setminus , \ opt \ 5]\!]$ — semicolon in parentheses

33 open math var_head intro → *open math*

$$[\![M_2 = M_1 \ math\_op \ cancel \ V\, \}]\!]$$ — **var** in parentheses

34 open proc intro → *open math* $\quad [\![M = math\_op \ cancel \ P\, \}]\!]$ — **procedure** in parentheses

35 open simp → *open math* — convert to math mode

36 open stmt close → *math* $\quad [\![M = O \ \$ \ cancel \ S \ cancel \ \$ \ C]\!]$ — field list

37 open var_head intro → *open math*

$$[\![M = math\_op \ cancel \ V\, \}]\!]$$ — **var** in parentheses

38 proc beginning close terminator → *stmt*

$$[\![S = P \ cancel \ outdent \ B \ C \ T]\!]$$ — end of procedure declaration

39 proc stmt → *proc* $\quad [\![P_2 = P_1 \ break\_space \ S]\!]$ — procedure declaration grows

40 record_head intro casey → *casey* $\quad [\![C_2 = R \ I \sqcup cancel \ C_1]\!]$ — **record case** ...

41 record_head → *case_head* $\quad [\![C = indent \ R \ cancel]\!]$ — other **record** structures

42 semi → *terminator* — semicolon after statement

43 simp close → *stmt close* — end of field list

44 simp colon → intro $\quad [\![I = \textit{force backup } S\,C]\!]$		simple label
45 simp math → math		simple concatenation
46 simp mod_scrap → mod_scrap		in emergencies
47 simp simp → simp		simple concatenation
48 simp terminator → stmt		simple statement
49 stmt stmt → stmt $\quad [\![S_3 = S_1 \textit{ break\_space } S_2]\!]$		adjacent statements
50 terminator → stmt		empty statement
51 var_head beginning → stmt beginning		end of variable declarations
52 var_head math colon → var_head intro $\quad [\![I = \$\,M\,\$\,C]\!]$		variable declaration
53 var_head simp colon → var_head intro		variable declaration
54 var_head stmt → var_head $\quad [\![V_2 = V_1 \textit{ break\_space } S]\!]$		variable declarations grow

Translations are not specified here when they are simple concatenations of the scraps that change. For example, the full translation of '*open math colon → open math*' is $O_2 = O_1$, $M_2 = M_1 C$.

The notation '*simp**', in the *exp*-related productions above, stands for a *simp* scrap that isn't followed by another *simp*.

144. Implementing the productions. When Pascal text is to be processed with the grammar above, we put its initial scraps $s_1 \ldots s_n$ into two arrays $cat[1 \mathrel{..} n]$ and $trans[1 \mathrel{..} n]$. The value of $cat[k]$ is simply a category code from the list above; the value of $trans[k]$ is a text pointer, i.e., an index into *tok_start*. Our production rules have the nice property that the right-hand side is never longer than the left-hand side. Therefore it is convenient to use sequential allocation for the current sequence of scraps. Five pointers are used to manage the parsing:

> pp (the parsing pointer) is such that we are trying to match the category codes designated by $cat[pp]\ cat[pp+1]\ldots$ to the left-hand sides of productions.

> *scrap_base*, *lo_ptr*, *hi_ptr*, and *scrap_ptr* are such that the current sequence of scraps appears in positions *scrap_base* through *lo_ptr* and *hi_ptr* through *scrap_ptr*, inclusive, in the *cat* and *trans* arrays. Scraps located between *scrap_base* and *lo_ptr* have been examined, while those in positions $\geq$ *hi_ptr* have not yet been looked at by the parsing process.

Initially *scrap_ptr* is set to the position of the final scrap to be parsed, and it doesn't change its value. The parsing process makes sure that $lo\_ptr \geq pp + 3$, since productions have as many as four terms, by moving scraps from *hi_ptr* to *lo_ptr*. If there are fewer than $pp + 3$ scraps left, the positions up to $pp + 3$ are filled with blanks that will not match in any productions. Parsing stops when $pp = lo\_ptr + 1$ and $hi\_ptr = scrap\_ptr + 1$.

The *trans* array elements are declared to be of type $0 \mathrel{..} 10239$ instead of type *text_pointer*, because the final sorting phase uses this array to contain elements of type *name_pointer*. Both of these types are subranges of $0 \mathrel{..} 10239$.

⟨ Globals in the outer block 9 ⟩ $+\equiv$
cat: **array** $[0 \mathrel{..} max\_scraps]$ **of** *eight_bits*; $\quad$ { category codes of scraps }
trans: **array** $[0 \mathrel{..} max\_scraps]$ **of** $0 \mathrel{..} 10239$; $\quad$ { translation texts of scraps }
pp: $0 \mathrel{..} max\_scraps$; $\quad$ { current position for reducing productions }
scrap_base: $0 \mathrel{..} max\_scraps$; $\quad$ { beginning of the current scrap sequence }
scrap_ptr: $0 \mathrel{..} max\_scraps$; $\quad$ { ending of the current scrap sequence }

lo_ptr: 0 .. *max_scraps*;   { last scrap that has been examined }
hi_ptr: 0 .. *max_scraps*;   { first scrap that has not been examined }
  stat *max_scr_ptr*: 0 .. *max_scraps*;   { largest value assumed by *scrap_ptr* }
  tats

145.   ⟨ Set initial values 10 ⟩ +≡
  scrap_base ← 1; *scrap_ptr* ← 0;
  stat *max_scr_ptr* ← 0; **tats**

146.   Token lists in *tok_mem* are composed of the following kinds of items for TEX output.

- ASCII codes and special codes like *force* and *math_rel* represent themselves;
- *id_flag* + *p* represents \\{identifier *p*};
- *res_flag* + *p* represents \&{identifier *p*};
- *mod_flag* + *p* represents module name *p*;
- *tok_flag* + *p* represents token list number *p*;
- *inner_tok_flag* + *p* represents token list number *p*, to be translated without line-break controls.

define *id_flag* = 10240   { signifies an identifier }
define *res_flag* = *id_flag* + *id_flag*   { signifies a reserved word }
define *mod_flag* = *res_flag* + *id_flag*   { signifies a module name }
define *tok_flag* ≡ *mod_flag* + *id_flag*   { signifies a token list }
define *inner_tok_flag* ≡ *tok_flag* + *id_flag*   { signifies a token list in '| ... |' }

define *lbrace* ≡ *xchr*["{"]   { this avoids possible Pascal compiler confusion }
define *rbrace* ≡ *xchr*["}"]   { because these braces might occur within comments }

debug procedure *print_text*(*p* : *text_pointer*);   { prints a token list }
var *j*: 0 .. *max_toks*;   { index into *tok_mem* }
  r: 0 .. *id_flag* − 1;   { remainder of token after the flag has been stripped off }
begin if *p* ≥ *text_ptr* **then** *print*(´BAD´)
else for *j* ← *tok_start*[*p*] **to** *tok_start*[*p* + 1] − 1 **do**
    begin *r* ← *tok_mem*[*j*] **mod** *id_flag*;
    case *tok_mem*[*j*] **div** *id_flag* **of**
    1: **begin** *print*(´\\´, *lbrace*); *print_id*(*r*); *print*(*rbrace*);
      end;   { *id_flag* }
    2: **begin** *print*(´\&´, *lbrace*); *print_id*(*r*); *print*(*rbrace*);
      end;   { *res_flag* }
    3: **begin** *print*(´<´); *print_id*(*r*); *print*(´>´);
      end;   { *mod_flag* }
    4: *print*(´[[´, *r* : 1, ´]]´);   { *tok_flag* }
    5: *print*(´|[[´, *r* : 1, ´]]|´);   { *inner_tok_flag* }
    othercases ⟨ Print token *r* in symbolic form 147 ⟩
    endcases;
    end;
  end;
  gubed

147.   ⟨ Print token *r* in symbolic form 147 ⟩ ≡
  case *r* **of**
  math_bin: *print*(´\mathbin´, *lbrace*);

$math\_rel$: $print(\text{`}\backslash\texttt{mathrel'}, lbrace)$;
$math\_op$: $print(\text{`}\backslash\texttt{mathop'}, lbrace)$;
big_cancel: $print(\text{`}\texttt{[ccancel]'})$;
$cancel$: $print(\text{`}\texttt{[cancel]'})$;
$indent$: $print(\text{`}\texttt{[indent]'})$;
$outdent$: $print(\text{`}\texttt{[outdent]'})$;
$backup$: $print(\text{`}\texttt{[backup]'})$;
opt: $print(\text{`}\texttt{[opt]'})$;
$break\_space$: $print(\text{`}\texttt{[break]'})$;
$force$: $print(\text{`}\texttt{[force]'})$;
big_force: $print(\text{`}\texttt{[fforce]'})$;
$end\_translation$: $print(\text{`}\texttt{[quit]'})$;
othercases $print(xchr[r])$
endcases

This code is used in section 146.

148.   The production rules listed above are embedded directly into the WEAVE program, since it is easier to do this than to write an interpretive system that would handle production systems in general. Several macros are defined here so that the program for each production is fairly short.

All of our productions conform to the general notion that some k consecutive scraps starting at some position j are to be replaced by a single scrap of some category c whose translations is composed from the translations of the disappearing scraps. After this production has been applied, the production pointer pp should change by an amount d. Such a production can be represented by the quadruple (j, k, c, d). For example, the production '$simp\ math \to math$' would be represented by '$(pp, 2, math, -1)$'; in this case the pointer pp should decrease by 1 after the production has been applied, because some productions with $math$ in their second positions might now match, but no productions have $math$ in the third or fourth position of their left-hand sides. Note that the value of d is determined by the whole collection of productions, not by an individual one. Consider the further example '$var\_head\ math\ colon \to var\_head\ intro$', which is represented by '$(pp + 1, 2, intro, +1)$'; the $+1$ here is deduced by looking at the grammar and seeing that no matches could possibly occur at positions $\leq pp$ after this production has been applied. The determination of d has been done by hand in each case, based on the full set of productions but not on the grammar of Pascal or on the rules for constructing the initial scraps.

We also attach a serial number of each production, so that additional information is available when debugging. For example, the program below contains the statement '$reduce(pp + 1, 2, intro, +1)(52)$' when it implements the production just mentioned.

Before calling $reduce$, the program should have appended the tokens of the new translation to the tok_mem array. We commonly want to append copies of several existing translations, and macros are defined to simplify these common cases. For example, $app2(pp)$ will append the translations of two consecutive scraps, $trans[pp]$ and $trans[pp + 1]$, to the current token list. If the entire new translation is formed in this way, we write '$squash(j, k, c, d)$' instead of '$reduce(j, k, c, d)$'. For example, '$squash(pp, 2, math, -1)$' is an abbreviation for '$app2(pp)$; $reduce(pp, 2, math, -1)$'.

The code below is an exact translation of the production rules into Pascal, using such macros, and the reader should have no difficulty understanding the format by comparing the code with the symbolic productions as they were listed earlier.

Caution: The macros *app*, *app1*, *app2*, and *app3* are sequences of statements that are not enclosed with **begin** and **end**, because such delimiters would make the Pascal program much longer. This means that it is necessary to write **begin** and **end** explicitly when such a macro is used as a single statement. Several mysterious bugs in the original programming of WEAVE were caused by a failure to remember this fact. Next time the author will know better.

> **define** *production*(#) ≡
> > **debug** *prod*(#)
> > **gubed**;
> > **goto** *found*
> **define** *reduce*(#) ≡ *red*(#); *production*
> **define** *production_end*(#) ≡
> > **debug** *prod*(#)
> > **gubed**;
> > **goto** *found*;
> > **end**
> **define** *squash*(#) ≡
> > **begin** *sq*(#); *production_end*
> **define** *app*(#) ≡ *tok_mem*[*tok_ptr*] ← #; *incr*(*tok_ptr*)
> > { this is like *app_tok*, but it doesn't test for overflow }
> **define** *app1*(#) ≡ *tok_mem*[*tok_ptr*] ← *tok_flag* + *trans*[#]; *incr*(*tok_ptr*)
> **define** *app2*(#) ≡ *app1*(#); *app1*(# + 1)
> **define** *app3*(#) ≡ *app2*(#); *app1*(# + 2)

149. Let us consider the big case statement for productions now, before looking at its context. We want to design the program so that this case statement works, so we might as well not keep ourselves in suspense about exactly what code needs to be provided with a proper environment.

The code here is more complicated than it need be, since some popular Pascal compilers are unable to deal with procedures that contain a lot of program text. The *translate* procedure, which incorporates the **case** statement here, would become too long for those compilers if we did not do something to split the cases into parts. Therefore a separate procedure called *five_cases* has been introduced. This auxiliary procedure contains approximately half of the program text that *translate* would otherwise have had. There's also a procedure called *alpha_cases*, which turned out to be necessary because the best two-way split wasn't good enough. The procedure could be split further in an analogous manner, but the present scheme works on all compilers known to the author.

⟨ Match a production at *pp*, or increase *pp* if there is no match 149 ⟩ ≡
> **if** *cat*[*pp*] ≤ *alpha* **then**
> > **if** *cat*[*pp*] < *alpha* **then** *five_cases* **else** *alpha_cases*
> **else begin case** *cat*[*pp*] **of**
> > *case_head*: ⟨ Cases for *case_head* 153 ⟩;
> > *casey*: ⟨ Cases for *casey* 154 ⟩;
> > *clause*: ⟨ Cases for *clause* 155 ⟩;
> > *cond*: ⟨ Cases for *cond* 156 ⟩;
> > *elsie*: ⟨ Cases for *elsie* 157 ⟩;
> > *exp*: ⟨ Cases for *exp* 158 ⟩;

mod_scrap: ⟨ Cases for *mod_scrap* 161 ⟩;
proc: ⟨ Cases for *proc* 164 ⟩;
record_head: ⟨ Cases for *record_head* 165 ⟩;
semi: ⟨ Cases for *semi* 166 ⟩;
stmt: ⟨ Cases for *stmt* 168 ⟩;
terminator: ⟨ Cases for *terminator* 169 ⟩;
var_head: ⟨ Cases for *var_head* 170 ⟩;
othercases *do_nothing*
endcases;
incr(*pp*);   { if no match was found, we move to the right }
found: **end**

This code is used in section 175.

150.   Here are the procedures that need to be present for the reason just explained.

⟨ Declaration of subprocedures for *translate* 150 ⟩ ≡
procedure *five_cases*;   { handles almost half of the syntax }
  label *found*;
  begin case *cat*[*pp*] **of**
  beginning: ⟨ Cases for *beginning* 152 ⟩;
  intro: ⟨ Cases for *intro* 159 ⟩;
  math: ⟨ Cases for *math* 160 ⟩;
  open: ⟨ Cases for *open* 162 ⟩;
  simp: ⟨ Cases for *simp* 167 ⟩;
  othercases *do_nothing*
  endcases;
  incr(*pp*);   { if no match was found, we move to the right }
found: **end**;

procedure *alpha_cases*;
  label *found*;
  begin ⟨ Cases for *alpha* 151 ⟩;
  incr(*pp*);   { if no match was found, we move to the right }
found: **end**;

This code is used in section 179.

151.   Now comes the code that tries to match each production that starts with a particular type of scrap. Whenever a match is discovered, the *squash* or *reduce* macro will cause the appropriate action to be performed, followed by **goto** *found*.

⟨ Cases for *alpha* 151 ⟩ ≡
  if *cat*[*pp* + 1] = *math* **then**
    begin if *cat*[*pp* + 2] = *colon* **then** *squash*(*pp* + 1, 2, *math*, 0)(1)
    else if *cat*[*pp* + 2] = *omega* **then**
        begin *app1*(*pp*); *app*("␣"); *app*("\$"); *app1*(*pp* + 1); *app*("\$"); *app*("␣");
        app(*indent*); *app1*(*pp* + 2); *reduce*(*pp*, 3, *clause*, −2)(2);
        end;
    end
  else if *cat*[*pp* + 1] = *omega* **then**
      begin *app1*(*pp*); *app*("␣"); *app*(*indent*); *app1*(*pp* + 1); *reduce*(*pp*, 2, *clause*, −2)(3);
      end

      else if $cat[pp+1] = simp$ **then** $squash(pp+1, 1, math, 0)(4)$

This code is used in section 150.

152. ⟨ Cases for *beginning* 152 ⟩ ≡

   if $cat[pp+1] = close$ **then**

     begin if $(cat[pp+2] = terminator) \lor (cat[pp+2] = stmt)$ **then** $squash(pp, 3, stmt, -2)(5)$;

     end

   else if $cat[pp+1] = stmt$ **then**

     begin $app1(pp)$; $app(break\_space)$; $app1(pp+1)$; $reduce(pp, 2, beginning, -1)(6)$;

     end

This code is used in section 150.

153. ⟨ Cases for *case_head* 153 ⟩ ≡

   if $cat[pp+1] = casey$ **then**

     begin if $cat[pp+2] = clause$ **then**

       begin $app1(pp)$; $app(outdent)$; $app2(pp+1)$; $reduce(pp, 3, case\_head, 0)(7)$;

       end;

     end

   else if $cat[pp+1] = close$ **then**

     begin if $cat[pp+2] = terminator$ **then**

       begin $app1(pp)$; $app(cancel)$; $app(outdent)$; $app2(pp+1)$; $reduce(pp, 3, stmt, -2)(8)$;

       end;

     end

   else if $cat[pp+1] = stmt$ **then**

     begin $app1(pp)$; $app(force)$; $app1(pp+1)$; $reduce(pp, 2, case\_head, 0)(9)$;

     end

This code is used in section 149.

154. ⟨ Cases for *casey* 154 ⟩ ≡

   if $cat[pp+1] = clause$ **then** $squash(pp, 2, case\_head, 0)(10)$

This code is used in section 149.

155. ⟨ Cases for *clause* 155 ⟩ ≡

   if $cat[pp+1] = stmt$ **then**

     begin $app1(pp)$; $app(break\_space)$; $app1(pp+1)$; $app(cancel)$; $app(outdent)$; $app(force)$;

     $reduce(pp, 2, stmt, -2)(11)$;

     end

This code is used in section 149.

156. ⟨ Cases for *cond* 156 ⟩ ≡

   if $(cat[pp+1] = clause) \land (cat[pp+2] = stmt)$ **then**

     if $cat[pp+3] = elsie$ **then**

       begin $app2(pp)$; $app(break\_space)$; $app2(pp+2)$; $app("\sqcup")$; $app(cancel)$;

       $reduce(pp, 4, clause, -2)(12)$;

       end

     else begin $app2(pp)$; $app(break\_space)$; $app1(pp+2)$; $app(cancel)$; $app(outdent)$;

     $app(force)$; $reduce(pp, 3, stmt, -2)(13)$;

     end

This code is used in section 149.

157.   ⟨ Cases for *elsie* 157 ⟩ ≡
   squash(*pp*, 1, *intro*, −3)(14)
This code is used in section 149.

158.   ⟨ Cases for *exp* 158 ⟩ ≡
   if *cat*[*pp* + 1] = *math* **then**
      begin if *cat*[*pp* + 2] = *simp* **then**
         if *cat*[*pp* + 3] ≠ *simp* **then**
            begin *app3*(*pp*); *app*("}"); *reduce*(*pp*, 3, *math*, −1)(15);
            end;
      end
   else if *cat*[*pp* + 1] = *simp* **then**
      if *cat*[*pp* + 2] ≠ *simp* **then**
         begin *app2*(*pp*); *app*("}"); *reduce*(*pp*, 2, *math*, −1)(16);
         end
This code is used in section 149.

159.   ⟨ Cases for *intro* 159 ⟩ ≡
   if *cat*[*pp* + 1] = *stmt* **then**
      begin *app1*(*pp*); *app*("␣"); *app*(*opt*); *app*("7"); *app*(*cancel*); *app1*(*pp* + 1);
      reduce(*pp*, 2, *stmt*, −2)(17);
      end
This code is used in section 150.

160.   ⟨ Cases for *math* 160 ⟩ ≡
   if *cat*[*pp* + 1] = *close* **then**
      begin *app*("$"); *app1*(*pp*); *app*("$"); *reduce*(*pp*, 1, *stmt*, −2)(18);
      end
   else if *cat*[*pp* + 1] = *colon* **then**
      begin *app*(*force*); *app*(*backup*); *app*("$"); *app1*(*pp*); *app*("$"); *app1*(*pp* + 1);
      reduce(*pp*, 2, *intro*, −3)(19);
      end
   else if *cat*[*pp* + 1] = *math* **then** *squash*(*pp*, 2, *math*, −1)(20)
      else if *cat*[*pp* + 1] = *simp* **then** *squash*(*pp*, 2, *math*, −1)(21)
         else if *cat*[*pp* + 1] = *stmt* **then**
            begin *app*("$"); *app1*(*pp*); *app*("$"); *app*(*indent*); *app*(*break_space*);
            app1(*pp* + 1); *app*(*cancel*); *app*(*outdent*); *app*(*force*); *reduce*(*pp*, 2, *stmt*, −2)(22);
            end
            else if *cat*[*pp* + 1] = *terminator* **then**
               begin *app*("$"); *app1*(*pp*); *app*("$"); *app1*(*pp* + 1);
               reduce(*pp*, 2, *stmt*, −2)(23);
               end
This code is used in section 150.

161.   ⟨ Cases for *mod_scrap* 161 ⟩ ≡
   if (*cat*[*pp* + 1] = *terminator*) ∨ (*cat*[*pp* + 1] = *semi*) **then**
      begin *app2*(*pp*); *app*(*force*); *reduce*(*pp*, 2, *stmt*, −2)(24);
      end
   else *squash*(*pp*, 1, *simp*, −2)(25)
This code is used in section 149.

162. ⟨ Cases for *open* 162 ⟩ ≡
  if (*cat*[*pp* + 1] = *case_head*) ∧ (*cat*[*pp* + 2] = *close*) **then**
    begin *app1*(*pp*); *app*("$"); *app*(*cancel*); *app1*(*pp* + 1); *app*(*cancel*); *app*(*outdent*);
    app("$"); *app1*(*pp* + 2); *reduce*(*pp*, 3, *math*, −1)(26);
    end
  else if *cat*[*pp* + 1] = *close* **then**
    begin *app1*(*pp*); *app*("\"); *app*(","); *app1*(*pp* + 1); *reduce*(*pp*, 2, *math*, −1)(27);
    end
  else if *cat*[*pp* + 1] = *math* **then** ⟨ Cases for *open math* 163 ⟩
    else if *cat*[*pp* + 1] = *proc* **then**
      begin if *cat*[*pp* + 2] = *intro* **then**
        begin *app*(*math_op*); *app*(*cancel*); *app1*(*pp* + 1); *app*("}");
        reduce(*pp* + 1, 2, *math*, 0)(34);
        end;
      end
    else if *cat*[*pp* + 1] = *simp* **then** *squash*(*pp* + 1, 1, *math*, 0)(35)
      else if (*cat*[*pp* + 1] = *stmt*) ∧ (*cat*[*pp* + 2] = *close*) **then**
        begin *app1*(*pp*); *app*("$"); *app*(*cancel*); *app1*(*pp* + 1); *app*(*cancel*);
        app("$"); *app1*(*pp* + 2); *reduce*(*pp*, 3, *math*, −1)(36);
        end
      else if *cat*[*pp* + 1] = *var_head* **then**
        begin if *cat*[*pp* + 2] = *intro* **then**
          begin *app*(*math_op*); *app*(*cancel*); *app1*(*pp* + 1); *app*("}");
          reduce(*pp* + 1, 2, *math*, 0)(37);
          end;
        end

This code is used in section 150.

163. ⟨ Cases for *open math* 163 ⟩ ≡
  begin if (*cat*[*pp* + 2] = *case_head*) ∧ (*cat*[*pp* + 3] = *close*) **then**
    begin *app2*(*pp*); *app*("$"); *app*(*cancel*); *app1*(*pp* + 2); *app*(*cancel*); *app*(*outdent*);
    app("$"); *app1*(*pp* + 3); *reduce*(*pp*, 4, *math*, −1)(28);
    end
  else if *cat*[*pp* + 2] = *close* **then** *squash*(*pp*, 3, *math*, −1)(29)
    else if *cat*[*pp* + 2] = *colon* **then** *squash*(*pp* + 1, 2, *math*, 0)(30)
      else if *cat*[*pp* + 2] = *proc* **then**
        begin if *cat*[*pp* + 3] = *intro* **then**
          begin *app1*(*pp* + 1); *app*(*math_op*); *app*(*cancel*); *app1*(*pp* + 2); *app*("}");
          reduce(*pp* + 1, 3, *math*, 0)(31);
          end;
        end
      else if *cat*[*pp* + 2] = *semi* **then**
        begin *app2*(*pp* + 1); *app*("\"); *app*(","); *app*(*opt*); *app*("5");
        reduce(*pp* + 1, 2, *math*, 0)(32);
        end
        else if *cat*[*pp* + 2] = *var_head* **then**
          begin if *cat*[*pp* + 3] = *intro* **then**
            begin *app1*(*pp* + 1); *app*(*math_op*); *app*(*cancel*); *app1*(*pp* + 2); *app*("}");
            reduce(*pp* + 1, 3, *math*, 0)(31);
            end;

```
                    end;
    end
```
This code is used in section 162.

164.   ⟨Cases for *proc* 164⟩ ≡
```
    if cat[pp + 1] = beginning then
        begin if (cat[pp + 2] = close) ∧ (cat[pp + 3] = terminator) then
            begin app1(pp); app(cancel); app(outdent); app3(pp + 1); reduce(pp, 4, stmt, −2)(38);
            end;
        end
    else if cat[pp + 1] = stmt then
            begin app1(pp); app(break_space); app1(pp + 1); reduce(pp, 2, proc, −2)(39);
            end
```
This code is used in section 149.

165.   ⟨Cases for *record_head* 165⟩ ≡
```
    if (cat[pp + 1] = intro) ∧ (cat[pp + 2] = casey) then
        begin app2(pp); app("␣"); app(cancel); app1(pp + 2); reduce(pp, 3, casey, −2)(40);
        end
    else begin app(indent); app1(pp); app(cancel); reduce(pp, 1, case_head, 0)(41);
        end
```
This code is used in section 149.

166.   ⟨Cases for *semi* 166⟩ ≡
```
    squash(pp, 1, terminator, −3)(42)
```
This code is used in section 149.

167.   ⟨Cases for *simp* 167⟩ ≡
```
    if cat[pp + 1] = close then squash(pp, 1, stmt, −2)(43)
    else if cat[pp + 1] = colon then
            begin app(force); app(backup); app2(pp); reduce(pp, 2, intro, −3)(44);
            end
        else if cat[pp + 1] = math then squash(pp, 2, math, −1)(45)
            else if cat[pp + 1] = mod_scrap then squash(pp, 2, mod_scrap, 0)(46)
                else if cat[pp + 1] = simp then squash(pp, 2, simp, −2)(47)
                    else if cat[pp + 1] = terminator then squash(pp, 2, stmt, −2)(48)
```
This code is used in section 150.

168.   ⟨Cases for *stmt* 168⟩ ≡
```
    if cat[pp + 1] = stmt then
        begin app1(pp); app(break_space); app1(pp + 1); reduce(pp, 2, stmt, −2)(49);
        end
```
This code is used in section 149.

169.   ⟨Cases for *terminator* 169⟩ ≡
```
    squash(pp, 1, stmt, −2)(50)
```
This code is used in section 149.

170. $\langle$ Cases for *var_head* 170 $\rangle \equiv$
if *cat*[*pp* + 1] = *beginning* then *squash*(*pp*, 1, *stmt*, −2)(51)
else if *cat*[*pp* + 1] = *math* then
    begin if *cat*[*pp* + 2] = *colon* then
      begin *app*("$"); *app1*(*pp* + 1); *app*("$"); *app1*(*pp* + 2);
      reduce(*pp* + 1, 2, *intro*, +1)(52);
      end;
    end
  else if *cat*[*pp* + 1] = *simp* then
    begin if *cat*[*pp* + 2] = *colon* then *squash*(*pp* + 1, 2, *intro*, +1)(53);
    end
  else if *cat*[*pp* + 1] = *stmt* then
      begin *app1*(*pp*); *app*(*break_space*); *app1*(*pp* + 1); *reduce*(*pp*, 2, *var_head*, −2)(54);
    end

This code is used in section 149.

171. The '*freeze_text*' macro is used to give official status to a token list. Before saying *freeze_text*, items are appended to the current token list, and we know that the eventual number of this token list will be the current value of *text_ptr*. But no list of that number really exists as yet, because no ending point for the current list has been stored in the *tok_start* array. After saying *freeze_text*, the old current token list becomes legitimate, and its number is the current value of *text_ptr* − 1 since *text_ptr* has been increased. The new current token list is empty and ready to be appended to. Note that *freeze_text* does not check to see that *text_ptr* hasn't gotten too large, since it is assumed that this test was done beforehand.

    define *freeze_text* $\equiv$ *incr*(*text_ptr*); *tok_start*[*text_ptr*] $\leftarrow$ *tok_ptr*

172. The '*reduce*' macro used in our code for productions actually calls on a procedure named '*red*', which makes the appropriate changes to the scrap list.

procedure *red*(*j* : *sixteen_bits*; *k* : *eight_bits*; *c* : *eight_bits*; *d* : *integer*);
  var *i*: 0 .. *max_scraps*; {index into scrap memory}
  begin *cat*[*j*] $\leftarrow$ *c*; *trans*[*j*] $\leftarrow$ *text_ptr*; *freeze_text*;
  if *k* > 1 then
    begin for *i* $\leftarrow$ *j* + *k* to *lo_ptr* do
      begin *cat*[*i* − *k* + 1] $\leftarrow$ *cat*[*i*]; *trans*[*i* − *k* + 1] $\leftarrow$ *trans*[*i*];
      end;
    lo_ptr $\leftarrow$ *lo_ptr* − *k* + 1;
    end;
  $\langle$ Change *pp* to max(*scrap_base*, *pp*+*d*) 173 $\rangle$;
  end;

173. $\langle$ Change *pp* to max(*scrap_base*, *pp*+*d*) 173 $\rangle \equiv$
  if *pp* + *d* $\geq$ *scrap_base* then *pp* $\leftarrow$ *pp* + *d*
  else *pp* $\leftarrow$ *scrap_base*

This code is used in sections 172 and 174.

174. Similarly, the '*squash*' macro invokes a procedure called '*sq*'. This procedure takes advantage of the simplification that occurs when *k* = 1.

```
procedure sq(j : sixteen_bits; k : eight_bits; c : eight_bits; d : integer);
  var i: 0 .. max_scraps;   { index into scrap memory }
  begin if k = 1 then
    begin cat[j] ← c; ⟨ Change pp to max(scrap_base,pp+d) 173 ⟩;
    end
  else begin for i ← j to j + k − 1 do
    begin app1 (i);
    end;
    red(j, k, c, d);
    end;
  end;
```

175.   Here now is the code that applies productions as long as possible. It requires two
local labels (*found* and *done*), as well as a local variable (*i*).

⟨ Reduce the scraps using the productions until no more rules apply 175 ⟩ ≡
```
  loop begin ⟨ Make sure the entries cat[pp .. (pp + 3)] are defined 176 ⟩;
    if (tok_ptr + 8 > max_toks) ∨ (text_ptr + 4 > max_texts) then
      begin stat if tok_ptr > max_tok_ptr then max_tok_ptr ← tok_ptr;
      if text_ptr > max_txt_ptr then max_txt_ptr ← text_ptr;
      tats
      overflow (`token/text`);
      end;
    if pp > lo_ptr then goto done;
    ⟨ Match a production at pp, or increase pp if there is no match 149 ⟩;
    end;
done:
```
This code is used in section 179.

176.   If we get to the end of the scrap list, category codes equal to zero are stored, since
zero does not match anything in a production.

⟨ Make sure the entries *cat*[*pp* .. (*pp* + 3)] are defined 176 ⟩ ≡
```
  if lo_ptr < pp + 3 then
    begin repeat if hi_ptr ≤ scrap_ptr then
        begin incr (lo_ptr);
        cat[lo_ptr] ← cat[hi_ptr]; trans[lo_ptr] ← trans[hi_ptr];
        incr (hi_ptr);
        end;
    until (hi_ptr > scrap_ptr) ∨ (lo_ptr = pp + 3);
    for i ← lo_ptr + 1 to pp + 3 do cat[i] ← 0;
    end
```
This code is used in section 175.

177.   If WEAVE is being run in debugging mode, the production numbers and current stack
categories will be printed out when *tracing* is set to 2; a sequence of two or more irreducible
scraps will be printed out when *tracing* is set to 1.

⟨ Globals in the outer block 9 ⟩ +≡
```
  debug tracing: 0 .. 2;   { can be used to show parsing details }
  gubed
```

178. The *prod* procedure is called in debugging mode just after *reduce* or *squash*; its parameter is the number of the production that has just been applied.

debug procedure *prod*($n : eight\_bits$); { shows current categories }
var k: 1 .. *max_scraps*; { index into *cat* }
begin if *tracing* = 2 **then**
  begin *print_nl*(n : 1, ´:´);
  for $k \leftarrow scrap\_base$ **to** *lo_ptr* **do**
    begin if $k = pp$ **then** *print*(´*´) **else** *print*(´␣´);
    print_cat(*cat*[k]);
    end;
  if *hi_ptr* $\leq$ *scrap_ptr* **then** *print*(´...´); { indicate that more is coming }
  end;
end;
gubed

179. The *translate* function assumes that scraps have been stored in positions *scrap_base* through *scrap_ptr* of *cat* and *trans*. It appends a *terminator* scrap and begins to apply productions as much as possible. The result is a token list containing the translation of the given sequence of scraps.

After calling *translate*, we will have $text\_ptr + 3 \leq max\_texts$ and $tok\_ptr + 6 \leq max\_toks$, so it will be possible to create up to three token lists with up to six tokens without checking for overflow. Before calling *translate*, we should have $text\_ptr < max\_texts$ and $scrap\_ptr < max\_scraps$, since *translate* might add a new text and a new scrap before it checks for overflow.

⟨ Declaration of subprocedures for *translate* 150 ⟩
function *translate*: *text_pointer*; { converts a sequence of scraps }
  label *done*, *found*;
  var i: 1 .. *max_scraps*; { index into *cat* }
    j: 0 .. *max_scraps*; { runs through final scraps }
    k: 0 .. *long_buf_size*; { index into *buffer* }
  begin $pp \leftarrow scrap\_base$; $lo\_ptr \leftarrow pp - 1$; $hi\_ptr \leftarrow pp$;
  ⟨ If tracing, print an indication of where we are 182 ⟩;
  ⟨ Reduce the scraps using the productions until no more rules apply 175 ⟩;
  if ($lo\_ptr = scrap\_base$) $\wedge$ (cat[lo_ptr] $\neq$ *math*) **then** *translate* $\leftarrow$ *trans*[lo_ptr]
  else ⟨ Combine the irreducible scraps that remain 180 ⟩;
  end;

180. If the initial sequence of scraps does not reduce to a single scrap, we concatenate the translations of all remaining scraps, separated by blank spaces, with dollar signs surrounding the translations of *math* scraps.

⟨ Combine the irreducible scraps that remain 180 ⟩ ≡
  begin ⟨ If semi-tracing, show the irreducible scraps 181 ⟩;
  for $j \leftarrow scrap\_base$ **to** *lo_ptr* **do**
    begin if $j \neq scrap\_base$ **then**
      begin *app*("␣");
      end;
    if cat[j] = *math* **then**
      begin *app*("$");

```
        end;
    app1 (j);
    if cat[j] = math then
        begin app("$");
        end;
    if tok_ptr + 6 > max_toks then overflow(`token´);
    end;
freeze_text; translate ← text_ptr − 1;
end
```

This code is used in section 179.

181. ⟨ If semi-tracing, show the irreducible scraps 181 ⟩ ≡
```
    debug if (lo_ptr > scrap_base) ∧ (tracing = 1) then
        begin print_nl(`Irreducible␣scrap␣sequence␣in␣section␣´, module_count : 1);
        print_ln(`:´); mark_harmless;
        for j ← scrap_base to lo_ptr do
            begin print(`␣´); print_cat(cat[j]);
            end;
        end;
    gubed
```
This code is used in section 180.

182. ⟨ If tracing, print an indication of where we are 182 ⟩ ≡
```
    debug if tracing = 2 then
        begin print_nl(`Tracing␣after␣l.´, line : 1, `:´); mark_harmless;
        if loc > 50 then
            begin print(`...´);
            for k ← loc − 50 to loc do print(xchr[buffer[k − 1]]);
            end
        else for k ← 1 to loc do print(xchr[buffer[k − 1]]);
        end
    gubed
```
This code is used in section 179.

183. Initializing the scraps.   If we are going to use the powerful production mechanism just developed, we must get the scraps set up in the first place, given a Pascal text. A table of the initial scraps corresponding to Pascal tokens appeared above in the section on parsing; our goal now is to implement that table. We shall do this by implementing a subroutine called *Pascal_parse* that is analogous to the *Pascal_xref* routine used during phase one.

Like *Pascal_xref*, the *Pascal_parse* procedure starts with the current value of *next_control* and it uses the operation *next_control* ← *get_next* repeatedly to read Pascal text until encountering the next '|' or '{', or until *next_control* ≥ *format*. The scraps corresponding to what it reads are appended into the *cat* and *trans* arrays, and *scrap_ptr* is advanced.

Like *prod*, this procedure has to split into pieces so that each part is short enough to be handled by Pascal compilers that discriminate against long subroutines. This time there are two split-off routines, called *easy_cases* and *sub_cases*.

After studying *Pascal_parse*, we will look at the sub-procedures *app_comment*, *app_octal*, and *app_hex* that are used in some of its branches.

⟨ Declaration of the *app_comment* procedure 195 ⟩
⟨ Declaration of the *app_octal* and *app_hex* procedures 196 ⟩
⟨ Declaration of the *easy_cases* procedure 186 ⟩
⟨ Declaration of the *sub_cases* procedure 192 ⟩
procedure *Pascal_parse*; { creates scraps from Pascal tokens }
  label *reswitch*, *exit*;
  var *j*: $0 .. long\_buf\_size$; { index into *buffer* }
    p: *name_pointer*; { identifier designator }
  begin while *next_control* < *format* **do**
    begin ⟨ Append the scrap appropriate to *next_control* 185 ⟩;
    next_control ← *get_next*;
    if (*next_control* = "|") ∨ (*next_control* = "{") **then return**;
    end;
exit: **end**;

184. The macros defined here are helpful abbreviations for the operations needed when generating the scraps. A scrap of category *c* whose translation has three tokens t_1, t_2, t_3 is generated by $sc3(t_1)(t_2)(t_3)(c)$, etc.

  define *s0*(#) ≡ *incr*(*scrap_ptr*); *cat*[*scrap_ptr*] ← #; *trans*[*scrap_ptr*] ← *text_ptr*; *freeze_text*;
      end
  define *s1*(#) ≡ *app*(#); *s0*
  define *s2*(#) ≡ *app*(#); *s1*
  define *s3*(#) ≡ *app*(#); *s2*
  define *s4*(#) ≡ *app*(#); *s3*
  define *sc4* ≡ **begin** *s4*
  define *sc3* ≡ **begin** *s3*
  define *sc2* ≡ **begin** *s2*
  define *sc1* ≡ **begin** *s1*
  define *sc0*(#) ≡
        begin *incr*(*scrap_ptr*); *cat*[*scrap_ptr*] ← #; *trans*[*scrap_ptr*] ← 0;
        end
  define *comment_scrap*(#) ≡
        begin *app*(#); *app_comment*;
        end

185. ⟨ Append the scrap appropriate to *next_control* 185 ⟩ ≡
  ⟨ Make sure that there is room for at least four more scraps, six more tokens, and four more texts 187 ⟩;
reswitch: **case** *next_control* **of**
  string, *verbatim*: ⟨ Append a string scrap 189 ⟩;
  identifier: ⟨ Append an identifier scrap 191 ⟩;
  TeX_string: ⟨ Append a TeX string scrap 190 ⟩;
  othercases *easy_cases*
  endcases
This code is used in section 183.

186. The *easy_cases* each result in straightforward scraps.

⟨ Declaration of the *easy_cases* procedure 186 ⟩ ≡
procedure *easy_cases*; { a subprocedure of *Pascal_parse* }

```
begin case next_control of
set_element_sign: sc3 ("\")("i")("n")(math);
double_dot: sc3 ("\")("t")("o")(math);
"#", "$", "%", "^", "_": sc2 ("\")(next_control)(math);
ignore, "|", xref_roman, xref_wildcard, xref_typewriter: do_nothing;
"(", "[": sc1 (next_control)(open);
")", "]": sc1 (next_control)(close);
"*": sc4 ("\")("a")("s")("t")(math);
",": sc3 (",")(opt)("9")(math);
".", "0", "1", "2", "3", "4", "5", "6", "7", "8", "9": sc1 (next_control)(simp);
";": sc1 (";")(semi);
":": sc1 (":")(colon);
⟨Cases involving nonstandard ASCII characters 188⟩
exponent: sc3 ("\")("E")("{")(exp);
begin_comment: sc2 ("\")("B")(math);
end_comment: sc2 ("\")("T")(math);
octal: app_octal;
hex: app_hex;
check_sum: sc2 ("\")(")")(simp);
force_line: sc2 ("\")("]")(simp);
thin_space: sc2 ("\")(",")(math);
math_break: sc2 (opt)("0")(simp);
line_break: comment_scrap(force);
big_line_break: comment_scrap(big_force);
no_line_break: begin app(big_cancel); app("\"); app("␣"); comment_scrap(big_cancel);
    end;
pseudo_semi: sc0 (semi);
join: sc2 ("\")("J")(math);
othercases sc1 (next_control)(math)
endcases;
end;
```
This code is used in section 183.

187.   ⟨Make sure that there is room for at least four more scraps, six more tokens, and four
        more texts 187⟩ ≡
```
if (scrap_ptr + 4 > max_scraps) ∨ (tok_ptr + 6 > max_toks) ∨ (text_ptr + 4 > max_texts) then
    begin stat if scrap_ptr > max_scr_ptr then max_scr_ptr ← scrap_ptr;
    if tok_ptr > max_tok_ptr then max_tok_ptr ← tok_ptr;
    if text_ptr > max_txt_ptr then max_txt_ptr ← text_ptr;
    tats
    overflow (´scrap/token/text´);
    end
```
This code is used in section 185.

188.   Some nonstandard ASCII characters may have entered WEAVE by means of standard
ones. They are converted to TeX control sequences so that it is possible to keep WEAVE from
stepping beyond standard ASCII.

⟨Cases involving nonstandard ASCII characters 188⟩ ≡
```
not_equal: sc2 ("\")("I")(math);
```

less_or_equal: *sc2* ("\")("L")(*math*);
greater_or_equal: *sc2* ("\")("G")(*math*);
equivalence_sign: *sc2* ("\")("S")(*math*);
and_sign: *sc2* ("\")("W")(*math*);
or_sign: *sc2* ("\")("V")(*math*);
not_sign: *sc2* ("\")("R")(*math*);
left_arrow: *sc2* ("\")("K")(*math*);

This code is used in section 186.

189. The following code must use *app_tok* instead of *app* in order to protect against overflow. Note that *tok_ptr* + 1 ≤ *max_toks* after *app_tok* has been used, so another *app* is legitimate before testing again.

Many of the special characters in a string must be prefixed by '\' so that TEX will print them properly.

⟨ Append a string scrap 189 ⟩ ≡
  begin *app*("\");
  if *next_control* = *verbatim* **then**
    begin *app*("=");
    end
  else begin *app*(".");
    end;
  app("{"); *j* ← *id_first*;
  while *j* < *id_loc* **do**
    begin case *buffer*[*j*] **of**
    "␣", "\", "#", "%", "$", "^", "'", "`", "{", "}", "~", "&", "_": **begin** *app*("\");
      end;
    "@": **if** *buffer*[*j* + 1] = "@" **then** *incr*(*j*)
      else *err_print*(`!␣Double␣@␣should␣be␣used␣in␣strings`);
    othercases *do_nothing*
    endcases;
    app_tok(*buffer*[*j*]); *incr*(*j*);
    end;
  sc1 ("}")(*simp*);
  end

This code is used in section 185.

190. ⟨ Append a TEX string scrap 190 ⟩ ≡
  begin *app*("\"); *app*("h"); *app*("b"); *app*("o"); *app*("x"); *app*("{");
  for *j* ← *id_first* **to** *id_loc* − 1 **do** *app_tok*(*buffer*[*j*]);
  sc1 ("}")(*simp*);
  end

This code is used in section 185.

191. ⟨ Append an identifier scrap 191 ⟩ ≡
  begin *p* ← *id_lookup*(*normal*);
  case *ilk*[*p*] **of**
  normal, *array_like*, *const_like*, *div_like*, *do_like*, *for_like*, *goto_like*, *nil_like*, *to_like*: *sub_cases*(*p*);
  ⟨ Cases that generate more than one scrap 193 ⟩
  othercases begin *next_control* ← *ilk*[*p*] − *char_like*; **goto** *reswitch*;

```
      end   { and, in, not, or }
    endcases;
    end
```

This code is used in section 185.

192.   The *sub_cases* also result in straightforward scraps.

⟨ Declaration of the *sub_cases* procedure 192 ⟩ ≡
procedure *sub_cases*(*p* : *name_pointer*);   { a subprocedure of *Pascal_parse* }
    begin case *ilk*[*p*] **of**
    normal: *sc1*(*id_flag* + *p*)(*simp*);   { not a reserved word }
    array_like: *sc1*(*res_flag* + *p*)(*alpha*);   { **array**, **file**, **set** }
    const_like: *sc3*(*force*)(*backup*)(*res_flag* + *p*)(*intro*);   { **const**, **label**, **type** }
    div_like: *sc3*(*math_bin*)(*res_flag* + *p*)("}")(*math*);   { **div**, **mod** }
    do_like: *sc1*(*res_flag* + *p*)(*omega*);   { **do**, **of**, **then** }
    for_like: *sc2*(*force*)(*res_flag* + *p*)(*alpha*);   { **for**, **while**, **with** }
    goto_like: *sc1*(*res_flag* + *p*)(*intro*);   { **goto**, **packed** }
    nil_like: *sc1*(*res_flag* + *p*)(*simp*);   { **nil** }
    to_like: *sc3*(*math_rel*)(*res_flag* + *p*)("}")(*math*);   { **downto**, **to** }
    end;
    end;

This code is used in section 183.

193.   ⟨ Cases that generate more than one scrap 193 ⟩ ≡
begin_like: **begin** *sc3*(*force*)(*res_flag* + *p*)(*cancel*)(*beginning*); *sc0*(*intro*);
    end;   { **begin** }
case_like: **begin** *sc0*(*casey*); *sc2*(*force*)(*res_flag* + *p*)(*alpha*);
    end;   { **case** }
else_like: **begin** ⟨ Append *terminator* if not already present 194 ⟩;
    sc3(*force*)(*backup*)(*res_flag* + *p*)(*elsie*);
    end;   { **else** }
end_like: **begin** ⟨ Append *terminator* if not already present 194 ⟩;
    sc2(*force*)(*res_flag* + *p*)(*close*);
    end;   { **end** }
if_like: **begin** *sc0*(*cond*); *sc2*(*force*)(*res_flag* + *p*)(*alpha*);
    end;   { **if** }
loop_like: **begin** *sc3*(*force*)("\")("~")(*alpha*); *sc1*(*res_flag* + *p*)(*omega*);
    end;   { **xclause** }
proc_like: **begin** *sc4*(*force*)(*backup*)(*res_flag* + *p*)(*cancel*)(*proc*); *sc3*(*indent*)("\")("␣")(*intro*);
    end;   { **function**, **procedure**, **program** }
record_like: **begin** *sc1*(*res_flag* + *p*)(*record_head*); *sc0*(*intro*);
    end;   { **record** }
repeat_like: **begin** *sc4*(*force*)(*indent*)(*res_flag* + *p*)(*cancel*)(*beginning*); *sc0*(*intro*);
    end;   { **repeat** }
until_like: **begin** ⟨ Append *terminator* if not already present 194 ⟩;
    sc3(*force*)(*backup*)(*res_flag* + *p*)(*close*); *sc0*(*clause*);
    end;   { **until** }
var_like: **begin** *sc4*(*force*)(*backup*)(*res_flag* + *p*)(*cancel*)(*var_head*); *sc0*(*intro*);
    end;   { **var** }

This code is used in section 191.

194. If a comment or semicolon appears before the reserved words **end**, **else**, or **until**, the *semi* or *terminator* scrap that is already present overrides the *terminator* scrap belonging to this reserved word.

⟨ Append *terminator* if not already present 194 ⟩ ≡
   if $(scrap\_ptr < scrap\_base) \vee ((cat[scrap\_ptr] \neq terminator) \wedge (cat[scrap\_ptr] \neq semi))$ **then**
      $sc0(terminator)$

This code is used in sections 193, 193, and 193.

195. A comment is incorporated into the previous scrap if that scrap is of type *omega* or *semi* or *terminator*. (These three categories have consecutive category codes.) Otherwise the comment is entered as a separate scrap of type *terminator*, and it will combine with a *terminator* scrap that immediately follows it.

The *app_comment* procedure takes care of placing a comment at the end of the current scrap list. When *app_comment* is called, we assume that the current token list is the translation of the comment involved.

⟨ Declaration of the *app_comment* procedure 195 ⟩ ≡
procedure *app_comment*;   { append a comment to the scrap list }
   begin *freeze_text*;
   if $(scrap\_ptr < scrap\_base) \vee (cat[scrap\_ptr] < omega) \vee (cat[scrap\_ptr] > terminator)$ **then**
      $sc0(terminator)$
   else begin $app1(scrap\_ptr)$;   { $cat[scrap\_ptr]$ is *omega* or *semi* or *terminator* }
      end;
   $app(text\_ptr - 1 + tok\_flag)$; $trans[scrap\_ptr] \leftarrow text\_ptr$; *freeze_text*;
   end;

This code is used in section 183.

196. We are now finished with *Pascal_parse*, except for two relatively trivial subprocedures that convert constants into tokens.

⟨ Declaration of the *app_octal* and *app_hex* procedures 196 ⟩ ≡
procedure *app_octal*;
   begin $app("\backslash")$; $app("0")$; $app("\{")$;
   while $(buffer[loc] \geq "0") \wedge (buffer[loc] \leq "7")$ **do**
      begin $app\_tok(buffer[loc])$; $incr(loc)$;
      end;
   $sc1("\}")(simp)$;
   end;

procedure *app_hex*;
   begin $app("\backslash")$; $app("H")$; $app("\{")$;
   while $((buffer[loc] \geq "0") \wedge (buffer[loc] \leq "9")) \vee ((buffer[loc] \geq "A") \wedge (buffer[loc] \leq "F"))$ **do**
      begin $app\_tok(buffer[loc])$; $incr(loc)$;
      end;
   $sc1("\}")(simp)$;
   end;

This code is used in section 183.

197. When the '|' that introduces Pascal text is sensed, a call on *Pascal_translate* will return a pointer to the TeX translation of that text. If scraps exist in the *cat* and *trans* arrays, they are unaffected by this translation process.

function *Pascal_translate*: *text_pointer*;
  var *p*: *text_pointer*; { points to the translation }
    save_base: $0 .. max\_scraps$; { holds original value of *scrap_base* }
  begin *save_base* ← *scrap_base*; *scrap_base* ← *scrap_ptr* + 1; *Pascal_parse*;
    { get the scraps together }
  if *next_control* ≠ "|" **then** *err_print*(´!␣Missing␣"|"␣after␣Pascal␣text´);
  app_tok(*cancel*); *app_comment*; { place a *cancel* token as a final "comment" }
  p ← *translate*; { make the translation }
  stat if *scrap_ptr* > *max_scr_ptr* **then** *max_scr_ptr* ← *scrap_ptr*; **tats**
  scrap_ptr ← *scrap_base* − 1; *scrap_base* ← *save_base*; { scrap the scraps }
  Pascal_translate ← *p*;
  end;

198.   The *outer_parse* routine is to *Pascal_parse* as *outer_xref* is to *Pascal_xref*: It constructs a sequence of scraps for Pascal text until $next\_control \geq format$. Thus, it takes care of embedded comments.

procedure *outer_parse*; { makes scraps from Pascal tokens and comments }
  var *bal*: *eight_bits*; { brace level in comment }
    p, q: *text_pointer*; { partial comments }
  begin while *next_control* < *format* **do**
    if *next_control* ≠ "{" **then** *Pascal_parse*
    else begin ⟨ Make sure that there is room for at least seven more tokens, three more texts,
        and one more scrap 199 ⟩;
      app("\\"); *app*("C"); *app*("{"); *bal* ← *copy_comment*(1); *next_control* ← "|";
      while *bal* > 0 **do**
        begin *p* ← *text_ptr*; *freeze_text*; *q* ← *Pascal_translate*;
          { at this point we have $tok\_ptr + 6 \leq max\_toks$ }
        app(*tok_flag* + *p*); *app*(*inner_tok_flag* + *q*);
        if *next_control* = "|" **then** *bal* ← *copy_comment*(*bal*)
        else *bal* ← 0; { an error has been reported }
        end;
      app(*force*); *app_comment*; { the full comment becomes a scrap }
      end;
  end;

199. ⟨ Make sure that there is room for at least seven more tokens, three more texts, and one
    more scrap 199 ⟩ ≡
  if $(tok\_ptr + 7 > max\_toks) \vee (text\_ptr + 3 > max\_texts) \vee (scrap\_ptr \geq max\_scraps)$ **then**
    begin stat if *scrap_ptr* > *max_scr_ptr* **then** *max_scr_ptr* ← *scrap_ptr*;
    if *tok_ptr* > *max_tok_ptr* **then** *max_tok_ptr* ← *tok_ptr*;
    if *text_ptr* > *max_txt_ptr* **then** *max_txt_ptr* ← *text_ptr*;
    tats
    overflow(´token/text/scrap´);
    end
This code is used in section 198.

200. Output of tokens.   So far our programs have only built up multi-layered token lists in WEAVE's internal memory; we have to figure out how to get them into the desired final form. The job of converting token lists to characters in the TeX output file is not difficult, although it is an implicitly recursive process. Three main considerations had to be kept in mind when this part of **WEAVE** was designed: (a) There are two modes of output, *outer* mode that translates tokens like *force* into line-breaking control sequences, and *inner* mode that ignores them except that blank spaces take the place of line breaks. (b) The *cancel* instruction applies to adjacent token or tokens that are output, and this cuts across levels of recursion since '*cancel*' occurs at the beginning or end of a token list on one level. (c) The TEX output file will be semi-readable if line breaks are inserted after the result of tokens like *break_space* and *force*. (d) The final line break should be suppressed, and there should be no *force* token output immediately after '\Y\P'.

201. The output process uses a stack to keep track of what is going on at different "levels" as the token lists are being written out. Entries on this stack have three parts:

end_field is the *tok_mem* location where the token list of a particular level will end;

tok_field is the *tok_mem* location from which the next token on a particular level will be read;

mode_field is the current mode, either *inner* or *outer*.

The current values of these quantities are referred to quite frequently, so they are stored in a separate place instead of in the *stack* array. We call the current values *cur_end*, *cur_tok*, and *cur_mode*.

The global variable *stack_ptr* tells how many levels of output are currently in progress. The end of output occurs when an *end_translation* token is found, so the stack is never empty except when we first begin the output process.

define *inner* = 0   { value of *mode* for Pascal texts within TEX texts }
define *outer* = 1   { value of *mode* for Pascal texts in modules }

⟨ Types in the outer block 11 ⟩ +≡
  mode = *inner* .. *outer*;
  output_state = **record** *end_field*: *sixteen_bits*;   { ending location of token list }
    tok_field: *sixteen_bits*;   { present location within token list }
    mode_field: *mode*;   { interpretation of control tokens }
    end;

202. **define** *cur_end* ≡ *cur_state.end_field*   { current ending location in *tok_mem* }
  define *cur_tok* ≡ *cur_state.tok_field*   { location of next output token in *tok_mem* }
  define *cur_mode* ≡ *cur_state.mode_field*   { current mode of interpretation }
  define *init_stack* ≡ *stack_ptr* ← 0; *cur_mode* ← *outer*   { do this to initialize the stack }

⟨ Globals in the outer block 9 ⟩ +≡
cur_state: *output_state*;   { *cur_end*, *cur_tok*, *cur_mode* }
stack: **array** [1 .. *stack_size*] **of** *output_state*;   { info for non-current levels }
stack_ptr: 0 .. *stack_size*;   { first unused location in the output state stack }
  stat *max_stack_ptr*: 0 .. *stack_size*;   { largest value assumed by *stack_ptr* }
  tats

203. ⟨ Set initial values 10 ⟩ +≡
  stat *max_stack_ptr* ← 0; **tats**

204. To insert token-list p into the output, the *push_level* subroutine is called; it saves the old level of output and gets a new one going. The value of *cur_mode* is not changed.

procedure *push_level*(p : *text_pointer*);   { suspends the current level }
  begin if *stack_ptr* = *stack_size* **then** *overflow*(´stack´)
  else begin if *stack_ptr* > 0 **then** *stack*[*stack_ptr*] ← *cur_state*;   { save *cur_end* ... *cur_mode* }
    incr(*stack_ptr*);
    stat if *stack_ptr* > *max_stack_ptr* **then** *max_stack_ptr* ← *stack_ptr*; **tats**
    cur_tok ← *tok_start*[p]; *cur_end* ← *tok_start*[$p + 1$];
    end;
  end;

205. Conversely, the *pop_level* routine restores the conditions that were in force when the current level was begun. This subroutine will never be called when *stack_ptr* = 1. It is so simple, we declare it as a macro:

define *pop_level* ≡
        begin *decr*(*stack_ptr*); *cur_state* ← *stack*[*stack_ptr*];
        end   { do this when *cur_tok* reaches *cur_end* }

206. The *get_output* function returns the next byte of output that is not a reference to a token list. It returns the values *identifier* or *res_word* or *mod_name* if the next token is to be an identifier (typeset in italics), a reserved word (typeset in boldface) or a module name (typeset by a complex routine that might generate additional levels of output). In these cases *cur_name* points to the identifier or module name in question.

  define *res_word* = ´201   { returned by *get_output* for reserved words }
  define *mod_name* = ´200   { returned by *get_output* for module names }

function *get_output*: *eight_bits*;   { returns the next token of output }
  label *restart*;
  var *a*: *sixteen_bits*;   { current item read from *tok_mem* }
  begin *restart*: **while** *cur_tok* = *cur_end* **do** *pop_level*;
  a ← *tok_mem*[*cur_tok*]; *incr*(*cur_tok*);
  if *a* ≥ ´400 **then**
    begin *cur_name* ← *a* **mod** *id_flag*;
    case *a* **div** *id_flag* **of**
    2: *a* ← *res_word*;   { *a* = *res_flag* + *cur_name* }
    3: *a* ← *mod_name*;   { *a* = *mod_flag* + *cur_name* }
    4: **begin** *push_level*(*cur_name*); **goto** *restart*;
      end;   { *a* = *tok_flag* + *cur_name* }
    5: **begin** *push_level*(*cur_name*); *cur_mode* ← *inner*; **goto** *restart*;
      end;   { *a* = *inner_tok_flag* + *cur_name* }
    othercases *a* ← *identifier*   { *a* = *id_flag* + *cur_name* }
    endcases;
    end;
  debug if *trouble_shooting* **then** *debug_help*;
  gubed
  get_output ← *a*;
  end;

207. The real work associated with token output is done by *make_output*. This procedure appends an *end_translation* token to the current token list, and then it repeatedly calls *get_output* and feeds characters to the output buffer until reaching the *end_translation* sentinel. It is possible for *make_output* to be called recursively, since a module name may include embedded Pascal text; however, the depth of recursion never exceeds one level, since module names cannot be inside of module names.

A procedure called *output_Pascal* does the scanning, translation, and output of Pascal text within '| ... |' brackets, and this procedure uses *make_output* to output the current token list. Thus, the recursive call of *make_output* actually occurs when *make_output* calls *output_Pascal* while outputting the name of a module.

procedure *make_output*; *forward*;

procedure *output_Pascal*;   { outputs the current token list }
   var *save_tok_ptr*, *save_text_ptr*, *save_next_control*: *sixteen_bits*;   { values to be restored }
     p: *text_pointer*;   { translation of the Pascal text }
   begin *save_tok_ptr* ← *tok_ptr*; *save_text_ptr* ← *text_ptr*; *save_next_control* ← *next_control*;
   next_control ← "|"; *p* ← *Pascal_translate*; *app*(*p* + *inner_tok_flag*); *make_output*;
     { output the list }
   stat if *text_ptr* > *max_txt_ptr* **then** *max_txt_ptr* ← *text_ptr*;
   if *tok_ptr* > *max_tok_ptr* **then** *max_tok_ptr* ← *tok_ptr*; **tats**
   text_ptr ← *save_text_ptr*; *tok_ptr* ← *save_tok_ptr*;   { forget the tokens }
   next_control ← *save_next_control*;   { restore *next_control* to original state }
   end;

208.   Here is WEAVE's major output handler.

procedure *make_output*;   { outputs the equivalents of tokens }
   label *reswitch*, *exit*, *found*;
   var *a*: *eight_bits*;   { current output byte }
     b: *eight_bits*;   { next output byte }
     k, *k_limit*: 0 .. *max_bytes*;   { indices into *byte_mem* }
     w: 0 .. *ww* − 1;   { row of *byte_mem* }
     j: 0 .. *long_buf_size*;   { index into *buffer* }
     string_delimiter: *ASCII_code*;   { first and last character of string being copied }
     save_loc, *save_limit*: 0 .. *long_buf_size*;   { *loc* and *limit* to be restored }
     cur_mod_name: *name_pointer*;   { name of module being output }
     save_mode: *mode*;   { value of *cur_mode* before a sequence of breaks }
   begin *app*(*end_translation*);   { append a sentinel }
   freeze_text; *push_level*(*text_ptr* − 1);
   loop begin *a* ← *get_output*;
   reswitch: **case** *a* **of**
     end_translation: **return**;
     identifier, *res_word*: ⟨ Output an identifier 209 ⟩;
     mod_name: ⟨ Output a module name 213 ⟩;
     math_bin, *math_op*, *math_rel*: ⟨ Output a \math operator 210 ⟩;
     cancel: **begin repeat** *a* ← *get_output*;
       until (*a* < *backup*) ∨ (*a* > *big_force*);
       goto *reswitch*;
       end;
     big_cancel: **begin repeat** *a* ← *get_output*;
       until ((*a* < *backup*) ∧ (*a* ≠ "␣")) ∨ (*a* > *big_force*);
       goto *reswitch*;
       end;

indent, *outdent*, *opt*, *backup*, *break_space*, *force*, *big_force*: ⟨Output a control, look ahead in
  case of line breaks, possibly **goto** *reswitch* 211⟩;
othercases *out*(*a*) {otherwise *a* is an ASCII character}
endcases;
end;
exit: **end**;

---

209. An identifier of length one does not have to be enclosed in braces, and it looks slightly
better if set in a math-italic font instead of a (slightly narrower) text-italic font. Thus we
output '\|a' but '\\{aa}'.

⟨Output an identifier 209⟩ ≡
 begin *out*("\");
 if *a* = *identifier* **then**
  if *length*(*cur_name*) = 1 **then** *out*("|")
  else *out*("\")
 else *out*("&"); {*a* = *res_word*}
 if *length*(*cur_name*) = 1 **then** *out*(*byte_mem*[*cur_name* **mod** *ww*, *byte_start*[*cur_name*]])
 else *out_name*(*cur_name*);
 end

This code is used in section 208.

---

210. ⟨Output a \math operator 210⟩ ≡
 begin *out5*("\")("m")("a")("t")("h");
 if *a* = *math_bin* **then** *out3*("b")("i")("n")
 else if *a* = *math_rel* **then** *out3*("r")("e")("l")
  else *out2*("o")("p");
 out("{");
 end

This code is used in section 208.

---

211. The current mode does not affect the behavior of WEAVE's output routine except
when we are outputting control tokens.

⟨Output a control, look ahead in case of line breaks, possibly **goto** *reswitch* 211⟩ ≡
 if *a* < *break_space* **then**
  begin if *cur_mode* = *outer* **then**
   begin *out2*("\")(*a* + −*cancel* + "0");
   if *a* = *opt* **then** *out*(*get_output*) {*opt* is followed by a digit}
   end
  else if *a* = *opt* **then** *b* ← *get_output* {ignore digit following *opt*}
  end
 else ⟨Look ahead for strongest line break, **goto** *reswitch* 212⟩

This code is used in section 208.

---

212. If several of the tokens *break_space*, *force*, *big_force* occur in a row, possibly mixed
with blank spaces (which are ignored), the largest one is used. A line break also occurs
in the output file, except at the very end of the translation. The very first line break is
suppressed (i.e., a line break that follows '\Y\P').

⟨Look ahead for strongest line break, **goto** *reswitch* 212⟩ ≡

```
begin b ← a; save_mode ← cur_mode;
loop begin a ← get_output;
  if (a = cancel) ∨ (a = big_cancel) then goto reswitch;   { cancel overrides everything }
  if ((a ≠ "␣") ∧ (a < break_space)) ∨ (a > big_force) then
    begin if save_mode = outer then
      begin if out_ptr > 3 then
        if (out_buf[out_ptr] = "P") ∧ (out_buf[out_ptr − 1] = "\") ∧ (out_buf[out_ptr − 2] =
            "Y") ∧ (out_buf[out_ptr − 3] = "\") then goto reswitch;
        out2("\")(b − cancel + "0");
        if a ≠ end_translation then finish_line;
        end
      else if (a ≠ end_translation) ∧ (cur_mode = inner) then out("␣");
      goto reswitch;
      end;
  if a > b then b ← a;   { if a = "␣" we have a < b }
  end;
end
```

This code is used in section 211.

213. The remaining part of *make_output* is somewhat more complicated. When we output a module name, we may need to enter the parsing and translation routines, since the name may contain Pascal code embedded in | . . . | constructions. This Pascal code is placed at the end of the active input buffer and the translation process uses the end of the active *tok_mem* area.

⟨ Output a module name 213 ⟩ ≡
```
  begin out2("\")("X"); cur_xref ← xref[cur_name];
  if num(cur_xref) ≥ def_flag then
    begin out_mod(num(cur_xref) − def_flag);
    if phase_three then
      begin cur_xref ← xlink(cur_xref);
      while num(cur_xref) ≥ def_flag do
        begin out2(",")("␣"); out_mod(num(cur_xref) − def_flag); cur_xref ← xlink(cur_xref);
        end;
      end;
    end
  else out("0");   { output the module number, or zero if it was undefined }
  out(":"); ⟨ Output the text of the module name 214 ⟩,
  out2("\")("X");
  end
```

This code is used in section 208.

214. ⟨ Output the text of the module name 214 ⟩ ≡
```
  k ← byte_start[cur_name]; w ← cur_name mod ww; k_limit ← byte_start[cur_name + ww];
  cur_mod_name ← cur_name;
  while k < k_limit do
    begin b ← byte_mem[w, k]; incr(k);
    if b = "@" then ⟨ Skip next character, give error if not '@' 215 ⟩;
    if b ≠ "|" then out(b)
    else begin ⟨ Copy the Pascal text into buffer[(limit + 1) . . j] 216 ⟩;
```

$save\_loc \leftarrow loc$; $save\_limit \leftarrow limit$; $loc \leftarrow limit + 2$; $limit \leftarrow j + 1$; $buffer[limit] \leftarrow$ "|";
$\quad$ $output\_Pascal$; $loc \leftarrow save\_loc$; $limit \leftarrow save\_limit$;
$\quad\quad$ **end**;
$\quad$ **end**

This code is used in section 213.

215. $\langle$ Skip next character, give error if not '@' 215 $\rangle \equiv$
$\quad$ **begin if** $byte\_mem[w, k] \neq$ "@" **then**
$\quad\quad$ **begin** $print\_nl($´!␣Illegal␣control␣code␣in␣section␣name:´$)$; $print\_nl($´<´$)$;
$\quad\quad$ $print\_id(cur\_mod\_name)$; $print($´>␣´$)$; $mark\_error$;
$\quad\quad$ **end**;
$\quad$ $incr(k)$;
$\quad$ **end**

This code is used in section 214.

216. The Pascal text enclosed in | ... | should not contain '|' characters, except within strings. We put a '|' at the front of the buffer, so that an error message that displays the whole buffer will look a little bit sensible. The variable *string_delimiter* is zero outside of strings, otherwise it equals the delimiter that began the string being copied.

$\langle$ Copy the Pascal text into $buffer[(limit + 1) .. j]$ 216 $\rangle \equiv$
$\quad$ $j \leftarrow limit + 1$; $buffer[j] \leftarrow$ "|"; $string\_delimiter \leftarrow 0$;
$\quad$ **loop begin if** $k \geq k\_limit$ **then**
$\quad\quad$ **begin** $print\_nl($´!␣Pascal␣text␣in␣section␣name␣didn´´t␣end:´$)$; $print\_nl($´<´$)$;
$\quad\quad$ $print\_id(cur\_mod\_name)$; $print($´>␣´$)$; $mark\_error$; **goto** $found$;
$\quad\quad$ **end**;
$\quad\quad$ $b \leftarrow byte\_mem[w, k]$; $incr(k)$;
$\quad\quad$ **if** $b =$ "@" **then** $\langle$ Copy a control code into the buffer 217 $\rangle$
$\quad\quad$ **else begin if** $(b =$ """") $\vee$ $(b =$ "´") **then**
$\quad\quad\quad$ **if** $string\_delimiter = 0$ **then** $string\_delimiter \leftarrow b$
$\quad\quad\quad$ **else if** $string\_delimiter = b$ **then** $string\_delimiter \leftarrow 0$;
$\quad\quad\quad$ **if** $(b \neq$ "|") $\vee$ $(string\_delimiter \neq 0)$ **then**
$\quad\quad\quad$ **begin if** $j > long\_buf\_size - 3$ **then** $overflow($´buffer´$)$;
$\quad\quad\quad$ $incr(j)$; $buffer[j] \leftarrow b$;
$\quad\quad\quad$ **end**
$\quad\quad$ **else goto** $found$;
$\quad\quad$ **end**;
$\quad$ **end**;
$found$:

This code is used in section 214.

217. $\langle$ Copy a control code into the buffer 217 $\rangle \equiv$
$\quad$ **begin if** $j > long\_buf\_size - 4$ **then** $overflow($´buffer´$)$;
$\quad$ $buffer[j + 1] \leftarrow$ "@"; $buffer[j + 2] \leftarrow byte\_mem[w, k]$; $j \leftarrow j + 2$; $incr(k)$;
$\quad$ **end**

This code is used in section 216.

218. Phase two processing. We have assembled enough pieces of the puzzle in order to be ready to specify the processing in WEAVE's main pass over the source file. Phase two is analogous to phase one, except that more work is involved because we must actually output the TEX material instead of merely looking at the WEB specifications.

⟨ Phase II: Read all the text again and translate it to TEX form 218 ⟩ ≡
   reset_input; *print_nl*(`Writing␣the␣output␣file...`); *module_count* ← 0; *copy_limbo*;
   finish_line; *flush_buffer*(0, *false*);   { insert a blank line, it looks nice }
   while ¬*input_has_ended* **do** ⟨ Translate the current module 220 ⟩

This code is used in section 261.

---

219. The output file will contain the control sequence \Y between non-null sections of a module, e.g., between the TEX and definition parts if both are nonempty. This puts a little white space between the parts when they are printed. However, we don't want \Y to occur between two definitions within a single module. The variables *out_line* or *out_ptr* will change if a section is non-null, so the following macros '*save_position*' and '*emit_space_if_needed*' are able to handle the situation:

   define *save_position* ≡ *save_line* ← *out_line*; *save_place* ← *out_ptr*
   define *emit_space_if_needed* ≡
        if (*save_line* ≠ *out_line*) ∨ (*save_place* ≠ *out_ptr*) **then** *out2*("\")("Y")

⟨ Globals in the outer block 9 ⟩ +≡
save_line: *integer*;   { former value of *out_line* }
save_place: *sixteen_bits*;   { former value of *out_ptr* }

---

220. ⟨ Translate the current module 220 ⟩ ≡
   begin *incr*(*module_count*);
   ⟨ Output the code for the beginning of a new module 221 ⟩;
   save_position;
   ⟨ Translate the TEX part of the current module 222 ⟩;
   ⟨ Translate the definition part of the current module 225 ⟩;
   ⟨ Translate the Pascal part of the current module 230 ⟩;
   ⟨ Show cross references to this module 233 ⟩;
   ⟨ Output the code for the end of a module 238 ⟩;
   end

This code is used in section 218.

---

221. Modules beginning with the WEB control sequence '@␣' start in the output with the TEX control sequence '\M', followed by the module number. Similarly, '@*' modules lead to the control sequence '\N'. If this is a changed module, we put * just before the module number.

⟨ Output the code for the beginning of a new module 221 ⟩ ≡
   out("\");
   if *buffer*[*loc* − 1] ≠ "*" **then** *out*("M")
   else begin *out*("N"); *print*(`*`, *module_count* : 1); *update_terminal*;   { print a progress report }
     end;
   out_mod(*module_count*); *out2*(".")("␣")

This code is used in section 220.

---

222. In the TEX part of a module, we simply copy the source text, except that index entries are not copied and Pascal text within | ... | is translated.

⟨ Translate the TEX part of the current module 222 ⟩ ≡
  repeat *next_control* ← *copy_TeX* ;
    case *next_control* **of**
    "|": **begin** *init_stack* ; *output_Pascal* ;
      end;
    "@": *out*("@");
    octal: ⟨ Translate an octal constant appearing in TEX text 223 ⟩;
    hex: ⟨ Translate a hexadecimal constant appearing in TEX text 224 ⟩;
    TeX_string, *xref_roman*, *xref_wildcard*, *xref_typewriter*, *module_name*: **begin** *loc* ← *loc* − 2;
      next_control ← *get_next* ;   { skip to @> }
      if *next_control* = *TeX_string* **then**
        err_print(´!␣TeX␣string␣should␣be␣in␣Pascal␣text␣only´);
      end;
    begin_comment, *end_comment*, *check_sum*, *thin_space*, *math_break*, *line_break*, *big_line_break*,
        no_line_break, *join*, *pseudo_semi*: *err_print*(´!␣You␣can´´t␣do␣that␣in␣TeX␣text´);
    othercases *do_nothing*
    endcases;
  until *next_control* ≥ *format*

This code is used in section 220.

223.   ⟨ Translate an octal constant appearing in TEX text 223 ⟩ ≡
  begin *out3*("\")("O")("{");
  while (*buffer*[*loc*] ≥ "0") ∧ (*buffer*[*loc*] ≤ "7") **do**
    begin *out*(*buffer*[*loc*]); *incr*(*loc*);
    end;   { since *buffer*[*limit*] = "␣", this loop will end }
  out("}");
  end

This code is used in section 222.

224.   ⟨ Translate a hexadecimal constant appearing in TEX text 224 ⟩ ≡
  begin *out3*("\")("H")("{");
  while ((*buffer*[*loc*] ≥ "0") ∧ (*buffer*[*loc*] ≤ "9")) ∨ ((*buffer*[*loc*] ≥ "A") ∧ (*buffer*[*loc*] ≤ "F")) **do**
    begin *out*(*buffer*[*loc*]); *incr*(*loc*);
    end;
  out("}");
  end

This code is used in section 222.

225.   When we get to the following code we have *next_control* ≥ *format*, and the token
memory is in its initial empty state.

⟨ Translate the definition part of the current module 225 ⟩ ≡
  if *next_control* ≤ *definition* **then**   { definition part non-empty }
    begin *emit_space_if_needed* ; *save_position* ;
    end;
  while *next_control* ≤ *definition* **do**   { *format* or *definition* }
    begin *init_stack* ;
    if *next_control* = *definition* **then** ⟨ Start a macro definition 227 ⟩
    else ⟨ Start a format definition 228 ⟩;
    outer_parse ; *finish_Pascal* ;

end

This code is used in section 220.

226. The *finish_Pascal* procedure outputs the translation of the current scraps, preceded by the control sequence '\P' and followed by the control sequence '\par'. It also restores the token and scrap memories to their initial empty state.

A *force* token is appended to the current scraps before translation takes place, so that the translation will normally end with \6 or \7 (the TₑX macros for *force* and *big_force*). This \6 or \7 is replaced by the concluding \par or by \Y\par.

procedure *finish_Pascal*; { finishes a definition or a Pascal part }
  var *p*: *text_pointer*; { translation of the scraps }
  begin *out2*("\")("P"); *app_tok*(*force*); *app_comment*; *p* ← *translate*; *app*(*p* + *tok_flag*);
  make_output; { output the list }
  if *out_ptr* > 1 **then**
    if *out_buf*[*out_ptr* − 1] = "\" **then**
      if *out_buf*[*out_ptr*] = "6" **then** *out_ptr* ← *out_ptr* − 2
      else if *out_buf*[*out_ptr*] = "7" **then** *out_buf*[*out_ptr*] ← "Y";
  out4("\")("p")("a")("r"); *finish_line*;
  stat if *text_ptr* > *max_txt_ptr* **then** *max_txt_ptr* ← *text_ptr*;
  if *tok_ptr* > *max_tok_ptr* **then** *max_tok_ptr* ← *tok_ptr*;
  if *scrap_ptr* > *max_scr_ptr* **then** *max_scr_ptr* ← *scrap_ptr*;
  tats
  tok_ptr ← 1; *text_ptr* ← 1; *scrap_ptr* ← 0; { forget the tokens and the scraps }
  end;

227. ⟨ Start a macro definition 227 ⟩ ≡
  begin *sc2*("\")("D")(*intro*); { this will produce '**define** ' }
  next_control ← *get_next*;
  if *next_control* ≠ *identifier* **then** *err_print*(´!␣Improper␣macro␣definition´)
  else *sc1*(*id_flag* + *id_lookup*(*normal*))(*math*);
  next_control ← *get_next*;
  end

This code is used in section 225.

228. ⟨ Start a format definition 228 ⟩ ≡
  begin *sc2*("\")("F")(*intro*); { this will produce '**format** ' }
  next_control ← *get_next*;
  if *next_control* = *identifier* **then**
    begin *sc1*(*id_flag* + *id_lookup*(*normal*))(*math*); *next_control* ← *get_next*;
    if *next_control* = *equivalence_sign* **then**
      begin *sc2*("\")("S")(*math*); { output an equivalence sign }
      next_control ← *get_next*;
      if *next_control* = *identifier* **then**
        begin *sc1*(*id_flag* + *id_lookup*(*normal*))(*math*); *sc0*(*semi*);
          { insert an invisible semicolon }
        next_control ← *get_next*;
        end;
      end;
    end;

if *scrap_ptr* $\neq$ 5 **then** *err_print*(´!␣Improper␣format␣definition´);
end

This code is used in section 225.

229.   Finally, when the TEX and definition parts have been treated, we have *next_control* $\geq$ *begin_Pascal*. We will make the global variable *this_module* point to the current module name, if it has a name.

⟨ Globals in the outer block 9 ⟩ +≡
this_module: *name_pointer*;   { the current module name, or zero }

230.   ⟨ Translate the Pascal part of the current module 230 ⟩ ≡
   this_module ← 0;
   if *next_control* $\leq$ *module_name* **then**
     begin *emit_space_if_needed*; *init_stack*;
     if *next_control* = *begin_Pascal* **then** *next_control* ← *get_next*
     else begin *this_module* ← *cur_module*; ⟨ Check that = or ≡ follows this module name, and
        emit the scraps to start the module definition 231 ⟩;
       end;
     while *next_control* $\leq$ *module_name* **do**
       begin *outer_parse*; ⟨ Emit the scrap for a module name if present 232 ⟩;
       end;
     finish_Pascal;
     end

This code is used in section 220.

231.   ⟨ Check that = or ≡ follows this module name, and emit the scraps to start the module
     definition 231 ⟩ ≡
   repeat *next_control* ← *get_next*;
   until *next_control* $\neq$ "+";   { allow optional '+=' }
   if (*next_control* $\neq$ "=") $\wedge$ (*next_control* $\neq$ *equivalence_sign*) **then**
     err_print(´!␣You␣need␣an␣=␣sign␣after␣the␣section␣name´)
   else *next_control* ← *get_next*;
   if *out_ptr* > 1 **then**
     if (*out_buf*[*out_ptr*] = "Y") $\wedge$ (*out_buf*[*out_ptr* − 1] = "\") **then**
       begin *app*(*backup*);   { the module name will be flush left }
       end;
   sc1(*mod_flag* + *this_module*)(*mod_scrap*); *cur_xref* ← *xref*[*this_module*];
   if *num*(*cur_xref*) $\neq$ *module_count* + *def_flag* **then**
     begin *sc3*(*math_rel*)("+")("}")(*math*);   { module name is multiply defined }
     this_module ← 0;   { so we won't give cross-reference info here }
     end;
   sc2("\")("S")(*math*);   { output an equivalence sign }
   sc1(*force*)(*semi*);   { this forces a line break unless '@+' follows }

This code is used in section 230.

232.   ⟨ Emit the scrap for a module name if present 232 ⟩ ≡
   if *next_control* < *module_name* **then**
     begin *err_print*(´!␣You␣can´´t␣do␣that␣in␣Pascal␣text´); *next_control* ← *get_next*;
     end

```
    else if next_control = module_name then
        begin sc1 (mod_flag + cur_module)(mod_scrap);  next_control ← get_next;
        end
```

This code is used in section 230.

233. Cross references relating to a named module are given after the module ends.

⟨ Show cross references to this module 233 ⟩ ≡
```
    if this_module > 0 then
        begin ⟨ Rearrange the list pointed to by cur_xref 235 ⟩;
        footnote(def_flag);  footnote(0);
        end
```

This code is used in section 220.

234. To rearrange the order of the linked list of cross references, we need four more variables that point to cross reference entries. We'll end up with a list pointed to by *cur_xref*.

⟨ Globals in the outer block 9 ⟩ +≡
next_xref, *this_xref*, *first_xref*, *mid_xref*: *xref_number*;   { pointer variables for rearranging a list }

235. We want to rearrange the cross reference list so that all the entries with *def_flag* come first, in ascending order; then come all the other entries, in ascending order. There may be no entries in either one or both of these categories.

⟨ Rearrange the list pointed to by *cur_xref* 235 ⟩ ≡
```
    first_xref ← xref[this_module];  this_xref ← xlink(first_xref);  { bypass current module number }
    if num(this_xref) > def_flag then
        begin mid_xref ← this_xref;  cur_xref ← 0;  { this value doesn't matter }
        repeat next_xref ← xlink(this_xref);  xlink(this_xref) ← cur_xref;  cur_xref ← this_xref;
            this_xref ← next_xref;
        until num(this_xref) ≤ def_flag;
        xlink(first_xref) ← cur_xref;
        end
    else mid_xref ← 0;   { first list null }
    cur_xref ← 0;
    while this_xref ≠ 0 do
        begin next_xref ← xlink(this_xref);  xlink(this_xref) ← cur_xref;  cur_xref ← this_xref;
        this_xref ← next_xref;
        end;
    if mid_xref > 0 then  xlink(mid_xref) ← cur_xref
    else xlink(first_xref) ← cur_xref;
    cur_xref ← xlink(first_xref)
```

This code is used in section 233.

236. The *footnote* procedure gives cross reference information about multiply defined module names (if the *flag* parameter is *def_flag*), or about the uses of a module name (if the *flag* parameter is zero). It assumes that *cur_xref* points to the first cross-reference entry of interest, and it leaves *cur_xref* pointing to the first element not printed. Typical outputs: '\A␣section 101.'; '\U␣sections 370 and 1009.'; '\A␣sections 8, 27*, and 64.'.

procedure *footnote*(*flag* : *sixteen_bits*);   { outputs module cross-references }
  label *done*, *exit*;
  var *q*: *xref_number*;   { cross-reference pointer variable }
  begin if *num*(*cur_xref*) ≤ *flag* **then return**;
  finish_line; *out*("\");
  if *flag* = 0 **then** *out*("U") **else** *out*("A");
  out4(" ")("s")("e")("c"); *out4*("t")("i")("o")("n");
  ⟨ Output all the module numbers on the reference list *cur_xref* 237 ⟩;
  out(".");
exit: **end**;

237.   The following code distinguishes three cases, according as the number of cross references is one, two, or more than two. Variable *q* points to the first cross reference, and the last link is a zero.

⟨ Output all the module numbers on the reference list *cur_xref* 237 ⟩ ≡
  q ← *cur_xref*;
  if *num*(*xlink*(*q*)) > *flag* **then** *out*("s");   { plural }
  out("~");
  loop begin *out_mod*(*num*(*cur_xref*) − *flag*); *cur_xref* ← *xlink*(*cur_xref*);
      { point to the next cross reference to output }
    if *num*(*cur_xref*) ≤ *flag* **then goto** *done*;
    if (*num*(*xlink*(*cur_xref*)) > *flag*) ∨ (*cur_xref* ≠ *xlink*(*q*)) **then** *out*(",");
        { not the last of two }
    out(" ");
    if *num*(*xlink*(*cur_xref*)) ≤ *flag* **then** *out4*("a")("n")("d")("~");   { the last }
    end;
done:

This code is used in section 236.

238.   ⟨ Output the code for the end of a module 238 ⟩ ≡
  out3("\")("f")("i"); *finish_line*; *flush_buffer*(0, *false*);   { insert a blank line, it looks nice }
This code is used in section 220.

239. Phase three processing.   We are nearly finished! WEAVE's only remaining task is to write out the index, after sorting the identifiers and index entries.

⟨ Phase III: Output the cross-reference index 239 ⟩ ≡
  phase_three ← *true*; *print_nl*(´Writing the index...´);
  if *change_exists* **then**
    begin *finish_line*; ⟨ Tell about changed modules 241 ⟩;
    end;
  finish_line; *out4*("\")("i")("n")("x"); *finish_line*; ⟨ Do the first pass of sorting 243 ⟩;
  ⟨ Sort and output the index 250 ⟩;
  out4("\")("f")("i")("n"); *finish_line*; ⟨ Output all the module names 257 ⟩;
  out4("\")("c")("o")("n"); *finish_line*; *print*(´Done.´);
This code is used in section 261.

240.   Just before the index comes a list of all the changed modules, including the index module itself.

⟨ Globals in the outer block 9 ⟩ +≡
k_module: 0 .. *max_modules*;   { runs through the modules }

241.   ⟨ Tell about changed modules 241 ⟩ ≡
  begin   { remember that the index is already marked as changed }
  k_module ← 1;   *out4*("\")("c")("h")("␣");
  while *k_module* < *module_count* **do**
    begin if *changed_module*[*k_module*] **then**
      begin *out_mod*(*k_module*);   *out2*(",")("␣");
      end;
    incr(*k_module*);
    end;
  out_mod(*k_module*);   *out*(".");
  end
This code is used in section 239.

242.   A left-to-right radix sorting method is used, since this makes it easy to adjust the collating sequence and since the running time will be at worst proportional to the total length of all entries in the index. We put the identifiers into 102 different lists based on their first characters. (Uppercase letters are put into the same list as the corresponding lowercase letters, since we want to have '$t <$ *TeX* $<$ **to**'.) The list for character *c* begins at location *bucket*[*c*] and continues through the *blink* array.

⟨ Globals in the outer block 9 ⟩ +≡
bucket: **array** [*ASCII_code*] **of** *name_pointer*;
next_name: *name_pointer*;   { successor of *cur_name* when sorting }
c: *ASCII_code*;   { index into *bucket* }
h: 0 .. *hash_size*;   { index into *hash* }
blink: **array** [0 .. *max_names*] **of** *sixteen_bits*;   { links in the buckets }

243.   To begin the sorting, we go through all the hash lists and put each entry having a nonempty cross-reference list into the proper bucket.
⟨ Do the first pass of sorting 243 ⟩ ≡
  for *c* ← 0 **to** 127 **do** *bucket*[*c*] ← 0;
  for *h* ← 0 **to** *hash_size* − 1 **do**
    begin *next_name* ← *hash*[*h*];
    while *next_name* ≠ 0 **do**
      begin *cur_name* ← *next_name*;   *next_name* ← *link*[*cur_name*];
      if *xref*[*cur_name*] ≠ 0 **then**
        begin *c* ← *byte_mem*[*cur_name* **mod** *ww*, *byte_start*[*cur_name*]];
        if (*c* ≤ "Z") ∧ (*c* ≥ "A") **then** *c* ← *c* + ´40;
        blink[*cur_name*] ← *bucket*[*c*];   *bucket*[*c*] ← *cur_name*;
        end;
      end;
    end
This code is used in section 239.

244.   During the sorting phase we shall use the *cat* and *trans* arrays from WEAVE's parsing algorithm and rename them *depth* and *head*. They now represent a stack of identifier lists for all the index entries that have not yet been output. The variable *sort_ptr* tells how many such lists are present; the lists are output in reverse order (first *sort_ptr*, then *sort_ptr* − 1, etc.). The *j*th list starts at *head*[*j*], and if the first *k* characters of all entries on this list are known to be equal we have *depth*[*j*] = *k*.

> **define** *depth* ≡ *cat*   { reclaims memory that is no longer needed for parsing }
> **define** *head* ≡ *trans*   { ditto }
> **define** *sort_ptr* ≡ *scrap_ptr*   { ditto }
> **define** *max_sorts* ≡ *max_scraps*   { ditto }

⟨ Globals in the outer block 9 ⟩ +≡
cur_depth: *eight_bits*;   { depth of current buckets }
cur_byte: 0 .. *max_bytes*;   { index into *byte_mem* }
cur_bank: 0 .. *ww* − 1;   { row of *byte_mem* }
cur_val: *sixteen_bits*;   { current cross reference number }
> **stat** *max_sort_ptr*: 0 .. *max_sorts*; **tats**   { largest value of *sort_ptr* }

245.   ⟨ Set initial values 10 ⟩ +≡
> **stat** *max_sort_ptr* ← 0; **tats**

246.   The desired alphabetic order is specified by the *collate* array; namely, *collate*[0] < *collate*[1] < · · · < *collate*[100].

⟨ Globals in the outer block 9 ⟩ +≡
collate: **array** [0 .. 100] **of** *ASCII_code*;   { collation order }

247.   ⟨ Local variables for initialization 16 ⟩ +≡
c: *ASCII_code*;   { used to initialize *collate* }

248.   We use the order null < ␣ < other characters < _ < A = a < · · · < Z = z < 0 < · · · < 9.

⟨ Set initial values 10 ⟩ +≡
>   *collate*[0] ← 0;   *collate*[1] ← "␣";
>   **for** *c* ← 1 **to** "␣" − 1 **do** *collate*[*c* + 1] ← *c*;
>   **for** *c* ← "␣" + 1 **to** "0" − 1 **do** *collate*[*c*] ← *c*;
>   **for** *c* ← "9" + 1 **to** "A" − 1 **do** *collate*[*c* − 10] ← *c*;
>   **for** *c* ← "Z" + 1 **to** "_" − 1 **do** *collate*[*c* − 36] ← *c*;
>   *collate*["_" − 36] ← "_" + 1;
>   **for** *c* ← "z" + 1 **to** 126 **do** *collate*[*c* − 63] ← *c*;
>   *collate*[64] ← "_";
>   **for** *c* ← "a" **to** "z" **do** *collate*[*c* − "a" + 65] ← *c*;
>   **for** *c* ← "0" **to** "9" **do** *collate*[*c* − "0" + 91] ← *c*;

249.   Procedure *unbucket* goes through the buckets and adds nonempty lists to the stack, using the collating sequence specified in the *collate* array. The parameter to *unbucket* tells the current depth in the buckets. Any two sequences that agree in their first 255 character positions are regarded as identical.

> **define** *infinity* = 255   { ∞ (approximately) }

procedure *unbucket*(*d* : *eight_bits*);   { empties buckets having depth *d* }
>   **var** *c*: *ASCII_code*;   { index into *bucket* }

begin for $c \leftarrow 100$ **downto** 0 **do**
    if $bucket[collate[c]] > 0$ **then**
        begin if $sort\_ptr > max\_sorts$ **then** $overflow(\text{'sorting'})$;
        $incr(sort\_ptr)$;
        stat if $sort\_ptr > max\_sort\_ptr$ **then** $max\_sort\_ptr \leftarrow sort\_ptr$; **tats**
        if $c = 0$ **then** $depth[sort\_ptr] \leftarrow infinity$
        else $depth[sort\_ptr] \leftarrow d$;
        $head[sort\_ptr] \leftarrow bucket[collate[c]]$; $bucket[collate[c]] \leftarrow 0$;
        end;
    end;

250. ⟨ Sort and output the index 250 ⟩ ≡
  $sort\_ptr \leftarrow 0$; $unbucket(1)$;
  while $sort\_ptr > 0$ **do**
    begin $cur\_depth \leftarrow cat[sort\_ptr]$;
    if $(blink[head[sort\_ptr]] = 0) \vee (cur\_depth = infinity)$ **then**
      ⟨ Output index entries for the list at $sort\_ptr$ 252 ⟩
    else ⟨ Split the list at $sort\_ptr$ into further lists 251 ⟩;
    end

This code is used in section 239.

251. ⟨ Split the list at $sort\_ptr$ into further lists 251 ⟩ ≡
  begin $next\_name \leftarrow head[sort\_ptr]$;
  repeat $cur\_name \leftarrow next\_name$; $next\_name \leftarrow blink[cur\_name]$;
    $cur\_byte \leftarrow byte\_start[cur\_name] + cur\_depth$; $cur\_bank \leftarrow cur\_name \bmod ww$;
    if $cur\_byte = byte\_start[cur\_name + ww]$ **then** $c \leftarrow 0$ { we hit the end of the name }
    else begin $c \leftarrow byte\_mem[cur\_bank, cur\_byte]$;
      if $(c \le \text{"Z"}) \wedge (c \ge \text{"A"})$ **then** $c \leftarrow c + '40$;
      end;
    $blink[cur\_name] \leftarrow bucket[c]$; $bucket[c] \leftarrow cur\_name$;
  until $next\_name = 0$;
  $decr(sort\_ptr)$; $unbucket(cur\_depth + 1)$;
  end

This code is used in section 250.

252. ⟨ Output index entries for the list at $sort\_ptr$ 252 ⟩ ≡
  begin $cur\_name \leftarrow head[sort\_ptr]$;
  debug if $trouble\_shooting$ **then** $debug\_help$; **gubed**
  repeat $out2(\text{"\textbackslash"})(\text{":"})$; ⟨ Output the name at cur_name 253 ⟩;
    ⟨ Output the cross-references at cur_name 254 ⟩;
    $cur\_name \leftarrow blink[cur\_name]$;
  until $cur\_name = 0$;
  $decr(sort\_ptr)$;
  end

This code is used in section 250.

253. ⟨ Output the name at cur_name 253 ⟩ ≡
  case $ilk[cur\_name]$ **of**
  $normal$: **if** $length(cur\_name) = 1$ **then** $out2(\text{"\textbackslash"})(\text{"|"})$ **else** $out2(\text{"\textbackslash"})(\text{"\textbackslash"})$;

> *roman*: *do_nothing*;
> *wildcard*: *out2*("\")("9");
> *typewriter*: *out2*("\")(".");
> **othercases** *out2*("\")("&")
> **endcases**;
> *out_name*(*cur_name*)

This code is used in section 252.

254.   Section numbers that are to be underlined are enclosed in '\[...]'.

⟨ Output the cross-references at *cur_name* 254 ⟩ ≡
   ⟨ Invert the cross-reference list at *cur_name*, making *cur_xref* the head 255 ⟩;
   repeat *out2*(",")("␣"); *cur_val* ← *num*(*cur_xref*);
     if *cur_val* < *def_flag* **then** *out_mod*(*cur_val*)
     else begin *out2*("\")("["); *out_mod*(*cur_val* − *def_flag*); *out*("]");
       end;
    cur_xref ← *xlink*(*cur_xref*);
   until *cur_xref* = 0;
   out("."); *finish_line*

This code is used in section 252.

255.   List inversion is best thought of as popping elements off one stack and pushing them onto another. In this case *cur_xref* will be the head of the stack that we push things onto.

⟨ Invert the cross-reference list at *cur_name*, making *cur_xref* the head 255 ⟩ ≡
   this_xref ← *xref*[*cur_name*]; *cur_xref* ← 0;
   repeat *next_xref* ← *xlink*(*this_xref*); *xlink*(*this_xref*) ← *cur_xref*; *cur_xref* ← *this_xref*;
    this_xref ← *next_xref*;
   until *this_xref* = 0

This code is used in section 254.

256.   The following recursive procedure walks through the tree of module names and prints them.

procedure *mod_print*(*p* : *name_pointer*);   { print all module names in subtree *p* }
  begin if *p* > 0 **then**
    begin *mod_print*(*llink*[*p*]);
    out2("\")(":");
    tok_ptr ← 1; *text_ptr* ← 1; *scrap_ptr* ← 0; *init_stack*; *app*(*p* + *mod_flag*); *make_output*;
    footnote(0);   { *cur_xref* was set by *make_output* }
    finish_line;
    mod_print(*rlink*[*p*]);
    end;
  end;

257.   ⟨ Output all the module names 257 ⟩ ≡ *mod_print*(*root*)
This code is used in section 239.

258.   Debugging.   The Pascal debugger with which **WEAVE** was developed allows breakpoints to be set, and variables can be read and changed, but procedures cannot be executed. Therefore a '*debug_help*' procedure has been inserted in the main loops of each phase of the program; when *ddt* and *dd* are set to appropriate values, symbolic printouts of various tables will appear.

The idea is to set a breakpoint inside the *debug_help* routine, at the place of '*breakpoint*:' below. Then when *debug_help* is to be activated, set *trouble_shooting* equal to *true*. The *debug_help* routine will prompt you for values of *ddt* and *dd*, discontinuing this when $ddt \leq 0$; thus you type $2n + 1$ integers, ending with zero or a negative number. Then control either passes to the breakpoint, allowing you to look at and/or change variables (if you typed zero), or to exit the routine (if you typed a negative value).

Another global variable, *debug_cycle*, can be used to skip silently past calls on *debug_help*. If you set *debug_cycle* > 1, the program stops only every *debug_cycle* times *debug_help* is called; however, any error stop will set *debug_cycle* to zero.

⟨ Globals in the outer block 9 ⟩ +≡
    debug *trouble_shooting*: *boolean*,   { is *debug_help* wanted? }
ddt: *integer*;   { operation code for the *debug_help* routine }
dd: *integer*;   { operand in procedures performed by *debug_help* }
debug_cycle: *integer*;   { threshold for *debug_help* stopping }
debug_skipped: *integer*;   { we have skipped this many *debug_help* calls }
term_in: *text_file*;   { the user's terminal as an input file }
    gubed

259. The debugging routine needs to read from the user's terminal.

⟨ Set initial values 10 ⟩ +≡
    debug *trouble_shooting* ← *true*; *debug_cycle* ← 1; *debug_skipped* ← 0; *tracing* ← 0;
    trouble_shooting ← *false*; *debug_cycle* ← 99999;   { use these when it almost works }
    reset(*term_in*, ˈTTY:ˈ, ˈ/Iˈ);   { open *term_in* as the terminal, don't do a *get* }
    gubed

260.   **define** *breakpoint* = 888   { place where a breakpoint is desirable }

  debug procedure *debug_help*;   { routine to display various things }
  label *breakpoint*, *exit*;
  var *k*: *integer*;   { index into various arrays }
  begin *incr*(*debug_skipped*);
  if *debug_skipped* < *debug_cycle* **then return**;
  debug_skipped ← 0;
  loop begin *write*(*term_out*, ˈ#ˈ); *update_terminal*;   { prompt }
    read(*term_in*, *ddt*);   { read a list of integers }
    if *ddt* < 0 **then return**
    else if *ddt* = 0 **then**
      begin goto *breakpoint*; @\   { go to every label at least once }
      breakpoint: *ddt* ← 0; @\
      end
    else begin *read*(*term_in*, *dd*);
      case *ddt* **of**
      1: *print_id*(*dd*);
      2: *print_text*(*dd*);
      3: **for** *k* ← 1 **to** *dd* **do** *print*(*xchr*[*buffer*[*k*]]);
      4: **for** *k* ← 1 **to** *dd* **do** *print*(*xchr*[*mod_text*[*k*]]);
      5: **for** *k* ← 1 **to** *out_ptr* **do** *print*(*xchr*[*out_buf*[*k*]]);

```
      6: for k ← 1 to dd do
           begin print_cat(cat[k]); print(´␣´);
           end;
        othercases print(´?´)
        endcases;
        end;
    end;
exit: end;
  gubed
```

261. The main program.   Let's put it all together now: WEAVE starts and ends here.

The main procedure has been split into three sub-procedures in order to keep certain Pascal compilers from overflowing their capacity.

procedure *Phase_I*;
  begin ⟨ Phase I: Read all the user's text and store the cross references 109⟩;
  end;

procedure *Phase_II*;
  begin ⟨ Phase II: Read all the text again and translate it to TeX form 218⟩;
  end;

  begin *initialize*; { beginning of the main program }
  print_ln(*banner*); { print a "banner line" }
  ⟨ Store all the reserved words 64⟩;
  Phase_I; *Phase_II*;
  ⟨ Phase III: Output the cross-reference index 239⟩;
  ⟨ Check that all changes have been read 85⟩;
end_of_WEAVE: **stat** ⟨ Print statistics about memory usage 262⟩; **tats**
{ here files should be closed if the operating system requires it }
  ⟨ Print the job *history* 263⟩;
  end.

262.   ⟨ Print statistics about memory usage 262⟩ ≡

  print_nl(´Memory␣usage␣statistics:␣´, *name_ptr* : 1, ´␣names,␣´, *xref_ptr* : 1,
      ´␣cross␣references,␣´, *byte_ptr*[0] : 1);
  for *cur_bank* ← 1 **to** *ww* − 1 **do** *print*(´+´, *byte_ptr*[*cur_bank*] : 1);
  print(´␣bytes;´); *print_nl*(´parsing␣required␣´, *max_scr_ptr* : 1, ´␣scraps,␣´,
      max_txt_ptr : 1, ´␣texts,␣´, *max_tok_ptr* : 1, ´␣tokens,␣´, *max_stack_ptr* : 1, ´␣levels;´);
  print_nl(´sorting␣required␣´, *max_sort_ptr* : 1, ´␣levels.´)

This code is used in section 261.

263.   Some implementations may wish to pass the *history* value to the operating system so that it can be used to govern whether or not other programs are started. Here we simply report the history to the user.

⟨ Print the job *history* 263⟩ ≡
  case *history* **of**
  spotless: *print_nl*(´(No␣errors␣were␣found.)´);
  harmless_message: *print_nl*(´(Did␣you␣see␣the␣warning␣message␣above?)´);
  error_message: *print_nl*(´(Pardon␣me,␣but␣I␣think␣I␣spotted␣something␣wrong.)´);
  fatal_message: *print_nl*(´(That␣was␣a␣fatal␣error,␣my␣friend.)´);

end { there are no other cases }

This code is used in section 261.

264. System-dependent changes. This module should be replaced, if necessary, by changes to the program that are necessary to make WEAVE work at a particular installation. It is usually best to design your change file so that all changes to previous modules preserve the module numbering; then everybody's version will be consistent with the printed program. More extensive changes, which introduce new modules, can be inserted here; then only the index itself will get a new module number.

265. Index. If you have read and understood the code for Phase III above, you know what is in this index and how it got here. All modules in which an identifier is used are listed with that identifier, except that reserved words are indexed only when they appear in format definitions, and the appearances of identifiers in module names are not indexed. Underlined entries correspond to where the identifier was declared. Error messages, control sequences put into the output, and a few other things like "recursion" are indexed here too.

Unknown control code: 87.

until_like: <u>42</u>, 64, 193.

up_to: <u>95</u>.

update_terminal: <u>22</u>, 31, 110, 221, 260.

var_head: <u>140</u>, 142, 143, 148, 149, 162, 163, 170, 193.

var_like: <u>42</u>, 64, 111, 193.

verbatim: <u>86</u>, 87, 100, 107, 185, 189.

Verbatim string didn't end: 107.

w: <u>44</u>, <u>58</u>, <u>66</u>, <u>69</u>, <u>131</u>, <u>208</u>.

WEAVE: <u>2</u>.

WEB file ended...: 79.

web_file: <u>2</u>, <u>23</u>, 24, 32, 71, 73, 79, 83, 85.

Where is the match...: 76, 80, 84.

wi: <u>40</u>, 41.

wildcard: <u>42</u>, 111, 253.

write: 20, 122, 124, 260.

write_ln: 20, 122.

ww: 8, <u>37</u>, 38, 39, 40, 41, 44, 50, 58, 61, 62, 66, 67, 68, 69, 131, 208, 209, 214, 243, 244, 251, 262.

xchr: <u>13</u>, 14, 16, 17, 18, 32, 44, 105, 122, 128, 146, 147, 182, 260.

xclause: 6.

xlink: <u>46</u>, 50, 51, 119, 213, 235, 237, 254, 255.

xlink_field: 46, <u>48</u>.

xmem: 46, <u>48</u>.

xord: <u>13</u>, 16, 18, 28.

xref: 36, <u>37</u>, 46, 49, 50, 51, 62, 67, 119, 213, 231, 235, 243, 255.

xref_number: <u>47</u>, 48, 50, 51, 118, 234, 236.

xref_ptr: 46, <u>48</u>, 49, 50, 51, 262.

xref_roman: <u>86</u>, 87, 93, 100, 111, 113, 186, 222.

xref_switch: 46, <u>48</u>, 49, 50, 93, 100, 101, 111, 113, 115.

xref_typewriter: <u>86</u>, 87, 93, 111, 113, 186, 222.

xref_wildcard: <u>86</u>, 87, 93, 111, 113, 186, 222.

You can't do that...: 222, 232.

You need an = sign...: 231.

⟨ Declaration of subprocedures for *translate* 150 ⟩   Used in section 179.
⟨ Declaration of the *app_comment* procedure 195 ⟩   Used in section 183.
⟨ Declaration of the *app_octal* and *app_hex* procedures 196 ⟩   Used in section 183.
⟨ Declaration of the *easy_cases* procedure 186 ⟩   Used in section 183.
⟨ Declaration of the *sub_cases* procedure 192 ⟩   Used in section 183.
⟨ Do special things when $c = $ "@", "\", "{","}"; **goto** *done* at end 92 ⟩   Used in section 91.
⟨ Do the first pass of sorting 243 ⟩   Used in section 239.
⟨ Emit the scrap for a module name if present 232 ⟩   Used in section 230.
⟨ Enter a new module name into the tree 67 ⟩   Used in section 66.
⟨ Enter a new name into the table at position *p* 62 ⟩   Used in section 58.
⟨ Error handling procedures 30, 31, 33 ⟩   Used in section 2.
⟨ Get a string 99 ⟩   Used in section 95.
⟨ Get an identifier 98 ⟩   Used in section 95.
⟨ Get control code and possible module name 100 ⟩   Used in section 95.
⟨ Globals in the outer block 9, 13, 20, 23, 25, 27, 29, 37, 39, 45, 48, 53, 55, 63, 65, 71, 73, 93, 108, 114,
         118, 121, 129, 144, 177, 202, 219, 229, 234, 240, 242, 244, 246, 258 ⟩   Used in section 2.
⟨ Go to *found* if *c* is a hexadecimal digit, otherwise set *scanning_hex* ← *false* 96 ⟩
         Used in section 95.
⟨ If end of name, **goto** *done* 104 ⟩   Used in section 103.
⟨ If semi-tracing, show the irreducible scraps 181 ⟩   Used in section 180.
⟨ If the current line starts with @y, report any discrepancies and **return** 80 ⟩
         Used in section 79.
⟨ If tracing, print an indication of where we are 182 ⟩   Used in section 179.
⟨ Invert the cross-reference list at *cur_name*, making *cur_xref* the head 255 ⟩
         Used in section 254.
⟨ Local variables for initialization 16, 40, 56, 247 ⟩   Used in section 2.
⟨ Look ahead for strongest line break, **goto** *reswitch* 212 ⟩   Used in section 211.
⟨ Make sure that there is room for at least four more scraps, six more tokens, and four more
         texts 187 ⟩   Used in section 185.
⟨ Make sure that there is room for at least seven more tokens, three more texts, and one
         more scrap 199 ⟩   Used in section 198.
⟨ Make sure the entries *cat*[*pp* .. (*pp* + 3)] are defined 176 ⟩   Used in section 175.
⟨ Match a production at *pp*, or increase *pp* if there is no match 149 ⟩   Used in section 175.
⟨ Move *buffer* and *limit* to *change_buffer* and *change_limit* 78 ⟩   Used in sections 75 and 79.
⟨ Output a control, look ahead in case of line breaks, possibly **goto** *reswitch* 211 ⟩
         Used in section 208.
⟨ Output a \math operator 210 ⟩   Used in section 208.
⟨ Output a module name 213 ⟩   Used in section 208.
⟨ Output all the module names 257 ⟩   Used in section 239.
⟨ Output all the module numbers on the reference list *cur_xref* 237 ⟩   Used in section 236.
⟨ Output an identifier 209 ⟩   Used in section 208.
⟨ Output index entries for the list at *sort_ptr* 252 ⟩   Used in section 250.
⟨ Output the code for the beginning of a new module 221 ⟩   Used in section 220.
⟨ Output the code for the end of a module 238 ⟩   Used in section 220.
⟨ Output the cross-references at *cur_name* 254 ⟩   Used in section 252.
⟨ Output the name at *cur_name* 253 ⟩   Used in section 252.

G.2 Modified Versions of TANGLE

The listings in this section illustrate how change files can be used to modify WEB programs.

Appendix G.2.1 is the result of applying the change file `tangle.wiz` (see Section F.2.1) to TANGLE, while Appendix G.2.2 corresponds to `paslines.ch` (see Section F.2.1).

G.2.1   Implementation Modification

1* Introduction.   This program converts a `WEB` file to a Pascal file. It is a modified form of a program written by D. E. Knuth in September, 1981.

For large `WEB` files one should have a large memory, since `TANGLE` keeps all the Pascal text in memory (in an abbreviated form). The program uses a few features of the local Pascal compiler that may need to be changed in other installations:

1) Case statements have a default.
2) Input-output routines may need to be adapted for use with a particular character set and/or for printing messages on the user's terminal.

These features are also present in the Pascal version of TeX, where they are used in a similar (but more complex) way. System-dependent portions of `TANGLE` can be identified by looking at the entries for 'system dependencies' in the index below.

The "banner line" defined here should be changed whenever `TANGLE` is modified.

We add a second decimal point and number to the main version number, so we can differentiate between changes to the standard `TANGLE` and changes local to the version for the hypothetical Whiz-Bang 5000 super-mini-micro-hyper-maxi-omni-computer.

define *banner* ≡ ´This␣is␣TANGLE,␣Whiz-Bang␣5000␣Version␣3.0.0´

2*   The program begins with a fairly normal header, made up of pieces that will mostly be filled in later. The `WEB` input comes from files *web_file* and *change_file*, the Pascal output goes to file *Pascal_file*, and the string pool output goes to file *pool*.

If it is necessary to abort the job because of a fatal error, the program calls the '*jump_out*' procedure, which aborts the program.

⟨Compiler directives 4⟩
program *TANGLE*;
  const ⟨Constants in the outer block 8⟩
  type ⟨Types in the outer block 11⟩
  var ⟨Globals in the outer block 9⟩
    ⟨Whiz-Bang 5000 procedures 190*⟩
    ⟨Error handling procedures 30⟩
  procedure *initialize*;
    var ⟨Local variables for initialization 16⟩
    begin ⟨Set initial values 10⟩
    end;

3*   Some of this code is optional for use when debugging only; such material is enclosed between the delimiters **debug** and **gubed**. Other parts, delimited by **stat** and **tats**, are optionally included if statistics about `TANGLE`'s memory usage are desired.

define *debug* ≡ @{   { change this to '*debug* ≡ ' when debugging }

define *gubed* ≡ @}   { change this to '*gubed* ≡ ' when debugging }
format *debug* ≡ *begin*
format *gubed* ≡ *end*

define *stat* ≡   { change this to '*stat* ≡ ' when gathering usage statistics }
define *tats* ≡   { change this to '*tats* ≡ ' when gathering usage statistics }
format *stat* ≡ *begin*
format *tats* ≡ *end*

7* We assume that **case** statements may include a default case that applies if no matching label is found. Thus, we shall use constructions like

> **case** x **of**
> 1: ⟨code for $x = 1$⟩;
> 3: ⟨code for $x = 3$⟩;
> **othercases** ⟨code for $x \neq 1$ and $x \neq 3$⟩
> **endcases**

since most Pascal compilers have plugged this hole in the language by incorporating some sort of default mechanism. For example, the compiler used to develop WEB and TEX allows '*others:*' as a default label, and other Pascals allow syntaxes like '**else**' or '**otherwise**' or '*otherwise:*', etc. The definitions of **othercases** and **endcases** should be changed to agree with local conventions. (Of course, if no default mechanism is available, the **case** statements of this program must be extended by listing all remaining cases. The author would have taken the trouble to modify TANGLE so that such extensions were done automatically, if he had not wanted to encourage Pascal compiler writers to make this important change in Pascal, where it belongs.)

define *othercases* ≡ *otherwise*   { default for cases not listed explicitly }
define *endcases* ≡ **end**   { follows the default case in an extended **case** statement }
format *othercases* ≡ *else*
format *endcases* ≡ *end*

12* The original Pascal compiler was designed in the late 60s, when six-bit character sets were common, so it did not make provision for lowercase letters. Nowadays, of course, we need to deal with both capital and small letters in a convenient way, so WEB assumes that it is being used with a Pascal whose character set contains at least the characters of standard ASCII as listed above. Some Pascal compilers use the original name *char* for the data type associated with the characters in text files, while other Pascals consider *char* to be a 64-element subrange of a larger data type that has some other name.

In order to accommodate this difference, we shall use the name *text_char* to stand for the data type of the characters in the input and output files. We shall also assume that *text_char* consists of the elements *chr*(*first_text_char*) through *chr*(*last_text_char*), inclusive. The following definitions should be adjusted if necessary.

define *text_char* ≡ *char*   { the data type of characters in text files }
define *first_text_char* = 0   { ordinal number of the smallest element of *text_char* }
define *last_text_char* = 127   { ordinal number of the largest element of *text_char* }
define *text_file* ≡ *text*

21* Different systems have different ways of specifying that the output on a certain file will appear on the user's terminal. Here is one way to do this when using Whiz-Bang Pascal:

⟨ Set initial values 10 ⟩ +≡
  assign(*term_out*, ´console_dev´); *rewrite*(*term_out*);   { send *term_out* output to the terminal }

22* The *update_terminal* procedure is called when we want to make sure that everything we have output to the terminal so far has actually left the computer's internal buffers and been sent. The Whiz-Bang always updates the terminal, so we will make the procedure null.

  define *update_terminal* ≡

26* The following code opens *Pascal_file* and *pool*.

⟨ Set initial values 10 ⟩ +≡
  ⟨ Set up all of the files, both input and output 191* ⟩;
  rewrite(*Pascal_file*); *rewrite*(*pool*);

28* The *input_ln* procedure brings the next line of input from the specified file into the *buffer* array and returns the value *true*, unless the file has already been entirely read, in which case it returns *false*. The conventions of TEX are followed; i.e., *ASCII_code* numbers representing the next line of the file are input into *buffer*[0], *buffer*[1], ..., *buffer*[*limit* − 1]; trailing blanks are ignored; and the global variable *limit* is set to the length of the line. The value of *limit* must be strictly less than *buf_size*.

We assume that none of the *ASCII_code* values of *buffer*[*j*] for $0 \le j < limit$ is equal to 0, ´177, *line_feed*, *form_feed*, or *carriage_return*.

```
function input_ln(var f : text_file): boolean;   { inputs a line or returns false }
  label done;
  var temp_buf: string[buf_size];   { intermediate input buffer }
    k: 0 .. buf_size;   { index into buffer }
  begin limit ← 0;
  if eof(f) then input_ln ← false
  else begin read_ln(f, temp_buf); limit ← length(temp_buf);
    if limit ≥ buf_size then
      begin print_nl(´!␣Input␣line␣too␣long´); loc ← 0; error; limit ← buf_size − 1;
      end;
    for k ← 1 to limit do buffer[k − 1] ← xord[temp_buf[k]];
    while limit > 1 do
      if buffer[limit − 1] = "␣" then decr(limit) else goto done;
  done: input_ln ← true;
    end;
  end;
```

34* The *jump_out* procedure just cuts across all active procedure levels and jumps out of the program. This is the only non-local **goto** statement in TANGLE. It is used when no recovery from a particular error has been provided.

Some Pascal compilers do not implement non-local **goto** statements. In such cases the code that appears at label *end_of_TANGLE* should be copied into the *jump_out* procedure, followed by a call to a system procedure that terminates the program. This is the case with the Whiz-Bang.

define *fatal_error*(#) ≡
   begin *new_line*; *print*(#); *error*; *mark_fatal*; *jump_out*;
   end

⟨ Error handling procedures 30 ⟩ +≡
procedure *jump_out*;
 begin stat ⟨ Print statistics about memory usage 186 ⟩; **tats**
 ⟨ Close the files since the Whiz-Bang 5000 requires it 189* ⟩;
 ⟨ Print the job *history* 187 ⟩;
 halt(*history*);
 end;

97* Here is a routine that is invoked when *out_ptr* > *line_length* or when it is time to flush out the final line. The *flush_buffer* procedure often writes out the line up to the current *break_ptr* position, then moves the remaining information to the front of *out_buf*. However, it prefers to write only up to *semi_ptr*, if the residual line won't be too long.

The Whiz-Bang 5000 allows us to use a '*string*' to write an entire line at once, rather than character by character. The maximum size of the string is fixed, but the current size is dynamic and can be set by accessing *temp_buf*.*length*, a simulated field within the string data type.

define *check_break* ≡
   if *out_ptr* > *line_length* **then** *flush_buffer*

procedure *flush_buffer*; { writes one line to output file }
 var *k*: 0 .. *out_buf_size*; { index into *out_buf* }
  b: 0 .. *out_buf_size*; { value of *break_ptr* upon entry }
  temp_buf: *string*[*out_buf_size*]; { intermediate input buffer }
 begin *b* ← *break_ptr*;
 if (*semi_ptr* ≠ 0) ∧ (*out_ptr* − *semi_ptr* ≤ *line_length*) **then** *break_ptr* ← *semi_ptr*;
 for *k* ← 1 **to** *break_ptr* **do** *temp_buf*[*k*] ← *xchr*[*out_buf*[*k* − 1]];
 temp_buf.*length* ← *break_ptr*; *write_ln*(*Pascal_file*, *temp_buf*); *incr*(*line*);
 if *line* **mod** 100 = 0 **then**
  begin *print*(´.´);
  if *line* **mod** 500 = 0 **then** *print*(*line* : 1);
  update_terminal; { progress report }
  end;
 if *break_ptr* < *out_ptr* **then**
  begin if *out_buf*[*break_ptr*] = "␣" **then**
   begin *incr*(*break_ptr*); { drop space at break }
   if *break_ptr* > *b* **then** *b* ← *break_ptr*;
   end;
  for *k* ← *break_ptr* **to** *out_ptr* − 1 **do** *out_buf*[*k* − *break_ptr*] ← *out_buf*[*k*];
  end;
 out_ptr ← *out_ptr* − *break_ptr*; *break_ptr* ← *b* − *break_ptr*; *semi_ptr* ← 0;
 if *out_ptr* > *line_length* **then**
  begin *err_print*(´!␣Long␣line␣must␣be␣truncated´); *out_ptr* ← *line_length*;
  end;
 end;

180* The debugging routine needs to read from the user's terminal.

⟨ Set initial values 10 ⟩ +≡
  debug *trouble_shooting* ← *true*; *debug_cycle* ← 1; *debug_skipped* ← 0;
  trouble_shooting ← *false*; *debug_cycle* ← 99999; { use these when it almost works }
  assign(*term_in*, ´console_dev´); *reset*(*term_in*); { open *term_in* as the terminal }
  gubed

182.*　The main program.　　We have defined plenty of procedures, and it is time to put the last pieces of the puzzle in place. Here is where TANGLE starts, and where it ends.

  begin *initialize*; ⟨ Initialize the input system 134 ⟩;
  print_ln(*banner*); { print a "banner line" }
  ⟨ Phase I: Read all the user's text and compress it into *tok_mem* 183 ⟩;
  stat for *zo* ← 0 **to** *zz* − 1 **do** *max_tok_ptr*[*zo*] ← *tok_ptr*[*zo*];
  tats
  ⟨ Phase II: Output the contents of the compressed tables 112 ⟩;
  if *string_ptr* > 128 **then** ⟨ Finish off the string pool file 184 ⟩;
  stat ⟨ Print statistics about memory usage 186 ⟩; **tats**
  ⟨ Close the files since the Whiz-Bang 5000 requires it 189* ⟩;
  ⟨ Print the job *history* 187 ⟩;
  halt(*history*);
  end.

188.*　System-dependent changes.　　Here will be the changes to the program that are necessary to make TANGLE work with the Whiz-Bang 5000.

⟨ Types in the outer block 11 ⟩ +≡
  str255 = *string*[255]; { long string type }

189.*　The Whiz-Bang 5000 doesn't automatically close files, so we have to close them manually to keep the output files from being truncated.

⟨ Close the files since the Whiz-Bang 5000 requires it 189* ⟩ ≡
  close(*web_file*); *close*(*change_file*); *close*(*Pascal_file*); *close*(*pool*);
This code is used in sections 34* and 182*.

190.*　This procedure appends a default file extension to a file name. We determine the file name based on the default extension, the base file name, and whatever was input on the command line. The *main* flag indiciates that this is the base file name that the others are derived from.

⟨ Whiz-Bang 5000 procedures 190* ⟩ ≡
procedure *setup_text_file*(**var** *the_file* : *text_file*; *def_ext* : *str255*; *descr_str* : *str255*;
      main : *boolean*); *extern*;
This code is used in section 2*.

191.*　⟨ Set up all of the files, both input and output 191* ⟩ ≡
  setup_text_file(*web_file*, ´web´, ´web´, *true*); *setup_text_file*(*change_file*, ´ch´, ´change´, *false*);
  setup_text_file(*Pascal_file*, ´pas´, ´Pascal´, *false*);
  setup_text_file(*pool*, ´pol´, ´string␣pool´, *false*);
This code is used in section 26*.

192* Index. Here is a cross-reference table for the TANGLE processor. All modules in which an identifier is used are listed with that identifier, except that reserved words are indexed only when they appear in format definitions, and the appearances of identifiers in module names are not indexed. Underlined entries correspond to where the identifier was declared. Error messages and a few other things like "ASCII code" are indexed here too.

The following sections were changed by the change file: 1, 2, 3, 7, 12, 21, 22, 26, 28, 34, 97, 180, 182, 188, 189, 190, 191, 192.

G.2.2   Enhancement Modification

1*   Introduction.   This program converts a `WEB` file to a Pascal file. It is a modified form of a program written by D. E. Knuth in September, 1981.

For large `WEB` files one should have a large memory, since `TANGLE` keeps all the Pascal text in memory (in an abbreviated form). The program uses a few features of the local Pascal compiler that may need to be changed in other installations:

1) Case statements have a default.
2) Input-output routines may need to be adapted for use with a particular character set and/or for printing messages on the user's terminal.

These features are also present in the Pascal version of TeX, where they are used in a similar (but more complex) way. System-dependent portions of `TANGLE` can be identified by looking at the entries for 'system dependencies' in the index below.

The "banner line" defined here should be changed whenever `TANGLE` is modified.

> **define** *banner* ≡ ´This␣is␣TANGLE,␣Line␣Numbers␣Version␣3´

122*   ⟨ Force a line break 122* ⟩ ≡
 begin *send_out*(*str*, 0);   { normalize the buffer }
 while *out_ptr* > 0 **do**
  begin if *out_ptr* ≤ *line_length* **then** *break_ptr* ← *out_ptr*;
  flush_buffer;
  end;
 if (*tok_mem*[*zo*, *cur_byte*] ≠ 0) ∨ (*tok_mem*[*zo*, *cur_byte* + 1] ≠ 0) **then**
  begin *n* ← *tok_mem*[*zo*, *cur_byte*];
  if *brace_level* = 0 **then** *send_out*(*misc*, "{")
  else *send_out*(*misc*, "[");
  if *n* ≥ ˝80 **then**
   begin *send_out*(*misc*, "C"); *n* ← (*n* − ˝80);
   end
  else *send_out*(*misc*, "W");
  n ← *n* ∗ ˝100 + *tok_mem*[*zo*, *cur_byte* + 1]; *send_val*(*n*);
  if *brace_level* = 0 **then** *send_out*(*misc*, "}")
  end;
 cur_byte ← *cur_byte* + 2; *out_state* ← *misc*;
 end

This code is used in section 113.

165*
procedure *scan_repl*(*t* : *eight_bits*);   { creates a replacement text }
 label *continue*, *done*, *found*;
 var *a*: *sixteen_bits*;   { the current token }

> b: $ASCII\_code$; { a character from the buffer }
> bal: $eight\_bits$; { left parentheses minus right parentheses }
> $saved\_line$: $integer$; $saved\_ch\_flag$: $boolean$;
> **begin** $bal \leftarrow 0$; $saved\_line \leftarrow -1$;
> **loop begin** $continue$: $a \leftarrow get\_next$;
>   **if** $((saved\_line \neq line) \vee (saved\_ch\_flag \neq changing)) \wedge (t = module\_name)$ **then**
>   **begin** $saved\_ch\_flag \leftarrow changing$; $saved\_line \leftarrow line$; $app\_repl(force\_line)$;
>   **if** $changing$ **then** $app\_repl((line \textbf{ div } "100) + "80)$
>   **else** $app\_repl(line \textbf{ div } "100)$;
> $app\_repl(line \textbf{ mod } "100)$;
>   **end**;
>   **case** a **of**
> $force\_line$: **begin** $app\_repl(force\_line)$; $app\_repl(0)$; $a \leftarrow 0$;
>   **end**,
> $"("$: $incr(bal)$;
> $")"$: **if** $bal = 0$ **then** $err\_print(\text{`}!\_\text{Extra}\_\text{)'})$
>   **else** $decr(bal)$;
> $"\text{`}"$: ⟨ Copy a string from the buffer to tok_mem 168 ⟩;
> $"\#"$: **if** $t = parametric$ **then** $a \leftarrow param$;
>   ⟨ In cases that a is a non-ASCII token ($identifier$, $module\_name$, etc.), either process it and
>   change a to a byte that should be stored, or **goto** $continue$ if a should be ignored, or
>   **goto** $done$ if a signals the end of this replacement text 167 ⟩
>   **othercases** $do\_nothing$
>   **endcases**;
> $app\_repl(a)$; { store a in tok_mem }
>   **end**;
> $done$: $next\_control \leftarrow a$; ⟨ Make sure the parentheses balance 166 ⟩;
>   **if** $text\_ptr > max\_texts - zz$ **then** $overflow(\text{`text'})$;
> $cur\_repl\_text \leftarrow text\_ptr$; $tok\_start[text\_ptr + zz] \leftarrow tok\_ptr[z]$; $incr(text\_ptr)$;
>   **if** $z = zz - 1$ **then** $z \leftarrow 0$ **else** $incr(z)$;
>   **end**;

189.* **Index.**   Here is a cross-reference table for the TANGLE processor. All modules in
which an identifier is used are listed with that identifier, except that reserved words are
indexed only when they appear in format definitions, and the appearances of identifiers in
module names are not indexed. Underlined entries correspond to where the identifier was
declared. Error messages and a few other things like "ASCII code" are indexed here too.

The following sections were changed by the change file: 1, 122, 165, 189.

G.3   MWEB **Processors**

G.3.1   Modified Listing for MANGLE

1.* Introduction.   This program converts a WEB file to a Modula-2 file. It is a modified form of a program written by D. E. Knuth in September, 1981.

For large WEB files one should have a large memory, since TANGLE keeps all the Pascal text in memory (in an abbreviated form). The program uses a few features of the local Pascal compiler that may need to be changed in other installations:

1) Case statements have a default.
2) Input-output routines may need to be adapted for use with a particular character set and/or for printing messages on the user's terminal.

These features are also present in the Pascal version of TeX, where they are used in a similar (but more complex) way. System-dependent portions of TANGLE can be identified by looking at the entries for 'system dependencies' in the index below.

The "banner line" defined here should be changed whenever TANGLE is modified.

For the Modula-2 versions of TANGLE, we add a second decimal point and number to the main version number, so we can differentiate between changes to the standard TANGLE and changes local to the Modula-2 version.

define *banner* ≡ ´This␣is␣MANGLE␣(Modula-2␣TANGLE)␣Version␣3.0.0´

8.* The following parameters are set big enough to handle TeX, so they should be sufficient for most applications of TANGLE.

⟨ Constants in the outer block 8* ⟩ ≡

$buf\_size = 100$;   { maximum length of input line }

$max\_bytes = 45000$;   { $1/ww$ times the number of bytes in identifiers, strings, and module names; must be less than 65536 }

$max\_toks = 50000$;

   { $1/zz$ times the number of bytes in compressed Pascal code; must be less than 65536 }

$max\_names = 4000$;   { number of identifiers, strings, module names; must be less than 10240 }

$max\_texts = 2000$;   { number of replacement texts, must be less than 10240 }

$hash\_size = 353$;   { should be prime }

$longest\_name = 400$;   { module names shouldn't be longer than this }

$line\_length = 72$;   { lines of Pascal output have at most this many characters }

$out\_buf\_size = 144$;   { length of output buffer, should be twice *line_length* }

$stack\_size = 50$;   { number of simultaneous levels of macro expansion }

$max\_id\_length = 31$;

   { long identifiers are chopped to this length, which must not exceed *line_length* }

$unambig\_length = 20$;   { identifiers must be unique if chopped to this length }

This code is used in section 2.

72.* If the first byte of a token is less than $'200$, the token occupies a single byte. Otherwise we make a sixteen-bit token by combining two consecutive bytes a and b. If $'200 \leq a < '250$, then $(a - \text{'}200) \times 2^8 + b$ points to an identifier; if $\text{'}250 \leq a < \text{'}320$, then $(a - \text{'}250) \times 2^8 + b$ points to a module name; otherwise, i.e., if $\text{'}320 \leq a < \text{'}400$, then $(a - \text{'}320) \times 2^8 + b$ is the number of the module in which the current replacement text appears.

Codes less than $\text{'}200$ are 7-bit ASCII codes that represent themselves. In particular, a single-character identifier like 'x' will be a one-byte token, while all longer identifiers will occupy two bytes.

Some of the 7-bit ASCII codes will not be present, however, so we can use them for special purposes. The following symbolic names are used:

param denotes insertion of a parameter. This occurs only in the replacement texts of parametric macros, outside of single-quoted strings in those texts.

begin_comment denotes @{, which will become either { or [.

end_comment denotes @}, which will become either } or].

octal denotes the @´ that precedes an octal constant.

hex denotes the @" that precedes a hexadecimal constant.

check_sum denotes the @$ that denotes the string pool check sum.

join denotes the concatenation of adjacent items with no space or line breaks allowed between them (the @& operation of WEB).

double_dot denotes '..' in Pascal.

verbatim denotes the @= that begins a verbatim Pascal string. It is also used for the end of the string.

force_line denotes the @\ that forces a new line in the Pascal output.

define *param* $= 0$ { ASCII null code will not appear }
define *verbatim* $= \text{'}2$ { extended ASCII alpha should not appear }
define *force_line* $= \text{'}3$ { extended ASCII beta should not appear }
define *begin_comment* $= \text{'}11$ { ASCII tab mark will not appear }
define *end_comment* $= \text{'}12$ { ASCII line feed will not appear }
define *octal* $= \text{'}14$ { ASCII form feed will not appear }
define *hex* $= \text{'}15$ { ASCII carriage return will not appear }
define *double_dot* $= \text{'}40$ { ASCII space will not appear except in strings }
define *check_sum* $= 1$ { this control code should not appear in normal text }
define *join* $= \text{'}177$ { ASCII delete will not appear }

115* Please don't ask how all of the following characters can actually get through TANGLE outside of strings. It seems that """" and "{" cannot actually occur at this point of the program, but they have been included just in case TANGLE changes.

If TANGLE is producing code for a Pascal compiler that uses '(.' and '.)' instead of square brackets (e.g., on machines with EBCDIC code), one should remove "[" and "]" from this list and put them into the preceding module in the appropriate way. Similarly, some compilers want '^' to be converted to '@'.

⟨ Other printable characters 115* ⟩ ≡
    "!", """", "#", "$", "%", "&", "(", ")", "*", ",", "/", ":", ";", "<", "=", ">", "?", "@", "[", "\", "]",
    "^", "_", "`", "{", "}", "|", "~"

This code is used in section 113.

121* Some Pascal compilers do not recognize comments in braces, so the comments must be delimited by '(*' and '*)'. In such cases the statement '*send_out*(*misc*, "{")' that appears here should be replaced by '**begin** $out\_contrib[1] \leftarrow$ "("; $out\_contrib[2] \leftarrow$ "*"; $send\_out(str, 2)$; **end**', and a similar change should be made to '$send\_out(misc, "$}$")$'.

Note: This is definitely the case with Modula-2, so the change must be made.

define $send\_left\_comment \equiv$
　　　　begin $out\_contrib[1] \leftarrow$ "("; $out\_contrib[2] \leftarrow$ "*"; $send\_out(str, 2)$;
　　　　end
define $send\_right\_comment \equiv$
　　　　begin $out\_contrib[1] \leftarrow$ "*"; $out\_contrib[2] \leftarrow$ ")"; $send\_out(str, 2)$;
　　　　end

$\langle$ Cases involving @{ and @} 121* $\rangle \equiv$
$begin\_comment$: **begin** $send\_left\_comment$; $incr(brace\_level)$;
　　end;
$end\_comment$: **if** $brace\_level > 0$ **then**
　　　begin $decr(brace\_level)$; $send\_right\_comment$;
　　　end
　else $err\_print(\text{`!}\sqcup\text{Extra}\sqcup\text{@}\}\text{'})$;
$module\_number$: **begin** $send\_left\_comment$;
　if $cur\_val < 0$ **then**
　　begin $send\_out(misc, ":")$; $send\_val(-cur\_val)$;
　　end
　else begin $send\_val(cur\_val)$; $send\_out(misc, ":")$;
　　end;
　$send\_right\_comment$;
　end;

This code is used in section 113.

142* $\langle$ Do special things when $c =$ "@", "\", "{", "}"; return at end 142* $\rangle \equiv$
　if $c =$ "@" **then**
　　begin $c \leftarrow buffer[loc]$;
　　if $(c \neq \text{"}\sqcup\text{"}) \wedge (c \neq tab\_mark) \wedge (c \neq \text{"*"}) \wedge (c \neq \text{"z"}) \wedge (c \neq \text{"Z"})$ **then** $incr(loc)$
　　else begin $err\_print(\text{`!}\sqcup\text{Section}\sqcup\text{ended}\sqcup\text{in}\sqcup\text{mid-comment'})$; $decr(loc)$; **return**;
　　　end
　　end
　else if $(c = \text{"\"}) \wedge (buffer[loc] \neq \text{"@"})$ **then** $incr(loc)$
　　else if $(c = \text{"("}) \wedge (buffer[loc] = \text{"*"})$ **then**
　　　　begin $incr(bal)$; $incr(loc)$;
　　　　end
　　　else if $(c = \text{"*"}) \wedge (buffer[loc] = \text{")"})$ **then**
　　　　　begin $incr(loc)$;
　　　　　if $bal = 0$ **then return**;
　　　　　$decr(bal)$;
　　　　　end

This code is used in section 141.

145* At the top level, get_next is a multi-way switch based on the next character in the input buffer. A new_module code is inserted at the very end of the input file.

function get_next: $eight\_bits$; { produces the next input token }
　label $restart, done, found$;

```
  var c: eight_bits;  { the current character }
    d: eight_bits;  { the next character }
    j, k: 0 .. longest_name;  { indices into mod_text }
  begin restart: if loc > limit then
    begin get_line;
    if input_has_ended then
      begin c ← new_module; goto found;
      end;
    end;
  c ← buffer[loc]; incr(loc);
  if scanning_hex then
    ⟨ Go to found if c is a hexadecimal digit, otherwise set scanning_hex ← false 146 ⟩;
  case c of
  "A", up_to("Z"), "a", up_to("z"): ⟨ Get an identifier 148 ⟩;
  """": ⟨ Get a preprocessed string 149 ⟩;
  "@": ⟨ Get control code and possible module name 150 ⟩;
  ⟨ Compress two-symbol combinations like ':=' 147* ⟩
  "␣", tab_mark: goto restart;  { ignore spaces and tabs }
  othercases do_nothing
  endcases;
found: debug if trouble_shooting then debug_help; gubed
  get_next ← c;
  end,
```

147* Note that the following code substitutes @{ and @} for the respective combinations '(*' and '*)'. Explicit braces should be used for TeX comments in Pascal text.

```
  define compress(#) ≡
            begin if loc ≤ limit then
              begin c ← #; incr(loc);
              end;
            end
⟨ Compress two-symbol combinations like ':=' 147* ⟩ ≡
".": if buffer[loc] = "." then compress(double_dot)
  else if buffer[loc] = ")" then compress("]");
":": if buffer[loc] = "=" then compress(left_arrow);
"=": if buffer[loc] = "=" then compress(equivalence_sign);
">": if buffer[loc] = "=" then compress(greater_or_equal);
"<": if buffer[loc] = "=" then compress(less_or_equal)
  else if buffer[loc] = ">" then compress(not_equal);
"(": if buffer[loc] = "*" then
      begin incr(loc); skip_comment; goto restart;
      end
  else if buffer[loc] = "." then compress("[");
```

This code is used in section 145*.

189* Index. Here is a cross-reference table for the TANGLE processor. All modules in which an identifier is used are listed with that identifier, except that reserved words are indexed only when they appear in format definitions, and the appearances of identifiers in module names are not indexed. Underlined entries correspond to where the identifier was declared. Error messages and a few other things like "ASCII code" are indexed here too.

The following sections were changed by the change file: 1, 8, 72, 115, 121, 142, 145, 147, 189.

G.3.2 Modified Listing for MWEAVE

1* Introduction.   This program converts a WEB file to a TeX file. It is a modified form of a program written by D. E. Knuth in October, 1981.

The code uses a few features of the local Pascal compiler that may need to be changed in other installations:

1) Case statements have a default.
2) Input-output routines may need to be adapted for use with a particular character set and/or for printing messages on the user's terminal.

These features are also present in the Pascal version of TeX, where they are used in a similar (but more complex) way. System-dependent portions of WEAVE can be identified by looking at the entries for 'system dependencies' in the index below.

The "banner line" defined here should be changed whenever WEAVE is modified.

For the Modula-2 versions of WEAVE, we add a second decimal point and number to the main version number, so we can differentiate between changes to the standard WEAVE and changes local to MWEAVE.

    define *banner* $\equiv$ `This␣is␣MWEAVE␣(Modula-2␣WEAVE)␣Version␣3.1.0`

42*   Several types of identifiers are distinguished by their *ilk*:

normal identifiers are part of the Pascal program and will appear in italic type.

roman identifiers are index entries that appear after `@^` in the WEB file.

wildcard identifiers are index entries that appear after `@:` in the WEB file.

typewriter identifiers are index entries that appear after `@.` in the WEB file.

array_like, *begin_like*, ..., *var_like* identifiers are Pascal reserved words whose *ilk* explains how they are to be treated when Pascal code is being formatted.

Finally, if *c* is an ASCII code, an *ilk* equal to *char_like* + *c* denotes a reserved word that will be converted to character *c*.

    define *normal* = 0   { ordinary identifiers have *normal* ilk }
    define *roman* = 1   { normal index entries have *roman* ilk }
    define *wildcard* = 2   { user-formatted index entries have *wildcard* ilk }
    define *typewriter* = 3   { 'typewriter type' entries have *typewriter* ilk }
    define *reserved*(#) $\equiv$ (*ilk*[#] > *typewriter*)   { tells if a name is a reserved word }
    define *array_like* = 4   { **array**, **file**, **set** }
    define *begin_like* = 5   { **begin** }
    define *case_like* = 6   { **case** }
    define *const_like* = 7   { **const**, **label**, **type** }
    define *div_like* = 8   { **div**, **mod** }
    define *do_like* = 9   { **do**, **then** }

define *else_like* = 10   { **else** }
define *end_like* = 11   { **end** }
define *for_like* = 12   { **for, if, while, with** }
define *goto_like* = 13   { **implementation, definition, packed** }
define *if_like* = 14   { not used for **MWEB** — see *for_like* }
define *in_like* = 15   { **in** }
define *nil_like* = 16   { **nil** }
define *proc_like* = 17   { **procedure, module** }
define *record_like* = 18   { **record** }
define *repeat_like* = 19   { **repeat** }
define *to_like* = 20   { **to** }
define *until_like* = 21   { **until, end** }
define *var_like* = 22   { **var** }
define *loop_like* = 23   { **loop** }
define *elsif_like* = 24   { **elsif** }
define *of_like* = 25   { **of** }
define *char_like* = 26   { **and, or, not, in** }

63* Initializing the table of reserved words.   We have to get Modula-2's reserved words into the hash table, and the simplest way to do this is to insert them every time **WEAVE** is run. A few macros permit us to do the initialization with a compact program. The maximum size of a reserved word had to be increased to accommodate words such as **implementation**.

define *sid14*(#) ≡ *buffer*[14] ← #; *cur_name* ← *id_lookup*
define *sid13*(#) ≡ *buffer*[13] ← #; *sid14*
define *sid12*(#) ≡ *buffer*[12] ← #; *sid13*
define *sid11*(#) ≡ *buffer*[11] ← #; *sid12*
define *sid10*(#) ≡ *buffer*[10] ← #; *sid11*
define *sid9*(#) ≡ *buffer*[9] ← #; *sid10*
define *sid8*(#) ≡ *buffer*[8] ← #; *sid9*
define *sid7*(#) ≡ *buffer*[7] ← #; *sid8*
define *sid6*(#) ≡ *buffer*[6] ← #; *sid7*
define *sid5*(#) ≡ *buffer*[5] ← #; *sid6*
define *sid4*(#) ≡ *buffer*[4] ← #; *sid5*
define *sid3*(#) ≡ *buffer*[3] ← #; *sid4*
define *sid2*(#) ≡ *buffer*[2] ← #; *sid3*
define *sid1*(#) ≡ *buffer*[1] ← #; *sid2*
define *id2* ≡ *id_first* ← 13; *sid13*
define *id3* ≡ *id_first* ← 12; *sid12*
define *id4* ≡ *id_first* ← 11; *sid11*
define *id5* ≡ *id_first* ← 10; *sid10*
define *id6* ≡ *id_first* ← 9; *sid9*
define *id7* ≡ *id_first* ← 8; *sid8*
define *id8* ≡ *id_first* ← 7; *sid7*
define *id9* ≡ *id_first* ← 6; *sid6*
define *id10* ≡ *id_first* ← 5; *sid5*
define *id11* ≡ *id_first* ← 4; *sid4*
define *id12* ≡ *id_first* ← 3; *sid3*
define *id13* ≡ *id_first* ← 2; *sid2*

define $id14 \equiv id\_first \leftarrow 1;\ sid1$

⟨ Globals in the outer block 9 ⟩ +≡
cur_name: *name_pointer*; { points to the identifier just inserted }

64* The intended use of the macros above might not be immediately obvious, but the riddle is answered by the following:

⟨ Store all the reserved words 64* ⟩ ≡
  $id\_loc \leftarrow 15$;
  $id3$("a")("n")("d")(*char_like* + *and_sign*);
  $id5$("a")("r")("r")("a")("y")(*array_like*);
  $id5$("b")("e")("g")("i")("n")(*begin_like*);
  $id2$("b")("y")(*to_like*);
  $id4$("c")("a")("s")("e")(*case_like*);
  $id5$("c")("o")("n")("s")("t")(*const_like*);
  $id3$("d")("i")("v")(*div_like*);
  $id2$("d")("o")(*do_like*);
  $id10$("d")("e")("f")("i")("n")("i")("t")("i")("o")("n")(*goto_like*);
  $id4$("e")("l")("s")("e")(*else_like*);
  $id5$("e")("l")("s")("i")("f")(*elsif_like*);
  $id3$("e")("n")("d")(*end_like*);
  $id4$("e")("x")("i")("t")(*goto_like*);
  $id6$("e")("x")("p")("o")("r")("t")(*goto_like*);
  $id3$("f")("o")("r")(*for_like*);
  $id4$("f")("r")("o")("m")(*goto_like*);
  $id2$("i")("f")(*for_like*);
  $id14$("i")("m")("p")("l")("e")("m")("e")("n")("t")("a")("t")("i")("o")("n")(*goto_like*);
  $id6$("i")("m")("p")("o")("r")("t")(*goto_like*);
  $id2$("i")("n")(*char_like* + *set_element_sign*);
  $id5$("l")("a")("b")("e")("l")(*const_like*);
  $id4$("l")("o")("o")("p")(*loop_like*);
  $id6$("m")("o")("d")("u")("l")("e")(*proc_like*);
  $id3$("m")("o")("d")(*div_like*);
  $id3$("n")("i")("l")(*nil_like*);
  $id3$("n")("o")("t")(*char_like* + *not_sign*);
  $id2$("o")("f")(*of_like*);
  $id2$("o")("r")(*char_like* + *or_sign*);
  $id7$("p")("o")("i")("n")("t")("e")("r")(*goto_like*);
  $id9$("p")("r")("o")("c")("e")("d")("u")("r")("e")(*proc_like*);
  $id9$("q")("u")("a")("l")("i")("f")("i")("e")("d")(*goto_like*);
  $id6$("r")("e")("c")("o")("r")("d")(*record_like*);
  $id6$("r")("e")("p")("e")("a")("t")(*repeat_like*);
  $id6$("r")("e")("t")("u")("r")("n")(*goto_like*);
  $id3$("s")("e")("t")(*array_like*);
  $id4$("t")("h")("e")("n")(*do_like*);
  $id2$("t")("o")(*to_like*);
  $id4$("t")("y")("p")("e")(*const_like*);
  $id5$("u")("n")("t")("i")("l")(*until_like*);
  $id3$("v")("a")("r")(*var_like*);
  $id5$("w")("h")("i")("l")("e")(*for_like*);

id4 ("w")("i")("t")("h")(*for_like*);
This code is used in section 261.

86*   Control codes in WEB, which begin with '@', are converted into a numeric code designed to simplify WEAVE's logic; for example, larger numbers are given to the control codes that denote more significant milestones, and the code of *new_module* should be the largest of all. Some of these numeric control codes take the place of ASCII control codes that will not otherwise appear in the output of the scanning routines. For Modula-2, special characters had to be added for regular comment delimiters, since these are two-character combinations in Modula-2.

> **define** *ignore* = 0   { control code of no interest to WEAVE }
> **define** *verbatim* = '2   { extended ASCII alpha will not appear }
> **define** *force_line* = '3   { extended ASCII beta will not appear }
> **define** *vertical_bar* = 15   { control code for vertical bar character }
> **define** *begin_regular_comment* = 16
> 　　　　　　{ control code for beginning of comments — Modula-2 only }
> **define** *end_regular_comment* = 17   { control code for ending of comments — Modula-2 only }
> **define** *begin_comment* = '11   { ASCII tab mark will not appear }
> **define** *end_comment* = '12   { ASCII line feed will not appear }
> **define** *octal* = '14   { ASCII form feed will not appear }
> **define** *hex* = '15   { ASCII carriage return will not appear }
> **define** *double_dot* = '40   { ASCII space will not appear except in strings }
> **define** *no_underline* = '175   { this code will be intercepted without confusion }
> **define** *underline* = '176   { this code will be intercepted without confusion }
> **define** *param* = '177   { ASCII delete will not appear }
> **define** *xref_roman* = '203   { control code for '@^' }
> **define** *xref_wildcard* = '204   { control code for '@:' }
> **define** *xref_typewriter* = '205   { control code for '@.' }
> **define** *TeX_string* = '206   { control code for '@t' }
> **define** *check_sum* = '207   { control code for '@$' }
> **define** *join* = '210   { control code for '@&' }
> **define** *thin_space* = '211   { control code for '@,' }
> **define** *math_break* = '212   { control code for '@|' }
> **define** *line_break* = '213   { control code for '@/' }
> **define** *big_line_break* = '214   { control code for '@#' }
> **define** *no_line_break* = '215   { control code for '@+' }
> **define** *pseudo_semi* = '216   { control code for '@;' }
> **define** *format* = '217   { control code for '@f' }
> **define** *definition* = '220   { control code for '@d' }
> **define** *begin_Pascal* = '221   { control code for '@p' }
> **define** *module_name* = '222   { control code for '@<' }
> **define** *new_module* = '223   { control code for '@␣' and '@*' }

92*   ⟨ Do special things when *c* = "@", "\", "{", "}"; **goto** *done* at end 92* ⟩ ≡
> **if** *c* = "@" **then**
> 　　**begin** *c* ← *buffer*[*loc*];
> 　　**if** (*c* ≠ "␣") ∧ (*c* ≠ *tab_mark*) ∧ (*c* ≠ "*") **then** *incr*(*loc*)
> 　　**else begin** *decr*(*loc*); *bal* ← 0; **goto** *done*;
> 　　　　**end**   { an error message will occur in phase two }

```
          end
      else if (c = "\") ∧ (buffer[loc] ≠ "@") then  incr(loc)
          else if c = begin_regular_comment then  incr(bal)
              else if c = end_regular_comment then
                  begin decr(bal);
                  if bal = 0 then goto done;
                  end
              else if (c = "(") ∧ (buffer[loc] = "*") then
                      begin incr(bal); incr(loc);
                      end
                  else if (c = "*") ∧ (buffer[loc] = ")") then
                          begin decr(bal); incr(loc);  c ← end_regular_comment;
                          if bal = 0 then goto done;
                          end
```

This code is used in section 91.

97* Note that the following code converts '(*' and '*)' to internal characters which are converted back to ASCII when output. Adjacent vertical bar characters (ˊ | | ˋ), which represent the Modula-2 usage of that character rather than that of WEB, are handled the same way.

```
define compress(#) ≡
            begin if loc ≤ limit then
                begin c ← #; incr(loc);
                end;
            end
```

⟨ Compress two-symbol combinations like ':=' 97* ⟩ ≡
```
".": if buffer[loc] = "." then  compress(double_dot)
    else if buffer[loc] = ")" then  compress("]");
":": if buffer[loc] = "=" then  compress(left_arrow);
"=": if buffer[loc] = "=" then  compress(equivalence_sign);
">": if buffer[loc] = "=" then  compress(greater_or_equal);
"<": if buffer[loc] = "=" then  compress(less_or_equal)
    else if buffer[loc] = ">" then  compress(not_equal);
"(": if buffer[loc] = "*" then  compress(begin_regular_comment)
    else if buffer[loc] = "." then  compress("[");
"*": if buffer[loc] = ")" then  compress(end_regular_comment);
"|": if buffer[loc] = "|" then  compress(vertical_bar);
```

This code is used in section 95.

111* The *Pascal_xref* subroutine stores references to identifiers in Pascal text material beginning with the current value of *next_control* and continuing until *next_control* is '{' or '|', or until the next "milestone" is passed (i.e., $next\_control \geq format$). If $next\_control \geq format$ when *Pascal_xref* is called, nothing will happen; but if $next_control = $ "|" upon entry, the procedure assumes that this is the '|' preceding Pascal text that is to be processed.

The program uses the fact that our internal code numbers satisfy the following relations:

$$xref\_roman = identifier + roman;$$

$$xref\_wildcard = identifier + wildcard;$$

$xref\_typewriter = identifier + typewriter$;

$normal = 0$.

An implied '`@!`' is inserted after **function**, **procedure**, **program**, and **var**.

procedure *Pascal_xref*; { makes cross references for Pascal identifiers }
    label *exit*;
    var *p*: *name_pointer*; { a referenced name }
    begin while *next_control* < *format* **do**
      begin if ($next\_control \geq identifier$) $\wedge$ ($next\_control \leq xref\_typewriter$) **then**
        begin $p \leftarrow id\_lookup(next\_control - identifier)$; $new\_xref(p)$;
        if ($ilk[p] = proc\_like$) $\vee$ ($ilk[p] = var\_like$) **then** $xref\_switch \leftarrow def\_flag$; { implied '`@!`' }
        end;
      $next\_control \leftarrow get\_next$;
      if ($next_control = $ "`|`") $\vee$ ($next\_control = begin\_regular\_comment$) **then return**;
      end;
  exit: **end**;

112* The *outer_xref* subroutine is like *Pascal_xref* but it begins with $next\_control \neq$ "`|`" and ends with $next\_control \geq format$. Thus, it handles Pascal text with embedded comments.

procedure *outer_xref*; { extension of *Pascal_xref* }
  var *bal*: *eight_bits*; { brace level in comment }
  begin while *next_control* < *format* **do**
    if $next\_control \neq begin\_regular\_comment$ **then** *Pascal_xref*
    else begin $bal \leftarrow skip\_comment(1)$; $next\_control \leftarrow$ "`|`";
      while $bal > 0$ **do**
        begin *Pascal_xref*;
        if $next_control = $ "`|`" **then** $bal \leftarrow skip\_comment(bal)$
        else $bal \leftarrow 0$; { an error will be reported in phase two }
        end;
      end;
  end;

124* In particular, the *finish_line* procedure is called near the very beginning of phase two. We initialize the output variables in a slightly tricky way so that the first line of the output file will be '`\input mwebmac`'.

⟨ Set initial values 10 ⟩ +≡
  $out\_ptr \leftarrow 1$; $out\_line \leftarrow 1$; $out\_buf[1] \leftarrow$ "`c`"; $write(tex\_file,$ `´\input␣mwebma´`$)$;

136* The *copy_comment* uses and returns a brace-balance value, following the conventions of *skip_comment* above. Instead of copying the TEX material into the output buffer, this procedure copies it into the token memory. The abbreviation *app_tok*(t) is used to append token t to the current token list, and it also makes sure that it is possible to append at least one further token without overflow.

define *app_tok*(**#**) ≡
      begin if $tok\_ptr + 2 > max\_toks$ **then** $overflow($ `´token´` $)$;
      $tok\_mem[tok\_ptr] \leftarrow$ **#**; $incr(tok\_ptr)$;
      end

function *copy_comment*(*bal* : *eight_bits*): *eight_bits*; { copies TeX code in comments }
   label *done*;
   var *c*: *ASCII_code*; { current character being copied }
   begin loop
     begin if *loc* > *limit* **then**
      begin *get_line*;
      if *input_has_ended* **then**
        begin *err_print*(´!␣Input␣ended␣in␣mid-comment´); *loc* ← 1;
        ⟨ Clear *bal* and **goto** *done* 138* ⟩;
        end;
      end;
     c ← *buffer*[*loc*]; *incr*(*loc*);
     if *c* = "|" **then goto** *done*;
     if (*c* = "*") ∧ (*buffer*[*loc*] = ")") **then**
      begin *incr*(*loc*); *c* ← *end_regular_comment*; *app_tok*("}");
      end
     else begin *app_tok*(*c*);
      end;
     ⟨ Copy special things when *c* = "@", "\", "{", "}"; **goto** *done* at end 137* ⟩;
     end;
done: *copy_comment* ← *bal*;
   end;

137* ⟨ Copy special things when *c* = "@", "\", "{", "}"; **goto** *done* at end 137* ⟩ ≡
  if *c* = "@" **then**
   begin *incr*(*loc*);
   if *buffer*[*loc* − 1] ≠ "@" **then**
    begin *err_print*(´!␣Illegal␣use␣of␣@␣in␣comment´); *loc* ← *loc* − 2; *decr*(*tok_ptr*);
    ⟨ Clear *bal* and **goto** *done* 138* ⟩;
    end;
   end
  else if (*c* = "\") ∧ (*buffer*[*loc*] ≠ "@") **then**
    begin *app_tok*(*buffer*[*loc*]); *incr*(*loc*);
    end
   else if *c* = *begin_regular_comment* **then** *incr*(*bal*)
    else if *c* = *end_regular_comment* **then**
     begin *decr*(*bal*);
     if *bal* = 0 **then goto** *done*;
     end
     else if (*c* = "(") ∧ (*buffer*[*loc*] = "*") **then**
      begin *incr*(*bal*); *incr*(*loc*);
      end

This code is used in section 136*.

138* When the comment has terminated abruptly due to an error, we output enough right braces to keep TeX happy.

⟨ Clear *bal* and **goto** *done* 138* ⟩ =
  app_tok("␣"); { this is done in case the previous character was '\' }
  repeat *app_tok*(*end_regular_comment*); *decr*(*bal*);

until $bal = 0$;
    goto *done*;
This code is used in sections 136* and 137*.

183* **Initializing the scraps.**   If we are going to use the powerful production mechanism just developed, we must get the scraps set up in the first place, given a Pascal text. A table of the initial scraps corresponding to Pascal tokens appeared above in the section on parsing; our goal now is to implement that table. We shall do this by implementing a subroutine called *Pascal_parse* that is analogous to the *Pascal_xref* routine used during phase one.

    Like *Pascal_xref*, the *Pascal_parse* procedure starts with the current value of *next_control* and it uses the operation *next_control* ← *get_next* repeatedly to read Pascal text until encountering the next '|' or '{', or until *next_control* ≥ *format*. The scraps corresponding to what it reads are appended into the *cat* and *trans* arrays, and *scrap_ptr* is advanced.

    Like *prod*, this procedure has to split into pieces so that each part is short enough to be handled by Pascal compilers that discriminate against long subroutines. This time there are two split-off routines, called *easy_cases* and *sub_cases*.

    After studying *Pascal_parse*, we will look at the sub-procedures *app_comment*, *app_octal*, and *app_hex* that are used in some of its branches.

⟨ Declaration of the *app_comment* procedure 195 ⟩
⟨ Declaration of the *app_octal* and *app_hex* procedures 196 ⟩
⟨ Declaration of the *easy_cases* procedure 186* ⟩
⟨ Declaration of the *sub_cases* procedure 192* ⟩
procedure *Pascal_parse*;   { creates scraps from Pascal tokens }
   label *reswitch*, *exit*;
   var *j*: 0 .. *long_buf_size*;   { index into *buffer* }
     p: *name_pointer*;   { identifier designator }
   begin while *next_control* < *format* **do**
     begin ⟨ Append the scrap appropriate to *next_control* 185 ⟩;
     next_control ← *get_next*;
     if (*next_control* = "|") ∨ (*next_control* = *begin_regular_comment*) **then return**;
     end;
exit: **end**;

186*   The *easy_cases* each result in straightforward scraps.

⟨ Declaration of the *easy_cases* procedure 186* ⟩ ≡
procedure *easy_cases*;   { a subprocedure of *Pascal_parse* }
   begin case *next_control* **of**
   set_element_sign: *sc3*("\")("i")("n")(*math*);
   double_dot: *sc3*("\")("t")("o")(*math*);
   "$", "%", "^", "_": *sc2*("\")(*next_control*)(*math*);
   "#": **if** *in_def_part* **then**
      begin *pound_found* ← *true*; *sc2*("\")("#")(*math*);
      end
     else *sc2*("\")("I")(*math*);
   "~": *sc2*("\")("R")(*math*);
   "&": *sc2*("\")("W")(*math*);
   ignore, *xref_roman*, *xref_wildcard*, *xref_typewriter*: *do_nothing*;

"(", "[": *sc1* (*next_control*)(*open*);
")", "]": *sc1* (*next_control*)(*close*);
"*": *sc4* ("\")("a")("s")("t")(*math*);
",": *sc3* (",")(*opt*)("9")(*math*);
".", "0", "1", "2", "3", "4", "5", "6", "7", "8", "9": *sc1* (*next_control*)(*simp*);
";": *sc1* (";")(*semi*);
"{": *sc2* ("\")("{")(*open*);
"}": *sc2* ("\")("}")(*close*);
"|", *vertical_bar*: *sc4* ("\")("V")("B")(*force*)(*semi*);
":": *sc1* (":")(*colon*);
⟨ Cases involving nonstandard ASCII characters 188* ⟩
exponent: *sc3* ("\")("E")("{")(*exp*);
begin_comment: *sc2* ("\")("B")(*math*);
end_comment: *sc2* ("\")("T")(*math*);
octal: *app_octal*;
hex: *app_hex*;
check_sum: *sc2* ("\")(")")(*simp*);
force_line: *sc2* ("\")("]")(*simp*);
thin_space: *sc2* ("\")(",")(*math*);
math_break: *sc2* (*opt*)("0")(*simp*);
line_break: *comment_scrap*(*force*);
big_line_break: *comment_scrap*(*big_force*);
no_line_break: **begin** *app*(*big_cancel*); *app*("\"); *app*("␣"), *comment_scrap*(*big_cancel*);
  end;
pseudo_semi: *sc0* (*semi*);
join: *sc2* ("\")("J")(*math*);
othercases *sc1* (*next_control*)(*math*)
endcases;
end;

This code is used in section 183*.

188* Some nonstandard ASCII characters may have entered WEAVE by means of standard ones. They are converted to TeX control sequences so that it is possible to keep WEAVE from stepping beyond standard ASCII.

⟨ Cases involving nonstandard ASCII characters 188* ⟩ ≡
not_equal: *sc2* ("\")("I")(*math*);
less_or_equal: *sc2* ("\")("L")(*math*);
greater_or_equal: *sc2* ("\")("G")(*math*);
equivalence_sign: **begin** *sc2* ("\")("S")(*math*);
  if ¬*pound_found* **then** *in_def_part* ← *false*;
  end;
and_sign: *sc2* ("\")("W")(*math*);
or_sign: *sc2* ("\")("V")(*math*);
not_sign: *sc2* ("\")("R")(*math*);
left_arrow: *sc2* ("\")("K")(*math*);

This code is used in section 186*.

191* ⟨ Append an identifier scrap 191* ⟩ ≡
  begin *p* ← *id_lookup*(*normal*);

case *ilk*[*p*] **of**
normal, *array_like*, *const_like*, *div_like*, *of_like*, *for_like*, *goto_like*, *nil_like*, *to_like*: *sub_cases*(*p*);
⟨Cases that generate more than one scrap 193*⟩
othercases begin *next_control* ← *ilk*[*p*] − *char_like*; **goto** *reswitch*;
   end   {and, in, not, or }
endcases;
end

This code is used in section 185.

192*   The *sub_cases* also result in straightforward scraps.

⟨Declaration of the *sub_cases* procedure 192*⟩ ≡
procedure *sub_cases*(*p* : *name_pointer*);   { a subprocedure of *Pascal_parse* }
  begin case *ilk*[*p*] **of**
  normal: *sc1*(*id_flag* + *p*)(*simp*);   { not a reserved word }
  array_like: *sc1*(*res_flag* + *p*)(*alpha*);   { **array**, **file**, **set** }
  const_like: *sc3*(*force*)(*backup*)(*res_flag* + *p*)(*intro*);   { **const**, **label**, **type** }
  div_like: *sc3*(*math_bin*)(*res_flag* + *p*)("}")(*math*);   { **div**, **mod** }
  for_like: *sc2*(*force*)(*res_flag* + *p*)(*alpha*);   { **for**, **if**, **while**, **with** }
  goto_like: *sc1*(*res_flag* + *p*)(*intro*);   { **packed** }
  nil_like: *sc1*(*res_flag* + *p*)(*simp*);   { **nil** }
  of_like: *sc1*(*res_flag* + *p*)(*omega*);   { **of** }
  to_like: *sc3*(*math_rel*)(*res_flag* + *p*)("}")(*math*);   { **to** }
  end;
  end;

This code is used in section 183*.

193*   ⟨Cases that generate more than one scrap 193*⟩ ≡
begin_like: **begin** *sc4*(*force*)(*backup*)(*res_flag* + *p*)(*force*)(*beginning*); *sc0*(*intro*);
  end;   { **begin** }
case_like: **begin** *sc0*(*casey*); *sc2*(*force*)(*res_flag* + *p*)(*alpha*);
  end;   { **case** }
do_like: **begin** *sc2*(*res_flag* + *p*)(*force*)(*omega*); *sc0*(*beginning*); *sc0*(*intro*);
  end;   { **do**, **then** }
elsif_like: **begin** ⟨Append *terminator* if not already present 194⟩;
  sc0(*close*); *sc0*(*terminator*); *sc1*(*res_flag* + *p*)(*alpha*);
  end;
else_like: **begin** *sc4*(*force*)(*backup*)(*res_flag* + *p*)(*force*)(*terminator*);
  end;   { **else** }
end_like: **begin** ⟨Append *terminator* if not already present 194⟩;
  sc4(*force*)(*backup*)(*res_flag* + *p*)(*break_space*)(*close*);
  end;   { **end** }
loop_like: **begin** *sc1*(*force*)(*alpha*); *sc2*(*res_flag* + *p*)(*force*)(*omega*); *sc0*(*beginning*); *sc0*(*intro*);
  end;   { **loop** }
proc_like: **begin** *sc4*(*force*)(*backup*)(*res_flag* + *p*)(*cancel*)(*proc*); *sc3*(*indent*)("\")("␣")(*intro*);
  end;   { **function**, **procedure**, **program** }
record_like: **begin** *sc1*(*res_flag* + *p*)(*alpha*); *sc0*(*omega*); *sc0*(*beginning*);
  end;   { **record** }
repeat_like: **begin** *sc4*(*force*)(*indent*)(*res_flag* + *p*)(*force*)(*beginning*); *sc0*(*intro*);
  end;   { **repeat** }

until_like: **begin** ⟨ Append *terminator* if not already present 194 ⟩;
  sc3 (*force*)(*backup*)(*res_flag* + *p*)(*close*); *sc0* (*clause*);
  end; { until }
var_like: **begin** *sc4* (*force*)(*backup*)(*res_flag* + *p*)(*cancel*)(*var_head*); *sc0* (*intro*);
  end; { var }
This code is used in section 191*.

198* The *outer_parse* routine is to *Pascal_parse* as *outer_xref* is to *Pascal_xref*: It constructs a sequence of scraps for Pascal text until *next_control* ≥ *format*. Thus, it takes care of embedded comments.

procedure *outer_parse*; { makes scraps from Pascal tokens and comments }
  var *bal*: *eight_bits*; { brace level in comment }
    p, q: *text_pointer*; { partial comments }
  begin while *next_control* < *format* **do**
    if *next_control* ≠ *begin_regular_comment* **then** *Pascal_parse*
    else begin ⟨ Make sure that there is room for at least seven more tokens, three more texts,
        and one more scrap 199 ⟩;
      app("\"); *app*("C"); *app*("{"); *bal* ← *copy_comment*(1); *next_control* ← *ignore*;
      while *bal* > 0 **do**
        begin *p* ← *text_ptr*; *freeze_text*; *q* ← *Pascal_translate*;
            { at this point we have *tok_ptr* + 6 ≤ *max_toks* }
        app(*tok_flag* + *p*); *app*(*inner_tok_flag* + *q*);
        if *next_control* = "|" **then**
          begin *next_control* ← *ignore*; *bal* ← *copy_comment*(*bal*);
          end
        else *bal* ← 0; { an error has been reported }
        end;
      app(*force*); *app_comment*; { the full comment becomes a scrap }
      end;
  end;

207* The real work associated with token output is done by *make_output*. This procedure appends an *end_translation* token to the current token list, and then it repeatedly calls *get_output* and feeds characters to the output buffer until reaching the *end_translation* sentinel. It is possible for *make_output* to be called recursively, since a module name may include embedded Pascal text, however, the depth of recursion never exceeds one level, since module names cannot be inside of module names.

A procedure called *output_Pascal* does the scanning, translation, and output of Pascal text within '| ... |' brackets, and this procedure uses *make_output* to output the current token list. Thus, the recursive call of *make_output* actually occurs when *make_output* calls *output_Pascal* while outputting the name of a module.

procedure *make_output*; *forward*;

procedure *output_Pascal*; { outputs the current token list }
  var *save_tok_ptr*, *save_text_ptr*, *save_next_control*: *sixteen_bits*; { values to be restored }
    p: *text_pointer*; { translation of the Pascal text }
  begin *save_tok_ptr* ← *tok_ptr*; *save_text_ptr* ← *text_ptr*; *save_next_control* ← *next_control*;
    next_control ← *ignore*; *p* ← *Pascal_translate*; *app*(*p* + *inner_tok_flag*); *make_output*;
      { output the list }

stat if $text\_ptr > max\_txt\_ptr$ **then** $max\_txt\_ptr \leftarrow text\_ptr$;
if $tok\_ptr > max\_tok\_ptr$ **then** $max\_tok\_ptr \leftarrow tok\_ptr$; **tats**
$text\_ptr \leftarrow save\_text\_ptr$; $tok\_ptr \leftarrow save\_tok\_ptr$; { forget the tokens }
$next\_control \leftarrow save\_next\_control$;   { restore $next\_control$ to original state }
end;

222* In the T_EX part of a module, we simply copy the source text, except that index entries are not copied and Pascal text within | . . . | is translated.

⟨ Translate the T_EX part of the current module 222* ⟩ ≡
  $in\_def\_part \leftarrow false$;
  repeat $next\_control \leftarrow copy\_TeX$;
    case $next\_control$ **of**
    `"|"`: **begin** $next\_control \leftarrow ignore$; $init\_stack$; $output\_Pascal$;
      end;
    `"@"`: $out(\texttt{"@"})$;
    $octal$: ⟨ Translate an octal constant appearing in T_EX text 223 ⟩;
    hex: ⟨ Translate a hexadecimal constant appearing in T_EX text 224 ⟩;
    $TeX\_string, xref\_roman, xref\_wildcard, xref\_typewriter, module\_name$: **begin** $loc \leftarrow loc - 2$;
      $next\_control \leftarrow get\_next$;   { skip to @> }
      if $next\_control = TeX\_string$ **then**
        $err\_print(\,\texttt{`!\_TeX\_string\_should\_be\_in\_Pascal\_text\_only'})$;
      end;
    $begin\_comment, end\_comment, check\_sum, thin\_space, math\_break, line\_break, big\_line\_break,$
        $no\_line\_break, join, pseudo\_semi$: $err\_print(\,\texttt{`!\_You\_can``t\_do\_that\_in\_TeX\_text'})$;
    othercases $do\_nothing$
    endcases;
  until $next\_control \geq format$
This code is used in section 220.

227* ⟨ Start a macro definition 227* ⟩ ≡
  begin $sc2(\texttt{"\\"})(\texttt{"D"})(intro)$;   { this will produce 'define ' }
  $in\_def\_part \leftarrow true$; $pound\_found \leftarrow false$; $next\_control \leftarrow get\_next$;
  if $next\_control \neq identifier$ **then** $err\_print(\,\texttt{`!\_Improper\_macro\_definition'})$
  else $sc1(id\_flag + id\_lookup(normal))(math)$;
  $next\_control \leftarrow get\_next$;
  end
This code is used in section 225.

229* Finally, when the T_EX and definition parts have been treated, we have $next\_control \geq begin\_Pascal$. We will make the global variable $this\_module$ point to the current module name, if it has a name.

⟨ Globals in the outer block 9 ⟩ +≡
$this\_module$: $name\_pointer$;   { the current module name, or zero }
$in\_def\_part, pound\_found$: $boolean$;
      { flags to determine context of use of pound sign and vertical bar }

230* ⟨ Translate the Pascal part of the current module 230* ⟩ ≡
  $this\_module \leftarrow 0$; $in\_def\_part \leftarrow false$;

if *next_control* ≤ *module_name* **then**
  begin *emit_space_if_needed*; *init_stack*;
  if *next_control* = *begin_Pascal* **then** *next_control* ← *get_next*
  else begin *this_module* ← *cur_module*; ⟨Check that = or ≡ follows this module name, and
      emit the scraps to start the module definition 231⟩;
    end;
  while *next_control* ≤ *module_name* **do**
    begin *outer_parse*; ⟨Emit the scrap for a module name if present 232⟩;
    end;
  finish_Pascal;
  end

This code is used in section 220.

265* Index.   If you have read and understood the code for Phase III above, you know what is in this index and how it got here. All modules in which an identifier is used are listed with that identifier, except that reserved words are indexed only when they appear in format definitions, and the appearances of identifiers in module names are not indexed. Underlined entries correspond to where the identifier was declared. Error messages, control sequences put into the output, and a few other things like "recursion" are indexed here too.

The following sections were changed by the change file: 1, 42, 63, 64, 86, 92, 97, 111, 112, 124, 136, 137, 138, 183, 186, 188, 191, 192, 193, 198, 207, 222, 227, 229, 230, 265.

G.4   Sample Programs

G.4.1   Knight's Tour

1. Introduction.   The following program is based on the "Knight's Tour" algorithm found on pages 137–142 of Niklaus Wirth's *Algorithms + Data Structures = Programs* (pages 148–152 in the 1986 edition, renamed *Algorithms and Data Structures*), translated into the WEB language.

2.   This program has no input, because we want to keep it rather simple. The result of the program will be the solution to the problem, which will be written to the *output* file.

In true top-down tradition, we lay out the entire program as a skeleton which will be filled in later.

```
program knights_tour (output);
   const ⟨ Constants of the program 6 ⟩
   type ⟨ Types of the program 7 ⟩
   var ⟨ Variables of the program 8 ⟩
      ⟨ Recursive procedure definitions 12 ⟩
      begin ⟨ Initialize the data structures 19 ⟩;
      ⟨ Perform the Knight's Tour and print the results 21 ⟩;
      end.
```

3.   Here are some macros for common programming idioms.

```
define incr (#) ≡ # ← # + 1    { increase a variable by unity }
define decr (#) ≡ # ← # − 1    { decrease a variable by unity }
```

4.   We shall proceed to build the program in pieces, following the text of Wirth's book and describing the structures and algorithms in more or less the same order in which he describes them. Part of the time we will be designing top-down; at other times, bottom-up; but always in the order that contributes more to the understanding of the program. One difference between this description and Wirth's is that we will use meaningful variable names (rather than names such as u, v, a, b, c). We can get away with this because we don't have to worry about the entire program's being listed in one place in narrow columns. It is broken up into small pieces and spread over several pages.

5. The Tour.   For those not familiar with the Knight's Tour, it is a classic computer science problem involving a knight, moving according to the rules of chess, which attempts to move to every square of a chessboard once and only once. To implement it, we use what is known as a "backtracking" algorithm, which is a trial-and-error search for a solution, sometimes referred to as a "brute force" approach. We start at a beginning position and try every path leading from that position (there are 8 possible knight moves from a given position) and then every path from each of those positions, etc. We follow every path until either a complete solution is found or the first failure occurs (the square is not on the board or has already been visited). If we get a failure, we "backtrack" to the previous good move and start again from there.

6. The board is a $max \times max$ square and the number of squares is max^2. Since this program has no input, we declare the value $max = 5$ as a compile-time constant.

⟨ Constants of the program 6 ⟩ ≡
  $max = 5$; $number\_of\_squares = 25$;

This code is used in section 2.

7. The obvious way to define the board is as a array of two dimensions where the indexes range from 1 to max.

⟨ Types of the program 7 ⟩ ≡
  $index = 1 \mathbin{.\,.} max$;

This code is used in section 2.

8. Boolean values for the squares would be sufficient if we only wanted to know which squares had been visited, but we also wish to know the *order* of the visits, so we define *board* as a two-dimensional array of ordinal values ranging from 0 to $number\_of\_squares$. If the value at $board[row, col] = 0$ then the square at that position has not been visited and is a candidate for a visit. Otherwise $board[row, col] = i$, which indicates that the square was visited on the ith move. The total number of moves (including the first one) $= number\_of\_squares$.

  define $empty = 0$

⟨ Variables of the program 8 ⟩ ≡
$board$: **array** $[index, index]$ **of** $empty \mathbin{.\,.} number\_of\_squares$;

See also sections 18 and 27.

This code is used in section 2.

9. Here we initialize all positions on the board to *empty*. This code is placed in a program scrap separate from all of the other initialization code for reasons explained later.

⟨ Initialize the Knight's Tour board 9 ⟩ ≡
  for $i \leftarrow 1$ **to** max **do**
    for $j \leftarrow 1$ **to** max **do** $board[i, j] \leftarrow empty$;

This code is used in sections 21, 22, and 23.

10. Two local variables, $targ\_row$ and $targ\_col$, are the coordinates of $target\_square$, the one to which we wish to move next. Before we attempt the move, we must first ensure that $target\_square$ is on the board ($1 \leq targ\_row \leq max$ and $1 \leq targ\_col \leq max$). Then we must determine whether it is available for knight placement ($target\_square = empty$). We provide some macros for manipulation of $target\_square$.

Side note: in Wirth's book, the $target\_position\_valid$ test is later changed to be a check for inclusion in the set $[1 \mathbin{.\,.} max]$ rather than discrete comparisons to 1 and max. While this is more efficient, it does not necessarily aid understanding of the algorithm, so we will not bother.

define *valid_row_or_column*(**#**) ≡ ((1 ≤ **#**) ∧ (**#** ≤ *max*))
define *target_position_valid* ≡ (*valid_row_or_column*(*targ_row*) ∧ *valid_row_or_column*(*targ_col*))
define *target_square* ≡ *board*[*targ_row*, *targ_col*]
define *target_empty* ≡ (*target_square* = *empty*)
define *set_square_to*(**#**) ≡ *target_square* ← **#**

⟨ Local variables of the Knight's Tour procedure 10 ⟩ ≡
targ_row, *targ_col*: *integer*;   { row and column of target square }

See also section 11.

This code is used in section 12.

11.   There are 8 possible knight moves from any given position. Since we normally are going to attempt all 8, we will define *candidate_move* to hold the move index.

define *number_of_legal_knight_moves* = 8

⟨ Local variables of the Knight's Tour procedure 10 ⟩ +≡
candidate_move: 0 .. *number_of_legal_knight_moves*;

12.   We are ready to define the procedure which actually does the search. It must be declared as a procedure rather than as simple inline code, since it is recursive. As the procedure is entered for a particular move number and current position, the moves possible from that position are attempted. The Boolean result *successful* is set if one of the 8 paths results in a solution. The procedure passes the value of *successful* back to the calling procedure, which will pass it to its own caller, etc., all the way back up to the original call.

⟨ Recursive procedure definitions 12 ⟩ ≡
procedure *try_knight_move*(*move_number* : *integer*; *row*, *col* : *index*; **var** *successful* : *Boolean*);
  var ⟨ Local variables of the Knight's Tour procedure 10 ⟩
    begin ⟨ Try the moves possible from the current position until solution is found or all have
        been tried 13 ⟩;
    end;

This code is used in section 2.

13.   Each of the 8 possible moves is attempted. If the move can be made, it is recorded and a move from the new position is attempted. If *successful* is ever *true*, it can only mean that a complete solution has been found and the search is terminated. If *successful* is false, the remaining candidate moves are tried.

define *no_more_candidates* ≡ (*candidate_move* = *number_of_legal_knight_moves*)

⟨ Try the moves possible from the current position until solution is found or all have been
    tried 13 ⟩ ≡
candidate_move ← 0;
repeat *incr*(*candidate_move*); *successful* ← *false*;
    ⟨ Set the coordinates of the next move as defined by the rules of chess 17 ⟩;
    ⟨ Record the move if acceptable and try to make further moves; set *successful* if solution is
        found 14 ⟩;
  until *successful* ∨ *no_more_candidates*;

This code is used in section 12.

14. The condition *move_is_acceptable* is equivalent to the combination of the conditions (*target_position_valid* ∧ *target_empty*). Because of the realities of computer memory addressing, if we find that the condition *target_position_valid* is not *true*, then we cannot perform the second test because the array indexes *targ_row* or *targ_col* are not valid and the contents of *target_square* cannot be accessed. We have to test these two conditions with separate nested **if** statements (" **if** *target_position_valid* **then if** *target_empty* **then**"). In the future, when the ANSI Extended Pascal Standard is adopted, its short-circuiting **and_then** operator will make this unnecessary, but we have to handle it manually in the meantime.

Once we have determined that the move is acceptable we record it. If *board_not_full* is true, we try the next knight move. If *board_not_full* is false (i.e., the board *is* full), it means we have found a solution to the problem, so we set *successful* to true, which will terminate the tour.

> **define** *board_not_full* ≡ *move_number* < *number_of_squares*
> **define** *record_move* ≡ *set_square_to*(*move_number*)

⟨ Record the move if acceptable and try to make further moves; set *successful* if solution is found 14 ⟩ ≡
>   **if** *target_position_valid* **then**
>   **if** *target_empty* **then**
>   **begin** *record_move*;
>   **if** *board_not_full* **then** ⟨ Try further knight moves and erase this move if not successful 15 ⟩
>   **else** *successful* ← *true*;
>   **end**;

This code is used in section 13.

15. Here we try the next move by having the procedure call itself recursively, with the *move_number* incremented by one and *targ_row*, *targ_col* as the position of the move. If a failure occurs on that move or any move that follows it (*successful* = *false*), we erase the move we just made (this is the "backtracking" part) and continue looking.

Important note: the **begin** and **end** statements are *critical* for this particular section, since it is used as a **then** clause in the previous section and the program text is simply inserted verbatim. Without the **begin** and **end** the call to the *try_knight_move* procedure alone becomes the **then** clause, which will cause a syntax error when the dangling **else** clause is processed.

> **define** *next_move* ≡ *move_number* + 1
> **define** *erase_move* ≡ *set_square_to*(*empty*)

⟨ Try further knight moves and erase this move if not successful 15 ⟩ ≡
>   **begin** *try_knight_move*(*next_move*, *targ_row*, *targ_col*, *successful*);
>   **if** ¬*successful* **then** *erase_move*;
>   **end**

This code is used in section 14.

16. We now consider the moves a knight is allowed to make. From any given position there are 8 possible moves, not all of which are necessarily on the board. A knight makes a two-part L-shaped move, where the first part is either one or two squares in a nondiagonal direction, and the second part is one or two squares in a direction perpendicular to the first. The number of squares is never the same for the two parts; if the knight is moved one square during the first part, then it is moved two squares during the second, and vice versa.

	⊙	⟷	⊙	
⊙		⇑		⊙
↕	⇐	♠	⇒	↕
⊙		⇓		⊙
	⊙	⟷	⊙	

The '♠' represents a knight. Doesn't it sort of look like one? (You have to use some imagination. Okay, a *lot* of imagination.) The '⊙' characters represent the legal destinations from the current position.

17. Rather than go through a complicated algorithm, we simply initialize a pair of tables, *row_deltas* and *col_deltas*, containing values to be added to the current position to get the target position. For each of the 8 moves which are possible from the current position, *row_deltas*[*candidate_move*] is added to the current row to get *targ_row* and *col_deltas*[*candidate_move*] provides the same service for *targ_col*.

⟨ Set the coordinates of the next move as defined by the rules of chess 17 ⟩ ≡
   targ_row ← *row* + *row_deltas*[*candidate_move*]; *targ_col* ← *col* + *col_deltas*[*candidate_move*];

This code is used in section 13.

18. If we are going to use these arrays, it might be helpful to define them to prevent the Pascal compiler from complaining bitterly.

⟨ Variables of the program 8 ⟩ +≡
row_deltas, *col_deltas*: **array** [1 .. *number_of_legal_knight_moves*] **of** −2 .. 2;

19. Even though the compiler is now happy, if we don't initialize the arrays with the proper delta values, we will take the knight on a route more like the Drunkard's Walk than the Knight's Tour.

⟨ Initialize the data structures 19 ⟩ ≡
   row_deltas[1] ← 2; *col_deltas*[1] ← 1; *row_deltas*[2] ← 1; *col_deltas*[2] ← 2; *row_deltas*[3] ← −1;
   col_deltas[3] ← 2; *row_deltas*[4] ← −2; *col_deltas*[4] ← 1; *row_deltas*[5] ← −2;
   col_deltas[5] ← −1; *row_deltas*[6] ← −1; *col_deltas*[6] ← −2; *row_deltas*[7] ← 1;
   col_deltas[7] ← −2; *row_deltas*[8] ← 2; *col_deltas*[8] ← −1;

This code is used in section 2.

20. Now it's time to start the tour. For starting position $x_0 y_0$ we select (1,1). Since this is the first move, we set *board*[1, 1] = 1. We then call the *try_knight_move* procedure with the proper parameters for move 2 to set events in motion. After all of the moves have been completed, we print out the board. The result should be the same as the first part of Table 3.1 on page 141 (page 151, 1986 edition) of Wirth's book, which is reproduced here.

1	6	15	10	21
14	9	20	5	16
19	2	7	22	11
8	13	24	17	4
25	18	3	12	23

21. We define a macro to initialize the first move and start the tour. Note: the call to *try_knight_move* in the definition of *do_the_tour_starting_at* appears to have the wrong number of parameters. This procedure requires four parameters and we seem to be passing only three. However, since a macro parameter is really just a simple string substitution, we will really be replacing the # character with two parameters at once: the row and column of the starting position. Since the comma is included in the substitution, the expanded text will have the proper four parameters.

> **define** *do_the_tour_starting_at*(#) ≡ *board*[#] ← 1; *try_knight_move*(2, #, *successful*);

⟨ Perform the Knight's Tour and print the results 21 ⟩ ≡
> ⟨ Initialize the Knight's Tour board 9 ⟩;
> *do_the_tour_starting_at*(1, 1); ⟨ Print the results of the Knight's Tour 26 ⟩;

See also sections 22 and 23.

This code is used in section 2.

22. Since Table 3.1 in the book shows a second solution obtained with a different first move (3,3),

23	10	15	4	25
16	5	24	9	14
11	22	1	18	3
6	17	20	13	8
21	12	7	2	19

we decide to run the tour again to duplicate that result as well. We decline the third test in Table 3.1, because it requires a different value of *max*, which we cannot change at run-time as the program is currently designed. Before rerunning the test, we must remember to reinitialize the board. This is the reason that the board initialization code was separated from all of the other initializations; it is executed more than once. We use the same name when defining the code for this section as for the previous section, which will cause the second test to follow immediately after the first in the Pascal program.

⟨ Perform the Knight's Tour and print the results 21 ⟩ +≡
> ⟨ Initialize the Knight's Tour board 9 ⟩;
> *do_the_tour_starting_at*(3, 3); ⟨ Print the results of the Knight's Tour 26 ⟩;

23. The 1986 edition shows yet another solution, with (2,4) as the starting move.

23	4	9	14	25
10	15	24	1	8
5	22	3	18	13
16	11	20	7	2
21	6	17	12	19

⟨ Perform the Knight's Tour and print the results 21 ⟩ +≡
  ⟨ Initialize the Knight's Tour board 9 ⟩;
  $do\_the\_tour\_starting\_at(2, 4)$; ⟨ Print the results of the Knight's Tour 26 ⟩;

24. The output phase.   The job of printing is not as interesting as the problem itself, but it must be done sooner or later, so we may as well get it over with.

25.   In order to keep this program reasonably free of notations that are uniquely Pascalesque, a few macro definitions for low-level output instructions are introduced here. All of the output-oriented commands in the remainder of the program will be stated in terms of three simple primitives called *new_line*, *print_string*, and *print_integer*.

  define *width* = 3   { width of an integer field }
  define *print_string*(#) ≡ *write*(#)   { put a given string into the *output* file }
  define *print_integer*(#) ≡ *write*(# : *width*)   { print an integer of *width* character positions }
  define *new_line* ≡ *write_ln*   { advance to a new line in the *output* file }

26.   ⟨ Print the results of the Knight's Tour 26 ⟩ ≡
  if *successful* **then**
    for $i \leftarrow 1$ **to** *max* **do**
      begin for $j \leftarrow 1$ **to** *max* **do** *print_integer*($board[i, j]$);
      new_line;
      end
  else *print_string*(´no␣solution´);
  new_line; *new_line*;
This code is used in sections 21, 22, and 23.

27.   We define a few more odd variables.
⟨ Variables of the program 8 ⟩ +≡
i, j: *index*;   { temporary index variables }
successful: *Boolean*;   { The Knight's Tour was successful }

28. A little math.   Just as the movies have gratuitous sex and violence, this program has gratuitous mathematics. The following sections in this group have nothing to do with the program and are here only to illustrate the power of TEX in typesetting mathematics. (This is an example, after all!) Since the problem of the Knight's Tour is more logical than mathematical, there was no need to tap the power of TEX math. Warning: the following formulas were lifted from several documents and are out of context, so they may or may not make sense. (They sure look nice, though.)

29. If this program had been mathematical in nature, we could have displayed the formula in its true form:

$$\sin[(2n + 1)\theta] = \Im(e^{(2n+1)i\theta})$$
$$= \Im\{[\cos(\theta) + i\sin(\theta)]^{2n+1}\}$$
$$= \sum_{k=0}^{n}(-1)^k \binom{2n + 1}{2k + 1} \sin^{2k+1}(\theta)\cos^{2(n-k)}(\theta)$$
$$= \left[\sum_{k=0}^{n}(-1)^k \binom{2n + 1}{2k + 1} \cot^{2(n-k)}(\theta)\right]\left[\sin^{2n+1}(\theta)\right]$$

rather than some line-printer approximation of it.

30. Since $\sin(\frac{k\pi}{2n+1}) \neq 0$ for $k = 1, \ldots, n$, the roots of $p(x) = \sum_{k=0}^{n}\binom{2n+1}{2k+1}(-1)^k x^{n-k}$ are exactly $\cot^2(\theta_k)$.

31. Matrices are fun (and good for you, too).

$$A = \begin{pmatrix} a_{11} & a_{12} & \cdots & a_{1n} \\ a_{21} & a_{22} & \cdots & a_{2n} \\ \vdots & \vdots & \ddots & \vdots \\ a_{m1} & a_{m2} & \cdots & a_{mn} \end{pmatrix}$$

32. I have heard that the risk-adjusted present discount value of firm j in period t, $MV_{j,t}$ is given by

$$MV_{j,t} = \sum_{r=0}^{\infty}\frac{E(cash\ payout)_{t+\tau}}{(1 + R_f)^r} - \theta\beta_j\sum_{r=0}^{\infty}\frac{K_{j,t+\tau}\left(\frac{1 - \delta^{2r}}{1 - \delta^2}\right)^{1/2}}{(1 + R_f)^r}$$

where R_f is the (assumed constant) risk-free discount rate and θ is the price of risk γ multiplied by $\sigma(\varepsilon_{mt})$.

33. Dividing both sides of equation 4 by the expected value of future cash flows allows Z for each firm to be calculated as a function of R_f and θ:

$$Z_{j,t}(R_f, \theta) \equiv \frac{MV_{j,t}}{\sum_{r=0}^{\infty}\frac{E(cash\ payout)_{t+\tau}}{(1 + R_f)^r}}$$

$$= 1 - \theta\frac{\beta_j\sum_{r=0}^{\infty}\frac{K_{j,t+\tau}\left(\frac{1 - \delta^{2r}}{1 - \delta^2}\right)^{1/2}}{(1 + R_f)^r}}{\sum_{r=0}^{\infty}\frac{E(cash\ payout)_{t+\tau}}{(1 + R_f)^r}}$$

I think that's wonderful.

34. Finally we have

$$e^x = \int_{-\infty}^{x} \sum_{n=0}^{\infty} \frac{\lambda^n}{n!} d\lambda$$

35. Index.   Every identifier used in this program is shown here together with a list of the section numbers where that identifier appears. The section number is underlined if the identifier was defined in that section. However, one-letter identifiers are indexed only at their point of definition, since such identifiers tend to appear almost everywhere.

This index also refers to other topics that appear in the documentation (e.g., 'backtracking algorithm').

G.4.2   Eight Queens

1.   Introduction.   The following program is based on the "Eight Queens" algorithm found on pages 143–147 of Niklaus Wirth's *Algorithms + Data Structures = Programs* (pages 153–157 in the 1986 edition, retitled *Algorithms and Data Structures*), translated into the WEB language.

2.   This program has no input, because we want to keep it rather simple. The result of the program will be the solution to the problem, which will be written to the *output* file.

In true top-down tradition, we lay out the entire program as a skeleton which will be filled in later.

program *eight_queens*(*output*);
   var ⟨ Variables of the program 5 ⟩
   ⟨ Recursive procedure definition 15 ⟩
     begin ⟨ Initialize the data structures 8 ⟩;
     ⟨ Place the queens on the board and print the results 17 ⟩;
     end.

3.   We shall proceed to build the program in pieces, following the text of Wirth's book and describing the structures and algorithms in more or less the same order that he describes them. Part of the time we will be designing top-down; at other times, bottom-up; but always in the order that contributes most to the understanding of the program. One difference between this description and Wirth's is that we will use meaningful variable names (rather than names such as u, v, a, b, c). We can get away with this because we don't have to worry about the entire program's being listed in one place in narrow columns. It is broken up into small pieces and spread over several pages.

4.   The Eight Queens.   Eight queens are to be positioned on a full-size (8×8) chessboard in such a way that no queen can "check" any other queen. This means that each queen must be placed so that it is not on the same row, column, or diagonal as any other queen. These restrictions allow us to get by with a set of small arrays containing pertinent information rather than a full-size chessboard that is mostly empty.

5.   Since each column has one and only one queen, we define an array *queen_pos* where *queen_pos*[*col*] is the position (row) of the queen in column *col*. This array ensures that we have only one queen per column. We make the queen number *queen* equivalent to the column number *col*. Since the column is now taken care of, we can concentrate on the other elements, the row and the two diagonals.

   define *number_of_queens* = 8
   define *queen* ≡ *col*

⟨ Variables of the program 5 ⟩ ≡
queen_pos: **array** [1 .. *number_of_queens*] **of** 1 .. 8;
See also sections 7, 10, and 19.
This code is used in section 2.

6.   A square is considered to be "safe," or available for queen placement, if there are no queens in the row or either of the diagonals of the current position. We define Boolean arrays to hold this information.

7.   Only one queen may be in a row, so we define the array *no_queen_in_row* where each element is a Boolean value which indicates the absence of a queen in that row. The macro *safe_row* is a shorthand to refer to the entry in *no_queen_in_row* for the current value of *row* and can be used in the remainder of the program as if it were a simple Boolean variable.

  define *safe_row* ≡ *no_queen_in_row*[*row*]

⟨ Variables of the program 5 ⟩ +≡
no_queen_in_row: **array** [1 .. *number_of_queens*] **of** *Boolean*;

8.   ⟨ Initialize the data structures 8 ⟩ ≡
  for $k \leftarrow 1$ **to** *number_of_queens* **do** *no_queen_in_row*[*k*] ← *true*;
See also section 11.
This code is used in section 2.

9.   Now to tackle the diagonals. We will define a left diagonal as one of the diagonals moving from top right to bottom left (╱), while a right diagonal goes from top left to bottom right (╲). We need an simple way to identify the diagonals. This turns out to be much easier than expected. Adding *row* + *col* will result in the same value for every square in a left diagonal, while *row* − *col* provides a number that can positively identify a right diagonal.

10.   By performing the calculations for each square, we can determine that for the index of the left diagonals, $2 \leq left\_diag \leq 16$ and, for the right diagonals, $-7 \leq right\_diag \leq 7$. We use these values to define the indexes of the diagonal arrays. We also define some macros for manipulation of the diagonals. The macros *safe_left_diag* and *safe_right_diag* can be treated as if they were simple Boolean variables.

  define *left_diag* ≡ *col* + *row*
  define *right_diag* ≡ *col* − *row*
  define *safe_left_diag* ≡ *left_diag_has_no_queen*[*left_diag*]
  define *safe_right_diag* ≡ *right_diag_has_no_queen*[*right_diag*]

⟨ Variables of the program 5 ⟩ +≡
left_diag_has_no_queen: **array** [2 .. 16] **of** *Boolean*;
right_diag_has_no_queen: **array** [−7 .. 7] **of** *Boolean*;

11.   Here we initialize the diagonal arrays.

⟨ Initialize the data structures 8 ⟩ +=
  for $k \leftarrow 2$ **to** 16 **do** *left_diag_has_no_queen*[*k*] ← *true*;
  for $k \leftarrow -7$ **to** 7 **do** *right_diag_has_no_queen*[*k*] ← *true*;

12.   To place a queen on the board, the row and diagonal *safe* indicators are set to *false*, indicating the presence of a queen. The row number is moved into the *queen_pos* array so we know where the queen was moved.

⟨ Set a queen on the board at the current position 12 ⟩ ≡
    queen_pos [*queen*] ← *row*; *safe_row* ← *false*; *safe_left_diag* ← *false*; *safe_right_diag* ← *false*;
This code is used in section 15.

13.   The reverse is used to remove a queen from the board. The three indicators are set to *true*.

⟨ Remove the queen from the board 13 ⟩ ≡
    safe_row ← *true*; *safe_left_diag* ← *true*; *safe_right_diag* ← *true*;
This code is used in section 15.

14.   A square is considered safe, or available for queen placement, if the row and both diagonals are safe.

    define *safe_square* ≡ *safe_row* ∧ *safe_left_diag* ∧ *safe_right_diag*

15.   The actual Eight Queens algorithm is defined as a procedure, since it is recursive. When the procedure is entered, all possible positions for the specified queen are checked. If a position is safe, the queen move is made. After checking for a solution, the move is erased. This particular algorithm performs backtracking on success or failure, because we want to find all solutions, which can't be done with old pieces lying all over the board.

⟨ Recursive procedure definition 15 ⟩ ≡
procedure *try_queen_move*(*queen* : *integer*);
    var *row*: *integer*;
    begin for *row* ← 1 **to** 8 **do**
        if *safe_square* **then**
            begin ⟨ Set a queen on the board at the current position 12 ⟩;
            ⟨ Print the solution if last queen; try next one if not 16 ⟩;
            ⟨ Remove the queen from the board 13 ⟩;
            end;
    end;
This code is used in section 2.

16.   If this is the last queen, we have found one of the solutions. If not, call *try_queen_move* recursively for the next queen.

⟨ Print the solution if last queen; try next one if not 16 ⟩ ≡
    if *queen* = *number_of_queens* **then** ⟨ Print one of the Eight Queens solutions 23 ⟩
    else *try_queen_move*(*queen* + 1);
This code is used in section 15.

17.   We start the action by calling the *try_queen_move* procedure for *queen* = 1.

⟨ Place the queens on the board and print the results 17 ⟩ ≡
    ⟨ Print a header line 22 ⟩;
    try_queen_move(1);
This code is used in section 2.

18. There are 192 different solutions generated by this program. If all of the symmetric duplicates were removed, there would be only 12, but the program doesn't realize that, so all 192 will be printed. The first 12 should match Table 3.2 on page 147 of Wirth's book (page 157 in 1986 edition). The first solution printed is (1,5,8,6,3,7,2,4), which looks like the figure 3.9 on page 144 (page 154):

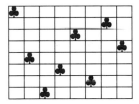

where ♣ represents a queen (yes, I know; wrong game. TEX doesn't have a chess queen character, although one could have been created with its companion program METAFONT if desired).

19. The variable *k* has to be defined somewhere.

⟨ Variables of the program 5 ⟩ +≡
k: *integer* ;

20. The output phase. The job of printing is not as interesting as the problem itself; but it must be done sooner or later, so we may as well get it over with.

21. In order to keep this program reasonably free of notations that are uniquely Pascalesque, a few macro definitions for low-level output instructions are introduced here. All of the output-oriented commands in the remainder of the program will be stated in terms of three simple primitives called *new_line*, *print_string*, and *print_integer* .

define *width* = 3   { width of an integer field }
define *print_string*(#) ≡ *write*(#)   { put a given string into the *output* file }
define *print_integer*(#) ≡ *write*(# : *width*)   { print an integer of *width* character positions }
define *new_line* ≡ *write_ln*   { advance to a new line in the *output* file }

22. A simple header is printed before the queen result lines. It consists of numbered column headers followed by a line of dashes.

⟨ Print a header line 22 ⟩ ≡
  new_line; *new_line*;
  for *k* ← 1 **to** 8 **do** *print_integer*(*k*);
  new_line;
  for *k* ← 1 **to** 8 **do** *print_string*(´---´);
  new_line;
This code is used in section 17.

23. Since every column contains one and only one queen, we only have to print the row number of the queen for each column. The **begin** and **end** statements are mandatory for this particular section, since it is used as a **then** clause.

⟨ Print one of the Eight Queens solutions 23 ⟩ ≡
  begin for $k \leftarrow 1$ **to** *number_of_queens* **do** *print_integer*(*queen_pos*[k]);
  new_line;
  end
This code is used in section 16.

24. Index.   Every identifier used in this program is shown here together with a list of the section numbers where that identifier appears. The section number is underlined if the identifier was defined in that section. However, one-letter identifiers are indexed only at their point of definition, since such identifiers tend to appear almost everywhere.

This index also refers to other topics that appear in the documentation (e.g., backtracking algorithm).

⟨Initialize the data structures 8, 11⟩   Used in section 2.
⟨Place the queens on the board and print the results 17⟩   Used in section 2.
⟨Print a header line 22⟩   Used in section 17.
⟨Print one of the Eight Queens solutions 23⟩   Used in section 16.
⟨Print the solution if last queen; try next one if not 16⟩   Used in section 15.
⟨Recursive procedure definition 15⟩   Used in section 2.
⟨Remove the queen from the board 13⟩   Used in section 15.
⟨Set a queen on the board at the current position 12⟩   Used in section 15.
⟨Variables of the program 5, 7, 10, 19⟩   Used in section 2.

G.4.3   WEB **Template**

1.   Introduction.   This is XXXXXX, a sample program.

    define *banner* ≡ ´This␣is␣XXXXXX,␣Version␣1.0´   { printed when the program starts }

2.   The program begins with a normal Pascal program heading, whose components will be filled in later, using the conventions of WEB. When this template is used for an actual program, all occurrences of **XXXXXX** should be replaced by the name of the real program.

program *XXXXXX*;
   label ⟨ Labels in the outer block 3 ⟩
   const ⟨ Constants in the outer block 0 ⟩
   type ⟨ Types in the outer block 11 ⟩
   var ⟨ Global variables 9 ⟩
   ⟨ Procedure and function definitions of the program 15 ⟩
   procedure *initialize*;   { this procedure gets things started properly }
     var ⟨ Local variables for initialization 0 ⟩
     begin ⟨ Initialize whatever XXXXXX might access 10 ⟩
     end;

3.   Three labels must be declared in the main program, so we give them symbolic names.

    define *start_of_prog* = 1   { go here when XXXXXX's variables are initialized }
    define *end_of_prog* = 9998   { go here to close files and terminate gracefully }
    define *final_end* = 9999   { this label marks the ending of the program }

⟨ Labels in the outer block 3 ⟩ ≡
   start_of_prog, *end_of_prog*, *final_end*;   { key control points }

This code is used in section 2.

4.   Here is the rest of the program body.

    begin *initialize*;   { set global variables to their starting values }
start_of_prog: ⟨ Do whatever it is that this program is supposed to do 0 ⟩;
end_of_prog: ⟨ Close any files opened by this program 0 ⟩;
   ⟨ Terminate the program normally 0 ⟩;
final_end: **end**.

5.   Debugging stuff.

    define *debug* ≡ @{   { change this to '*debug* ≡ ' when debugging }
    define *gubed* ≡ @}   { change this to '*gubed* ≡ ' when debugging }
    format *debug* ≡ *begin*
    format *gubed* ≡ *end*

6. Set up the **case** statement.

    define *othercases* ≡ *others*:   { default for cases not listed explicitly }
    define *endcases* ≡ **end**   { follows the default case in an extended **case** statement }
    format *othercases* ≡ *else*
    format *endcases* ≡ *end*

7. Set up labels.

    define *exit* = 10   { go here to leave a procedure }
    define *restart* = 20   { go here to start a procedure again }
    define *reswitch* = 21   { go here to start a case statement again }
    define *continue* = 22   { go here to resume a loop }
    define *done* = 30   { go here to exit a loop }
    define *found* = 40   { go here when you've found it }
    define *not_found* = 45   { go here when you've found nothing }

8. Here are some macros for common programming idioms.

    define *incr*(#) ≡ # ← # + 1   { increase a variable by unity }
    define *decr*(#) ≡ # ← # − 1   { decrease a variable by unity }
    define *negate*(#) ≡ # ← −#   { change the sign of a variable }
    define *loop* ≡ **while** *true* **do**   { repeat over and over until a **goto** happens }
    format *loop* ≡ *xclause*   { WEB's **xclause** acts like 'while *true* do' }
    define *do_nothing* ≡   { empty statement }
    define *return* ≡ **goto** *exit*   { terminate a procedure call }
    format *return* ≡ *nil*
    define *empty* = 0   { symbolic name for a null constant }

9. Set up the global variable *history*.

    define *spotless* = 0   { *history* value for normal jobs }
    define *harmless_message* = 1   { *history* value when nonserious info was printed }
    define *error_message* = 2   { *history* value when an error was noted }
    define *fatal_message* = 3   { *history* value when we had to stop prematurely }
    define *mark_harmless* ≡ **if** *history* = *spotless* **then** *history* ← *harmless_message*
    define *mark_error* ≡ *history* ← *error_message*
    define *mark_fatal* ≡ *history* ← *fatal_message*

⟨ Global variables 9 ⟩ =
history: *spotless* .. *fatal_message*;   { how bad was this run? }

This code is used in section 2.

10. ⟨ Initialize whatever XXXXX might access 10 ⟩ ≡
    history ← *spotless*;

This code is used in section 2.

11. Set up the character set, if the programmer wishes to make this program readily portable between a wide variety of computers.

⟨ Types in the outer block 11 ⟩ ≡
    ASCII_code = 0 .. 127;   { 7-bit numbers }

See also section 13.

This code is used in section 2.

12.   And so on.

   define *text_char* ≡ *char*   { the data type of characters in text files }
   define *first_text_char* = 0   { ordinal number of the smallest element of *text_char* }
   define *last_text_char* = 127   { ordinal number of the largest element of *text_char* }

13.   Set up generic input and output.

   define *width* = 3   { width of an integer field }
   define *print_string*(#) ≡ *write*(#)   { put a given string into the *output* file }
   define *print_integer*(#) ≡ *write*(# : *width*)   { print an integer of *width* character positions }
   define *new_line* ≡ *write_ln*   { advance to a new line in the *output* file }
⟨ Types in the outer block 11 ⟩ +≡
   eight_bits = 0 .. 255;   { unsigned one-byte quantity }
   alpha_file = **packed file of** *text_char*;   { files that contain textual data }
   byte_file = **packed file of** *eight_bits*;   { files that contain binary data }

14.   The various input and output procedures for binary and text files should be defined
here.

15.   A template procedure.
⟨ Procedure and function definitions of the program 15 ⟩ ≡
procedure *whatever*(**var** *p1* : *integer*; *p2* : *integer*);
   var ⟨ Generic local variables for procedures and functions 17 ⟩
   begin *statement*;
   end;
See also section 16.

This code is used in section 2.

16.   A template function.
⟨ Procedure and function definitions of the program 15 ⟩ +≡
function *whichever*(**var** *p1* : *integer*; *p2* : *integer*): *integer*;
   var ⟨ Generic local variables for procedures and functions 17 ⟩
   begin *statement*; *whichever* ← 1;
   end;

17.   ⟨ Generic local variables for procedures and functions 17 ⟩ ≡
i, j, k, l, m, n: *integer*;   { assorted loop index variables }
count: *integer*;   { a counter to use for various things }
ch: *char*;   { an anonymous character variable }
This code is used in sections 15 and 16.

18.   System-dependent changes.   This section should be replaced, if necessary,
by changes to the program that are necessary to make XXXXXX work at a particular
installation.

19.   Index.

⟨Close any files opened by this program 0⟩   Used in section 4.

⟨Constants in the outer block 0⟩   Used in section 2.

⟨Do whatever it is that this program is supposed to do 0⟩   Used in section 4.

⟨Generic local variables for procedures and functions 17⟩   Used in sections 15 and 16.

⟨Global variables 9⟩   Used in section 2.

⟨Initialize whatever XXXXXX might access 10⟩   Used in section 2.

⟨Labels in the outer block 3⟩   Used in section 2.

⟨Local variables for initialization 0⟩   Used in section 2.

⟨Procedure and function definitions of the program 15, 16⟩   Used in section 2.

⟨Terminate the program normally 0⟩   Used in section 4.

⟨Types in the outer block 11, 13⟩   Used in section 2.

G.4.4   Bad Example

1.   The program.   This program has only marginally been adapted to WEB.

program *knights_tour* (*output*);
       { The following program is based on the "Knight's Tour" algorithm }
      { found on pages 137–142 of Niklaus Wirth's "Algorithms + Data }
      { Structures = Programs". }
      { This program has no input, because we want to keep it rather simple. }
      { The result of the program will be the solution to the problem, which }
      { will be written to the output file. }
  const *max* = 5; *number_of_squares* = 25;
  type *index* = 1 .. *max*;
  var *board*: **array** [*index*, *index*] **of** 0 .. *number_of_squares*;
   row_deltas, *col_deltas*: **array** [1 .. 8] **of** −2 .. 2;
   i, *j*: *index*; *successful*: *boolean*;

  procedure *try_knight_move* (*move_number* : *integer*; *row*, *col* : *index*; **var** *successful* : *boolean*);
      { This the procedure which actually does the search. It must be declared }
     { as a procedure rather than as simple inline code, since it is recursive. }
     { As the procedure is entered for a particular move number and current }
     { position, the moves possible from that position are attempted. The }
     { boolean result *successful* is set if one of the eight paths results }
     { in a solution. The procedure passes the value of *successful* back to }
     { the calling procedure, which will pass it to its own caller, etc., all }
     { the way back up to the original call. }
   var *targ_row*, *targ_col*: *integer*; *candidate_move*: 0 .. 8;
   begin   { of *try_knight_move* }
   candidate_move ← 0;
   repeat *candidate_move* ← *candidate_move* + 1; *successful* ← *false*;
    targ_row ← *row* + *row_deltas*[*candidate_move*]; *targ_col* ← *col* + *col_deltas*[*candidate_move*];
     if (((1 ≤ *targ_row*) ∧ (*targ_row* ≤ *max*)) ∧ ((1 ≤ *targ_col*) ∧ (*targ_col* ≤ *max*))) **then**
      if (*board*[*targ_row*, *targ_col*] = 0) **then**
        begin *board*[*targ_row*, *targ_col*] ← *move_number*;
        if *move_number* < *number_of_squares* **then**
          begin *try_knight_move* (*move_number* + 1, *targ_row*, *targ_col*, *successful*);
          if ¬*successful* **then** *board*[*targ_row*, *targ_col*] ← 0;
          end
        else *successful* ← *true*;
        end;
   until *successful* ∨ (*candidate_move* = 8);
   end; { of *try_knight_move* }

```
begin    { of main program }
row_deltas[1] ← 2;  col_deltas[1] ← 1;  row_deltas[2] ← 1;  col_deltas[2] ← 2;
row_deltas[3] ← −1;  col_deltas[3] ← 2;  row_deltas[4] ← −2;  col_deltas[4] ← 1;
row_deltas[5] ← −2;  col_deltas[5] ← −1;  row_deltas[6] ← −1;  col_deltas[6] ← −2;
row_deltas[7] ← 1;  col_deltas[7] ← −2;  row_deltas[8] ← 2;  col_deltas[8] ← −1;
for i ← 1 to max do
    for j ← 1 to max do board[i, j] ← 0;
board[1, 1] ← 1;  try_knight_move(2, 1, 1, successful);
if successful then
    for i ← 1 to max do
        begin for j ← 1 to max do  write(board[i, j] : 3);
        writeln;
        end
else write('no solution');
writeln;  writeln;
for i ← 1 to max do
    for j ← 1 to max do board[i, j] ← 0;
board[3, 3] ← 1;  try_knight_move(2, 3, 3, successful);
if successful then
    for i ← 1 to max do
        begin for j ← 1 to max do  write(board[i, j] : 3);
        writeln;
        end
else write('no solution');
writeln;  writeln;
for i ← 1 to max do
    for j ← 1 to max do board[i, j] ← 0;
board[2, 4] ← 1;  try_knight_move(2, 2, 4, successful);
if successful then
    for i ← 1 to max do
        begin for j ← 1 to max do  write(board[i, j] : 3);
        writeln;
        end
else write('no solution');
writeln;  writeln;
end.    { of main program }
```

2. Index.

G.5 Modula-2 Programs

G.5.1 Table Handler Library Module

1. Introduction. This general-purpose symbol table handler is based on the Table-Handler module in Niklaus Wirth's *Programming in Modula-2*. It allows a calling program to build a table of symbols with a cardinal value associated with each.

2. A library module in the Modula-2 language consists of two parts: a definition module and an implementation module. The language specification does not permit the two to be present in the same source file, although this would be convenient for coordination purposes.

3. The code for use when generating a implementation module is enclosed between the beginning delimiter **impmod** and ending delimiter **endimp**. Since the implementation module is modified and compiled many more times than the definition module, generation of the implementation module is the default for the MWEB file.

> **define** *impmod* ≡   (∗ change this to '*impmod* ≡ @{' for definition module ∗)
> **define** *endimp* ≡   (∗ change this to '*endimp* ≡ @}' for definition module ∗)
> **format** *impmod* ≡ *begin*
> **format** *endimp* ≡ *end*

4. Similarly, the delimiters **defmod** and **enddef** enclose the code for generating a definition module.

> **define** *defmod* ≡ @{   (∗ change this to '*defmod* ≡ ' for definition module ∗)
> **define** *enddef* ≡ @}   (∗ change this to '*enddef* ≡ ' for definition module ∗)
> **format** *defmod* ≡ *begin*
> **format** *enddef* ≡ *end*

5. Here is where the code for the modules will be inserted. The code for both the definition module and the implementation module is present, although only one or the other will actually be compiled.

> impmod
>   ⟨ Implementation module of *table_handler* 8 ⟩
> endimp
> defmod
>   ⟨ Definition module of *table_handler* 6 ⟩
> enddef

6. This is the definition module, which specifies the interface between the module and a client program; it consists of only the elements which are visible outside the module.

> ⟨ Definition module of *table_handler* 6 ⟩ ≡
>   **definition module** *table_handler*;

⟨Export List 7⟩
const ⟨Constants to be exported 11⟩
type ⟨Types to be exported 10⟩
⟨Procedure heading declarations of the definition module 18⟩
end *table_handler*.

This code is used in section 5.

7. These are the symbols we are exporting. They are the only ones visible outside the module. In the most recent edition of Modula-2, the export list was dropped; all symbols in the definition module are exported. To support existing code, most compilers still accept an export list. If necessary, this section can be removed.

⟨Export List 7⟩ ≡
export qualified *symbol_length*, *undefined_symbols_in_table*, *symbol_string_ptr*, *symbol_string*,
search_symbol_table, *delete_symbol_table*, *create_symbol_table*, *set_error_handler*, *table_proc*,
error_proc, *symbol_table_error_code*, *symbol_table*, *symbol_is_defined*, *set_value_of_symbol*,
get_value_of_symbol;

This code is used in section 6.

8. This is the implementation module.

⟨Implementation module of *table_handler* 8⟩ ≡
implementation module *table_handler*;
⟨Import list of the implementation module 16⟩
const ⟨Constants local to the module 20⟩
type ⟨Types local to the module 9⟩
⟨Full procedure declarations of the implementation module 19⟩
end *table_handler*.

This code is used in section 5.

9. Data Structures. This is the format of an entry in the symbol table tree. As we define the record type, we define a few symbols to make it easier to access the fields.

define *symbol_ptr* ≡ $p\uparrow.str$
define *symbol_defined* ≡ $p\uparrow.defined$
define *symbol_value* ≡ $p\uparrow.num$
define *left_sub_tree* ≡ $p\uparrow.left$
define *right_sub_tree* ≡ $p\uparrow.right$

⟨Types local to the module 9⟩ ≡
treeptr = **pointer to** *tree_record*;
tree_record = **record**
    str: *symbol_string_ptr*; (* pointer to the actual string *)
    num: *cardinal*; (* number to be stored with the entry *)
    defined: *Boolean*; (* this symbol has been defined, not just referenced *)
    left, *right*: *treeptr*; (* left and right subtrees *)
    end ;

See also sections 14 and 29.

This code is used in section 8.

10.   Types are defined in the definition module rather than in the implementation module when they are either needed for the exported procedure definitions or are to be exported themselves or both. A *symbol_string* is defined to be of length *symbol_length*. A pointer to the string is defined.

⟨ Types to be exported 10 ⟩ ≡
    symbol_string = **array** [0 .. *symbol_length* − 1] **of** *char*;
    symbol_string_ptr = **pointer to** *symbol_string*;

See also sections 12, 13, 15, and 43.

This code is used in section 6.

11.   ⟨ Constants to be exported 11 ⟩ ≡
    symbol_length = 200;

This code is used in section 6.

12.   We define the following error codes.

⟨ Types to be exported 10 ⟩ +≡
    symbol_table_error_code = (*undefined_symbol*, *duplicate_symbol*, *memory_exhausted*,
        unknown_error);

13.   Modula-2 provides a mechanism whereby a procedure, complete with parameters, can be defined as a data type and stored in memory or passed to another procedure as any other parameter can. We define a error handler procedure type, which is called whenever an error occurs. When one of these procedures is called, the type of error and the symbol involved are passed as parameters.

⟨ Types to be exported 10 ⟩ +≡
    error_proc = **procedure** (*symbol_table_error_code*, **array of** *char*);

14.   We define a structure containing information applying to an entire table.
    define *head_of_table* ≡ *the_table*↑.*the_tree*↑.*right*
    define *report_error* (**#**) ≡ *the_table*↑.*user_err_routine* (**#**);

⟨ Types local to the module 9 ⟩ +≡
    table_record = **record**
      next_entry: *cardinal*;
      the_tree: *treeptr*;   (∗ pointer to head of tree ∗)
      user_err_routine: *error_proc*;   (∗ procedure to call if errors occur ∗)
      last_entry_found: *treeptr*;
      case_sensitive: *Boolean*;
      end ;
    tableptr = **pointer to** *table_record*;
    symbol_table = *tableptr*;

15.   For export, we define *symbol_table* again, this time as an *opaque* type, since the details of its structure are hidden. The caller does not need to know anything about the type in order to use it. All that is needed is the capability to declare variables of the type and pass them as parameters to procedures.

⟨ Types to be exported 10 ⟩ +≡
    symbol_table;

16. We are going to be doing some string handling, so we need to import some identifiers from the Logitech module *Strings*. The boxes signify words that must not be forced to uppercase when the program is MANGLED, since Modula-2 is case-sensitive.

> **define** *length_of_string* ≡ ⌞Length⌟   (∗ get the length of a string ∗)
> **define** *copy_string* ≡ ⌞Assign⌟   (∗ assign one string to another ∗)
> **define** *string_module* ≡ ⌞Strings⌟   (∗ library module for handling strings ∗)

⟨ Import list of the implementation module 16 ⟩ ≡

> **from** *string_module* **import** *length_of_string*, *copy_string*;

See also section 26.

This code is used in section 8.

17. Main Table Lookup Procedure. In this section, we introduce the notation that will be used for all of the procedures which are to be made visible outside the module. The procedure heading is defined independently of the body, to be included in both the definition module and the implementation module.

This is the main symbol table lookup procedure, the one visible to the calling program. If the entry does not exist it is created.

⟨ Procedure heading of the *get_value_of_symbol* procedure 17 ⟩ ≡

procedure *get_value_of_symbol* (*the_table* : *symbol_table*; *target_symbol* : **array of** *char*;
     this_is_a_definition: *Boolean*; **var** *string_ptr*: *symbol_string_ptr*) : *cardinal*;

This code is used in sections 18 and 19.

18. For the definition module, we need only the procedure heading.

⟨ Procedure heading declarations of the definition module 18 ⟩ ≡
> ⟨ Procedure heading of the *get_value_of_symbol* procedure 17 ⟩

See also sections 33, 36, 39, 44, 48, 52, and 56.

This code is used in section 6.

19. For the implementation module, we need the procedure heading again, and this time we add a body to it.

⟨ Full procedure declarations of the implementation module 19 ⟩ ≡
⟨ Procedure heading of the *get_value_of_symbol* procedure 17 ⟩
> ⟨ Procedures local to *get_value_of_symbol* 24 ⟩

var *p*: *treeptr*; *n*: *cardinal*; *current_symbol*: *symbol_string*;
begin
     the_table↑.*last_entry_found* ← **nil**; *copy_string*(*target_symbol*, *current_symbol*);
     ⟨ If table is not case-sensitive, force string to uppercase 21 ⟩;
     p ← *search*(*the_table*↑.*the_tree*);
     if *p* = **nil then**
         report_error(*memory_exhausted*, ´⌞´);
         return *max_card*;
     else
         ⟨ If this is a definition, check for duplicates 22 ⟩
         ⟨ If name has been referenced before definition, reset the value 23 ⟩
         string_ptr ← *symbol_ptr*; *the_table*↑.*last_entry_found* ← *p*;
         return *symbol_value*;

```
    end ;
end get_value_of_symbol;
```

See also sections 34, 37, 40, 45, 49, 50, 53, and 57.

This code is used in section 8.

20.   ⟨ Constants local to the module 20 ⟩ ≡
```
    max_card = 65535;
```
This code is used in section 8.

21.   ⟨ If table is not case-sensitive, force string to uppercase 21 ⟩ ≡
```
    if ¬the_table↑.case_sensitive then
       for n ← 0 to length_of_string(current_symbol) − 1 do
          current_symbol[n] ← cap(current_symbol[n]);
       end ;
    end ;
```
This code is used in section 19.

22.   ⟨ If this is a definition, check for duplicates 22 ⟩ ≡
```
    if this_is_a_definition then
       if symbol_defined then
          report_error(duplicate_symbol, current_symbol);
          return max_card;
       else
          symbol_defined ← true;
       end ;
    end ;
```
This code is used in section 19.

23.   ⟨ If name has been referenced before definition, reset the value 23 ⟩ ≡
```
    if symbol_value = max_card then
       symbol_value ← the_table↑.next_entry;  inc(the_table↑.next_entry);
    end ;
```
This code is used in section 19.

24.   This function procedure returns with a pointer to either the entry matching the target symbol or a newly created entry if no match is found.
⟨ Procedures local to *get_value_of_symbol* 24 ⟩ ≡
```
procedure search(p : treeptr): treeptr;
    var q: treeptr; r: relation; i: cardinal; slen: cardinal;
    begin
       q ← right_sub_tree;  r ← greater;
       while q ≠ nil do
          p ← q;  r ← relation_of(symbol_ptr);
          ⟨ If r is equal, return p; otherwise follow proper subtree 25 ⟩;
       end ;
       ⟨ Create new table entry 27 ⟩;
       return q;
    end search;
```
See also section 30.

This code is used in section 19.

25. ⟨ If r is *equal*, **return** p; otherwise follow proper subtree 25 ⟩ ≡
  if $r = equal$ **then**
    return p
  elsif $r = less$ **then**
    $q \leftarrow left\_sub\_tree$
  else
    $q \leftarrow right\_sub\_tree$
  end

This code is used in section 24.

26. Since we intend to do heap operations, it may help to import the *allocate* and *deallocate* procedures from standard module *Storage*. We define a macro to determine whether a given amount of space is available.

  define $mcm\_available$ ≡ $\boxed{\text{␣Available␣}}$
  define $enough\_memory(\#)$ ≡ $mem\_available(\#)$

⟨ Import list of the implementation module 16 ⟩ +≡
  from $\boxed{\text{␣Storage␣}}$ **import** *allocate*, *deallocate*, *mem_available*;
  from *system* **import** *tsize*;

27. We have to create a new entry in the symbol table. First we allocate the space for the entry by using the standard function *new*. Then we initialize the fields. Finally we allocate space for the string itself and copy it.

  define $initialize\_entry(\#)$ ≡
        $\# \leftarrow$ **nil**;
        if $enough\_memory(tsize(tree\_record))$ **then**
          $new(\#)$;
          with $\#\uparrow$ **do**
            $str \leftarrow$ **nil**; $left \leftarrow$ **nil**; $right \leftarrow$ **nil**; $defined \leftarrow false$; $num \leftarrow max\_card$;
          end ;
        else
          $report\_error(memory\_exhausted, \acute{~}{␣}\acute{~})$;
        end ;
⟨ Create new table entry 27 ⟩ ≡
  $q \leftarrow$ **nil**; $slen \leftarrow length\_of\_string(current\_symbol) + 1$;
  if $enough\_memory(tsize(tree\_record) + slen)$ **then**
    $initialize\_entry(q)$;
    with $q\uparrow$ **do**
      $allocate(str, slen)$; $copy\_string(current\_symbol, str\uparrow)$;
    end ;
    ⟨ Put this new entry on proper subtree 28 ⟩;
  else
    $report\_error(memory\_exhausted, \acute{~}{␣}\acute{~})$;
  end ;

This code is used in section 24.

28. ⟨ Put this new entry on proper subtree 28 ⟩ ≡
  if $r = less$ **then**
    $left\_sub\_tree \leftarrow q$;

```
    else
        right_sub_tree ← q;
    end ;
```
This code is used in section 27.

29.   ⟨ Types local to the module 9 ⟩ +≡
relation = (less, equal, greater);

30.   This function procedure determines the relationship (*less*, *equal*, *greater*) of the string
current_symbol to that of the current table entry (pointed to by *k*).
⟨ Procedures local to *get_value_of_symbol* 24 ⟩ +≡
```
procedure relation_of (k : symbol_string_ptr): relation;
    var i: cardinal; r: relation; x, y: char;
    begin
        i ← 0;  r ← equal;
        loop
            x ← current_symbol[i];  y ← k↑[i];
            if cap(x) ≠ cap(y) then
                exit ;
            end ;
            if x ≤ ´␣´ then
                return r
            end ;
            if x < y then
                r ← less
            elsif x > y then
                r ← greater
            end ;
            i ← i + 1;
        end ;
        ⟨ Return the result of the comparison 31 ⟩;
    end relation_of;
```

31.   ⟨ Return the result of the comparison 31 ⟩ ≡
```
    if cap(x) > cap(y) then
        return greater
    else
        return less
    end ;
```
This code is used in section 30.

32.   We provide a procedure to set the table entry to a specific value.
⟨ Procedure heading of the *set_value_of_symbol* procedure 32 ⟩ ≡
```
procedure  set_value_of_symbol ( the_table : symbol_table; target_symbol : array of char;
        this_is_a_definition: Boolean;  var  string_ptr: symbol_string_ptr; the_val: cardinal ) ;
```
This code is used in sections 33 and 34.

33.   ⟨ Procedure heading declarations of the definition module 18 ⟩ +≡
    ⟨ Procedure heading of the *set_value_of_symbol* procedure 32 ⟩

34. ⟨Full procedure declarations of the implementation module 19⟩ +≡
⟨Procedure heading of the *set_value_of_symbol* procedure 32⟩
var *ent*: *cardinal*;
begin
   the_table↑.*last_entry_found* ← **nil**;
   ent ← *get_value_of_symbol*(*the_table*, *target_symbol*, *this_is_a_definition*, *string_ptr*);
   if *the_table*↑.*last_entry_found* ≠ **nil then**
      the_table↑.*last_entry_found*↑.*num* ← *the_val*;
   end ;
end *set_value_of_symbol*;

35. We provide a function procedure to determine whether a particular symbol has been defined.

⟨Procedure heading of the *symbol_is_defined* function procedure 35⟩ ≡
procedure *symbol_is_defined*(*the_table* : *symbol_table*; *target_symbol* : **array of** *char*): *Boolean*;
This code is used in sections 36 and 37.

36. ⟨Procedure heading declarations of the definition module 18⟩ +≡
   ⟨Procedure heading of the *symbol_is_defined* function procedure 35⟩

37. ⟨Full procedure declarations of the implementation module 19⟩ +≡
⟨Procedure heading of the *symbol_is_defined* function procedure 35⟩
var *ent*: *cardinal*; *string_ptr*: *symbol_string_ptr*;
begin
   the_table↑.*last_entry_found* ← **nil**;
   ent ← *get_value_of_symbol*(*the_table*, *target_symbol*, *false*, *string_ptr*);
   if *the_table*↑.*last_entry_found* ≠ **nil then**
      return *the_table*↑.*last_entry_found*↑.*defined*;
   else
      return *false*;
   end ;
end *symbol_is_defined*;

38. Undefined Symbol Check. The purpose of this function procedure it to check the integrity of the table by searching for entries that have been referenced, but never defined. If undefined symbols are found, the user-supplied error routine is called for each one and a value of *true* is returned for the procedure.

⟨Procedure heading of the *undefined_symbols_in_table* function procedure 38⟩ ≡
procedure *undefined_symbols_in_table*(*the_table* : *symbol_table*;
        undefined_symbol_handling_routine : *error_proc*): *Boolean*;
This code is used in sections 39 and 40.

39. ⟨Procedure heading declarations of the definition module 18⟩ +≡
   ⟨Procedure heading of the *undefined_symbols_in_table* function procedure 38⟩

40. This procedure calls *this_node_is_undefined* with the pointer to the root node, and *this_node_is_undefined* will recursively check each entry in the tree for undefined symbols, eventually returning with a Boolean value containing the result of the search.

⟨ Full procedure declarations of the implementation module 19 ⟩ +≡
⟨ Procedure heading of the *undefined_symbols_in_table* function procedure 38 ⟩
    ⟨ Procedure to check an individual node 41 ⟩
begin
    return *this_node_is_undefined* (*head_of_table*);
end *undefined_symbols_in_table* ;

41.   This procedure checks an individual tree entry for undefined symbols. It also calls
itself recursively to check the subtrees below it for the same condition. If this node or any
subnodes have an undefined symbol, then the result for this node is true. This procedure
must be declared local to *undefined_symbols_in_table* , because the user-supplied procedure
to be called exists only within the scope of *undefined_symbols_in_table* .

⟨ Procedure to check an individual node 41 ⟩ ≡
procedure *this_node_is_undefined* (*p* : *treeptr*): *Boolean* ;
    var *undefined_was_found* , *undefined_symbol_in_left_subtree* , *undefined_symbol_in_right_subtree* :
          Boolean ;
    begin
       undefined_was_found ← *false* ;
       if *p* ≠ **nil then**
          if *symbol_defined* **then**
             undefined_symbol_in_left_subtree ← *this_node_is_undefined* (*left_sub_tree*);
             if ¬*undefined_symbol_in_left_subtree* **then**
                undefined_symbol_in_right_subtree ← *this_node_is_undefined* (*right_sub_tree*);
             end ;
          else
             undefined_symbol_handling_routine (*undefined_symbol* , *symbol_ptr* ↑);
          end ;
          undefined_was_found ← (¬*symbol_defined*) ∨ *undefined_symbol_in_left_subtree* ∨
                undefined_symbol_in_right_subtree ;
       end ;
       return *undefined_was_found* ;
    end *this_node_is_undefined* ;
This code is used in section 40.

42.   Table Search Procedures.   This purpose of this procedure is to perform a user-
provided operation on every entry in the table. As each entry is processed, a user-provided
procedure is called, and the value stored with this name is passed as a parameter. The user
procedure is free to perform any operation it wishes. The nodes are processed alphabetically.

⟨ Procedure heading of the *search_symbol_table* procedure 42 ⟩ ≡
procedure *search_symbol_table* (*the_table* : *symbol_table* ; *user_action_routine* : *table_proc*);
This code is used in sections 44 and 45.

43.   We define a procedure type *table_proc* , which is used as one of the parameters of
the *search_symbol_table* procedure. The user is allowed to specify his own procedure to
perform some action on each entry in the table. The value stored in the entry, a pointer
to the symbol, and a Boolean variable indicating that the symbol is defined are passed as
parameters.

⟨ Types to be exported 10 ⟩ +≡
    table_proc = **procedure** (*cardinal* , *symbol_string_ptr* , *Boolean*);

44. ⟨ Procedure heading declarations of the definition module 18 ⟩ +≡
⟨ Procedure heading of the *search_symbol_table* procedure 42 ⟩

45. ⟨ Full procedure declarations of the implementation module 19 ⟩ +≡
⟨ Procedure heading of the *search_symbol_table* procedure 42 ⟩
⟨ Procedure to search an individual node 46 ⟩
begin
   search_a_node(*head_of_table*);
end *search_symbol_table*;

46. This procedure searches an individual node and all of the nodes below it. As each node is processed, a user-provided procedure is called, and the value corresponding to this name is passed to the user procedure as a parameter. The user procedure is free to perform any operation it wishes. The nodes are processed alphabetically, because this procedure will perform the processing on its left subtree before its own processing then on the right subtree. This procedure must be declared as a procedure local to *search_symbol_table*, because the user-supplied *user_action_routine* only exists within the scope of *search_symbol_table*.

⟨ Procedure to search an individual node 46 ⟩ ≡
procedure *search_a_node*(*p* : *treeptr*);
   begin
      if $p \neq$ **nil then**
         search_a_node(*left_sub_tree*), *user_action_routine*(*symbol_value*, *symbol_ptr*, *symbol_defined*);
         search_a_node(*right_sub_tree*);
      end ;
   end *search_a_node*;
This code is used in section 45.

47. Table Deletion Procedures.   This procedure is used to delete the table and free the memory allocated to it.

⟨ Procedure heading of the *delete_symbol_table* procedure 47 ⟩ ≡
procedure *delete_symbol_table*(**var** *the_table* : *symbol_table*);
This code is used in sections 48 and 49.

48. ⟨ Procedure heading declarations of the definition module 18 ⟩ +≡
⟨ Procedure heading of the *delete_symbol_table* procedure 47 ⟩

49. ⟨ Full procedure declarations of the implementation module 19 ⟩ +≡
⟨ Procedure heading of the *delete_symbol_table* procedure 47 ⟩
begin
   if *the_table* $\neq$ **nil then**
      delete_a_node(*head_of_table*); *dispose*(*the_table*); *the_table* ← **nil**;
   end ;
end *delete_symbol_table*;

50. This procedure first deletes the subtrees below the input node, then deletes the node itself.

⟨ Full procedure declarations of the implementation module 19 ⟩ +≡
procedure *delete_a_node*(**var** *p* : *treeptr*);

```
    var slen: cardinal;
    begin
      if p ≠ nil then
        with p↑ do
          delete_a_node(left);  delete_a_node(right);  slen ← length_of_string(str↑) + 1;
          deallocate(str, slen);
        end ;
        dispose(p);  p ← nil;
      end ;
    end delete_a_node;
```

51. Table Initialization.   This procedure is used to create a symbol table. An error procedure can be supplied by the user in case errors occur during symbol manipulation. Case sensitivity is optional for table keys. If *case_sens = true* then junk, Junk, and JUNK are considered different symbols.

⟨ Procedure heading of the *create_symbol_table* procedure 51 ⟩ ≡
procedure *create_symbol_table*(**var** *the_table* : *symbol_table*; *case_sens* : *Boolean*;
              user_error_routine : *error_proc*);

This code is used in sections 52 and 53.

52.   ⟨ Procedure heading declarations of the definition module 18 ⟩ +≡
    ⟨ Procedure heading of the *create_symbol_table* procedure 51 ⟩

53.   ⟨ Full procedure declarations of the implementation module 19 ⟩ +≡
⟨ Procedure heading of the *create_symbol_table* procedure 51 ⟩
begin
    ⟨ Initialize the symbol table 54 ⟩
end *create_symbol_table*;

54.   To initialize the symbol table, we create a root node with initialized fields. The right node of this entry is the head of the table.

⟨ Initialize the symbol table 54 ⟩ ≡
    if *enough_memory*(*tsize*(*table_record*) + *tsize*(*tree_record*)) **then**
      new(*the_table*);
      with *the_table*↑ **do**
        user_err_routine ← *user_error_routine*; *initialize_entry*(*the_tree*); *next_entry* ← 0;
        case_sensitive ← *case_sens*;
      end ;
    else
      user_error_routine(*memory_exhausted*, ´␣´);
    end ;

This code is used in section 53.

55.   An error procedure can be supplied by the user in case errors occur during symbol manipulation. This procedure is used to change the error handler for a particular table after it has been created.

⟨ Procedure heading of the *set_error_handler* procedure 55 ⟩ ≡
procedure *set_error_handler*(*the_table* : *symbol_table*; *user_error_routine* : *error_proc*);

This code is used in sections 56 and 57.

56. ⟨ Procedure heading declarations of the definition module 18 ⟩ +≡
⟨ Procedure heading of the *set_error_handler* procedure 55 ⟩

57. ⟨ Full procedure declarations of the implementation module 19 ⟩ +≡
⟨ Procedure heading of the *set_error_handler* procedure 55 ⟩
begin
    the_table↑.*user_err_routine* ← *user_error_routine*;
end *set_error_handler*;

58. Index. Here is the index of names.

⟨Constants local to the module 20⟩   Used in section 8.
⟨Constants to be exported 11⟩   Used in section 6.
⟨Create new table entry 27⟩   Used in section 24.
⟨Definition module of *table_handler* 6⟩   Used in section 5.
⟨Export List 7⟩   Used in section 6.
⟨Full procedure declarations of the implementation module 19, 34, 37, 40, 45, 49, 50, 53, 57⟩
   Used in section 8.
⟨If name has been referenced before definition, reset the value 23⟩   Used in section 19.
⟨If table is not case-sensitive, force string to uppercase 21⟩   Used in section 19.
⟨If this is a definition, check for duplicates 22⟩   Used in section 19.
⟨If *r* is *equal*, **return** *p*; otherwise follow proper subtree 25⟩   Used in section 24.
⟨Implementation module of *table_handler* 8⟩   Used in section 5.
⟨Import list of the implementation module 16, 26⟩   Used in section 8.
⟨Initialize the symbol table 54⟩   Used in section 53.
⟨Procedure heading declarations of the definition module 18, 33, 36, 39, 44, 48, 52, 56⟩
   Used in section 6.
⟨Procedure heading of the *create_symbol_table* procedure 51⟩   Used in sections 52 and 53.
⟨Procedure heading of the *delete_symbol_table* procedure 47⟩   Used in sections 48 and 49.
⟨Procedure heading of the *get_value_of_symbol* procedure 17⟩   Used in sections 18 and 19.
⟨Procedure heading of the *search_symbol_table* procedure 42⟩   Used in sections 44 and 45.
⟨Procedure heading of the *set_error_handler* procedure 55⟩   Used in sections 56 and 57.
⟨Procedure heading of the *set_value_of_symbol* procedure 32⟩   Used in sections 33 and 34.
⟨Procedure heading of the *symbol_is_defined* function procedure 35⟩
   Used in sections 36 and 37.
⟨Procedure heading of the *undefined_symbols_in_table* function procedure 38⟩
   Used in sections 39 and 40.
⟨Procedure to check an individual node 41⟩   Used in section 40.
⟨Procedure to search an individual node 46⟩   Used in section 45.
⟨Procedures local to *get_value_of_symbol* 24, 30⟩   Used in section 19.
⟨Put this new entry on proper subtree 28⟩   Used in section 27.
⟨Return the result of the comparison 31⟩   Used in section 30.
⟨Types local to the module 9, 14, 29⟩   Used in section 8.
⟨Types to be exported 10, 12, 13, 15, 43⟩   Used in section 6.

G.5.2   ScanTEX

1.   Introduction.   This program takes a TEX file generated by **WEAVE** and strips out the sections which have not been changed, outputting the changed sections to a second, greatly reduced TEX file. The index, section names, and table of contents are dropped as well.

The major or "starred" sections normally start a new page. Since this is not meaningful with the abbreviated listing, the TEX macro that handles starred sections ('\N') is redefined to operate in a manner similar to that of regular sections ('\M').

The program uses a few features of the Modula-2 compiler used in its development (Logitech MS-DOS) that may need to be changed in other installations. System-dependent portions of ScanTEX can be identified by looking at the entries for 'system dependencies' in the index below.

The "banner line" defined here should be changed whenever ScanTEX is modified.

> **define** *banner* ≡ ´This␣is␣SCANTeX,␣Version␣1.1´

2.   The program begins with a fairly normal header, made up of pieces that will mostly be filled in later. The TEX input comes from file *TEX_file* and the new TEX output goes to file *out_TEX_file*. Unlike Pascal, Modula-2 does not require the constant, type, and variable sections to be placed here in the program header in a rigidly specified order, but we will do it anyway, since **WEB** makes it so easy.

module *scan_TEX* ;
   ⟨ Import List 5 ⟩
   const ⟨ Constants in the outer block 7 ⟩
   type ⟨ Types in the outer block 8 ⟩
   var ⟨ Globals in the outer block 9 ⟩
   ⟨ Procedures and functions of the program 3 ⟩
   begin
      ⟨ Create *out_TEX_file* and copy the changed sections from *TEX_file* to it 33 ⟩;
   end *scan_TEX* .

3.   This procedure initializes the module.
⟨ Procedures and functions of the program 3 ⟩ ≡
procedure *initialize* ;
   var ⟨ Local variables for initialization 22 ⟩
   begin
      ⟨ Set initial values 10 ⟩
      ⟨ Initialize the file system 23 ⟩;
   end *initialize* ;
See also sections 17, 20, and 21.
This code is used in section 2.

4. A few macro definitions for low-level output instructions are introduced here. All of the terminal-oriented commands in the remainder of the module will be stated in terms of simple primitives.

5. First we will define macros corresponding to Modula-2's procedure names. The boxes signify words that must not be forced to uppercase when the program is **MANGLED**, since Modula-2 is case-sensitive.

define *pr_char* ≡ ⌞Write⌞   (∗ library procedure to output a character ∗)

define *pr_string* ≡ ⌞WriteString⌞   (∗ library procedure to output a string ∗)

define *rd_string* ≡ ⌞ReadString⌞   (∗ library procedure to input a string ∗)

define *pr_card* ≡ ⌞WriteCard⌞   (∗ library procedure to output a cardinal number ∗)

define *new_line* ≡ ⌞WriteLn⌞   (∗ a new line ∗)

⟨ Import List 5 ⟩ ≡

   from ⌞InOut⌞ **import** *pr_string*, *rd_string*, *pr_char*, *pr_card*, *new_line*;

See also sections 13 and 14.

This code is used in section 2.

6. Then we will define macros for I/O handling on the basis of the new names that are not case-sensitive.

define *print_string*(**#**) ≡ *pr_string*(**#**)   (∗ put a given string to the terminal ∗)

define *read_string*(**#**) ≡ *rd_string*(**#**)   (∗ read a given string from the terminal ∗)

define *print_cardinal*(**#**) ≡ *pr_card*(**#**, 1)   (∗ put a given cardinal to the terminal, in decimal

          notation, using only as many digit positions as necessary ∗)

define *print_ln*(**#**) ≡ *pr_string*(**#**); *new_line*;

          (∗ put a given string to the terminal, followed by a new line ∗)

define *print_char*(**#**) ≡ *pr_char*(**#**)   (∗ put a given character to the terminal ∗)

7. Let's define a few constants.

⟨ Constants in the outer block 7 ⟩ ≡

   buf_size = 1000;   (∗ maximum length of input line ∗)

   file_name_len = 200;   (∗ length of a file name ∗)

This code is used in section 2.

8. A global variable called *history* will contain one of four values at the end of every run: *spotless* means that no unusual messages were printed, *harmless_message* means that a message of possible interest was printed but no real errors were detected; *error_message* means that at least one error was found; *fatal_message* means that the program terminated abnormally. The value of *history* does not influence the behavior of the program; it is simply computed for the convenience of systems that might want to use such information.

⟨ Types in the outer block 8 ⟩ ≡

   error_level = (*spotless*, *harmless_message*, *error_message*, *fatal_message*);

This code is used in section 2.

9. ⟨ Globals in the outer block 9 ⟩ ≡

history: *error_level*;   (∗ how bad was this run? ∗)

See also sections 16, 25, and 31.

This code is used in section 2.

10.   ⟨ Set initial values 10 ⟩ ≡
history ← *spotless*;

See also section 24.

This code is used in section 3.

11.   We don't really have to worry about errors much in this particular program because
the input is machine-generated by WEAVE and we assume that this program is not run if
errors occurred during the WEAVE run. The error likeliest to occur is failure during file
opens.

    define *mark_harmless* ≡
          if *history* = *spotless* **then**
            history ← *harmless_message*;
          end ;
    define *mark_error* ≡ *history* ← *error_message*
    define *mark_fatal* ≡ *history* ← *fatal_message*
    define *err_print*(#) ≡ *print_ln*(#); *mark_error*;

12.   Some implementations may wish to pass the value of the *history* variable to the
operating system so that it can be used to govern whether or not other programs are started.
The *doscall* procedure passes a program status value back to DOS. We use *fatal_error* to
terminate the program abnormally.

    define *print_fatal_message* ≡ *print_string*(´(That␣was␣a␣fatal␣´);
        print_ln(´error,␣my␣friend.)´)
    define *fatal_error*(#) ≡ *mark_fatal*; *print_ln*(#); *print_fatal_message*; *doscall*("4C, *history*);

⟨ Terminate program, converting *history* to program exit status 12 ⟩ ≡
    doscall("4C, *history*);

This code is used in section 33.

13.   If we are going to use *doscall* from the Logitech library we have to import it from the
module *system*.

⟨ Import List 5 ⟩ +≡
    from *system* **import** *doscall*;

14.   File Handling.   Here we define the symbols for use with file handling. As before,
we define the names which are case-sensitive first.

    define *lookup* ≡ ␣Lookup␣   (∗ library procedure to open a file ∗)
    define *close* ≡ ␣Close␣   (∗ library procedure to close a file ∗)
    define *failure*(#) ≡ (#. res ≠ done)   (∗ last file operation sucessful ? ∗)
    define *end_file* ≡ eof
    define *null_char* ≡ ␣nul␣
    define *read_char* ≡ ␣ReadChar␣
    define *write_char* ≡ ␣WriteChar␣
    define *text_file* ≡ ␣File␣

⟨ Import List 5 ⟩ +≡
    from ␣FileSystem␣ **import** *lookup*, Response , *read_char*, *write_char*, *text_file*, *close*;
    from *ascii* **import** *eol*, *null_char*;

15. Then we define the rest of the names based on those.

> **define** *abort_if_open_error* (**#**) ≡
>   **if** *failure* (**#**) **then**
>   *print_string* (´unable␣to␣open␣´); *fatal_error* (*filename*);
>   **end** ;
> **define** *open_input_file* (**#**) ≡ *lookup* (**#**, *filename* , *false*); *abort_if_open_error* (**#**)
> **define** *open_output_file* (**#**) ≡ *lookup* (**#**, *filename* , *true*); *abort_if_open_error* (**#**)
> **define** *close_file* (**#**) ≡ *close* (**#**);
> **define** *end_of_line* (**#**) ≡ (*ch* = *eol*)
> **define** *end_of_file* (**#**) ≡ (**#**.*end_file*)
> **define** *input_char* (**#**) ≡ *read_char* (**#**, *ch*);
> **define** *output_char* (**#**) ≡ *write_char* (**#**, *ch*)
> **define** *read_ln* (**#**) ≡
>   **while** ¬*end_of_line* (**#**) **do**
>   *input_char* (**#**);
>   **end** ;
> **define** *write_ln* (**#**) ≡ *write_char* (**#**, *eol*);

16. Input goes into an array called *buffer*.

⟨ Globals in the outer block 9 ⟩ +≡
buffer : **array** [0 .. *buf_size*] **of** *char* ;
TEX_file , *out_TEX_file* : *text_file* ;

17. The *input_ln* procedure brings the next line of input from the specified file into the *buffer* array and returns the value *true*, unless the file has already been entirely read, in which case it returns *false*. Under normal conditions, we will never reach true end-of-file, for reasons discussed in later sections, but we will handle it anyway. Trailing blanks are ignored and the global variable *current_line_len* is set to the length of the line. The value of *current_line_len* must be strictly less than *buf_size*.

⟨ Procedures and functions of the program 3 ⟩ +≡
procedure *input_ln* (**var** *f* : *text_file*): *boolean* ; (∗ inputs a line or returns *false* ∗)
  var *actual_size* : [0 .. *buf_size*]; (∗ *current_line_len* without trailing blanks ∗)
    ch : *char* ; (∗ current input character ∗)
    line_pres : *boolean* ; (∗ temporary result of procedure ∗)
  begin
    current_line_len ← 0; *actual_size* ← 0;
    if *end_of_file* (*f*) **then**
      line_pres ← *false*
    else
      input_char (*f*); ⟨ Input characters until end-of-line 18 ⟩;
      read_ln (*f*); *current_line_len* ← *actual_size* ; *line_pres* ← *true* ;
    end ;
    return *line_pres* ;
  end *input_ln* ;

18. ⟨ Input characters until end-of-line 18 ⟩ ≡
  while ¬*end_of_line* (*f*) **do**
    if *ch* = *null_char* **then**

```
      return false
   end  ;
   buffer[current_line_len] ← ch;  inc(current_line_len);
   if buffer[current_line_len − 1] ≠ ´␣´ then
      actual_size ← current_line_len
   end  ;
   ⟨ If the input line is too long, report an error and return  19⟩;
   input_char(f);
end  ;
```

This code is used in section 17.

19.   ⟨ If the input line is too long, report an error and **return** 19⟩ ≡

```
   if current_line_len = buf_size then
      read_ln(f);  dec(current_line_len);  err_print(´!␣Input␣line␣too␣long´);  return true;
   end  ;
```

This code is used in section 18.

20.   The *output_ln* procedure writes the next line of output from the *buffer* array to the specified file.

⟨ Procedures and functions of the program 3⟩ +≡

```
procedure output_ln(var f : text_file);
   var ch: char;  (∗ current output character ∗)
      temp: [0 .. buf_size];
   begin
      if current_line_len > 0 then
         for temp ← 0 to current_line_len − 1 do
            ch ← buffer[temp];  output_char(f);
         end  ;
      end  ;
      write_ln(f);
   end output_ln;
```

21.   The *output_canned_line* procedure writes *the_line* as the next line of output to the specified file.

⟨ Procedures and functions of the program 3⟩ +≡

```
procedure output_canned_line(var f : text_file; the_line : array of  char);
   var ch: char;  (∗ current output character ∗)
      temp: cardinal;
   begin
      for temp ← 0 to high(the_line) do
         ch ← the_line[temp];  output_char(f);
      end  ;
      write_ln(f);  inc(out_TEX_line);
   end output_canned_line;
```

22.   We define *filename* local to the initialization procedure because it is used only during file open.

⟨ Local variables for initialization 22⟩ ≡

filename: **array** $[0 .. file\_name\_len - 1]$ **of** *char*;

This code is used in section 3.

23. The code in this section attempts to get the names of the two text files and open them in a generic Modula-2 manner. If it doesn't work with a particular Modula-2 environment, it must be modified.

> **define** *next_file*(#) ≡ *filename*[0] ← ´␣´; *print_ln*(#); *read_string*(*filename*); *new_line*;
>   *print_ln*(*filename*); *new_line*;

⟨ Initialize the file system 23 ⟩ ≡
  next_file(´TeX␣file:´); *open_input_file*(*TEX_file*); *next_file*(´output␣TeX␣file:´);
  open_output_file(*out_TEX_file*);

This code is used in section 3.

24. Here we initialize most of the variables. The *output_enabled* flag is initialized to *true* so that the lines in the header of the WEAVE-generated TEX file, known as *limbo text*, are picked up in addition to the changed sections.

⟨ Set initial values 10 ⟩ +≡
  TEX_line ← 0; *out_TEX_line* ← 0; *current_line_len* ← 0; *buffer*[0] ← ´␣´;
  input_has_ended ← *false*; *output_enabled* ← *true*;

25. Since we just initialized the variables, it may be helpful to define them before the compiler notices they're not there.

⟨ Globals in the outer block 9 ⟩ +≡
TEX_line: *cardinal*; (∗ the number of the current line in the main TEX file ∗)
out_TEX_line: *cardinal*; (∗ the number of the line in the output TEX file ∗)
current_line_len: $[0 .. buf\_size]$; (∗ the last character position occupied in the buffer ∗)
input_has_ended: *boolean*; (∗ there is no more input ∗)
output_enabled: *boolean*; (∗ we are copying input lines to output ∗)

26. Main Input Loop. This is the main processing loop of ScanTEX. We simply read lines until told to stop reading by the setting of the *input_has_ended* flag. The scanning code will determine the setting of the *output_enabled* flag. If set, we copy the line to the output file.

⟨ Read the input from *TEX_file* and copy selected lines to *out_TEX_file* 26 ⟩ ≡
  while ¬*input_has_ended* **do**
    ⟨ Get the next input line and scan it 28 ⟩;
    if *output_enabled* **then**
      output_ln(*out_TEX_file*); *inc*(*out_TEX_line*);
      if *out_TEX_line* = 1 **then**
        ⟨ Output the redefinition of '\N' and the the running head 27 ⟩
      end ;
    end ;
  end ;

This code is used in section 33.

27. After the first line, normally '\input webmac', we generate some special code to redefine some things defined by webmac.

define *out_line*(#) ≡ *output_canned_line*(*out_TEX_file*, #);

⟨ Output the redefinition of '\N' and the the running head 27 ⟩ ≡
 out_line(´\def\rhead{Modified␣Sections␣Only}´);
 out_line(´\def\N#1.#2.{\MN#1.\ifon\vfil´); *out_line*(´\penalty-100\vfilneg␣´);
 out_line(´\vskip12ptminus3pt\startsection%´); *out_line*(´{\bf\ignorespaces#2.\quad}´);
 out_line(´\ignorespaces}´);

This code is used in section 26.

28.   This section reads in the next line and scans it. We will output an "I'm alive!" dot to the terminal every 100 input lines and a new line every 2000.

⟨ Get the next input line and scan it 28 ⟩ ≡
 input_has_ended ← ¬*input_ln*(*TEX_file*);
 if *input_has_ended* **then**
   output_enabled ← *false*;
 else
   inc(*TEX_line*); ⟨ Output an "I'm alive!" dot if needed and maybe a new line 29 ⟩;
   ⟨ Scan the line 30 ⟩;
   buffer[*current_line_len*] ← ´␣´;
 end ;

This code is used in section 26.

29.   ⟨ Output an "I'm alive!" dot if needed and maybe a new line 29 ⟩ ≡
 if (*TEX_line* **mod** 100) = 0 **then**
   print_char(´.´);
   if (*TEX_line* **mod** 2000) = 0 **then**
     new_line;
   end ;
 end ;

This code is used in section 28.

30.   In this section we determine whether the current line is the beginning of a section ('\M' or '\N' at beginning of line, followed immediately by a section number) and, if so, whether the section has been modified ('*.' following the number). We update the *output_enabled* flag according. Additionally, the index section ('\inx') is considered end-of-file. If it is detected, we set the flag *input_has_ended* to terminate the program and set *output_enabled* to false to prevent the '\inx' command from being copied to the output file.

  define *numeric_digit_at*(#) ≡ ((*buffer*[#] ≤ ´9´) ∧ (*buffer*[#] ≥ ´0´))
  define *third_char_matches*(#) ≡ (*buffer*[*scan_index* + 2] = #)
  define *second_char_matches*(#) ≡ (*buffer*[*scan_index* + 1] = #) ∧ *third_char_matches*
  define *char_matches*(#) ≡ (*buffer*[*scan_index*] = #)
  define *three_chars_match*(#) ≡ *char_matches*(#) ∧ *second_char_matches*

⟨ Scan the line 30 ⟩ ≡
 scan_index ← 1;   (* preset comparison index to second character position *)
 if (*current_line_len* > 3) ∧ (*buffer*[0] = ´\´) **then**
   if (*char_matches*(´M´) ∨ *char_matches*(´N´)) ∧ *numeric_digit_at*(2) **then**
     ⟨ Search for '*.'; set *output_enabled* if found 32 ⟩;
   elsif *three_chars_match*(´i´)(´n´)(´x´) **then**
     output_enabled ← *false*; *input_has_ended* ← *true*;

```
      end ;
   end ;
```
This code is used in section 28.

---

31. ⟨Globals in the outer block 9⟩ +≡
keep_looking: *boolean*;
scan_index: *cardinal*;

---

32. Starting at the first digit of the section number, search for '*.', which indicates that this is a changed section. Discontinue the search if '*.' is found or the current position is no longer a numeric digit, which means we have moved past the section number without finding it.

⟨Search for '*.'; set *output_enabled* if found 32⟩ ≡
   output_enabled ← *false*; *keep_looking* ← *true*; *scan_index* ← 3;
   while (¬*output_enabled*) ∧ *keep_looking* **do**
      output_enabled ← *three_chars_match*(´\´)(´*´)(´.´);
      keep_looking ← *numeric_digit_at*(*scan_index*); *inc*(*scan_index*);
   end ;

This code is used in section 30.

---

33. Main Program. This is the main program.

⟨Create *out_$T_{E}X$_file* and copy the changed sections from $T_{E}X$_file to it 33⟩ ≡
   print_ln(*banner*); *initialize*;
   ⟨Read the input from $T_{E}X$_file and copy selected lines to *out_$T_{E}X$_file* 26⟩;
   ⟨Add '\bye' command to end of output and close both files 36⟩;
   ⟨Print statistics about line counts 35⟩;
   ⟨Print the job *history* 34⟩;
   ⟨Terminate program, converting *history* to program exit status 12⟩;

This code is used in section 2.

---

34. Here we simply report the history to the user.

⟨Print the job *history* 34⟩ ≡
   case *history* **of**
   spotless: *print_ln*(´(No␣errors␣were␣found.)´) |
   harmless_message: *print_string*(´(Did␣you␣see␣the␣´);
      print_ln(´warning␣message␣above?)´) |
   error_message: *print_string*(´(Pardon␣me,␣but␣I␣think␣I␣´);
      print_ln(´spotted␣something␣wrong.)´) |
   fatal_message: *print_fatal_message*
   end ; (∗ there are no other cases ∗)

This code is used in section 33.

---

35. ⟨Print statistics about line counts 35⟩ ≡
   new_line; *print_ln*(´Line␣count␣statistics:´); *print_cardinal*($T_{E}X$_line);
   print_ln(´␣lines␣in␣input␣TeX␣file´); *print_cardinal*(*out_$T_{E}X$_line*);
   print_ln(´␣lines␣in␣output␣TeX␣file´);

This code is used in section 33.

36.   The command to generate the table of contents ('\con') is normally the last line in a TEX file generated by **WEAVE**. Part of its function is to terminate TEX gracefully by generating a '\bye' command or equivalent after generating the table of contents. Since we are dropping the '\con' command, we must issue the '\bye' command directly, just before closing the input and output files.

⟨ Add '\bye' command to end of output and close both files 36 ⟩ ≡
　　out_line(´\bye´); *close_file*(*TEX_file*); *close_file*(*out_TEX_file*);

This code is used in section 33.

37. Index.

⟨ Add '\bye' command to end of output and close both files 36 ⟩   Used in section 33.

⟨ Constants in the outer block 7 ⟩   Used in section 2.

⟨ Create *out_TEX_file* and copy the changed sections from *TEX_file* to it 33 ⟩
        Used in section 2.

⟨ Get the next input line and scan it 28 ⟩   Used in section 26.

⟨ Globals in the outer block 9, 16, 25, 31 ⟩   Used in section 2.

⟨ If the input line is too long, report an error and **return** 19 ⟩   Used in section 18.

⟨ Import List 5, 13, 14 ⟩   Used in section 2.

⟨ Initialize the file system 23 ⟩   Used in section 3.

⟨ Input characters until end-of-line 18 ⟩   Used in section 17.

⟨ Local variables for initialization 22 ⟩   Used in section 3.

⟨ Output an "I'm alive!" dot if needed and maybe a new line 29 ⟩   Used in section 28.

⟨ Output the redefinition of '\N' and the the running head 27 ⟩   Used in section 26.

⟨ Print statistics about line counts 35 ⟩   Used in section 33.

⟨ Print the job *history* 34 ⟩   Used in section 33.

⟨ Procedures and functions of the program 3, 17, 20, 21 ⟩   Used in section 2.

⟨ Read the input from *TEX_file* and copy selected lines to *out_TEX_file* 26 ⟩
        Used in section 33.

⟨ Scan the line 30 ⟩   Used in section 28.

⟨ Search for '*.'; set *output_enabled* if found 32 ⟩   Used in section 30.

⟨ Set initial values 10, 24 ⟩   Used in section 3.

⟨ Terminate program, converting *history* to program exit status 12 ⟩   Used in section 33.

⟨ Types in the outer block 8 ⟩   Used in section 2.

G.6   Design Documents for ScanTEX

G.6.1   High-level Design Document

1.   Introduction.   This program takes a TEX file generated by `WEAVE` and strips out the sections which have not been changed, outputting the changed sections to a second, greatly reduced TEX file. The index, section names, and table of contents are dropped as well.

The major or "starred" sections normally start a new page. Since this is not meaningful with the abbreviated listing, the TEX macro that handles starred sections ('\N') is redefined to operate in a manner similar to that of regular sections ('\M').

2.   In the main processing loop, we simply read lines until told to stop reading by the setting of the *input_has_ended* flag. The scanning code will determine the setting of the *output_enabled* flag. If set, we copy the line to the output file.

3.   This section reads in the next line and scans it. We will output an "I'm alive!" dot to the terminal every 100 input lines and a new line every 2000.

4.   In this section we determine whether the current line is the beginning of a section ('\M' or '\N' at beginning of line, followed immediately by a section number) and, if so, whether the section has been modified ('*.' following the number). We update the *output_enabled* flag according. Additionally, the index section ('\inx') is considered end-of-file. If it is detected, we set the flag *input_has_ended* to terminate the program and set *output_enabled* to false to prevent the '\inx' command from being copied to the output file.

5. Index.

G.6.2 Detail Design Document

1. Introduction. This program takes a TeX file generated by WEAVE and strips out the sections which have not been changed, outputting the changed sections to a second, greatly reduced TeX file. The index, section names, and table of contents are dropped as well.

The major or "starred" sections normally start a new page. Since this is not meaningful with the abbreviated listing, the TeX macro that handles starred sections ('\N') is redefined to operate in a manner similar to that of regular sections ('\M').

2. In the main processing loop, we simply read lines until told to stop reading by the setting of the *input_has_ended* flag. The scanning code will determine the setting of the *output_enabled* flag. If set, we copy the line to the output file.

⟨ Read the input from *TeX_file* and copy selected lines to *out_TeX_file* 2 ⟩ ≡
    while ¬*input_has_ended* **do**
        ⟨ Get the next input line and scan it 3 ⟩;
        if *output_enabled* **then**
            ⟨ Output the line and increment the line count 0 ⟩
            if *first_line* **then**
                ⟨ Output the redefinition of '\N' and the the running head 0 ⟩
            end ;
        end ;
    end ;

This code is used in section 5.

3. This section reads in the next line and scans it. We will output an "I'm alive!" dot to the terminal every 100 input lines and a new line every 2000.

⟨ Get the next input line and scan it 3 ⟩ ≡
    ⟨ Input a line and set *input_has_ended* accordingly 0 ⟩
    if *input_has_ended* **then**
        ⟨ Set the *output_enabled* flag to *false* 0 ⟩
    else
        ⟨ Scan the line 4 ⟩;
    end ;

This code is used in section 2.

4. In this section we determine whether the current line is the beginning of a section ('\M' or '\N' at beginning of line, followed immediately by a section number) and, if so, whether the section has been modified ('*.' following the number). We update the *output_enabled* flag according. Additionally, the index section ('\inx') is considered end-of-file. If it is detected, we set the flag *input_has_ended* to terminate the program and set *output_enabled* to false to prevent the '\inx' command from being copied to the output file.

⟨ Scan the line 4 ⟩ ≡
    if ⟨ The line length is greater than three and the line starts with a '\' character 0 ⟩ **then**
      if ⟨ The second character is ´M´ or ´N´ and the third is a digit 0 ⟩ **then**
        ⟨ Search for '*.'; set *output_enabled* if found 0 ⟩;
      elsif ⟨ This is the index ('\inx') command 0 ⟩ **then**
        ⟨ Set *output_enabled* to *false* and *input_has_ended* to *true* 0 ⟩
      end ;
    end ;
This code is used in section 3.

5.   This is the main program.

⟨ Create *out_TEX_file* and copy the changed sections from *TEX_file* to it 5 ⟩ ≡
    ⟨ Initialize, open *TEX_file*, and create *out_TEX_file* 0 ⟩
    ⟨ Read the input from *TEX_file* and copy selected lines to *out_TEX_file* 2 ⟩;
    ⟨ Add '\bye' command to end of output and close both files 0 ⟩;
    ⟨ Terminate program 0 ⟩;

6. **Index.**

*. : 4.
\inx : 4.
\M : 1, 4.
\N : 1, 4.
first_line : 2.
input_has_ended : 2, 3, 4.
output_enabled : 2, 4.

⟨ Add '\bye' command to end of output and close both files 0 ⟩   Used in section 5.

⟨ Create *out_TEX_file* and copy the changed sections from *TEX_file* to it 5 ⟩

⟨ Get the next input line and scan it 3 ⟩   Used in section 2.

⟨ Initialize, open *TEX_file*, and create *out_TEX_file* 0 ⟩   Used in section 5.

⟨ Input a line and set *input_has_ended* accordingly 0 ⟩   Used in section 3.

⟨ Output the line and increment the line count 0 ⟩   Used in section 2.

⟨ Output the redefinition of '\N' and the the running head 0 ⟩   Used in section 2.

⟨ Read the input from *TEX_file* and copy selected lines to *out_TEX_file* 2 ⟩   Used in section 5.

⟨ Scan the line 4 ⟩   Used in section 3.

⟨ Search for '*.'; set *output_enabled* if found 0 ⟩   Used in section 4.

⟨ Set the *output_enabled* flag to *false* 0 ⟩   Used in section 3.

⟨ Set *output_enabled* to *false* and *input_has_ended* to *true* 0 ⟩   Used in section 4.

⟨ Terminate program 0 ⟩   Used in section 5.

⟨ The line length is greater than three and the line starts with a '\' character 0 ⟩
      Used in section 4.

⟨ The second character is ´M´ or ´N´ and the third is a digit 0 ⟩   Used in section 4.

⟨ This is the index ('\inx') command 0 ⟩   Used in section 4.

G.7   Sample C Program—Homotopy

1.   Introduction.   This program illustrates the Whitney-Graustein theorem, that two closed curves (immersions of the circle) in the plane can be deformed into one another without letting go of the immersion property if and only if their turning numbers are the same. (These terms are defined below.)

This program was originally written in C by David Dobkin and Bill Thurston; Silvio Levy rewrote it in WEB, adding new features.

Let the two curves be described by the maps $f : S^1 \to \mathbf{R}^2$ and $g : S^1 \to \mathbf{R}^2$, where S^1 is the circle. We can also think of them as periodic maps defined on $\mathbf{R}$; for concreteness, let their period be 1. Saying that $f : \mathbf{R} \to \mathbf{R}^2$ is an immersion means that f is differentiable, and that the derivative f' is never zero; in particular, the curve has a tangent everywhere.

Deforming f into g means that we can find a family h_s of immersions, parametrized by a real number $s \in [0, 1]$, so that $h_0 = f$, $h_1 = g$ and all the members of the family are also immersions. Of course, the family should be continuous, that is, if $H : [0, 1] \times S^1 \to \mathbf{R}^2$ is defined by $H(s,t) = h_s(t)$, then H is a continuous map.

2.   Now it's very easy to find a family of curves h_s to mediate between f and g that satisfies the continuity condition: one can just take weighted averages of f and g, say $h_s(t) = sg(t) + (1 - s)f(t)$. It's also easy to see that the members of this family are differentiable. What may go wrong here, however, is that some of them may not be immersions: since $h_s' = sg' + (1 - s)f'$, there may very well be values of s and t for which $h_s'(t)$ is zero.

In fact there *must* be such values if the turning numbers of f and g are different. The turning number of an immersion $f : S^1 \to \mathbf{R}^2$ is the number of times that the tangent to f turns around, or, in fancier terms, the degree of the map $\dfrac{f'}{\|f'\|} : S^1 \to S^1$. (This map makes sense because f' is never zero.) For instance, if f is just the unit circle described counterclockwise, the tangent vector keeps turning left as we go along, and when we come back to the starting point it will have turned 360°: the turning number is 1. If the circle is described clockwise, the turning number is -1. If f is a skater's 8 the turning number is zero: the tangent is turning left for half of the time, and right for the other half, and the net amount of turning is zero.

Now since our family h_s gives rise to a homotopy between $f'/\|f'\|$ and $g'/\|g'\|$, and homotopic maps have the same degree, it follows that h_s cannot exist if the turning numbers of f and g are different. For instance, there is no way to deform a circle into an 8 according to the rules of our game. On the other hand, if the two curves do have the same turning number, the theorem of Whitney-Graustein says that they can be deformed into one another, but we have to do better than just averaging the two curves.

There are several ways to make the construction of the h_s more sophisticated, to guarantee that they are immersions. The idea implemented here is due to Bill Thurston, and it basically consists in first deforming f and g in a controlled way, by adding eight-shaped bumps to them, so that their derivatives become so big that there is no danger that they will vanish when we average them (in the right way). But first let's create some structures, so we can explain the process as we present the actual code.

3. Structures. We will represent our maps $S^1 \to \mathbf{R}^2$ by large, but finite, arrays of points, since it would be too hard to do otherwise. The arrays will be allocated dynamically, but for each run they will have constant size n_pts, the same for all curves.

We will need to store information about the direction of tangent vectors as well as positions. Sometimes the direction is best thought of as being an angle, sometimes a complex number of absolute value 1. For this reason our **tangent_vector** structure will contain redundant information.

#define $make\_curve(size)$ $(curve)malloc((\mathbf{unsigned})\,(size*\mathbf{sizeof}\,(point)))$
#define $make\_tang\_map(size)$ $(tang\_map)malloc((\mathbf{unsigned})\,(size*\mathbf{sizeof}\,(tang\_vector)))$
#define $subt\_vec(a,b,c)$ $(a).x = (b).x - (c).x, (a).y = (b).y - (c).y$
#define $add\_vec(a,b,c)$ $(a).x = (b).x + (c).x, (a).y = (b).y + (c).y$
#define $smult\_vec(a,r,b)$ $(a).x = (b).x * r, (a).y = (b).y * r$ /* scalar multiplication */

⟨ External variables and types 3 ⟩ ≡
  char $*malloc(\,)$, $*sprintf(\,)$; /* this keeps lint happy */
  typedef struct {
    double x, y,
  } **point**; /* a point in $\mathbf{R}^2$ */
  typedef point $*$**curve**; /* a map $S^1 \to \mathbf{R}^2$ */
  typedef point cis; /* a direction in Cartesian coordinates ("cos $+i$ sin") */
  typedef struct {
    cis $cis\_$; /* info in Cartesian coordinates */
    double arg; /* argument of preceding */
  } **tang_vector**; /* a direction in S^1 */
  typedef tang_vector $*$**tang_map**; /* a map $S^1 \to S^1$ */
  int n_pts; /* number of points representing a curve */

See also sections 4, 9, and 34.

This code is used in section 33.

4. Those curves that are input by the user are not read in at their final resolution: the user inputs a few of their points, and the others are interpolated by means of splines. In order to keep together the "coarse" version of a curve, its splined version, and the corresponding tangent map, we create a structure to hold this information.

⟨ External variables and types 3 ⟩+ ≡
  typedef struct {
    curve $coarse$; /* unsplined version of curve */
    int $input\_pts$; /* number of points in preceding */
    curve $fine$; /* splined version of curve, containing n_pts points */
    tang_map $prime$; /* derivative of preceding */
  } **CURVE**;
  CURVE F, G; /* we store f in $F.fine$, g in $G.fine$ */

5. We may as well see the code to display our curves. We normally plot two related curves at a time, using the *snapshot* routine, whose arguments include, in addition to the curves, flags saying whether each curve should be plotted in color and whether the snapshot should be saved for later playback.

#define *in_color* 0

⟨ Function definitions 5 ⟩ ≡
   snapshot(*beta*, *flag1*, *gamma*, *flag2*, *record*)
   curve *beta*, *gamma*;   /∗ curves to be plotted ∗/
   int *flag1*, *flag2*;   /∗ black or color? ∗/
   int *record*;   /∗ are we to record this frame? ∗/
   {
      char *temp*[*BUFSIZ*];

      ⟨ Draw *beta* and *gamma* 6 ⟩;
      if (*animate* ∧ *record*) *graf_store_frame*( );
      if (*waiting*) (**void**) *fgets*(*temp*, *BUFSIZ*, *stdin*);
      else *usleep*((**unsigned**) (1 · 10^6 ∗ *delay*));
      graf_clear_screen( );
   }

See also sections 7, 8, 12, 21, 23, 24, 25, 26, 27, 28, and 36.

This code is used in section 33.

6. Self-intersecting curves can be easier to understand if they're drawn bit by bit, with their color changing as we go along; on the other hand, drawing is generally much quicker when only one color is used, since it can be done by using a single function call. For this reason we give the user a choice: when the variable *oomph* is 0, color curves are monochromatic; otherwise they're iridescent (rainbowlike).

The rainbow colors are chosen from an array made up of three scales in succession, one going from red to green, the next from green to blue, and the last back to red. This array is filled at startup time by some kind of interpolation rule, which depends on the graphics device (since some devices have very nonlinear color response). The high-level graphics routines *graf_line* and *graf_polygon* take as their last argument a number in [0, 1], indicating a position in this array (in terms of the size of the array); in this way they can maintain system independence. This argument can also be negative, in which case the line or curve is drawn in black.

⟨ Draw *beta* and *gamma* 6 ⟩ ≡
   {
      int *i*, *j*;
      if (*oomph*)
         for (*i* = 0, *j* = 1; *i* < *n_pts*; *i*++, *j* = (*j* + 1)%*n_pts*)
            graf_line(*beta*[*i*], *beta*[*j*], *flag1* ≡ *in_color* ?(**double**) *i*/*n_pts* : −1.), *graf_line*(*gamma*[*i*],
               gamma[*j*], *flag2* ≡ *in_color* ?(**double**) *i*/*n_pts* : −1.);
         else *graf_polygon*(*n_pts*, *beta*, *flag1* ≡ *in_color* ? 0. : −1.), *graf_polygon*(*n_pts*, *gamma*,
               flag2 ≡ *in_color* ? 0. : −1.);
   }

This code is used in section 5.

7. The homotopy. We start with *calc_turning_no*, a function that takes a **tang_map**

whose *arg* components are known up to multiples of 2π and computes the turning number. Starting with the second vertex, at each vertex we compute a *turning angle*, which is by convention the angle of smallest absolute value required to turn from the direction of the previous side to that of the next side. That is, the turning angle is a number in the interval $(-\pi, \pi)$, if we rule out the case of a 180° turn (this is necessary, since this case is inherently ambiguous). We fix the direction angle of the next side by adding a multiple of 2π, so the direction of each side reflects the direction of the previous side plus the turning angle. After we've done this for the last vertex we do it (conceptually) for the first, and the accumulated turning angle will be registered as the difference between the direction angle of the first side when we left and its direction angle when we arrive. This accumulated turning angle is, by definition, 2π times the turning number.

```
#define  pi  3.1415916535897
#define  poltoc(a, r, theta)  (a).x = r * cos(theta), (a).y = r * sin(theta);
⟨ Function definitions 5 ⟩+ ≡
  calc_turning_no(prime)
  tang_map prime;    /* derivative map of curve under consideration */
  {
    int i;

    for (i = 1; i < n_pts; i++)
      prime[i].arg -= 2 * pi * rint((prime[i].arg - prime[i - 1].arg)/(2 * pi));
    return -(int) rint((prime[0].arg - prime[n_pts - 1].arg)/(2 * pi));
  }
```

8. Next we tackle the homotopy proper. It's easiest to think of the intermediate curves h_s as the sum of a "base" curve, which is either f or g or an average of them, and a curve made up of "eights." A single eight, of half-width w_8 and half-height h_8 and centered at the origin, is parametrically described by $x = -w_8 \sin 2\theta$, $y = h_8 \sin \theta$, where θ ranges from 0 to 2π as we go around the eight once. If we're adding n eights to the base curve, the phase angle θ along the eights curve is $\theta = 2\pi nt$, where t is the parameter along the base curve.

However, the eights are not all drawn standing up: for each s and t they have a direction $\alpha(s, t)$, so in general what we'll be adding to the base curve is the vector $(-w_8 \sin 2\theta, h_8 \sin \theta)$, rotated α. We set *two_wh_ratio* $= 2w_8/h_8$.

```
⟨ Function definitions 5 ⟩+ ≡
  eight(theta, in, alpha, out)
  cis theta;    /* exponential of phase angle along eight */
  cis alpha;    /* direction of pinching of eight */
  point *in, *out;    /* point on base curve and point after deformation */
  {
    out → x = in → x + theta.y * h_8 * (-two_wh_ratio * theta.x * alpha.x - alpha.y);
    out → y = in → y + theta.y * h_8 * (-two_wh_ratio * theta.x * alpha.y + alpha.x);
  }
```

9. The reason for the eights is that if their size is big enough, the derivative associated with them is also big, and when added to the derivative of the base curve it will guarantee a nonzero overall derivative. A sufficient condition for this masking effect to occur, then, is that the smallest possible speed of the eights be bigger than the largest possible speed of either f or g (this will also be bigger than the speed of any weighted average, with positive weights, of f and g).

The derivative of the eights itself can be written as the sum of two components, from the variations in θ and α, respectively. The length of the second of these is no more than $\|\alpha'\| \max(w_8, h_8)$. The length of the first is $2\pi n\sqrt{4w_8^2 \cos^2 2\theta + h_8^2 \cos^2 \theta}$; either the square root is $\geq 2w_8$, or we have $4w_8^2 \sin^2 2\theta > h_8^2 \cos^2 \theta$, whence $16w_8^2 \sin^2 \theta > h_8^2$ and $16w_8^2 > h_8^2$. In this case a small calculation show that the square root is $\geq .5h_8$, so we can say that the length of the first component is never less than $2\pi n \min(2w_8, .5h_8)$.

Let's assume h_8 and w_8 were chosen so that the length of the second component is, say, no more than half the length of the first; then as long as $.5 \cdot 2\pi n \min(2w_8, .5h_8) > \max(\|f'\|, \|g'\|)$, our intermediate steps will be immersions.

The function α is not very significant when h_8 and w_8 are big, except that $\|\alpha'\|$ shouldn't be too big, as we've just seen. But how about small values of h_8 and w_8? After all, we have to provide a homotopy between f without eights and f with eights. The answer is that, if α is parallel to the derivative of the base curve, we're OK, no matter what the size of the eights. To see why, assume for a moment that the point where we are has a horizontal velocity. With $\alpha = 0$, the velocity along the eight is $2\pi n(-2w_8 \cos 2\theta, h_8 \cos \theta)$, plus a component due to the variation in α, of length no more than $\|\alpha'\| \max(w_8, h_8)$. With the same reasoning as above, one shows that the condition $\|\alpha'\| \max(w_8, h_8) < .5 \cdot 2\pi n \min(2w_8, .5h_8)$ implies that the velocity along the eight avoids the negative x-axis, so it can never cancel out with the velocity along the base curve.

To summarize, we compute from f and g the maximum value of $\|\alpha'\|$, of $\|f'\|$ and of $\|g'\|$, then we choose w_8, h_8 and n in such a way that

$$\alpha' \max(w_8, h_8) < .5 \cdot 2\pi n \min(2w_8, .5h_8),$$
$$\max(\|f'\|, \|g'\|) < .5 \cdot 2\pi n \min(2w_8, .5h_8).$$

We now turn to the implementation of the ideas above. We need variables for the maximum velocity and angular velocity or f and g, and for the "milestones" in the homotopy, namely f and g with full-size eights added.

⟨ External variables and types 3 ⟩+ ≡
 double *max_omega* = 0; /∗ upper bound for $\omega = \|\alpha'\|$ ∗/
 double *max_speed* = 0; /∗ upper bound for $\|f'\|$ and $\|g'\|$ ∗/
 curve *f_with_eights*; /∗ intermediate step: f with eights added ∗/
 curve *g_with_eights*; /∗ ditto for g ∗/

10. The homotopy, then, consists of four parts. First we deform the initial curve f (stored in *F.fine*) by adding increasingly bigger eights to it; we display *lin_frames* snapshots of this action. The resulting curve is called *f_with_eights*; actually, we can save a bit of time by calculating *f_with_eights* beforehand and taking weighted averages of f and *f_with_eights*. The base curve so far is still f. Next we deform the base curve from f to g, without changing the direction of the eights; we show *twist_frames* frames of this action. Then we rotate the eights as necessary to get *g_with_eights*, which is to g as *f_with_eights* is to f; by shrinking the eights we finally get to g.

All four phases are carried out by calls to the same function, *homotopy*. The last argument to this function tells what part we're in: if positive, we're adding eights, if negative we're smoothing away eights, and if zero we're doing something else.

⟨ Homotope between f and g 10 ⟩ ≡
  ⟨ Make f_with_eights and g_with_eights 11 ⟩;
  $snapshot(F.fine, in\_color, F.fine, in\_color, 1)$;   /* save first frame */
  $homotopy(lin\_frames, F.fine, F.prime, f\_with\_eights, F.prime, 1)$;
  $homotopy(twist\_frames, F.fine, F.prime, G.fine, F.prime, 0)$;
  $homotopy(twist\_frames, G.fine, F.prime, G.fine, G.prime, 0)$;
  $homotopy(lin\_frames, g\_with\_eights, G.prime, G.fine, G.prime, -1)$;

This code is used in section 33.

11. An efficient way to generate the eights is to update the first parameter to *eight* at each point along the curve, by multiplying it by an exponential increment $exp(2\pi n\_eights/n\_pts)$.

#define $rot\_mult(a, b, c)$
        { **double** $temp = b.x * c.x - b.y * c.y;\ a.y = b.x * c.y + b.y * c.x;\ a.x = temp;$ }

⟨ Make f_with_eights and g_with_eights 11 ⟩ ≡
  $f\_with\_eights = make\_curve(n\_pts)$;
  $g\_with\_eights = make\_curve(n\_pts)$;
  {
    int k;
    cis $theta$;   /* exponential of phase angle of eight */
    cis $incr$;   /* increment in $theta$ between consecutive points */
    $poltoc(incr, 1., 2. * pi * n\_eights/(\textbf{double})\ n\_pts)$;
    $poltoc(theta, 1., 0.)$;
    for $(k = 0;\ k < n\_pts;\ k{+}{+})$ {
      $eight(theta, \&F.fine[k], F.prime[k].cis\_, \&f\_with\_eights[k])$;
      $eight(theta, \&G.fine[k], G.prime[k].cis\_, \&g\_with\_eights[k])$;
      $rot\_mult(theta, theta, incr)$;
    }
  }

This code is used in section 10.

12. When $part\_code$ is zero, beg and end are interpreted as base curves and beg_dir and end_dir as directions of eights; *homotopy* must average base curves and directions and add the eights to the averaged base curve in the averaged direction. If $part\_code$ is nonzero, *homotopy* just averages between the curves beg and end, ignoring beg_dir and end_dir.

⟨ Function definitions 5 ⟩+ ≡
  $homotopy(n\_steps, beg, beg\_dir, end, end\_dir, part\_code)$
  int n_steps; /* number of steps in homotopy */
  curve beg, end; /* initial and final curves */
  tang_map beg_dir, end_dir; /* initial and final angles for eights */
  int $part\_code$; /* what part of overall process are we in? */
  {
    static curve ave; /* weighted average of beg and end */
    static curve $delta$; /* increment in ave */
    static curve $scratch$; /* a scratch area */
    static tang_map ave_dir; /* weighted average of beg_dir and end_dir */
    static tang_map $delta\_dir$; /* increment in ave_dir */
    int i, j; /* counters over points and steps, respectively */
    cis $theta$; /* exponential of phase angle of eight */

```
   cis incr;     /* increment in theta between consecutive points */
   double frac= 1./n_steps;     /* for arithmetic convenience */
   if (part_code ≡ 1) {    /* allocate vectors */
      ave_dir = make_tang_map(n_pts);  delta_dir = make_tang_map(n_pts);
        ave = make_curve(n_pts);  delta = make_curve(n_pts);  scratch = make_curve(n_pts);
   }
   ⟨Initialize ave and set delta and incr 13⟩;
   if (part_code ≡ 0) ⟨Fill in ave_dir and delta_dir 14⟩;
   for (j = 0; j < n_steps; j++) {
      if (beg ≠ end) ⟨Increment ave 15⟩;
      if (part_code ≡ 0) {
         ⟨Add eights to ave, put result in scratch, and increment ave_dir 16⟩;
            snapshot(scratch, in_color, ave, ¬in_color, 1);
      }
      else snapshot(ave, in_color, part_code > 0 ? beg : end, ¬in_color, 1);
   }
}
```

13.   We set $delta = (end - beg)/n\_steps$, so later we can increment ave by adding $delta$.
⟨Initialize ave and set $delta$ and $incr$ 13⟩ ≡
```
   for (i = 0; i < n_pts; i++) {
      ave[i] = beg[i];
      if (beg ≠ end) subt_vec(delta[i], end[i], beg[i]), smult_vec(delta[i], frac, delta[i]);
   }
   poltoc(incr, 1., 2 * pi * n_eights/(double) n_pts);
```
This code is used in section 12.

14. ave_dir is an average between beg_dir and end_dir, just as ave is an average between
beg and end. However, the $\_dir$ variables are **tang_map**s, which stand for direction-valued
maps on S^1, so the averaging doesn't make sense unless we choose a *determination* for
the direction angles. Such a determination is, quite conveniently, available in the arg
component of beg_dir and end_dir; in symbols, we will set $delta\_dir.arg = (end\_dir.arg -$
$beg\_dir.arg)/n\_steps$ and $ave\_dir.arg = beg\_dir.arg + (j/n\_steps) * delta\_dir.arg$. It is here
that the assumption that beg and end have the same turning number is essential, for it
implies that the difference $end\_dir.arg - beg\_dir.arg$ can be seen not only as a direction-
valued map on S^1 but also as a (continuous) real-valued function on S^1, so that $delta\_dir.arg$
makes sense.

Notice that adding to beg_dir or to end_dir a multiple of 2π has no effect on those maps,
but if affects $delta\_dir$, which means the eights will turn faster or more slowly. We will
adjust the difference $end\_dir.arg - beg\_dir.arg$ by a constant *adjustment*, a multiple of 2π,
so that $delta\_dir$ is, on the whole, as small as possible.

⟨Fill in ave_dir and $delta\_dir$ 14⟩ ≡
```
   {
      double diff, min_diff = 0, max_diff = 0;
      double adjustment;
      for (i = 0; i < n_pts; i++) {
         diff = end_dir[i].arg - beg_dir[i].arg;
```

```
      if (diff < min_diff) min_diff = diff;
      else if (diff > max_diff) max_diff = diff;
   }
   adjustment = 2 * pi * rint((min_diff + max_diff)/(2 * 2 * pi));
   for (i = 0; i < n_pts; i++) {
      ave_dir[i] = beg_dir[i];
      poltoc(delta_dir[i].cis_, 1., (end_dir[i].arg − beg_dir[i].arg − adjustment) * frac);
   }
}
```

This code is used in section 12.

15. ⟨Increment *ave* 15⟩ ≡
  for (*i* = 0; *i* < *n_pts*; *i*++) *add_vec*(*ave*[*i*], *ave*[*i*], *delta*[*i*]);

This code is used in section 12.

16. ⟨Add eights to *ave*, put result in *scratch*, and increment *ave_dir* 16⟩ ≡

```
   {
      poltoc(theta, 1., 0.);
      for (i = 0; i < n_pts; i++) {
         rot_mult(ave_dir[i].cis_, ave_dir[i].cis_, delta_dir[i].cis_);
         eight(theta, &ave[i], ave_dir[i].cis_, &scratch[i]);
         rot_mult(theta, theta, incr);
      }
   }
```

This code is used in section 12.

17. Inputting the curve. As mentioned above, the curves input by the user go to the *coarse* component of the **CURVE**s *F* and *G*. At most *max_input_pts* per curve should be input.

#define *max_input_pts* 60   /* *F.input_pts* and *G.input_pts* must be less than this */

⟨Make *f* and *g* 17⟩ ≡
  graf_window(1.);   /* window now covers [−1, 1] × [−1, 1] */
  F.coarse = *make_curve*(*max_input_pts*); *G.coarse* = *make_curve*(*max_input_pts*);
  ⟨Read representative points on *f* and *g*, interpolate between them, and compute the maximum
     speed and angular velocity 19⟩;
  if (*verbose*)
    message2("**max_speed=%f\n**", *max_speed*), *message2*("**max_omega=%f\n**", *max_omega*);
  if (¬*user*) ⟨Check whether current parameters will ensure that all steps in the homotopy are
     immersions; if not, fix them accordingly 18⟩;
  graf_window(1.1 * (1 + *h_8*));   /* so all curves will fit in window */
  snapshot(*F.fine*, *in_color*, *G.fine*, *in_color*, 0);   /* don't save this frame */
  if (*waiting* ∧ *filter*) (**void**) *freopen*("**/dev/tty**","**r**", *stdin*);

This code is used in section 33.

18. Here we implement the equations relating *n_eights*, *max_speed*, *max_omega* and *h_8*.

⟨Check whether current parameters will ensure that all steps in the homotopy are immersions; if
    not, fix them accordingly 18⟩ ≡
  if (*n_eights* < 1 + 1.5 * *max_omega*/*pi*) {

$n\_eights = 1 + 1.5 * max\_omega / pi;$
$free\_CURVE(F); \ free\_CURVE(G);$
⟨ Reinterpolate with more points 20 ⟩;
}
$h\_8 = max\_speed / (pi * n\_eights * .67081);$
$two\_wh\_ratio = 2 * .559017;$
if (*verbose*) {
  $message2("$**number**$_\sqcup$**of**$_\sqcup$**eights=%d\n**", n_eights);
  $message2("$**height**$_\sqcup$**of**$_\sqcup$**eights=%f\n**", h_8);
}

This code is used in section 17.

19.   The next two modules are very similar and so can be subsumed under a single function whose last argument says whether or not we should read in *F.coarse* and *G.coarse*.

⟨ Read representative points on *f* and *g*, interpolate between them, and compute the maximum speed and angular velocity 19 ⟩ ≡
  $process\_curves(\&F, \&G, 1);$

This code is used in section 17.

20.   ⟨ Reinterpolate with more points 20 ⟩ ≡
  $process\_curves(\&F, \&G, 0);$

This code is used in section 18.

21.   We start by computing the size *n_pts* of our *fine* curves and allocating room for them. If *inputting* = 1, we input *F.coarse*, spline it, and compute its turning number. Then we do the same thing for *G*.

#define $alloc\_CURVE(a) \ a \rightarrow fine = make\_curve(n\_pts), a \rightarrow prime = make\_tang\_map(n\_pts)$
#define $free\_CURVE(a) \ free((\mathbf{char} *) \ a.fine), free((\mathbf{char} *) \ a.prime)$
#define $spline\_and\_turning\_no(a) \ (spline(a \rightarrow coarse, a \rightarrow fine, a \rightarrow input\_pts, n\_pts),$
           $calc\_tang\_map(*a), calc\_turning\_no(a \rightarrow prime))$
⟨ Function definitions 5 ⟩+ ≡
  $process\_curves(pF, pG, inputting)$
  CURVE $*pF, *pG;$ /* pointers to the **CURVE**s we'll be processing */
  int *inputting*;   /* are we inputting points on the curves? */
  {
    int *turning_no*;

    $n\_pts = n\_eights * pts\_per\_eight;$
    $alloc\_CURVE(pF); \ alloc\_CURVE(pG);$
    if (*inputting*) $pF \rightarrow input\_pts = get\_curve(pF \rightarrow coarse);$
    $turning\_no = spline\_and\_turning\_no(pF);$
    if (*inputting*) ⟨ Read in *G.coarse* or make it equal to a circle 22 ⟩;
    if ($turning\_no \neq spline\_and\_turning\_no(pG)$)
      $message1("$**turning**$_\sqcup$**numbers**$_\sqcup$**don't**$_\sqcup$**match!\n**"), exit(0);$
  }

22.   If the user is not supplying *G.coarse*, we make it equal to a circle drawn *turning_no* times. We supply 16 points to the circle to get a reasonable approximation.

Actually, if $|turning\_no| > 1$, we don't want the default curve to be an exact circle, because it becomes difficult to see what's going on when two parts of the curve coincide. For this reason we perturb the curve a bit with a radial term that oscillates around 1.

⟨ Read in *G.coarse* or make it equal to a circle 22 ⟩ ≡

```
   if (¬g_is_circle)  pG → input_pts = get_curve(pG → coarse);
   else {
      int k;    /* ranges from 0 to pG → input_pts */
      int sign = (turning_no > 0 ? 1 : −1);
      double r, theta;    /* polar coordinates of point on "circle" */

      pG → input_pts = 16 * turning_no * sign;
      if (pG → input_pts > max_input_pts)  pG → input_pts = max_input_pts;
      for (k = 0; k < pG → input_pts; k++) {
         theta = 2 * pi * turning_no * k/(double) pG → input_pts;
         r = (.8 + .2 * sin(2 * pi * (turning_no − 1) * k/(double) pG → input_pts));
         poltoc(pG → coarse[k], r, theta);
      }
   }
```

This code is used in section 21.

---

23.   ⟨ Function definitions 5 ⟩+ ≡

```
   calc_tang_map(gamma)
   CURVE gamma;
   {
      point side;     /* difference between each vertex and the previous one */
      int i;

      for (i = 0; i < n_pts; i++) {
         subt_vec(side, gamma.fine[(i + 1)%n_pts], gamma.fine[i]);
         gamma.prime[i].arg = atan2(side.y, side.x);
         poltoc(gamma.prime[i].cis_, 1., gamma.prime[i].arg);
      }
   }
```

---

24.   Here is the code that reads in a polygon. It returns the number of points read. Since we're assuming that our curves are immersions, we disallow consecutive points that are too close to one another.

#define *epsilon* .0000001

⟨ Function definitions 5 ⟩+ ≡

```
   get_curve(gamma)
   curve gamma;
   {
      point side;     /* line from one vertex to previous one */
      int i = −1;
      int is_not_last;

      if (verbose)
         if (filter)  message1("reading␣from␣standard␣input\n");
         else graf_mouse_message();
      do {
         i++;
```

```
      is_not_last = (i < max_input_pts) ∧ get_point(&gamma[i]);
      if (i > 0) {
          subt_vec(side, gamma[i * is_not_last], gamma[i − 1]);
          if (side.x * side.x + side.y * side.y < epsilon) message2("vertex␣%d␣too␣close␣to␣",
                  i−−), message2("%d␣one␣will␣be␣ignored\n", is_not_last ? i : 0);
          else graf_line(gamma[i * is_not_last], gamma[i − 1], 0.);
      }
  } while (is_not_last) ;
  message2("read␣%d␣points", i);
  if (i ≡ max_input_pts) message1("␣(the␣maximum)\n");
  else if (i < 3) message1("␣(too␣few)\n"), exit(0);
    else message1("\n");
  return i;
}
```

25.   *get_point* gets the coordinates of the next point (from the standard input or from a mouse click) or returns 0.

⟨ Function definitions 5 ⟩+ ≡

```
  get_point(t)
  point *t;
  {
      char temp[BUFSIZ];

      if (¬filter) return graf_read_mouse(t);
      else return fgets(temp, BUFSIZ, stdin) ∧ (sscanf(temp,"%F%F", &t → x, &t → y) ≡ 2);
  }
```

26.   The interpolation is done with cubic splines. While doing it we estimate the maximum velocity and angular velocity of each curve.

```
#define find_coeffs(t)  d.t = in[i].t, c.t = .5 * (in[(i + 1)%n_in].t − in[(n_in + i − 1)%n_in].t),
              b.t = 3.*(in[(i+1)%n_in].t−(c.t+d.t))−((in[(i+2)%n_in].t−in[(i)%n_in].t)/2.−c.t),
              a.t = in[(i + 1)%n_in].t − (b.t + c.t + d.t)
```
⟨ Function definitions 5 ⟩+ ≡

```
  spline(in, out, n_in, n_out)
  curve in, out;     /* original and interpolated polygons */
  int n_in;     /* number of points on in */
  int n_out;     /* number of points on out */
  {
      point a, b, c, d;     /* coefficients of degree-three polynomial */
      int i;     /* index into input vector */
      int j = 0;     /* index into output vector */
      int k;     /* roughly n_out/n_in */
      int l;     /* roughly j%i */
      double t, omega, speed;     /* temporary values */
      for (i = 0; i < n_in; i++) {
        find_coeffs(x);
        find_coeffs(y);
        k = (n_out + i)/n_in;
        for (l = 0; l < k; l++, j++) {
```

```
      t =((double) l)/k;
      out[j].x = d.x + t * (c.x + t * (b.x + t * a.x));
      out[j].y = d.y + t * (c.y + t * (b.y + t * a.y));
    }
    a.x = 3 * a.x;  a.y = 3 * a.y;  b.x = 2 * b.x;  b.y = 2 * b.y;
    find_extrema(a, b, c, &speed, &omega);
    if ((speed *= n_out/k) > max_speed)  max_speed = speed;
    if ((omega *= n_out/k) > max_omega)  max_omega = omega;
  }
}
```

27. Numerical estimates. We finally look at *find_extrema*, a routine that examines a vector function (f_x, f_y) defined on $[0, 1]$ by two quadratic polynomials $f_x = a_x t^2 + b_x t + c_x$ and $f_y = a_y t^2 + b_y t + c_y$, and returns two numbers associated with them: the maximum length, given by $\sqrt{\max(f_x^2 + f_y^2)}$, and an upper bound for the angular velocity (speed of change of direction), given by

$$\frac{\max\left(|f_y' f_x - f_x' f_y|\right)}{\min(f_x^2 + f_y^2)}.$$

By elementary calculus these maxima and minima occur at points where the derivative of the relevant function is zero, or else at either endpoint of the interval $[0, 1]$ of interest. The derivative of $f_x^2 + f_y^2$ is a cubic polynomial, and we find its real zeros by using standard formulas; the derivative of $f_y' f_x - f_x' f_y$ is a linear function.

⟨ Function definitions 5 ⟩+ ≡

```
find_extrema(a, b, c, p_max_length, p_max_omega)
  point a, b, c;    /* where f_x = a_x t^2 + b_x t + c, and similarly for y */
  double *p_max_length, *p_max_omega;    /* addresses of results */
{
    double coeff_length[4];    /* coefficients of derivative of length */
    double coeff_numerator[2];    /* coefficients of derivative of numerator above */
    double root[3];    /* real roots of derivative of length */
    int n_roots;    /* number of roots of ditto */
    double max_numerator;    /* maximum value of numerator */
    double sq_length( ), sq_max_length, sq_min_length;    /* squared length */
    double temp;    /* temporary register */

    ⟨ Find coefficients of derivatives 29 ⟩;
    ⟨ Find real zeros of derivative of length 30 ⟩;
    ⟨ Examine extreme points 0 and 1 31 ⟩;
    ⟨ Examine zeros of derivatives in the interval [0, 1] 32 ⟩;
    *p_max_length = sqrt(sq_max_length);
    *p_max_omega = max_numerator / sq_min_length;    /* should test for zero division */
}
```

28. Here are routines to evaluate our two polynomials:

```
#define numerator(a, b, c, t)
    fabs((((b.x * a.y - a.x * b.y) * t + 2 * (c.x * a.y - a.x * c.y)) * t + c.x * b.y - b.x * c.y)
```

⟨ Function definitions 5 ⟩+ ≡

```
double sq_length (a, b, c, t)
point a, b, c;
double t;
{
    double x= (a.x * t + b.x) * t + c.x, y= (a.y * t + b.y) * t + c.y;
    return x * x + y * y;
}
```

29.   We calculate the coefficients of the derivatives explicitly. The index of the array of coefficients indicates the exponent.

⟨ Find coefficients of derivatives 29 ⟩ ≡

$coeff\_length[0] = 2 * (b.x * c.x + b.y * c.y);$

$coeff\_length[1] = 2 * (b.x * b.x + b.y * b.y) + 4 * (a.x * c.x + a.y * c.y);$

$coeff\_length[2] = 6 * (b.x * a.x + b.y * a.y);$

$coeff\_length[3] = 4 * (a.x * a.x + a.y * a.y);$

$coeff\_numerator[0] = 2 * (c.x * a.y - a.x * c.y);$

$coeff\_numerator[1] = 2 * (b.x * a.y - a.x * b.y);$

This code is used in section 27.

30.   The function *solve3* is coded elsewhere; it takes (the addresses of) a vector of coefficients and one of roots, fills in the vector of roots (in no particular order, but without repetition), and returns the number of roots found.

⟨ Find real zeros of derivative of length 30 ⟩ ≡

$n\_roots = solve3 (coeff\_length, root);$

This code is used in section 27.

31.   ⟨ Examine extreme points 0 and 1 31 ⟩ ≡

```
{
    sq_max_length = sq_min_length = c.x * c.x + c.y * c.y;     /* i.e., sq_length(a, b, c, 0.) */
    if ((temp = sq_length(a, b, c, 1.)) < sq_min_length)  sq_min_length = temp;
    else if (temp > sq_max_length)  sq_max_length = temp;
    max_numerator = fabs(c.x * b.y - b.x * c.y);     /* i.e., fabs(numerator(a, b, c, 0.)) */
    if ((temp = numerator(a, b, c, 1.)) > max_numerator)  max_numerator = temp;
}
```

This code is used in section 27.

32.   ⟨ Examine zeros of derivatives in the interval [0, 1] 32 ⟩ ≡

```
{
    int i;
    for (i = 0; i < n_roots; i++)
        if (root[i] > 0. ∧ root[i] < 1.) {
            if ((temp = sq_length(a, b, c, root[i])) < sq_min_length)  sq_min_length = temp;
            else if (temp > sq_max_length)  sq_max_length = temp;
        }
    if (coeff_numerator[1] ≠ 0.) {
        root[0] = −coeff_numerator[0]/coeff_numerator[1];
        if (root[0] > 0. ∧ root[0] < 1.)
            if ((temp = numerator(a, b, c, root[0]) > max_numerator))  max_numerator = temp;
```

```
      }
    }
```
This code is used in section 27.

33.   The main routine and the command line.   We now put everything together:

```
#include <stdio.h>
#include <math.h>
  ⟨ External variables and types 3 ⟩
  ⟨ Function definitions 5 ⟩;
  main ( argc, argv )
  int argc;
  char **argv;
  {
    ⟨ Parse command line 35 ⟩;
    graf_begin( );     /* initialize graphics */
    ⟨ Make f and g 17 ⟩;
    ⟨ Homotope between f and g 10 ⟩;
    graf_animate( );     /* play back animation, if desired */
    graf_end( );     /* terminate graphics */
  }
```

34.   Here are the user-definable quantities and their default values. The defaults for the size and number of eights are used only if $user = 1$, that is, if the user does not want the program to compute values for them that will ensure the validity of the homotopy process.

```
#define   def_animate  10
#define   def_delay  0.1
#define   def_lin_frames  4
#define   def_twist_frames  8
#define   def_pts_per_eight  14

#define   def_n_eights  20
#define   def_wh_ratio  0.4
#define   def_h_8  0.3
```
⟨ External variables and types 3 ⟩+ ≡

```
  typedef int boolean;

  boolean filter = 0;     /* should the curve be entered interactively? */
  boolean oomph = 0;     /* should we plot curves slowly or quickly? */
  boolean user = 0;     /* should the user have control over parameters? */
  boolean verbose = 0;     /* should we print lots of messages? */
  boolean waiting = 0;     /* should we wait for <CR> between frames? */
  boolean g_is_circle = 1;     /* should g be a circle? */

  int animate = 0;     /* should the frames be saved and played back? */
  float delay = def_delay;     /* delay between frames, in seconds */
  int lin_frames = def_lin_frames;     /* number of frames in linear part of homotopy */
  int twist_frames = def_twist_frames;     /* number of frames in twist part of homotopy */
  int pts_per_eight = def_pts_per_eight;     /* number of points per eight */

  float two_wh_ratio = 2 * def_wh_ratio;     /* twice the width/height ratio of eights */
  float h_8 = def_h_8;     /* maximum height of eights */
  int n_eights = def_n_eights;     /* number of eights added to curve */
```

35.   The command line syntax is straightforward. Each argument sets a variable, corresponding exactly to the list above. For the non-**boolean** variables the argument should consist of a letter followed by the desired value of the variable.

```
#define read_int()  atoi((∗argv) + 1)
#define read_float()  atof((∗argv) + 1)
⟨ Parse command line 35 ⟩ ≡
  while (++argv, −−argc > 0)
  reswitch:
    switch (∗∗argv) {
    case 'f': filter = 1; break;
    case 'o': oomph = 1; break;
    case 'u': user = 1; break;
    case 'v': verbose = 1; break;
    case 'w': waiting = 1; break;
    case '2': g_is_circle = 0; break;

    case 'a': if ((animate = read_int()) ≤ 0)  animate = def_animate; break;
    case 'd': if ((delay = read_float()) ≤ 0)  delay = def_delay; break;
    case 'e': if ((n_eights = read_int()) ≤ 0)  n_eights = def_n_eights; break;
    case 'h': if ((h_8 = read_float()) ≤ 0)  h_8 = def_h_8; break;
    case 'l': if ((lin_frames = read_int()) ≤ 0)  lin_frames = def_lin_frames; break;
    case 'p': if ((pts_per_eight = read_int()) ≤ 0)  pts_per_eight = def_pts_per_eight; break;
    case 'r': if (2 ∗ ((two_wh_ratio = read_float()) ≤ 0))  two_wh_ratio = def_wh_ratio; break;
    case 't': if ((twist_frames = read_int()) ≤ 0)  twist_frames = def_twist_frames; break;

    case '?': usage(); exit(0);
    case '-': (∗argv)++; goto reswitch;
    default: message2("Unknown␣option␣%s\n", ∗argv); break;
    }
```

This code is used in section 33.

36.   ⟨ Function definitions 5 ⟩+ ≡
  usage()
  {
```
    message1("Options␣should␣separated␣by␣blanks;\n");
    message1("those␣that␣say␣`to␣set'␣should␣be␣followed␣by␣a␣number\n");
    message1("\n");
    message1("␣f␣(filter)␣to␣read␣curve␣from␣standard␣input\n");
    message1("␣o␣to␣draw␣curves␣with␣more␣oomph␣(but,␣alas,␣more␣slowly)\n");
    message1("␣u␣to␣give␣user␣control␣over␣parameters\n");
    message1("␣v␣to␣turn␣on␣verbose␣mode\n");
    message1("␣w␣to␣wait␣between␣frames\n");
    message1("␣2␣to␣homotope␣between␣two␣user-defined␣curves\n");
    message1("\n");
    message1("␣a␣to␣set␣number␣of␣times␣for␣animation␣playback\n");
    message2("␣␣␣default=0,␣but␣'a'␣by␣itself␣sets␣it␣to␣%d\n", def_animate);
    message1("␣d␣to␣set␣delay␣between␣frames␣(with␣'a'␣option)\n");
    message2("␣␣␣default=%f\n", def_delay);
    message1("␣e␣to␣set␣number␣of␣eights␣(with␣'u'␣option)\n");
    message2("␣␣␣default=%d\n", def_n_eights);
    message1("␣h␣to␣set␣height␣of␣eights␣(with␣'u'␣option)\n");
```

```
message2 ("␣␣␣default=%f\n", def_h_8 );
message1 ("␣l␣to␣set␣number␣of␣frames␣in␣linear␣part␣of␣homotopy\n");
message2 ("␣␣␣default=%d\n", def_lin_frames );
message1 ("␣p␣to␣set␣number␣of␣interpolated␣points␣per␣eight\n");
message2 ("␣␣␣default=%d\n", def_pts_per_eight );
message1 ("␣r␣to␣set␣width/length␣ratio␣of␣eights␣(with␣'u'␣option)\n");
message2 ("␣␣␣default=%f\n", def_wh_ratio );
message1 ("␣t␣to␣set␣number␣of␣frames␣in␣twist␣part␣of␣homotopy\n");
message2 ("␣␣␣default=%d\n", def_twist_frames );
message1 ("\n");
message1 ("␣?␣to␣print␣this␣blurb\n");
}
```

37. The printing macros used above (and elsewhere in the program) are defined here The graphics functions, whose names all start with *graf_*, are of necessity system-dependent and we do not include them in this file. Their syntax is explained in the modules where they're used, when appropriate.

#define *message1* (*a*) (**void**) *fprintf* (*stderr* , *a*)
#define *message2* (*a*, *b*) (**void**) *fprintf* (*stderr* , *a*, *b*)

38. Index.

a: 26, 27, 28.
add_vec: 3, 15.
adjustment: 14.
alloc_CURVE: 21.
alpha: 8.
animate: 5, 34, 35.
arg: 3, 7, 14, 23.
argc: 33, 35.
argv: 33, 35.
atan2: 23.
atof: 35.
atoi: 35.
ave: 12, 13, 14, 15, 16.
ave_dir: 12, 14, 16.
b: 26, 27, 28.
beg: 12, 13, 14.
beg_dir: 12, 14.
beta: 5, 6.
boolean: 34, 35.
BUFSIZ: 5, 25.
bumps: 2.
c: 26, 27, 28.
calc_tang_map: 21, 23.
calc_turning_no: 7, 21.
circles: 2.

cis: 3, 8, 11, 12.
cis_: 3, 11, 14, 16, 23.
coarse: 4, 17, 19, 21, 22.
coeff_length: 27, 29, 30.
coeff_numerator: 27, 29, 32.
cos: 7.
curve: 3, 4, 5, 9, 12, 24, 26.
CURVE: 4, 17, 21, 23.
d: 26.
def_animate: 34, 35, 36.
def_delay: 34, 35, 36.
def_h_8: 34, 35, 36.
def_lin_frames: 34, 35, 36.
def_n_eights: 34, 35, 36.
def_pts_per_eight: 34, 35, 36.
def_twist_frames: 34, 35, 36.
def_wh_ratio: 34, 35, 36.
delay: 5, 34, 35.
delta: 12, 13, 15.
delta_dir: 12, 14, 16.
diff: 14.
eight: 8, 11, 16.
eights: 2.
end: 12, 13, 14.
end_dir: 12, 14.

⟨ Add eights to *ave*, put result in *scratch*, and increment *ave_dir* 16 ⟩   Used in section 12.

⟨ Check whether current parameters will ensure that all steps in the homotopy are
    immersions; if not, fix them accordingly 18 ⟩   Used in section 17.

⟨ Draw *beta* and *gamma* 6 ⟩   Used in section 5.

⟨ Examine extreme points 0 and 1 31 ⟩   Used in section 27.

⟨ Examine zeros of derivatives in the interval [0, 1] 32 ⟩   Used in section 27.

⟨ External variables and types 3, 4, 9, 34 ⟩   Used in section 33.

⟨ Fill in *ave_dir* and *delta_dir* 14 ⟩   Used in section 12.

⟨ Find coefficients of derivatives 29 ⟩   Used in section 27.

⟨ Find real zeros of derivative of length 30 ⟩   Used in section 27.

⟨ Function definitions 5, 7, 8, 12, 21, 23, 24, 25, 26, 27, 28, 36 ⟩   Used in section 33.

⟨ Homotope between *f* and *g* 10 ⟩   Used in section 33.

⟨ Increment *ave* 15 ⟩   Used in section 12.

⟨ Initialize *ave* and set *delta* and *incr* 13 ⟩   Used in section 12.

⟨ Make *f* and *g* 17 ⟩   Used in section 33.

⟨ Make *f_with_eights* and *g_with_eights* 11 ⟩   Used in section 10.

⟨ Parse command line 35 ⟩   Used in section 33.

⟨ Read in *G.coarse* or make it equal to a circle 22 ⟩   Used in section 21.

⟨ Read representative points on *f* and *g*, interpolate between them, and compute the
    maximum speed and angular velocity 19 ⟩   Used in section 17.

⟨ Reinterpolate with more points 20 ⟩   Used in section 18.

Appendix H

How to Get the Software

The WEB system is in the public domain and can be acquired from a number of sources. In general, the sources of the WEB software are the same as for TEX. In fact, most of the TEX distributions have WEB bundled in for no extra charge. However, the TEX distributors are listed here even if they do not provide WEB, because TEX is necessary in order to run WEB anyway.

The primary source of information on WEB and related TEXnology is

TEX Users Group (TUG)
c/o American Mathematical Society
P. O. Box 9506
Providence, RI 02940–9506
(401)751-7760
tug@math.ams.com

Ordering *information* for both the actual software (on mag tape) and the documentation (including [Knu86d,Knu86b,Knu83,KF86,KRS89,Knu86a]) can be obtained from TUG. Anyone enquiring about TUG will be sent an information packet, including forms for acquiring TEX, joining TUG, and ordering publications

TUG does not handle the software or documentation itself. The Stanford distribution is available from a commercial duplication service:

Maria Code
Data Processing Services
1371 Sydney Drive
Sunnyvale, CA 94087
(408)735-8006

The distribution is available in the following formats: VMS Backup, TOPS 20 Dumper, IBM VM/CMS, IBM MVS, generic ASCII, and generic EBCDIC. The

535

latter two contain only sources. Other implementations, such as UNIX, must be acquired directly from the applicable site coordinator (see below).

The DECUS Program Library is another source for people with VAX computers. The DECUS distribution is basically the same as the Stanford distribution. The order number for TEX/LATEX/WEB is V-SP-58. Another library package, WEB Pack (VAX-294), contains MWEB, ScanTEX, and WEBMERGE.

> DECUS (BP02)
> Library Order Processing
> 219 Boston Post Road
> Marlboro, MA 01752–1850
> (508)480-3418
> (508)480-3315

The TUG Site Coordinators provide information about specific implementations and/or handle the standard distribution for that implementation.

VAX/VMS:

> David Kellerman
> Northlake Software
> 812 SW Washington Street
> Suite 1100
> Portland, OR 97205–3215
> (503)228-3383
> Fax: (503)228-5662

UNIX:

> Pierre A. MacKay
> Northwest Computer Support Group
> University of Washington
> Mail Stop DW-10
> Seattle, WA 98195
> (206)543-6259
> (206)545-2386
> MacKay@June.CS.Washington.edu

IBM VM/CMS:

> Dean Guenther
> Computing Service Center

Washington State University
Pullman, WA 99164–1220
(503)335-0411
Bitnet: `Guenther@WSUVM1`

IBM MVS:

Craig Platt
Department of Math & Astronomy
Machray Hall
University of Manitoba
Winnipeg R3T 2N2, Manitoba, Canada
(204)474-9832
CSnet: `Platt@uofm.cc.cdn`
Bitnet: `Platt@uofmcc`

Data General & Cray:

Bart Childs
Department of Computer Science
Texas A & M University
College Station, TX 77843–3112
(409)845-5470
`bart@cssun.tamu.edu`
Bitnet: `Bart@TAMLSR`

The PC implementations tend to be commercial products (which, of course, means more expensive), I suppose because of the extreme difficulty of porting TeX to limited architectures (see Chapter 12).

Macintosh:

Blue Sky Research (Product: TeXTURES)
534 SW Third Avenue
Portland, OR 97204
(800)622-8398
(503)222-9571
Telex: 9102900911

Rosetta, Inc. (Product: MacWEB)
2502 Robinhood
Houston, TX 77005
(713)528-8350

IBM PC:

ArborText (Product: MicroTEX)
535 West William Street, Suite 300
Ann Arbor, MI 48103
(313)996-3566
FAX: (313)996-3573

The Kinch Computer Company (Product: TurboTEX)
501 South Meadow Street
Ithaca, NY 14850
(607)273-0222

Micro Publishing Systems (Product: CTEX)
Suite 300, 1120 Hamilton Street
Vancouver, B. C., V6B 2S2, Canada
(604)687-0354

Personal TEX (Product: PC TEX)
12 Madrona Avenue
Mills Valley, CA 94941
(415)388-8853
FAX: (414)388-8865

ScripTek, Inc.
Sales Department
P. O. Box 5310
Kansas City, Missouri 64131
(800)383-5022

Amiga:

Radical Eye Software (Product: AmigaTEX)
Box 2081
Stanford, CA 94309
(415)326-5312

The addresses and phone numbers listed above were correct at the time this book was published. As always when dealing with such ephemeral data in something as non-real-time as a book, there is a possibility they are no longer correct by the time you read this. If you can contact TUG, you should be able to get current names and numbers. If the address of TUG itself is no longer valid, try the American Mathematical Society, TUG's parent (ideally, the AMS will be around for a while).

Bibliography

[AH86]   Wolfgang Appelt and Karin Horn. Multiple changefiles in WEB. *TUGboat*, 7(1):20–21, March 1986. A description of KNIT and TWIST.

[Ben86] Jon Bentley. Programming pearls. *Communications of the ACM*, May and June 1986.

[Bre88] Peter Breitenlohner. Still another aspect of multiple change files. *TUGboat*, 9(1):11, April 1988. A description of PATCH.

[Bro88] Marcus Brown. *Literate Programming Tool*. PhD thesis, Texas A & M University, College Station, Texas, May 1988. A description of the Literate Programming Tool.

[Dam86] R. M. Damerell. Error detecting changes to TANGLE. *TUGboat*, 7(1):22–24, March 1986. How to add error detection to the TANGLE processor.

[GR86]   Klaus Guntermann and Wolfgang Rülling. Another approach to multiple changefiles. *TUGboat*, 7(3):134, October 1986. A description of TIE.

[GS86]   Klaus Guntermann and Joachim Schrod. WEB adapted to C. *TUGboat*, 7(3), October 1986. A version of WEB using C and TeX.

[Kel87] Kellerman & Smith (now Blue Sky Research). *TeXTURES User Guide*, 1987. User's guide for the Macintosh version of TeX.

[KF86]   Donald E. Knuth and David R. Fuchs. TeXware. Computer Science Report 1097, Stanford University, Stanford, California, April 1986. WEB source for four TeX utilities.

[KLR88] Donald E. Knuth, Tracy Larrabee, and Paul M. Roberts. Mathematical writing. Computer Science Report 1193, Stanford University, Stanford, California, January 1988. Transcripts of lectures from course of same name.

[Knu83]   Donald E. Knuth. The WEB system of structured documentation. Computer Science Report 980, Stanford University, Stanford, California, September 1983. Definition of WEB.

[Knu84]   Donald E. Knuth. Literate programming. *The Computer Journal*, 27:97–111, 1984. An expository introduction to WEB.

[Knu86a] Donald E. Knuth. *The TEXbook*, volume A of *Computers and Typesetting*. Addison-Wesley, Reading, Massachusetts, 1986. User's guide for TEX.

[Knu86b] Donald E. Knuth. *METAFONT: The Program*, volume D of *Computers and Typesetting*. Addison-Wesley, Reading, Massachusetts, 1986. WEB source code for METAFONT.

[Knu86c] Donald E. Knuth. Remarks to celebrate the publication of *Computers and Typesetting*. *TUGboat*, 7(2):95–97, June 1986.

[Knu86d] Donald E. Knuth. *TEX: The Program*, volume B of *Computers and Typesetting*. Addison-Wesley, Reading, Massachusetts, 1986. WEB source code for TEX.

[KRS89]   Donald E. Knuth, Tomas G. Rokicki, and Arthur L. Samuel. METAFONTware. Computer Science Report 1255, Stanford University, Stanford, California, April 1989. WEB source for four METAFONT utilities.

[KV88]   Richard J. Knich and Jennifer L. Vollbrecht. TurboTEX: A new port in C for Unix and MS-DOS. *TUGboat*, 9(1):48–52, April 1988.

[Lev87]   Silvio Levy. WEB adapted to C, another approach. *TUGboat*, 8(1):12–13, April 1987. A version of WEB using C and TEX.

[Mor88]   Tim Morgan. TEX to C converter. *TUGboat*, 9(1):44–45, April 1988.

[Nor88]   Northlake Software. *The TEX Guide*, 1988. User's guide for the VAX/VMS version of TEX.

[Ram88]   Norman Ramsey. A SPIDER user's guide. Technical report, Princeton University, September 1988. User guide for the SPIDER program generator.

[Rei87]   Thomas J. Reid. TANGLE mod causes problems in METAFONT and PK files. *TUGboat*, 8(3):264–265, November 1987. A discussion of problems caused by a particular modification to TANGLE.

[Sew87a] Wayne Sewell. How to MANGLE your software: The WEB system for Modula-2. *TUGboat*, 8(2):118–128, July 1987. A description of MWEB (Modula-2 WEB).

[Sew87b] Wayne Sewell. Multiple change files: The adventure continues. *TUGboat*, 8(2):117–118, July 1987. A description of WEBMERGE.

[Spi86] Michael D. Spivak. *The Joy of TEX*. American Mathematical Society, Providence, Rhode Island, 1986. User's guide for $\mathcal{A}_{\mathcal{M}}\mathcal{S}$-TEX.

[Thi86a] Harold Thimbleby. Cweb. Technical report, University of York, October 1986. A version of WEB using C and Ntroff.

[Thi86b] Harold Thimbleby. Cweb manual. Technical report, University of York, July 1986. Users guide for Cweb.

[Thi86c] Harold Thimbleby. Experiences of "literate programming" using Cweb. *The Computer Journal*, 29:201–211, 1986.

[Zir87] Daniel M. Zirin. *TEX Made Easy—Using TEX With the PLAIN Macro Package*. ZAR Limited, 1987. Training manual for introductory TEX course.

Glossary

Ada   A language developed for the Department of Defense to apply software engineering concepts to software development.

Almost Modern fonts   An earlier vintage of the Computer Modern fonts, considered obsolete but still in use at many sites. See **Computer Modern fonts**.

AM fonts   See **Almost Modern fonts**.

ASCII   The American Standard Code for Information Interchange. The standard character set for nearly all non-IBM computers.

banner line   A line output to a terminal identifying the particular version of a program.

change file   A file containing changes to be dynamically applied to a WEB file. The WEB file itself is not modified.

change section An entry in a change file, consisting of '@x', lines to match the main WEB file, '@y', lines to replace the matched text, and '@z'.

CLD file   Command Language Definition source file. Used to add a command to the VAX/VMS system. See also **foreign command**.

CM fonts   See **Computer Modern fonts**.

CMS   Conversational Monitor System. One of the operating systems of IBM mainframes.

code section   The fundamental unit of the WEB language. Consists of a description part, a definition part, and a code part. The code part is sometimes referred to as a **module**.

Computer Modern fonts   The final version of the fonts used by TeX. If possible, these fonts should be used instead of the Almost Modern fonts.

control sequence   A character or group of characters, starting with a backslash character, that performs a particular function in TeX. Includes TeX macros, control symbols, and primitives.

control symbol   A TeX control sequence consisting of the TeX escape character and a nonalphabetic ASCII character. Used for elements such as accents on words in foreign languages ('\"{o}' would print as 'ö').

control text   A WEB command that is variable in length and consists of a starting WEB command and an undetermined amount of text, followed by the '@>' command.

control word   A TeX control sequence consisting of the TeX escape character and an alphabetic name. Can be either a macro or a primitive.

CWEB   A version of the WEB system modified for the C language.

DCL   Digital Command Language. The command language for the VMS operating system.

DECUS   Digital Equipment Computer User's Society. The user group for DEC computers.

definition module   In Modula-2, the part of a module containing the interface to the module, the only part visible on the outside. Contained in a source file completely separate from the implementation module.

EBCDIC   The Extended Binary Coded Decimal Interchange Code. The character set typically used by IBM mainframes.

executable image   A file containing executable instructions which, when activated, will run a program.

finder   The system program which performs all file system operations on the Macintosh and operates the desktop.

font   A distinct style of character shapes.

foreign command	An alternate mechanism for adding commands to the VMS command language. See **CLD file**.
implementation module	In Modula-2, the part of a module containing the actual code to implement the module. Contained in a source file completely separate from the interface (definition module).
JCL	Job Control Language. The command language for the MVS operating system.
kerning	Adjustment of character position by distances of less than character width.
launching	On the Macintosh, the act of starting an application program, especially if done automatically by selecting a data file bound to that application.
ligature	A multiple-character combination that is treated as a single character, such as 'fi'.
limbo text	Setup TEX code at the beginning of a WEB file, used to define macros, load fonts, etc.
literate programming	The concept of computer programs as literature, the idea that someone should be able to read a program as if it were a book. The fundamental concept of WEB.
load module	See **executable image**.
macro	A symbol or command that equates to a variable amount of text, with or without parameters. When the macro is "expanded" or "invoked" by using its name, the name of the macro is replaced by the text it represents. See **TEX macro** and **WEB macro**.
major section	A code section that starts a new group of related code sections. Also known as a **starred section**.
MANGLE	The Modula-2 version of **TANGLE**.
markup language	A batch-oriented methodology for typesetting documents in which a text file containing text and embedded formatting commands is used to create a document, which is then "marked up" with changes to be made for the next run. Opposite of **WYSIWYG**.

match line   In a change section, the first line of the match text, just after '@x'. This is the line that is compared to every line of the main WEB file. See **change section** and **match text**.

match text   In a change section, the lines between '@x' and '@y' used to match the main WEB file. See **change section**.

math mode   An operational mode of TEX designed for the typesetting of mathematics. Spacing and font defaults are different from those of normal mode, and special control sequences for mathematical symbols are available.

meta-comments   Special comments in WEB used to implement conditional compilation.

METAFONT   The program that creates the typefaces that TEX uses. While TEX can use any typeface, it requires metric information on the characters. METAFONT will provide the metrics as well as the bit maps when it builds a font.

Modula-2   A language designed by Niklaus Wirth to be the successor to Pascal. Contains modules with separate compilation, low-level machine access, and a simpler syntax.

module   A separately compiled program unit, usually containing a group of related procedures and data structures. This term is sometimes used for the code part of a code section.

MS-DOS   An operating system for the IBM PC.

MVS   One of the operating systems of IBM mainframes.

MWEAVE   The Modula-2 version of WEAVE.

MWEB   A version of the WEB system modified for the Modula-2 language.

null device   A pseudodevice found on many computer systems. It is used to throw away output which would otherwise have to go somewhere or to simulate a file that is always empty.

object module   A binary file containing the result of one compilation of a program file. When combined with other such modules, becomes an executable image. See **executable image**.

package	The Ada version of a module.
package body	In Ada, the part of a package containing the actual code to implement the package. Can be contained in a source file completely separate from the interface (package specification).
package specification	In Ada, the part of a package containing the interface to the package, the only part visible on the outside. Can be contained in a source file completely separate from the package body.
Pascal	A computer language invented by Niklaus Wirth to teach structured programming concepts. Named after the French mathematician Blaise Pascal.
PDL	Program Design Language. A pseudocode used to design computer programs.
porting	The action of transporting a program from one computer, operating system, or compiler to another, ideally without rewriting the whole program.
preprocessed string	A string which is to be inserted into the string pool, a separate text file created by TANGLE to be read in by the program at run-time. Manipulated within the program as a numeric constant instead of a character string.
process	In a multitasking system, a serial instruction stream independent of any other stream.
replacement text	The text which will be inserted inline when a macro or code section is expanded; or, when referring to a change section, the lines between '@y' and '@z'. See **change section**.
reserved word	An identifier with special meaning in a computer language. Typeset by WEB in **bold font**.
running heads	The left and right header lines that appear on every page of a document, containing page numbers, chapter names, etc. Normally, the left and right headers on odd pages are reversed from those on even pages.

separate compilation	The capability of compiling components of a computer program separately, with or without type checking, and combining the components into a single executable image. See **module**.
SPIDER	A program used to generate language-specific WEB systems from a text file containing a language specification.
starred section	A code section that starts a new group of related code sections. Also known as a **major section**.
string pool	A WEB construct for strings. The strings are written to a separate text file and read into the program at run-time.
system dependencies	The portions of a WEB program that are specific to a particular computer system and must be modified to run the program on a different computer system.
TANGLE	The preprocessor that creates a Pascal source file from a WEB file and optional change file; when used as a verb, the action of running this processor.
TANGLEized **identifier**	An identifier that has been forced to uppercase, stripped of underscore characters, and truncated to max_id_size before being output to the Pascal file to make it compatible with all Pascal compilers
task	See **process**.
TEX	A program designed by Donald Knuth for high-quality computerized typesetting, especially for mathematical texts; when used as a verb, the action of running this program.
TEX macro	A variable amount of text and TEX control sequences assigned to a name. See **macro**.
TEX primitive	One of TEX's built-in, low-level functions.
TUG	TEX Users Group, the primary source of information on TEX and related TEXnology.
tugboat	Newsletter of the TEX Users Group. See TUG.
unnamed section	A catchall code section (indicated by '@p') containing all Pascal code not in a regular named section. Constitutes the "main program."

VAX   Virtual Address eXtended. The primary computer of Digital Equipment Corporation.

VMS   Virtual Memory System. The primary operating system of the VAX.

WEAVE   The preprocessor that creates a T_EX source file from a WEB file and optional change file; when used as a verb, the action of running this processor.

WEB   A system for structured documentation.

WEB file   The source file of a WEB program, containing WEB commands, T_EX code, and Pascal code, used to create a Pascal file and a T_EX file.

WEB macro   One of three types of macro provided by WEB: numeric, simple, or parametric. Numeric macros are replaced by a decimal number when expanded; the others are replaced by text, like the macros of T_EX. See **T_EX macro** and **macro**.

WYSIWYG   What You See Is What You Get, sometimes known as What You See Is What You Deserve. Pronounced *whizzy-wig*. The formatting of text on a page is manually adjusted by an operator one page at a time. Opposite of a **markup language**.

Index

– D –

– E –

– N –